Source Code Secrets
The Basic Kernel

Lynne Greer Jolitz
and William Frederick Jolitz

Peer-to-Peer Communications
San Jose, California

Published by Peer-to-Peer Communications, Inc.
P.O. Box 640218
San Jose California 95164-0218, U.S.A.
Phone: 800-420-2677
Fax: 408-435-0895
E-mail: info@peer-to-peer.com

Cover Design: Susan Wilson, Palo Alto, CA
Production: Barclay Press, Newberg, OR
Printing: Paramount Graphics, Beaverton, OR

Printed in the United States of America
2   3   4   5   6   7   8   9   10

ISBN 1-57398-026-9

Peer-to-Peer offers discounts on this book when ordered in bulk
quantities. For more information, contact the Sales Deptartment
at the address above.

For a catalog of Peer-to-Peer Communications' other titles,
please contact the publisher.

This book is
Volume I

of
Operating System
Source Code Secrets

This Book is Dedicated to
William Leonard Jolitz (dec.)

An engineer whose knowledge
and dreams have traveled
beyond the solar system.

An operating system is more than just a set of simple running modules—it is actually a complicated mechanism. The *heart* of an operating system is the basic kernel. Like a human heart, the basic kernel provides a complex operating system a fundamental means to distribute resources to all other subsystems in order for them to function independently. Without the basic kernel, no other portion of the operating system can "live." The virtual memory system, on the other hand, is the *brain* of an operating system, since it is through the virtual memory system that temporary and permanent memory is stored and accessed. Like a human brain, temporary memory is used as a workspace to assemble a new item before it is stored into permanent memory.

The modules and subsystems of the kernel, like biological ones, are also *interdependent.* Even "illnesses" which arise in one module and subsystem can manifest themselves in another. For example, in biological systems, if blood circulation is inadequate, the problem can appear as a neurologic disorder (i.e. dizziness or blurred vision). Likewise, if in the basic kernel (heart) interrupts are blocked for too long, the networking software (the nervous system) will not be able to acknowledge fast enough, resulting in service which is inefficient or fails. If the kernel memory allocator in the basic kernel has been misdesigned so that it suffers memory "leaks" (a common problem in commercial operating systems), the virtual memory system (brain) will suffer memory "loss," eventually resulting in system failure. As such, a thorough understanding of the *entire* kernel is crucial to proper operating system design.

Other modules and systems in the kernel have similar analogs in biological systems. The filesystem forms the *skeletal* structure of the operating system. Sockets, acting as conduits for information, outline a nervous system structure for the operating system as a whole, while the Internet networking protocols act as neurotransmitters for this information. The combination of these two modules complete the central nervous system for the operating system.

A biological analogy to operating systems design has its limits, since the primary motivation of biological systems is to survive and replicate. Neither of these functions can yet be done by any operating system, since our knowledge of control dynamics is still in its infancy.[1] The point of this analogy is not to achieve complete similarity but instead to foster an understanding of the roles, responsibilities, and interdependencies of the portions of the kernel, just as an anatomy text organizes the study of the human body as a means for exposition. With this series we undertake to organize a complete understanding of an operating system kernel in order to give the reader the ability to evaluate and evolve any operating system.

---

[1] Error recovery and clustering are two simple mechanisms discussed throughout this series that attempt to replicate a portion of these functions, but these are still primitive means compared with the elegance of biological systems.

PREFACE

Obtaining an understanding of the core operating system kernel is not as simple as might appear—even if one has access to source code. Real world operating systems, unlike their academic paper counterparts, are trendy beasts, loaded down with mounds of additional hacks, functions, files, and other superfluous items with no regard for design, flexibility, extensibility, or future technology needs. The only thing that matters (and the only thing that a team of overloaded programmers have time for) is responding to customer demands in a timely manner.

Wading through all of this additional code to find the gems is a daunting task. However, there is a basic structure and rational design at the heart of even the most bloated operating system, but, like an archeologist searching for that elusive fossil, it may be buried so deeply that one could spend a lifetime trying to find it.

The **386BSD Operating System Reference Series** describes in detail the design and implementation decisions affecting key kernel source files made during the development of an operational kernel—386BSD. By discussing these basic components in detail and cross-referencing them to other components in the 386BSD kernel, the interwoven and complex structure of the kernel begins to take shape in a form which emphasizes its minimalist roots in a comprehensible manner. Through a rigorous discussion of these kernel files, the strengths and flaws of the various components of each file are revealed.

This agonizing reappraisal directly results in either new design or redesign (some of which appears in 386BSD Release 1.0), or a strengthened justification for the current design based on meticulous scrutiny—not assumption. Finally, a thorough understanding of current implementation feeds directly back into an understanding of the basic *levels of abstraction* which describe the kernel at its most elemental.[1]

Future direction and specific implementation suggestions to the reader are discussed in detail for these files. By gaining insight into the past, present, and future directions of 386BSD development, the reader now has enough information to explore the kernel

---

[1] See Chapter 2, **386BSD From the Inside-Out** (due 1997), for a detailed discussion of kernel level of abstraction.

further by working independently towards the future and not wasting time reinventing or reincorporating obsolete code from the past.

Among the volumes already written or in progress in this reference series are: **The Basic Kernel, The Virtual Memory Subsystem, The Filesystem, POSIX and Windows Sockets, The Internet Protocol Suite**, and **The UFS Filesystem**. It is from the basic files and subsystems discussed in these volumes that a modern operating system is made.

Isn't Source Code Enough?

The question which begs at this point is typically something along the lines of "Why should I bother reading about how the system kernel is constructed and designed when I already have the source code and an operational system to play with—after all, don't I already have everything I need to understand, fix, and modify it?" In particular, the wealth of 386BSD source code (including utilities and applications programs) must appear to answer all the dreams of the user previously denied any access to source code and system software.

Although the authors have been working with operating systems source code for a fair number of years (count in the decades), even we find new surprises with a kernel which has changed over 20 years of development and has had literally thousands of man-years put into it. As such, while having the source code is a powerful thing, it is not nearly enough to provide an overview of its many designers' intentions. If this were true, for example, Landau's landmark book on **Classical Mechanics**[2] would provide all the information required for the beginning physics student to derive all classical mechanics formulas (including Hamiltonian equations) with no further need for additional texts, lectures, or other information. While there are probably a few genius physicists out there who might claim to be able to do just this, the vast majority generally require a greater degree of insight from a variety of sources. In sum, it is a difficult area to comprehend immediately—even if you are a genius.

It is no longer enough to possess an operational operating system. Instead, it is imperative that its details be documented, examined and explained so that rational revision and extension is possible. Otherwise, it becomes difficult to determine if an operating system is correctly architected and implemented because the arcane details overwhelm the structure and obliterate the fine points of its design. In those cases, it may be impossible to tell the difference between an improvement in an artifact of the implementation and an improvement in a fundamental operating system paradigm shift. Indeed, the source code may even unintentionally obfuscate the paradigm beyond recognition, if it were not for other "sources" of information on the given system.

---

[2] L. D. Landau, & E.M. Liftshitz, **Mechanics**, Pergamon Press, Oxford (1960).

A modern operating system is far more than just a body of code—it must have well-justified reasons for being. If the rationale behind it is not firm, probably neither is the implementation. As such, both may require considerable revision to better approximate the ideal case.

Structure of This Book

Source Code Secrets Volume 1 examines the basic kernel source files required for a minimalist kernel design. Every operating system has a "simplest" model of form and structure, and many of them use similar mechanisms to deal with similar requirements. The primitive mechanics of the kernel and details of the kernel program as implemented on a target computer processor must be described in order to adapt the rest of the kernel program to that processor. The kernel itself is a program that benefits from a set of services that are used to make the program easier to manage and more concise. Not only must the kernel run a single application program, but it must allow for many application programs to be run concurrently through the concept of a process. And finally, the interface to each of these processes must reflect the POSIX standard operating system interface which, in this implementation, is directly implemented by the kernel.

This book is divided into five sections: **Introduction to the Basic Kernel (Chapter 1)**, **The Machine-Dependent Kernel (Chapters 2** and **3)**, **Internal Kernel Services (Chapter 4)**, **The Process Object (Chapters 5, 6, 7, and 8)**, and **POSIX Operating System Functionality (Chapter 9)**.

An instructor's guide containing course outline and lecture notes for this entire series is in progress. Contact the publisher for further information.

How to Use This Book

Since this book describes the actual implementation of a working basic operating system kernel, it is intended to be used in tandem with an operating systems structure and design book such as **386BSD From the Inside-Out**. Examples and laboratory assignments should:

- Make concrete the concepts presented in each chapter.
- Illustrate the competing choices and the cost trade-offs implied.
- Clearly delimit how far the implementation may be extended.

In addition, code should be examined from the very beginning, from chapter to chapter, as we see the basic kernel built from the lowest level of abstraction layers of the basic kernel to the highest levels.

386BSD Source Code and Other Information

In 1989, 386BSD was begun by the authors as a means to encourage new ideas in operating systems and networking design and has gone through a number of major and minor releases. The port of BSD to the 386 PC was chronicled in a 17-part feature series published in **Dr. Dobbs Journal** called *Porting UNIX to the 386.*[3] This series is still one of the best references to understanding the genesis of 386BSD, as well as applying the methodology of an operating systems port to a new architecture.

The complete 386BSD operating system is now available as a bootable Window/UNIX CD-ROM containing over 574 Mbytes of source and binary. It also contains the complete text of the article series as will as other hyperlinked information on 386BSD by the authors in Windows help files. The **386BSD Reference CD-ROM** can be ordered using the order form at the very back of the book. It is strongly recommended for any serious study of operating systems. In addition, up-to-date information on 386BSD can be had by examining the 386BSD web site http://www.386bsd.org/

Acknowledgements

386BSD has been a continuing work since its genesis in 1989 by the authors, and while it might appear complete, there is still much more to explore. The basis work of 386BSD actually owes its lineage to the talents of a great many people over the last thirty years, from the contributions of those who worked on prior operating systems projects such as CTSS, the Berkeley TimeSharing System, MULTICS, UNIX, MACH, and of course Berkeley UNIX, coupled with more recent contributions (primarily in the areas of utilities and applications) by people on the Internet.

This current project would not have been possible without the help and encouragement of many people who wanted to see this legacy continued into the future. We would especially like to thank Thos Sumner for his critical review and suggestions while we wrote this book. We would also like to thank Peter Hutchinson, Manny Sawit, and Stan Barnes of Miller-Freeman for their unstinting support of this documentation project, and Jon Erickson and Ray Valdéz of **Dr. Dobbs Journal** for their support of our early porting efforts (resulting in an article series). Finally, we would like to thank Paul Fronberg for his encouragement in talking about and teaching this material.

In the production of this book and formulation of the rest of this series, we would like to thank Dan Doernberg and Rachel Unkefer, Chris MacIntosh (production coordination), Darwin Melnyk and Darren Gilroy (production), and Susan Wilson (cover art), Daniel Hobbs (proofing and word list), and Hank Kennedy (contracts).

---

[3] January through November 1991 and February through July 1992. Follow-on articles on 386BSD have since appeared in this magazine as well.

Perspective: 386BSD and the "Real World"

The perspective of these writings is a combined set of views reflecting stability, standards compatibility, raw "bit-level" performance, and extensibility/scalability. No attempt is made to extend this perspective to other areas, such as providing compatibility with arbitrary commercial products, nor are testing or support isolation a portion of this work since this is not intended as a commercial quality operating system. While the quality of most commercial systems may be in decline, this should not be viewed as a permanent condition but instead one that will be eventually remedied by market forces when the customer has become sufficiently educated to see through the smoke and haze. As a result, providing enough perspective to see through the marketing smokescreen to the actual work which underlies it is another key portion of this work (something which may not necessarily be appreciated by those proffering commercial systems).

Acuity is thus a deft tool to separate operating system fact from fancy. We hope our work here helps you to hone your edge—if just a bit sharper. If so, please use it in a positive and productive direction.

> Finally: It was stated at the outset, that this system would not be here, and at once, perfected. You cannot but plainly see that I have kept my word. But I now leave my cetological System standing thus unfinished, even as the great Cathedral of Cologne was left, with the crane still standing upon the top of the uncompleted tower. For small erections may be finished by their first architects; grand ones, true ones, ever leave the copestone to posterity. God keep me from ever completing anything. This whole book is but a draught - nay, but the draught of a draught. Oh, Time, Strength, Cash, and Patience!
>
> —Herman Melville, *Moby Dick*, Chapter 32

CONTENTS

CREDENTIALS AND PRIVILEGES (kern/cred.c, kern/priv.c)

1 INTRODUCTION TO THE BASIC KERNEL

The 386BSD system (excluding debuggers and diagnostic modules) contains approximately 374 kernel source files, with over 50% of these files header files (essentially cross-references to other files). With such a large number of files (and approximately 100,000 lines of code) from which to choose, selecting key files which best exemplify a minimalist example system becomes a very subtle task. Yet correct selection and discussion of these files is critical for a detailed understanding of modern operating system design and development.

The kernel files discussed in this book form the "core" of a modern research system. Any basic kernel must perform the following functions: multiprogramming, file implementation, and program execution. In a modern setting it must afford the ability to schedule programs based on the availability of resources, processor time, and memory. These basic kernel files are also responsible for the creation, operation, and destruction of processes—the most fundamental objects in this operating system, and around which everything is built.

User programs are executed by a mechanism called **execve()** (see **kern/execve.c**), which is documented here as well. It is an example which fits in alongside many other functions of the kernel accessible by user programs through the system call applications program interface. POSIX and BSD system calls are also documented in this book to provide a view of the semantics of the kernel from the user program's perspective. These system calls frequently reference other subsystems in the kernel. Process exception handling (also known as signals) provides a means by which user programs can be notified or aborted of possibly terminal events. Finally, the machine-dependent underpinnings of the system are documented regarding processor-dependent and system-dependent functions down to the machine code primitive level (see **i386/locore.s**).

This book documents the implementation of the basic kernel, so that it becomes possible to understand the "why" behind just the code. It displays the dependencies between different portions of the kernel implementation, documents limitations of the implementation, shows alternatives directions of implementation or locations where the kernel may be extended, and demonstrates the current choice of implementation.

1.1 The Machine-Dependent Kernel

It would be nice to have a kernel program that could be written entirely in terms of a high-level programming language and not have to incorporate any machine-dependent characteristics. But since the purpose of the kernel is to create such a programming environment, one point of which is to "hide" such characteristics, the kernel must contain machine-dependent and processor-specific code in order to make it function. The kernel must frequently adopt very machine-dependent characteristics since these characteristics are what the architect of the processor chose to make most efficient in the first place.

Among the necessary machine-dependent details are the bootstrap of how the kernel is loaded into the computer and enters operation. In addition, interrupts and exception handling are frequently very different across architectures, as are the mechanisms used by user programs to request service from the kernel. Of lesser significance in the modern day but still an important difference is the details of the memory management hardware used to implement the virtual memory feature,[1] as well as to protect and isolate programs in individual processes. Most of these differences cannot be easily described by a high-level language (like C), so the universal fallback of expressing them in the machine's native assembly language is necessary (see **i386/locore.s**).

Besides machine-dependent functionality that must be implemented for the kernel to operate, there are functions that are implemented in a machine-dependent way simply for efficiency's sake. This code could have been implemented in a high-level language, but instead has been arranged to take best advantage of an architecture by being written in a highly machine-dependent way. While everything could be distilled down to a very few primitives that would be exploited by machine-independent code, this may not be as efficient as code tailored explicitly for the need. This is especially the case in a UNIX system in areas of frequent use, including system call and exception handling (**i386/trap.c**) and context switching, interrupt handling, and signal delivery (see **i386/cpu.c**).

1.2 The Internal Kernel Services

The kernel program itself is large enough to require its own bevy of support functions and services to maxmimize uniformity and in some cases indirectly increase efficiency. By centralizing these core support needs of the kernel program, the kernel program becomes more manageable for a programmer to use and extend. One of the most basic kernel support needs is to allocate kernel memory for use in a variety of circumstances. The general purpose kernel memory allocator (see **kern/malloc.c**) serves this function of providing access to the kernel's most critical resource in a

---

[1] See Chapter 5, **386BSD From the Inside-Out**, for a discussion of the physical address translation map.

universal fashion whereby memory resource can be obtained by any part of the kernel on an equal basis.

Not only is the kernel required to adapt itself to a specific architecture using machine-dependent code, but it must also adapt itself to the peripherals with which it may be used at any given time, along with the additional filesystems, protocols, and other software options required.[2] These items ancillary to the kernel may greatly exceed the size of the core kernel module itself. The management of these options itself requires a need for more kernel services. In this case, the kernel service of configuration is used as an organized means to add and adapt a module that provides access to hardware or software functionality for use with the core kernel module (**kern/config.c**).

1.3 The Process Object

The principle concurrent object in a UNIX-like system is the process.[3] Processes contain instances of programs to be run (commands, daemons, and so forth). They are a general purpose object that is created by the invocation of a POSIX function interface (see **kern/fork.c**), and loaded by a program (see **kern/execve.c**) which then ultimately terminates, causing the process to be destroyed (see **kern/exit.c**).

While a process is executing, it may need to gain exclusive use of a portion of potentially shared memory or other resource. In this case, it may have to *lock* the affected area so that other processes cannot gain access to it (see **kern/lock.c**). Processes may also encounter exceptions, generated either from other processes (the outside world) or from conditions internal to the process (see **kern/sig.c**). Since all the processes share a single processor, there must be a means to schedule and switch among processes so that all of them may appear to be executing simultaneously on a single processor (**kern/synch.c**).

Another aspect of a UNIX-like operating system is the concept of ownership of processes and other objects on the system. Since the early UNIX systems were usually used as timesharing systems, multiple different users were distinguished with a user identification (for an individual user) and group identification (for a collection of users like students in a class). Collectively, the information used to indentify a user may be thought of as a set of *credentials*—a property of processes passed on to all objects attached to the process. This protection model regulates access to shared objects (like files) among these potentially different users. An additional feature present only in UNIX-like systems is the concept of the so-called **setuserid/setgroupid** programs that use a privilege to bypass these protection rules for users otherwise unable to gain access. Thus, without altering the system or the protections on the files themselves, the

---

[2] See Chapter 10, **386BSD From the Inside-Out**, discussing user-level services and hierarchy.
[3] See Chapter 1, **386BSD From the Inside-Out**.

program can gateway access on an as-needed basis. This is an example of a selectable privilege based on credentials (see **kern/cred.c**).

In addition, 386BSD has extended the concept of a privilege from this simplistic form to a more general form which provides verification orthogonally to the traditional approach of passwords and credentials (**kern/priv.c**). By use of a role, privileges can become geographically isolated to ensure integrity even if there is subversion.[4]

1.4 POSIX Operating System Functionality

An operating system must have a basic applications program interface (API) on which to build its higher level functions and services. In 386BSD, a series of system calls are implemented via system call handlers to provide access to a basic POSIX/BSD set of functional API interfaces, which are extended by means of a user mode object library (*libc.a*). Some aspects of the kernel are explicitly written to allow efficient implementation of the most common elements of this API (files and file descriptors—see **kern/descrip.c**), while others are written for convenience of implementation as kernel system calls (e.g. program loading via **execve()**).

1.5 Structure of the Kernel Program

There are many other kernel files not discussed here which are important to the operation of a complete system. An overview of the entire kernel source tree hierarchy, **The 386BSD Kernel Program Source Organization**, is provided in **Appendix A** to give the reader an idea of the larger structure of the kernel program. In addition, the modular program Makefiles used to construct the kernel program are fully discussed in **Appendix C: A Dynamic Make Environment for Large Scale Applications Development**.

1.6 Structure of the Annotations

Each chapter file discussion briefly describes the contents of each source file and breaks up discussion into the functions present. Ocassionally, historical legacies of earlier systems and the different ways that they were implemented are discussed to provide additional context regarding the intent of the functions.

Each function starts with a short definition of its content and role in the 386BSD kernel and describes the calling conventions, net effects, and side effects of the function. This is followed by a description of fragments of code that implement the function, how it achieves its effects, and how it interacts with other functions and subsystems in the kernel.

---

[4] See **Appendix B: A Blueprint for Role-Based Network-Level Security**.

The code fragments chosen do not include every portion of the function or file—only the parts deemed necessary to clearly illustrate the function's action. It may prove helpful to display a copy of the actual source file via a computer or have a printout of the file nearby, to see better more of the surrounding context than is present in the annotation. Intentionally, many comments, diagnostic code, and other irrelevant matter are excluded from the fragments so as to minimize clutter and confusion. In some cases, extraneous material is left in simply because it would be too confusing to take it out, break up the fragments, and otherwise disrupt the discussion. In any event, the code fragments always represent the contents of that portion of the file verbatim, so that it is possible to know with certainty where the code is in a file.

The descriptions, however, cover every function in the file—even many functions that have similar effects but different interfaces or implementation. We allow for some redundancy as the price paid to achieve complete coverage of these key files, so that the reader has a chance to see the large grain details of kernel composition as well as the fine grain ones.

Finally, some of the functions have an additional section describing potential improvements to the implementation that are being considered or that have been withdrawn awaiting other coincident improvements.

1.7 Perspective: Why Write Annotations?

One of the major goals behind the 386BSD effort is to establish structure and clarity in the kernel. These annotations illustrating kernel architecture and implementation represent our *best effort* thus far in providing a raison d'etre, so that critical work done to improve it is also structured and justified. A historical examination of earlier work is provided, not to *take* from the past just to roll it into the future, but to *learn* from the past as we head towards the future. While this information can also be used for other purposes, such as improving the quality of other systems through relative understanding, we prefer to focus our work towards refinement of these ideas in subsequent releases. As such, thoughtful commentary, suggestions, alternatives or perspectives to that end are always read, as they help us speed towards the next release of this material.

Achieving critical mass for 386BSD's operating systems research dimension requires establishment of a framework with which we can measure progress against. It may be pleasant to think that ideas can be clearly seen in naked code or in papers on specific topics, but this is a simplistic notion in a project of such as large scale. Unfortunately, the academic community's disinterest towards communicating the intent behind the structure of an operating system implementation and the goals motivating its development has terminally wounded many research projects of this nature. This is simply due to the fact that these projects are of such great complexity that even accomplished experts, lacking an organized and interlinked structure of information, have difficulty evaluating the worth (or weakness) of various components. The current requirement that one can only learn by directly working on such unusual and infrequent projects is too high a requirement for most people. To allow greater understanding, the meaning behind the work must be conveyed beyond that rare individual or group.

Hopefully, this book helps to capture our history of the work on 386BSD, so that the reader can more easily follow the changes between revisions without having to learn everything over from scratch each time, while developing and accumulating a basic understanding of why it has changed in the first place.

2 ASSEMBLY ENTRY AND PRIMITIVES (i386/locore.s)

In undertaking the design of an operating system, the architect is faced with a daunting number of conflicting responsibilities. All high-level abstractions present in any operating system design must be reconciled and delineated—not only between the operating system itself (kernel, utilities, and so forth) and the user programs which run under it, but also within the operating system as well (filesystems, drivers, the applications interface, etc.).

Coupled with these abstract design demands are the pragmatic realities of the hardware design itself on which this operating system runs. The manner in which the operating system can make use of the processor's architecture, or even something as mundane as how to load the program that is the operating system into memory to start the ball rolling, must be built into the design as well, in order for the system to operate.

This decision-making process becomes especially complicated when one is a pioneer in a new area, as was the case with 386BSD. Until the development of 386BSD, no one else had proffered a nonproprietary and documented port of Berkeley UNIX (or any other kind of UNIX, for that matter) to the 386 architecture, and there was no guide available to consult for doing this port (even though we had experience doing the PDP-11, VAX, 68000, and 32000 architectures for other prior ports).

Since every architecture and computer design handles these areas in a different manner, the initial design choices become critical. At some point, the juncture between the machine-independent design and the fact that we are running code on a particular specific architecture requires that many tough and far-reaching decisions be made from the beginning of the port. Unfortunately, many of these choices may appear on the surface to be contradictory.

2.1 Locore.s Development Decisions

Prior to the start of this port, the first question from Berkeley was "How long would it take to write the locore?" since the sequence of development is the **locore.s** file, the machine-dependent code (**machdep.c**), and the drivers, with the locore itself the big stopping point. Why this is so difficult to accomplish is because many decisions must be made correctly in providing a basic framework to build an operating system kernel.

This file contains the initial assembly language that expands the core machine dependencies of the architecture of 386/486/Pentium processors. When we set forth back in 1989 to create a new version of Berkeley UNIX on the 386, we had no master copy of a file like this to start from. We also had no experience with the 386 architecture and could not obtain any example from other 386 UNIX versions, those being very tightly controlled in access—even some of the secrets to writing a file like this were controlled. As such, we had to invent our own **locore.s**.

2.1.1 Historical Origins

The original Bell Laboratories PDP-11/45 UNIX system had two assembly language files—**low.s** and **mch45.s**. **low.s** contained startup and interrupt vector interface code that resided at the lowest word of memory in the computer (the 64-word bootstrap would load programs at location 0 and start them, and the PDP-11's interrupts were wired to specific low memory *vectors*). **mch45.s** contained the assembly language support code for interfacing to the processor (**spl's**, **copyin/copyout**, **fu/suword**, etc.). On the VAX, a single **locore.s** file contained the primary machine-dependent code, and conditionally included vector catcher arrays to intercept interrupts from its multiple buses.

Many of these functions are similar to their PDP-11 counterparts, since there are still many similarities in kernel bootstrap and start-up. Since **locore.s** occupies the bottom of memory on the 386, the name makes at least a little sense, if you ignore the whimsy in the fact that core memory has now been obsolete for two decades. Traditions definitely endure.

2.1.2 System Initialization and Operation

The first function in this file is the **start** routine. **start** is the entry point for the system to begin operation after it is loaded into memory, and is the very first portion of code that is run. This code is located at the very bottom of the text image that makes up the kernel program. It is used to initialize the processor with memory management turned on so that the remainder of the kernel can manage to initialize all of its subsystems and enter operation by loading the very first process (*/sbin/init*).

While appearing innocuous, many design decisions are made in the course of implementing this particular function. Six different versions of this code have been written by us alone, and will probably evolve further as demands change. Not only does this code reflect processor-specific, system-dependent, virtual memory system-dependent, and context switch-dependent portions—it also interacts with the bootstrap environment that in turn loads the program.

Thus, **start** involves certain degrees of compromise at any given point in time. Other functions in this file, while nonetheless important, have a more minor impact. The prototype hand-crafted first user process is originated here, as is the signal code used to process signal entry in every user process, the communications routines that allow portions of memory to be passed between kernel and user processes, and the nonlocal goto subroutines used by the system's debugger.

2.1.3 The Context Switch Mechanism

The second section in this file is concerned with the system's context switch mechanism. In 386BSD, as with most UNIX-like systems, concurrent operation occurs by explicit context switch operations invoked by a process to pass control to the next runable process waiting in line for the processor. The **swtch** function (and its alternate incarnation that allows the running process to probe for the existence of a higher priority process—**qswtch**) implement context switches as a coroutine call to another kernel-mode process that is awaiting a return from a prior call to **swtch**. In the case where no process is available, the processor is left to idle in a loop awaiting a runable process.

2.1.4 Entry to / Exit from the Kernel

The last section in this file is concerned with the code used to implement entry and exit to the kernel from user mode. The kernel can only be entered from a user process by one of three means: called explicitly via a system call (on the 386 this is done via a *call gate*); or implicitly via a *processor exception* or a *peripheral device interrupt*. The *interrupt set processor level* (splXX) functions are used to adjust the Interrupt Control Units (ICU) to filter a desired set of interrupts.

2.2 Kernel Program as Loaded by the Bootstrap

The kernel program is loaded into memory as a sequence of segments embedded in an ordinary 386BSD a.out format executable file.[1] The segment lengths are described by fields in the executable file format header that the bootstrap uses to deposit the program into memory. Thus, the kernel program's segments can be presented in logical order (see Figure 2.1).

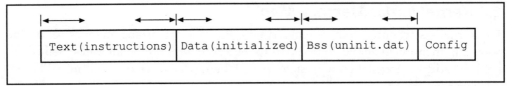

Figure 2.1: Program Symbolic Addresses

The kernel program is loaded by the bootstrap into the PC's memory starting with the first word of RAM. Following the end of the program, the bootstrap tacks on configuration strings from the configuration file (/.config). Since 386BSD makes use of the full 32-bit address space of the X86 processor, the bootstrap enters 32-bit protected mode in order to load the kernel program and allow it to initialize the entire complement of physical memory of the computer (see Figure 2.2).

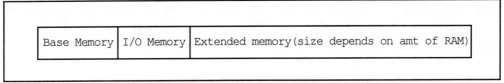

Figure 2.2: X86 PC Physical Memory Map

RAM program memory is broken into two segments, base and extended memory (expanded memory is bank-switched memory, referenced via portions of I/O device memory, and is not usable by 386BSD because it is not directly addressable). The base memory holds up to 640 KBytes of RAM. Since the kernel can exceed the size of the base memory, the 386BSD kernel program can be loaded by the bootstrap in both base and extended memory. The remainder of the Kernel Program not loadable into base memory is placed in the beginning of the extended memory (see Figure 2.3).

---

[1] See *The Berkeley a.out File Format* in **Chapter 9.**

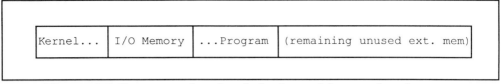

Figure 2.3: Bootstrap has loaded a kernel larger than base memory

2.3 Kernel Initial Memory Map

The kernel's **start** entry point is entered with the memory arrangement as set by the bootstrap mentioned above. In addition to the kernel program, it allocates memory to hold the address translation map state (page tables, page directory) and initial kernel stack (see Figure 2.4).

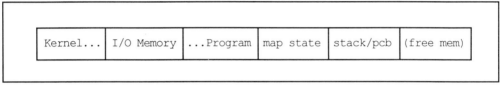

Figure 2.4: Physical memory layout during start()

start creates the initial address translation state to allow the program to run in a virtual address space at a different base address (KERNBASE). By iBCS convention, the kernel runs at the top of the 4 GByte virtual address space, even though its physical memory contents are located at the lowest part of physical address space (see Figure 2.5).

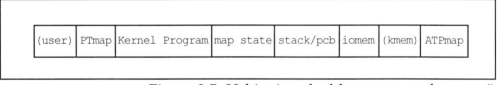

Figure 2.5: 32-bit virtual address space, after start()

The kernel program also has its process control block (pcb) initialized partially (located at the base of its kernel stack) so that the initial kernel program can become the statically created ancestor process, allowing all subsequent processes to be created by kernel **fork()** operations. Remaining virtual address space above the kernel program (*kmem* or kernel memory) is unallocated by **start**, and managed by the kernel virtual memory allocator (**kmem_alloc()**, see **vm/kmem.c**), which is used by **malloc()**[2]. Memory at the bottom of the address space (user) is reserved for use with user program run by the kernel program in operation. These programs are multiplexed by

---

[2] See the discussion on **malloc()** in **Chapter 4**.

context switches (see **swtch**) through the lower portion of address space, while the kernel program remains fixed at the top of the virtual address space at all times.

Two sets of indirect address translation page tables are present at the top of the user program portion of virtual address space (*PTmap*), and at the top of the kernel address space (*APTmap*). The lower set always refers to the current address space, including user program, while the upper set is used to refer to an alternate address space that is not mapped. The alternate page tables are a convenience for the kernel to be able to create a new address space without altering the current address space. [3]

The virtual memory system manages both the single kernel and multiple user virtual address spaces via program interface. In addition, remaining physical extended memory not used by the kernel is organized into a managed pool of memory that is allocated and reclaimed by the virtual memory system to allow the operating system to achieve its function of running multiple user program.

The memory map of the kernel changes considerably during operation, as memory is dynamically allocated and freed from the kernel heap, and as different user processes run, occupying different portions of virtual memory and different pages from the physical memory free pool.

2.4 locore.s Functions and Terminology

The following functions appear in **locore.s**:

start

reloc

rfillkpt

fillkpt

icode

sigcode

copyout

copyout_4

copyout_2

copyout_1

copyoutstr

ssdtosd

swtch

idle

qswtch

---

[3] Which is useful in performing a **fork()** operation to create another address space.

start is the machine-dependent program used to begin kernel operation, while **reloc**, **rfillkpt**, and **fillkpt** are internal functions called only from system initialization used in setting up the processor. A plethora of other minor routines handle various processor functions as well.

In addition to **start**, the most performance-sensitive portion of the system, the **swtch** context switch mechanism, is implemented in this file, as well as the *trap* and *exception* and *interrupt handling* for the processor and the system call interface. These discrete functions implement the mechanisms on the X86 family that control how the kernel is entered and exited:

- Processor Exceptions
- Peripheral Device Interrupts
- Set Processor Level Functions
- System Call 'Call Gates'

2.4.1 What is start?

start is the runtime startoff of the kernel. The kernel is a standalone program loaded into the computer and started via this entry point, while **start** achieves the effect of entering into kernel operation. Since the kernel is written to assume certain characteristics[4] of operation from the beginning, **start** must achieve this effect for machine-independent operation and device initialization to occur. Similarly, **start** presumes that the bootstrap has loaded the kernel program and entered 32-bit protected mode instead of the real mode in which the processor begins operation.

start creates an initial virtual address space resembling other address spaces created by the kernel in which to run user processes. In this way, the kernel's machine-independent initialization routine **main()** will be entered as if the operating system had always been running, and it will not need to differentiate between operations performed on the initial kernel address space and operations performed on any other address space.[5]

A hallmark of good kernel design is to avoid redundant mechanisms whenever possible—in this case we reuse the same mechanism. This design approach is a technique used again and again in other portions of 386BSD as well, and one against which other systems approaches can be measured.

2.4.1.1 What Does start Expect of the Bootstrap?

start expects that the bootstrap will load the kernel program into memory starting at address zero and successively occupying space in physical memory. Since the IBM PC

---

[4] E.g., that initialization is done with memory management on and, in the case of the 386, running at a high virtual address.

[5] It can use exactly the same primitives without distinction.

has its I/O bus memory mapped as the last third of the first megabyte, for kernels larger than 640 KBytes the bootstrap will continue to load memory above this *hole* successively. It will be up to the **start** code then to rejoin this hole in virtual address space.[6]

The bootstrap passes in three arguments: the boot flags that indicate how the kernel is to be booted; the boot device which indicates from what device, kind of filesystem, partition, or other details the system is loaded; and where the hole starts. The boot device is used to determine where the initial root filesystem may be found.

locore.s now allows the kernel to compensate for systems set up with small base memories. Older versions of 386BSD assumed the presence of 640 KBytes of base memory and would not load large kernels properly when such systems were configured with smaller amounts of base memory. In particular, a certain brand of AT&T PC defaulted to 512 KBytes of base memory, even though it had the ability to map base memory as 640 KBytes. This is a good example of the idiosyncratic characteristics of the bootstrap preventing initial operation of the kernel. Unfortunately, an inexperienced user might not be able to tell the difference between a simple matter of misconfiguration of base memory or a more complex failure in this case—since the program loaded will just issue a reset or hang. And so it goes for assumptions in the bootstrap.

Currently, the bootstrap assumes that the kernel is loaded at address zero. Since the PC manages to store its BIOS (Basic I/O System) ROM's data area in the lower portion of memory, the kernel overwrites this area, and thus destroys the information.

2.4.1.2 Future Design Considerations in the Bootstrap

In future versions of the system, the kernel will be loaded above this data area so that the BIOS operation will be unaffected. There is no major design reason which precludes BIOS operation or even DOS/Windows coexistence with 386BSD. The technical problems arise only in eliding the bootstrap dependencies upon initialization. For the moment, the only interaction with the BIOS within this file is to set a warm boot flag so that diagnostics won't be rerun when the system resets and reboots.[7]

One area for future consideration in the bootstrap environment is whether or not this **start** routine should run self-relocating. By self-relocating we mean to say that the bootstrap could load the kernel anywhere in any sequence of physical pages, and this kernel program startup code would sense the address it was executed from and allocate its page tables appropriately (not assuming that it starts at address zero). This

---

[6] Since some PCs can be set to have 256 KBytes or 512 KBytes of memory for base memory, this boundary should actually be determined by the bootstrap and passed in as an argument—this will be done in the next release of the system.

[7] To save time on reboot by avoiding power-on diagnostics.

would allow the system to run adjacent to another operating system where the memory reserved for 386BSD could then be independently managed by that of another operating system present in the same machine. Thus, both 386BSD and Windows, for example, would coexist (with care). Preliminary work has already begun in this area, but it is a very touchy area of design, since both 386BSD and Windows are currently architected to control all memory resources—they wish to play in their own ponds alone, so to speak. Thus, the technical limitations of such a change is more one of conventions and conformance, rather than some obscure reason.

Another area for future design consideration regarding the bootstrap environment is determining just what surrounds the initial load of the system. A system bootstrap might, for example, have the ability to stay resident as a kind of underlying operating system that could, for example, use the BIOS to demand-load drivers as the system is configured. Unfortunately, the early UNIX systems never had as rich a run-time environment to take advantage of this as did the simplest DOS system[8]. The BIOS offers a considerable programming environment, allowing the operating system to avoid the chicken-and-egg situation of loading the system before configuring the system. Since this system can be loaded using the BIOS, its configuration would then be discovered and the root devices driver, say, loaded from the filesystem before the root filesystem is mounted. Thus we can have an entirely dynamically loaded system from the start. The debugger for the system could even be loaded ahead of the operating system, so that we could debug this entry code by single-stepping from the beginning. To achieve this, multiple modules besides just the kernel would need to be loaded into the system and dynamically relocated.

Obviously, all this would require much additional work, but this future design discussion is intended to provide the reader some idea of the scope compromised by the design of the runtime startup, which otherwise is considered to be a relatively straightforward process.

2.4.1.3 How is start Implemented?

... [File: /usr/src/kernel/kern/i386/locore.s, line: 127]

```
        .globl  start
start:
        movw    $0x1234, 0x472  /* warm boot */
        jmp     1f
        .space  0x500           /* skip over bios data region */
1:
    ...
```

The very first instruction of the kernel is described by the **start** entry point. The kernel first assigns a BIOS magic value to the BIOS data region that has been overwritten by

---

[8] Usually, a ROM would just load a boot block from a disk containing a simple disk driver to load a larger bootstrap and, ultimately, the kernel program.

loading the kernel. This magic flag will keep the BIOS from running diagnostics on the system again if the system is rebooted.[9]

The area for the BIOS variables is kept in place, although the state is not preserved. This is done so that other entries can be made in the BIOS data region to change the warm boot operation. This region is skipped over on initialization.

... [File: /usr/src/kernel/kern/i386/locore.s, line: 140]

```
        movl    12(%esp), %ebp   /* must be obtained first */
        movl    4(%esp), %edx
        movl    $_boothowto-KERNBASE, %eax
        call    reloc
        movl    %edx, (%eax)
        movl    8(%esp), %edx
        movl    $_bootdev-KERNBASE, %eax
        call    reloc
        movl    %edx, (%eax)
...
```

At the point where **start** is called, the bootstrap has placed the kernel into consecutive physical memory at the start of RAM. If the kernel is larger than the base memory of the system, the bootstrap will continue to place the remainder of the kernel into extended memory, beginning above the first physical megabyte of storage (skipping over the hole). Since the kernel may be larger than memory immediately addressable by the one megabyte limitation of real mode, the kernel is entered by the bootstrap already in 32-bit flat protected mode,[10] with its segment selectors referencing segments that correspond to the full physical address space.[11]

The stack pointer is above the kernel and contains three arguments passed in from the bootstrap. All interrupts are disabled by the bootstrap (this is the state as it enters the kernel), since the interrupt's descriptor table entry state has not yet been created and an interrupt would immediately cause a *processor shutdown*.

We extract the parameters on the stack before the stack is overwritten. Since the kernel has been entered at the program's address of zero, yet the kernel is linked to run relocated high at virtual address space, the manifest constant of KERNBASE is subtracted from the address associated with the variable where we will store the arguments from the bootstrap. One of the arguments of the bootstrap is the location where the kernel is bisected by its overflowing of base memory. This address, while the third argument, must be obtained first, since it is used to relocate the virtual address (to which the program was compiled) to the physical address where the page

---

[9] The only point of this instruction is to save a little time on doing a warm boot.
[10] See *Creating a Software Specification* (January 1991), *Three PC Utilities* (February 1991), and *The Standalone System* (March 1991), among others, in **Dr. Dobbs Journal**.
[11] 2^{32} bytes or 4 GBytes.

may be located. If the variable to be set has its address in the segment above the hole, this would need to be compensated for here.

PCs vary in how they may be configured to break up their many megabytes of physical memory into base and extended memory. For our purposes, the break is irrelevant since the kernel only believes that it is loaded into a set of physical pages. Earlier Berkeley systems relied much more on the fact that physically contiguous kernel memory was consecutive with kernel virtual memory. However, as 386BSD evolves, it relies less and less on this, since the I/O system checks to see if memory is physically contiguous anyway and shuffles it appropriately. It would be possible to run all of the kernel on physically discontiguous arbitrarily assigned memory, if that were to be of value for some purpose (such as running 386BSD as a subsidiary operating system to Windows or OS/2. We leave it as an exercise to the reader to figure out what would be necessary in order to accomplish this).

Both the boot flags and boot device values are taken from the stack. The physical address where their contents are currently stored in physical memory is computed by the **reloc** subroutine and stored there.

... [File: /usr/src/kernel/kern/i386/locore.s, line: 151]

```
        movl    $_end - KERNBASE, %eax
        addl    $NBPG, %eax
        andl    $~(NBPG - 1), %eax
        call    reloc
        movl    %eax, %edx
        movl    $0, 0               /* insure bottom does not hold pattern */
        movl    $-NBPG, %ecx
        cmpl    $640*1024 - NBPG, %eax
        jg      1f
        movl $640*1024, %ecx
...
```

Next the total amount of memory is probed for by this startoff code. While we could have used the contents of the BIOS or the CMOS memory descriptions of the PC itself, configuration dependent problems arise when doing so, so we instead manually check for the presence of memory, taking care to look for address rollover.

On some PCs, not all physical memory address space is implemented—some PCs only implement the lower 16 MBytes of physical address space; thus, the next 16 MBytes refer to the same 16 MBytes, and so on.[12] Luckily, these inadequate PCs are fast becoming rare since 16 MBytes is considered "small" when running Windows NT and other advanced commercial operating systems looming on the horizon.

To avoid rollover, we clear the first word to ensure it does not hold a pattern. For our check of the end of the kernel, we then take the starting address from the _end address that has been rounded up to the next physical page of memory (and relocated in the

---

[12] One PC didn't even implement over 8 MBytes, but that's another story.

case it is above the hole in extended memory). We do not check to see that the memory loaded for the kernel does exist—that is the bootstrap's responsibility.

If this starting address is below the hole, we start looking from below the hole; otherwise, we start at the address of the end of the kernel. In either case, we check up until the page before the last page of memory (4 GBytes less 4 KBytes). The reason that we don't check the last page is that some PCs implement the top pages of memory as control registers. Compaqs, for example, actually allow for special use of the top portion of memory as well, as in control registers for the memory system.

... [File: /usr/src/kernel/kern/i386/locore.s, line: 163]

```
#define PAT 0xa55a5aa5
1:      movl    $PAT, (%eax)    /* write test pattern */
        cmpl    $PAT, (%eax)    /* does test pattern work? */
        jne     2f
        cmpl    $PAT, 0         /* have we rolled over to bottom of memory ? */
        je      2f
        movl    $0, (%eax)      /* force word to zero */
        addl    $NBPG, %eax
        cmpl    %ecx, %eax
        jne     1b
2:
        cmpl    %eax, %edx      /* nothing in this segment? */
        je      3f
...
```

We check for the presence of memory by writing a pattern and checking to see if the pattern is still present after we wrote it. If it is, the memory exists. However, if the pattern has been written to the zeroth location, we know that a rollover has occurred. We don't save the contents of the memory we are checking because this causes some PC caches to simulate the presence of memory at that location, thus defeating the whole point of this operation.[13]

We may wish to preserve memory on probing in the case that we wish to preserve its contents. One clever trick that can be done to make a fault-tolerant log-based filesystem is to check to see if the data buffers on restarting the system happen to be consistent before they are reinitialized. Thus, one could immediately reuse the contents of a previous power failure or crash since the freshly loaded kernel program will refer to memory exactly the same way as it did before—all of memory is then used as if it was a giant delayed-write buffer. Unfortunately, most PCs don't permit this capability, since they scrupulously scrub the memory clean.[14] In addition, on X86 processor shutdowns[15] the processor is reset and forced to rerun the BIOS before a program can intercept to find out why, and the BIOS then scrubs the memory clean,

---

[13] For Example, 386 Systems with 82385 Cache Control Chip, which "cache" nonexistent memory!
[14] N.B. If 386BSD is booted from DOS, memory is **not** clean.
[15] Occurring when the processor can no longer continue to execute instructions.

SOURCE CODE SECRETS: THE BASIC KERNEL

destroying any record of what went wrong. This makes debugging of shutdowns very difficult.

The test pattern word is forced back to zero to be consistent with this clearing of memory and we continue on to the next page.

... [File: /usr/src/kernel/kern/i386/locore.s, line: 167]

```
        shrl    $12, %eax
        movl    %eax, %edx
        movl    $_maxmem - KERNBASE, %eax
        call    reloc
        movl    %edx, (%eax)
3:
        /* need to do extended mem? */
        cmpl    $640*1024, %ecx
        movl    $1*1024*1024, %eax
        movl    %eax, %edx
        movl    $-NBPG, %ecx
        je      1b
    ...
```

We check up to two segments as described above—the base memory and the extended memory. When we have finished with one particular segment, we will iterate to the next segment, saving the last probed page frame in the variable *maxmem*.

We probed for the presence of memory before turning on translation because all of the memory is accessible without mapping entries successively, so it is convenient to check for it at this point. We do not need the size of memory for starting up—it is just a side-effect of this process. In the future, we may wish to scale various data structures based on the size of memory, and this may affect data structures that the runtime startup manages to use, so in anticipation of this, probing for memory is the very first thing we do before we write any data structure.

... [File: /usr/src/kernel/kern/i386/locore.s, line: 192]

```
        movl    $_etext-KERNBASE, %edi
        andl    $~(NBPG-1), %edi

        /* find end of kernel image, round to integral page size */
        movl    $_end-KERNBASE,%esi
        addl    $NBPG-1,%esi
        andl    $~(NBPG-1),%esi
/* number of pages of system map. n.b APTmap steals one. */
#define NSYSMAP (1024 - SYSPDROFF - 1)
    ...
```

Now that we know the amount of memory, we find the location of the end of the kernel text and the end of the kernel's image, and save these in the EDI and ESI registers, respectively, in preparation for building the initial kernel address translation maps.

Note that these registers hold endpoints that are logical (not physical) addresses, since they do not yet take into account the hole. The kernel's address translation maps will be comprised of the top few page directory entries, starting with the SYSPDROFF (system page directory offset) entries. These entries correspond to the NSYSMAP entries that will be initialized[16] (see Figure 2.6).

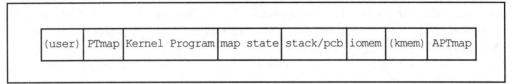

Figure 2.6: 32-bit virtual address space, after **start()**

The kernel program is presented here (in the middle of Figure 2.6) as three successive segments of text, data, and zero initialized blank storage. Below it in virtual address space lies the page table map (*PTmap*), which is actually a recursive address translation page map of the active user process at the bottom and the kernel's entries at the very top. Above the kernel program lies the initialization and mapping state information that will be built by this startup code.

Both the page directory and its map of page table entries (*sysmap*) actually will be used after setup only from the *PTmap* address space. Before we set up the initial address space, it must have an adjacent portion of address space so the it can come into existence. We leave it mapped in the address space afterwards as a convenience and also because some older Berkeley subsystems refer to a historical *sysmap* linear kernel map—this is easier than converting them.

This initial virtual address space resembles what we are about to build. Virtual addresses above this diagram of kernel virtual address space will be managed by the virtual memory system on behalf of the kernel program, as will all of the virtual address space of a user process in the address space not initialized by this startup code.

Between the page directory and the kernel's page tables lies the first initial kernel stack of length UPAGES. This initial stack is allocated at this point in time to simulate the appearance of the initialization of the kernel as part of the zeroth process (you have to have a stack somewhere—it might as well correspond to the kernel stack of the zeroth process). Like most other aspects of the zeroth hand-crafted process, it is statically initialized and never deallocated.

---

[16] Note that one is stolen for use in the alternate page table map (APT map) which is used to access the page tables of an alternate address space—the alternate address space is defined as the one not currently mapped.

Also, as mentioned earlier, the page tables of this initial process are allocated forever—they are the page tables of the zeroth process as well as the archetypal copy of all processes' page directories, as all process page directories will have the NSYSMAP page directory entries pointing to the same page tables (*sysmap*).

While we could have dynamically grown the kernel's page tables (by faulting entries on demand), the benefits obtained by faulting the eight pages of possible page table entries were found not to be worth the trouble—it actually induced errors and underlying dependencies not discussed here.[17] However, if the kernel needed to grow in size to several hundred megabytes for its address space, the situation may change, but this is not within the scope of our minimalist kernel—the current 32 MBytes of default address space for the kernel seems plenty big.[18]

... [File: /usr/src/kernel/kern/i386/locore.s, line: 228]

```
        movl    %esi, %eax
        call    reloc
        movl    %eax, %edx
        movl    $_KernelPTD-KERNBASE, %eax
        call    reloc
        movl    %edx, (%eax)

        /* virtual address of Kernel PTD */
        movl    %esi, %edx
        addl    $KERNBASE, %edx
        movl    $_VAKernelPTD-KERNBASE, %eax
        call    reloc
        movl    %edx, (%eax)

        /* logical address of proc 0 pcb/stk */
        lea     NBPG(%esi), %eax
        lea     KERNBASE(%eax), %edx
        movl    $_proc0paddr - KERNBASE, %eax
        call    reloc
        movl    %edx, (%eax)

        /* logical address of kernel PT */
        lea     (UPAGES+1)*NBPG(%esi), %ebx
        movl    $_KPTphys - KERNBASE, %eax
        call    reloc
        movl    %ebx, (%eax)
    ...
```

The physical address of the kernel page table directory is stored within its associated variable *KernelPTD*, as well as the virtual address of the page table directory

---

[17] With "wiring", see Chapter 5, **386BSD From the Inside-Out,** and **Volume II** of this reference series.

[18] To increase the size of the kernel address space, all that is required is that the system be recompiled with a lower KERNBASE manifest constant. This was used, for example, by Los Alamos National Laboratories to increase the size of the virtual address space to 64 MBytes to hold two special I/O maps of 16 MBytes apiece for a very high speed networking application. See *Very High-Speed Networks: HiPPi and SIGNA* (Winter 1994), **Dr. Dobbs Journal**, Volume 19, Issue 14, Pages 32 - 35.

VAKernelPTD. These addresses will later become useful in deciphering the page tables in postmortem debugging.[19] In addition, the address of the process zero virtual address, placed in its *p_addr* field, is passed to the kernel initialization routine via the *proc0.p_addr* field.

Finally, the physical address of the page tables is recorded in the *KPTphys* variable. This address cannot necessarily be determined from the others because it may be different than the other relocations in the case of a kernel that spans the base-to-extended memory gap. This occurs, for example, in the boundary case where the page tables have just overlapped the top of physical memory.[20]

... [File: /usr/src/kernel/kern/i386/locore.s, line: 260]

```
        movl    %edi, %ecx              /* this much virtual address space */
        shrl    $PGSHIFT, %ecx
        movl    $PG_V|PG_KR, %edx       /* read-only (for 486) */
        xorl    %eax, %eax              /*  starting at this address - 0 XXX */
        call    rfillkpt

        /* kernel data pages - covers data, bss, and initial state */
        movl    %esi, %ecx
        subl    %edi, %ecx              /* remaining data pages */
        shrl    $PGSHIFT, %ecx
        addl    $UPAGES+1+NSYSMAP, %ecx /* include initial state */
        movl    $PG_V|PG_KW, %edx       /* read-write */
        call    rfillkpt

        /* map I/O memory map XXX */
        movl    $_atdevphys-KERNBASE, %eax /* record relative pte base */
        call    reloc
        movl    %ebx, (%eax)
        movl    $0x100-0xa0, %ecx       /* pages to map hole */
        movl    $PG_V|PG_KW, %edx       /* read-write */
        movl    $0xa0000, %eax          /* beginning with the base of the hole*/
        call    fillkpt
...
```

Next, we construct the page tables themselves, starting with the kernel text pages. Since the kernel program itself is broken up into text and data, the kernel text is made read-only by assigning read-only page table entries to its portion of address space. These will only affect a 486 or better processor, since the 386 does not honor the write protect page table bit in kernel mode.

Kernel text pages occupy space in the range of zero to the contents of the EDI register. This is placed in the counter register and turned into a number of pages by a left shift.

---

[19] They are used to locate the inital page table directory in a dump of physical memory so that the kernel's address translation information can be extracted prior to decoding the contents of the kernel program, its stacks and variables—see the user mode **libutil** object library, and the **kvn** functions.
[20] The rest of the kernel lies below the base memory, but the page tables start as the first part of extended memory (if they are allocated just off the end of the kernel image in base memory).

The page table entry's attribute bits are set to the EDX register and its physical address starting at zero set to the EAX register, where the subroutine **rfillkpt** is called to fill the kernel page table with the appropriate number of page table entries.

rfillkpt fills the set of page tables by doing a logical address relocation for the address of the PTE itself and the physical page associated with it, since the addresses referred to in the kernel text segment may not only transit the hole in this memory but also transit the actual page tables themselves (they may be split across the page table hole). We have no way of knowing just where the hole will come since the hole can differ on every machine on which the kernel is loaded and, depending on how big the kernel is, it may overlap into the hole at any point.

Similarly, we initialize the successive kernel data pages but instead of setting the read-only page attribute, we set the read/write attribute for these pages. They are allocated to consecutive physical addresses following the kernel text, as the EAX register has been updated successively by the **rfillkpt** subroutine to refer to successive memory pages as well as page table entries. The kernel data region for these entries includes both the initialized data, the uninitialized but zeroed bss region, and the initialization mapping state.

After the kernel data pages initialization, the hole itself is mapped so that drivers can get access to it. The starting physical address currently held in the EBX register in the *atdevphys* variable holds the relative physical location of the kernel page table entry associated with the region of virtual memory that maps the hole. The **fillkpt** function is thus called to add these page table entries referring to the hole. We cannot use the **rfillkpt** function to do this because, as it attempts to bypass the hole, it would immediately jump over the area of physical memory we are trying to map.

At this point, all of the kernel's page tables are initialized. We can now obtain a page table directory, since we know the address and length of the kernel page tables.

... [File: /usr/src/kernel/kern/i386/locore.s, line: 287]

```
        lea     (UPAGES+1)*NBPG(%esi), %eax /* logical address of kernel */
                                            /* page table */
        movl    $PG_V|PG_KW, %edx          /* read-write */
        movl    $1, %ecx                   /* a single entry */
        movl    %esi, %ebx                 /* at the start of the page directory */
        call    rfillkpt

        /* install a set of entries for the kernel's page tables */
        lea     (UPAGES+1)*NBPG(%esi), %eax /* logical address of kernel */
                                            /* page table */
        movl    $NSYSMAP, %ecx             /* for this many directory entries */
        lea     SYSPDROFF*4(%esi), %ebx    /* offset into page directory of */
                                            /* kernel program */
        call    rfillkpt                   /* install an entry recursively */
                                            /* mapping the page directory as a */
                                            /* page table */
        movl    %esi, %eax                 /* logical address of PTD in proc 0 */
        movl    $1, %ecx                   /* a single entry */
```

```
        lea     PDRPDROFF*4(%esi), %ebx /* below the kernel entries */
        call    rfillkpt
...
```

The very first entry in the page table directory refers to the bottom 4 MBytes of memory. This entry is initialized to point to the kernel page tables and mark the attributes of the directory entry as writable. The **rfillkpt** function is used to initialize the page directory elements, since these elements have an identical format to page table entries, and it performs all of the same functions to mitigate the existence of the hole (just in case the boundary case of allocating the page table directory immediately adjacent to the hole occurs). This page directory entry will thus map the first 4 MBytes of address space to coincide with the kernel's base address of the first 4 MBytes—thus, memory translation can be turned on running at a low address. A program will continue to run, as it has been mapped in this region already, then jump high to the portion of the virtual address space where it has been linked to run as the second step of initializing operation in a high kernel virtual address.

The kernel is placed at the top of virtual address space because there is only one virtual address space on the 386 to be shared between kernel and user. The standard for UNIX on the Intel architecture iBCS mandates that the bottom of the address space be reserved for kernel programs. This is similar to the arrangement on the VAX where all programs ran in the low addresses of a shared address space and the kernel ran in the high portion of this shared virtual address space.

After we have effectively relocated the kernel to run in high virtual address space (where it will permanently run), we destroy the temporary entry to catch any indirections through the user's address space before any operations on user processes begin. Note that we do not prevent indirections through null pointers during ordinary kernel operations past this point, because a user process could be present and thus will have the bottom of address space allocated. It is possible to come up with an executable image which leaves the bottom unmapped to catch these attempts, either by use of a special executable format, or by having a running program unmap its first page of memory.

Next, we initialize the kernel's page directory elements to point successively to the kernel page table. These seven entries (one reserved for the *PTmap*), are consecutively assigned to the just-created page tables—this time with write access.

Finally, an entry corresponding to the physical address of the page table directory itself is placed within the page table directory at the entry corresponding to the virtual address of the *PTmap*; hence, we have a page table directory entry which in turn has a physical address referring to the page table directory itself—thus, recursively mapping itself. This step is the basis of the entire virtual address translation mechanism used in this implementation. The physical memory associated with the address translation will now always appear in a region of virtual address space in consecutive order corresponding to the relative virtual address mapped, regardless of what page the physical memory holds in the page table.

... [File: /usr/src/kernel/kern/i386/locore.s, line: 306]

```
        movl    %esi, %eax              /* logical address of PTD in proc 0 */
        call    reloc
        movl    %eax, %ebx
        movl    %eax, %cr3              /* load ptd addr into mmu */
        movl    %cr0, %eax              /* get control word */
        orl     $CR0_PG, %eax           /* turn on paging mode bit */
        movl    %eax, %cr0              /* enter paged mode with this instr. */
        ...
```

The memory management unit (MMU) now has page tables that it can use to function. The address of the page directory entry is loaded into the MMU at the base address specified with the control register 3 (CR3) and the MMU is enabled by setting its paging mode bit in the control register 0 (CR0).

At the end of this listing, the processor is now referencing the page tables. Should the page tables be incorrectly set up for the lower portion of virtual address space, the processor will either jam or shut down.

... [File: /usr/src/kernel/kern/i386/locore.s, line: 315]

```
        movl    _proc0paddr, %eax
        addl    $UPAGES*NBPG-4*12, %eax /* XXX 4*12 is for printf's sake */
        movl    %eax, %esp

        /* relocate program counter to high addresses */
        pushl   $begin
        ret
        ...
```

The end of the kernel stack region is assigned as the stack pointer for this process. An address corresponding to the high virtual address space of the kernel program is pushed onto this stack and a return issued. This is then loaded as our new program counter, and control is transferred to the high virtual address region (where the kernel has been linked to run). As one person has described it, this is the "jump to hyperspace," where the memory management hardware must work correctly.

At this point, we no longer have to manually relocate entries because the system symbols are relocated at this address. This is the initial access to the top page directory entries corresponding to the kernel. If the page tables or directory entries have been improperly set up, a shutdown will occur at this point. Note that up to this point we have been depending on the protected mode segment descriptors created in the bootstrap. If the size of the bootstrap's segment descriptors do not cover the kernel base address, a general protection violation will also occur, thus preventing the kernel from operating at this address.

One amusing idiosyncrasy (see line 316) is that if a function references more arguments than it actually has, it may reference off the top of the kernel stack. Some dummy calls to **printf()** preserve a set of arguments larger than they might ever use—thus, an early page fault may be induced if a printout routine used for diagnostic or device purposes during early initialization is activated where it references above the end of the stack and underflows it.

... [File: /usr/src/kernel/kern/i386/locore.s, line: 318]

```
        movl    _Crtat, %eax
        subl    $0xfe0a0000, %eax
        movl    _atdevphys, %edx        /* get pte PA */
        subl    _KPTphys, %edx  /* remove virt base of ptes */
        shll    $PGSHIFT-2, %edx
        addl    $KERNBASE, %edx
        movl    %edx, _atdevbase        /* save virt addr */
        addl    %eax, %edx
        movl    %edx, _Crtat
...
```

The base of the console's memory for its frame buffer address is manually adjusted to correspond to the new virtual address of the hole. This a holdover of console initialization currently done to allow use of the kernel's **printf()** routine from an early point, as might be used during the machine initialization routine prior to when consoles are initialized. This is only an artifice inserted for the convenience of the debugger and will not persist in later versions.

... [File: /usr/src/kernel/kern/i386/locore.s, line: 339]

```
        movl    $_end, %ecx     /* find end of kernel image */
        movl    $_edata, %edi
        subl    %edi, %ecx
        xorl    %eax, %eax
        cld
        rep
        stosb

        /* clear first kernel stack */
        movl    $(UPAGES * NBPG)/4, %ecx
        movl    _proc0paddr, %edi
        xorl    %eax, %eax
        cld
        rep
        stosl
...
```

The BSS (Blank Storage Segment) starts at the location _edata and ends at the location _end. The kernel's uninitialized data space and its first kernel stack are both cleared to zero, in preparation for use. Since most PCs zero memory anyway, the only time this actually comes into play is when booting from an operating system such as DOS, where memory isn't initialized to zero to begin with. Note that BSS is redundantly zeroed in both bootstrap and kernel, since there exist some other bootstraps used by others with 386BSD that cannot reliably clear BSS.

The kernel stack is zeroed for any initial variable reference depending on zero. Since the process control block lies at the bottom of the stack, all fields within it are initialized to zero as well.

... [File: /usr/src/kernel/kern/i386/locore.s, line: 356]

```
        lea     (UPAGES+1+NSYSMAP)*NBPG(%esi), %eax
        call    reloc
        pushl   %eax

        /* set up bootstrap frame */
        xorl    %eax, %eax
        movl    %eax, %ebp      /* top most frame pointer points to unmapped */
        movw    %ax, %fs        /* bootstrap could have used these, zero */
        movw    %ax, %gs

        movl    $0, _PTD        /* blow away temporary "low" directory entry? */

        /* bootstrap processor - void init386(int firstphys) */
        call    _init386
        popl    %esi

        /* void main(void) */
        call    _main
...
```

The first physical page of memory past the end of the kernel program and its initialized mapping state is placed on the stack frame to pass to the machine initialization function for the X86 architecture family. The rest of the bootstrap frame is touched up by clearing the base pointer so as to indicate the first frame for use with the machine-independent portion of the kernel. Since the bootstrap could have used the extended selectors FS and GS, they are also cleared and the temporary double-mapped directory entry is zeroed.

After the processor is initialized, the machine-independent initialization of the kernel is started by calling the **main()** function. In the case of the 386, many processor characteristics must be initialized to catch early faults that could show up in debugging the kernel proper. Thus, the machine-dependent initialization is always arranged ahead of the machine-independent initialization, so that it is possible to catch errors at an earlier point.

It is also imperative that the kernel debugger be able to run as early as possible in this cycle, so as much of the initialization process as possible can be debugged without postponing debugger initialization itself. If an interrupt or exception is not caught appropriately by the machine-dependent initialization, a processor shutdown will likely result, causing the screen to flash and the system to reboot. This allows no opportunity for system debugging.

... [File: /usr/src/kernel/kern/i386/locore.s, line: 375]

```
        .globl  __ucodesel, _udatasel
        movzwl  __ucodesel, %eax
```

```
    movzwl    __udatasel, %ecx

    /* build an outer stack frame to enter user mode to execute proc 0 */
    pushl    %ecx              /* user ss */
    pushl    $USRSTACK - 4     /* user esp */
    pushl    %eax              /* user cs */
    pushl    $0                /* user ip */
    movw %cx, %ds              /* user ds */
    movw %cx, %es              /* user es */
    movw %cx, %gs              /* XXX and ds to gs */
    lret                       /* goto user */
...
```

After the kernel machine-independent initialization has been completed, it is assumed that we will transfer to the first user process to be executed, and that a program has already been loaded into the user virtual address space.[21]

The user's code selector and data selector are set and an outer stack frame is constructed on the stack in place to simulate an arrived entry into the kernel via a call gate. Embedded in the outer stack frame are the code selector and stack selector for the user process as well as its new program instruction pointer address. All other selectors are manually initialized by the kernel prior to executing the return from the call gate that will send this process into user mode. Note that at the point that the call gate return occurs, this current kernel stack pointer will be lost.

On entry to the kernel the next time around, the kernel stack pointer is obtained from this process's current task structure (tss) initialized during the **init386()** initialization function (see **i386/machdep.c**). An amusing consequence of this is that if the tss is not set up correctly, the process will be entered for the first time in user mode but on reentry to the kernel a shutdown will probably occur, since it has an invalid kernel stack and nowhere to go.

2.4.1.4 Design Considerations for start

Alternatively, instead of having this code present, this runtime startup routine could have been intermixed with the call gate associated with system calls, so that the common code on return and the layout of the stack would resemble an ordinary outbound system call. This approach was thought to be too complicated to arrange and too obtuse to explain.

Another consideration for the design of **start** could be presenting a structure containing the arrangement of the outer stack frame. This would allow for a more general handling of initialization, which might be useful in the case that we allow another kind of operating system interface in addition to a POSIX applications program interface. In this case, one might want to interpose a layer that allows the discovery, attachment, and implementation of an initial emulation library binding for

---

[21] Actually, all that is assumed is that the virtual address space has been set up to use the process, as it may fault within the virtual address space just as well. All that is necessary is that the bookkeeping for the virtual address fault be correctly established by this time.

the bootstrap process that would necessarily be run. The semantics of the descriptors associated with the bootstrap process would then be determined between the time the kernel dispatches to the emulation library—thus, there would be an additional layer not discussed here. Other choices for implementation of **start** might involve implementing more of this in C, allowing for multiple modules, and changing the nature of the bootstrap environment.

2.4.2 What is reloc?

reloc is a simple function used by kernel startup which determines if the given argument in the EAX register is at or above the hole, and if so, adjusts the address to bypass the hole. In effect, this *glues* the top of the base memory to the bottom of extended memory by successive assignment.

reloc has one argument: the EAX register value. It returns the relocated address, bypassing the hole.

2.4.2.1 How is reloc Implemented?

... [File: /usr/src/kernel/kern/i386/locore.s, line: 402]

```
reloc:
        cmpl    %eax, %ebp              /* if at or above start of hole, */
        ja      1f
        subl    %ebp, %eax              /* use physical pages above hole */
        addl    $ENDHOLE, %eax
1:      ret
    ...
```

The function checks to see if its argument appearing in the EAX register is at or above the start of the hole. If it is, then it adjusts its address to bypass the hole. Note that the argument is value result and that it is modified inline.

2.4.3 What is rfillkpt?

rfillkpt relocates and fills a page table element. It is used by kernel startup to create a kernel page table entry for a page of the kernel program. **rfillkpt** relocates both the PTE address and the physical page address used by the PTE. It calls **reloc**, or's the protection bits, and stuffs the new PTE into place.

2.4.3.1 How is rfillkpt Implemented?

... [File: /usr/src/kernel/kern/i386/locore.s, line: 411]

```
rfillkpt:
        pushl   %ebx                    /* save relative physical address "pointers" */
        pushl   %eax

        movl    %ebx, %eax              /* do logical address reloc for pte addr */
        call    reloc
        movl    %eax, %ebx

        popl    %eax                    /* restore page address */
```

```
        pushl   %eax                /* and relocate logical page address */
        call    reloc

        movl    %eax, (%ebx)        /* stuff pte */
        orl     %edx, (%ebx)        /* add protection bits to pte */

        popl    %eax
        popl    %ebx
        addl    $NBPG, %eax         /* increment logical page frame address */
        addl    $4, %ebx            /* and look to next logical pte */
        loop    rfillkpt
        ret
...
```

The function increments the physical address and the PTE address for as many PTEs as it has been asked to fill. Thus, it is converting logically addressed[22] items to actual physically assigned addresses and seamlessly jumps the hole with both page tables and physical pages as well.

Logical addresses may also be viewed as the offset from the start of virtual address space. Thus, the page's logical address corresponds to its the virtual address, but only because of the presence of the hole, and doesn't necessarily correspond to the physical offset.

2.4.4 What is fillkpt?

fillkpt, like **rfillkpt**, relocates the pages table to which the PTE belong (but not the pages mapped by the PTE). It is used by kernel startup to map the I/O memory *hole* that bisects physical memory. **fillkpt** relocates the PTE address, since the page tables to which the PTE belongs may still potentially span the hole.

2.4.4.1 How is fillkpt Implemented?

... [File: /usr/src/kernel/kern/i386/locore.s, line: 435]

```
fillkpt:
        pushl   %ebx                /* save relative physical address "pointers" */
        pushl   %eax

        movl    %ebx, %eax          /* do physical address reloc for pte addr */
        call    reloc
        movl    %eax, %ebx
        popl    %eax

        movl    %eax, (%ebx)        /* stuff pte */
        orl     %edx, (%ebx)        /* add protection bits to pte */

        addl    $NBPG, %eax         /* increment physical address */
        popl    %ebx
        addl    $4, %ebx            /* next pte */
        loop    fillkpt
        ret
...
```

---

[22] Where it is load-ordered logically addressed.

SOURCE CODE SECRETS: THE BASIC KERNEL

The function simply relocates the page tables to span the hole, in the same manner as described in **rfillkpt**.

2.4.4.2 386BSD fillkpt Design Choices and Trade-Offs

fillkpt is necessary only because we have to map the hole itself. We could have put off mapping the hole until processor initialization, but we prefer to map all of the page tables at the same time—both for consistency and because with the I/O space initialized early, we can insert instructions to write the console display's frame buffer with diagnostic display codes. This allows us to more easily debug this portion of the system. Debugging bootstraps and kernel runtime initialization is always very touchy because too much context is lacking to run a debugger.

2.4.5 What is icode?

icode is effectively the user mode bootstrap for the system. **icode** is simply a prototype hand-crafted user program that executes the initialization process *init* from a system call. The kernel's only use of this function is to copy it in the first process's user space so that the first process can bootstrap the system. This code is never executed by the kernel itself.

2.4.5.1 How is icode Implemented?

... [File: /usr/src/kernel/kern/i386/locore.s, line: 456]

```
        .set    execve, 59
        .set    exit, 1
        .globl  _icode
        .globl  _szicode

/*
 * Icode is copied out to process 1 to exec /sbin/init
 * If the execve() fails, process 1 exits
 */
_icode:
        pushl   $0                      /* empty env, for now */
        movl    $argv, %eax
        subl    $_icode, %eax
        pushl   %eax

        movl    $init, %eax
        subl    $_icode, %eax
        pushl   %eax

        pushl   %eax                    /* place holder for return address */

        movl    %esp, %ebp
        movl    $execve, %eax
        lcall   $iBCSSYSCALLSEL, $0     /* execve("/sbin/init", argv, 0); */
        pushl   $0
        movl    $exit, %eax
        pushl   %eax                    /* place holder for return address */
        lcall   $iBCSSYSCALLSEL, $0     /* exit(0); */

init:
        .asciz  "/sbin/init"
```

```
        .align  2
argv:
        .long   init+6-_icode    /* argv[0] = "init" ("/sbin/init" + 6) */
        .long   eicode - _icode  /* argv[1] follows icode after copyout */
        .long   0
eicode: /* main appends a string(s) here ... */
        _szicode:
        .long   _szicode - _icode
   ...
```

icode builds a stack frame of arguments for the **execve()** system call,[23] then calls the kernel using the iBCS system call gate (like all system calls do under 386BSD). The arguments to **execve()** include the argument vector that specifies that the program */sbin/init* be executed in place of **icode**.

The contents of the argument pointed to by *arg* (argv[1]) will be set during kernel initialization to point to a string indicating how the kernel was booted via the *boothowto* boot flags. This is done precisely at the end of this code fragment, so that it is possible to append the string immediately to the end of this sequence of instructions.

Since this program will run starting at the zero virtual address of a user process (even though it is assembled at the kernel high virtual address), care must be taken to generate addresses that are relative to the bottom virtual address in which it will actually be executed. Since the addresses in the code are all relative to the program's instruction pointer, they do not need to be manually relocated. However, the addresses of the arguments are self-relocated relative to the beginning of the program manually.

Because the assembler does not support in certain cases the ability to subtract relative addresses, some symbolic address calculations are done with instructions that would otherwise not need to be done.

2.4.5.2 Improvements to the Current Implementation of icode

Some of the information regarding how the kernel was initialized and configured should be conveyed into the *init* process in a more general way, such as by encoding the environment variable for this initial bootstrap program. This would allow the kernel to make up for a long standing UNIX idiosyncrasy of not being able to tell which kernel was loaded if it was not the default kernel image from the system.

It would also be useful if we could discover aspects of kernel configuration to determine conflicts present in configuring the system. By passing the information to the initialization process, a higher level configuration could be done either in the init process or in a subprocess (e.g. a program like */sbin/config*). This might also be a more

---

[23] See *What is execve()?* in **Chapter 9.**

elegant solution to the autoconfiguration dilemmas present with UNIX systems in general.[24]

2.4.6 What is sigcode?

sigcode is used to communicate a signal action from the kernel program to the user process. **sigcode**, like **icode**, is not executed by the kernel directly but is maintained by the kernel. This code is copied to the end of a process (usually in the top of its stack frame). It is used to bounce off signals for entry and exit of the signal action in the user process.

2.4.6.1 How is sigcode Implemented?

... [File: /usr/src/kernel/kern/i386/locore.s, line: 501]

```
        .globl  _sigcode, _szsigcode
_sigcode:
        call    12(%esp)
        xorl    %eax, %eax              /* smaller movl $103, %eax */
        movb    $103, %al
        /* enter kernel with args on stack */
        lcall   $iBCSSYSCALLSEL, $0     /* sigreturn(); */
        hlt                             /* never gets here */

_szsigcode:
        .long   _szsigcode - _sigcode
...
```

sigcode is entered with the signal's stack frame instantiated on the stack. It immediately calls the handler associated with the signal and on return from the handler forces the process to reenter the kernel using the **sigreturn()** system call (see **kern/sig.c** in **Chapter 6**) and the processor-dependent signal delivery mechanism (see **Chapter 3**, **cpu_signal()** in i386/cpu.c). This code is executed in user mode on entry to the program's signal handler.

2.4.6.2 386BSD sigcode Design Choices and Trade-Offs

The whole point of this routine is to ensure that the signal handler reenters the kernel after every signal before going back to the point in the user program where the user program was prior to the signal. This procedure thus allows the signal mask to be updated by the kernel without interruption.

This mechanism is actually an artifact of signal processing. It will change in subsequent versions of the system when emulation libraries are added, since there will be provinces of code in the emulation library that will alleviate the need for this function being managed by the kernel.

---

[24] See the discussion regarding configuration in **Chapter 4**.

2.4.7 What is ssdtosd?

ssdtosd is a processor-specific function which converts a software description of a segment descriptor to the hardware-specific format used by the processor. **ssdtosd** is a convenient function used to convert a software description of a segment descriptor to a hardware usable form. This implementation is the suggested procedure.[25]

2.4.7.1 How is ssdtosd Implemented?

... [File: /usr/src/kernel/kern/i386/locore.s, line: 518]

```
ENTRY(ssdtosd)
        pushl   %ebx
        movl    8(%esp),%ecx
        movl    8(%ecx),%ebx
        shll    $16,%ebx
        movl    (%ecx),%edx
        roll    $16,%edx
        movb    %dh,%bl
        movb    %dl,%bh
        rorl    $8,%ebx
        movl    4(%ecx),%eax
        movw    %ax,%dx
        andl    $0xf0000,%eax
        orl     %eax,%ebx
        movl    12(%esp),%ecx
        movl    %edx,(%ecx)
        movl    %ebx,4(%ecx)
        popl    %ebx
        ret
   ...
```

For purposes of compatibility with the 286 descriptor form, the 386 and successor processors extended this descriptor by adding fields on the end instead of redefining the contents of the descriptor. As a result, the bit fields are rather contorted and not the nice convenient ones used in software. For consistency during initialization, these fields are kept in a software format and translated before use with this function.

This function uses Chinese rotation to shuffle the "extended" word fields that exceed the 286 descriptor form. 386BSD presumes a "rational" format for descriptors in software, then converts them before use (see **i386/machdep.c** for an example of its use).

This function could also be written in C, except for the fact that it would appear just as contorted in appearance. In other words, writing it in C would not improve its understandability nor efficiency.

---

[25] Cited in the book **80386 System Software Writers Guide** (Intel publication, page 215, figure 2-6).

2.4.8 What is copyout?

copyout is a kernel function used to pass a segment of data from the kernel program to a user process. This function is only concerned with the 386—for the 486, an inline assembler version is used instead for speed. In addition, the inlined version does not need to reconcile the 386's lack of write protection from kernel mode.

copyout checks to see that the portion of user address space associated with the segment both exists and is writable before transferring the contents from kernel to user space. If it is not possible to do this operation, the function will return an error (EFAULT); otherwise, it returns zero to indicate no error occurred in performing the transfer.

While **copyout** is implemented in assembler and does not have any function entry description, if it were implemented in C it would appear of the form:

```
int copyout (struct proc *p, void *ksrc, void *udest, u_int sz);
```

copyout has four arguments: a pointer to a process to which the function will pass the contents of the segment; a pointer to a region of memory in the kernel; a pointer in the user process's address space; and the byte count of how many bytes to transfer. The side-effect of this function can result in an address space fault which may or may not be transparent, depending on whether or not the fault manages to make the address space valid to receive the transfer.

Currently, the first argument is always the current process and is just used to gain access to the fault vector. However, in subsequent versions, this function may also gain access to a process that might be another process other than the current one in the system or on another network host system entirely.

2.4.8.1 How is copyout Implemented?

... [File: /usr/src/kernel/kern/i386/locore.s, line: 552]

```
ENTRY(copyout)
        movl    4(%esp), %eax           /* p */
        movl    $9f, PMD_ONFAULT(%eax)  /* in case we fault */
        pushl   %esi
        pushl   %edi
        pushl   %ebx
        movl    20(%esp), %esi          /* ksrc */
        movl    24(%esp), %edi          /* udest */
        movl    28(%esp), %ebx          /* sz */

        cmpl    $_PTmap, %edi           /* out of user space */
        jae     9f
        movl    %edi, %eax
        addl    %ebx, %eax
        cmpl    $_PTmap, %eax
        jae     9f
...
```

The process argument is used to set a default trap vector to the end of this routine in the case that a terminating exception might be found. Rather than implement this as a two-pass algorithm of checking protections and then doing the transfer, only one pass is done, while the MMU is relied upon to detect a write to either a write-protected portion of valid memory or to an invalid address. If there is a write attempt to an invalid address, the virtual memory system may successfully fault a page into this area. In this case, the fault will be silently ignored as it will have allocated the address space to receive the information (e.g. made it valid).

The arguments for this transfer are loaded into registers appropriate for use with a string copy instruction, which is used to do the bulk of the work. The destination argument is checked to see that it fits within the range of the user address space immediately below the *PTmap*. It is checked both at the beginning and at the end of its segment to ensure that wraparound does not occur (as the kernel is located at the end of the address space).

... [File: /usr/src/kernel/kern/i386/locore.s, line: 570]

```
1:      movl    %edi, %eax
        shrl    $IDXSHIFT, %eax /* fetch pte associated with address */
        andb    $0xfc, %al
        movl    _PTmap(%eax), %eax

        andb    $7, %al         /* if we are the one case that won't trap... */
        cmpb    $5, %al
        jne     2f

        /* ... then simulate the trap! */
        pushl   %edi
        call    _trapwrite      /* trapwrite(addr) */
        testl   %eax %eax
        popl    %eax

        jne     9f              /* if not ok, return */

        /* otherwise, continue with reference */
...
```

Before the copy is attempted, a code check is done for the PTE associated with this address to be transferred to see if it is a valid page marked for read-only access. This step makes up for a deficiency in the 386 which would not honor the write-protect bit from supervisor mode.

In the case where the write-protect bit would not be honored, the trap is forced by calling the **trapwrite()** handler on this address (see **Chapter 3, i386/trap.c**). If **trapwrite()** detects a failed write fault (a nonzero return), then **copyout** terminates with a fault. This check is done at the beginning of every page across the span of the **copyout** segment. This implies that we limit the amount that we transfer to the amount remaining in the destination page so that we may check every destination page's PTE to see if it is writable.

SOURCE CODE SECRETS: THE BASIC KERNEL

In the case of 486 processors which trap write-protected pages for both supervisor and user mode, no check needs to be done since the fault will occur in either case. Thus, this routine is not used for the 486 and its followers; instead, a string copy inline is used[26] (see **init386()** in **i386/machdep.c**).

... [File: /usr/src/kernel/kern/i386/locore.s, line: 587]

```
2:        movl      %edi, %eax       /* calculate the remainder in this page */
          andl      $NBPG-1, %eax
          movl      $NBPG, %ecx
          subl      %eax, %ecx
          cmpl      %ecx, %ebx
          jg        3f

          movl      %ebx, %ecx
3:        subl      %ecx, %ebx
          movl      %ecx, %edx

          shrl      $2, %ecx         /* move a page fragment */
          cld;      rep; movsl
          movl      %edx, %ecx
          andl      $3, %ecx
          rep;      movsb

          cmpl      $0, %ebx         /* any remainder? */
          jne       1b
...
```

The segment size of the transfer is limited to the amount remaining in the page that it addresses. Thus, the function iterates over a large transfer checking at the beginning of each page's boundary to see if the protection is different for each page. We then attempt to transfer in units of words (using a move string long instruction which transfers in units of 4 bytes) as much as possible of this segment and transfer any residual number of bytes with the move string byte instruction.

If there is any more remaining to be done requiring yet another pass, we loop back to the beginning to check the protection on the page table entry associated with the next page address.

... [File: /usr/src/kernel/kern/i386/locore.s, line: 607]

```
          popl      %ebx
          popl      %edi
          popl      %esi
          xorl      %eax, %eax
          movl      4(%esp), %edx
          movl      %eax, PMD_ONFAULT(%edx)
          ret

9:        popl      %ebx             /* detected a fault, return error */
          popl      %edi
          popl      %esi
```

---

[26] As long as the write-protect feature in the control register zero is set with the WP bit.

```
        movl    4(%esp), %edx
        xorl    %eax, %eax
        movl    %eax, PMD_ONFAULT(%edx)
        movl    $EFAULT, %eax
        ret
...
```

Otherwise, we restore all registers saved on the stack. The return value is cleared to indicate success, the fault vector is cleared so that we don't unintentionally trap a valid exception, and the function returns. In the case that an error occurred, the same type of return processing is done, except that an EFAULT value is passed back as a return value.

2.4.8.2 386BSD copyout Design Choices and Trade-Offs

In the 2.8 BSD PDP-11 implementation, six functions were used to communicate between the user process and the kernel: **fuword, suword, fubyte, subyte, copyin**, and **copyout**. **fuword** and **suword** were used to fetch integer-sized values used by system calls. **fubyte** and **subyte** were used to fetch incrementally characters for strings or to place characters from the terminal driver into the user process. **copyin** and **copyout** were used for mass transfer of a block of memory from a disk memory, say to, be returned as part of a read operation. Now only one of these functions, **copyout**, remains and it is substantially different. These functions were all implemented in assembly language—both for efficiency and because the simple C compiler used at the time provided no facility for inlining instructions special to the architecture.

The Berkeley system for the VAX architecture required a new set of paired functions (**fusword** and **susword**), since profiling was still done with 16-bit counters even though the word size was now 32-bits for integers. In addition, it was found that the filename strings were a significant burden in the use of **fubyte**. This was especially painful because the per-function overhead (the "calls" instruction) was exceedingly slow on the VAX. This burden was reduced by the addition of the **copyinstr** function, which allowed whole strings to be read in from the user process in a more efficient manner. Its companion function **copyoutstr** (a much less used function) mimicked the same property in the case where they might otherwise have used **subyte**.

copyinstr and **copyoutstr** also ameliorated the burden caused by the strings in finite sized buffers. While **copyoutstr** (et. al.) had similar calling conventions to **copyout**, the older functions used (**fubyte, subyte, fuword**, and **suword**) had different calling conventions. From this point on, *all* UNIX systems used this approach, including System V, ports of BSD to architectures other than the VAX (Sparc, HP), and older versions of 386BSD. Even Solaris still uses this approach.

The only purpose in using the older small sized functions was to gain convenient and quick access to constant regions. In this version of 386BSD, they have been replaced with a constant form of **copyin** and **copyout** (see **copyin** and **copyout**) whose only semantic difference is that the length is a constant value. The optimizing compiler can now discern which of the constant lengths is being transferred and remove all other "dead" code, thus selecting uniquely the minimal amount of code from an inline procedure to use.

In 386BSD Release 1.0, many assembly language enhanced functions have been replaced with inline assembler. The compiler itself can now tailor the assembly language function even better than the writer, since it can handcraft the function's usage depending upon its use and the surrounding context of the code from which it is called.

On the 386 (and even more so with the Pentium), extremely tailored optimizations can be done to exploit the processor's speed more effectively. In 4.3BSD, an attempt to do just this was tried with a postpass of the compiler through an inline program that would attempt to edit out the *call/save* return sequence and manually insert the assembly language. This was found to be somewhat cumbersome to maintain and almost impossible to debug—it was hence obsoleted (removed) in subsequent versions of Berkeley UNIX and not taken further.

Now, the **copyout** and **copyin** functions have complements in constant length analogues which replace entirely the need for the **fu/su** functions completely. In the future, if the C language is extended to allow for determination of the constant properties of the arguments in a more elaborate way, the constant functions themselves would just become a subcase of **copyin** and **copyout**.

The explicit copy functions (**copyout, copyoutstr, copyout_1, copyout_2,** and **copyout_4**) are used only to maintain 386 compatibility. The write-protection deficiency on 386 processors requires us to examine every page table entry to determine if the improperly implemented case is encountered by checking the page table entries. There is no sense in inlining any of these functions for the 386, since the advantage gained in avoiding the procedure call is lost in the excessive overhead needed to conduct these checks.

However, even the 386 version benefits from the inlining of all **copyin** functions, because the inline functions will never generate a write fault (since they only read). The only time where this might not be the case would be if copy-on-write were allowed within the kernel itself (in this case, the same problem would arise with the receiving buffers in the kernel for the **copyin** cases). Note this would still not present a problem for 486 and Pentium, since the copy-on-write feature works correctly on these processors (whether it is a kernel page or a user page). Since the efficient handling of copy-on-write pages is imperative for implementing a zero-copy high speed TCP implementation, there are no plans to further extend support to 386 processors beyond these functions, as the 386 itself will soon become obsolete.

In addition, note that all of these functions now have an argument that describes the process to be read from or written to in an explicit form. In the future, remote processes on another processor may be detected and the request passed to the processor for evaluation.

2.4.9 What are copyout_4, copyout_2, and copyout_1?

The **copyout_X** functions are almost identical functions which implement the constant region **copyout** function for the 386. These functions enumerate one of the three constant region inlines possible that are used in the 486. The constant region inline relies upon an optimizing C compiler to select one of these three cases to provide the most efficient code generation for access to a user process.

Since the compiler cannot optimize in an assembler subroutine, we preoptimize the four cases of the constant copyout functions into three separate cases implemented here as the separate assembly language functions **copyout_4**, **copyout_2**, and **copyout_1**. Since the most optimized form would be to copyout to the current user process, only two arguments are passed on the stack: the value to be stored and the address to be stored within the current user process. All functions return zero if successful and an error (EFAULT) otherwise.

2.4.9.1 How is copyout_4 Implemented?

... [File: /usr/src/kernel/kern/i386/locore.s, line: 628]

```
ENTRY(copyout_4)
        movl    _curproc, %ecx
        movl    $copyout_fault1, PMD_ONFAULT(%ecx)    /* in case of fault */
        movl    8(%esp), %edx
        cmpl    $_PTmap, %edx                         /* out of user space */
        jae     copyout_fault1
    ...
```

The fault vector in the current process is set to the shared copyout fault processing for all of these routines. The only point at which the fault can occur is at the single instruction that modifies the word—this is the point of this function. The address is checked to see if it is within the user's address space. If not, the fault routine is called directly to terminate this function.

... [File: /usr/src/kernel/kern/i386/locore.s, line: 635]

```
        shrl    $IDXSHIFT, %edx /* fetch pte associated with address */
        andb    $0xfc, %dl
        movl    _PTmap(%edx), %edx

        andb    $7, %dl         /* if we are the one case that won't trap... */
        cmpb    $5, %dl
        jne     1f

        /* ... then simulate the trap! */
        pushl   8(%esp)
        call    _trapwrite      /* trapwrite(addr) */
        popl    %edx
        movl    _curproc, %ecx
        testl   %eax, %eax      /* if not ok, return */
```

```
          jne      copyout_fault1

1:
          movl     8(%esp), %edx
          movl     4(%esp), %eax
          movl     %eax, (%edx)
          exorl    %eax, %eax
          movl     %eax, PMD_ONFAULT(%ecx)
          ret
...
```

The PTE associated with the address is examined to see if it is a valid protected page. In this case, a write fault is simulated using **trapwrite()**. If an error is present the fault routine is directly called to end this transfer. The arguments for the value of the address are received from the stack and the word is modified in the user process. If the memory is not mapped as valid, a transparent page fault may occur.

After the modification has been made, the fault vector is cleared and a zero is returned, indicating success. If a fault had been induced either from one of the above explicit cases or from the the implicit case of a transparent fault, the fault mechanism will terminate the function and the return value of EFAULT will be passed back.

2.4.9.2 How is copyout_2 Implemented?

... [File: /usr/src/kernel/kern/i386/locore.s, line: 663]

```
ENTRY(copyout_2)
          movl     _curproc, %ecx
          movl     $copyout_fault1, PMD_ONFAULT(%ecx)    /* in case of fault */
          movl     8(%esp), %edx
          cmpl     $_PTmap, %edx                         /* out of user space */
          jae      copyout_fault1
...
```

The fault vector in the current process is set to the shared copyout fault processing for all of these routines. The only point at which the fault can occur is at the single instruction that modifies the half word—this is the point of this function. The address is checked to see if it is within the user's address space. If not, the fault routine is called directly to terminate this function.

... [File: /usr/src/kernel/kern/i386/locore.s, line: 670]

```
          shrl     $IDXSHIFT, %edx /* calculate pte address */
          andb     $0xfc, %dl
          movl     _PTmap(%edx), %edx

          andb     $7, %dl          /* if we are the one case that won't trap... */
          cmpb     $5, %dl
          jne      1f

          /* ... then simulate the trap! */
          pushl    8(%esp)
          call     _trapwrite       /* trapwrite(addr) */
          popl     %edx
          movl     _curproc, %ecx   /* restore trashed register */
          testl    %eax, %eax       /* if not ok, return */
```

```
        jne        copyout_fault1

1:
        movl       8(%esp), %edx
        movl       4(%esp), %eax
        movw       %ax, (%edx)
        xorl       %eax, %eax
        movl       %eax, PMD_ONFAULT(%ecx)
        ret
...
```

The PTE associated with the address is examined to see if it is a valid protected page. In this case, a write fault is simulated using **trapwrite()**. If an error is present the fault routine is directly called to end this transfer. The arguments for the value of the address are received from the stack and the half word is modified in the user process. If the memory is not mapped as valid, a transparent page fault may occur.

After the modification has been made, the fault vector is cleared and a zero is returned, indicating success. If a fault had been induced either from one of the above explicit cases or from the the implicit case of a transparent fault, the fault mechanism will terminate the function and the return value of EFAULT will be passed back.

2.4.9.3 How is copyout_1 Implemented?

... [File: /usr/src/kernel/kern/i386/locore.s, line: 698]

```
ENTER(copyout_1)
        movl       _curproc,%ecx
        movl       $copyout_fault1, PMD_ONFAULT(%ecx)    /* in case of fault */
        movl       8(%esp),%edx
        cmpl       $_PTmap, %edx                         /* out of user space */
        jae        copyout_fault1
...
```

The fault vector in the current process is set to the shared copyout fault processing for all of these routines. The only point at which the fault can occur is at the single instruction that modifies the byte—this is the point of this function. The address is checked to see if it is within the user's address space. If not, the fault routine is called directly to terminate this function.

... [File: /usr/src/kernel/kern/i386/locore.s, line: 705]

```
        shrl       $IDXSHIFT, %edx /* calculate pte address */
        andb       $0xfc, %dl
        movl       _PTmap(%edx), %edx

        andb       $7, %dl          /* if we are the one case that won't trap... */
        cmpb       $5, %dl
        jne        1f

        /* ... then simulate the trap! */
        pushl      8(%esp)
        call       _trapwrite       /* trapwrite(addr) */
        popl       %edx
        movl       _curproc, %ecx   /* restore trashed register */
        testl      %eax, %eax       /* if not ok, return */
```

```
        jne       copyout_fault1

1:
        movl      8(%esp),%edx
        movl      4(%esp),%eax
        movb      %al, (%edx)
        xorl      %eax, %eax
        movl      %eax, PMD_ONFAULT(%ecx)
        ret
copyout_fault1:
        xorl      %eax, %eax
        movl      %eax, PMD_ONFAULT(%ecx)
        movb      $EFAULT, %al
        ret
    ...
```

The PTE associated with the address is examined to see if it is a valid protected page. In this case, a write fault is simulated using **trapwrite()**. If an error is present the fault routine is directly called to end this transfer. The arguments for the value of the address are received from the stack and the byte is modified in the user process. If the memory is not mapped as valid, a transparent page fault may occur.

After the modification has been made, the fault vector is cleared and a zero is returned, indicating success. If a fault had been induced either from one of the above explicit cases or from the the implicit case of a transparent fault, the fault mechanism will terminate the function and the return value of EFAULT will be passed back.

2.4.10 What is copyoutstr?

copyoutstr copies a null terminated string of characters (e.g. a filename) back to a user process. This function is only concerned with the 386—for the 486, an inline assembler version is used instead for speed. In addition, the inlined version does not need to reconcile the 386's lack of write protection from kernel mode.

Like **copyout** above, **copyoutstr** checks to see that the portion of user address space associated with the segment both exists and is writable before transferring the contents from kernel to user space. If it is not possible to do this operation, the function will return an error (EFAULT); otherwise, it returns zero to indicate no error occurred in performing the transfer.

While is implemented in assembler and does not have any function entry description, if this function were implemented in C it would appear of the form:

```
        int copyoutstr(struct proc *p, void *from, void *to, u_int size,
              u_int *lencopied);
```

copyoutstr has five arguments: the process pointer to which it is transferring the string; the address of the string in the kernel that is the source of the operation; the address in the user process receiving the string; the size of the portion of user memory in the process reserved for the string; and an argument to return optionally the

---

number of characters transferred. The side-effect of this function is to copy this string to the user process.

2.4.10.1 How is copyoutstr Implemented?

... [File: /usr/src/kernel/kern/i386/locore.s, line: 740]

```
ENTER(copyoutstr)
        movl    4(%esp), %eax           /* p */
        movl    $9f, PMD_ONFAULT(%eax)  /* in case we fault */
        pushl   %esi
        pushl   %edi
        pushl   %ebx
        movl    20(%esp), %esi          /* from */
        movl    24(%esp), %edi          /* to */
        movl    28(%esp), %ebx          /* size */

        cmpl    $_PTmap, %edi           /* out of user space */
        jae     9f

        movl    %edi, %eax
        addl    %ebx, %eax
        cmpl    $_PTmap, %eax
        jae     9f
...
```

Like **copyout**, the bounds of the buffer that will receive the string in the user process are checked to see that they fall within acceptable limits for the user process space, and the arguments are set into register variables appropriate for use with string instructions.

... [File: /usr/src/kernel/kern/i386/locore.s, line: 758]

```
1:      movl %edi, %eax
        shrl    $IDXSHIFT, %eax /* fetch pte associated with address */
        andb    $0xfc, %al
        movl    _PTmap(%eax), %eax

        andb    $7, %al         /* if we are the one case that won't trap... */
        cmpb    $5, %al
        jne     2f

        /* ... then simulate the trap! */
        pushl   %edi
        call    _trapwrite      /* trapwrite(addr) */
        testl   %eax, %eax
        popl    %eax
        jne     9f              /* if not ok, return */
...
```

Again like **copyout**, the operation is performed in terms of integral number of page table element segments so that each affected destination page table element may be checked to see if write protection fault may be present that won't trap. This is determined by checking the page table entry corresponding to the address to see if it is a valid but read-only entry. If so, then we simulate the trap by calling **trapwrite()** on the associated address. If the write fault did not succeed successfully, the routine is terminated with an error (EFAULT), since a portion of the memory was not effectively writable. If the fault was successful, the condition discovered is no longer present.

... [File: /usr/src/kernel/kern/i386/locore.s, line: 773]

```
2:      movl    %edi, %eax      /* calculate the remainder in this page */
        andl    $NBPG-1, %eax
        movl    $NBPG, %ecx
        subl    %eax, %ecx
        cmpl    %ecx, %ebx
        jg      3f
        movl    %ebx, %ecx
3:      subl    %ecx, %ebx

        cld                     /* process a dest. page fragement */
5:      cmpb    $0, (%esi)
        movsb
        loopne  5b
        lahf
        je      4f              /* null? normal termination. */

        cmpl    $0, %ebx        /* any remainder? */
        jne     1b
...
```

Next, the amount of memory within this destination page that we can process is calculated before another page table entry is checked for write protection. We then operate on this section of destination memory, filling it with a string from the kernel and checking to see if there is a null byte signalling the end of our transfer.

The null byte is transferred before the processing of this segment is complete. If we don't encounter a null, we check to see if any remainder string information needs to be transferred. If so, the associated page table entry is examined to make sure that the address space is writable.

... [File: /usr/src/kernel/kern/i386/locore.s, line: 792]

```
        sahf
        jne     7f      /* out of space */
...
```

An additional case must be tested here—that of determining if the destination string buffer ran out of space before we ran into the null byte signalling termination. This is the third terminating case of this routine.

... [File: /usr/src/kernel/kern/i386/locore.s, line: 795]

```
        /* found null, normal termination */
4:      xorl    %eax, %eax

        /* termination processing */
8:
        popl    %ebx
        popl    %edi
        popl    %esi
        movl    4(%esp), %edx            /* p */
```

```
        movl    $0, PMD_ONFAULT(%edx)

        /* termination count needs to be returned? */
        movl    20(%esp), %edx          /* lencopied */
        cmpl    $0, %edx
        je      1f
        subl    %ecx, 16(%esp)          /* size */
        movl    16(%esp), %ecx
        movl    %ecx, (%edx)
1:      ret
...
```

In the common case of performing a successful transfer of a null-terminated string, the return value of zero is passed back to signal success. The registers are restored and the fault vector is cleared.

If the termination count was requested, it is calculated as the residual of what wasn't processed versus what wasn't requested. Otherwise, nothing is returned for this termination count.

... [File: /usr/src/kernel/kern/i386/locore.s, line: 815]

```
7:      movl    $ENAMETOOLONG, %eax     /* ran out of space in user process */
        jmp     8b

9:      movl    $EFAULT, %eax           /* detected a fault, return error */
        jmp     8b
...
```

Two errors are possible during the processing of this routine. The first error is that we ran out of space in the user process destination buffer, in which case an ENAMETOLONG error is returned. The second error occurs if we detect a fault while transferring, and an EFAULT error is returned. This fault case may stem from either the discovery of a nonwritable portion of memory found during the mandatory examination of page table entries or from a fault that occurred during the string instruction's transfer when access was attempted to an invalid page.

2.4.11 What is swtch?

swtch is the explicit context switch mechanism, implemented as a coroutine call to the next schedulable process (or to **idle** until there is one). **swtch** is a coroutine call in that it saves the context of the current process and locates the next runable process, reloading that process's context in place of the previous one. This function has no arguments and returns nothing. Thus, the side-effect of **swtch** is to switch processes.

The caller to **swtch** will not return until the process is next runable. If the process is not allowed to be set runable, and **swtch** has been called, this routine will never return in that process. This is how a process termination occurs.

2.4.11.1 How is swtch Implemented?

... [File: /usr/src/kernel/kern/i386/locore.s, line: 832]

```
ENTRY(swtch)
ALTENTRY(final_swtch)
        PROC_ENTRY
        incl    _cnt+V_SWTCH

        /* mark as not in a process, remembering "old" process */
        xorl    %eax, %eax
        xchgl   %eax, _curproc
        pushl   %eax

        /* now find highest priority full process queue or idle */
        pushl   %ebx
        pushl   %esi
...
```

The context switch is accounted for in the statistics counter array (displayed by the **vmstat** utility) and the current process variable is marked as not active in a process (*curproc* is now set equal to zero). The contents of the current process are saved on the stack for use later. We also save an additional two registers for use in attempting to locate the next highest priority process.

... [File: /usr/src/kernel/kern/i386/locore.s, line: 851]

```
swtch_selq:
        bsfl    _whichqs, %eax   /* find a full queue */
        jz      Idle             /* if none, idle */

        btrl    %eax, _whichqs   /* clear queue full status */
        jnc     swtch_selq       /* if it was clear, look for another */
        cli                      /* interrupts off until after swtch() */
        movl    %eax, %ebx       /* save queue head index */
        shll    $3, %eax         /* select associated queue */
        addl    $_qs, %eax
        movl    %eax, %esi       /* save queue head pointer */
...
```

The status of all 32 run queues is checked to discover if any might already have a process in them (a bit in this variable indicates true if the queue has something in it). A bit scan instruction is used to find the highest priority queue among those set.

If the *whichqs* variable is not set at all, we branch to the **idle** routine where the processor does nothing while waiting for a runable process to become available. In this case, it reenters the process at the *swtch_selq* label.

If there is a queue, the full status of the queue is cleared since we may pull off the last entry. If it had been cleared earlier, a race condition is in progress—the process has just been pulled off the queue by another part of the system (like **schedcpu()**, see **Chapter 8** on **kern/synch.c**). In this case, we branch back to the *swtch_selq* label to look for another full queue.

Since we know for certain that the one that we just examined is now empty, we turn off interrupts so as to protect the run queue from competition with other interrupts (mainly the clock). We then locate the associated queue head with the queue bit we just cleared and save it in a register.

... [File: /usr/src/kernel/kern/i386/locore.s, line: 870]

```
        movl    P_LINK(%eax), %ecx
        movl    P_LINK(%ecx), %edx
        movl    %edx, P_LINK(%eax)
        movl    P_RLINK(%ecx), %eax
        movl    %eax, P_RLINK(%edx)
    ...
```

We proceed to unlink the first process attached to the queue head by removing it from the doubly linked list to which it is attached on the queue heads, so that the next consecutive process after this one that we are removing will be the first one on the queue head. Thus, processes are consumed from the run queue in a strictly FIFO fashion. If the run queue only contained one entry, the queue header will now point to itself, signalling it is now empty.

... [File: /usr/src/kernel/kern/i386/locore.s, line: 877]

```
        cmpl    P_LINK(%ecx), %esi
        je      1f
        btsl    %ebx, _whichqs

1:
        xorl    %eax, %eax
    ...
```

The forward pointer of the process that we just removed off the queue head is checked to see if it points back to the queue header or elsewhere. If it is pointed to the queue header, we know it was the only process on the queue and the queue must now be empty and consistent with the status accounted for in the *whichqs* status variable. Otherwise, we set the bit associated with the queue so that it still indicates the presence of other processes on the queue. The register is then cleared in order to isolate the process's remaining reverse link.

... [File: /usr/src/kernel/kern/i386/locore.s, line: 892]

```
        movl    %eax, P_RLINK(%ecx)      /* isolate process to run */

        /* recover state of previous register contents */
        popl    %esi
        popl    %ebx

        /* recover previous process pointer */
        popl    %eax
        PROC_EXIT

        /* if process is switching to itself then don't ljmp */
```

```
        cmpl    %ecx, %eax
        je      1f
...
```

As part of the steps in preparing this new process to run, the run link must be cleared and the state recovered from the two saved registers used to scan and select a new process. The original process pointer that we entered **swtch** on is also recovered and compared against the one that we are about to do a context switch to. If the two are the same, we don't bother doing the context switch.

... [File: /usr/src/kernel/kern/i386/locore.s, line: 906]

```
        ljmp    PMD_TSEL - 4(%ecx)

1:
        movl    %eax, _curproc          /* into next process */
        ret
...
```

The context switch is implemented as a "ljmp" jump to the tss (task switch state) at the beginning of the new process's kernel stack in the process control block. Since the descriptor address itself is composed of a six-byte quantity and the selector in the field of the process is of two-byte width, we offset the address to fetch the selector segment pair by four (the size of the ignored segment address) so that now the selector field to be activated will be fetched instead.

With this single instruction, the old context (all registers included) is atomically saved in the previous process's task switch state and the new context is loaded in its place from the new process. Because the state of the tss changes only after this operation completes, the same process context cannot be loaded and saved to itself. Thus, if the previous comparison had not been done, not only would **swtch** take more time but it would also fail because the "jump tss" instruction would detect the state of the wrong tss (e.g. one that was busy and active which we are attempting to load as inactive) and the kernel would panic. The "jump tss" instruction is not a quick instruction, as it loads and unloads 108 bytes of memory at a time; however, it is faster than the older code used in prior 386BSD releases.[27]

After performing the context switch, the EAX register contains the saved address from the previous call to **swtch** of the process. This is placed back into *curproc* to indicate we are running on that particular process. Finally, we return back from the coroutine call and pick up where we last left off in this process.

---

[27] We attempted to avoid using it earlier because of all of the unresolved contradictions that resulted (e.g., the process's kernel stack and task state were not in the kernel's address space, each process's stack was at the same virtual address space when active, threads could not be constituted out of processes in a nestable arrangement, and termination of processes could not recover address space when in the terminating context—see **i386/cpu.c** for details of the design change).

2.4.11.2 386BSD swtch Design Choices and Trade-Offs

It is mandatory that every call to **swtch** have a *splXX* call to reset the interrupt level priority which had been externally saved. Older versions of Berkeley UNIX also saved the context of the interrupt level priority. Versions of Berkeley UNIX after 4.3 Reno moved away from this because the machine-dependent characteristics and local optimization details varied greatly from machine to machine in this area. Thus, interrupts cannot be enabled and correctly initialized until the *splXX* call is done.

2.4.12 What is qswtch?

qswtch combines the functions of the inline **setrq** and **swtch** so that it remembers that this process asking for a context switch should be enqueued as well. **qswtch** inserts the current process on the run queue and atomically switches to another process. It will never idle and in the worse case will only switch back to itself.

qswtch is optimized for the case where there is only one process running that has been asked to reschedule itself. However, since there is nothing else to run, it has to "run" itself instead.

2.4.12.1 How is qswtch Implemented?

... [File: /usr/src/kernel/kern/i386/locore.s, line: 925]

```
ENTRY(qswtch)
        PROC_ENTRY
        incl    _cnt+V_SWTCH

        /* mark as not in a process, remembering "old" process */
        xorl    %eax, %eax
        xchgl   %eax, _curproc
        pushl   %eax

        pushl   %ebx
        pushl   %esi
        cli
    ...
```

Like **swtch**, **qswtch** accounts for a context switch and clears the current process (*curproc*) to indicate there is no running process at the moment. It saves the old process pointer on the stack and also saves two register variables that will be used for processing this request. Interrupts are turned off. This code is written to mimic **swtch** as much as possible so that the two can become more intimate.

... [File: /usr/src/kernel/kern/i386/locore.s, line: 944]

```
        andl    $~MDP_RESCHED, PMD_FLAGS(%eax)
        movzbl  P_PRI(%eax), %edx
        shrl    $2, %edx
        btsl    %edx, _whichqs          /* set q full bit */
        shll    $3, %edx
        addl    $_qs, %edx              /* locate q hdr */
        movl    %edx, P_LINK(%eax)      /* link process on tail of q */
        movl    P_RLINK(%edx), %ecx
```

```
        movl      %ecx, P_RLINK(%eax)
        movl      %eax, P_RLINK(%edx)
        movl      %eax, P_LINK(%ecx)
        jmp       swtch_selq
...
```

The rescheduling and signal flags of the machine-dependent process definition are cleared to indicate that there are no more outstanding reschedule requests for this process. Unlike earlier versions of Berkeley UNIX, rescheduling and signaling are now done relative to a thread/process context state.[28] This is necessary for both clustering and shared memory multiprocessors.

The priority of the current process is extracted and used to insert the process into the appropriate run queue with the queue status bit for that run queue set to indicate that it contains something (full). We don't need to check the status because we are placing a new entry. The process is linked onto the tail of the existing queue and the reverse links for the corresponding previous entry are set and appended to the end of the run queue.

A call is made to the switch select queue label for the switch selection process to begin. Since we have already ensured an entry, we know that there will be a process on the return journey. The whole point of going through this is to see if preemption is possible. Thus, **qswtch** can be used to handle preemption—possibly even for limited real-time purposes.

2.4.13 What is idle?

idle causes the processor to wait until there is a process available to be run. **idle** is called from the explicit context switch mechanism **swtch**. While the processor is still executing in a process context (even one that may be on a terminating process), **idle** hovers it until another process becomes runable.

2.4.13.1 How is idle Implemented?

... [File: /usr/src/kernel/kern/i386/locore.s, line: 968]

```
Idle:
        call      _splnone       /* idle with all interrupts unmasked */
        cmpl      $0, _whichqs    /* if any process ready on queue, */
        jne       swtch_selq     /*  reenter scheduler after saves. */
        cmpl      $0, _dma_active /* don't use hlt if DMA is active */
        jne       Idle
        hlt                       /* wait for interrupt */
        jmp       Idle
...
```

During the time the processor is idled, interrupts are unmasked by a call to **splnone** so that any interrupt activity can now take place. A check of the *whichqs* queue status variable is done to see if a process has become available that can be run. If so, the

---

[28] See *Threads versus Processes* in **Chapter 3** on **i386/cpu.c**.

swtch routine is returned (via *swtch_selq*) to to find the process which has just become available. Otherwise, the *"dma_active"* word is checked to see if any DMA channel activity is occurring.

On some laptops and power-saving versions of the PC, the DMA channels may require that the address buffers have power constantly applied to them. One of the power-saving features of many laptop and power-saving chipsets is that if the "hlt" (halt) instruction is executed, the machine enters a powerdown loop which removes power from the address buffers to save energy. As a result, the DMA requests fail since they can't gain access to the processor's bus. This failure may appear mysterious since it is not predictable just when we might hit the **idle** loop.

If there is no active DMA outstanding, the "hlt" instruction is issued to stop all activity on the processor, conserve energy, and wait until an interrupt comes in to reactivate the processor. If this is the case, then the **idle** loop is restarted.

2.5 What are Processor Exceptions?

Processor exceptions result from some condition in the processor that requires software intervention. Common examples of conditions which result in processor exceptions are improper "divide by zero" instructions or MMU address faults. These conditions usually occur synchronously with what the processor is running—meaning that the program immediately operating is the one that generated the fault.[29]

On the 386 architecture, the first 32 interrupt descriptor table entries are special descriptors (trap gates) that connect processor exceptions to the code that should be executed if the exception occurs. The interrupt descriptor table is an array of descriptors, each of which have a vector that points to a location in the kernel program where that exception will be fielded. Exceptions are not masked; thus, they are always active at anytime.

2.5.1 How are Processor Exceptions Implemented?

... [File: /usr/src/kernel/kern/i386/locore.s, line: 1002]

```
#define IDTVEC(name) .align 4; .globl _X/**/name; _X/**/name:
#define TRAP(a)  pushl $(a) ; jmp common_traps

IDTVEC(div)    pushl $0; TRAP(T_DIVIDE)
IDTVEC(dbg)    pushl $0; TRAP(T_TRCTRAP)
IDTVEC(nmi)    pushl $0; TRAP(T_NMI)
IDTVEC(bpt)    pushl $0; TRAP(T_BPTFLT)
```

---

[29] One important exception in the case of the 386 is that of the coprocessor exception. Since the coprocessor handling floating point exceptions runs asynchronously to the rest of the processor, it is better thought of as being a kind of peripheral device in many cases.

```
IDTVEC(ofl)      pushl $0; TRAP(T_OFLOW)
IDTVEC(bnd)      pushl $0; TRAP(T_BOUND)
IDTVEC(ill)      pushl $0; TRAP(T_PRIVINFLT)
IDTVEC(dna)      pushl $0; TRAP(T_DNA)
IDTVEC(dble)     TRAP(T_DOUBLEFLT)
IDTVEC(fpusegm)  pushl $0; TRAP(T_FPOPFLT)
IDTVEC(tss)      TRAP(T_TSSFLT)
IDTVEC(missing)  TRAP(T_SEGNPFLT)
IDTVEC(stk)      TRAP(T_STKFLT)
IDTVEC(prot)     TRAP(T_PROTFLT)
IDTVEC(page)     TRAP(T_PAGEFLT)
IDTVEC(rsvd)     pushl $0; TRAP(T_RESERVED)
IDTVEC(fpu)      pushl $0; TRAP(T_ARITHTRAP)
...
```

The trap vector table is an assembly of these code entry points. For the convenience of this discussion, they are grouped together as a table (but don't have to be). They are actually separate vectors hanging off of an array of descriptor table entries (see **init386()** in **i386/machdep.c** to see how they are initialized). In fact, they could be initialized individually over separate modules. However, since all of them are currently grouped together to a single trap handler, there is little advantage gained since they are treated in a like fashion.

Each vector is named by a macro that prepends a prefix to make the name relatively unique, as well as a symbolic name referring to the function to which it is coupled. Each entry in this table starts the build of a trap stack frame.[30] The trap stack frame begins at the end (it grows down) with an error code and an integer word tag denoting the type of trap that this corresponds to. Since not all of the traps have error codes, the ones missing error codes push a dummy error code of zero onto the stack so that the frame will be consistently built for all of the entries.

After making the unique portion of the stack frame, each entry jumps to the common trap processing code. The first sixteen entries refer to common processor faults. The arrangement of these faults is historical—the original 8086 processor only had the first seven of these implemented, the 80286 had still more, and so on.

... [File: /usr/src/kernel/kern/i386/locore.s, line: 1023]

```
IDTVEC(rsvd0)    pushl $0; TRAP(17)
IDTVEC(rsvd1)    pushl $0; TRAP(18)
IDTVEC(rsvd2)    pushl $0; TRAP(19)
IDTVEC(rsvd3)    pushl $0; TRAP(20)
IDTVEC(rsvd4)    pushl $0; TRAP(21)
IDTVEC(rsvd5)    pushl $0; TRAP(22)
IDTVEC(rsvd6)    pushl $0; TRAP(23)
IDTVEC(rsvd7)    pushl $0; TRAP(24)
IDTVEC(rsvd8)    pushl $0; TRAP(25)
IDTVEC(rsvd9)    pushl $0; TRAP(26)
IDTVEC(rsvd10)   pushl $0; TRAP(27)
IDTVEC(rsvd11)   pushl $0; TRAP(28)
IDTVEC(rsvd12)   pushl $0; TRAP(29)
```

[30] See the include file **i386/frame.h**, struct trapframe.

```
IDTVEC(rsvd13)   pushl $0; TRAP(30)
IDTVEC(rsvd14)   pushl $0; TRAP(31)
...
```

The second sixteen exceptions are reserved for future processors. Interestingly, many of these exceptions also correspond to vector entries for valid INT instructions used by DOS. An INT instruction (short for software interrupt) was the original system call instruction used on the 8086 and is heavily used by DOS. It simulates an exception in one of the 255 possible exceptions in the IDT table.

The only way to tell the difference between a processor exception and an INT instruction is to mark the IDT descriptor as not being accessible from the user process at Ring 3. In this way, an attempt to reference an INT instruction will generate a general protection violation, whereby the software will check to see what caused the exception and find that one of the IDT entries is responsible for the associated interrupt instruction (in **trap.c**—currently not implemented).

... [File: /usr/src/kernel/kern/i386/locore.s, line: 1040]

```
common_traps:
        pushal
        nop
        push    %ds
        push    %es
        movw    $KDSEL, %ax
        movw    %ax,%ds
        movw    %ax,%es

        incl    _cnt+V_TRAP
        call    _trap
        movl    _cpl, %ecx
        jmp     trap_exit
...
```

Each trap executes the common code for all the traps after tagging the stack frame as mentioned. At this point, the code selector and stack selector are known to refer to the kernel program; however, the data selector could either be referring to the kernel (if the exception occurred from within the kernel) or from the current running user process. The register state is pushed immediately onto the stack to free up the use of the registers for the kernel, saving the previous values for reuse when the trap processing has been completed.[31]

Since the kernel will make use of the ES and DS segment selectors, these will be pushed onto the stack and reloaded with the kernel data selector. The data selector is used by all instructions to refer to where to fetch data from, while the ES or extra selector refers to string instruction destinations. (These are the same in 386BSD.)

---

[31]A flaw with some versions of the 386 is that the contents of the stack can sometimes be corrupted if an instruction modified memory immediately after the **pushal** instruction. A **nop** follows the **pushal** in this case to correct this situation.

From this point on, data references can be made by the kernel to variables, so the trap counter statistic is incremented and the rest of the trap processing is done off of this freshly created trap frame by the higher level trap handler **trap()** (see **Chapter 3, i386/trap.c**). Even though this code is very machine dependent, the remainder of the processor exception handling for the kernel is done in a mostly machine-independent manner as most trap handlers in UNIX systems look very similar.

After returning from the trap handler, the current priority level for interrupts is loaded in the ECX register and the trap exit is made by jumping to the common code shared with interrupt processing. While it is known that interrupts are not masked during trap calls from user processes, traps actually can occur from interrupt level in 386BSD, such as during the initial fault on demand allocation of a buffer.

2.5.2 386BSD Processor Exception Design Choices and Trade-Offs

To minimize redundant code, traps and interrupts share the same code on processing because traps and certain kinds of software interrupt simulations for network packet traffic are rather closely intertwined. Since traps and system calls are *value/result* functions, they behave differently than ordinary C function calls. In an ordinary C function call, any modification made to an argument will not be seen by its caller because the portion of stack used to store the argument will not be used again. The semantics of C is call by value.

However, with system calls and traps, the processor state is reloaded from the arguments passed to the **trap()** and **syscall()** system call handlers. Thus, any modifications that the handlers make to the registers stored on the stack will be made to the registers to which they correspond. This is, for example, how an exception would be bypassed if this was part of that particular machine architecture's method of restarting.[32]

2.6 What are Peripheral Device Interrupts?

Device interrupts are similar to processor exceptions, in that an external condition occurs while a program was running, causing a special exception to be generated. In this case, however, a peripheral device caused the exception to be signalled based on completion of some operation totally unrelated to whatever process was running on the computer at the time. Thus, peripheral device interrupts occur asynchronous to the processor.

Since many peripheral device interrupts may be handled at various priorities and levels, the mechanism which processes these interrupts at any given point in time

---

[32] Some older machines would deal with floating point exceptions by forcing the software in the trap entry to actually move the program counter past the offending instruction.

itself requires an interface. Processor exceptions and system calls, on the other hand, require only the most minimal interface to the largely machine-independent handlers to which they belong.

Interrupts in the X86 family make use of an external peripheral device that organizes interrupts. This device, which actually emulates or is an Intel 8259 Priority Interrupt Control Unit (ICU), is accessed via I/O instructions. Some older 386 and 486 systems use devices which require a certain amount of "recovery time" between successive I/O operations. In these cases, a sequence of instructions in a macro is used to provide this recovery time.

One oddity of this I/O port control device is that some processor bus chipsets buffer writes to improve performance—that is, they hold the contents of the last write to memory and/or output operation until an appropriate idle time develops on the processor's bus. This permits the bus to operate more efficiently, since the processor does not stall waiting for the slow write operation to complete. However, this also means that the writes don't always occur when they absolutely must. As such, it is imperative that the masks are received by the ICU before interrupts are reenabled; otherwise, the interrupts recurse, the kernel stack overflows, and the processor shuts down and resets.

There are two kinds of interrupt vector tables used in 386BSD. One table is a stray interrupt catcher table containing entries that catch and extract the values of the ICU, Interrupt In-Service Register (ISR), and Interrupt Request Register (IRR). The other table is an interrupt vector table used to dispatch the interrupt to an associated function. The interrupt vector table connects device interrupts with the particular device driver that makes use of that interrupt, while the stray table of entries corresponds to interrupts that should not ever be received (corresponding to a nonexistent device).

Two ICUs are present on a standard ISA bus machine to receive these interrupts. Each ICU has eight interrupts present on it. The primary (or first) ICU has one of its interrupts dedicated to cascading the second ICU—thus, the interrupts from the first unit need only interact with that unit, while interrupts from the second unit must interact with both the primary unit that holds the cascade interrupt and the second ICU that the interrupt arrived on.

2.6.1 How are Peripheral Device Interrupts Implemented?

... [File: /usr/src/kernel/kern/i386/locore.s, line: 1074]

```
/*
 * If this is an old 386 that requires recovery time on the 8259,
 * add nops via a -DNOP="inb $0x84, %al". New processors don't
 * require NOP's, thus NOP is a null macro by default.
 */
```

```
/* Processor/Bus chip set has write buffers to be forced out. */
#define WRPOST inb $0x84, %al
    ...
```

I/O instructions are used to organize the interrupts. For older 386 and 486 systems, the **NOP** macro is used to provide the recovery time required for operation. Early 8088 processors needed only one "nop" instruction. This was optimized out by newer 386 processors, so a jump to a successive address is used to force the processor to flush its prefetch queue[33], thus allowing enough recovery time for the ICU. On 486 and newer machines, the branch is optimized out by the processor. Since these machines have caches, the delay is thus masked.[34]

If the chipset buffers writes, these writes are forced out with an input operation. An input operation on an unused port is used as the write posting operation because it will not alter any registers that would otherwise lose information by reading them, yet it has the side-effect of forcing write-posted chipsets to write their buffers out for no other reason than the fact that the buffers must be written in order to obtain the correct value on a read (e.g. it has to hit the device). This way, we don't need specifically to probe for a certain kind of chipset or implement a mechanism for each to achieve the posting (this is not a configuration-dependent item).

... [File: /usr/src/kernel/kern/i386/locore.s, line: 1083]

```
#define INTRSTRAY1(unit, mask, offst) \
        pushl   $0 ; \
        pushl   $T_ASTFLT ; \
        pushal  ; \
        NOP     ;                       /* wait for 8259 recovery */ \
        movb    $3, %al ;               /* select ISR ... */ \
        outb    %al, $IO_ICU1 ;         /* in 8259 unit 1 ...*/ \
        NOP     ;                       /* wait for 8259 recovery */ \
        inb     $IO_ICU1, %al ;         /* grab ISR */ \
        movb    %al, %dl ;              /* save ISR */ \
        NOP     ;                       /* ... ASAP */ \
        movb    $2, %al ;               /* reselect IRR ... */ \
        outb    %al, $IO_ICU1 ;         /* ... ...*/ \
        NOP     ;                       /* ... ASAP */ \
        movb    $(0x60 | unit), %al ;   /* next, as soon as can send EOI */ \
        outb    %al, $IO_ICU1 ;         /* ... so in service bit may be cleared ...*/ \
        pushl   %ds ;                   /* save our data and extra segments ... */ \
        pushl   %es ; \
        movw    $KDSEL, %ax ;           /* ... and reload with kernel's own */ \
        movw    %ax, %ds ; \
        movw    %ax, %es ; \
        movl    _cpl, %eax ; \
        pushl   %eax ; \
        shll    $8, %edx ; \
        movb    $unit, %dl ; \
        pushl   %edx ; \
```

---

[33] E.g. "jmp 1f ; 1: ".
[34] One alternative is to use an input from a known nonexistent port different from that of the ICU to force a period of recovery time.

```
orw       mask, %ax ; \
movl      %eax,_cpl ; \
orw       _imen, %ax ; \
outb      %al, $IO_ICU1+1 ; \
movb      %ah, %al ; \
outb      %al, $IO_ICU2+1 ; \
WRPOST    ;                    /* do write post */ \
sti       ; \
call      _isa_strayintr ; \
jmp       common_int_return
...
```

Both the primary and secondary ICU use separate macros for interrupt entry processing. The **INTSTRAY** macro for unit one processes a stray interrupt associated with the first ICU. It records a dummy error code and trap type (since interrupt stack frames are a special case of trap interrupt frames) and completes the content of the trap frame by saving all of the registers. It then issues a NOP (dealing with any potential recovery time required for the ICU to become ready), since the ICU has already been referenced by the processor to have arrived at the vector with which this stray macro is associated.

The ICU is sent a command to request that the ISR be made available on output, and is read bracketed with NOP's to allow recovery time for the chip. The ISR contains the bits corresponding to each of the interrupt vectors that have presented a request and sampled them at the time that the processor honored the interrupt. In some cases, an interrupt pulse will be so brief as to be lost by the processor before the vector dispatch is done; thus, the "in-service" bit will not be set and it will instead be assigned to the lowest priority (highest numbered) interrupt for this unit (e.g. IRQ 7, for the primary ICU). The whole purpose of the **INTSTRAY** macro is to capture this information, so that it may be determined by higher level routines whether or not this interrupt was meant for another interrupt vector on this unit.

The interrupt request register is then reselected as the default value for when the ICU's port is read. In this way, the interrupt request lines can be monitored for active interrupt activity at any time—even for interrupts that are not masked.[35]

The end of interrupt acknowledgement is sent to the ICU so that the "in-service" register bit associated with the interrupt can be cleared and the interrupt thus reissued. The data and extra selectors are saved and the kernel data selector loaded into both, so that data references and string references may be done by interrupt level code.

The current interrupt priority level mask is stored on the stack and the contents of the "in-service" register, along with the interrupt vector number, is incorporated into another word stored as an argument to the stray interrupt handler. The current interrupt mask (*cpl*) is updated with the contents of the current mask for this interrupt

---

[35] This feature is not yet thoroughly implemented in the system.

and assigned to both ICUs to ensure that the interrupt will not recurse (by masking it) during the period of the interrupt handler's operation, and a write posting is done to ensure that the masks are updated prior to reenabling interrupts. Interrupts are thus allowed to be nested—higher priority interrupts that are unmasked may take precedence over the current interrupt processing handled outside of these macros by higher level code.

Obviously, since the interrupts can mask themselves, no more than a level of 16 interrupts is allowed to be nested. Since the average PC has eight or fewer devices, this level of nesting is considered adequate for most purposes.

After reenabling interrupts and this macro concluding, the stray interrupt handler[36] is called with a jump to the common interrupt return code that will take the processor out of kernel mode and return it back to where it came from before the interrupt occurred.

... [File: /usr/src/kernel/kern/i386/locore.s, line: 1079]

```
#define INTRSTRAY2(unit, mask, offst) \
        pushl   $0 ; \
        pushl   $T_ASTFLT ; \
        pushal  ; \
        NOP     ;               /* wait for 8259 recovery */ \
        movb    $3, %al ;       /* select ISR ... */ \
        outb    %al, $IO_ICU2 ; /* in 8259 unit 2 ...*/ \
        NOP     ;               /* wait for 8259 recovery */ \
        inb     $IO_ICU2, %al ; /* grab ISR */ \
        xorb    %dl, %dl ;   \
        movb    %al, %dh ;      /* save ISR */ \
        NOP     ;               /* ... ASAP */ \
        movb    $2, %al ;       /* reselect IRR ... */ \
        outb    %al, $IO_ICU2 ; /* ... ...*/ \
        movb    $0x62, %al ;    /* next, as soon as possible send EOI ... */ \
        outb    %al, $IO_ICU1 ; /* ... so in service bit may be cleared ...*/ \
        movb    $(0x60|(unit-8)), %al ; /* next, as soon as can send EOI... */ \
        outb    %al, $IO_ICU1 ; /* ... so in service bit may be cleared ...*/ \
        outb    %al, $IO_ICU2 ; /* ... ...*/ \
        pushl   %ds ;           /* save our data and extra segments ... */ \
        pushl   %es ; \
        movw    $KDSEL, %ax ;   /* ... and reload with kernel's own */ \
        movw    %ax, %ds ; \
        movw    %ax, %es ; \
        movl    _cpl, %eax ; \
        pushl   %eax ; \
        shll    $8, %edx ; \
        movb    $unit, %dl ; \
        pushl   %edx ; \
        orw     mask, %ax ; \
        movl    %eax,_cpl ; \
        orw     _imen, %ax ; \
        outb    %al, $IO_ICU1+1 ; \
        movb    %ah, %al ; \
```

[36] Written in C—see **isa.c**, a bus device driver.

```
outb    %al, $IO_ICU2+1 ; \
WRPOST  ;                       /* do write post */ \
sti     ; \
call    _isa_strayintr ; \
jmp     common_int_return
```
...

The **INTSTRAY2** macro functions identically to the proceeding macro, except that this macro refers to the second ICU, and the ISR for the second ICU is obtained. For consistency, the bits associated with the ISR from the second ICU is kept in the higher 8-bits of this 16-bit field associated with the "in-service" registers passed to the **INTSTRAY2** routine.

Another difference between this macro and the previous one is that the end of interrupt acknowledge is sent to both ICUs—the primary ICU so that the cascaded interrupt can be reset and the second ICU so that it can clear its "in-service" bit.

... [File: /usr/src/kernel/kern/i386/locore.s, line: 1168]

```
IDTVEC(intr0)   INTRSTRAY1(0, _highmask, 0)
IDTVEC(intr1)   INTRSTRAY1(1, _highmask, 1)
IDTVEC(intr2)   INTRSTRAY1(2, _highmask, 2)
IDTVEC(intr3)   INTRSTRAY1(3, _highmask, 3)
IDTVEC(intr4)   INTRSTRAY1(4, _highmask, 4)
IDTVEC(intr5)   INTRSTRAY1(5, _highmask, 5)
IDTVEC(intr6)   INTRSTRAY1(6, _highmask, 6)
IDTVEC(intr7)   INTRSTRAY1(7, _highmask, 7)
IDTVEC(intr8)   INTRSTRAY2(8, _highmask, 8)
IDTVEC(intr9)   INTRSTRAY2(9, _highmask, 9)
IDTVEC(intr10)  INTRSTRAY2(10, _highmask, 10)
IDTVEC(intr11)  INTRSTRAY2(11, _highmask, 11)
IDTVEC(intr12)  INTRSTRAY2(12, _highmask, 12)
IDTVEC(intr13)  INTRSTRAY2(13, _highmask, 13)
IDTVEC(intr14)  INTRSTRAY2(14, _highmask, 14)
IDTVEC(intr15)  INTRSTRAY2(15, _highmask, 15)
/* all interrupts after first 16 */
IDTVEC(intrdefault)     INTRSTRAY2(255, _highmask, 255)
```
...

The stray interrupt catcher table is comprised of entries for each of the possible device interrupts, coupled with an appropriate **INTSTRAY** macro to generate the code to process that stray interrupt. These vector entries handle an incoming interrupt if it is not assigned to a device driver and is thus left dangling. It processes, records, and clears these interrupts.

If an interrupt not pointing to a device driver was left uninitialized, it would cause a random execution or fault. If the interrupt descriptor table entry for an interrupt is left uninitialized, that interrupt would cause a general protection violation in the kernel (usually signalled by a panic). Normally, interrupts not used by device drivers are masked anyway. However, even masked interrupts can cause interrupts, as in the case of a lost interrupt. The lowest priority interrupt in the interrupt controller (IRQ 7 or IRQ 15) receives this interrupt, which will be honored even though it is masked. The primary reason for this table is to catch these interrupts.

Finally, while there are only two ICUs, implying that we should only receive interrupts and exceptions on the first 48 interrupt descriptor table entries, the interrupt descriptor table itself may be as large as 256 entries. Certain chip bugs and steppings of older 386's and some clones may actually generate spurious stray interrupts for the topmost interrupt or any above this point. To deal with this case, a generic vector is set that covers this range and initializes all of the remaining interrupt descriptor table entries, forestalling any unforeseen panics caused by a spurious interrupt launched by these sources.[37]

... [File: /usr/src/kernel/kern/i386/locore.s, line: 1194]

```
#define INTR1(offst) \
        pushl   $0; \
        pushl   $T_ASTFLT; \
        pushal; \
        NOP     ; \
        movb    $(0x60|offst), %al;     /* next, as soon as can send EOI... */ \
        outb    %al, $IO_ICU1;          /* so in service bit is cleared...*/ \
        pushl   %ds;                    /* save data and extra segments ... */ \
        pushl   %es; \
        movw    $0x10, %ax;             /* ... and reload with kernel's own */ \
        movw    %ax, %ds; \
        movw    %ax, %es; \
        incl    _cnt+V_INTR;            /* tally interrupts */ \
        incl    _intrcnt+offst*4; \
        movl    _cpl, %eax; \
        pushl   %eax; \
        pushl   _isa_unit+offst*4; \
        orw     _isa_mask+offst*2, %ax; \
        movl    %eax, _cpl; \
        orw     _imen, %ax; \
        NOP     ; \
        outb    %al, $IO_ICU1+1; \
        movb    %ah, %al; \
        outb    %al, $IO_ICU2+1; \
        WRPOST  ;                       /* do write post */ \
        sti; \
        call    *(_isa_vec+(offst*4)); \
        jmp     common_int_return
...
```

Alongside of the stray interrupt vector table lies the interrupt vector table. It is made up of macro entries for the primary and secondary ICUs. These entries do not bother to save the status of the "in-service" register, but instead build their trap frame, acknowledge the interrupt, and tally the statistics of this interrupt against both a global counter and a per-interrupt counter.

---

[37] This type of stray interrupt occurred approximately once a day on the old 386 machine (a "Sigma-Sigma" chip) to which 386BSD was originally ported—see *Creating a Software Specification*, **Dr. Dobbs Journal** (January 1991) and *386BSD: A Modest Proposal* on the **386BSD Reference CD-ROM**.

From a table associated with this interrupt entry, the device unit and interrupt mask are obtained. The device unit is the argument to be passed to the device driver interrupt handler, and the mask corresponds to all of the set of interrupts which must be masked if this interrupt is present. Since some of the interrupts share resources, they may be masked at the same time that this particular device interrupt is masked. Thus, before the interrupt handler is entered, the new interrupt mask is added to the existing interrupt mask and both ICUs are updated, since the mask may contain entries which affect both.

After updating the mask in both ICU's, the write post is done to ensure that the mask made it to the ICUs before reenabling interrupts. The device driver interrupt handler for this interrupt vector is called by indirecting through a vector of functions to find the appropriate address of the one to execute.

The association between the interrupt vector and its device driver handler is made by the bus driver when it attaches the device driver into the system—thus, it is done dynamically to allow device drivers to be loaded or unloaded independent of when the kernel is loaded. After the device driver interrupt handler has concluded, the common interrupt code is called to turn the processor back to user mode.

... [File: /usr/src/kernel/kern/i386/locore.s, line: 1224]

```
#define INTR2(offst) \
        pushl   $0; \
        pushl   $T_ASTFLT; \
        pushal; \
        NOP     ; \
        movb    $0x62, %al;    /* next, as soon as possible send EOI ... */ \
        outb    %al, $IO_ICU1; /* ... so in service bit may be cleared ...*/ \
        movb    $(0x60|(offst-8)), %al; /* next, as soon as can send EOI... */ \
        outb    %al, $IO_ICU1; /* ... so in service bit may be cleared ...*/ \
        outb    %al, $IO_ICU2; \
        pushl   %ds;           /* save our data and extra segments ... */ \
        pushl   %es; \
        movw    $0x10, %ax;    /* ... and reload with kernel's own */ \
        movw    %ax, %ds; \
        movw    %ax, %es; \
        incl    _cnt+V_INTR;   /* tally interrupts */ \
        incl    _intrcnt+offst*4; \
        movl    _cpl,%eax; \
        push    %eax; \
        pushl   _isa_unit+offst*4; \
        orw     _isa_mask+offst*2, %ax; \
        movl    %ax, _cpl; \
        orw     _imen, %ax; \
        outb    %al, $IO_ICU1+1; \
        movb    %ah, %al; \
        outb    %al, $IO_ICU2+1; \
        WRPOST  ;               /* do write post */ \
        sti; \
        call    *(_isa_vec+offst*4); \
        jmp     common_int_return
...
```

The interrupt handler for the second ICU is almost identical to the interrupt vector macro discussed above and processes the interrupt in the same fashion. However, it acknowledges the interrupt on both ICUs instead of just the first ICU, so that the cascaded controller is reset as well.

... [File: /usr/src/kernel/kern/i386/locore.s, line: 1258]

```
IDTVEC(irq0)     INTR1(0)
IDTVEC(irq1)     INTR1(1)
IDTVEC(irq2)     INTR1(2)
IDTVEC(irq3)     INTR1(3)
IDTVEC(irq4)     INTR1(4)
IDTVEC(irq5)     INTR1(5)
IDTVEC(irq6)     INTR1(6)
IDTVEC(irq7)     INTR1(7)
IDTVEC(irq8)     INTR2(8)
IDTVEC(irq9)     INTR2(9)
IDTVEC(irq10)    INTR2(10)
IDTVEC(irq11)    INTR2(11)
IDTVEC(irq12)    INTR2(12)
IDTVEC(irq13)    INTR2(13)
IDTVEC(irq14)    INTR2(14)
IDTVEC(irq15)    INTR2(15)
```
...

The interrupt vector table contains the entry points for the interrupt vector associated with the particular hardware interrupt. Like the stray interrupt table, there is a vector entry for every possible hardware interrupt. Also like the vector table, the cascade interrupt IRQ2 is redundantly mentioned, since the actual hardware interrupt arrives on the second interrupt controller as IRQ9. No interrupt should ever make it to IRQ2, nor should an interrupt ever arrive at the associated stray interrupt counter. The stray interrupt counter is left attached in this way just in case the ICU should glitch and generate an IRQ or be configured in such a way as to generate an impossible interrupt.

... [File: /usr/src/kernel/kern/i386/locore.s, line: 1330]

```
common_int_return:
        /* turn interrupt frame into a trap frame */
        popl    %eax            /* remove intr number */
        popl    %eax            /* get previous priority */

        /* return to previous priority level */
        movl    %eax, %ecx
        cli
        movl    %eax, _cpl
        orw     _imen, %ax
        outb    %al, $IO_ICU1+1 /* re-enable intr? */
        NOP
        movb    %ah, %al
        outb    %al, $IO_ICU2+1
        WRPOST;                 /* write post before restoring interrupts */
```
...

The common interrupt return code handles all interrupt processing, effectively stripping away the part of the stack frame that makes it an interrupt stack frame. It

---

removes the device driver interrupt handler's unit argument, extracts the previous priority level mask from the stack, and sets about returning the interrupt mask back to what it was before the interrupt came in.

The interrupt mask is taken and combined with the mask enable word *imem* of interrupts. This word contains a bit for each interrupt. If an interrupt is enabled, its corresponding bit is of value zero. If disabled, the bit is set to one. Thus, the current priority level only has bits set within it for actively masked interrupts, and the interrupt mask enable variable holds the set of inactive interrupts (which are always masked).

The newly constructed mask is set into the ICUs, the writes are posted, and the interrupts are reenabled so that nested interrupts may arrive. At this point, we are back at the previous interrupt level, even though we are still within the interrupt service routine. Technically, an interrupt could nest from the current level at this point. Thus a portion of the kernel's stack is taken up in storing this interrupt. The remainder of the processing required to escape back from this interrupt is handled the same way as trap processing, so the two are combined.

... [File: /usr/src/kernel/kern/i386/locore.s, line: 1346]

```
trap_exit:
        testl   %ecx, %ecx        /* returning to zero? */
        je      9f
        /* returning to greater than basepri */
trap_return:
        pop     %es               /* returning to previous context */
        pop     %ds
        popal
        nop
        addl    $8, %esp
        .globl  _iret
_iret:
        iret
...
```

If the level we are returning to is the zero priority interrupt level, then some additional checking must be done before we can return from either this trap or interrupt. Otherwise, if we are returning to a nested interrupt or a situation in the kernel where interrupts are masked, no further processing needs to be done.

The return from the trap or interrupt proceeds by recovering the state of the extra segment in the data selector and returning all of the registers back to the contents that were saved on entry to the trap or interrupt. The two words associated with the trap and error code are then removed on the very top portion of the stack frame and an interrupt return is issued. The interrupt return instruction itself has a label attached to it so that the trap handling mechanism can gain access to it and use it for special handling of invalid CS register faults (see **Chapter 3**, **trap()** in **i386/trap.c** for further information).

... [File: /usr/src/kernel/kern/i386/locore.s, line: 1361]

```
9:
        movl    $0, _cpl         /* force back to ipl 0 */

        /* first, see if we can look for asts ... */
#define SEL_UPL 3                /* XXX */
        movw    13*4(%esp), %ax
        andw    $3, $ax
        cmpw    $SEL_UPL, %ax
        jne     1f               /* nope, ignore checking for asts */
        movl    _curproc, %edx   /* have we a process? */
        testl   %edx, %edx
        je      1f
        btrl    $0, PMD_FLAGS(%edx)
        jc      4f

1:
        /* then network software interrupts */
        xorl    %ebx, %ebx
        xchgl   %ebx, _netisr
        testl   %ebx, %ebx
        jne     2f

        /* next, look for softclocks. */
        xorl    %eax, %eax
        xchgl   %eax, _sclkpending
        testl   %eax, %eax
        jne     3f
        jmp     trap_return      /* return at base pri */
    ...
```

In the case where we are returning back to a non-interrupt state of the processor, we check to see if we are returning back to a user process by determining if the code selector is the user's code selector. If so, then we need to check to see if there are any outstanding signals present by examining the current process's (*curproc*) machine-dependent flags. We then check to see whether or not a network software interrupt (*netisr*) is present. If so, then we process this separately as well. Finally, if there is a software clock request (*sclkpending*), we process that as one of our entries. Note that the contents of the network software interrupts and software clock requests are captured with a bus interlock instruction which exchanges the contents of the variable with a register uninterruptably so that this thread of execution can sample any outstanding software clocks or network interrupts to be processed on this thread alone. Subsequent interrupts or softclocks will be sampled by other threads. All of these interrupts must be processed prior to returning to the system at a base level of priority. These three cases are covered separately.

... [File: /usr/src/kernel/kern/i386/locore.s, line: 1390]

```
2:
        movl    $IRNET|IRSCLK, _cpl     /* mask net and softclock */
        sti

#define DONET(isr, tmp) ; \
1: \
```

```
        bsfl    isr , tmp ;              /* find a software interrupt */ \
        jz      1f ; \

        btrl    tmp , isr ;   \
        jnc     1f ; \
        incl    _cnt+V_SOFT ; \
        call    *_netintr(, tmp ,4) ; \
        testl   isr , isr ; \
        jne     1b ; \
1:
        DONET(%ebx, %eax)
        jmp     9b
    ...
```

The **DONET** macro checks for the presence of bits in the software interrupt service register corresponding to a given network interrupt service routine. If present, it increments the appropriate accounting counter for software interrupts and calls the protocol processing network interrupt handler so that it may service the next packet that has been enqueued. The software interrupt levels associated with the clock and network are masked so that subsequent nested interrupts will not process these software interrupts but instead be processed by this particular instantiation of the interrupt code.

The **DONET** macro successively checks all outstanding service requests for protocols which may have a bit set in the network software interrupt register (sampled in the previous code fragment). Only one of these is currently implemented in the system— that associated with IP packets. After processing the network software interrupt, the mask is cleared for software interrupts, and the processing for network software interrupts is completed.

Network software interrupts are triggered on arrival of a packet which is enqueued by a network packet driver. When the interrupt returns and eventually attempts to return to zero priority level, the software interrupt is checked and the protocol processing done. No blocking of the arrival of another packet is done. Thus, it allows the nesting of successive packet interrupts without blocking interrupts off and possibly losing them—this is the whole point of network software interrupts.

... [File: /usr/src/kernel/kern/i386/locore.s, line: 1409]

```
3:
        /* simulate a hardware interrupt for softclock() */
        movl    $IRSCLK, _cpl            /* mask softclock */
        sti
        incl    _cnt+V_SOFT

        pushl   13*4(%esp)               /* cs */
        pushl   13*4(%esp)               /* eip */
        pushl   $0                       /* basepri */
        call    _softclock               /* softclock(clockframe); */
        addl    $12, %esp
        jmp     9b
4:
        /* have an AST to deliver */
```

```
        sti
        incl    _cnt+V_TRAP
        movl    $T_ASTFLT, 10*4(%esp)
        call    _trap                      /* trap(struct trapframe); */
        jmp     9b
...
```

Like network software interrupts, a separate software interrupt simulates a hardware interrupt to the soft clock function in the kernel. This is a special, dedicated device driver that accepts an interrupt from the soft clock interrupt control processing mechanism when scheduled by the hardware interrupt processing mechanism to keep the overhead low on clock interrupts.[38]

The hardware clock interrupt itself does only the minimum amount of work necessary, postponing events like rescheduling so that they may be performed away from interrupt level. This postponement schedules the software clock interrupts when there is additional work to be done that can be processed away from interrupt level, such as rescheduling and timeout processing. In this case, before the interrupt returns to a zero priority level, it checks for the presence of a soft clock interrupt.

If the soft clock interrupt is present, it simulates a hardware interrupt directed at the soft clock function. A minimal clock frame is constructed corresponding to the code selector, program counter, or instruction pointer, and the interrupt level priority (in this case zero) of where the processor will be returning to. This frame is then used to call the soft clock routine to process the necessary requested event by the hardware clock routine.

Both soft clock as well as network software interrupts are software simulations of hardware mechanisms used to downgrade the priority of software processing to a level between the hardware levels and no interrupt at all. A stack record is present prior to return in the preceding interrupt level which contains the total overhead required to register such a mechanism for interrupt processing.

Finally, if a signal or rescheduling of this process has been requested, a trap is simulated for the delivery of an asynchronous system trap (AST) to the current process by calling the trap handler. If necessary, this will instigate a check for an outstanding signal to be delivered to the process or for the process to be exchanged with yet another one. In the case where a user has interrupted the processing (say, by typing CNTL-Z), the terminal driver will request the signal be sent to the process and arrange for an AST to be sent to the process.

As in the case of the network software interrupt, upon return from the interrupt as we travel back to the user process, this AST request will be honored by a call to trap which will instantiate the signal in the user process. When the user process is

---

[38] This is really appropriate only on large timesharing or systems, where it soaks up a measurable amount.

reentered immediately after the interrupt, it will reenter its signal handler to process the interrupt signal. Thus, the time delay between the hardware arrival of the character which results in the signal and the actual processing of the signal by the user program will be as short as is possible for this architecture. This is a major consideration for the design of this level of interrupt handling.

2.7 What are Set Processor Level Functions?

The interrupt priority control mechanism uses the set processor level (*splXX*) functions to adjust the priority interrupt controllers so that interrupts of a certain class may come in at varied times. It thus acts as a filter for a desired set of interrupts. The name "spl" is historically derived—it comes from a PDP-11/45 instruction that would set the interrupt priority level for the processor to mask all interrupts below a certain priority level.

On the PDP-11 that ran the original UNIX system from Bell Labs, the interrupts were jumpered on peripheral boards to respond to a certain priority and supply a particular interrupt vector when they interrupted the processor. Four priority levels were implemented out of eight possible (in the range 0-7, where 7 indicated no interrupts allowed and 0 indicated that any priority level interrupt was allowed). All terminal devices resided at one priority level while all disk or network devices resided at different priority levels. By adjusting the priority level, one could guarantee that a certain class of devices would be kept from interrupting.

Since all of the disks would share buffer storage (and thus compete for it on an equal basis), and since terminal devices would use a common pool of character buffers (c-lists) to keep access to the shared resources from contending with the multiple devices present, the original UNIX system would temporarily set the interrupt level above that which would allow an interrupt to come in during the time that the shared structure was being modified. This was done in lieu of a more elaborate locking mechanism which would take up many more instructions on a PDP-11.

This archaic mechanism was continued through all Berkeley and commercial UNIX systems. More modern systems like Solaris don't use this mechanism; instead, they isolate the interrupts from the driver, and contention is based on threads (in this case interrupt threads), so that the actual control of interrupts is built into the property of launching an interrupt thread.

Compared to an old PDP-11, the 386's interrupt control situation is quite different. First, the processor itself does not implement vectored interrupts built as tightly into its architecture. It instead uses an external peripheral device for this purpose. Thus, there are no interrupt priority control instructions. The 386 simply uses ordinary I/O instructions to gain access to the device (see *What are Peripheral Device Interrupts*).

This external ICU does not have the ability to disable interrupts based on class. Instead, it can disable them on a device-by-device basis, where each device has a fixed priority associated with that bit. In addition, since there are more than one of these ICUs cascaded off of the primary ICU, the actual priorities are nonconsecutive.[39]

Finally the ICU has a variety of different modes in which it can operate. Unlike the PDP-11, which was oriented more towards timeshared use, the X86 interrupt architecture is designed for embedded control applications which may require guaranteed real-time response. Thus, the priority schemes are somewhat simplistic and not at all intended for use with a system like UNIX (but perfect for, say, controlling a robot or milling machine).

All other BSD and UNIX systems (excepting modern systems like Solaris), including those ported to the 386, still rely upon the old PDP-11 approach described above—they just simulate (rather poorly) the old PDP-11 by emulating the priority levels at interrupt time.[40] In 386BSD, interrupt mask sets are used (instead of interrupt levels) corresponding to all of the devices which need to share a level with which to be blocked.[41]

The tty mask corresponds to all of the interrupts which need to be masked when an interrupt or a **spltty** must be asserted by the software to keep the common code from accessing an interrupt level object. In the case of ttys, there are no longer any shared pool c-lists since we use ring buffers allocated on a per driver basis (see **subr/rlist.c**). In practice, all that needs to occur is that the device interrupt must be masked, and this is done automatically by the hardware anyway during an interrupt.

splbio uses *biomask* to block all other block I/O devices such as, for example, the floppy and the hard disk when referencing a buffer or performing a disk operation. Currently, the only real need for this in the shared case is so that we can set and clear the busy bit associated with the buffer.

In the case of protocol processing, the purpose of the **splimp** and **splnet** operations is to block any interface or the shared software network interrupt temporarily to prevent contention among multiple network interfaces and/or competition when supplying packets to the input queue for protocol processing. [42]

---

[39] E.g. while interrupt IRQ0 has a higher priority than IRQ1, IRQ9 has a higher priority than IRQ3).

[40] The author is quite familiar with the PDP-11, managing variations of this code for 2.8 BSD, and notes that it still hangs on even as the technology has changed. It is a good example of the importance of re-evaluating ideas—as no one else will do your thinking for you. See *386BSD Research Directions and Guidelines* on the **386BSD Reference CD-ROM** for more information.

[41] This reliance on mask sets is decreasing, however, as 386BSD evolves, but a mask set roughly corresponding to a PDP-11 interrupt level still remains in this release.

[42] Since these are only used by the interrupt level memory allocators, this ensures unique access to the interrupt memory allocators.

These *splXX* functions, which once provided so much for us so conveniently on the PDP-11, could now be done at a much lower cost with other locking primitives. In fact, in the case of very high speed networking, the last thing we would ever want is to be forced to manage any part of the interrupt or I/O transfer characteristics of a device when we don't have to manage it. Since these characteristics may not scale with the quantity of I/O obtained from a device, it would just become yet another bottleneck. As such, this mechanism is scheduled for replacement in future versions of 386BSD (perhaps by interrupt threads).

2.7.1 How are Set Processor Level Functions Implemented?

... [File: /usr/src/kernel/kern/i386/locore.s, line: 1433]

```
#define COMMON_SPL          \
        movl    %eax, %edx ;        \
        orw     _imen, %ax ;      /* mask off those not enabled yet */ \
        outb    %al, $IO_ICU1+1 ;        /* update icu's */  \
        NOP ; \
        movb    %ah, %al ;        \
        outb    %al, $IO_ICU2+1 ;        \
        WRPOST  ;                 /* write post before restoring interrupts */ \
        xchgl   %edx, _cpl ;     /* exchange old/new priority level */ \
        movl    %edx, %eax ; \
        sti     ;                 /* enable interrupts */  \
        ret
    ...
```

This macro contains the common code for all the spl functions. It saves the new level into a separate temporary register and "or's" in the mask of non-enabled devices to the new interrupt level, assigning the new mask to each ICU. A write posting operation is done to ensure that the masks make it to the devices. The new interrupt level is then exchanged with the current priority level kept in the variable *cpl* (current priority level). The old value is returned to the caller with the interrupts reenabled. This common code requires that the interrupts be off and the new desired priority level be left in the EAX register.

... [File: /usr/src/kernel/kern/i386/locore.s, line: 1446]

```
ENTRY(splhigh)
        movl    $IRHIGH, %eax   /* set new priority level with interrupts off */
        cli
        COMMON_SPL
    ...
```

The first example of the use of this common code is in the **splhigh** function. The **splhigh** function forces the priority level to have all interrupts disabled. This is achieved by assigning the interrupt mask corresponding to all hardware and software interrupts to the EAX register. The interrupt bit is then cleared, and the common code discussed above is implemented. Regardless of the interrupt level the processor was in, it will return with interrupts disabled.

... [File: /usr/src/kernel/kern/i386/locore.s, line: 1451]

```
ENTRY(splclock)
        movl    _cpl, %eax
        orb     $IRQ0, %al      /* set new priority level with interrupts off */
        cli
        COMMON_SPL
    ...
```

The function **splclock** disables the clock interrupt associated with process scheduling. The least significant bit corresponding to the clock interrupt is added to the current priority mask. Then, the interrupt is forced off prior to invoking the common code to update the interrupt mask register.

Note that the effect of changing the interrupt priority mask is to add to the existing mask instead of just assigning the mask outright (like in **splhigh**). This is done to deal with the case of nested spl's (common within the code). For example, one function may call another with the tty mask present, and within that function another function may require that the clock interrupt be blocked. If an assignment were done, the tty mask settings would be undone when the clock was masked.

On the PDP-ll and VAX, the software was originally arranged so that ascendancy of nested levels would always work, since the only way one could increase in level would be to nest successively more restrictive levels as the hardware itself was arranged to operate at such levels (the jumpers were set). Since we can't run around and reassign the priorities of all PC hardware (most of it isn't even jumperable anymore), this "or'ing" of levels causes the constraints to be kept.

Note that when the levels are removed (by means of the outgoing *splXX*'s recovering the previous priority level and assigning it back to the ICU), the level will now contain the mask value priority. Thus, the mask value semantics are maintained.

... [File: /usr/src/kernel/kern/i386/locore.s, line: 1457]

```
ENTRY(spltty)
        movl    _cpl, %eax
        orw     _ttymask, %ax
        cli
        COMMON_SPL
ENTRY(splimp)
        movl    _cpl, %eax
        orw     _netmask, %ax
        cli
        COMMON_SPL
ENTRY(splbio)
        movl    _cpl, %eax
        orw     _biomask, %ax
        cli
        COMMON_SPL
    ...
```

spltty, **splimp**, and **splbio** all work in this same fashion by selectively masking off devices associated with the tty mask, net mask, and bio mask (for terminal devices, network packet interfaces, and block I/O devices, e.g. disk and tapes), respectively.

The name **splimp** is historically derived. Early versions of 4BSD required an interface message processor[43] to gain access to the Arpanet. Since the primary allocator of memory at interrupt level is network packet devices, blocking at **splimp** is associated in the code with defeating any attempted memory allocations from interrupt level.

... [File: /usr/src/kernel/kern/i386/locore.s, line: 1475]

```
ENTRY(splsoftclock)
        movl    $IRSCLK, %eax
        cli
        COMMON_SPL

ENTRY(splnet)
        movl    $IRNET|IRSCLK, %eax
        cli
        COMMON_SPL
    ...
```

splsoftclock and **splnet** function very much like the hardware interrupt-related spl's, except that they block software interrupts only. Since their effect on hardware is to allow hardware interrupts to come in while keeping certain software interrupts from being emulated by the return from interrupt processing, they are implemented as assignments and do not allow nesting of spl's (as occurs in the prior cases). Thus, it would be a mistake to have, for example, the nesting of **splimp** and within it **splnet**, since the effect would be to abandon hardware interrupt priority as if the two spanning regions were adjacent rather than nested.

The only effect of **splsoftclock** or **splnet** (other than to drop hardware interrupt masks) is to force software interrupts to not be processed. On earlier versions of 386BSD, this was done by stealing IRQ15 and assigning it for use in blocking out low priority hardware interrupts. Not only did this tie up an IRQ (which are scarce), but it also did not work correctly in all cases, because IRQ15 actually resides above the level of many interrupts (especially the serial port interrupts).

By implementing these software interrupts orthogonally to the hardware interrupts, all of the IRQs may be used on a PC. In addition, since IRQ 7 and IRQ 15 perform a special function in catching lost interrupts, this special function now can be implemented without interaction from the network.

For a recap: the **splsoftclock** just blocks the rescheduling of processes and timeouts and is at a slightly lower priority than protocol processing (which is blocked by **splnet**). The effect of blocking network software interrupt processing is to prevent

---

[43] Essentially a small Honeywell minicomputer used as a network interface.

---

further additions to the input queue of a protocol. It is primarily used to allow the queue to be manipulated exclusively.

... [File: /usr/src/kernel/kern/i386/locore.s, line: 1485]

```
ENTRY(splnone)
        PROC_ENTRY
        cli
        pushl   _cpl                /* save old priority */
        movw    _imen, %ax          /* mask off those not enabled yet */
        outb    %al, $IO_ICU1+1 /* update icu's */
        NOP
        movb    %ah, %al
        outb    %al, $IO_ICU2+1
        WRPOST                      /* write post before restoring interrupts */

        pushl   %ebx                /* save register contents before use */

9:
        xorl    %ebx, %ebx
        xchgl   %ebx, _netisr
        movl    $IRNET|IRSCLK, _cpl     /* set new priority level */

        testl   %ebx, %ebx
        je      5f
        sti
        DONET(%ebx, %eax)
        cli
        jmp     9b
5:
        movl    $IRSCLK, _cpl           /* set new priority level */
        xorl    %ebx, %ebx
        xchgl   %ebx, _sclkpending

        testl   %ebx, %ebx
        je      1f

        /* create a softclock interrupt frame */
        sti
        pushl   $KCSEL                  /* cs */
        pushl   3*4(%esp)               /* eip */
        pushl   $0                      /* basepri */
        call    _softclock              /* softclock(clockframe); */
        addl    $12, %esp
        cli
        jmp     9b

1:
        movl    $0, _cpl                /* set new priority level */
        sti
        popl    %ebx
        popl    %eax                    /* return old priority */
        PROC_EXIT
        ret
...
```

splnone unmasks any enabled interrupts. It is implemented differently than all other spl functions, because in returning to a noninterrupt level it must first check to see if

---

software interrupts must be implemented (as in the case of the interrupt return code already discussed).

splnone forces the processor to be at **splnet** priority level. If any hardware interrupts are pending, they will arrive at this point, but they will be blocked when they exit from implementing any of the software clock or network interrupt processing. If there are any network interrupts present, they are processed; otherwise, the priority level is adjusted to correspond to the software clock level, since from now on any subsequent network interrupts will be processed by the return to low priority level.

The software clock is then examined to see if any of these requests are pending. If so, a call to the software clock is arranged by assembling a clock frame and calling the **softclock** routine. Finally, the software clock mask is removed and we have arrived at our base level. We then retrieve the previous priority level and return it to the caller.

... [File: /usr/src/kernel/kern/i386/locore.s, line: 1537]

```
ENTRY(splx)
        movl    4(%esp), %eax    /* new priority level */
        testl   %eax, %eax
        je      _splnone         /* going to "zero level" is special */

        cli
        COMMON_SPL
    ...
```

splx takes a priority as an argument and assigns that level. It commonly is used to return the mask back to the current priority level. It first checks to see if we are returning to zero priority level (e.g. none are blocked). If so, it then jumps to the **splnone** function which implements returning to the base level. Otherwise, it calls the interrupt common code and assigns the appropriate level.

2.8 What are System Call 'Call Gates'?

The system call *"call gate"* is the entry point for a local descriptor table entry known to all user processes. In the Intel iBCS2 specification, it is denoted as the system call selector which all system calls must use. A system call "call gate" is actually nothing more than a controlled entry into the kernel program via a descriptor, which allows the appropriate exchange of user stack for kernel stack. This is done in the form of a special stack frame known as an *outer stack frame.*

Unlike traps and interrupts, call gates use a different format as befits a subroutine call mechanism instead of an exception handler. Most notably, the processor status word (or "EFLAGS") register is not saved, as it is automatically during trap handling. This is inconvenient when implementing the iBCS2 system calls, which specify that an error return will be passed back to the user process as a change in the status of the flags. As such, we save the flags along with all of the registers at the start of this routine.

It might be possible to use the value returned from **syscall()** to assign the carry bit at the end of this routine instead of at the beginning; however, there are other uses of the status word in variations on POSIX/UNIX system calls that become part of 386BSD in future versions. Even though this code is scheduled to become part of an emulation library (one of many to support different applications program interfaces), this problem will still persist. This area is hence more one of the scope of the binary programmable program interface itself than anything else.

Because of the format difference between call gates and traps and interrupts, it is difficult to reconcile the trap and system call stack frame formats. This additional complexity permeates parts of the system and could be jettisoned by clever reformatting of the trap stack—this is a task left to the reader. We prefer not to alter the system call handler processing, since it occurs much more frequently than trap handling. For comparison, interrupts occur much more frequently than trap handling.

2.8.1 How are System Call Gates Implemented?

... [File: /usr/src/kernel/kern/i386/locore.s, line: 1549]

```
IDTVEC(syscall)
_SYSCALL_ENTRY:
        pushfl
        pushal
        nop
        movw    $KDSEL, %ax      /* reload kernel selectors */
        movw    %ax, %ds
        movw    %ax, %es
        movw    __udatasel, %ax /* reload user selectors */
        movw    %ax, %gs
        incl    _cnt+V_SYSCALL
        call    _syscall
...
```

The flags and all registers are first saved. Then, like traps and interrupts, the data and extra selectors are assigned to the kernel values. We don't bother to save the user, data, and extra selectors because we can reconstruct their value anyway upon return. The statistics for the number of system calls is incremented and the generic system call handler is then called.

... [File: /usr/src/kernel/kern/i386/locore.s, line: 1562]

```
9:
        /* snatch values for softints */
        cli
        movl    _curproc, %edx
        btrl    $0, PMD_FLAGS(%edx)

        /* an ast? */
        jc      7f

        /* any network software interrupts present? */
        xorl    %ebx, %ebx
        xchgl   %ebx, _netisr
```

```
        testl   %ebx, %ebx
        jne     5f

        /* need a software clock interrupt? */
        xorl    %edi, %edi
        xchgl   %edi, _sclkpending
        testl   %edi, %edi
        jne     6f
...
```

Upon return from this system call, we mask interrupts and check for any outstanding events (like network level, asynchronous trap, or software clock interrupts) and check to see if any need to be done prior to return of this system call. If there is an outstanding network interrupt, we dispatch to process it at this time.

After implementing the requests (if any), the interrupts are cleared for the period of time that the final return back to the user process is arranged. This is done so that an interrupt doesn't arrive which might be connected to a signal, since we would no longer be checking for signals in this process before making it back into the user process that called this system call handler.

... [File: /usr/src/kernel/kern/i386/locore.s, line: 1583]

```
        movl    $0, _cpl
        movw    __udatasel, %ax  /* reload user selectors */
        movw    %ax, %ds
        movw    %ax, %es
        movw    %ax, %gs
        popal
        nop
        popfl

_syscall_lret:
        lret
...
```

If no special event processing needs to be done prior to return to the user process's program, the return to user mode is made. First, the user selectors are reloaded. The processor flags are the last values of the user's context to be reloaded prior to the "lret" (long return—to user selector) instruction that will reload the outer stack frame, causing the processor to reenter the user process from the kernel. The effect of the reload of the flags will only take place after the "lret" instruction is issued, thus avoiding the problem of an interrupt entering before reentering user space.[44]

The remainder code fragments implement the event handling functions prior to return to user mode.

---

[44] Note that any interrupt that may instigate a signal will be held off until the processor returns to user mode, thereby eliminating the race with signal evaluation due to a late AST delivery.

SOURCE CODE SECRETS: THE BASIC KERNEL

```
5:
        movl    $IRNET|IRSCLK, _cpl
        sti
        DONET(%ebx, %eax)
        jmp     9b
    ...
```

If there is an outstanding network interrupt, we process it at this time (using the **DONET** macro discussed above) at the network software interrupt level.

```
6:      /* simulate a hardware interrupt */
        incl    _cnt+V_SOFT
        movl    $IRSCLK, _cpl
        sti

        pushl   10*4(%esp)              /* cs */
        pushl   10*4(%esp)              /* eip */
        pushl   $0                      /* basepri */
        call    _softclock              /* softclock(clockframe); */
        addl    $12, %esp
        jmp     9b
    ...
```

If a software clock event is scheduled, a clock frame is constructed and the software clock routine is called to implement the request. After calling the interrupt service handler, the frame is dismantled and entry to the common event.

```
7:
        sti
        incl    _cnt+V_TRAP
        call    _systrap                /* systrap(struct syscframe); */
        jmp 9b

    ...
```

If a late AST is present, a special function, **systrap()**, is called to process a signal or reschedule an event prior to return to the user program. This function is necessary only because in this implementation system call stack frames are of different format than trap stack frames.

Exercises

2.1 **a)** Why do system calls occur more frequently than traps?
b) Why do interrupts occur more frequently than traps?

2.2 Why is the software interrupt status sampled with interlocked instructions in the interrupt, trap, and system call entry functions?

2.3 In what way do trap, interrupt, and system call stack frames differ and why?

2.4 **a)** Why does the "PTmap" portion of kernel address space always appear as an ordered array of page table entries, regardless of the physical memory address holding the page tables?
b) Why is this useful for the kernel and its virtual memory system?

2.5 What happens if the kernel's MMU tables are not set up correctly upon the "jump to hyperspace"?

2.6 Why do we use 32 run queues instead of just one single run queue?

3 CPU SPECIFIC PRIMITIVES (i386/trap.c, i386/cpu.c)

Since the kernel is written in a machine-independent form, it must adapt itself to a specific machine by means of files with machine-specific data types, structures, constant values, macros, and inline functions. The kernel also relies on mandatory, generic machine-dependent facilities present in all implementations.[1] In all, the basic kernel must achieve five primary machine-specific functions:

- Kernel thread creation and destruction.

- User process signal delivery and return.

- User program entry.

- Address location of a stored user processor register.

- Processor forced reset.

In addition, due to the machine-dependent nature of processor exception handling and system call entry, these mechanisms common to most computer systems have extraordinarily machine-dependent details which render the implementation of such handlers again machine specific.

Earlier UNIX systems intermixed the machine-dependent and independent portions more extensively. The earliest example of these simply copied the entire process to the disk[2] in order to achieve the effect of replicating state (in this case, as a cheap way to deal with this problem in terms of code size). Signals evolved out of a simulated interrupt mechanism which originally only reflected hardware exceptions into the user program.

---

[1] See **i386/machdep.c** for some of these functions which are defined in **sys/kernel.h**.
[2] CTSS, early versions of UNIX, MINI-UNIX ... 4BSD even did "expansion" swaps for this reason.

3.1 Processor Exception and System Call Entry Handling: i386/trap.c

The file **i386/trap.c** contains the code to handle both processor exception handling and system call entry. Almost every UNIX or UNIX-like variant for any architecture has such functions, but the exact implementation of each differs quite widely, since many of the fundamental assumptions of a kernel implementation greatly impact the actual operation. In addition, since the number, kind, and structure of processor exceptions depends on architectural considerations beyond the needs of a pure UNIX system, much of the trap handling reflects support for the overall processor architecture itself. Finally, system call entry code is frequently heavily optimized so as to reduce the overhead common to all system calls. Since UNIX systems are very system call intensive, this means better management of a critical resource.

One oddity of the X86 processor family is that system call handling is done via a special kind of system call called a *call gate*.[3] Call gates do not inherently save a portion of the status during its operation. Thus, in order to correctly process the delivery of a user level exception an artifice must be added. This artifice also deals with some of the problems encountered in **locore.s** dealing with delivery of processor signals and race exceptions. Machine-dependent workarounds which compensate for idiosyncracies in specific processors[4] are also present in this file.

While much of this file is very similar on different processors, it is edited in places to favor a particular processor family—in this case the X86 family. **trap.c** is written with intimate knowledge of **locore.s**. It is coded, however, entirely in C with small enhancements in inline assembler.

3.1.1 Functions Contained in the File i386/trap.c

The following functions appear in the file i386/trap.c:

> **trap()**
> **trapexcept()**
> **trapwrite()**
> **copyin3()**
> **syscall()**
> **systrap()**

The largest function in this file is the **trap()** routine, followed in size by **syscall()**. **trap()** is a generalized process exception handler that all process exception handlers in

---

[3] See *What are System Call 'Call Gates'?* in **Chapter 2, locore.s.**
[4] For example, in the case of the 386 a mechanism to bypass an inability of the processor to honor write-protection from kernel mode—see **Chapter 2, locore.s.**

locore.s call.[5] **syscall()** is a specialized call gate handler that processes an Intel BCS system call and dispatches to the appropriate system call handler.

The other functions **trapexcept()**, **trapwrite()**, **copyin3()**, and **systrap()** are simply artifacts of the X86 processor family. **trapexcept()** remedies a problem in signal processing when a corrupt CS register causes a forever terminating process (it gets an exception, goes to terminate, than gets another exception, and so forth). **trapwrite()** specifically makes up for the write protection mechanism left off the 386.[6] **copyin3()** is an inline function private to this module that transfers three words of arguments, since the vast majority of system calls use three arguments—it is, in sum, an optimization. Finally, **systrap()** processes an AST found just prior to returning from system mode from a system call.

3.1.2 What is trap()?

trap() is the generic processor exception handler. All processor exceptions are funneled through this single function. **trap()** receives all exception requests and dispatches them to the appropriate portion of the kernel for handling. In the case of machine-specific faults that do not require involvement of any other portion of the kernel, **trap()** handles them internally to this file.

trap() has a most unusual calling arrangement:

... [File: /usr/src/kernel/kern/i386/trap.c, line: 99]

```
void
trap(struct trapframe frame)
  ...
```

trap() has one argument—a multiword structure (or *frame*). It returns no value other than through modification to the arguments. The frame is the description of the top of stack on entry from the processor exception.[7] This frame is partially constructed by the processor itself upon encountering an exception and partially assembled by the trap handler's functions that are written in assembly language.[8] Except for **locore.s**, no other reference to **trap()** is made in the rest of the kernel.

Since the stack frame is a structure, its arguments are bulk loaded on top of the stack.[9] One of the oddities of this structure assignment is that the contents of these variables may be modified and values returned to the caller (instead of the normal case of them

---

[5] See *What are Processor Exceptions?* in **Chapter 2, i386/locore.s.**
[6] It will never be used on a more advanced processor.
[7] See **i386/frame.h.**
[8] See *How are Processor Exceptions Implemented?* in **Chapter 2, i386/locore.s.**
[9] Actually, this is true in the case of a C function calling it. However, since this function is called by assembly language in **i386/locore.s,** the contents of the structure are placed on the stack and later restored to the hardware registers from whence they came.

---

being discarded). The contents of this frame include all of the register values at the time the trap occurred. This register contents may be changed on the stack frame image, which will in turn change the contents of the register upon return from the stack. This is the primary way by which very primitive communications to the processor occur (such as stepping over an illegal instruction which may have been emulated).

3.1.2.1 How is trap() Implemented?

... [File: /usr/src/kernel/kern/i386/trap.c, line: 107]

```
        frame.tf_eflags &= ~PSL_NT;      /* clear nested trap XXX */
        type = frame.tf_trapno;
...
```

The nested trap bit in the processor's status flag (tf_eflags) is unconditionally cleared. In the case of this processor family, it is possible to nest traps between one address space and another. Because the register may be accessed via user mode (and is thus settable), the bit may have been legitimately set incorrectly, causing the processor on return to panic if the secondary address space is not present.[10] The type of trap is extracted from the stack frame and held in a local variable for reference by the rest of the function.

... [File: /usr/src/kernel/kern/i386/trap.c, line: 111]

```
        if (p = curproc) {

                /* record trap evaluation start time */
                syst = p->p_stime;

                /* engage this instantiation of fault handling */
                onfault = (int)p->p_md.md_onfault;
                p->p_md.md_onfault = 0;

#ifdef DDB
                /* if an anticapated fault with a handler */
                if (onfault)
                        switch (frame.tf_trapno) {

                        case T_BPTFLT:  /* always pass to debugger regardless */
                        case T_TRCTRAP:
                        if (kdb_trap (frame.tf_trapno, frame.tf_err, &frame))
                                return;
                        break;
                }
#endif
        }
...
```

---

[10] Address spaces via TSS's can be nested into a chain of list entries. Support for this is not yet implemented for handling multiple operating systems so it is outright defeated on any cases of traps to avoid crashing the system by accident.

Traps can occur when a user process is active or when the processor is idling and no process is active. A local variable *p* contains the contents of the current process or thread active at that moment in time. If *p* is zero, the thread or process is inactive and the processor is idling.[11] However, if there is a process or thread active we record the amount of time the trap will take to evaluate and attempt to locate if the process has a fault handler (p->p_md.md_onfault). A nonzero value in this field corresponds to the address of the temporary "overriding" fault handler where the trap should be handled in place of this the current fault handler. Since only one process can have one on-fault handler per every fault that may occur, the field is cleared in the process so that a subsequent fault may chain to a different handler recursively.

If a kernel debugger is being used, breakpoint and single-stepping (T_TRCTRAP) faults will be handled specially so as to force entry into the debugger before the trap is evaluated. This allows potential debugger traps to be discovered and filtered out from traps encountered in normal operation. Thus, the debugger can be used to debug code that induces on-fault traps. If these faults are not present, the **trap()** function will handle the exception.

In effect, the on-fault and debugger trap mechanism are a way of permitting the exception to be *inherited* by another layer of the kernel ahead of the generic trap handling mechanism. If one were to write an operating system using object inheritance, this would be handled by the shared inheritance mechanism built into the exception object.

... [File: /usr/src/kernel/kern/i386/trap.c, line: 135]

```
    if ((frame.tf_eip == (int)&iret || frame.tf_eip == (int)&syscall_lret)){
        trapexcept(&frame, &frame.tf_esp);
        return;
    }
...
```

Next, we check for unusual machine-dependent exceptions. If the fault occurred while attempting to execute the "iret" instruction (determined by checking for the labeled address *iret* as being the address where the program counter or instruction pointer (tf_eip) is located or comparably checking for the location of the lret instruction on return from the system call (*syscall_lret()*), then the trap is an exception due to a botched CS register. The function **trapexcept()** is then called to alter the characteristics of the trap so that the trap can be unwound and returned safely back to the user with a safe CS value restored and the state reassembled. **trap()** then stops its processing. Currently, the only way this special case could occur is when the contents of the CS register have been intentionally destroyed to provoke this condition.

---

[11] Few traps are honored when the processor is idling or at interrupt level, as most traps are synchronous with the processor and extraordinary events. Among those honored are some address space faults, floating point, and debugger traps (for the kernel debugger).

... [File: /usr/src/kernel/kern/i386/trap.c, line: 141]

```
            if (ISPL(frame.tf_cs) == SEL_UPL) {

#ifdef  DIAGNOSTIC
                    if (p == 0)
                            panic(trap: no process, yet from user mode);
#endif

                    type |= T_USER;
                    p->p_md.md_regs = (int *)&frame;
                    p->p_addr->u_pcb.pcb_flags |= FM_TRAP;  /* XXX used by
cpu_signal() */

#ifdef DIAGNOSTIC
                    if (cpl)
                            panic (trap: #1 user mode at interrupt level);
#endif
            }
    ...
```

Traps can come from either a kernel source or from a program running in user mode. This is determined by checking the contents of the code selector (tf_cs). The least significant two bits correspond to the protection level of the code segment executing. A selector executing at the user protection level (SEL_UPL) indicates that a user mode process generated this exception. Since it must be the case that a process or thread must be present and that the processor must not be at an interrupt level (e.g. the current priority level must be equal to zero), two diagnostic checks can be conditionally compiled to check for both of these events.

If this trap came from a user process, the trap type is updated with an additional bit (T_USER). In addition, the pointer to the base of the trap stack frame is left in the machine-dependent process region so that it might be found by the **ptrace()** mechanism which will decode the registers in the stack frame (*md_regs*). Finally, for backwards compatibility the process's flags (*pcb_flags*) are updated with a trap entry indication (FM_TRAP) so that the processor-dependent code (see **i386/cpu.c**) can be informed of the necessity to decode a trap frame entry instead of a system call entry.

... [File: /usr/src/kernel/kern/i386/trap.c, line: 158]

```
        code = frame.tf_err;
        switch (type) {
    ...
```

Each exception entry of the processor is typed by a number indicated in the trap frame *tf_trapno* and kept in a local variable type. Since the trap subroutine determined if the trap came from the kernel or user program, a flag has been added to this local variable. A dispatch is then made to these different traps to handle the particular trap exception.

... [File: /usr/src/kernel/kern/i386/trap.c, line: 168]

```
          default:
          we_re_toast:
#ifdef DDB
                  /* always pass to debugger regardless */
                  if ((type == T_BPTFLT || type == T_TRCTRAP || enterddb)
                      && kdb_trap(type, code, &frame))
                          return;
#endif

                  printf(trap %d code %x eip %x cs %x eflags %x ,
                          frame.tf_trapno, frame.tf_err, frame.tf_eip,
                          frame.tf_cs, frame.tf_eflags);
                  if (p)
                          printf(comm %s , p->p_comm);
                  printf(cr2 %x cpl %x\n, rcr(2), cpl);
                  panic(trap);
          ...
```

For traps that are not handled by this handler or for traps known to be terminal (*we_re_toast*), terminal fault handling is arranged. If support for the debugger is present (DDB) and if the trap is a breakpoint or trace trap, the trap is always passed to the debugger; otherwise, if the variable *enterddb* is present the debugger is entered unconditionally at this point by calling its trap entry function **kdb_trap()** in **ddb/db_trap.c**. Note that the trap may return after a debugging session and the trap dismissed outright. This presumes of course that the condition caused by the trap has been removed by the debugger as in the case of a breakpoint or a single step fault. If the exception has not been removed, it is likely that the exception will reoccur and a subsequent trap will place the kernel into the debugger yet again.

Otherwise, terminal processing of the exception will occur. Information from the trap is displayed on the console and a panic undertaken by calling the **panic()** function (see **subr/printf.c**). **panic()** will attempt to save a copy of all of the processor's memory to disk and reboot the system. There is never a return from **panic()** as it is an unhandleable fault resulting from either a software flaw or a severe hardware problem.

... [File: /usr/src/kernel/kern/i386/trap.c, line: 189]

```
          case T_SEGNPFLT|T_USER:          /* segment not present fault */
          case T_STKFLT|T_USER:            /* stack protection fault */
          case T_PROTFLT|T_USER:           /* general protection fault */
          case T_FPOPFLT|T_USER:           /* coprocessor operand fault */
                  ucode = code + BUS_SEGM_FAULT;
                  signo = SIGSEGV;
                  break;
          ...
```

The X86 family has a series of segment protection faults. One fault T_SEGNPFLT indicates that the segment is not present. Another fault T_STKFLT indicates that the stack's segment selector is pointed to an invalid segment. The fault T_PROTFLT is a general protection fault indicating that the characteristics of this particular segment selector were not appropriate (this is the catchall case). Finally, T_FPOPFLT is the coprocessor or floating point operand fault—which means in simple language that the coprocessor has failed. Since 386BSD makes little use of segments in user mode, these should never happen. Should one occur, a signal will be sent to the process in which they occur (SIGSEGV) indicating that a segmentation violation has resulted. An additional class of segment faults (BUS_SEGM_FAULT) records the kind and class of machine-dependent faults occurring.

... [File: /usr/src/kernel/kern/i386/trap.c, line: 200]

```
            case T_PRIVINFLT:
            case T_PRIVINFLT|T_USER:

                    /*
                     * Attempt to emulate some 486 instructions on 386, to
                     * allow a 486-only kernel to at least function.
                     */

                    /* check if a two byte 486-only instruction */
                    ins = *(u_short *)frame.tf_eip;

                    /* bswap %eax */
                    if (ins == 0xc80f) {
                            frame.tf_eax = htonl(frame.tf_eax);
                            frame.tf_eip += 2;
                            break;
                    } else
                    /* wbinvd, invd */
                    if (ins == 0x090f || ins == 0x080f) {
                            frame.tf_eip += 2;
                            break;
                    }

                    /* 3 byte instructions: */
                    ins = *(int *)frame.tf_eip & 0xffffff;
                    /* invlpg (%eax) */
                    if (ins == 0x38010f) {
                            lcr(3, rcr(3));
                            frame.tf_eip += 3;
                            break;
                    }
...
```

The unimplemented instruction exception T_PRIVINFLT checks to see if there are certain cases of 486 and successor processor instructions used by the kernel or in user program that cannot be run on a 386. These instructions are the byte swap instruction "bswap", write back invalidate instruction "wbinvd", invalidate instruction "invd", and a special case of the invalidate page instruction "invlpg". This function emulates them inline rather than panic the kernel unnecessarily or terminate the user program. The point here is just to allow a system to run even if the software was not configured for the correct processor, so that the situation may be potentially rectified.

If the instruction that caused the fault is not any of these special case instructions, the kernel will panic, or in the case of a user process it will receive an illegal instruction

---

signal (SIGILL) and the additional code associated with the signal will point to the specific cause—again without regard to the user or supervisor mode since it is obvious.

... [File: /usr/src/kernel/kern/i386/trap.c, line: 243]

```
        case T_ASTFLT|T_USER:              /* Allow process switch */
        case T_ASTFLT:
                goto out;
...
```

The transparent fault T_ASTFLT is used to signal a context switch. It is used by signal generation code from interrupt level to indicate that the process in the context we are running has received a signal and that it should make a pass through **trap()** for signal evaluation and a possible process context switch. This fault name comes from the VAX/PDP-11 asynchronous trap or "ast" used to automatically generate a fault prior to returning to user mode from the kernel on an interrupt fault.

... [File: /usr/src/kernel/kern/i386/trap.c, line: 247]

```
        case T_DNA:
        case T_DNA|T_USER:

                /* hardware floating point context switch? */
                if (cpu_dna && (*cpu_dna)((void *)&frame))
                        break;

                /* software floating point? */
                else if (cpu_dna_em) {
                        if ((*cpu_dna_em)((void *)&frame) == 0)
                                break;
                }
                signo = SIGFPE;
                ucode = FPE_FPU_NP_TRAP;
                break;
...
```

Attempts to access the floating point coprocessor (which may or may not be a separate chip from the processor die) will generate a device not available fault T_DNA. If there is a hardware floating point unit, this fault may signal the presence of a context switch, thus calling the registered fault handler. If no hardware is present, however, the software floating point emulator is checked to see if it can emulate the instruction causing the fault—if so, the trap dispatch loop is exited. If neither of these two routines are present or have not succeeded, a floating point-related signal (SIGFPE) will be sent to the process with the additional machine-dependent indication that it was generated by a processor not present trap (FPE_FPU_NP_TRAP).

... [File: /usr/src/kernel/kern/i386/trap.c, line: 263]

```
        case T_BOUND|T_USER:
                /* ucode = SEGV_BOUND_TRAP; */
```

```
            signo = SIGSEGV;
            break;
...
```

If the bounds instruction of the X86 found that the value it was checking for is out of bounds, it will generate a trap. This will send the process a segmentation violation signal. Since this signal is shared by many others, a special code indicating that it is a bound trap SEGV_BOUND_TRAP is passed along in the trap source field.

... [File: /usr/src/kernel/kern/i386/trap.c, line: 268]

```
    case T_OFLOW|T_USER:
            ucode = SEGV_OFLOW_TRAP;
            signo = SIGSEGV;
            break;
...
```

If the overflow state of the X86 found that the value calculated has overflowed the numeric range, it will generate a trap. This will send the process a segmentation violation signal. Since this signal is shared by many others, a special code indicating that it is an overflow state trap SEGV_OFLOW_TRAP is passed along in a trap source field.

... [File: /usr/src/kernel/kern/i386/trap.c, line: 273]

```
    case T_ALIGN|T_USER:
            ucode = BUS_ALIGN_TRAP;
            signo = SIGBUS;
            break;
...
```

If the processor is a 486 or better and the alignment fault feature is enabled (see control register zero definitions), then the alignment fault T_ALIGN is intercepted and sent to the process as a bus error signal SIGBUS. At the moment there are no other ways to generate a bus error signal (but there may be in the future). So as to disambiguate it from any other use of SIGBUS the processor source field is tagged as a BUS_ALIGN_TRAP.

... [File: /usr/src/kernel/kern/i386/trap.c, line: 278]

```
    case T_DIVIDE|T_USER:
            ucode = FPE_INTDIV_TRAP;
            signo = SIGFPE;
            break;
...
```

If the X86 has attempted to do an integer divide by zero, it will generate a T_DIVIDE trap. This will send the process a floating point exception signal (SIGFPE). Since this signal is shared by many others, a special code indicating that it is an integer divide by zero FPE_INTDIV_TRAP is passed along. Note that even though it is an integer divide by zero that causes the problem, there is no standard integer divide by zero signal—it is piggybacked on the floating point exception signal. This is done because the PDP-11

---

did not have an integer division instruction, so it used the floating point exception signal as well. Old habits appear to die hard.

... [File: /usr/src/kernel/kern/i386/trap.c, line: 283]

```
        case T_ARITHTRAP|T_USER:
                ucode = npxerror();
                signo = SIGFPE;
                break;
...
```

If the X86's floating point coprocessor generated an exception, the specific nature of the fault is obtained by calling the coprocessor's driver error decode function. It will then return an appropriate machine and coprocessor specific fault.

... [File: /usr/src/kernel/kern/i386/trap.c, line: 288]

```
        case T_PAGEFLT:                  /* kernel page fault */
        case T_PAGEFLT|T_USER:           /* user page fault */
            {
                vm_offset_t va;
                struct vmspace *vm = 0;
                vm_map_t map;
                extern vm_map_t kernel_map;
                unsigned nss = 0;

                eva = rcr(2);
                va = trunc_page((vm_offset_t)eva);
...
```

The next trap kind handled by the trap handler is the most elaborate trap—the page fault trap. On the X86 family, both page not present and page protection exceptions are shared through this same fault. In addition, both user and kernel page faults are treated with the same shared case, since the kernel can indirectly generate page faults on the user address space (e.g. by referencing a user page not present). The faulting address is recovered from the contents of the processor's control register 2 (eva) since this address is the one that caused the fault (it is not necessarily caused by the associated page) and the base page address is separately determined.

... [File: /usr/src/kernel/kern/i386/trap.c, line: 301]

```
                if (type == T_PAGEFLT && va >= KERNBASE)
                        map = kernel_map;

                /* otherwise, either a user address or page table fault */
                else {
                        if (p == 0 || (vm = p->p_vmspace) == 0)
                                panic (trap: invalid user space fault);
                        map = &vm->vm_map;

                        /* are we a page table reference */
                        if (type == T_PAGEFLT && va >= PT_MIN_ADDRESS) {
                                pmap_ptalloc(&vm->vm_pmap, vm->vm_pmap.pm_pdir
```

```
                          + i386_btop(va - PT_MIN_ADDRESS));
              return; /* XXX */
        }
  }
...
```

If the fault corresponds to one generated from kernel mode and the address is above the boundary between kernel and user space, the address space corresponds to the one associated with the kernel for use in evaluating the trap. Otherwise, the address space associated with the current executing process is located. If there is no process or no address space associated with the process, the kernel will panic indicating that an attempt is being made to reference a nonexistent address space. Otherwise, the address of the map is located. Notice that at this point the kernel program could also be referencing a user address space since user address spaces are allowed to fault on demand page tables in a reserved region of virtual address space, but only from kernel mode.[12]

A check is made to see if a legal page table reference is being made. In this case, the address translation level of the virtual memory system is called via the **pmap_ptalloc()** call (see **i386/pmap.c**). This function force-allocates an appropriate page of page tables so that the page table fault will not reoccur. The function immediately returns from **trap()** following the allocation since it is known by the rest of the virtual memory system that no page table allocation blocks will occur (e.g. intervening context switches). Note this is a slight inefficiency that should be dealt with and has thus been left as an exercise to the reader. At this point all of the details of the fault are known to pass to the virtual memory system.

... [File: /usr/src/kernel/kern/i386/trap.c, line: 319]

```
        if (vm && vm->vm_ssize && (caddr_t)va >= vm->vm_maxsaddr) {

                /* has the stack exceeded the limit bounds? */
                nss = clrnd(btoc((unsigned)vm->vm_maxsaddr
                        + MAXSSIZ - (unsigned)va));
                if (nss > btoc(p->p_rlimit[RLIMIT_STACK].rlim_cur))
                        goto nogo;

                /* does more stack need to be allocated? */
                if (nss > vm->vm_ssize) {
                        vm_offset_t oldtospage = (vm_offset_t)
                            vm->vm_maxsaddr + MAXSSIZ - ctob(vm->vm_ssize);
                        vm_offset_t sz =  oldtospage - va;

                        /* fail if the idiot mapped it already */
                        if (vmspace_allocate(vm, &va, sz, FALSE)
                            != KERN_SUCCESS)
                                goto nogo;
```

---

[12] Page tables can only be referenced from kernel mode.

```
                          vm->vm_ssize = nss;
                      }
            }
  ...
```

The special case of a growable user process stack is implemented inline. Eventually, this will be done as a portion of the virtual memory system once address space can be typed by function.[13] If there is a process address space associated with the fault, and this address space has a stack that needs to be bounded by a given size (a zero size means that there may be a stack but that it is unbounded and does not need to be checked) and if the faulting address lies within the range of the region, then stack limit checking will be done.

The reference is examined to see if it falls within the current range of the stack. If the number of stack pages present exceeds the resource limit for this process (a limit associated with the index RLIMIT_STACK), then the stack size has grown too large and the fault will be failed without attempting it. This check accounts for the virtual size of the stack segment seen by the user process and managed by the user process itself.

If the number of pages to be mapped into the growable region is larger than what is currently present, the stack will be allocated to cover this new portion inclusively. The size of the new section is determined from the location of the old top of stack's page *oldtospage* less the current faulting page. If the stack cannot be grown (probably because there is something there already), the fault fails. Otherwise, the expansion will succeed and the size of the address space of the stack is recorded as being the full desired expanded size. All that has been done up to this point is just the bookkeeping of allocating address space, as no memory has actually been allocated. This code fragment allows us to avoid allocating the full user stack all at once, reducing the size of a core dump file should a fault occur.

Note that at the level of abstraction of the kernel top half, individual page divisibility of active pages is not present—only active virtual regions. Thus, the majority of trap handling code deals with artifacts of how the kernel virtual memory system is attached to the kernel.

... [File: /usr/src/kernel/kern/i386/trap.c, line: 343]

```
        if (vm_fault(map, va, (code & PGEX_W) ?
            VM_PROT_READ | VM_PROT_WRITE : VM_PROT_READ,
            FALSE) != KERN_SUCCESS) {
        nogo:
                /* handle via prearranged kernel handler */
                if (onfault) {
                        frame.tf_eip = onfault;
                        return;
```

---

[13] The special function of an "expand-down" region managed by an emulator outside of the kernel's address space.

```
                    }

                    /* kernel fault panic */
                    if (type == T_PAGEFLT) {
                            printf(MMU %s fault at 0x%x\n,
                                    (code & PGEX_W) ? write : read, eva);
                            goto we_re_toast;
                    }
            /* ucode = SEGV_PAGE_TRAP; */
                    signo = SIGSEGV;
            }
        }
...
```

The fault is finally passed to the virtual memory system's fault handler **vm_fault()** (see **Volume II** on **vm/fault.c**). The address space associated with the process or the kernel is passed in as the first argument, the page generating the fault passed in as the second argument, and the protection level of the fault that occurred is passed in as the third argument. The fourth parameter on this fault call indicates if it is a fault for wiring or not.[14]

Note that the exception code (code) can only distinguish between write and read faults, with the read fault categorized by the absence of the write fault. Thus, the write fault is turned into a potential read modify write fault with the conventions shifted from the hardware to the virtual memory system's nomenclature (VMPROT_XXX).

If the response from **vm_fault()** is to return the value KERN_SUCCESS, the trap has been handled successfully and the trap handling function is successfully exited (e.g. no signal will be generated). Otherwise, an exception case where the trap is to be failed has occurred. In this case a prearranged kernel fault handler is searched for and located. Since the fault is being handled by the kernel as has been anticipated by the code generating the fault, a safe return is made but with the return address altered to the handler that has inherited control. These are the cases in general where attempted modification or reference of the address space has failed and the calling code must handle recovery. No context switch or other fault handling is allowed to occur since the error may be transparent or at a point where a context switch would not be safe to occur. Note that this is a case where the generic fault handler takes precedence over the inherited fault handler (see above).

If no fault handler is present and the trap occurred from kernel mode, a terminal[15] condition is present. A message is printed on the console and terminal fault handling is begun. If no fault handler is present and the trap occurred from mode, a segmentation violation (SIGSEGV) occurred, the associated processor specific fault indication SEGV_PAGE_TRAP is assigned, and common trap handling is done.

---

[14] Wiring is an internal fault used by the virtual memory system—see **Volume II** for more information.

[15] There is no fault recovery mechanism present to deal with this condition.

... [File: /usr/src/kernel/kern/i386/trap.c, line: 365]

```
        case T_TRCTRAP:

                /* trace trap - someone single stepping lcall's */
                if (frame.tf_eip == (int)&syscall_entry) {
                        frame.tf_eflags &= ~PSL_T;
                        p->p_md.md_flags |= MDP_SSTEP;
                } else
                        goto we_re_toast;
                break;

        case T_BPTFLT|T_USER:           /* bpt instruction fault */
        case T_TRCTRAP|T_USER:          /* trace trap */
                frame.tf_eflags &= ~PSL_T;
                signo = SIGTRAP;
                break;
...
```

An optional mode of the processor (set with a bit in the processor's EFLAGS register) can generate an instruction trace trap following the processing of every instruction. One consequence of instruction single-stepping on the X86 is that one can actually single-step system call entry into the kernel. This will inadvertently cause a kernel panic because the kernel is not written in an entirely re-entrant manner. Thus, if a trace trap occurs from kernel mode and is associated with the call gate for a system call, the trace condition is cleared, and an indication of this event MDP_SSTEP is left on the process as a machine-dependent characteristic.

If the trace trap has occurred elsewhere then it is an unexpected occurrence apparently not found by the debugger filter earlier in this routine and is thus considered a terminal error. If either breakpoints (T_BPTFLT) or trace exceptions (T_TRCTRAP) are entered from user mode, a debugger signal case is simulated by sending a sigtrap signal which will, in the case of a debugged **ptrace()**'d child process, be intercepted by the debugger and used as a transparent entry into stopping the child process. If the breakpoint is also being traced, the trace bit PSL_T in the process's EFLAGS register is cleared so that a second trap to the same instruction will not reoccur.

... [File: /usr/src/kernel/kern/i386/trap.c, line: 381]

```
#ifdef nope
#include isa.h
#if     NISA > 0
        case T_NMI:
        case T_NMI|T_USER:
#ifdef  FAILSAFE
                if (inb(0x61) & 0x40) {
                        extern int splstart;
                        failsafe_cancel();
                        printf(|%x %x:%x. , splstart,
                                frame.tf_eip, frame.tf_cs & 0xffff);
                        return;
                }
#endif
#ifdef DDB
```

```
                /*
                 * NMI can be hooked up to a pushbutton for debugging
                 * (in a pinch, a meduim flat-blade screwdriver can be
                 *  used to short NMI accross to ground in an ISA slot
                 *  -- be very careful! -wfj)
                 */
                printf(NMI ... going to debugger\n);
                if (kdb_trap(type, code, &frame))
                        return;
#endif
                /* machine/parity/power fail/kitchen sink faults */
                if(isa_nmi(code) == 0)
                        return;
                else
                        goto we_re_toast;
#endif
#endif
        ...
```

The NMI (Non-Maskable Interrupt) exception handler is present here. The NMI is used on many processors as a catchall for other processor exception characteristics. In the case of IBM PCs, the NMI can be generated by many sources in a vendor-specific way. Many different kinds of motherboard faults (for example, failsafe timeout, refresh timeout, and bus timeout) as well as memory parity errors all pass through this function. Most laptops generate their power failure exceptions through this line as well. Finally, on an ISA bus machine the NMI can be generated by pulling the I/O channel check signal to ground. The code for dealing with some of these faults is present here since the Compaq SystemPro allows us to implement a failsafe timer that is conditionally compiled in—however, this is by no means generic to all ISA bus machines.

In addition, code for forcing the kernel into the debugger is present in the case that the I/O channel check is generated,[16] along with code to funnel the exception through to the bus adapter and exceptions for battery power (to determine if the processor should be reset or the fault ignored). A more elaborate mechanism really should be implemented here, with the responsibility going to portions of the system other than the kernel, but this is not completed yet.

This ends the fault-specific code handling for this trap handler. We now return to generic handling of the fault.

... [File: /usr/src/kernel/kern/i386/trap.c, line: 416]

```
        if (p == 0)
                return;
    ...
```

---

[16] By the extremely crude method of sticking a flat blade screwdriver into an ISA slot to short the NMI to ground momentarily. This is a very delicate operation, and one had best count pins on the connector carefully.

If there is no process present, then there is nothing more to be done with this fault as there is no way to check signals on a nonexistent process context. Thus processing for interrupt level or idle faults is completed, and the handler returns to the site of the exception (or to an inherited handler).

... [File: /usr/src/kernel/kern/i386/trap.c, line: 420]

```
trap:
        p->p_md.md_flags |= MDP_SIGPROC;
        if (signo)
                trapsignal(p, signo, ucode);
npxerr:
        if (p->p_md.md_flags & MDP_NPXCOLL) {
                p->p_md.md_flags &= ~MDP_NPXCOLL;
                trapsignal(p, SIGFPE, npxlasterror);
        }
        p->p_md.md_flags &= ~MDP_SIGPROC;

        if ((type & T_USER) == 0)
                return;
    ...
```

Signals will now be evaluated on the process. During the pass to evaluate and possibly send the signal to the process, a machine-dependent flag (MDP_SIGPROC) is asserted on the process to deal with the case of asynchronously delivered processor faults.[17] This avoids potential race conditions for an unmaskable event (and also allows us to avoid implementing a **spl_npx** function). This flag indicates that the process has entered into a point where the signal is being evaluated and possibly delivered; thus, external handlers that deliver signals (see **npx/npx.c**) may use this flag to indicate that a npx-generated signal cannot be sent directly to the trap layer.

Should a npx exception come in during the execution of the **trapsignal()** function, the npx routine will not call the **trapsignal()** routine again; it will instead set a machine-dependent flag (NDP_NPXCOLL) to indicate that a collision occurred with the processing of **trapsignal()** and the occurrence simultaneously of an exception from the numeric coprocessor. Following the detection of this flag, the flag will be cleared and the signal passed to the process.

If the process was in kernel mode the signal processing for this trap exception handler is at an end. If the process was in user mode, however, the process will be checked for other outstanding signals and potentially context switched.

... [File: /usr/src/kernel/kern/i386/trap.c, line: 434]

```
out:
        cpu_signals(p = curproc);
        cpu_preempt(p);
    ...
```

---

[17] Such as the case of the floating point coprocessor where the signal may come in after we have switched to a completely different processor.

The process is evaluated for any outstanding signals present. The check of signals is made unconditionally since special cases involved with the tracing of the process[18] may need to be done. These artifacts result from the distinction between the top half of the kernel and interrupt-derived signal generation (see **Chapter 3, cpu_signal()** in **i386/cpu.c**).

After evaluating the process for signals, the process is checked to see if it might be preempted by another using the **cpu_preempt()** function in **i386/inline/kernel/preempt.h**. Notice that both signal and preemption are done only for user mode code. The user mode process itself is always preemptible since it is known that all user code runs without any critical sections or locks held on any kernel data structure. The same is not true for the kernel, however, so preemption cannot be done in the generic case of kernel code. (Note that if kernel mode sections were identified as preemptible and not entered from interrupt level, it would be possible to execute this code. This is in fact how some kinds of real-time UNIX implementations finesse this UNIX design choice.)

... [File: /usr/src/kernel/kern/i386/trap.c, line: 439]

```
        if (p->p_stats->p_prof.pr_scale) {
                int ticks;
                struct timeval *tv = &p->p_stime;

                ticks = ((tv->tv_sec - syst.tv_sec) * 1000 +
                        (tv->tv_usec - syst.tv_usec) / 1000) / (tick / 1000);
                if (ticks)
                        addupc(frame.tf_eip, &p->p_stats->p_prof, ticks);
        }
...
```

If the process executing is making use of the profiling feature of the kernel (pr_scale), the elapsed time spent processing the signal will be billed to the process by recording the time in the process's histogram with the **addupc()** function. The time is calculated in units of rescheduling clock intervals called *ticks*. One side effect of this is when a context switch takes a considerable period of time, an unusual amount of time may be indicated in that histogram entry, depending on the aliasing effects of the boundaries of the histogram counters.

... [File: /usr/src/kernel/kern/i386/trap.c, line: 450]

```
        curpri = p->p_pri;
        p->p_addr->u_pcb.pcb_flags &= ~FM_TRAP; /* XXX used by cpu_signal() */
...
```

Since the process that is executing may not be the process that **trap()** entered with, the priority (*curpri*) is loaded from this current process. This priority will be used to judge potential preemptibility by other processes of the current process. The process's stack

---

[18] Handled as an artifact of signal evaluation.

---

frame type FM_TRAP (which is different from the system call stack frame) is cleared so that the signal code will know that the outstanding trap frame no longer differs (as in the case of employing a trap stack frame on entry to the kernel). This obviates the need for similar code in the system call handler, thus speeding it up.

3.1.2.2 Improvements to the Current Implementation of trap()

One of the weakest aspects of the UNIX kernel architecture is that of error recovery. This is in part due to the lack of a general purpose nestable error recovery interface that can be used throughout the kernel. While the current "on-error" mechanism can be used in a nested fashion, a general purpose "unwinding" or dependency interface has yet to be implemented (e.g. avoid panic). More mundane is the need to support X86 architectural features such as the intXX instructions, virtual 86 real mode, and multiple segments, as well as interfaces to emulators and signals.

3.1.3 What is trapexcept()?

trapexcept() is a special trap handler used in the case of a user code selector-induced reload exception unique to the X86 family. trapexcept() reorganizes the trap frame to allow a safe return to the user process while forcing a terminal signal to the process causing the condition. In addition, the function ensures that no recursively occurring trap will be induced that otherwise might jam the system.[19]

The X86 processor family supports a multisegmented architecture[20] that directly impacts the method by which the segment registers are exchanged in the handling of a trap exception. When the user mode segment selector for instructions is reloaded, the processor is actually running in kernel mode. As such, if the selector has been written with an impossible value, the processor will generate a kernel mode fault since an attempt was made to reference a selector in kernel mode that does not exist or is inappropriate. However, this exception occurs at a point when a portion of the stack frame has yet to be unwound from the stack, and if it were unwound information would be lost. Thus we must carefully restructure the contents of the state of the trap frame so that it will be appropriate in appearance to generate a signal conveying what happened to the process and then reformat the stack so that an appropriate set of selectors is present and the kernel's trap exception can be transformed into a recoverable user segmentation violation.

... [File: /usr/src/kernel/kern/i386/trap.c, line: 460]

```
void
trapexcept(struct trapframe *tf, int *sp) {
 ...
```

---

[19] This is necessary in the case of multithreaded operation.
[20] Which we make little use of with 386BSD.

---

trapexcept() has two arguments: the pointer to the trap entry stack frame; and a pointer to the address of the entry's stack pointer. It returns nothing but has the side-effect of restructuring the trap entry so that a kernel exception will be turned into an ordinary user process exception.

3.1.3.1 How is trapexcept() Implemented?

... [File: /usr/src/kernel/kern/i386/trap.c, line: 467]

```
eip = tf->tf_eip;
eflags = tf->tf_eflags;
...
```

The program counter and processor status word are saved in temporary variables so that they may be used to reconstruct the frame later on (they will be overwritten).

... [File: /usr/src/kernel/kern/i386/trap.c, line: 471]

```
tf->tf_eip = *sp++;
tf->tf_cs = *sp++;
if (eip == (int)&iret)
        tf->tf_eflags = *sp++;
tf->tf_esp = *sp++;
tf->tf_ss = *sp;
...
```

The current outstanding trap frame is overwritten with the values abstracted from the kernel mode fault for the program counter and its corresponding code segment selector. Should the location where the fault occurred result from a return from interrupt (iret) instruction, then the value for the processor's status is overloaded. Otherwise it is assumed that the error occurred with an lret instruction, and the stack pointer and stack's segment selector will also be reloaded. The stack frame is now formatted so that a signal can be sent to the process that incurred this fault.

... [File: /usr/src/kernel/kern/i386/trap.c, line: 479]

```
p->p_md.md_flags |= MDP_SIGPROC;
trapsignal(p, SIGSEGV, 0);
...
```

A segmentation violation signal is forced on the process. As with all entries to signal generation processing, access to these functions is bracketed with a machine-dependent flag (MDP_SIGPROC) to isolate them from races with the numeric coprocessor.

... [File: /usr/src/kernel/kern/i386/trap.c, line: 483]

```
cpu_signals(p);
cpu_preempt(p);
...
```

In addition, checks are made for signals much like in **trap()** above. In fact, the successive two code fragments are also identical to the **trap()** handler as the net effect is the same.

... [File: /usr/src/kernel/kern/i386/trap.c, line: 487]

```
    *sp = _udatasel;        /* force a sane value */
    *--sp = tf->tf_esp;
    if (eip == (int)&iret) {
        *--sp = tf->tf_eflags;
        tf->tf_eflags = eflags;
    }
    *--sp = _ucodesel;      /* force a sane value */
    *--sp = tf->tf_eip;
    ...
```

Since the trap stack frame has been determined to be appropriate for a user exception, the changes made on the stack frame are reversed in place. The user data and code selectors are then restored to their respective spots along with the entry stack pointer and program counter. If the exception was due to a return from interrupt instruction, the flags are similarly updated.

... [File: /usr/src/kernel/kern/i386/trap.c, line: 497]

```
    tf->tf_eip = eip;
    tf->tf_cs = KCSEL;
    tf->tf_es = tf->tf_ds = _udatasel;
    ...
```

Once the stack is reformatted for entry back into user mode, the trap frame is forced to be consistent with the values necessary to reexecute the previously failing instruction (to reenter user mode). Thus, when trap returns from what was initially a kernel mode fault due to a bad user mode context, the kernel fault will restart and attempt to reload a correct user mode context.

3.1.4 What is trapwrite()?

trapwrite() allows a 386 to write-protect pages from supervisor mode write operations, thus correcting a poor design choice which was rectified (as an option) in subsequent processors. This choice was made by the designers of the 386 to compel the use of segments for protection purposes (which we and everyone else got around anyway). **trapwrite()** is called when an attempt is made to write to a read-only page of a user process. It simulates a write operation with the virtual memory system to upgrade the page to write access. The success or failure of this operation is then returned to the caller.

... [File: /usr/src/kernel/kern/i386/trap.c, line: 511]

```
int
trapwrite(unsigned addr) {
    ...
```

---

trapwrite() has one argument: the read-only address that we are attempting to write. It returns true if successful, false otherwise.

Since the process of making a page writeable may cause a copy-on-write fault to occur,[21] the page being accessed prior to the call of this function may not be the same page present afterwards. Indeed, with a copy-on-write fault, a substantial delay may occur between such references (see **Volume II** on **vm/fault.c**).

3.1.4.1 How is trapwrite() Implemented?

... [File: /usr/src/kernel/kern/i386/trap.c, line: 515]

```
        va = trunc_page((vm_offset_t)addr);
        if (va > VM_MAX_ADDRESS)
                return(1);

        if (vm_fault(&curproc->p_vmspace->vm_map, va,
            VM_PROT_READ | VM_PROT_WRITE, FALSE) == KERN_SUCCESS)
                return(0);
        else
                return(1);
...
```

The beginning address of the page is isolated from the address of the effectively virtual fault. Should the address lie in kernel mode, the function fails immediately since it is outside of the user's address space and can never be made writable. The address is then passed to the **vm_fault()** fault handler (in **vm/fault.c**) along with the address of the process's address space map (vm_map) and the attempted reference protection. The fourth parameter indicates that this is not a software induced fault for wiring. Should **vm_fault()** return success, indicating that the page is now writeable, the function returns successfully (zero); otherwise it fails (one).

3.1.5 What is copyin3()?

copyin3() is an optimized inline function used to load, in the most efficient manner possible, three words from the user address space. If there are more than three words to load into the kernel, the function defers to the generic **copyin** inline function. Since the majority of UNIX system calls have three arguments or less, this inline copy routine shaves a handful of microseconds off of almost every system call. **copyin3()** obtains the parameters for a UNIX system call as efficiently as possible.

... [File: /usr/src/kernel/kern/i386/trap.c, line: 531]

```
extern inline int
copyin3(struct proc *p, void *fromaddr, void *toaddr, u_int sz) {
...
```

copyin3() has four arguments: the pointer to the process from whose address space we will obtain information; the address in the process from which to obtain the

---

[21] See *Copy-on-Write in a Nutshell* in **Volume II** on **vm/object.c**.

information; the address in the kernel in which to store the information; and the number of bytes of information to return from the process to the kernel. It returns either zero if successful or an error code EFAULT if unable to load the information into the kernel.

3.1.5.1 How is copyin3() Implemented?

... [File: /usr/src/kernel/kern/i386/trap.c, line: 535]

```
        if (sz > 3 * sizeof(int)) {
                return (copyin(p, fromaddr, toaddr, sz));
    ...
```

If the number of bytes to be transferred is larger than three, the generic inline function **copyin** is called to perform the operation. Otherwise, the copy operation will be performed inline.

... [File: /usr/src/kernel/kern/i386/trap.c, line: 537]

```
        } else {
                /* set fault vector */
                asm ( movl      $4f, %0 : : m (p->p_md.md_onfault));

                /* copy the arguments */
                *((int *) toaddr)|| = *((int *) fromaddr)||;
                *((int *) toaddr)++ = *((int *) fromaddr)++;
                *((int *) toaddr)++ = *((int *) fromaddr)++;

                /* catch the possible fault */
                asm (\
                        xorl %0, %0 ;                   \
                        jmp 5f ;                        \
                4:      movl %1, %0 ;                   \
                5:
                        : =r (rv)
                        : I (EFAULT));

                /* clear the fault vector */
                p->p_md.md_onfault = 0;

                return (rv);
        }
    ...
```

The address of the fault handler within this procedure is recorded in the process's inherited fault handler field (md_onfault). Then, the three words of arguments are copied inline as word moves from successive addresses. Should a fault occur during this operation, control will be transferred indirectly from the main fault handler **trap()** to the fault handler within this function. The assembly language-inherited fault handler will catch the fault and set an EFAULT value into the returning value. Otherwise a value of zero will be placed into the return value variable (rv). In either case the inherited fault handler is cleared and the value returned.

3.1.6 What is syscall()?

syscall() is the generic system call handler for all iBCS, POSIX, and BSD system calls. It is implemented for the X86 architecture as a system call *call gate* interface[22] connected to descriptor selector 7.[23] Unlike other machines which generally encode a system call as a kind of exception or fault, the X86 implements it as a special kind of procedure call which is then filtered by this function and redirected to a specific system call handler (many of which are documented in **kern/descrip.c**). **syscall()** accepts a specially formatted stack and series of arguments from its assembly language entry code (see **locore.s**). It takes this kernel stack frame of information and extracts the relevant information to determine the standardized semantics of the system call, validates that it exists, locates and transfers to the kernel all pertinent system call parameters, and returns generic exceptions in the case it cannot compose a suitable request to a system call handler.

Upon completion of a system call, **syscall()** (like **trap()**) evaluates the process to discover if any new signals are present so that the process may be made aware of them. It also checks for any other processes waiting to preempt the current process. In addition, **syscall()** performs a special obligation for the **fork()** system call (see **Chapter 5** on **kern/fork.c**) whereby it detects the presence of a new process formed from the old process.

... [File: /usr/src/kernel/kern/i386/trap.c, line: 568]

```
void
syscall(volatile struct syscframe frame)
...
```

syscall() has one argument of unusual type: a system call stack frame passed in as a value-result structure (much like **trap()**). The contents of the structure are turned into a series of values which provide input and output from the system call. However, unlike **trap()**, this structure is marked as a **volatile** type in ANSI C indicating that all references must be made to main memory and not cached in a register. This is done because the parameters in the stack frame might be altered by other functions called by **syscall()**, aliased by other subtle means, or even change entirely due to stack relocation.[24]

3.1.6.1 How is syscall() Implemented?

... [File: /usr/src/kernel/kern/i386/trap.c, line: 591]

```
        syst = p->p_stime;
        idx = frame.sf_eax;
        params = (caddr_t)frame.sf_esp + sizeof (int) ;
```

---

[22] See *What are System Call 'Call Gates'?* in **i386/locore.s**.
[23] Local descriptor table entry number 0 at ring 3 access.
[24] As in the case of the fork primitive **cpu_fork()** in **cpu.c**. See **Chapter 3** for more information.

```
    p->p_addr->u_pcb.pcb_flags &= ~FM_TRAP; /* XXX used by cpu_signal() */
    p->p_md.md_regs = (int *)&frame;
...
```

The time of entry into the system call is recorded into the local variable *syst*. This marks the beginning of the processing time spent in the kernel for the system call. As part of the calling convention for an iBCS system call, the index associated with this system call handler is located in the EAX register extracted from the stack frame. Since there are multiple stack frame formats on entry,[25] the stack format is signalled by a bit in the processor control block flags guaranteed not to conflict with a similar bit used by the **trap()** call. This bit has been kept in the same location (pcb_flags) from the earliest implementation of 386BSD only for compatibility reasons, since external system code unfortunately knows about it and should have been migrated to the machine-dependent proc_flags field. However, there are now steps underway to eliminate the pcb_flags field entirely (along with other things) through a significant reorganization of the **locore.s** trap entry code to achieve entry format standardization.

Another holdover from the past is the **ptrace**-related machine-dependent process register's description field md_regs, which is set to point at the base of the kernel's stack entry frame. The parameters of an iBCS system call are located on the user process stack whose contents in turn are located in the stack entry frame (sf_esp) corresponding to the ESP register value when the user program was last running. Since a word on the top of stack is associated with the address of the caller to the system call handler, it is bypassed and all of the parameters begin from that point on up in ascending order.

... [File: /usr/src/kernel/kern/i386/trap.c, line: 598]

```
    if (p->p_md.md_flags & MDP_SSTEP) {
            p->p_md.md_flags &= ~MDP_SSTEP;
            frame.sf_eflags |= PSL_T;
    }
...
```

Should the system call be single-stepped into the kernel (which is possible), the condition is noticed by the presence of a machine-dependent process flag MDP_SSTEP. In this case the flag is cleared and the single-step bit in the processor status register is set (PSL_T), thus ensuring that single-stepping will continue in the instruction following the system call (where it will not cause a problem). This artifact exists because our X86 system call is an extended function call mechanism and not an exception mechanism.

---

[25] The system call mechanism of the X86, like most system call mechanisms, doesn't bother to save the processor status—exception handlers do, however.

... [File: /usr/src/kernel/kern/i386/trap.c, line: 604]

```
          callp = (idx >= nsysent) ? &sysent[0] : &sysent[idx];
      ...
```

The index to the appropriate system call handler is used to locate a table entry describing the system call. If the system call's index is larger than the number of entries in the linear table, then the first system call entry is returned. This call entry corresponds to the nonexistent system call handler **nosys()** (see **Chapter 6, kern/sig.c**). This simple manner of locating system calls in a single linear table was employed in the very earliest UNIX systems.

In iBCS system calls, some indexes with very large values are used to describe extensions to the original set of UNIX system calls (which were arranged in a fairly dense format), allowing the implementation of multiple tables hanging off the same handler with separate spans of value of the index. This is not implemented in 386BSD, since 386BSD is evolving an emulation library to handle system call formats external to the kernel. This ensures that compatibility need not slow down operation.

For the moment, however, the current mechanism described here is quite adequate for a simple system. However, it and the system calls specific to BSD, POSIX, and iBCS are subjects for migration out of the kernel as the kernel evolves separate implementations of operating system personalities.

... [File: /usr/src/kernel/kern/i386/trap.c, line: 607]

```
      if (callp == sysent) {
              if (error = copyin_(p, (void *)params, (void *)&idx,
                  sizeof(idx)))
                     goto err;
              params += sizeof (int);
              callp = (idx >= nsysent) ? &sysent[0] : &sysent[idx];
      }
  ...
```

A special case system call is the *indirect* system call implemented inline. The system call indirect handler corresponds to the very first entry and so overloads the previously mentioned **nosys()** handler, allowing for the arguments (including the system call index) to be located from yet another address—resulting in a variable system call number. Thus, a new index is located as the first parameter in the indirect system call handler. Should an error occur, the system call terminates early with an illegal faulting parameter (EFAULT); otherwise, the new address of the parameters is loaded and used to bypass the index value, and another pointer into the table of system call entries is located.[26]

---

[26] N.B. Not all system call handlers work in this frame, since some require special handling on the user mode side. Thus, care must be taken when selecting which system calls are used with this indirect system call handler—the interface is not general purpose.

```
        if ((i = callp->sy_narg * sizeof (int)) &&
            (error = copyin3(p, params, (caddr_t)args, (u_int)i))) {
        err:
                frame.sf_eax = error;
                frame.sf_eflags |= PSL_C;         /* carry bit */
#ifdef KTRACE
                if (KTRPOINT(p, KTR_SYSCALL))
                        ktrsyscall(p->p_tracep, idx, callp->sy_narg, &args);
#endif
                goto done;
        }
    ...
```

The next step, once we have a system call to evaluate, is to load any arguments necessary for the system call from the user mode address space of the process. Since these arguments are in units of words, the number of bytes of arguments is calculated. If no arguments are needed, no reference to the user address space will be made. A special version of **copyin** is used to load the parameters into a statically allocated array of local variables called *args*. **copyin3()** optimally attempts to copy in three words because the majority of system calls are three words of arguments or less. Should the arguments not be fetched successfully, then an EFAULT error is returned and the system call terminated. By convention, the error in the system call has its error value returned in the EAX register as well as a value-result parameter using the stack frame argument. In addition, the error is signalled by setting the carry bit of the processor status (PSL_C). Control is then transferred to the common conclusion of the system call handler.

It is not necessary to copy the parameters of a system call into the kernel for an architecture such as the X86, since the system call is being performed in the context of the process. Even if the processor did not have the context directly referenceable (as is true for some other architectures), the parameters could still be incrementally copied on demand. One problem with doing this, however, is that the parameters may have addresses of the parameters embedded in them. If a cunning programmer knew that the validation checks on a portion of the arguments might be done before a modification and fetch of the subsequent arguments, he might arrange to bypass the checking by overwriting the checked parameters, thus getting the kernel to compromise security of parameters before they are used.[27] Copying all of the parameters forestalls this possibility, since the address of where the parameters lie is expressly off-limits to any valid address of parameters (since it lies in the kernel's address space).

---

[27] This actually happened with early timesharing systems and was a significant security flaw.

... [File: /usr/src/kernel/kern/i386/trap.c, line: 633]

```
        rval[0] = 0;
        rval[1] = frame.sf_edx;
        error = (*callp->sy_call)(p, args, rval);
...
```

As part of the common format for all system call handlers, the arguments, context, and area to return values to the user are prepared. Return values are buffered in an array of up to two values in size, corresponding to the two temporary registers containing the values to be returned to the user process. Since a few system calls may override these values, preliminary initialized values are left in place corresponding to the common return value of zero (success) in the EAX register, while the EDX register holds the state previously in the register. Only a few system calls return both values (like the **pipe()** system call). By leaving unmodified the EDX register, it need not always be saved by user mode system call handlers.[28] With the parameters for the return buffer arguments and a pointer to the process present, the system call handler can be called, and its address is recovered from the table entry (sy_call). All system calls have the same conventions regardless of the number of arguments, number of return values, or process with which they were called.

This calling convention for system call handlers ensures that all references to elements of the process's context are made relative to the supplied context pointer and not a global variable. Similarly, the arguments may also be supplied and return values obtained separately. One advantage to this arrangement becomes clear when multiprocessing is added to the kernel. With loosely coupled multiprocessing, an alternative system call handler invoked across a network connection can engage the same system call indirectly on its address space (via messages) that a local system call may then make use of. In the case of tightly coupled multiprocessing, thread locking primitives with shared datastructures can resolve exclusive access restrictions based solely on information contained in the unshared portion of the process context. The return values from such system calls are also orthogonal to the return values potentially returned by the system call. Thus, the parameters can be returned sans specific items reflecting the processor format of the system call itself and how that format might be locally implemented. This allows for the machine-independent system call formats necessary for heterogeneous clustering to become possible.

... [File: /usr/src/kernel/kern/i386/trap.c, line: 638]

```
        if (error == ERESTART)
                frame.sf_eip -= 7;      /* backup pc, size of lcall $0x7,0 */
        else if (error != EJUSTRETURN) {
                if (error) {
                        frame.sf_eax = error;
                        frame.sf_eflags |= PSL_C;        /* carry bit */
```

---

[28] Thus corresponding to conventions of user mode C code in the process.

```
        } else {
                frame.sf_eax = rval[0];
                frame.sf_edx = rval[1];
                frame.sf_eflags &= ~PSL_C;        /* carry bit */
        }
    }           /* otherwise, don't modify return register state */
...
```

After completing the system call, the results of the system call must be placed back into the standardized format of the user mode conventions for an iBCS system call. In particular, any errors returned must be correctly passed back to the process along with any return values in a machine-dependent fashion. Two errors of note here are unique to this implementation of the kernel—they are *pseudo-errors* meant to signal special processing. The ERESTART error indicates that the system call should be arranged to reoccur (e.g. be backed up). This is done on restartable system calls where a signal may have been passed to the user process while the kernel had been waiting for a system call to complete. In this case, the system call has silently aborted so that the signal may be discovered at the "bottom" of a system call handler, delivered to the user (via **syscall()**), and entry made back into user mode so that the signal may be processed. After the signal completes and the kernel is reentered, the system call restarts from the point that it left off, in effect calling itself yet again. Since it is known that the system call is always entered via a seven-byte instruction[29] in all cases, the instruction pointer is backed up by seven bytes.

Another pseudo-error, EJUSTRETURN, forces the kernel not to modify the state of any registers at all. This special return is used by a hidden system call in signal processing called **sigreturn()** (see **Chapter 6** on **kern/sig.c**) that forces reentry into the kernel on conclusion of a user signal handler. Since the handler appears as an interrupt and cannot modify any registers on return (for it would corrupt the program running), it makes no modifications but only returns (not modifying register contents). This kind of system call handler either works completely or generates a signal itself to indicate an error. If neither of these pseudo-errors is present, an ordinary system call return is done. It is possible to add more pseudo-errors to deal with other special case situations in the kernel. These pseudo-errors are a way of specifying a different class of system call return treatment and are artifacts of the kernel not being written in an object-oriented language.

Should the system call handler return an error, a nonzero value will be returned by convention in the EAX register with the carry bit set in the processor status word. If no error is present, however, both return values will be returned unconditionally in the user process's EDX and EAX registers, respectively. The carry bit of the processor status word is forced to zero in case it already was set, ensuring that the return value not be interpreted as an error.

[29] And the instruction is **lcall $ 0x7, 0**.

... [File: /usr/src/kernel/kern/i386/trap.c, line: 652]

```
        p = curproc;
...
```

In the case of a **fork()** system call (see **Chapter 5** on **kern/fork.c**) returning in the child context, the local variable *p* holding the pointer to the current process may have become stale, so it is reloaded from the global variable. Since the kernel stack is a copy of the parent process (including registers), the value must be reloaded with the new process's address. It makes no sense to add a conditional test to save the cost of the load.

... [File: /usr/src/kernel/kern/i386/trap.c, line: 655]

```
done:
        cpu_signals(p = curproc);
        cpu_preempt(p);
...
```

The process is evaluated for any outstanding signals which must be delivered prior to returning from the system call. These signals will be delivered by the **cpu_signal()** function. Following the mandatory delivery of any signals, a call will be made to the preemption function **cpu_preempt()** in **i386/mdproc.h** which checks to see if the process is preemptible by another process. Note that during the time that a process has become preempted and then made runable again, additional signals may have occurred. Thus, **cpu_preempt()** must also detect any additional signals and return them. Since system calls are only allowed to come from user mode, these checks may be done at any time

... [File: /usr/src/kernel/kern/i386/trap.c, line: 660]

```
        if (p->p_stats->p_prof.pr_scale) {
                int ticks;
                struct timeval *tv = &p->p_stime;

                ticks = ((tv->tv_sec - syst.tv_sec) * 1000 +
                        (tv->tv_usec - syst.tv_usec) / 1000) / (tick / 1000);
                if (ticks)
                        addupc(frame.sf_eip, &p->p_stats->p_prof, ticks);
        }
...
```

If the process executing is making use of the profiling feature of the kernel (pr_scale), the elapsed time spent processing the system call will be billed to the process by recording the time in the process's histogram with the **addupc()** function. The time is calculated in units of rescheduling clock intervals called *ticks*. One side effect of this is when a context switch takes a considerable period of time, an unusual amount of time may be indicated in that histogram entry, depending on the aliasing effects of the boundaries of the histogram counters.

... [File: /usr/src/kernel/kern/i386/trap.c, line: 676]

```
        curpri = p->p_pri;
    ...
```

Since the process that is executing may not be the process that **syscall()** entered with, the priority (*curpri*) is loaded from this current process. This priority will be used to judge potential preemptibility by other processes of the current process.

3.1.7 What is systrap()?

systrap() handles an asynchronous trap (AST) that has arrived just as the system call handler returned to the user address space. It is an artifact of the X86 implementation. **systrap()** exists because there is no way to call a nonexistent system call with the current system handler to resample signals transparently. In addition, because network software interrupts require returning to a processor mask level where such an interrupt could generate an AST, a signal could be posted in a race after the system call handler had completed but before return to the process could be done. In this case, the signal would otherwise be postponed until the next entry to the kernel had occurred, which might take a considerable period of time.

systrap() is called when a short noninterruptible portion of the kernel has determined that an AST has occurred before the last few instructions returned to the user process, thus greatly reducing the window of the race to no instructions at all.[30] Thus, the latency of delivery of a signal is at most the cost of kernel entry plus the overhead of signal delivery.

... [File: /usr/src/kernel/kern/i386/trap.c, line: 687]

```
void
systrap(volatile struct syscframe frame) {
    ...
```

systrap() has one argument: a structure containing the kernel stack entry frame of a system call. It returns nothing. Like the **syscall()** function, the structure argument is a value-result parameter used only by signals associated with the AST that caused **systrap()** to be called in the first place. **systrap()** relies heavily on the fact that it is only called after a **syscall()** invocation, so it assumes that the values that **syscall()** has set up (e.g. md_regs) are correct values.

---

[30] E.g. an interrupt that would cause a signal must now occur after the process has made it into user mode—thus generating its own trap entry.

3.1.7.1 How is systrap() Implemented?

... [File: /usr/src/kernel/kern/i386/trap.c, line: 693]

```
        syst = p->p_stime;

        cpu_preempt(p = curproc);
...
```

Since signals may take a considerable amount of time which must be accounted for, the time of entry is loaded into a local variable. Signals and any outstanding rescheduling request which may also have arrived with the AST are interpreted by a call to **cpu_preempt()** (see **i386/mdproc.h**). Note that no call to **cpu_signal()** is done as with **syscall()** since the only reason for a signal to be present regardless of the artifacts induced by the tracing of a process is the delivery of an asynchronous system call generated from the lower levels of the system. Thus, this is an optimization.

Another optimization present is the apparent redundancy in electing to call **cpu_preempt()** in the system call handler above. It is commonly the case that rescheduling an AST will occur during the course of a system call handler event, and **cpu_preempt()** handles all ASTs usually associated with the system call handler. Thus, the only times that **systrap()** will be called are in those rare cases where a race condition is present. The inefficiency induced from multiple calls to a system call handler is small due to infrequency of occurrence, which is why this implementation has been designed in this fashion.

... [File: /usr/src/kernel/kern/i386/trap.c, line: 698]

```
        if (p->p_stats->p_prof.pr_scale) {
                int ticks;
                struct timeval *tv = &p->p_stime;

                ticks = ((tv->tv_sec - syst.tv_sec) * 1000 +
                        (tv->tv_usec - syst.tv_usec) / 1000) / (tick / 1000);
                if (ticks)
                        addupc(frame.sf_eip, &p->p_stats->p_prof, ticks);
        }
...
```

If the process executing is making use of the profiling feature of the kernel (pr_scale), the elapsed time spent processing the system call will be billed to the process by recording the time in the process's histogram with the **addupc()** function. The time is calculated in units of rescheduling clock intervals called *ticks*. One side effect of this is when a context switch takes a considerable period of time, an unusual amount of time may be indicated in that histogram entry, depending on the aliasing effects of the boundaries of the histogram counters.

... [File: /usr/src/kernel/kern/i386/trap.c, line: 709]

```
        curpri = p->p_pri;
...
```

Since the process that is executing may not be the process that **systrap()** entered with, the priority (*curpri*) is loaded from this current process. This priority will be used to judge potential preemptibility by other processes of the current process.

3.2 CPU Kernel Facilities: i386/cpu.c

The file **i386/cpu.c** contains the code specific to the Central Processing Unit (CPU) which implements at the bottom level of abstraction a variety of kernel facilities, including kernel thread creation and destruction, user process signal delivery and return, and user program entry. Processor-dependent functions prefaced with **cpu_** are implicitly called from the kernel to implement the machine-dependent portions of specific kernel subsystems. These functions are optionally defined to implement parts of the kernel as needed by a specific implementation.

3.2.1 Threads versus Processes

Processes and threads are the lowest level of abstraction concurrent objects in the kernel. The *threads* used in this implementation are actually slimmed down processes sharing process structures with fewer and/or shared entries. We use the term *threads* in places where both processes and threads are appropriate. The only exception to this convention is where the word "process" is used for historical reasons even though it also applies to threads, such as in the process structure (see **sys/proc.h** for struct proc) and process control block (see **i386/pcb.h**). The term *process* is used for operations relevant only to processes and not threads. Since we have found no compelling need to complicate matters by either increasing the number of data objects, nor renaming them yet again, we have chosen to deal with this dichotomy through name conventions only.

This implementation of **i386/cpu.c** is responsible for generating and destroying the basic portion of kernel resident state for either of these concurrent entities. Higher level routines in the machine-independent kernel and virtual memory subsystem are responsible for the remaining portions of the generation of process or thread. These functions implement the lowest level of abstraction of concurrent function; below this lies only the processor itself.

3.2.2 POSIX Signals

Signals are POSIX exception handling mechanisms. They are implemented using BSD-specific data structures,[31] managed by the kernel (see **kern/sig.c**), and instigated by various other kernel services (see **kern/tty.c**, **kern/proc.c**, **kern/exit.c**, **kern/descrip.c**, and so forth).

---

[31] See **sys/signal.h** and **sys/signalvar.h**.

The functions responsible for signals in this file add and remove the special stack frames in the user process that achieve the net effect of the signal itself. Higher level portions of the machine-independent kernel maintain the interface and additional POSIX semantics of the signal mechanism.

3.2.3 Functions Contained in the File i386/cpu.c

The file **i386/cpu.c** contains those portions which can be built out of other facilities private to the machine-dependent kernel. Corresponding to this file, the file **i386/cpu.h** defines these functions for reference by other portions of the kernel.

Within this file are contained the functions:

cpu_tfork()

cpu_texit()

cpu_signal()

cpu_signalreturn()

cpu_execsetregs()

cpu_ptracereg()

cpu_reset()

The names are indicative of the kernel function they provide for the machine-dependent implementation. **cpu_tfork()** and **cpu_texit()** provide the thread creation and destruction mechanism used in the kernel to implement kernel support threads and user processes.[32] **cpu_signal()** and **cpu_signalreturn()** implement the POSIX signal mechanism on user processes, by stacking and unstacking a signal, respectively. **cpu_execsetregs()** prepares a user program's initial register set for execution inside a process.[33] **cpu_reset()** is used in rebooting the system to request that the computer restart, thus entering bootstrap operations. Finally, **cpu_ptracereg()** locates the address of a desired register in a process's stored state for use by the **ptrace()** debugging facility.

3.2.4 What is cpu_tfork?

cpu_tfork(), the machine-dependent thread fork operation, implements at the lowest level of abstraction the creation of all concurrent objects in 386BSD. Each user and kernel process possesses a thread of execution that is present in the kernel. This thread

---

[32] Via the **fork()** and **exit()** system calls.
[33] Via the **execve()** system call.

consists of a unique kernel stack and a process control block (struct pcb, see **i386/pcb.h**) that holds the processor state when the thread becomes inactive.

cpu_tfork() creates a new thread by copying an existing thread into the blank state of the new thread. Since each stack is allocated out of a unique portion of kernel virtual address space, the copy must relocate any references to the kernel stack itself to be relative to the address of the "new" stack instead of the address of the "old" stack. Since the new thread is not yet running, a valid pcb must be built out of the current thread's active register state. This allows the thread to begin execution by having its state reloaded via the principal concurrency mechanism, the thread context switch. Finally, since the thread is a copy of an existing thread, it is different in one way—it is denoted as a "copy."

... [File: /usr/src/kernel/kern/i386/cpu.c, line: 81]

```
int
cpu_tfork(struct proc *p1, register struct proc *p2)
...
```

The function is *first* called with pointers to two threads: the one to be copied (p1); and the new copy (p2). This function returns *twice*; once in the process making the copy, and once returning in the new copy process. If it is returning from the new copy, it returns a "true" value; "false" otherwise. The new thread (p2) is allocated but not scheduled for execution.

In sum, **cpu_tfork()** fills in a blank thread state that has already been allocated, allowing the thread to be context-switchable. Unlike thread destruction, where we must deallocate state from a running thread, state allocation for creation is machine-independent because the thread is not yet running. It is important to remember that threads don't need to create like-sized objects—a thread can create a process and a process can create a thread.

3.2.4.1 How is cpu_tfork() Implemented?

For the hardware (the 386 processor family) to access the pcb state itself, **cpu_tfork()** creates a new concurrent object by using the 386 TSS (Task Switch State, see **i386/tss.h**) descriptor, a processor-dependent data structure that makes use of a special hardware mechanism to exchange the contents of a thread or task state with the next one to run.

[File: /usr/src/kernel/kern/i386/cpu.c, line: 93]

```
        p2->p_stksz = ctob(UPAGES);
        /* if (p2->p_stksz >= NBPG) */
              p2->p_addr = up = (struct user *)
                    kmem_alloc(kernel_map, ctob(UPAGES), M_WAITOK);
        /* else
              p2->p_addr = up = (struct user *)
                    malloc((u_long)ctob(UPAGES), M_KSTACK, M_NOWAIT); */
...
```

Thread state is a variable length record which is known to be a contiguous segment of kernel virtual address with a pcb located at the start and a program stack at the end. Some thread states only contain stack and pcb; they are *naked* threads launched by the kernel to perform housekeeping functions on global kernel state. Others may have larger thread states to hold additional information used to maintain larger and more elaborate objects (like a POSIX process). The additional space is present above the pcb and below the bottom of the kernel stack. Since any concurrent object can create other classes of concurrent objects,[34] freshly created threads may be of different size then the original thread. Relocation between the stacks is determined by the ends of the stacks, each of which may be of different size.

As a shorthand, since all we will be concerned with in the new thread is the new state, a variable is allocated to bypass numerous indirections and obtain the address of the new thread state (up).

... [File: /usr/src/kernel/kern/i386/cpu.c, line: 102]

```
        diff = ((caddr_t)p2->p_addr + p2->p_stksz)
                - ((caddr_t)p1->p_addr + p1->p_stksz);
...
```

The address relocation of the new kernel stack is first calculated from the old one. From this value, we can relocate any of the existing thread's kernel stack relative addresses to the nascent thread's stack frame.

... [File: /usr/src/kernel/kern/i386/cpu.c, line: 106]

```
        up->u_pcb = p1->p_addr->u_pcb;

        /* update the new pcb to reflect this process current status. */
                asm volatile ("movl %%esp, %0" : "=m"
                        (up->u_pcb.pcb_tss.tss_esp));
                asm volatile ("movl %%ebp, %0" : "=m"
                        (up->u_pcb.pcb_tss.tss_ebp));
        /* } */
...
```

The contents of the pcb is now copied by structure assignment to the new thread state. These values will be current as of the last **swtch()** away from this process, and it constitutes a way of initializing a empty process state conveniently, by loading all inactive state information into the new process control block. If this task is found to be the current task, some of the fields in the process control block contain stale information on registers used in executing **cpu_tfork()**, so the "new" pcb must be updated with its current register state. Inline assembly code is used for efficiency to access the processor register contents required for this update. In this implementation, the frame (EBP) and stack (ESP) pointers are updated at this point, while the

---

[34] For example, a POSIX process could indirectly create some kernel threads by opening a device driver.

remaining registers will either be updated later in this function,[35] or will never be referenced again.[36]

Note that this function may later be used to generate a new thread from another unrelated context entirely. In this case, the state would not need to be updated from the running context. Code appearing in comments reflects the additional changes necessary when this step in the kernel's evolution occurs.

... [File: /usr/src/kernel/kern/i386/cpu.c, line: 115]

```
        up->u_pcb.pcb_tss.tss_esp += diff;
        up->u_pcb.pcb_tss.tss_ebp += diff;
...
```

Now, having copied the stack, the pcb's contents must be adjusted to reflect the new stack location. The kernel's stack can have absolute address references to itself that will no longer be valid with the new location. As such, it is unwise to record the address of C automatic variables in global variables and data structures, since the frames to which they belong could become deallocated and the addresses would then point at unpredictable contents. Thus, the kernel program avoids this possible complication in stack relocation.

To minimize stack relocation overhead, the kernel program is constructed to avoid holding any references to stack variables, even within the stack itself, where a possible thread creation could occur. At this point in the kernel's evolution, this is not a major limitation in implementation.

... [File: /usr/src/kernel/kern/i386/cpu.c, line: 119]

```
        asm volatile ("  cld ; repe ; movsl " : :
            "D" ((caddr_t)up->u_pcb.pcb_tss.tss_esp
            "S" ((caddr_t)up->u_pcb.pcb_tss.tss_esp - diff),
            "c" (((unsigned)p1->p_addr + p1->p_stksz
                - up->u_pcb.pcb_tss.tss_esp + diff) ) / sizeof(int)));
...
```

The active portion of the kernel stack is now copied into place in the "new" task. Usually, this is a small (32-word) region containing a few C function frames on top of a kernel entry frame (trap, syscall, or interrupt). Since this is always an aligned field of integral word size, a special inline copy is used to streamline replication on this architecture.

---

[35] Such as the registers EBX, ESI, and EDI, that the compiler uses to hold permanent values per function call.
[36] Such as the temporary registers EAX, EDX, and ECX, which are known not to be preserved by the compiler after a function call.

```
        fp = (unsigned *) up->u_pcb.pcb_tss.tss_ebp;
        while ((nfp = *fp) >= (unsigned) fp - (unsigned) diff) {
                nfp += diff;
                *fp = nfp;
                fp = (unsigned *)nfp;
        }
...
```

In addition to the program visible state mentioned above, the compiler can also interpose state into the stack that can have stack references. With the 386, the GCC compiler uses the EBP register to denote function stack frames, which are then recorded as a list of absolute stack addresses embedded in the stack frame. These frame pointers are located and relocated on the stack, by following them back from the original recorded in the task state. The last frame pointer is discovered by the fact that the last frame contains a kernel entry frame, which has a frame pointer that points to a frame in the user program portion of address space, instead of the ascending order of frames as expected.

Alternatively, one could check for both order and bounds of the top of the thread state. On other architectures that don't use frame pointers (such as RISC), no such relocation is needed. However, different support may be required at this point to deal with other "invisible" stack references.[37]

... [File: /usr/src/kernel/kern/i386/cpu.c, line: 134]

```
        (int)p2->p_md.md_regs = (int) p1->p_md.md_regs + diff;
        p2->p_md.md_flags = 0;
...
```

One notable exception to the programming discipline mentioned above is the case of a pointer to the user program register state saved in the kernel entry frame (mentioned above) which is saved in the machine-dependent portion of the proc structure. This must be separately relocated to be kept consistent in the new thread.[38] In addition to the register pointer, the machine-dependent flags are cleared for the new thread.

... [File: /usr/src/kernel/kern/i386/cpu.c, line: 138]

```
        alloctss(p2);
...
```

For the 386 hardware to save and reload this process control block, the **alloctss()** inline function is called to assign an unused TSS to this new space. The TSS is a segment of kernel virtual address space that overlays the thread state and allows atomic

---

[37] For example, the SPARC's register windows.
[38] N.B. This "feature" will be deprecated in future releases of 386BSD when the format of the entry stack is fixed. This item will then become a fixed structure ending at the exact end (top) of the kernel stack (p_addr + p_stksz).

exchanges of program state by a segmented jump instruction to the TSS descriptor so assigned. Descriptors are designated by indexes called selectors that denote a unique descriptor in the global descriptor table. The selector associated with the new thread is kept in the task state itself (pcb_tss_sel) for use during context switches. **alloctss()** is a short inline procedure that calls an ordinary function if it cannot conveniently allocate a new TSS in the simple case. Almost always the new TSS is allocated without the need for a function call.

... [File: /usr/src/kernel/kern/i386/cpu.c, line: 141]

```
        up->u_pcb.pcb_tss.tss_esp0 = (unsigned) up + p2->p_stksz;
    ...
```

One unique aspect of the 386 architecture comes into play now. Unlike other processors which have dedicated registers to hold supervisor program state, to change from user to kernel mode the processor consults the TSS to obtain the contents of the initial stack pointers on entry to supervisor mode. Since there are three modes (Rings 0, 1, 2) that can be entered from the outermost (Ring 3 or user mode), each has an entry stack pointer. For entry into the kernel (Ring 0), ESP0 must be set to the top of stack of the new thread.[39]

... [File: /usr/src/kernel/kern/i386/cpu.c, line: 144]

```
        up->u_pcb.pcb_ptd = KernelPTD;
    ...
```

Another x86 hardware detail lies in the address translation information. In this implementation, all threads share a single kernel address space (KernelPTD) until an attempt is made to allocate or modify a user address space. This technique improves the speed to context switch among kernel-mode threads, since the context switch hardware observes that the switch is to the same address space and can thus avoid the cost imposed in flushing stale address translations to the previous space.

... [File: /usr/src/kernel/kern/i386/cpu.c, line: 148]

```
            asm volatile ("movl %%ebx, %0" : "=m"
                    (up->u_pcb.pcb_tss.tss_ebx));
            asm volatile ("movl %%edi, %0" : "=m"
                    (up->u_pcb.pcb_tss.tss_edi));
            asm volatile ("movl %%esi, %0" : "=m"
                    (up->u_pcb.pcb_tss.tss_esi));
        /* } */
    ...
```

The register state for the child process must be updated by updating the registers that might hold values used in processing the ending portion of this function in the new thread. The additional registers updated in this version allow the inline functions

---

[39] Currently, only rings 0 and 3 are used.

---

called in this function to be transparently compiled as non-inlined functions for use with the debugger.[40]

... [File: /usr/src/kernel/kern/i386/cpu.c, line: 154]

```
        asm volatile ("movl $1f, %0; 1:" : "=m" (up->u_pcb.pcb_tss.tss_eip));

        /* are we the new thread? */
        if (curproc == 0) { asm(".globl _tfork_child ; _tfork_child: ");
                curproc = p2;
                splnone();
                return (1);      /* child */
        }
        return (0);              /* parent */
    ...
```

Finally, the function must start the new thread (child). This new thread starts executing at the end of the function and evaluates the return statement differently in the new thread. Access to the assembler via an asm statement allows us to grab the next instruction's address to stuff in the child's EIP register. The return from the creator of the thread will set the global variable *curproc*. In the child the value is zero because the jump TSS instruction in **swtch** has been called with the "no process running" indication set. This is the only point where the thread is made known to the system as a whole, since the child must write the address of its own process into the variable denoting the current running process (*curproc*).[41]

3.2.4.2 386BSD cpu_tfork() Evolutionary History

Earlier versions of 386BSD avoided use of the TSS entirely for context switching, in a vain attempt to reduce the cost of the process context switch. The kernel stack was kept as a portion of the user program's address space, so that by exchanging the address space the context would also change. This behavior was a hold-over from the VAX/CCI implementation that worked in identical fashion, since the original port of 386BSD was done using the older VAX virtual memory subsystem. To be fair, an advantage of this remapping approach is that it consumes less kernel virtual address space, which is limited on other architectures such as the VAX and SPARC.

Unfortunately, for the 386 processor family the cost of maintaining the process context completely swamped any savings gained by trimming cycles in the context switch. On second glance, the apparently "expensive" 386 context switch mechanism was overall more efficient when the machine-dependent implementation was adjusted to better fit the processor instead of perpetuating the characteristics of the VAX. The new machine-dependent code which eventually resulted was simpler, but achieving this consumed far more time and effort than might otherwise be apparent. Sometimes simpler is more agonizing to achieve.

---

[40] All functions are forced non-inline to allow breakpoints to be set in any function.

The earlier 386BSD version was also careful to step around interactions with the virtual memory system, and was dependent on special treatment to avoid conflicts (such as reclaiming the memory of an active kernel stack or page table). The newer version is independent of the virtual memory system implementation, so that machine dependencies no longer need to be present inside the virtual memory system. This resulted in a much cleaner virtual memory system design as well.

3.2.4.3 386BSD cpu_tfork() Design Choices and Trade-Offs

The key objectives of this implementation are to: a) reduce overhead, b) facilitate thread generalization, c) increase interface portability, d) introduce the use of 386 TSS, and e) allow prototyping of a processor-clustering remote execution mechanism. By streamlining the code, the cost of assembling a new concurrent object was reduced, even though the actual complexity of replication was increased (e.g. the object must now be relocated). No additional function calls are required inside this routine.[42] Tiny amounts of inline assembler are used to gain access to the native instruction set to eliminate the need for excess overhead in copying the stack, and to minimize the amount of assembly code in the machine-dependent portion of the kernel.

With this release of the kernel, support was also increased for additional classes of concurrent objects that can be of *lighter* or *heavier* weight, as denoted by the size and complexity of the per-object state (which itself is now variable in size). In the smallest case, a thread can be created that has only a process control block and a kernel stack, and can fit in substantially less than a page in size. The bound of the number of such threads is no longer the size of the thread, nor the time of creation, but instead is limited by the number of descriptors that a 386 processor can have at a time (currently 16,000).

Since a process may desire an arbitrary number of threads per process, the older notion of holding the state in a fixed location of a user process was abandoned. A consequence of this action is that the POSIX **ptrace()** facility must discover the kernel virtual address of the process's thread that it is debugging to discover thread state information (such as register contents), since it is dynamically assigned on thread creation. Thread generalization means that this same code is used for all concurrent object generation—the choice of the exact underlying object, be it process or kernel thread, is made at a higher level of abstraction than this routine.

Earlier implementations left ambiguous the requirements for concurrent object creation. This was intentional to allow for machines with limited kernel virtual address space (i.e. VAX, CCI, older SPARC's) to selectively map per-process and kernel stack information, and required an address space modification to access a new

---

[41] N.B. On multiprocessor systems, this is the point where the individual processor assigned to the start of the thread is chosen.

[42] A single inline function creates almost all new TSS descriptors, calling an embedded external function only if short on descriptor space—a rare occurrence.

object's information. Since the information has now been minimized anyways (cf. threads), and the cost of the modification is significant, the benefit of this design choice becomes questionable. In this release of 386BSD, we have abandoned this practice, and chosen to standardize on keeping all thread state information in paged kernel virtual address space as a requirement for the machine-dependent layer. Thus, for any ports of this software, it is assumed that the state is always present and addressable, and that the context switch mechanism does not necessarily alter the address space of the process associated with a thread.[43]

This function has been written to allow the creation of a new thread where a clone of either the current or a non-running thread could be obtained. At the moment, it is only used to clone a running thread. However, this mechanism can be used as part of a cluster thread generation mechanism, where we may do a "sideways" creation of special prototype threads as needed as a part of a distributed "remote" execution mechanism. In this case, the thread may be created from an unrelated event (like from a protocol on an interrupt stack).

3.2.4.4 Improvements to the Current Implementation of cpu_tfork()

If the kernel was run in Ring 1 or 2 and the interrupt code run in Ring 0, one could use a single large stack (ESP0) and a smaller stack per thread (ESP1/ESP2). To do this, extensive changes to the machine-dependent code would be necessary and some means to partition the top half of the kernel from calling bottom half code would be required.[44]

To enforce the programming discipline mentioned above, a diagnostic that checks the entire contents of the stack for pointers falling within the stack's subrange, as well as for any remaining references to the rest of the thread state, should also be present as a conditional compilation flag.

3.2.5 What is cpu_texit ?

The function **cpu_texit()** releases any address space-related resources when the thread terminates. It controls the final stages of the thread prior to the last context switch to the next thread, which *never* returns. Any special treatment of address space management by the specific process architecture must be implemented at this point. **cpu_texit()** is additionally given the responsibility to free any associated address space and the kernel stack, and thus is not symmetrical with **cpu_tfork()**.

---

[43] It may, for example, postpone the context switch to the next attempted reference of the user address space by setting a flag on the newly switched thread.

[44] Many instructions only work in ring 0, however.

Generally, **cpu_tfork()**, **cpu_texit()**, and **swtch()** must carefully coordinate operations to allow creation, context destruction, and context switching of threads, and are hence written in terms of each of the others.

... [File: /usr/src/kernel/kern/i386/cpu.c, line: 169]

```
volatile void
cpu_texit(register struct proc *p)
...
```

cpu_texit() is passed the address of the process state that is being terminated. Note that since it never returns, it has no return value.

3.2.5.1 How is cpu_texit() Implemented?

On the 386, this function releases cpu resources and cuts over to a special stack and context assigned for the purpose of a terminating context switch before releasing the kernel stack and transferring control to the next process.

... [File: /usr/src/kernel/kern/i386/cpu.c, line: 175]

```
        if (p == npxproc)
                npxproc = 0;
...
```

The thread is checked to see if it has the floating point unit attached to it. If the global variable *npxproc* points to this thread, the association is broken by assigning the value of NULL to it to cancel any saves to this thread on the next allocation (on an *npxdna* fault) to another thread. Currently, only user processes are allowed to use the floating point unit.

... [File: /usr/src/kernel/kern/i386/cpu.c, line: 179]

```
        freetss((sel_t)p->p_md.md_tsel);
...
```

Next, the TSS descriptor associated with this thread is released via an inline function call.[45] Since we will need a TSS until finished with this thread, we have reserved a statically assigned descriptor for the purpose of an exiting thread. Only one is necessary since the descriptor will be used only until the next thread is executed, upon which time the context switch hardware mechanism will free the descriptor. Nor do we need to check if it is free with DIAGNOSTIC code, because the mechanism will also check to see that the *exit_tss* is free before being loaded as the current TSS.[46]

... [File: /usr/src/kernel/kern/i386/cpu.c, line: 182]

```
        asm ("movl $%0, %%esp" : : "m"(Exit_stack));
...
```

---

[45] See **i386/segments.h** for the definitions.
[46] A hardware fault would then occur.

Not only do we need a current TSS, but we also need a stack to handle interrupts on and to hold state during context switches. We assign a new stack via inline assembly, noting that no further references will be made to any stack-relative objects.[47] Note, however, that frame pointer-relative (e.g. C automatic) variables are still accessible.

... [File: /usr/src/kernel/kern/i386/cpu.c, line: 185]

```
    /* if (p->p_stksz >= NBPG) */
            kmem_free(kernel_map, (vm_offset_t)p->p_addr, p->p_stksz);
    /* else
            free(p->p_addr, M_TEMP); */
...
```

Now that we no longer need our thread's allocated stack and pcb, we free the thread state that contains them. Since our automatic variables are in this frame, we can't access them any more after this call. If our thread state is a fraction of a page in size, we return space to the **malloc()** allocator via **free()** instead of via the faster but page granularity-sized allocator of the virtual memory system, in a speed versus size decision.[48]

... [File: /usr/src/kernel/kern/i386/cpu.c, line: 191]

```
    final_swtch();
...
```

Totally stripped of its resources and only running on either the kernel shared resources (address translation and kernel program) or the special purpose thread exit state (pcb and kernel stack), the thread context switch routine is called, never to return. On entry to the next thread, the static state is deallocated, and the termination is complete.

3.2.5.2 386BSD cpu_texit() Evolutionary History

Earlier implementations of 386BSD could not free all of the state from the running process, and so used yet another function, **cpu_wait()**, to free the remaining state in the calling process. This was due in part to the fact that the kernel stack was left as part of the user's virtual address space, so as to keep a fixed virtual address for the per-process information that would be switched on the fly. This is consistent with UNIX systems, but greatly complicated matters on process creation and destruction, since the user address space was no longer orthogonal to the kernel in all ways.

3.2.5.3 386BSD cpu_texit() Design Choices and Trade-Offs

This implementation attempted to minimize interactions with the virtual memory system and other subsystems. Also, the entire thread state was reaped from the running thread, instead of putting it off till the parent collects status. The maximum return now occurs as soon as possible, undelayed by a reschedule.

---

[47] We don't bother copying the old stack as we don't need it anymore.

3.2.5.4 Improvements to the
Current Implementation of cpu_texit()

Like **cpu_tfork()**, a separate interrupt stack would be a bonus here, since only the per-thread task need be deallocated in that case. In addition, extending thread state to a resource-free call might allow a thread to be terminated cleanly from the context of another thread, thus allowing forced termination of threads.

3.2.6 What is cpu_execsetregs()?

The function **cpu_execsetregs()** prepares the process's register state for execution of the newly loaded program. The machine-independent portion of the kernel passes the addresses of the program's starting location (obtained from the executable file) and the base of the new stack frame.[49] This function then sets these arguments into place in the process so that the program may begin.

... [File: /usr/src/kernel/kern/i386/cpu.c, line: 198]

```
void
cpu_execsetregs(struct proc *p, caddr_t eip, caddr_t esp)
...
```

cpu_execsetregs() is passed the process state pointer, new instruction pointer (EIP) and stack (ESP). No error can be passed back.

3.2.6.1 How is cpu_execsetregs() Implemented?

... [File: /usr/src/kernel/kern/i386/cpu.c, line: 204]

```
        p->p_md.md_regs[sESP] = (int) esp;
        p->p_md.md_regs[sEBP] = 0;      /* bottom of the fp chain */
        p->p_md.md_regs[sEIP] = (int) eip;
        p->p_addr->u_pcb.pcb_flags = 0; /* no fp at all */
...
```

cpu_execsetregs() implements the mandatory assignment of stack and instruction pointer. In addition, it zeros the frame or base pointer so that the first frame in the program can be identified when following the frame pointers backwards in user stack unwinding. The machine-dependent flags for the process are also initialized (in this case, clearing the AST signal, rescheduling, and floating point flags).

3.2.6.2 Improvements to the
Current Implementation of cpu_execsetregs()

Program initialization would be more elaborate than provided for here if an entry point could be passed for alternate initialization of the user program prior to execution. Shared libraries then might not require special assistance in the user program's run time start-off entry.

---

[48] N.B. The thread state is similarly allocated in the kernel's thread creation.
[49] Allocated by **execve()** to contain the contents of the passed arguments to the new program.

3.2.7 What is cpu_signal()?

cpu_signal() is the lowest level layer of abstraction of signal processing. It is the agent through which a signal to a user program is delivered, by adjusting the program's state (registers and stack) so that a signal handler in the user program will be run. In effect, the signal will appear to the user program as if a hardware interrupt mediated by the signal mechanism has occurred.

cpu_signal() builds a stack frame that can allow the system to restore program state to exactly what it was before the **cpu_signal()** function executed. Since many signals may be sent at once, **cpu_signal()** could be executed for each signal outstanding (conceivably for as many as NSIG signals) before the first of these have their associated handlers run. So, while **cpu_signal()** itself need not be reentrant, the stack frames it creates in the user program must be nestable.

... [File: /usr/src/kernel/kern/i386/cpu.c, line: 225]

```
int
cpu_signal(struct proc *p, int sig, int mask)
    ...
```

cpu_signal() has three arguments: the process pointer of the process receiving the signal; the signal to be delivered; and the state of the signal mask. If the signal cannot be delivered to the process, the function returns failure with an appropriate error value.

3.2.7.1 How is cpu_signal() Implemented?

On the 386, the user and kernel program share the 32-bit linear virtual address space, so it is possible to directly reference the user program's stack frame with the program. This function makes extensive use of this feature by building a new stack frame in place on the user stack instead of constructing a new frame in the kernel program's address space and copying it into place using the **copyout()** primitive.[50]

... [File: /usr/src/kernel/kern/i386/cpu.c, line: 242]

```
        catcher = ps->ps_sigact[sig];
        regs = p->p_md.md_regs;
        oonstack = ps->ps_onstack;
        frmtrap = p->p_addr->u_pcb.pcb_flags & FM_TRAP;
    ...
```

Four local variables hold values relevant to the delivery of a signal: the address of the user program's signal action handler (catcher), the address of the array holding the user program's register contents (regs), the "old" value of the alternate signal stack (oonstack), and a boolean indicator specifying whether the user program's registers are in a trap frame organization or a system call layout.

---

[50] This would be necessary in the case of an architecture with independent 32-bit address spaces for kernel and user programs (examples: MC680X0 or NS32000 architectures).

```
        if (ps->ps_onstack == 0 && (ps->ps_sigonstack & sigmask(sig))) {
                fp = (struct sigframe *)
                    (ps->ps_sigsp - sizeof(struct sigframe));
                ps->ps_onstack++;
        } else {
                /* could be in one of two places */
                if (frmtrap)
                        fp = (struct sigframe *)(regs[tESP]
                                - sizeof(struct sigframe));
                else
                        fp = (struct sigframe *)(regs[sESP]
                                - sizeof(struct sigframe));
        }
}
...
```

The function begins by locating the base of the new stack frame (FP). In addition to the user program's stack pointer, which can be found in one of two different locations depending on whether the kernel was entered with a trap (or interrupt) or system call, a signal can optionally be selected to be processed on a reserved stack (so that it won't affect the program stack).[51]

```
        if (catcher == BADSIG
           || (unsigned) fp + sizeof(struct sigframe) >  USRSTACK) {
                asm("cpu_signal_err:");
                p->p_md.md_onfault = 0;
                return(EFAULT);
        }
    ...
```

Next, the new stack frame is checked to see if it is within the bounds of the program's address space. If not, the signal can't be delivered, and an EFAULT (invalid address) error is returned. A special assembler label is inserted here to refer to a function return sequence to be used if an error occurs when building the rest of the new signal stack frame. Note that we don't check to see if the stack is allocatable, or writable for that matter, but instead rely on the virtual memory system's fault handler to handle the reference and possible fault. In addition, we don't even attempt delivery on the specially denoted BADSIG address by convention.

```
        asm ("movl $cpu_signal_err, %0 "
            : "=o" (p->p_md.md_onfault));
    ...
```

---

[51] In this case, it could actually be implemented as a list or spaghetti stack by an application that could reshuffle the program stack in such a way that it would be interfered with if the signal frame was also present on the same stack.

If the reference is invalid, the virtual memory system will pass control (via **trap()**, see previous chapter) to the error return sequence mentioned above. It does this by noticing the pcb's fault field is not null.[52]

... [File: /usr/src/kernel/kern/i386/cpu.c, line: 285]

```
        fp->sf_code = ps->ps_code;
        fp->sf_scp = &fp->sf_sc;
        fp->sf_handler = catcher;
    ...
```

With the error handler in place, we now build the new stack frame in place in the user stack. We first construct the program visible portion of the stack frame. This part builds the POSIX function call corresponding to the function prototype:

```
        void handler(int signalno);
```

In a BSD system, we also supply additional arguments so that it resembles the function prototype:

```
        void handler(int signalno, int code, struct sigcontext *scp);
```

These additional arguments are used to pass machine-dependent details regarding the fault that may be used by machine-dependent code in debuggers and in the program libraries to qualify the exact reason for the signal and the details regarding how the state is retained.

... [File: /usr/src/kernel/kern/i386/cpu.c, line: 290]

```
    if(frmtrap) {
            fp->sf_eax = regs[tEAX];
            fp->sf_edx = regs[tEDX];
            fp->sf_ecx = regs[tECX];
            fp->sf_ebx = regs[tEBX];
            fp->sf_edi = regs[tEDI];
            fp->sf_esi = regs[tESI];
            fp->sf_cs = regs[tCS];
            fp->sf_ss = regs[tSS];
            fp->sf_ds = regs[tDS];
            fp->sf_es = regs[tES];
            fp->sf_fs = regs[tFS];
            fp->sf_gs = regs[tGS];
    } else {
            fp->sf_eax = regs[sEAX];
            fp->sf_edx = regs[sEDX];
            fp->sf_ecx = regs[sECX];
            fp->sf_ebx = regs[sEBX];
            fp->sf_edi = regs[sEDI];
            fp->sf_esi = regs[sESI];
            fp->sf_cs = regs[sCS];
            fp->sf_ss = regs[sSS];
```

---

[52] N.B. The field is cleared on all returns from the function so as to avoid catching spurious traps to this function after it completes.

```
        fp->sf_ds = regs[sDS];
        fp->sf_es = regs[sES];
        fp->sf_fs = regs[sFS];
        fp->sf_gs = regs[sGS];
    }
...
```

In addition to the program-visible portion of the stack frame, we need to preserve the contents of the temporary registers not normally saved by the compiler in an opaque portion of the stack frame (not visible to the user program). Since we have two different kinds of stack frames, we need to insert them separately.

... [File: /usr/src/kernel/kern/i386/cpu.c, line: 319]

```
        fp->sf_sc.sc_onstack = oonstack;
        fp->sf_sc.sc_mask = mask;
        memcpy((caddr_t)fp->sf_sigcode, &sigcode, szsigcode);
        if(frmtrap) {
                fp->sf_sc.sc_sp = regs[tESP];
                fp->sf_sc.sc_fp = regs[tEBP];
                fp->sf_sc.sc_pc = regs[tEIP];
                fp->sf_sc.sc_ps = regs[tEFLAGS];
                regs[tESP] = (int)fp;
                regs[tEIP] = (int)fp->sf_sigcode;
        } else {
                fp->sf_sc.sc_sp = regs[sESP];
                fp->sf_sc.sc_fp = regs[sEBP];
                fp->sf_sc.sc_pc = regs[sEIP];
                fp->sf_sc.sc_ps = regs[sEFLAGS];
                regs[sESP] = (int)fp;
                regs[sEIP] = (int)fp->sf_sigcode;
        }
...
```

Another opaque portion of information contains a snapshot of the program's state for returning from the signal (see **cpu_signalreturn()** below). Included in this are the stack frame, instruction pointer and processor status word. With the frame now in place, we adjust the program counter (EIP) and stack (ESP) to point at the new function entry address and stack base. If a memory reference error occurred during any user program stack reference, none of the registers would be modified, and any partial contents would only occur in the unallocated portion of the stack. The signal entry/exit code (see **sigcode**) is then copied into the base of the new frame for immediate execution.

... [File: /usr/src/kernel/kern/i386/cpu.c, line: 339]

```
        p->p_md.md_onfault = 0;
        return(0);
...
```

With the stack frame in place, all that remains is to cancel the fault handler and return success (e.g., no error).

3.2.7.2 386BSD cpu_signal() Evolutionary History

In earlier versions of 386BSD, the **sendsig()** function provided this functionality, using the manual segment extension of the stack and break regions of a user process. It also made use of functions to check the accessibility of the memory under the stack. These were holdovers from the earlier 4BSD virtual memory system and were responsible for significant excess overhead.

3.2.7.3 386BSD cpu_signal() Design Choices and Trade-Offs

This implementation attempts to minimize the cost of signal delivery, which was such a significant overhead bane for certain signal-intensive operations (such as network-based applications using non-blocking I/O). The decision to lazy evaluate memory access was the most significant and controversial choice here. By simplifying the interface and organization of this routine, it was possible to layer it in such a way as to isolate functionality to the respective interface (user program, kernel program).

3.2.7.4 Improvements to the Current Implementation of cpu_signal()

The most significant missing item here is support for the 386 page modification misfeature (the read-only bit does not work from the kernel). As this significantly slows and complicates the implementation, it has been intentionally left out (signal stack frames rarely occur in shared memory that is labeled copy-on-write). The drawback is one of security, since a shared text program can be altered by successfully taking a signal with a signal stack directed at an already referenced text memory.

Another missing item here is the ability to deliver a signal to an unrelated process (or to a kernel thread). Since the rest of the system cannot handle this either, it is of little consequence in this implementation. The oddity of having two stack frames is also of little advantage, and perhaps more trouble than it is worth.[53]

Another change possible is to improve the signal code (sigcode) copied into user space. Due to backwards compatibility issues with earlier versions, this expedite was added to the system and may warrant minimization.

3.2.8 What is cpu_signalreturn()?

The companion to **cpu_signal()**, **cpu_signalreturn()** removes the signal frame off the stack and returns to the program state prior to the signal occurrence. This function is eventually called in response to reentering the kernel from the user program on return from the signal handler (back to the sigcode mentioned above, which calls a system call to reenter the system).

This function must recognize a valid signal frame (generated by **cpu_signal()** above) and restore the saved program state.

---

[53] Ten instructions additional to the critical path in system call evaluation.

... [File: /usr/src/kernel/kern/i386/cpu.c, line: 351]

```
int
cpu_signalreturn(struct proc *p)
...
```

The function is called with the process pointer of the current process which is returning from processing a signal. If either the frame is not recognized (EINVAL) or cannot be referenced (EFAULT), the appropriate error value is returned.

3.2.8.1 How is cpu_signalreturn() Implemented?

This function resembles **cpu_signal()** considerably, which is not surprising given the fact it unloads the frame that **cpu_signal()** originally built.

[File: /usr/src/kernel/kern/i386/cpu.c, line: 354]

```
        struct sigframe *fp;
        int *regs = p->p_md.md_regs;

        /* signal state is current top of stack contents */
        fp = (struct sigframe *) regs[sESP];
...
```

The location of the frame is implicitly known to be the current user program top-of-stack, and entry into the kernel is known to be via a system call. This function is written assuming that it may be called either through a reserved system call (BSD) or via a reserved gate descriptor,[54] and thus assumes nothing more about the user program register contents.[55]

... [File: /usr/src/kernel/kern/i386/cpu.c, line: 361]

```
        if ((unsigned) fp + sizeof(struct sigframe) > USRSTACK) {
                asm("cpu_signalreturn_err:");
                p->p_md.md_onfault = 0;
                return(EFAULT);
        }
...
```

The frame is checked to ensure that it is within the range for the user program to assign. Like **cpu_signal()**, it labels an error return that is used by the fault handler if any exceptions occur while referencing the user program stack.

... [File: /usr/src/kernel/kern/i386/cpu.c, line: 372]

```
        asm ("movl $cpu_signalreturn_err, %0 " : "=o" (p->p_md.md_onfault));
...
```

Again like **cpu_signal()**, this function enables a fault handler for any exceptions caused by the following direct references to the user program. From this point until

[54] See the Intel BCS specification.
[55] In the case of the iBCS, the frame is not the same as a system call!

the time the field is cleared, any unrecoverable exception will terminate this function via the above error return.

... [File: /usr/src/kernel/kern/i386/cpu.c, line: 375]

```
        if (fp->sf_scp != &fp->sf_sc) {
                p->p_md.md_onfault = 0;
                return(EINVAL);
        }
        scp = fp->sf_scp;
        if ((scp->sc_ps & PSL_MBZ) != 0 || (scp->sc_ps & PSL_MBO) != PSL_MBO) {
                p->p_md.md_onfault = 0;
                return(EINVAL);
        }
...
```

We next directly reference the contents of the stack frame in place to decide if it is a valid signal stack frame that we can restore. The frame is checked for consistency before any modification of program state is allowed. To be consistent, the signal frame must have a consistent pointer to itself and contain a program status word that has appropriate bits set or cleared for "normal" operation. In this way, privileged bits that must be present or absent are ensured to be proper to prevent program misbehavior.

... [File: /usr/src/kernel/kern/i386/cpu.c, line: 386]

```
        p->p_sigacts->ps_onstack = scp->sc_onstack & 1;
        p->p_sigmask = scp->sc_mask & ~sigcantmask;
        regs[sEBP] = scp->sc_fp;
        regs[sESP] = scp->sc_sp;
        regs[sEIP] = scp->sc_pc;
        regs[sEFLAGS] = (scp->sc_ps | PSL_USERSET) & ~PSL_USERCLR;
...
```

Program state and signal state are next recovered from the signal context. The previous state of the signal stack, clamped to a boolean value, is restored, and the signal mask is restored, taking care to disallow any attempts to mask the unmaskable signals. Frame, stack, and instruction pointers are restored without bounds checking, as out of bounds values will just cause a user program trap to occur.

... [File: /usr/src/kernel/kern/i386/cpu.c, line: 394]

```
        regs[sEAX] = fp->sf_eax;
        regs[sEDX] = fp->sf_edx;
        regs[sECX] = fp->sf_ecx;
        regs[sEBX] = fp->sf_ebx;
        regs[sEDI] = fp->sf_edi;
        regs[sESI] = fp->sf_esi;

        /* restore selectors */
        regs[sCS] = fp->sf_cs | SEL_UPL;
        regs[sSS] = fp->sf_ss | SEL_UPL;
        regs[sDS] = fp->sf_ds | SEL_UPL;
        regs[sES] = fp->sf_es | SEL_UPL;
        regs[sFS] = fp->sf_fs | SEL_UPL;
```

```
        regs[sGS] = fp->sf_gs | SEL_UPL;
  ...
```

Compiler temporary registers and selectors are restored as the first step towards restoring processor state; this is done early solely to minimize compiler overhead.

... [File: /usr/src/kernel/kern/i386/cpu.c, line: 409]

```
        p->p_md.md_onfault = 0;
        return (EJUSTRETURN);
  ...
```

Finally, we clear the fault handler vector now that we've successfully referenced the user program stack, and return a special error value (EJUSTRETURN) that instructs the system call handler to overwrite any program state with return values or error indication and "just return."

3.2.8.2 386BSD cpu_signalreturn()
Design Choices and Trade-Offs

The primary design choice for this implementation was to offer minimal functionality coupled with maximum efficiency. However, this function could be written considerably differently if we had wished to support the nested exception handlers present in other operating systems specifications besides POSIX. In that case, stack unwinding, verification, and transient error conditions would need to be much more elaborate than what is presently implemented here. The question then becomes how to stratify exception handling across the different systems.[56]

3.2.9 What is cpu_reset()?

cpu_reset() is a function to force the processor to reset. It is independent of I/O bus, system architecture, or processor mother board.

... [File: /usr/src/kernel/kern/i386/cpu.c, line: 416]

```
void
cpu_reset(void) {
  ...
```

cpu_reset() is called with no arguments and never returns.

3.2.9.1 How is cpu_reset() Implemented?

... [File: /usr/src/kernel/kern/i386/cpu.c, line: 420]

```
        (void)memset((caddr_t) PTD, 0, NBPG);

        /* "good night, sweet prince .... <THUNK!>" */
        tlbflush();
```

---

[56] While this area is one of interest and merits futher exploration, it is beyond the scope of this book.

```
asm("   movl    $0, %esp ");
```
...

cpu_reset() does an inline zero fill of the top-level page directory of the address translation for this processor, unmapping the entire address space. Thus, any address not in the translation look-aside cache will cause a processor double fault and a mandatory processor reset. Next, the address translation entries are all flushed. At this point, the processor is running solely out of the instruction queue. We reload the stack pointer with 0, and attempt a return from the function, forcing both a page fault from the stack contents, and a stack segment error due to rollover of address space from low to high. Depending on the version of X86, the processor will reset at a different point in this sequence.

3.2.9.2 386BSD cpu_reset() Design Choices and Trade-Offs

cpu_reset() was needed because keyboard controller reset functions are implemented differently in various manufacturer's BIOS ROMs. It was necessary to have a mechanism that would work on any X86 implementation, regardless of choice or future implementation.

3.2.10 What is cpu_ptracereg()?

cpu_ptracereg() returns the address of a stored user register of a child process undergoing a **ptrace()** operation.

... [File: /usr/src/kernel/kern/i386/cpu.c, line: 438]

```
int *
cpu_ptracereg(struct proc *p, int reg) {
...
```

cpu_ptracereg() is passed a pointer to the process and a register index. It returns a pointer to an integer buffer describing the register contents of the desired register.

3.2.10.1 How is cpu_ptracereg() Implemented?

... [File: /usr/src/kernel/kern/i386/cpu.c, line: 441]

```
        /* if (p->p_addr->u_pcb.pcb_flags & FM_TRAP)
                return (p->p_md.md_regs + ipcreg[reg]);
        else
                return (p->p_md.md_regs + sipcreg[reg]); */
        return (p->p_md.md_regs + reg);
...
```

This function selects the appropriate trap frame and indexes the register through one of two separate relocation tables, depending on whether the kernel was entered from user mode by a trap or a system call.

3.2.10.2 386BSD cpu_ptracereg() Design Choices and Trade-Offs

Prior versions of 386BSD embedded this information in the machine-independent code. The separate trap and system call frames are a historical legacy that is on the way out in future versions.

Exercises

3.1 The "on-fault" mechanism allows for an alternative exception handler, but 386BSD currently uses only a single-level mechanism that can be used re-entrantly. Why would one extend this and how?

3.2 Why does **trap()** process an address space fault (e.g. **vm_fault**) before it checks for an alternative fault handler?

3.3 In restarting a system call, why don't we simply branch to the top of the system call handler to re-issue the request?

3.4 What are the elements contained in a 386BSD kernel thread?

3.5 Which TSS descriptor is used when the processor idles following an exiting thread?

4 *INTERNAL KERNEL SERVICES (kern/config.c, kern/malloc.c)*

The 386BSD kernel program, like any other major program, has intrinsic needs separate from the dedicated subsystems it makes use of. While many of these needs could be handled in an ad-hoc manner[1] throughout the kernel, a refined, common set of *internal kernel services* provide a concise programming environment through which the kernel can be made more consistent in implementation and more extensible in scope of function. Hence, these internal kernel services form the nucleus of a system programming taxonomy.

Two examples of internal kernel services are memory allocation and software configuration. Within a program as complicated as an operating system kernel, small[2] portions of memory are needed to hold a variety of objects. A single kernel *memory allocator* provides a common kernel service to fill that need. In addition, since the kernel is just an intermediary that routes information to a variety of kernel subsystems, filesystems, protocols, and drivers, many of which may in turn depend on other modules, the kernel also has significant *software configuration* requirements— allowing the kernel to be adaptable without becoming intertwined with non-kernel code or extensions. Both of these examples are present in this chapter, as we examine the **kern/config.c** file containing the current configuration mechanism, and the **kern/malloc.c** file containing the top-level memory allocator used by the kernel.

4.1 Issues in Configuration

The primary motivation for beginning the process of developing new approaches in combined hardware and software configuration has fallen directly out of the demands instigated by supplying a modern operating system on a so-called "PC-compatible" system. Two issues thus arise which must be addressed by *any* operating system purporting to operate efficiently and correctly on the PC: the combinatorial increase in PC devices, and the increasing obsolescence of the PC hardware itself.

---

[1] And historically have been handled in this manner for earlier kernels.
[2] Less than 64 KBytes, typically.

4.1.1 PC Device Conflicts

Firstly, it must be noted that a direct result of the success of the PC *compatible* architecture has been an explosion in the number of possible configurations of devices that can be used with the PC. Thus, PC configurability (unlike large systems, for which UNIX[3] was developed) deals with the *average* user of this system, because this user is much more likely than the user of other architectures (such as the Apple Macintosh or Sun Sparc workstation) to use a different configuration from that of the developer of the software. However, since there are now in the case of the PC literally thousands of boards that can potentially interact in different combinations, millions of unique cases can never be fully tested by the system's developer prior to use.

One of the unique characteristics of BSD (adopted by other commercial UNIX systems) had been its ability to configure itself to better suit the hardware, albeit in a simplistic manner, but it is now demonstrably inadequate to the demands of the PC customer. As such, the naive constraints of the past must be abandoned. A different approach based more on dynamic runtime environment and less on compile-time tables, conditional compilation, and elaborate (often wrong) static kernel build configuration programs must be designed.[4]

A secondary consideration falls out of PC configuration, however. PC compatibility itself is based on obsolete[5] technology which relies upon manual resolution of configuration conflicts by the user, usually by permuting the jumper combinations until the configuration appears to work. This economic arrangement, while suitable for small numbers of configurations (and actually possible to improve upon given one discerns the conflicts symbolically) is totally inadequate in meeting the needs of thousands and thousands of boards which may not correspond perfectly to the rules described for each and every class of device. In sum, the amount of time required to locate the conflict may be too great.

For example, many ne2000 Ethernet network controller clones decode register banks slightly differently from that of the original ne2000 card, saving a few gates and possibly a nickel in the process. Since these cards appear to function in place of the original, the average user who replaces a ne2000 Ethernet card with a clone may not see a problem. However, with the increase in the number of add-in cards, drives, and peripherals, the chance that an overlap exists with another board increases—in this case, while the system may become destabilized, it may be impossible to determine if and where a conflict exists, since the hardware assumptions by the software may also be flawed.

---

[3] The "UNIX Timesharing System," frequently used with 10–100 users per system
[4] However, HP workstations for example find this acceptable.
[5] Effectively, the PC has the heritage of the original Apple II.

In sum, there are less than 1000 ports, 15 interrupts, and 7 DMA ports available for use—the same as when the PC/AT first came out. Yet there are now thousands of types of boards available. With such limited resources, one has two choices: uniquely allocate them (as one does with Ethernet, assigning unique 48-bit addresses), or use a conflict avoidance mechanism.

4.1.2 The Built-in Obsolescence of PC Static Configuration Mechanisms

The origin of this problem stemmed from simple platform economics. At the time of the PC's design, there were many bus designs which actually used conflict resolution mechanisms. The original NuBus, for example, provided an elegant but costly mechanism[6] dealing with conflict discovery and avoidance.[7] In the case of the IBM PC AT, however, the designers preferred to assume (in retrospect very foolishly) that a handful of boards would suffice, even though it was intended to be an open architecture and had literally thousands of eager developers lined up waiting to get their hands on the bus. Through the choice of static configuration, the immediate cost was reduced.[8]

An even more damning situation developed when both Apple and IBM chose not to immediately publish the criteria of compatibility for their respective bus architectures[9], thus disallowing any means for qualifying new products (and hence avoid configuration problems). In the case of IBM, it was tacitly acknowledged that it would be preferred that the customer not desire a third-party product, but only IBM's. While this was not an unreasonable thought from a business point of view, it was found to be unrealistic in practice, since IBM could not keep up with the rapid pace of development. As such, customers inevitably went for the most immediate solution available anyway, thus forcing IBM itself to follow other board manufacturer's defacto standards.[10]

Compatibility conflicts were less of a problem with Apple's closed architecture (which had a more narrow-minded view of configurability). Instead of slip-streaming or otherwise leveraging the PC, however, Apple preferred a high-margin but often needlessly incompatible approach. As such, the processor and operating system

---

[6] Mailbox interrupts replaced by a fixed interrupt per slot.

[7] Which Apple chose not to use in its products because of the cost of doing a single customized IC, a trivial item nowadays.

[8] Ironically, the Apple II that IBM copied had a more effective strategy for hardware configuration than the PC or AT.

[9] This was done to combat "clone" products, since a solid external specification is a key element of the cloning process. The proliferation of multiple ad hoc standards finally forced them to disclose some of this information, but vagueness persists to this day.

[10] One example of this is the Hercules graphics "standard."

dependence engineered into Apple's peripheral market would forever doom it to second-class status in the huge PC marketplace.[11]

4.2 Plug and Play: A Growing Necessity

Another factor in the development of new configuration approaches in modern systems such as 386BSD is the increased demand for *plug and play* technology. Plug and play has been considered by some to be more of a *usability* improver, and not something required in a development system. However, it should be made clear to anyone working with operating systems technology that if the basic infrastructure does not even support from the beginning the state-of-the-art in commercial systems usability, then it is not really a modern operating system. This file begins the process of driving 386BSD towards a plug and play configurable system by the end user.

This is not an easy task for any BSD system. When visiting Intel in 1989, our contacts there regarded our porting project as uninteresting and BSD as an obsolete relic, partly because of its heavy reliance upon relatively naive configuration software.[12] Intel was acutely aware of the inability of UNIX systems to penetrate much of the PC marketplace—primarily because integration of drivers, networks, and filesystems is much harder on UNIX systems than on the most primitive of operating systems available: MS-DOS.

Having praised DOS, however, we must also scrutinize its shortcomings carefully to learn from experience. DOS configuration, while head-and-shoulders better than that provided on any UNIX system in existence,[13] is still for all practical purposes a ludicrous toy. This is mostly due to the de-evolutionary choices in design made by its architects. The DOS configuration process (among other things) is order-dependent, has no bounds to its use, and follows no rules regarding its employment on the PC. It is simply left up the user to vary the configuration until an adequate arrangement can be found. Even if an apparently working[14] configuration is found, there is no way to confirm that all parts of the computer's operating system are functional. As such, it may be the case that an unused interface is still fouled by a configuration flaw that will only be discovered during use an arbitrary period of time later.[15]

---

[11] The fact that both companies now embrace more modern and better public configurable architectures, such as PCMCIA and PCI, suggests that they may learn their lesson yet.

[12] See *Device Autoconfiguration*, **Dr. Dobbs Journal** (November 1991) for a discussion of the older BSD autoconfiguration software methodology.

[13] The closest best one is Solaris, and even it is a bear.

[14] E.g., the configuration appears stable when used with an application.

[15] Windows also has similar problems with their own unique flavor, as exemplified in a 1994 Apple commercial showing parents attempting to configure a PC to run a DOS game for a children's Christmas present. Aspersions aside, many Mac games suffer from similar conflicts with messaging (e.g., System 7.5 extensions).

Finally, in addition to the configuration of software (drivers) used to gain access to hardware, software-only modules must themselves resolve intricate configuration dilemmas to arrive at a stable and desirable configuration. This area is almost entirely ignored.

These shortcomings have really been brought to the fore with the popularity of CDROM drives, sound cards, and other accouterments of multimedia—with failures due to petty and arcane configuration or compatibility conflicts among the complement of PC software drivers and hardware increasingly common. As the PC is pushed to support another generation of technology, its hardware and popular software are not up to the task.

It should be possible with any configurable system to determine *by entirely automatic means* hardware and software conflicts and dependencies at all times. At the moment, this is not done by any PC operating system[16] or bus architecture. Thus, in a sense, any PC extended beyond the original traditional PC AT complement of devices is in effect a potential pathologic case.

4.3 Configuration in 386BSD: kern/config.c

The file **kern/config.c** contains the machine-independent code that configures the software modules of the kernel and reconciles a shared configuration file with the configuration scripts in every module. The configuration scripts themselves allow for symbolic reconfiguration of the kernel without altering its contents.[17] This file also contains the device-independent device interfaces used by the kernel exclusively to access devices.

The configuration scripts themselves are composed of a very simple byte string language used to describe symbolically the configuration details of every module. The exact meaning of the terms in the language are relative to every module.

A communications primitive module ties together the devices with the configuration strings and the device interfaces. This module discovers kernel modules and signals them to configure themselves into the kernel. To support this mechanism from the driver level, configuration calls employing the configuration scripts uniquely register each module symbolically with the device interfaces.

There is only one location in the configuration script per each module where the actual name of a module appears. Thus, it is possible symbolically to alter the names and characteristics of the devices in the shared configuration script for use with other

---

[16] Although Windows 95 attempts this, by intensively analyzing the hardware during installation/upgrade, and ferreting out the details over the course of hitting many brick walls. While the internals approach taken is incorrect, resulting often in failure and frustration, it should be noted that these guys are the only ones that take the topic seriously.

[17] By redefinition or redirection in place of modification.

kernel facilities and have the modules *learn* their new characteristics without altering them in any special way. This allows one, for example, to operate a new device driver alongside of another older one without conflict.

4.3.1 How Levels of Abstraction and Hierarchy Impact Configuration Issues

A commonly held misconception regarding configuration in the operating system is that configuration can be solved at a single level of abstraction. This is a great fallacy. In truth, configuration for an operating system, much like network management (to the network layer model), is an issue that impacts all levels of abstraction in an operating system.

At the lowest levels of abstraction, detection and conflict avoidance are the prime objectives. At increasing levels of abstraction, however, administration and resource utilization are bound together with the needs of the corresponding layer of the operating system to which they are attached (which also increase at successive layers).

At some point as the layers are ascended, the system's administrator of the particular host computer running the operating system is made aware of the existence of configurable subsystems within the operating system. These are identified by the *role* they play from the perspective of the administrator, regardless of the actual subentities from which they are assembled that may exist on many of the lower levels of abstraction. In the past, many operating system designs dealing with configuration sought to take these levels of abstraction and compact them to a single level so as to create a flat arrangement that would be more manageable by a systems administrator. While this is an expedient approach, it is important always to realize that it is a fiction that could be broken in certain cases.[18]

In the formation of the 386BSD operating systems kernel, the kernel itself is composed of several modules, each of which may perform various actions at different levels in the hierarchy of level of abstraction. Originally (in earlier versions of BSD), an attempt was made to segregate portions of these modules into like categories to make them more manageable.[19] The problem with this approach is that the topology of the filesystem could not do justice to the layering and levels of abstraction as implemented in an operating system of these modules. Thus, they are kept as even peers in the current version of 386BSD. (This is an example of where visualization of layering may not necessarily provide an immediate benefit).

---

[18] Due to interactions between modules made opaque by the enforced lack of hierarchy
[19] In 4.1d, the kernel program was divided up into separate groups, one per directory. This was a futile attempt at organizing the kernel functionally. This idea returned in 4.4BSD, to the same problems.

Nevertheless, the hierarchy is necessary, as many of these modules have different interfaces to different parts of the hierarchy. During initialization and configuration, dependency usually requires an order of initialization. Thus, before higher level entities can be initialized, many details of lower levels must be found.

In recent years, depth-first analysis of configuration has been seen as the strongest mechanism to solving this dilemma. By successively examining every element from the top-down to its atomic dependencies, configuration conflicts for a particular top level resource could be found. However, in the case where this top down hierarchy itself is impossible to establish (such as in a clustered system where there is no "top"), it is not possible to tell if one can proceed in this manner. Of more immediate concern is the plethora of new operating systems facilities and the fact that older modules might have to "know" about newer module hierarchies before they can configure themselves or otherwise must be taken into account in this manner.

In the current scheme of configuration for 386BSD, the operating system's kernel itself is responsible for ensuring that the depth-first approach to configuration order is maintained, so that new kernel abstractions will be configured at the appropriate order in the hierarchy—independent of an actual configuration-specific event itself. In this way, the depth-first analysis within a specific module becomes *independent* of the evolution of the rest of the operating system and other modules which might be incorporated in after the fact. Thus, the hierarchy itself becomes independent of kernel development and operating systems implementation.

4.3.2 The Configuration "Objects": Future Direction & Evolution

The specific configuration implementation in this file is oriented towards developing the details of *core objects* embedded in the configuration process and on the *methods* which surround them. In the course of this work, many design considerations relating to module interfaces in the kernel have thus been exposed as a first step towards its reconstitution as an *extensible class library*. In its present form, this file succeeds in placing the configurable (and possibly brokerable) kernel object into the kernel, extending the scope of the kernel itself. As such, this file could easily be reworked into an object-oriented language (such as C++ or objective C). However, since the need to provide backwards compatibility with UNIX and BSD device driver interfaces is fundamentally at odds with the need to develop an abstract interface mechanism requiring less operating system specific code, its ultimate resolution is still a matter for future work.

4.3.3 Provisioning and Tailoring

The configuration process is broken up into two stages: *provisioning* and *tailoring*. Provisioning implies that we load enough modules into a kernel to cover all uses to which the kernel may be applied. Tailoring, on the other hand, deals with the

---

resolution of per-system conflicts and differences at boot time, thus allowing the modules in a kernel to be correctly used on a particular host.

A practical example of this is that now all of the author's internal 386BSD systems use a single kernel program, even though the hardware devices, buses, and add-in cards differ tremendously. Each system and bootstrap is then tailored by use of a few line files to suit our needs. As a result, 386BSD is now tailorable to an individual PC without requiring recompilation.

4.3.3.1 Configuration Language Conventions

cfg_XX functions are primitives for interpreting the syntax of the configuration script language. The configuration script language is an extremely simple language built up of *tokens*. These tokens are one of three categories: *character*, *string* or *number*. White space is used as a delimiter (as is done in the C-shell).

Each configuration script consists of a set of tokens terminated by a period, with arbitrary amounts of white space in between. Comments may be included in the form of pound sign characters (#) with arbitrary text up to the next newline character. The first token is always the module name, followed by any parameters required by its associated kernel interfaces, followed by any external module-related details (like information to pass to a bus driver to allow the driver to configure a hardware device), and finished up with per-driver details. By default, provisioned drivers usually install themselves per an embedded script which can be overridden by the configuration file, or defeated with an exclaimation character (!) to prevent interaction.

It should be noted that the syntax is reserved to substitute drivers symbolically, using the equal character "=." For example, as used in the pair of script strings ("driver=olddriver ... .", "newdriver=driver ... ."), this would have the effect of replacing "driver" with "newdriver." The implementation of this has been postponed until after dynamic driver loading and relocation, to decide if there is a point to providing this capability after dynamic reloading of drivers is present.

Each line is individually parsed as it is evaluated. The syntax is determined by the routine that calls and extracts fields. It is possible to write specific configuration script language sequences not covered in this language definition. (This is done in the case of the bus driver **isa/isa.c**, which uses descriptions of ISA device characteristics as parenthetical expressions.)

4.3.3.2 An Example Configuration Script

Figure 4.1 contains a configuration script written for a server host.

```
#
# Server host aslan; avoid ethernet port conflicts for port banks 300 & 320
# and irq 5.
#
ed 2 (0x300 5 -1 0xd8000 8192 1)
(0x320 9 -1 0xd0000 8192 0).     # two specific ethernet cards
as 4 13 (0x230).                 # adaptec 1542 SCSI at a nonstandard I/O port
```

```
console com 1 9600.          # serial console com1 at 9600 baud
!wt.                         # defeat wangtek driver
```

In this configuration script, two Ethernet cards at specific locations and interrupts are being probed for. Since no parameters are needed by the system, all of these are specific to the driver. In this case, provision is made for two devices, located with ISA device strings for units ed1 and ed0. A SCSI card at a nonstandard port is also described; it has block major number 4 and character major number 13 for interface "names." A serial port has been chosen as a console device, and the "wt" driver has been defeated. This file has tailored use of the kernel to avoid known port/interrupt conflicts, and to select use of a serial console for operation.

4.3.3.3 What the Configuration Script Language is Not!

A configuration script is used to tailor the 386BSD kernel to adapt it to nonstandard or conflicting configurations. As such, the configuration script used by **kern/config.c** is not intended as a generic configuration or initialization file, but instead is used only to deal with incidental configuration conflicts or incompatibilities.

Specifically, this file is not akin to the MS-DOS CONFIG.SYS file. That function should only be performed by supervisory programs that can do a more capable job because they can use the resources of a full-blown user program to resolve all of the significant problems that occur with configurations. Instead, the purpose of this file is to resolve Gordian Knot problems (e.g., we can't get the system to run the configuration program because we need the configuration program to run before we can boot the system).

In general, 386BSD configuration is headed towards a model where extensions are dynamically loaded and configured when requested for use by a user of the kernel. Analogous to the way the command shell finds commands on demand from a search path of directories, the kernel itself can also incorporate modules as needed. Thus, the only long-term need for a ".config" file is to assemble enough of a viable configuration to then access a root filesystem.

In the earlier configuration script example (see *An Example Configuration Script* above), a conflict would have prevented the system from booting, because the default (non-invasive) probe touched a register on an Ethernet card that immediately jammed the machine. This conflict was known by the machine operator, but unavoidable because the particular selection of cards did not allow a non-overlapping default case. The operator compensated for this problem with the file entries mentioned above. Since the remaining cards used the standard configuration (ide, com, lpt, npx, ...), none of them needed to be mentioned in the file, nor did a specially configured kernel need to be created.

In sum, this language is intended to be as simple as possible, since we don't want to overload the kernel with an overly elaborate mechanism. Attempts to expand this mechanism without significant justification are strongly discouraged.

4.3.4 Configuration Module Class Types

Modules are identified as having a unique name and an embedded identifier that can be found by the module communications mechanism to allow self-configuration. The unique identifier inside of the module is actually a configuration script and name—as such, there is only *one* location where the symbolic name is present for the module. Every other instance of the name in the operating system for that module stems from this source.[20]

The only *name* used internally for module communications is the module *class* type, as all modules within a class are considered peers. It is impossible to distinguish which should take precedence over another within the class—that is up to the configuration script and the configuration process that is instigated by asking a module to configure itself.

Configuration classes exist solely as a way of implying configuration *order* to the process of configuration. A configuration class identifies all modules of a specific level of abstraction to be configured at a given point in time. The actual order of configuration of each of these classes is determined by the order of implicit calls to initialize a given class in the kernel itself. Thus, very low level of abstraction configuration requests (i.e. the bus and console) occur very early in the bootstrap of the kernel, while very high level configuration requests (i.e. the filesystems and protocols) occur later. When a module responds to a initialization request, the module's interfaces are engaged for possible use by the kernel. At this point, whatever is required for that level of abstraction configuration request is implemented by the corresponding module.

The point of this classification scheme is to disallow a module from intertwining itself with other modules, since that would imply an ordering between modules which we cannot assure. In addition, we cannot assure that all the modules necessary for an intermodule communications set to be present are present at the time that the initialization occurs. In effect, module initialization is *stateless* with respect to other modules, but *stateful* with respect to the kernel and to class order.[21]

In some cases, order itself creates loops or dependencies that cannot easily be resolved. In these cases, an *external symbol binding* mechanism[22] is used. This redefinable binding mechanism, called *"fuzzy binding"*, facilitates resolution of the conflict by permitting

---

[20] A possible improvement contemplated for modules is to allow the name to be renamed in the configuration file, so that it is possible to exchange drivers symbolically—it is not obvious yet if this is a sensible addition at this point.

[21] This contrasts with the mechanism used by Novell Netware Loadable Kernel Modules, for example, which require order—in this case, severe problems can result if resources are allocated out of order.

[22] Called an "esym".

an incomplete configuration knowing that a subsequent revision will occur which will complete the configuration process.

One example of dependence involves bus versus driver initialization. In sum, the bus must be configured before the device, yet to complete the configuration of the bus we need to have all devices configured ahead of time; thus, a chicken-and-egg scenario develops. 386BSD resolves this dilemma by splitting the bus configuration into two levels of abstraction, with the low-level bus configuration considered a separate class from the high-level bus configuration which occurs after driver initialization is complete.

The upshot of this organization of classes is that a configuration script is unordered. The lines that describe a particular module can appear in any order in the configuration file without causing any difference in operation, since they will be examined and parsed only when their class comes up for evaluation.[23]

4.3.4.1 Broadcast Mechanism For Module Communications

One of the consequences of the way modules are organized is the reliance on a broadcast mechanism for module communications—where a single request message to initialize the modules may hit from none to many different modules all at the same time. Currently, there is only one message. This is considered adequate for 386BSD Release 1.0.

In the future, we would like to broadcast more kinds of messages. However, because of the many-to-one mapping, it becomes difficult to design parameters to exchange with a module initialization or other communication request, due to the dilemma of sorting out the return replies and selecting specific modules to take effect. By decoupling the dependencies through the use of two separate mechanisms (e.g., the message itself and the configuration semantics embedded in the configuration scripts), we have elided this problem.

However, if we wish to introduce a program-driven configuration control mechanism, this current approach is inadequate. In this case, in order to expand the number of messages that we are able to send to the modules, the broadcast mechanism itself must be changed. Alternatives to do just this include making the module communications mechanism more heavyweight, or using an IPC mechanism (like a communications domain) to provide the configuration and parameter selection mechanisms used for a programmatic interface.

4.3.5 Interfaces to Device Drivers

The device drivers are interfaced to the system via a set of functions that gain access to methods and characteristics of a device driver. The current implementation of this

---

[23] See Exercise 4.2 on configuration order.

interface is intended to hide the details of the actual implementation in the layer between the kernel and the particular device drivers.

The device drivers are responsible for connecting their interfaces to the kernel, while the kernel is responsible for indicating when the device drivers should do this and only makes use of the device drivers through this procedural interface only. As such, they are not to get intimate with the contents of the device interface structures themselves, since it may be the case that the contents of the structures have changed and the actual mapping of devices to function requests may differ from what the kernel request might have guessed. For example, a logical device may actually be built up of many physical devices, or there may exist a device that converts, say, Unicode characters to ISO Latin I character devices transparently.

This architecture of kernel interface to device drivers is extensible in three independent directions. To the kernel interface itself, additional functions could be added to support new requirements by the kernel. Similarly, the actual implementation of the device interface structure could be extended to provide different device types or methods of interaction with the kernel (the way in which the functions are implemented that attach new functionality). Finally, within the kernel interface layer, the layer could be extended to allow for transparent filtering and/or logical device management which may create different pseudo-devices composed of possibly multiple physical devices in the lower level of abstraction. Thus, for example, a disk array could be implemented as appearing like a single disk without changing any of the underlying device driver characteristics.[24] Again, while this is provisioned, none of these extensions has yet been done, but have instead been left as an exercise to the reader.

4.3.5.1 386BSD Line Disciplines

386BSD line disciplines are a class of *superdrivers* used to implement more elaborate functionality on top of a character device. They are a predecessor to the streams mechanism and have been used in Berkeley UNIX to provide multiple tty driver support, as well as SLIP, ppp, and access to pointing devices. Their presence in the current release of 386BSD is simply that of a holdover of older technology that hopefully will be replaced in the future by a streams-like mechanism (not yet ready for widespread use) called *currents*.

Line disciplines are implemented much in the same way as device drivers, in that they are dynamically configured during system initialization and accessed by other drivers in the kernel via a procedural interface. The procedural interface is the registered means of gaining access to a line discipline. If the line discipline is unimplemented in

---

[24] See the swap driver in the virtual memory system **vm/swap.c** for an example of how this is currently achieved using the older architecture.

the system, an attempt to reference it will be denied as a request to an unconfigured module.

Line disciplines are currently known by their *global index number* only. However, the system tracks their allocation and use by means of a module name. Like the device interface, the methods that they support are incorporated into an embedded structure in the line discipline (currently referenced by an array of pointers) that converts the line discipline's index to a pointer to the appropriate line discipline interface (ldiscif) method structure *ldiscif_XX*.

No line disciplines are mandatory for system operation. However, usually at least one line discipline is present as a user terminal interface. By virtue of the modular compartmentalization of the system, it is possible to change the line disciplines independent from the kernel and develop new functionality in them as if they were separate programs—just like device drivers.

A series of support routines for managing line disciplines is present in the kernel as a central facility for use by all of the subsequent line disciplines. It is written in such a fashion as to use the line disciplines themselves for underlying characteristics of implementation, such as character size and semantics of action.

The intent of this arrangement is to obviate the need to modify the core kernel to support arbitrarily functionality within a line discipline. Thus, the line discipline interface and kernel dependencies on that interface will remain constant over at least one more major revision of the system. Also, any changes to the kernel to improve the efficiency or to expand the top-level semantics of all line disciplines can thus be uniformly implemented across all line disciplines solely by changing the kernel's functionality in the file **kern/ldisc.c**.

Implicit within the idea of a line discipline is the existence of a terminal device structure (struct tty) which contains the per-open characteristics of a given line discipline. Inside of the tty structure is a hidden pointer to the particular line discipline in use. This is managed internally by the line discipline interface to refer to the line discipline associated with the particular open device.

Unlike earlier UNIX and BSD implementations, line disciplines in 386BSD are implemented as a sparse list. Thus, this pointer is used to find the unique line discipline—the line discipline number is no longer an index into a table.

4.3.5.2 Driver Names

Like the famous poem "The Naming of Cats" (by T. S. Eliot), drivers in the current implementation also have up to three different names. First and foremost is the device driver module name itself. This name is a character string which describes the module.

To reconcile the naming conventions of older UNIX systems, which denoted drivers by their character major device number and block major device number, these number indexes can also be used to find a module supporting that particular function. It would be easy enough to remove the restriction of these two additional separate names, except for the fact that they still have some historic identification with supporting programs elsewhere. Eventually, however, these two names may very well be removed as the need to maintain backwards compatibility decreases.

4.3.5.3 Driver Methods

Every driver has a set of methods embedded within it, which the kernel employs indirectly via the device driver interface functions (**devifXXX()**). These methods are registered with the kernel by means of a pointer to a device interface structure.

Two arrays are hidden within the device interface implementation that convert character or block major numbers to the corresponding device interface pointer values. This could alternatively have been done with a linked list of device interfaces, whereby the list could be scanned to find a particular character or block major device name. If implemented as a linked list, there would be no upper bound on devices; however, a scan on reference of the list would be required.[25] Alternatively, a variable-sized array could be maintained, grown and compressed as needed. However, this approach would imply a certain degree of memory space inefficiency if the names were sparsely allocated.

At the time of implementation, the simplest possible mechanism of a fixed array was used. This allows for an upper limit of one hundred entries. This mechanism is adequate for the current system, but may be revisited if the linked list or other sparse mechanism becomes more desirable.

4.3.5.4 Portals

An alternative naming convention for device drivers is a *portal*. A portal is a file-like object which transforms its file operations into program operations transparently. Thus, it is a way of transforming file semantics into program action. While the concept of a portal is not rigorously defined (primarily because most operating systems don't implement them as yet), it is still a convenient form for translating the semantics of a program file to a device driver or protocol.[26]

Indeed, if interfaced via this method, a device driver may become a program file that is *mounted* so as to make it configured into the kernel for use. The semantics of the file would then be transformed into driver operations (a read or a write would accept or send characters on a UART, for example). As with all new work, the devil is in the details of how the semantics are arranged.

---

[25] Similar to the way the virtual memory system scans for map entries in a map—see **vm_map_lookup()** in **vm/map.c**, **Volume II**, for more information.

[26] Or even a filesystem—see *386BSD namei() Design Choices and Trade Offs* in the discussion of **fs/lookup.c** on the **386BSD Reference CD-ROM**. Plan 9 also uses multiple filesystem semantics.

The abstraction of a portal could be used to hide the differences between a driver developed as a user program and possibly migrated to the kernel as a way of avoiding the cost of context switching (if relevant). While there are a number of touchy situations that will result in bootstrapping such a system (and, of course, the development costs incurred in building such as system), portals could avoid many of the naming conundrums present in the device drivers and filesystems (stacking, inheritance, transparency, and so forth).

Note that a portal is actually a general concept (actually, more general than what is inferred here), and has many uses in other areas of IPC/networking (as, for example, a means to allow our streams-like mechanism to bind to its namespace(s)).

4.3.6 Configuration Resolution

No system yet available manages to solve configuration deterministically with real live autonomous programs, because no one wants to take the trouble of finishing and maintaining such programs. As such, we tend to fall back on letting users configure things with arcane strings because eventually we figure they will make it work somehow. However, to allow plug and play systems, we need to bite the bullet and resolve the conflicts in an automated program.

This configuration program is a start in this direction. It moves configuration out of the province of compile time and moves it into the run-time environment—this is its best virtue. However, it is still incomplete, in that it doesn't provide a program interface to the administration, configuration, and conflict resolution programs that should exist and make use of the symbolic interface to modules.

As a result, all that is actually left is the appendix (so to speak) of a configuration file used to tailor the system. This incomplete area is a bit of a problem, since it might leave the user the impression that all the configuration information must reside in this file. This will not be the case in the future (so don't start elaborating on this—those who don't learn from the past are condemned to repeat it).

One place to improve this mechanism is the program interface to the configuration process, so that an automatic program can oversee the process of configuration as an intermediary. Once this is in place, another area of improvement is to write programs that tenderly examine the device hardware (not being tender means that you hang or crash the machine—treat it as you would like to be treated during a colonoscopy) and from this inspection suggest that devices may be configured at certain port interrupts and/or DMA assignments.

Since unpleasant events can occur (like formatting the disk accidentally in probing for it), care must be taken to determine the degree to which intrusive operations can be performed or the degree to which examining BIOS strings in device ROMs can prove useful in discovering the presence of random pieces of PC hardware (provided, of course, that they bought the BIOS ROMs for their SCSI card and didn't get cheap).

Thus, those programs that manage the database of higher level configuration extending upward into the more elaborate peripheral characteristics might be used to condition drivers in the system to work more efficiently. This would be the most portable and elegant solution to resolving the dilemmas that plague present systems software and allow for rather elaborate and successful plug and play.

4.3.7 Future Directions in 386BSD Configuration

This configuration work is in the preliminary stages, and not at the end of the process. Several stages of design are planned for which would move the system more towards the plug and play environment required in today's world.

The current design is actually positioned towards the second stage of allowing provisioning at boot time. In this case, the tailoring process itself can also be used to select the modules needed for the kernel on that very machine. It would then be possible to supply new drivers *independent* of operating systems (for an operating system version). This would, for example, allow peripheral manufacturers to economically offer a 386BSD driver alongside a Windows driver and an OS/2 driver for use with the system.

The third stage in this development sequence is to allow dynamically the reprovisioning or exchange of device drivers after loading the system. This allows for driver development without resorting to rebooting the processor (which on some machines costs a significant period of time). While it is currently possible to do this with far simpler mechanisms which overload existing driver tables, it is impossible with these mechanisms to catch aberrant situations which will cause crashes (as for example, in the common case where a reference exists to an older driver that now refers to a new driver at an inappropriate place). It is possible to develop a crash-proof driver mechanism which allows for driver debugging, but this requires a much more elaborate and elegant solution to this problem—one involving the use of *portals* (see the discussion on **Portals** above).

The fourth stage involves fleshing out the higher level of abstractions of configuration by means of integration with the rest of the operating system. At this point, all the kernel is responsible for in configuration is to be an intermediary that receives revised methods from the configuration programs running as user processes.

While this program has the function of evaluating the computer's hardware (looking for any remaining devices not configurable by the kernel), the first program, **/sbin/config**, must be run by the initialization process (**/sbin/init**) to finish the job begun by this file in getting the kernel to the point where it can run user program.

The fifth and last stage of development involves developing a registry of interfaces that allow for multiple operating system interface convergence. This registry, for example, might allow 386BSD (and other research operating systems) to make use of other operating system drivers and standard interfaces and by means of conversion protocols make use of the resources of these different operating systems interchangeable with its own private standard.

This co-mingling of kernel programming environments could result in both competition of interfaces as well as seamless intercompatibility with existing popular operating system environments to the benefit of the average user. Thus, the user would be free to select the best hardware for use and not have to wait for a 386BSD-specific driver to be developed (if one ever is).

4.3.8 Configuration Topology and Clustering

Another consideration with configuration looking towards the future is that of the topology of the items being configured. Currently, all of the software modules and hardware devices can be thought of as being described by a simple directed acyclic graph—this is adequate to meet the needs of the current system. However, as we discovered on the VAX with its dual-ported controllers (e.g. two controllers pointing to the same device), a considerable problem develops when more elaborate configurations can only be described by a cyclic or a non-directed graph (or both).

In the case of a processor cluster architecture, for example, the complement of devices may actually be a combination of shared cyclic graphs describing the connectivity of each of the modules and devices that they manage. For this kind of architecture, configuration order and interdependence must be managed by a mechanism that can sort out the details and costs inherent in the I/O architecture, since there may be multiple choices as to how the modules may be connected in order to allow access to modules and devices to take place. [27]

An example by which this could be accomplished (in terms of simple configuration detection) is through the use of a "mark and sweep" operation, thus allowing the topology to be taken into account. However, in the general case of a completely configurable cluster architecture that allows process migration, many configuration-related problems can result that are variations on the "traveling salesman" problem. Thus, the elements of an advanced configuration scheme for this stage of complexity of computer architecture absolutely requires a *dynamic* management entity and cannot

---

[27] E.g., "Which disk controller do I use this time to access a disk when I have more than one option?"

be solved by a static configuration mechanism. This represents a challenging research topic opportunity in the area of configuration in the operating system.[28]

4.3.9 Functions Contained in kern/config.c

The following functions are contained in the **kern/config.c** file:

cfg_skipwhite()
isdigit()
isalphanum()
valdigit()
cfg_number()
cfg_string()
cfg_char()
cfg_namelist()
config_scan()
modscaninit()
devif_name()
devif_root()
devif_open()
devif_close()
devif_ioctl()
devif_read()
devif_write()
devif_select()
devif_mmap()
devif_strategy()
devif_psize()
devif_dump()
devif_config()
ldiscif_open()
ldiscif_close()
ldiscif_read()
ldiscif_write()
ldiscif_ioctl()

---

[28] To the author's knowledge, the only system which dealt with even the first level of complexity is VAX VMS, with its ability to build systems which shared controllers using multiple processors, but even this system had very significant limits.

ldiscif_rint()

ldiscif_put()

ldiscif_start()

ldiscif_modem()

ldiscif_qsize()

ldiscif_config()

console_putchar()

console_getchar()

console_config()

These functions fall into five groups. The **cfg_XX()** functions, **isdigit()**, **isalphanum()**, and **valdigit()** are all configuration string handling functions. The module configuration mechanism is handled by both **config_scan()** and **modscaninit()**. The kernel interface to device drivers and line disciplines are handled by the **devif_XX()** and **ldiscif_XX()** functions, respectively, while the console kernel interface is handled by the **putchar()**, **getchar()**, and **config()** functions.

The **devif_XXX** functions implement a series of object method calls to a UNIX device driver interface object. By interposing a layer between the kernel and device drivers, requests to device drivers can be filtered and potentially redirected (remote, cluster, and logical device mappings). One use of this would be to "stripe" disk drives by reassigning operations to different drives, subunits, or controllers, depending on the request.

Like the **devif_XXX** functions, the **ldisk_XXX** functions manage access to line disciplines. Line disciplines are a temporary class driver-like mechanism used to provide common terminal and network functionality to serial communciations drivers. In addition, the console interface functions allow the kernel to read/write one of many different console interfaces embedded in certain drivers.

Many of these functions could be combined using macros to reduce code redundancy. This was not done intentionally in this file at this time, since some of these files may be modified in later versions. As such, macroization is left as an exercise for the reader.

4.3.10 What is cfg_skipwhite()?

cfg_skipwhite() is a trivial function which skips over any white space in a configuration string. The supplied reference to a string is updated by **cfg_skipwhite()** to point to the next non-white space character. By definition, this includes any content in a comment string. Thus, white space in this system is used as a delimiter.

... [File: /usr/src/kernel/kern/config.c, line: 77]

```
char *
cfg_skipwhite(char **ptr) {
    ...
```

cfg_skipwhite() has one argument: a pointer to a character string. It returns a character string. The side-effect of this function is that it updates the string pointer to the next non-white space character.

4.3.10.1 How is cfg_skipwhite() Implemented?

... [File: /usr/src/kernel/kern/config.c, line: 81]

```
rescan:
        /* white space is any blanks, tabs, newlines or returns */
        while (*p == ' ' || *p == '\t' || *p == '\n' || *p == '\r')
                p++;

        /* comments are treated as white space, terminated by a newline */
        if (*p == '#') {
                while (*p && *p != '\n')
                        p++;
                goto rescan;
        }

        return (*ptr = p);
    ...
```

The pointer to a string is fetched into a temporary value which is then examined character by character and any blanks, tabs, newlines or returns are skipped over. If the character that it stops on is the beginning of a comment (#), the string is skipped over until after the next newline or until the end of the string. At that point, the string is again rescanned for any additional white space. The routine terminates with a non-white space character not corresponding to a comment, and the string pointer is updated with the argument's address.

4.3.11 What is isdigit()?

isdigit() is a trivial internal function which checks to see if a character is a digit in the supplied *base* variable. **isdigit()** recognizes that a character is a digit. It returns a boolean value if the character falls within the given base.

... [File: /usr/src/kernel/kern/config.c, line: 97]

```
static int
isdigit(char c, int base) {
    ...
```

isdigit() has two arguments: the character to be examined; and the base to check it for. It returns a boolean value—true if a character is a digit in that base, false otherwise. The character in all cases is an ordinary ASCII character.

4.3.11.1 How is isdigit() Implemented?

... [File: /usr/src/kernel/kern/config.c, line: 100]

```
    if (base == 10)
            return ((c >= '0' && c <= '9') ? 1 : 0);
    if (base == 8)
            return ((c >= '0' && c <= '7') ? 1 : 0);
    if (base == 16) {
            if (c >= '0' && c <= '9')
                    return (1);
            if (c >= 'a' && c <= 'f')
                    return (1);
            if (c >= 'A' && c <= 'F')
                    return (1);
    }
    return (0);
...
```

The character is checked to see if it falls within the bounds of the *base* variable (base 8, 10, 16). If it does, a true is returned, and a false (zero) otherwise.

4.3.12 What is isalphanum()?

isalphanum() is an internal trivial function which checks to see if a character is a valid alphanumeric character. **isalphanum()** recognizes that a character is a alphanumeric character and returns a boolean value as a result.

... [File: /usr/src/kernel/kern/config.c, line: 116]

```
static int
isalphanum(char c) {
 ...
```

isalphanum() has one argument: the character to be examined. It returns a boolean value—true if a character is a alphanumeric, and false otherwise. The character in all cases is an ordinary ASCII character.

4.3.12.1 How is isalphanum() Implemented?

... [File: /usr/src/kernel/kern/config.c, line: 119]

```
    if (c >= 'a' && c <= 'z')
            return (1);
    if (c >= 'A' && c <= 'Z')
            return (1);
    if (c >= '0' && c <= '9')
            return (1);

    return (0);
...
```

The character is checked to see if it is a lower case or upper case alpha character or a numeric character. If it is, a true is returned, and false otherwise.

4.3.13 What is valdigit()?

valdigit() is an internal trivial function which returns the value of a digit in the appropriate base. The value of the ASCII character is returned by **valdigit()** as a decimal or hexadecimal digit.

... [File: /usr/src/kernel/kern/config.c, line: 130]

```
static int
valdigit(char c) {
    ...
```

valdigit() has one argument: the character to be examined. It returns the value of the character as a digit.

4.3.13.1 How is valdigit() Implemented?

... [File: /usr/src/kernel/kern/config.c, line: 133]

```
        if (c >= '0' && c <= '9')
                return (c - '0');
        if (c >= 'a' && c <= 'f')
                return (c - 'a' + 10);
        if (c >= 'A' && c <= 'F')
                return (c - 'A' + 10);

        return (0);
    ...
```

A decimal digit is identified and its numeric digit value is returned. If it is a hexadecimal digit, only the first six alpha characters are returned as the corresponding hexadecimal value. It should never be the case that this function will need to be used on anything other than these cases. If supplied with an out-of-range value, the function will return false (zero) by default.

4.3.14 What is cfg_number()?

cfg_number() parses a configuration string looking for a number. If a number is present, **cfg_number()** obtains the value of the number and returns it, passing over any characters. Otherwise, the function indicates that no number was present and does not alter the position of the supplied pointer to the character string.

... [File: /usr/src/kernel/kern/config.c, line: 143]

```
int
cfg_number(char **ptr, int *pval) {
    ...
```

cfg_number() has two arguments: a pointer to the character string; and a pointer to an integer to receive the value of the number. It returns true as a value if a number was successfully found and returned as a value, and false otherwise. The side-effect of this function is that if a number is found, the pointer is updated to point after the found number.

4.3.14.1 How is cfg_number Implemented?

... [File: /usr/src/kernel/kern/config.c, line: 149]

```
p = cfg_skipwhite(ptr);

/* sign? */
if (*p == '-') {
        p++;
        sign = 1;
}
```
...

Any white space in the configuration string is skipped over with the **cfg_skipwhite()** function call. The first character of the string is then checked to see if it is a signed character; if so, the state of the sign is recorded.

... [File: /usr/src/kernel/kern/config.c, line: 158]

```
if (isdigit(*p, 10)) {

        /* base of number */
        if (p[0] == '0') {
                if (p[1] == 'x') {
                        p += 2; base = 16;
                } else {
                        p++ ; base = 8;
                }
        }

        /* accumulate number value. */
        while (isdigit(*p, base))
                val = base * val + valdigit(*p++);

        /* return found number, and advance string pointer */
        *pval = sign ? -val : val;
        *ptr = p;
        return (1);

} else
        return (0);
```
...

The next character is checked to see if it corresponds to a decimal numeric character. All numbers in a configuration string must start with at least one decimal number, even if it is not a decimal number. In the C tradition of octal and hexadecimal numbers, base 8 and base 16 numbers begin with a 0 or a 0x respectively. This is recognized in the character string (if present), and the base is adjusted appropriately.

The number is then evaluated as a successive string of digits in the decided base. The end of the number is determined by the first non-digit character. When this is found, the value is returned after adjusting it with the appropriate sign. The string pointer in the supplied argument is then updated and a true returned. If the string did not begin with a numeric digit, a boolean value of zero is returned (false) and the string is not updated.

4.3.15 What is cfg_string()?

cfg_string() matches an alphanumeric string token of a supplied finite length. A string is examined by **cfg_string()** to see if it is not parsable as a number. The string is then returned in a buffer supplied by the caller untranslated.

... [File: /usr/src/kernel/kern/config.c, line: 183]

```
int
cfg_string(char **ptr, char *sp, int szval) {
    ...
```

cfg_string() has three arguments: the pointer to the character string; the buffer in which the character string is returned; and the size of the buffer. It returns a true if it found a character string, false otherwise.

4.3.15.1 How is cfg_string() Implemented?

... [File: /usr/src/kernel/kern/config.c, line: 189]

```
        lp = p = cfg_skipwhite(ptr);

        /* reserve place in buffer for null */
        szval -= 1;

        /* accumulate alphanumeric string value. */
        while (isalphanum(*p)) {
                if (szval- > 0)
                        *rsp++ = *p;
                p++;
        }
    ...
```

The string has its white space skipped over and a place in the return buffer is reserved for a null to terminate the terminating string. An alphanumeric string is accumulated in the supplied string buffer to the size present in the string buffer (any exceeding the string will be scanned and ignored). A non-alphanumeric value will be used as a delimiter to determine the end of the alphanumeric string.

... [File: /usr/src/kernel/kern/config.c, line: 202]

```
        if (rsp != sp) {

                /* return found string, adding terminating null */
                *rsp = 0;
                *ptr = p;
                return (1);

        } else
                return (0);
    ...
```

The return buffer is examined to see if anything was accumulated in the return string. If there was, the pointer to the string is updated to skip over the string argument just found and a null is added to the return string. A true is then returned by the function; otherwise, a false is returned and the pointer to the string of tokens is left unchanged.

4.3.16 What is cfg_char()?

cfg_char() tests the configuration string for the presence of a particular character token. It returns true and advances the pointer if one is found. The supplied string is scanned by **cfg_char()** for the next character (beyond any white space) and tested for the presence of the supplied character. This mechanism is the principal way an external parsing routine determines the syntax of the string for building an external expression.

... [File: /usr/src/kernel/kern/config.c, line: 214]

```
int
cfg_char(char **ptr, char t) {
        char *p;
    ...
```

cfg_char() has two arguments: a pointer to a character string; and a character to examine it for. It returns true if the character is found; false otherwise. The side-effect of this function is that it advances the string pointer if it finds the character.

4.3.16.1 How is cfg_char() Implemented?

... [File: /usr/src/kernel/kern/config.c, line: 218]

```
        p = cfg_skipwhite(ptr);

        if (*p++ == t) {
                *ptr = p;
                return (1);
        } else
                return (0);
    ...
```

Again, white space is skipped over and the next character is examined to see if it corresponds to the supplied character. If it does, the pointer to the string is advanced, and a true is returned. Otherwise, a false is returned, and the pointer is not advanced. The purpose of this function is to parse a particular character so as to build an external parsing routine.[29]

4.3.17 What is cfg_namelist()?

cfg_namelist() parses the configuration string for a sequence of (name,token) pairs and returns their respective values in a supplied *namelist* structure. This function is the method by which a set of alphanumeric parameters (names) can be assigned to values obtained from a configuration string.

---

[29] For another example, see the function **cfg_isadev()** in **isa/isa.c**. It is a routine private to the ISA bus which parses the bus-dependent details of an ISA bus.

cfg_namelist() scans the entries in the configuration string corresponding to the supplied patterns of a *namelist* structure. If any are found, the function updates the corresponding values appropriately and returns a true, indicating success.

... [File: /usr/src/kernel/kern/config.c, line: 228]

```
int
cfg_namelist(char **cfg, struct namelist *nmp) {
 ...
```

cfg_namelist() has two arguments: a pointer to the configuration string; and a pointer to a *namelist* structure. It returns true if any elements of the name list are found; false otherwise. The side-effect of this function is that the values in the *namelist* structure are changed depending on the values found in the configuration string. In addition, the configuration string is consumed for any found entries.

The term *namelist* comes from the Fortran NAMELIST feature which allowed a programmer to set variables symbolically from input.

4.3.17.1 How is cfg_namelist() Implemented?

... [File: /usr/src/kernel/kern/config.c, line: 235]

```
        while (cfg_string(&lcfg, val, sizeof(val))) {
                for (n = nmp; n->name ; n++)
                        if (strcmp(n->name, val) == 0)
                                goto found;
                return (any);
 ...
```

The configuration string is examined for the presence of a string token. If one is found, the token is searched for in all of the entries in the supplied *namelist* array. The *namelist* array is terminated by a zero-valued name pointer. If the string is not found in this array, the function returns with the value corresponding to any *namelist* entries that had been previously found.

If this is the first entry examination to be attempted and it is not found, the value of zero is returned.

... [File: /usr/src/kernel/kern/config.c, line: 240]

```
        found:
                switch (n->type) {
                case NUMBER:
                        if (cfg_number(&lcfg, (int *)n->value) == 0)
                                return (any);
                        break;

                case STRING:
                        /* XXX do I really want a length? */
                        if (cfg_string(&lcfg, (char *)n->value, 80) == 0)
                                return (any);
                        break;

                default:
```

```
                    return (any);
          }
          *cfg = lcfg;     /* reduce */
          any++;
      }
      return (any);
...
```

If an entry is found, the entry's *type* is examined. It then attempts to match the next token with the appropriate corresponding kind of token. If the type is a number, a number is looked for and returned in the configuration string, with its value returned in the *namelist* associated value pointer. Otherwise, if a string was requested, a string is returned in like manner. Currently, no length is present in the *namelist* structure, as strings are assumed to be set to appropriately sized lengths.

If the type is unimplemented, the function immediately returns with the string fields unparsed, as it will similarly do if neither type is successfully parsed. Otherwise, if this *namelist* entry has been successfully parsed and the value returned, the configuration string pointer is updated to eliminate the associated two tokens, and the fact that we have successfully found the *namelist* pair is recorded. We then attempt to find the next successive pair. Note that *namelist* entries can be found in any order and can even redundantly appear in definite succession. The *namelist*, therefore, is usually placed at the end of a *namelist* string, where a non-blank delimiter will be found. If no *namelist* name is present, the loop terminates and the status of any found *namelist* entries is returned.

4.3.18 What is config_scan()?

config_scan() begins the module's configuration process and is the source of configuration strings from the module's perspective. It examines both the shared configuration file loaded by the bootstrap of the system as well as the supplied default configuration string by a module to determine whether or not the module should be configured and if there is a corresponding string in the shared configuration file that will override the default configuration embedded in the module. If the module is to be configured, the function will return true, indicating success, as well as a pointer to the remaining portion of the configuration string meant to be parsed by the module containing its symbolic configuration parameters.

... [File: /usr/src/kernel/kern/config.c, line: 265]

```
int
config_scan(char *cfg, char **cfg_sp) {
    ...
```

config_scan() has two arguments: a pointer to the module's default configuration string; and pointer to return a string pointer to the configuration string to be evaluated by the module (if successful). The side-effect of this function is to evaluate the

---

configuration string and possibly supply a different string from the shared configuration file.

During normal use, configuration should be done quietly—without any console printout or interaction—since it is usually the case that configuration is debugged once and then the system is booted afterwards without change. This differs from current and prior versions of 386BSD and all other BSD variants, which instead present a lengthy discourse on configuration during bootstrap. Unfortunately, this console printout may become so long and so verbose that it overwhelms the user and actually hides a configuration conflict.

In the next revision to 386BSD, we will attempt to highlight true configuration flaws as always being made visible, and leave the configuration inventory to a separate user program for those interested in discovering the complement of hardware and software in the system.

4.3.18.1 How is config_scan() Implemented?

... [File: /usr/src/kernel/kern/config.c, line: 273]

```
        (void)cfg_string(&cfg, arg, sizeof(arg));

        /* if starting string matches, signal configuration state */
next_entry:
        exclaim = cfg_char(&lp, '!');
        if (cfg_string(&lp, strbuf, 32) && strcmp(arg, strbuf) == 0 &&
            query("config: override %s", arg)) {

                /* return config string? */
                if (cfg_sp)
                        *cfg_sp = lp;

                return (exclaim == 0);
        }
    ...
```

The default configuration is first examined to find the name of the module as the beginning token in the configuration script string. This argument token will be used to search for the shared configuration file that has been loaded into the kernel at the address located at the end of the kernel image (end).

For every entry in the shared configuration script file, the beginning entry will be checked to see if it corresponds to the name of this module. If it does, but the name is prefaced with a "!", the string will be ignored and the module not allowed to be loaded.

If the module is found in the shared configuration string, a request is made to the operator to decide whether or not the shared configuration file should override the default configuration embedded in the module. This facility (query) is activated if the system is booted with the *specify* option set which allows the user to view and

---

potentially alter the configuration process as it occurs as a way of discovering and debugging potential conflicts due to improper setting of the shared configuration file.

If the entry was found in the shared configuration file but marked as not to be configured, the scan stops immediately and the state of whether or not a "!" is present is returned as an indication of whether or not this module should be configured.

... [File: /usr/src/kernel/kern/config.c, line: 289]

```
        for (;; lp++) {

                /* consume either kind of token */
                while (cfg_number(&lp, &dummy) || cfg_string(&lp, strbuf, 32))
                        ;
                /* done with string */
                if (cfg_char(&lp, 0))
                        goto done_all;

                /* done with entry */
                if (cfg_char(&lp, '.'))
                        break;
        }
goto next_entry;
...
```

If the entry does not contain the module we are looking for, we consume the remaining portions of the entry so as to find the beginning of the next entry to examine. Since entries are composed of different token types, we consume any of the token types and check to see if we have either come to the end of the string (by finding a null) or come to the end of the entry (by finding a "." character). If there are any more entries, we turn to the *next_entry* label and scan this entry to determine whether or not it is the one we are seeking.

... [File: /usr/src/kernel/kern/config.c, line: 304]

```
done_all:
        /* if not found, and not to be configured if not found, ignore */
        if (cfg_char(&cfg, '.'))
                return(0);

        if (cfg_sp)
                *cfg_sp = cfg;

        return(query("config: default %s", arg));
...
```

If we have made a pass through the entire string, we return the supplied configuration string as the configuration string to use. If this string itself has no entries, then there is nothing to configure. However, if there are entries, the user is queried from the console to see if the default configuration of a module is to be allowed (in the case of a *specify* option supplied at boot time). Thus, the *specify* option is used as a filter by the user to discover or change the configuration.

4.3.18.2 Improvements to the Current Implementation of config_scan()

In successive versions of 386BSD, which will allow multiple program files to be loaded and relocated at boot time, the configuration string will be evaluated by file type. Its discovery will thus occur by scanning the list of files loaded and looking for a file of the configuration type, within which the configuration string may be discovered.

4.3.19 What is modscaninit()?

modscaninit() sends a broadcast message to all modules of a given class type to initialize themselves. **modscaninit()** discovers all modules of a supplied type and calls their corresponding initialization functions so as to allow them to register their interfaces with the system.

... [File: /usr/src/kernel/kern/config.c, line: 322]

```
void
modscaninit(modtype_t modtype) {
    ...
```

modscaninit() has one argument: the module class type to be initialized. It returns nothing.

Each module has an embedded record that details an initialization entry point, its module class type, and a recognizable signature. These records can be found in the data segments of any loaded kernel module. Currently, there is only one module, and only that module is scanned to find any entries.[30] This mechanism allows the modules to avoid direct links to the kernel and instead permits them to be loaded independently. The kernel also has no semantic knowledge of the symbols of a module—thus, their symbol tables are independent (or nonexistent).

4.3.19.1 How is modscaninit() Implemented?

... [File: /usr/src/kernel/kern/config.c, line: 326]

```
        for (sigp = &etext; sigp < &edata; sigp++)

                /* if valid signature ... */
                if (*sigp == MODULE_SIGNATURE) {
                        struct modconfig *mcp = (struct modconfig *)sigp;

                        /* ... and a valid type ... */
                        if (MODT_ISVALID(mcp->mod_type)) {

                                /* either to the supplied arg, or to all */
                                if ((mcp->mod_type == modtype
                                    || modtype == __MODT_ALL__)
                                    && mcp->mod_init)
                                        (mcp->mod_init)();
```

---

[30] See *Configuration Module Class Types* for more information.

```
                                                         }
                              }
    ...
```

In scanning for a module, an aligned signature is searched for. A record is said to be found when a corresponding record is attached adjacent to a signature holding a valid type and a valid initialization function. If the module class type corresponds to either the selected class type or the denoted broadcast to all class type, the associated initialization function is called.

While the choice for implementation initializes things by order of load address within the data segment, this fact is hidden from the view of the modules and could be done in various other ways. The net effect of the initialization calls themselves is not unlike that of a hidden C++ static constructor of interface structures.

4.3.20 What is devif_name()?

devif_name() returns the canonical name of a particular device determined by its device and device type. **devif_name()** evaluates the corresponding device interface. It then assembles a unique name for this device that can be used to denote it to both user and kernel programs as a recognizable name against which to reference a specific device associated with a device driver (see *Driver Names*).

... [File: /usr/src/kernel/kern/config.c, line: 374]

```
int
devif_name(dev_t dev, devif_type_t typ, char *name, int namelen) {
    ...
```

devif_name() has four arguments: the device identifier and type; and the name buffer and its length. It returns an error code on failure or zero if it is successful. The side-effect of this function is that a name is loaded into the supplied buffer.

A future variation on **devif_name()** could be used to locate drivers dynamically configured into a directory /name lookup request.

4.3.20.1 How is devif_name() Implemented?

... [File: /usr/src/kernel/kern/config.c, line: 381]

```
        switch (typ) {
        case CHRDEV:
                if (major > sizeof chrmajtodevif / sizeof chrmajtodevif[0] ||
                    (dif = chrmajtodevif[major]) == 0)
                        return (ENODEV);
                break;

        case BLKDEV:
                if (major > sizeof blkmajtodevif / sizeof blkmajtodevif[0] ||
                    (dif = blkmajtodevif[major]) == 0)
                        return (ENODEV);
                break;

        default:
```

```
            panic("devif_name");    /* unimplemented device type */
    }
...
```

The device interface is located for the supplied device and type by examining either of
the device types and its associated device interface pointer. If the supplied device does
not have a device interface, an error (NODEV) is returned. If the device type is not
implemented, the system panics.

... [File: /usr/src/kernel/kern/config.c, line: 399]

```
    fp = dif->di_name;
    while (namelen) {
            *name++ = *fp++;
            namelen--;
    }
...
```

The device interface's name is inserted at the start of the buffer. If the buffer is
overflowed, the remaining portion of the name is not saved.

... [File: /usr/src/kernel/kern/config.c, line: 406]

```
    minor = minor(dev);
    tmpbuf[0] = 0;
    if (dif->di_minor_unit_mask && dif->di_minor_subunit_mask)
            sprintf(tmpbuf,"%d%c",
                    (minor & dif->di_minor_unit_mask)
                        >> dif->di_minor_unit_shift,
                    ((minor & dif->di_minor_subunit_mask)
                        >> dif->di_minor_subunit_shift) + 'a');

    /* ... or construct minor device name with unit */
    else if (dif->di_minor_unit_mask && dif->di_minor_subunit_mask)
            sprintf(tmpbuf,"%d",
                    (minor & dif->di_minor_unit_mask)
                        >> dif->di_minor_unit_shift);

    /* put into name */
    fp = tmpbuf;
    while (namelen && *fp) {
            *name++ = *fp++;
            namelen--;
     }
...
```

If the device supports minor units and possibly subunits, these additional fields are
tacked on after the name by composing them based on the portion of the device field
assigned to that use.

4.3.21 What is devif_root()?

devif_root() takes a bootstrap's device parameters and creates a root device if it can.
devif_root() evaluates the supplied parameters based on the contents of the associated
device interfaces.

... [File: /usr/src/kernel/kern/config.c, line: 430]

```
int
devif_root(unsigned major, unsigned unit, unsigned subunit, dev_t *rd)
 ...
```

devif_root() has four arguments: the major device, unit, and subunit of the boot device parameters; and a pointer to a buffer to return a boot device. If a valid boot device can be found based on those parameters, the root device is returned in a pointer and a true value returned. Otherwise, a false value is returned to indicate failure.

Improvements to **devif_root()** are possible. After the kernel adds dynamically loadable drivers at boot time, **devif_root()** could scour all devices capable of being the root filesystem, instead of solely presuming the stated boot device.

4.3.21.1 How is devif_root() Implemented?

... [File: /usr/src/kernel/kern/config.c, line: 436]

```
        if (query("devif_root: major %d unit %d sub %d\n",
              major, unit, subunit) == 0)
                    return (0);

        /* is there a device driver for the root? */
        if (major >= NDEVIF || (dif = blkmajtodevif[major]) == 0)
              return (0);
 ...
```

The operator is optionally queried to see if this device should be the one that should be configured as the root device. If it is not, or if the device is outside the bounds of a valid device interface, or if the device interface has not been registered at the appropriate block device name, a false is returned (which will generally cause the system to panic).

... [File: /usr/src/kernel/kern/config.c, line: 445]

```
        *rd = makedev(major, ((unit) << dif->di_minor_unit_shift)
              + ((subunit) << dif->di_minor_subunit_shift));
        return (1);
 ...
```

Otherwise, the device interface is used to build a root device by composing its unit and subunit parameters into an appropriate minor device to be used in the root device. The root device is returned in the pointer and a true value is also returned, indicating that a valid root device is present.

4.3.22 What is devif_open()?

devif_open() calls the device driver **open()** method associated with this device driver. **devif_open()** locates the appropriate function to call given the device and device type and calls it with the supplied parameters, returning the result. Otherwise, if the device is not present, it will return an error value indicating the device is not configured. If an unimplemented device type is encountered, the **devif_open()** routine will cause a panic.

... [File: /usr/src/kernel/kern/config.c, line: 452]

```
int
devif_open(dev_t dev, devif_type_t typ, int flag, struct proc *p) {
    ...
```

devif_open() has four arguments: the device identifier and type of device; the parameters of the **open()** flag; and the process for which the **open()** is being performed. It returns an error indication from the **open()** routine of the device driver itself or an error (ENXIO) indicating that the device has not been configured; otherwise, success is indicated.

4.3.22.1 How is devif_open() Implemented?

... [File: /usr/src/kernel/kern/config.c, line: 458]

```
    if (typ == CHRDEV &&
        major < sizeof chrmajtodevif / sizeof chrmajtodevif[0]) {
            dif = chrmajtodevif[major];
            if (dif == console_devif)
                    dev = makedev(major, console_minor);
            if (dif)
                    return ((dif->di_open)(dev, flag, S_IFCHR, p));
            return (ENXIO);
    }
    ...
```

If the type of the device is a BSD UNIX character device, it is found by examining the character major number-to-device interface array to locate the corresponding device interface pointer. If the device happens to be the console device, the appropriate console minor device is reincorporated into the device name so as to select the correct unit and subunit.

If there is a device associated with the supplied device identifier, the device **open()** method is called with the arguments appropriate for a BSD UNIX character device. Otherwise, an unconfigured device error code (ENXIO) is returned.

... [File: /usr/src/kernel/kern/config.c, line: 470]

```
    if (typ == BLKDEV &&
        major < sizeof blkmajtodevif / sizeof blkmajtodevif[0]) {
            if (dif = blkmajtodevif[major])
                    return ((dif->di_open)(dev, flag, S_IFBLK, p));
            return (ENXIO);
    }
    ...
```

Similarly, if the block device type is encountered, the associated device interface pointer is found in the block major-to-device interface array and, if present, the associated **open()** method is called. Otherwise, an unconfigured device error code (ENXIO) is returned.

... [File: /usr/src/kernel/kern/config.c, line: 498]

```
        panic("devif_open"); /* unimplemented type */
    ...
```

If neither of these device types is the device type called, the kernel will panic to indicate that an unimplemented type has been encountered.

4.3.23 What is devif_close()?

devif_close() calls the device driver **close()** method associated with this device driver. **devif_close()** locates the appropriate function to call given the device and device type and calls it with the supplied parameters, returning the result. Otherwise, if the device is not present, it returns an error value (ENODEV). If an unimplemented device type is encountered, the **devif_close()** routine will cause a panic. (Device **close()** routines usually ignore their results).

... [File: /usr/src/kernel/kern/config.c, line: 502]

```
int
devif_close(dev_t dev, devif_type_t typ, int flag, struct proc *p) {
    ...
```

devif_close() has four arguments: the device identifier and type of device; the parameters of the **open()** flag; and the process for which the **close()** is being performed. It returns an error indication from the **close()** routine of the device driver itself or an error (ENODEV) indicating that the device is not present; otherwise, success is indicated.

Since an **open()** requires a device to be present, the only way an ENODEV error could occur is if the device was translated by the device interface layer to a device that did not implement a **close()** routine (e.g., it was never intended to be closed—no such mechanism currently exists in the system, however, and all devices all should have a device interface associated with them at this point).

4.3.23.1 How is devif_close() Implemented?

... [File: /usr/src/kernel/kern/config.c, line: 508]

```
        if (typ == CHRDEV &&
            major < sizeof chrmajtodevif / sizeof chrmajtodevif[0]) {
                dif = chrmajtodevif[major];
                if (dif == console_devif)
                        dev = makedev(major, console_minor);
                if (dif)
                        return ((dif->di_close)(dev, flag, S_IFCHR, p));
                return (ENODEV);
        }
    ...
```

If the type of the device is a BSD UNIX character device, it is found by examining the character major number-to-device interface array to locate the corresponding device interface pointer. If the device happens to be the console device, the appropriate console minor device is reincorporated into the device name so as to select the correct unit and subunit.

If there is a device associated with the supplied device identifier, the device **close()** method is called with the arguments appropriate for a BSD unit character device. Otherwise, a device error code (ENODEV) is returned.

... [File: /usr/src/kernel/kern/config.c, line: 520]

```
      if (typ == BLKDEV &&
          major < sizeof blkmajtodevif / sizeof blkmajtodevif[0]) {
              if (dif = blkmajtodevif[major])
                      return ((dif->di_close)(dev, flag, S_IFBLK, p));
              return (ENODEV);
      }
  ...
```

Similarly, if the block device type is encountered, the associated device interface pointer is found in the block major-to-device interface array and, if present, the associated **close()** method is called. Otherwise, an error is returned.

... [File: /usr/src/kernel/kern/config.c, line: 546]

```
      panic("devif_close"); /* unimplemented type */
  ...
```

If neither of these device types is the device type called, the kernel will panic to indicate that an unimplemented type has been encountered.

4.3.24 What is devif_ioctl()?

devif_ioctl() calls the device driver **ioctl()** method associated with this device driver. **devif_ioctl()** locates the appropriate function to call given the device and device type and calls it with the supplied parameters, returning the result. Otherwise, if the device is not present, it returns an error value (ENODEV). If an unimplemented device type is encountered, the **devif_ioctl()** routine will cause a panic.

... [File: /usr/src/kernel/kern/config.c, line: 550]

```
int
devif_ioctl(dev_t dev, devif_type_t typ, int cmd, caddr_t data, int flag,
  ...
```

devif_ioctl() has six arguments: the device identifier and type of device; the **ioctl()** command and its associated data pointer; the **open()** flag; and the process for which the **ioctl()** is being performed. It returns an error from the **ioctl()** routine of the device driver or an error (ENODEV) indicating the device is not present.

4.3.24.1 How is devif_ioctl() Implemented?

... [File: /usr/src/kernel/kern/config.c, line: 557]

```
if (typ == CHRDEV &&
    major < sizeof chrmajtodevif / sizeof chrmajtodevif[0]) {
chrcase:
        dif = chrmajtodevif[major];
        if (dif == console_devif)
                dev = makedev(major, console_minor);
        if (dif)
                return ((dif->di_ioctl)(dev, cmd, data, flag, p));
        return (ENODEV);
}
...
```

If the type of the device is a BSD UNIX character device, it is found by examining the character major number-to-device interface array to locate the corresponding device interface pointer. If the device happens to be the console device, the appropriate console minor device is reincorporated into the device name so as to select the correct unit and subunit.

If there is a device associated with the supplied device identifier, the device **ioctl()** method is called with the arguments appropriate for a BSD unit character device. Otherwise, a device error code (ENODEV) is returned.

... [File: /usr/src/kernel/kern/config.c, line: 570]

```
if (typ == BLKDEV &&
    major < sizeof blkmajtodevif / sizeof blkmajtodevif[0]) {
        if (dif = blkmajtodevif[major])
                return ((dif->di_ioctl)(dev, cmd, data, flag, p));
        return (ENODEV);
}
...
```

Similarly, if the block device type is encountered, the associated device interface pointer is found in the block major-to-device interface array and, if present, the associated **ioctl()** method is called. Otherwise, an error is returned.

... [File: /usr/src/kernel/kern/config.c, line: 585]

```
panic("devif_ioctl"); /* unimplemented type */
...
```

If neither of these device types is the device type called, the kernel will panic to indicate that an unimplemented type has been encountered.

4.3.25 What is devif_read()?

devif_read() calls the device driver **read()** method associated with this device driver. **devif_read()** locates the appropriate function to call given the device and device type and calls it with the supplied parameters, returning the result. Otherwise, if the device is not present, it will return an error value (ENODEV). If an unimplemented device type is encountered, the **devif_read()** routine will panic.

... [File: /usr/src/kernel/kern/config.c, line: 589]

```
int
devif_read(dev_t dev, devif_type_t typ, struct uio *uio, int flag) {
...
```

devif_read() has four arguments: the device identifier and type of device; the parameters of the **open()** flag; and the process for which the **read()** is being performed. It returns an error indication from the **read()** routine of the device driver itself or an error (ENODEV) indicating that the device is not present; otherwise, success is indicated.

4.3.25.1 How is devif_read() Implemented?

... [File: /usr/src/kernel/kern/config.c, line: 595]

```
    if (typ == CHRDEV &&
        major < sizeof chrmajtodevif / sizeof chrmajtodevif[0]) {
            dif = chrmajtodevif[major];
            if (dif == console_devif)
                    dev = makedev(major, console_minor);
            if (dif)
                    return ((dif->di_read)(dev, uio, flag));
            return (ENODEV);
    }
...
```

If the type of the device is a BSD UNIX character device, it is found by examining the character major number-to-device interface array to locate the corresponding device interface pointer. If the device happens to be the console device, the appropriate console minor device is reincorporated into the device name so as to select the correct unit and subunit.

If there is a device associated with the supplied device identifier, the device **read()** method is called with the arguments appropriate for a BSD unit character device. Otherwise, a device error code (ENODEV) is returned.

... [File: /usr/src/kernel/kern/config.c, line: 624]

```
        panic("devif_read"); /* unimplemented type */
...
```

If the character device type is not found, the kernel will panic to indicate that an unimplemented type has been encountered.

4.3.26 What is devif_write()?

devif_write() calls the device driver **write()** method associated with this device driver. **devif_write()** locates the appropriate function to call given the device and device type and calls it with the supplied parameters, returning the result. Otherwise, if the device

---

is not present, it returns an error (ENODEV). If an unimplemented device type is encountered, the **devif_write()** routine will panic.

... [File: /usr/src/kernel/kern/config.c, line: 628]

```
int
devif_write(dev_t dev, devif_type_t typ, struct uio *uio, int flag) {
...
```

devif_write() has four arguments: the device identifier and type of device; the parameters of the **open()** flag; and the process for which the **write()** is being performed. It returns an error indication from the **write()** routine of the device driver itself or an error (ENODEV) indicating that the device is not present; otherwise, success is indicated.

4.3.26.1 How is devif_write() Implemented?

... [File: /usr/src/kernel/kern/config.c, line:634]

```
        if (typ == CHRDEV &&
            major < sizeof chrmajtodevif / sizeof chrmajtodevif[0]) {
                dif = chrmajtodevif[major];
                if (dif == console_devif)
                        dev = makedev(major, console_minor);
                if (dif)
                        return ((dif->di_write)(dev, uio, flag));

                return (ENODEV);
        }
...
```

If the type of the device is a BSD UNIX character device, it is found by examining the character major number-to-device interface array to locate the corresponding device interface pointer. If the device happens to be the console device, the appropriate console minor device is reincorporated into the device name so as to select the correct unit and subunit.

If there is a device associated with the supplied device identifier, the device **write()** method is called with the arguments appropriate for a BSD unit character device. Otherwise, a device error code (ENODEV) is returned.

... [File: /usr/src/kernel/kern/config.c, line: 663]

```
        panic("devif_write"); /* unimplemented type */
...
```

If the character device type is not found, the kernel will panic to indicate that an unimplemented type has been encountered.

4.3.27 What is devif_select()?

devif_select() calls the device driver **select()** method associated with this device driver. **devif_select()** locates the appropriate function to call given the device and

---

device type and calls it with the supplied parameters, returning the result. Otherwise, if the device is not present, it will return an error (ENODEV). If an unimplemented device type is encountered, the **devif_select()** routine will panic.

... [File: /usr/src/kernel/kern/config.c, line: 667]

```
int
devif_select(dev_t dev, devif_type_t typ, int rw, struct proc *p) {
    ...
```

devif_select() has four arguments: the device identifier and type of device; the parameters of the **select()** call (read/write); and the process for which the **select()** is being performed. It returns an error indication from the **select()** routine of the device driver itself or an error (ENODEV) indicating that the device has not been configured; otherwise, success is indicated.

4.3.27.1 How is devif_select() Implemented?

... [File: /usr/src/kernel/kern/config.c, line: 673]

```
        if (typ == CHRDEV &&
            major < sizeof chrmajtodevif / sizeof chrmajtodevif[0]) {
        chrcase:
                dif = chrmajtodevif[major];
                if (dif == console_devif)
                        dev = makedev(major, console_minor);
                if (dif)
                        return ((dif->di_select)(dev, rw, p));

                return (ENODEV);
        }
    ...
```

If the type of the device is a BSD UNIX character device, it is found by examining the character major number-to-device interface array to locate the corresponding device interface pointer. If the device happens to be the console device, the appropriate console minor device is reincorporated into the device name so as to select the correct unit and subunit.

If there is a device associated with the supplied device identifier, the device select method is called with the arguments appropriate for a BSD unit character device. Otherwise, a device error code (ENODEV) is returned.

... [File: /usr/src/kernel/kern/config.c, line: 692]

```
        panic("devif_select"); /* unimplemented type */
    ...
```

If the character device type is not found, the kernel will panic to indicate that an unimplemented type has been encountered.

4.3.28 What is devif_mmap()?

devif_mmap() calls the device driver **mmap()** method associated with this device driver. **devif_mmap()** locates the appropriate function to call given the device and device type and calls it with the supplied parameters, returning the result. Otherwise, if the device is not present, it will return an error value (-1) indicating that there are no physical addresses associated with the device (thus, the supplied device should not be used by **vm/mmap.c**). If an unimplemented device type is encountered, **devif_mmap()** will cause a panic.

... [File: /usr/src/kernel/kern/config.c, line: 696]

```
int
devif_mmap(dev_t dev, devif_type_t typ, int offset, int nprot) {
...
```

devif_mmap() has four arguments: the device identifier and type of device; the parameters of the offset; and the protection used with the **mmap()** method call. It returns the physical address associated with the device. If no physical device exists or if the offset does not correspond to any physical device, an error (-1) is returned.

4.3.28.1 How is devif_mmap() Implemented?

... [File: /usr/src/kernel/kern/config.c, line: 702]

```
        if (typ == CHRDEV &&
            major < sizeof chrmajtodevif / sizeof chrmajtodevif[0]) {
                dif = chrmajtodevif[major];
                if (dif == console_devif)
                        dev = makedev(major, console_minor);
                if (dif)
                        return ((dif->di_mmap)(dev, offset, nprot));

                return (-1);
        }
    ...
```

If the type of the device is a BSD UNIX character device, it is found by examining the character major number-to-device interface array to locate the corresponding device interface pointer. If the device happens to be the console device, the appropriate console minor device is reincorporated into the device name so as to select the correct unit and subunit.

If there is a device associated with the supplied device identifier, the device **mmap()** method is called with the arguments appropriate for a BSD unit character device. Otherwise, a device error code (-1) is returned.

... [File: /usr/src/kernel/kern/config.c, line: 714]

```
        panic("devif_mmap"); /* unimplemented type */
    ...
```

If the character device type is not found, the kernel will panic to indicate that an unimplemented type has been encountered.

4.3.29 What is devif_strategy()?

devif_strategy() locates and calls the device driver **strategy()** routine associated with the requested device embedded in a buffer pointer. **devif_strategy()** locates the appropriate device interface pointer by consulting the device field embedded in a buffer argument, and then calls the **strategy()** method associated with this device.

... [File: /usr/src/kernel/kern/config.c, line: 718]

```
int
devif_strategy(devif_type_t typ, struct buf *bp) {
    ...
```

devif_strategy() has two arguments: the device type; and a buffer structure pointer. It returns either an error value from the **strategy()** routine or an error (ENODEV) if no corresponding device is implemented; otherwise, it returns a success indication.

4.3.29.1 How is devif_strategy() Implemented?

... [File: /usr/src/kernel/kern/config.c, line: 724]

```
        if (typ == CHRDEV &&
            major < sizeof chrmajtodevif / sizeof chrmajtodevif[0]) {
                if (dif = chrmajtodevif[major])
                        return ((dif->di_strategy)(bp));

                return (ENODEV);
        }
    ...
```

If the type is a BSD character device and it has a device interface associated with it, the **strategy()** method is called on this buffer pointer. Otherwise, a ENODEV error is returned.

... [File: /usr/src/kernel/kern/config.c, line: 733]

```
        if (typ == BLKDEV &&
            major < sizeof blkmajtodevif / sizeof blkmajtodevif[0]) {
                if (dif = blkmajtodevif[major])
                        return ((dif->di_strategy)(bp));

                return (ENODEV);
        }
    ...
```

Likewise, if the type is a BSD block device and it has a device interface associated with it, the **strategy()** method is called on this buffer pointer. Otherwise, a ENODEV error is returned.

... [File: /usr/src/kernel/kern/config.c, line: 741]

```
        panic("devif_strategy"); /* illegal type */
    ...
```

If neither of these device types is the device type called, the kernel will panic to indicate that an unimplemented type has been encountered.

4.3.30 What is devif_psize()?

devif_psize() locates and calls the device driver partition size routine. **devif_psize()** calls the partition size method associated with this device, and returns the result. If there is no device present, a value of zero for the size of the device is returned. If the device is not an implemented block device, **devif_psize()** causes a panic.

... [File: /usr/src/kernel/kern/config.c, line: 745]

```
int
devif_psize(dev_t dev, devif_type_t typ) {
    ...
```

devif_psize() has two arguments: the device; and the device type. It returns the value of the partition size method of the driver.

It should be noted that partition size routines in drivers are not used in later versions of 386BSD. Their use is supplanted by an **ioctl()** method. However, it has been kept in this version of 386BSD for backward compatibility with other obsolete Berkeley systems.

4.3.30.1 How is devif_psize() Implemented?

... [File: /usr/src/kernel/kern/config.c, line: 751]

```
        if (typ == BLKDEV &&
            major < sizeof blkmajtodevif / sizeof blkmajtodevif[0]) {
                if (dif = blkmajtodevif[major])
                        return ((dif->di_psize)(dev));

                return (0);
        }

        panic("devif_psize"); /* illegal type */
    ...
```

If the device is a BSD block device, and there is an associated device interface pointer, the device method for peripheral size is called and its value returned. If there is no block device present, a zero value is returned. Otherwise, if the device is not a block device type, then the routine will cause a panic.

4.3.31 What is devif_dump()?

devif_dump() locates and calls the device driver crash dump routine. **devif_dump()** calls the crash dump method associated with this device. If the device is an incorrect or unimplemented block device, an ENODEV error is returned.

... [File: /usr/src/kernel/kern/config.c, line: 763]

```
int
devif_dump(dev_t dev, devif_type_t typ) {
    ...
```

devif_dump() has two arguments: the device; and the device type. It returns the error status of the crash dump method of the driver or an error (ENODEV).

Since this function is is called as a result of a system panic, it would make no sense to differentiate between an error due to an incorrect block device type or to an unimplemented device type, as there is no way to signal the difference. Hence, an ENODEV error is returned in all cases.

4.3.31.1 How is devif_dump() Implemented?

... [File: /usr/src/kernel/kern/config.c, line: 769]

```
        if (typ == BLKDEV &&
            major < sizeof blkmajtodevif / sizeof blkmajtodevif[0]) {
                if (dif = blkmajtodevif[major])
                        return ((dif->di_dump)(dev));
        }

        return (ENODEV);
    ...
```

If the device is a BSD block device, and there is an associated device interface pointer, the device method for crash dump is called and its value returned. Otherwise, an ENODEV error is returned in all other cases.

4.3.32 What is devif_config()?

devif_config() attempts to configure a device using a supplied *devif* pointer and configuration string, by registering its interface in the device interface registration arrays. It is only used by device drivers upon receiving an initialization message to bind symbolically their method function interfaces into the kernel proper.

devif_config() examines the supplied configuration string to determine if the device can and should be configured, and if it contains the correct parameters to allow a device to be linked into the kernel. Assuming that the device supplies an appropriate configuration string and device interface pointer, the function will also initialize the various names for the device (module name, character major number, block major number) into the device interface structure (see *Driver Names*). In this way, only one source of the configuration information (e.g. the configuration's string) will define all of the kernel-dependent parameters of the driver.

... [File: /usr/src/kernel/kern/config.c, line: 779]

```
int
devif_config(char **cfg, struct devif *dif)
...
```

devif_config() has two arguments; the pointer to a configuration string; and a device interface pointer. It returns a success or fail indication.

This function also checks to see if there are any conflicts in configuring this device and will warn the user of such conflicts. In addition, it checks the sanity of the supplied device interface structures to ensure that they contain complete entries that point to valid function names.

4.3.32.1 How is devif_config() Implemented?

... [File: /usr/src/kernel/kern/config.c, line: 787]

```
        if (dif->di_name[0] == 0) {
                if (!config_scan(*cfg, cfg))
                        return (0);
                memcpy(dif->di_name, arg, sizeof(arg));
        }
...
```

If there is no name for the device module, the device module is attempted to be configured by the **config_scan()** function that evaluates all device configurations. If it cannot configure the device to obtain the name, then we obviously cannot continue, and the function returns a failure indication.

Otherwise, the argument that describes the module name is copied into the device interface module name location for further reference. This section of code is included to eliminate redundant code in all of the configuration entry points for all of the drivers, and to minimize the impact of modularity on the system. It also has the side-effect of allowing a single string in the driver to describe the name and configuration parameters of the device, since we get the name by using the very first entry of the configuration string as the argument of what to configure in **config_scan()**. It should be noted that as a result of finding an entry in the configuration string table, the value of the *cfg* variable may change at this point from that with which the program was called.

... [File: /usr/src/kernel/kern/config.c, line: 794]

```
        if (dif->di_bmajor == -1 && !cfg_number(cfg, &dif->di_bmajor))
                return (0);

        /* configure character device? */
        if (dif->di_cmajor == -1 && !cfg_number(cfg, &dif->di_cmajor))
                return (0);
...
```

The device interface structure is checked to see if either its block and/or character device names have been requested to be automatically configured (again this is done a shorthand way of reducing the overhead of the code in each driver). If so, the number is pulled from the configuration string and inserted, replacing the impossible value of -1 used to signal this in either of the two name fields. If either option is requested and neither number is found, a false return is immediately passed back, and the function terminates due to an error in the configuration string request.

... [File: /usr/src/kernel/kern/config.c, line: 802]

```
        if ((bmaj = dif->di_bmajor) >= 0) {
                struct devif *odif;

                /* device number out of range */
                if (bmaj >= NDEVIF) {
                        printf("%s: blkdev %d too big, not configured.\n",
                                arg, bmaj);
                        return (0);
                }

                /* device already in use? */
                if (odif = blkmajtodevif[bmaj]) {
                    printf("%s: blkdev %d already used by %s, not configured.\n",
                        arg, bmaj, odif->di_name);
                    return (0);
                }

                if (query("devif: config %s blkdev", arg) == 0)
                        return(0);

                blkmajtodevif[bmaj] = dif;
        }
...
```

If there is a block device name to be configured, the proposed block major number is examined to see if it is within a range of an implementable device, that there is no other block device in use at that major number, and that the operator does not want to block the configuration of the device. If none of those exceptions exist, then the driver's device interface pointer is assigned to this block major number at its appropriate array location.

Otherwise, the configuration of the device is aborted early with a false return. In the case of the two possible configuration errors, an appropriate message is always displayed on the console.

... [File: /usr/src/kernel/kern/config.c, line: 826]

```
        if ((cmaj = dif->di_cmajor) >= 0) {

                /* device number out of range */
                if (cmaj >= NDEVIF) {
                        printf("%s: chrdev %d too big, not configured.\n",
                                arg, cmaj);
                        return (0);
                }

                /* device already in use? */
```

```
            if (odif = chrmajtodevif[cmaj]) {
                printf("%s: chrdev %d already used by %s, not configured.\n",
                    arg, cmaj, odif->di_name);
                return (0);
            }

            if (query("devif: config %s chrdev", arg) == 0)
                    return(0);

            chrmajtodevif[cmaj] = dif;
        }
    ...
```

If there is a character device name to be configured, the proposed character major number is examined to see if it is within a range of an implementable device, that there is no other character device in use at that major number, and that the operator does not want to block the configuration of the device. If none of those exceptions exist, then the driver's device interface pointer is assigned to this character major number at its appropriate array location.

Otherwise, the configuration of the device is aborted early with a false return. In the case of the two possible configuration errors, an appropriate message is always displayed on the console.

... [File: /usr/src/kernel/kern/config.c, line: 849]

```
    if (cmaj >= 0 || bmaj >= 0) {
            if ((int)dif->di_open == 0)
                    (int *) dif->di_open = (int *)nullop;
            if ((int)dif->di_close == 0)
                    (int *) dif->di_close = (int *)nullop;
            if ((int)dif->di_ioctl == 0)
                    (int *) dif->di_ioctl = (int *)enodev;
    }
...
```

If the device being configured has a block or character name, the **open()**, **close()**, and **ioctl()** methods in the supplied device interface structure are all checked to see if there is a corresponding function (not null). Null in these function pointers indicates an unimplemented function, whereby the driver does not implement the function because it does not make use of the facility or expects a default action.

Very simple device drivers often don't even have an **open()** and **close()** method, since there is nothing for the driver to do during them. In these cases, a null function is present that exists only to return a zero value.

If a null **ioctl()** method is implemented, a function that always returns an ENODEV error supplants the **ioctl()** method. Thus, any attempts to use **ioctl()** methods in these cases will be met with the statement that the operation is not implemented for the device.

... [File: /usr/src/kernel/kern/config.c, line: 859]

```
if (cmaj >= 0) {
        if (dif->di_strategy) {
                if (dif->di_read == 0)
                        dif->di_read = rawread;
                if (dif->di_write == 0)
                        dif->di_write = rawwrite;
        }
        if ((int)dif->di_select == 0)
                dif->di_select = seltrue;
        if (dif->di_write == 0)
                (int *)dif->di_write = enodev;
        if (dif->di_read == 0)
                (int *)dif->di_read = enodev;
}
...
```

In the case of character devices, the **strategy()**, **select()**, **write()**, and **read()** methods are examined. If the character device has a **strategy()** method, it is assumed that the device is capable of (in UNIX parlance) *physical I/O* (e.g. the ability to directly read information into a process address space). If either of the **read()** or **write()** methods are not implemented, the default physical I/O functions raw read and/or raw write will be placed into those methods.

If the **select()** method is not present, the default select true function *seltrue* is used. It always returns true if the device has a **select()** operation performed on it (it is always ready to receive or send information).

Finally, if either the **read()** or **write()** method is still unset (the strategy method was not present and this device is not capable of physical I/O), the **read()** or **write()** methods are replaced with the ENODEV function to return errors on attempts to either read or write, respectively, the device. (Obviously the device in this case is something like a line printer, which only works in one direction.)

... [File: /usr/src/kernel/kern/config.c, line: 875]

```
if (bmaj >= 0) {
        if ((int)dif->di_strategy == 0) {
                blkmajtodevif[bmaj] = 0;
                printf("%s: blkdev %d no strategy, not configured.\n",
                        arg, bmaj);
                return (0);
        }
        if ((int)dif->di_dump == 0)
                (int *) dif->di_dump = (int *)enodev;
        if ((int)dif->di_psize == 0)
                (int *) dif->di_psize = (int *)enodev;
}
...
```

If we are configuring a block device, we check to see if there is a **strategy()** method. Since block devices only work via the **strategy()** method to achieve I/O, there is no point in having a block device if this method is not present. If it does not have a

strategy() method, the device is not configured, and an error message is returned with a false return value.

If the block device does not have a **dump()** or **psize()** method, then the ENODEV function is substituted to return an appropriate lack of operation for this method.

... [File: /usr/src/kernel/kern/config.c, line: 888]

```
      return (1);
 ...
```

Otherwise, the device configuration function returns true, having successfully evaluated the device configuration and validated a device interface set of function methods. Note that at this point the configuration string has been consumed up to the point where all kernel-dependent fields have been found. Any fields beyond this point in the string are bus or device-specific, and the remaining syntax of the string is left up to the implementer (within reason, of course).

4.3.33 What is ldiscif_open()?

ldiscif_open() opens and initializes the terminal structure associated with this device's use of a line discipline. It is used by device drivers to gain access to a line discipline named by the number in the tty structure supplied. The device driver expects **ldiscif_open()** to locate the line discipline and call its **open()** method to instantiate the terminal structure passed in with this pointer.

... [File: /usr/src/kernel/kern/config.c, line: 896]

```
int
ldiscif_open(dev_t dev, struct tty *tp, int flag) {
 ...
```

ldiscif_open() has three arguments: the device identifier used with the line discipline; its terminal structure; and the **open()** flag supplied with the line discipline. It returns either the error status from the line discipline's **open()** method call or an error (ENXIO) indicating no line discipline is present for this terminal.

4.3.33.1 How is ldiscif_open() Implemented?

... [File: /usr/src/kernel/kern/config.c, line: 903]

```
      for (lif = ldisc; lif && lif->li_disc != line ; lif = lif->li_next)
            ;

      /* not found */
      if (lif == 0)
            return (ENXIO);

      /* if a BSD UN*X line discipline ... */
      val = (lif->li_open)(dev, tp, flag);
      tp->t_ldiscif = (void *) lif;
      return (val);
 ...
```

The configured line discipline list of devices is linearly scanned to locate the line discipline corresponding to the one associated with the terminal structure's line discipline entry. If there is not a matching entry in the list of line disciplines, an unconfigured device error is returned (ENXIO).

Otherwise, the line discipline's **open()** method is called with the supplied parameters and the terminal structure is updated to point to this particular line discipline for this terminal structure. The value of the **open()** method is then returned.

Note that the terminal is associated with the line discipline regardless of the success or failure of the **open()** routine. Also note that the line discipline interface is an opaque part of the tty structure and is implemented in this way simply for convenience of access.

4.3.34 What is ldiscif_close()?

ldiscif_close() forces a close on the terminal structure. It is used by the device to detach the terminal structure from the device. The device driver expects **ldiscif_close()** to call the associated line discipline's **close()** method. The terminal structure is then disassociated from the line discipline.

... [File: /usr/src/kernel/kern/config.c, line: 917]

```
void
ldiscif_close(struct tty *tp, int flag) {
...
```

ldiscif_close() has two arguments: the pointer to the terminal's structure; and the original **open()** flag. It returns nothing.

4.3.34.1 How is ldiscif_close() Implemented?

... [File: /usr/src/kernel/kern/config.c, line: 922]

```
        if (lif == 0)
                panic("ldiscif_close");

        /* if a BSD UN*X line discipline ... */
        (lif->li_close)(tp, flag);
        tp->t_ldiscif = (void *) 0;
...
```

If the terminal is not already associated with the line discipline, the system panics, since it should never be the case that a **close()** is done on an already closed line discipline. Otherwise, the line discipline's **close()** method is called, and the terminal is disassociated from the line discipline.

4.3.35 What is ldiscif_read()?

ldiscif_read() performs a device **read()** on a terminal device. It is used by a device driver to pass control to the device driver with a device **read()** method to use the line

---

discipline's capabilities to manipulate the device and obtain the desired effect of a read operation. The device driver expects **ldiscif_read()** to invoke the line discipline's **read()** method on the supplied arguments.The status is returned so that it may pass this back in turn to the kernel.

... [File: /usr/src/kernel/kern/config.c, line: 931]

```
int
ldiscif_read(struct tty *tp, struct uio *devuio, int devflag) {
 ...
```

ldiscif_read() has three arguments: the pointer to the terminal structure; the pointer to the device's read user I/O structure; and the device **read()** method's flag parameters. It returns the value of a line discipline's **read()** method return value.

4.3.35.1 How is ldiscif_read() Implemented?

... [File: /usr/src/kernel/kern/config.c, line: 936]

```
        if (lif == 0)
                panic("ldiscif_read");

        /* if a BSD UN*X line discipline ... */
        return ((lif->li_read)(tp, devuio, devflag));
 ...
```

The terminal structure's line discipline interface pointer is checked to see if it already has been **closed()**; if it has, then the system panics. Otherwise, the line discipline's **read()** method is invoked with the supplied parameters. It returns the value returned by the line interface's **read()** method that was called.

4.3.36 What is ldiscif_write()?

ldiscif_write() performs a device write on a terminal device. It is used by a device driver to pass control to the device driver with a device **write()** routine to use the line discipline's capabilities to manipulate the device and obtain the desired effect of a write operation. The device driver expects **ldiscif_write()** to invoke the line discipline's **write()** method on the supplied arguments. The status is returned, so that it may pass this back in turn to the kernel.

... [File: /usr/src/kernel/kern/config.c, line: 945]

```
int
ldiscif_write(struct tty *tp, struct uio *devuio, int devflag) {
 ...
```

ldiscif_write() has three arguments: the pointer to the terminal structure; the pointer to the device's write user I/O structure; and the device **write()** method's flag parameter. It returns the value of a line discipline's **write()** method return value.

4.3.36.1 How is ldiscif_write() Implemented?

... [File: /usr/src/kernel/kern/config.c, line: 949]

```
        if (lif == 0)
                panic("ldiscif_write");

        /* if a BSD UN*X line discipline ... */
        return ((lif->li_write)(tp, devuio, devflag));
  ...
```

The terminal structure's line discipline interface pointer is checked to see if it already has been closed; if it has, then the system panics. Otherwise, the line discipline's **write()** method is invoked with the supplied parameters. It returns the value returned by the line interface's **write()** method that was called.

4.3.37 What is ldiscif_ioctl()?

ldiscif_ioctl() performs a device **ioctl()** operation on the associated terminal structure and device. It is used by a device driver to implement a line discipline-specific **ioctl()** operation. The device driver expects **ldiscif_ioctl()** to invoke the line discipline's **ioctl()** method on the supplied parameters and return the value of the function to it.

... [File: /usr/src/kernel/kern/config.c, line: 958]

```
int
ldiscif_ioctl(struct tty *tp, int cmd, caddr_t data, int flag, struct proc *p)
{
  ...
```

ldiscif_ioctl() has five arguments: the terminal structure pointer; the **ioctl()** command to be implemented and its data pointer; the associated device flag; and the pointer to the process for which the **ioctl()** is being performed. It returns the error status of the **ioctl()** method invoked.

4.3.37.1 How is ldiscif_ioctl() Implemented?

... [File: /usr/src/kernel/kern/config.c, line: 962]

```
        if (lif == 0)
                panic("ldiscif_ioctl");

        /* if a BSD UN*X line discipline ... */
        return ((lif->li_ioctl)(tp, cmd, data, flag, p));
  ...
```

If the line discipline has already been disassociated from the terminal structure, the kernel will panic indicating an impossible situation has occurred. Otherwise, the line discipline's **ioctl()** method is invoked to evaluate this ioctl for this particular line discipline, and the return value of the line discipline's **ioctl()** method is returned to the caller.

4.3.38 What is ldiscif_rint()

ldiscif_rint() is used by a terminal device to pass an incoming character to a line discipline. The device driver expects **ldiscif_rint()** to locate the line discipline and pass a character to it. The function is usually called from interrupt level to deliver a character to the line discipline along with the terminal structure associated with the device that is interrupting. If the line discipline is still associated with the terminal, the character will be passed to the line discipline.

... [File: /usr/src/kernel/kern/config.c, line: 970]

```
void
ldiscif_rint(unsigned ch, int flags, struct tty *tp) {
    ...
```

ldiscif_rint() has three arguments: the character to be passed to the line discipline; the flags associated with the character; and the terminal structure associated with the device that had received the character. It returns nothing.

4.3.38.1 How is ldiscif_rint() Implemented?

... [File: /usr/src/kernel/kern/config.c, line: 975]

```
    if (lif)
            (lif->li_rint)(ch, flags, tp);
    ...
```

If there is a line discipline associated with the terminal structure, the **rint()** (receiver interrupt) method is called to pass the character and its associated flags to the terminal structure. Note that it is always possible that an interrupt might come in prior to the setup or after the close of a line discipline—this is not an error in the case of a line discipline not being allocated.

4.3.39 What is ldiscif_put()?

ldiscif_put() is used by the kernel's generic line discipline routines to pass a character through the line discipline routines for output. **ldiscif_put()** calls the line discipline's associated **put()** character routine method on the associated terminal structure and passes the supplied character.

... [File: /usr/src/kernel/kern/config.c, line: 980]

```
unsigned
ldiscif_put(unsigned ch, struct tty *tp) {
    ...
```

ldiscif_put() has two arguments: the character; and the terminal structure to be passed the character. It returns the character if it could not be output, and a "-1" otherwise. The return value semantics are from old UNIX conventions for line disciplines.

4.3.39.1 How is ldiscif_put() Implemented?

... [File: /usr/src/kernel/kern/config.c, line: 985]

```
    if (lif)
            return((lif->li_put)(ch, tp));
    else
            return (ch);
...
```

If there is a line discipline associated with the terminal structure, the line discipline's **put()** method is called to place the character on the terminal structure. Otherwise, the character is immediately returned back to the caller.

4.3.40 What is ldiscif_start()?

ldiscif_start() is used by the driver and the kernel to initiate output on a terminal-related device. **ldiscif_start()** calls the line discipline's **start()** method if a line discipline is present.

... [File: /usr/src/kernel/kern/config.c, line: 992]

```
void
ldiscif_start(struct tty *tp) {
 ...
```

ldiscif_start() has one argument: the terminal structure. It returns nothing.

4.3.40.1 How is ldiscif_start() Implemented?

... [File: /usr/src/kernel/kern/config.c, line: 997]

```
    if (lif)
            (lif->li_start)(tp);
...
```

A line discipline's **start()** method is called if a line discipline is associated with a terminal. Since this function is also called from interrupt level, a line discipline may not be associated with a terminal at the time this is called.

4.3.41 What is ldiscif_modem()?

ldiscif_modem() informs a line discipline of the change in status of modem control associated with the particular terminal structure. The device driver expects that **ldiscif_modem()** will call the line discipline's **modem()** method to update the status of the modem control for the terminal structure.

... [File: /usr/src/kernel/kern/config.c, line: 1002]

```
int
ldiscif_modem(struct tty *tp, int flag) {
 ...
```

ldiscif_modem() has two arguments: the terminal structure; and a flag indicating the state of the modem lines. It returns the value from the call to the **modem()** method of the line discipline.

4.3.41.1 How is ldiscif_modem() Implemented?

... [File: /usr/src/kernel/kern/config.c, line: 1007]

```
    if (lif)
            return ((lif->li_modem)(tp, flag));

    return (1);
...
```

If there is a line discipline associated with the terminal, the **modem()** method is called with this function's arguments and the value returned. Otherwise, a default value of "1" is returned to indicate that the line is still active for this particular non-allocated line discipline.

4.3.42 What is ldiscif_qsize()?

ldiscif_qsize() returns the size of a line discipline's implementation-specific queue of *character* elements. It is used by the kernel's line discipline support functions to determine the size of queues that may be implemented with implementation-specific sized characters. **ldiscif_qsize()** calls the associated line discipline's **qsize()** method. If no line discipline is allocated, a default queue size of zero is returned, indicating that an unbound line discipline is always of length zero (e.g. empty).

... [File: /usr/src/kernel/kern/config.c, line: 1014]

```
int
ldiscif_qsize(struct tty *tp, void *q) {
 ...
```

ldiscif_qsize() has two arguments: the pointer to the terminal structure; and an opaque pointer to a terminal queue within that structure. It returns the value of the **qsize()** method called on the line discipline.

4.3.42.1 How is ldiscif_qsize() Implemented?

... [File: /usr/src/kernel/kern/config.c, line: 1019]

```
    if (lif)
            return ((lif->li_qsize)(tp, q));

    return (0);
...
```

If there is a line discipline associated with the terminal structure, the line discipline's **qsize()** method is called and the value returned. If there is no associated line discipline, a value of zero is returned indicating that the queue is empty.

4.3.43 What is ldiscif_config()?

ldiscif_config() is used to register a line discipline for use in the kernel. It is called from the line discipline's module initialization entry. The line discipline expects that **ldiscif_config()** will take and optionally configure the line discipline, using the shared configuration string, and assign its symbolic parameter to the line discipline interface supplied with the function. It then attempts to insert it into the kernel for use as a registered line discipline interface.

... [File: /usr/src/kernel/kern/config.c, line: 1026]

```
int
ldiscif_config(char **cfg, struct ldiscif *lif)
    ...
```

ldiscif_config() has two arguments: a pointer to the configuration string associated with the line discipline; and a pointer to the line discipline interface of the line discipline. It returns a true or false value indicating whether or not the discipline was successfully configured.

4.3.43.1 How is ldiscif_config() Implemented?

... [File: /usr/src/kernel/kern/config.c, line: 1034]

```
        if (lif->li_name[0] == 0) {
                if (!config_scan(*cfg, cfg))
                        return (0);
                memcpy(lif->li_name, arg, sizeof(arg));
        }

        /* configure line index? */
        if (lif->li_disc == -1 && !cfg_number(cfg, &lif->li_disc))
                return (0);
    ...
```

If the name for the line discipline is uninitialized, the line discipline's module is configured into the system by calling the **config_scan()** function, using the first string in the configuration as the name of the module to be configured. If the configuration is not successful, the routine terminates unsuccessfully. Otherwise, it records the name of the line discipline in its interface structure.

Likewise, if the line discipline's index name is uninitialized, a configuration string is examined to return the line discipline number associated with the line discipline and placed in the interface structure.

... [File: /usr/src/kernel/kern/config.c, line: 1045]

```
        if ((line = lif->li_disc) >= 0) {

                /* attempt to find line discipline */
                for (olif = ldisc; olif && olif->li_disc != line ;
                    olif = lif->li_next)
                        ;
```

```
                  /* device already in use? */
                  if (olif)
                      printf("%s: ldisc %d already used by %s, not configured.\n",
                          arg, line, olif->li_name);
                      return (0);
                  }

                  if (query("ldiscif: config %s", arg) == 0)
                          return(0);

                  lif->lif_next = ldisc;
                  ldisc = lif;
            } else
                  return (0);
      ...
```

If the line discipline index is a positive number (valid line discipline indexes must always be positive), an attempt is made to find the line discipline of the same number already allocated by walking the line discipline interface list.

If there is a device already using the line discipline number, an error message is displayed on the console and the line discipline is not allowed to be configured. In this case, the function terminates. The line discipline can also be conditionally checked by the operator to see if it can be configured on the system by querying the operator.

If it can be configured, it is linked into the head of the list of line disciplines. However, if the line discipline is not a positive number, the line discipline will fail to be configured, since it is out of the range of allowable line disciplines, and the function terminates.

... [File: /usr/src/kernel/kern/config.c, line: 1067]

```
      /* check sanity */
      if ((int)lif->li_open == 0)
              (int *) lif->li_open = (int *)enodev;
      if ((int)lif->li_close == 0)
              (int *) lif->li_close = (int *)enodev;
      if ((int)lif->li_read == 0)
              (int *) lif->li_read = (int *)enodev;
      if ((int)lif->li_write == 0)
              (int *) lif->li_write = (int *)enodev;
      if ((int)lif->li_ioctl == 0)
              (int *) lif->li_ioctl = (int *)enodev;
      if ((int)lif->li_rint == 0)
              (int *) lif->li_rint = (int *)enodev;
      if ((int)lif->li_start == 0)
              (int *) lif->li_start = (int *)enodev;
      if ((int)lif->li_modem == 0)
              (int *) lif->li_modem = (int *)enodev;
      if ((int)lif->li_qsize == 0)
              (int *) lif->li_qsize = def_qsize;

      return (1);
  ...
```

The line discipline's entries are checked to see if any of them are unimplemented. If any are, an ENODEV function is substituted so as to return an error condition if a request on the associated method is made. In the case of the **qsize()** method, the default **qsize()** method is called instead.

After conducting a sanity check of the entry, a "1" is returned to indicate success of the line discipline being configured.

4.3.44 What is console_putchar()?

console_putchar() sends a character to the console. If there is a console device configured, **console_putchar()** invokes its **putchar()** method, using the console's major and minor number to output a character on a console device.

... [File: /usr/src/kernel/kern/config.c, line: 1091]

```
void
console_putchar(unsigned c) {
    ...
```

console_putchar() has one argument: the character to be output on the console. It returns nothing.

4.3.44.1 How is console_putchar() Implemented?

... [File: /usr/src/kernel/kern/config.c, line: 1104]

```
        if (console_devif)
            (console_devif->di_putchar)(
                makedev(console_devif->di_cmajor, console_minor), c);
    ...
```

If the console device has been allocated, the console device's device interface is used to find the console's **putchar()** method to output the character to the console device. The console device itself is selected by a supplied device specification built out of the device interface's major number and the console minor number (configured separately).

4.3.45 What is console_getchar()?

console_getchar() waits uninterruptibly for a character from the console. **console_getchar()** defeats interrupts and uses the console device interface's **getchar()** method to get a character from the console interface device and returns it.

... [File: /usr/src/kernel/kern/config.c, line: 1100]

```
unsigned
console_getchar(void) {
    ...
```

console_getchar() has no arguments. It returns the character.

4.3.45.1 How is console_getchar() Implemented?

... [File: /usr/src/kernel/kern/config.c, line: 1104]

```
        if (console_devif) {
                s = splhigh();
                ch = (console_devif->di_getchar)
                        (makedev(console_devif->di_cmajor, console_minor));
                splx(s);
                return (ch);
        } else
                return (0);
...
```

If there is a configured console device, interrupts are disabled and the console device's console character method is used to obtain a character from the device driver. To select the appropriate device within the driver, a device identifier is constructed for the console device and passed as an argument to the method. After obtaining the character, the device interrupts are restored and the character is returned to the caller. If the console is not configured, a value of zero is returned to indicate that there is no character to be returned.

4.3.46 What is console_config()?

console_config() configures a device driver module as a console device. **console_config()** takes the console configuration string and driver module configuration string, along with the device interface pointer, and determines if this is the console that should be configured for use with the system. Since multiple consoles can be configured, **console_config()** must decide if this is a console that has been configured for use and is associated with a configurable module. Otherwise, it needs to select a default console for use in the case that no console is selected for primary use.

... [File: /usr/src/kernel/kern/config.c, line: 1115]

```
int
console_config(char **cons_cfg, char **mod_cfg, struct devif *dif) {
    ...
```

console_config() has three arguments: the pointer to the console configuration string; the pointer to the module configuration string; and the pointer to the module's device interface. It returns true or false based on the success or failure of configuring the console.

4.3.46.1 How is console_config() Implemented?

... [File: /usr/src/kernel/kern/config.c, line: 1122]

```
        cfg = *cons_cfg;

        /* is there a console defined? */
```

```
        if (config_scan(cfg, cons_cfg) == 0)
                return (0);
...
```

The console configuration string is first evaluated to determine if there is a console present in the shared configuration string. If the console is not defined to be allocated, then the routine prematurely returns unsuccessfully.

... [File: /usr/src/kernel/kern/config.c, line: 1129]

```
        if (cfg_string(cons_cfg, modname1, sizeof(modname1)) == 0)
                return(0);

        /* is the requested console module configurable? */
        cfg = *mod_cfg;
        if (config_scan(cfg, mod_cfg) == 0)
                return (0);
...
```

The module to be used with the console is found as the next token in the console configuration string. If it is not present, the configuration is also terminated unsuccessfully.

Having retrieved the effective console module that the system expects should be configured, the supplied module is scanned to see if it is configurable. If it is not, then this particular console configuration attempt is unsuccessful.

... [File: /usr/src/kernel/kern/config.c, line: 1138]

```
        if (strcmp(modname1, "default") == 0)
                default_console_devif = dif;

        /* is it the same module? */
        else if (strcmp(modname1, arg) != 0)
                return(0);
...
```

If the module to be configured as the console is to be the default console, this value is saved in a separate global variable to indicate that default console configuration has occurred. Otherwise, if the console is not the module to be configured as a console, then we know that it is not the correct console—that it is another module in the system. The function then returns unsuccessfully.

At this point, if none of these unsuccessful situations has occurred, we have found the correct device to configure. It may either be the default console or the specified console in the shared configuration string.

... [File: /usr/src/kernel/kern/config.c, line: 1146]

```
        console_minor = 0;
        (void)cfg_number(cons_cfg, &console_minor);

        /* consume major unit */
        (void)cfg_number(mod_cfg, &dummy);
```

```
      /* set console device interface */
      console_devif = dif;
      chrmajtodevif[0] = dif;

      /* if not default console, record use of console */
      if (default_console_devif == 0) {
              DELAY(10000);
              printf("using console %s\n", dif->di_name);
      }

      return (1);
...
```

The console's minor device number is obtained from the console configuration string as the third token. The major unit number for the module to be configured as a console is then consumed in the module configuration string, so that the remaining bus and device parameters can be used to configure the device early for operation. The device's interface structure is recorded as the console device interface and by convention is always associated with the character major number of zero.

If the device is not a default console, a message indicating which console is in use is output on the console so as to indicate that this is not the default console. Prior to outputting the message, a delay of one character's worth is made to compensate for devices with slow initialization times. The function then returns true, indicating that a console has been configured.

4.3.47 Postscript: Limits to Configuration

We cannot do the impossible with configuration software—there is no magical mind-reading capability that we can implement. The ISA bus cannot, for example, allow us to determine that an overlapping configuration of I/O ports, interrupt requests, DMA requests, BIOS ROM assignments, or frame buffer exists. This lack of information is an inherent flaw of the bus design itself.

It is the writer's objective architectural consideration that given the economies of scale of the computer industry, the 35 to 50 cents additional cost of a computer bus architecture which could supply or make unnecessary this problem is economically feasible for all future bus designs. If the end users only knew how ludicrous this penny-wise pound-foolish manner of bus design is, they would be much less receptive to new bus designs which didn't provide for this most obvious set of needs.

One way this could be accomplished is to add enough decoding information within the bus such that all boards become unique, by, for example, using a board address reservation of address space and guaranteeing, say, 16 bits tacked onto the exiting address (to define uniquely multiple address spaces per each board manufacturer issuing a unique board address). While this incredibly simplistic suggestion has lots of commercially detrimental details, it is only supplied here as an example to illustrate that this is not a rocket science type of problem, and the refusal to address it in modern computer systems is based on a flawed short-term economics decision that should never have been made in the first place (before the first IBM PC even went out the door).

4.4 The Kernel Memory Allocator: kern/malloc.c

There are precisely three memory allocators in use in the 386BSD system. **malloc()** is the *primary memory allocator* used to allocate frequently reused or perpetual objects. The **mbuf** cluster allocator **mclget()** allocates *packet-related memory* which will be copied by reference. Finally, the *virtual memory system's allocator* **kmem_alloc()** is used to allocate actual pages of memory from the pool of free pages inside of the virtual memory system.

Prior versions of Berkeley UNIX had quite a few more memory allocators than in 386BSD—in fact, it began to seem like every new version of a Berkeley kernel had some new memory allocator. While occasionally adding more memory allocators in a program is unavoidable (because the characteristics of the program may require many special purpose memory allocators), this short-term convenience should never become a habit.

Ultimately, multiple memory allocators interfere with each other's operation, because they all must reconcile their memory pools. These artificial barriers between memory allocators directly result in wasted resources.[31] In addition, disagreements arising between memory allocators over precedence becomes a limiting factor in the design of the system. As such, following the 386BSD design objectives of minimalism and reuse of existing functionality whenever possible, the 386BSD kernel uses only one primary memory allocator: **kern/malloc.c**.

4.4.1 Functions Contained in the File kern/malloc.c

The file **kern/malloc.c** contains the machine-independent code for the primary dynamic memory allocator of the kernel. It is composed of three functions:

malloc()

free()

kmeminit()

malloc() is the memory allocator proper which returns a portion of memory of a desired size and type to the caller. In addition, it can pass optional flags to control how it allocates memory. **free()** is the corresponding function which returns storage to the kernel's free memory arena. The free memory arena consists of a number of hash buckets containing fragments of varying size. **kmeminit()** is the initialization function that creates the initial arena used by both **malloc()** and **free()**.

All three functions interact with and rely upon the virtual memory system to obtain or release actual amounts of memory. In fact, this memory allocator operates only as an intermediary interceding between the requestor and the source of memory in the system.

4.4.1.1 Hash Buckets

Both **malloc()** and **free()** use hash buckets. Hash buckets are lists of free segments of memory all of the same size (the bucket is the list header of the list). These buckets are arranged in an ascending sequence (of power of two) in size. Thus, the smallest bucket might contain sixteen elements (e.g. 16, 32, ..., 64 Kbytes), with the maximum segment size of 64 Kbytes set by the number of buckets in the array.

4.4.1.2 Allocation Algorithm

The memory allocator algorithm itself is a modified Knuth buddy allocator[32] that finds a free portion of memory from the nearest power of two that will fit—thus, a 65-byte request will be given a 128-byte fragment to use. Like a Knuth "buddy" allocator, **malloc()** manages an arena of hash buckets of binary-increasing size. Unlike a Knuth "buddy" allocator, however, **malloc()** and **free()** don't successively refragment/coa‐ lesce hash buckets to satisfy requests from larger buckets when smaller buckets are

---

[31] Because each has to obtain a separate parcel of memory to manage.
[32] See Knuth's **Art of Computer Programming, Volume I** for further information.

empty. Thus, storage allocated to a bucket stays associated with the bucket until a surplus of memory in the buckets allows storage to be released from the arena.

4.4.1.3 Types of Memory

One of **malloc()**'s supplied arguments is the *type* of memory allocated. The type is used to record statistics of use by **malloc()** so that it is possible both to trace the amount of memory allocated at any given time to the particular type and also to restrict the amount of memory allocated for every type to prevent runaway allocation of memory. In this way, simple memory leaks can be caught before they entirely overrun the kernel's operating complement of memory.

This mechanism was a stopgap measure added to both 4.3BSD Reno and Net/2 systems when the use of **malloc()** by the rest of the kernel was dramatically increased, causing many overrun situations to occur from incorrect code. As such, type is not essential for the current operation of the memory allocator and is conditional in use, depending on the conditional compilation flag KMEMSTATS.[33]

4.4.1.4 Overhead and Precedence

Overhead and precedence are very simply determined. **malloc()**'s job as a primary memory allocator is to reduce fragmentation loss, and to reduce overhead of memory allocation in terms of time. Thus, **malloc()** controls only a portion of memory as big as is needed for it to subdivide the pages that the virtual memory system allocates.

If the allocated fragment is smaller than a page, **malloc()** controls a free list as large as needed to coalesce fragments together, returning the memory resource back to the memory allocator of the virtual memory system. If the portion of memory is larger than a page in size, it simply barters the transaction to the virtual memory system (fragmentation loss is no longer an issue in this case), since the virtual memory system has to obtain it for use anyway. Thus, **malloc()** has precedence over the virtual memory system's allocation only for fragments smaller than a page size.

For anything including and especially portions of memory that dwell within **malloc()**'s control that can be coalesced into a page to be returned to the virtual memory system, it maintains precedence and control over that memory. Otherwise, the virtual memory system has precedence. In effect, this means that the virtual memory system always holds onto a free list of page-granularity memory.

The concept of precedence is important because memory can now be used for any purpose inside the kernel[34] without a loss of generality while keeping conflicts

---

[33] These statistics can be found by using the **vmstat -m** command, which displays the information in a tabular format.

[34] Either in a process as a buffer, or allocated to a data structure in a driver or to a filesystem to hold direct locks, or to a table of address translation entries, a message buffer as part of a packet, and so forth.

between memory allocators in this system to a minimum.[35] Another advantage of this approach is that in adding a new subsystem for the kernel, one can immediately decide when to use an allocator and when not to.[36]

4.4.2 Minimalism and Memory Allocation

One of the advantages of this current memory allocator is its simplicity. It deals with its mission of minimizing memory fragmentation while still allowing the virtual memory system the latitude of reusing the pool of memory as it sees fit. In further elaboration upon the basic theme, it is easy to lose the essence of a lightweight kernel memory allocator. Thus, this is one area of the kernel where compulsive featurism is more a curse than a virtue. With the possible exception of a conditional compiled feature to locate[37] misuse of dynamically allocated portions of memory supposedly freed, extensive improvements to the current design may not be warranted.

However, when 386BSD is expanded for use in a multithreaded environment, a less restrictive mechanism will be necessary to provide exclusion when allocating portions of memory to multiple threads (other than the spl mechanism). This in-progress redesign impacts many other areas of the system as well and as such is not a trivial hack.

4.4.3 What is malloc()?

malloc() requests a portion of memory in the kernel's virtual address space of a desired size and type. This function can be used anywhere in the system's operation, including at interrupt level. To prevent **malloc()** from blocking at interrupt level, one of its many options (M_NOWAIT) can request that it not block. In these cases, if no memory is available, **malloc()** will return a null pointer to indicate no memory is available without blocking.

... [File: /usr/src/kernel/kern/malloc.c, line: 54]

```
void *
malloc(u_long size, int type, int flags)
 ...
```

malloc() has three arguments: the size of the requested section of memory; the type of memory requested; and the options flags to **malloc()** as to how to allocate memory. It returns a pointer to the new region of memory.

---

[35] Note that conflict is just minimized, not eliminated, as a pathologic case like leaving allocated just one fragment of a page of every managed page could still occur and use up the kernel's memory resource.
[36] In prior Berkeley systems, new or altered subsystems usually had arbitrary memory allocators added as well, whose use propagated elsewhere—for example, network/IPC mbufs were used to hold process termination state.

malloc() allocates memory as a side-effect of the function, which may or may not require it to block or to request additional memory from the virtual memory system, which is the source of the resource that **malloc()** manages. **malloc()** does not always need to request memory from the virtual memory system, as it uses its own private list of hash buckets to allocate memory out of as well. Since the amount of memory that **malloc()** uses is finite, this resource must be returned with the corresponding **free()** function in this file.

4.4.3.1 How is malloc() Implemented?

... [File: /usr/src/kernel/kern/malloc.c, line: 69]

```
        indx = BUCKETINDX(size);
        kbp = &bucket[indx];
        s = splimp();
...
```

malloc() first finds the associated hash bucket to handle a request of this size with the (rather elaborate) macro **BUCKETINDX**, which converts a size request into the appropriate power-of-two sized bucket index.

... [File: /kernel/kern/malloc.c, line: 73]

```
        while (ksp->ks_memuse >= ksp->ks_limit) {
                if (flags & M_NOWAIT) {
                        splx(s);
                        return ((void *) NULL);
                }
                if (ksp->ks_limblocks < 65535)
                        ksp->ks_limblocks++;
                tsleep((caddr_t)ksp, PSWP+2, memname[type], 0);
        }
...
```

The associated statistics for this type are checked to see whether or not the amount of memory in use exceeds a fixed limit associated with the type. If it does, no memory is allocated, and, if the memory allocator did not allow blocking, a null pointer is immediately returned indicating no memory is available for allocation. Otherwise, **malloc()** blocks waiting for memory of this type to become available for allocation (e.g., someone else freed another block of this type). In this way, runaway allocation results in either memory denials or blocks.

... [File: /usr/src/kernel/kern/malloc.c, line: 83]

```
        if (kbp->kb_next == NULL) {
                if (size >= MAXALLOCSAVE)
                        allocsize = roundup(size, CLBYTES);
                else
                        allocsize = 1 << indx;
                npg = clrnd(btoc(allocsize));
```

---

[37] E.g., via garbage collection "mark and sweep."

```
            va = (caddr_t) kmem_malloc(kmem_map,(vm_size_t)ctob(npg),
                    flags);
...
```

The hash bucket list is examined to see if a free bucket is already present to allocate to the requestor. If the head of this list is null (no entries on the list), a new bucket must be allocated. If the bucket size is larger than the size allowed to persist in the memory allocator (e.g. page-size granularity), the memory is allocated directly from the virtual memory system in a multiple of the page size (rounded up to the next logical page size). If the size is less than a multiple of page-size granularity, then the next power-of-two larger than the size of the requested chunk is allocated. Since the hash bucket index is setup in terms of powers-of-two, the calculation of page size only requires a left shift of the hash bucket index.

Occasionally a larger page size is desired. In this case, the page granularity of blocks that will persist in the **malloc()** memory allocator is set by the manifest constant MAXALLOCSAVE (currently set to two pages in size or 8192 bytes). It should be noted that this just happens to be the same size as the largest allowed size of a block in the buffer cache. This is no accident. Since only pages can be allocated from the virtual memory system's memory allocator, this size is rounded up to the next integral number of pages that can be allocated and that number of pages is requested from the virtual memory system's allocator.[38]

... [File: /usr/src/kernel/kern/malloc.c, line: 91]

```
        if (va == NULL) {
                splx(s);
                return ((void *) NULL);
        }
...
```

The virtual memory system's memory allocator takes full responsibility for the allocation of the memory and any blocks which might be incurred as a result. If it cannot return memory, for whatever reason, the attempt at allocating memory for this requestor is aborted and the null pointer is returned. Since the virtual memory system's memory allocator will block when allowed (if the flags are set to allow blocking), it should never return null in that case, even if that means never returning.

... [File: /usr/src/kernel/kern/malloc.c, line: 95]

```
#ifdef KMEMSTATS
                kbp->kb_total += kbp->kb_elmpercl;
#endif
                kup = btokup(va);
                kup->ku_indx = indx;
...
```

---

[38] Note that this means that for a fractional page allocation (e.g. one less than 4096 bytes), we will allocate more than one bucket entry at a time.

If the memory was allocated successfully by the virtual memory system's memory allocator **kmem_alloc()**, the statistics for the bucket indicating the number of elements associated with the bucket is increased and the bucket instance associated with this address is assigned to this particular hash bucket. For every portion of the arena, there is a corresponding in-use array element that is allocated on a per-page basis (obviously, since memory is only allocated in units of pages).

One consequence of this one-for-one correspondence between pages of memory in the arena and their usage structures instance is that the arena is of fixed size, set either upon compilation or during run-time configuration. It cannot grow itself. Thus, the structure is not recursively allocatable.

It is possible to do variable length hashing, if one had a need for a variable sized arena. However, since the size of RAM memory is fixed, simply setting aside a portion of virtual address space for use with the dynamic memory allocator is no great limitation. Currently, the default size of the virtual address space associated with **malloc()**'s arena is set to 4 MBytes. Note this is not a physical memory limit but virtual address space, so none of it needs to be allocated if desired.

The only time one might want to make a variable sized portion of virtual address space is when such a dynamic range of memory allocation is required that it could not be anticipated ahead of time. The only extant case of this is that of the memory consumed by a program itself (this is why we have a virtual memory system for programs), and it doesn't sit in the kernel.

... [File: /usr/src/kernel/kern/malloc.c, line: 100]

```
                if (allocsize >= MAXALLOCSAVE) {
                        if (npg > 65535)
                                panic("malloc: allocation too large");
                        kup->ku_pagecnt = npg;
#ifdef KMEMSTATS
                        ksp->ks_memuse += allocsize;
#endif
                        goto out;
                }
    ...
```

If the freshly allocated bucket is larger than the page granularity, then the size of this fragment and its usage entry is recorded and it is returned to the user. At this point, **malloc()** no longer has any management responsibilities, as it has turned over such responsibilities for these fragments to the virtual memory system, and they do not persist in its arena. In addition, since they are of integral size, only one per allocation is received, so that every time there is a **malloc()** of a large object, it always follows the path outlined above. As such, **malloc()** becomes a trivial front-end that monitors the allocation of memory from the virtual memory system.

Note that a usage entry corresponding to a page consists of the index size (which is a 16-bit quantity) and the amount of memory allocated (also a 16-bit quantity), which together form a 4-byte overhead for every page allocated from the virtual memory system. The size of the new allocated piece either corresponds to the number of pages allocated for page granularity allocations that we just described, or to the number of elements that the page granularity chunk that we are going to allocate elements out of. Thus, for example, if a new 128-byte entry is needed, the virtual memory system is asked for 4 KBytes of memory (one page), that will be subdivided up into 32 128-byte elements to be added to this bucket's chain—one will be immediately used and 31 will be left over for succeeding allocations.

... [File: /usr/src/kernel/kern/malloc.c, line: 109]

```
#ifdef KMEMSTATS
                kup->ku_freecnt = kbp->kb_elmpercl;
                kbp->kb_totalfree += kbp->kb_elmpercl;
#endif
                /*
                 * Just in case we blocked while allocating memory,
                 * and someone else also allocated memory for this
                 * bucket, don't assume the list is still empty.
                 */
                savedlist = kbp->kb_next;
                kbp->kb_next = va + (npg * NBPG) - allocsize;
                for (cp = kbp->kb_next; cp > va; cp -= allocsize)
                        *(caddr_t *)cp = cp - allocsize;
                *(caddr_t *)cp = savedlist;
        }
    ...
```

The count of the number of elements associated with this allocation is recorded, and the number of elements associated with this bucket is incremented. Note that two sets of books are kept on the size of memory in the buckets—the amount of pages of allocated space, as well as the number of byte-granularity items associated with this space in the case of subpage allocations.

This new reserve of memory is then added to the hash bucket's free list by successively dividing the page into fragments. As each ascending fragment is placed onto the list, care is taken to place the contents of the head of the list unconditionally on the end of the list instead of overwriting it, thus averting a race condition where two allocations of the same bucket occur simultaneously because we blocked. In this case, while we got the new page from memory, someone else also allocated another page before we got there, so our free list is already allocated and we need to add our contribution back in.[39]

[39] Alternatively, we could have detected this case and freed the just allocated block, but we didn't bother here because the **free()** function will right this temporary upset anyways, and we don't wish to unnecessarily complicate memory allocation.

Once allocated, blocks stay on the same hash bucket chain and are not further subdivided.[40] Thus, this allocator will have fragmentation loss associated with overallocation for small granularity blocks.[41] If no more than 100 entries are ever used, more than half this block is wasted and will never be allocated to any of the other memory classes. This is in contrast to that of a buddy allocator, which would fragment the page into a smaller binary fragment (128 bytes) closer in fit with less wastage. However, the cost of using the latter method would lie in the greatly increased complexity of both **malloc()** and **free()**. The design bias here leans towards many allocations of similarly sized objects, which just happens to be the common case in 386BSD. Hence, the emphasis here is on making it faster and not worrying overly much about fragmentation loss, since we tend to use many entries of the same size.

... [File: /usr/src/kernel/kern/malloc.c, line: 124]

```
        va = kbp->kb_next;
        kbp->kb_next = *(caddr_t *)va;
    ...
```

Once the hash bucket is refilled with fresh entries, the first entry on the bucket list is allocated to be returned. The free list is moved down by passing over the currently allocated entry. The first word of the memory area is now the pointer to the next entry on the free list.

... [File: /usr/src/kernel/kern/malloc.c, line: 126]

```
#ifdef KMEMSTATS
        kup = btokup(va);
        if (kup->ku_indx != indx)
                panic("malloc: wrong bucket");
        if (kup->ku_freecnt == 0)
                panic("malloc: lost data");
        kup->ku_freecnt−;
        kbp->kb_totalfree−;
        ksp->ks_memuse += 1 << indx;
out:
        kbp->kb_calls++;
        ksp->ks_inuse++;
        ksp->ks_calls++;
        if (ksp->ks_memuse > ksp->ks_maxused)
                ksp->ks_maxused = ksp->ks_memuse;
#else
out:
#endif /* KMEMSTATS */
    ...
```

If statistics are being recorded, the usage pointer associated with this bucket is located, and the number of free elements associated with it, and the bucket's total list of free

---

[40] This differs from a buddy allocator in that blocks are not recursively subdivided and reassembled.
[41] E.g. at least a 4 KByte block for the smallest size of 16 bytes, allowing 256 entries from that page.

entries for the type associated with this bucket are reduced. The amount of memory in use is incremented by the size of the fragment allocated to it (not the size of the allocation requested). The number of calls and the number of in-use segments (both by per-bucket as well as per-type of allocation registered) are tallied for both page granularity and fragment allocations. If we have managed to exceed the previous maximum amount of memory allocated to this type, the new high amount is recorded so we can tell what the peak usage was for this type.

... [File: /usr/src/kernel/kern/malloc.c, line: 144]

```
        splx(s);

        /* clear memory? */
        if (flags & M_ZERO_IT)
                memset((void *)va, 0, size);

        return ((void *) va);
}
    ...
```

This function now ends by returning an address to the freshly allocated portion of memory. During the time we actually manipulated the contents of the bucket, interrupts that might allocate memory were blocked out by use of the spl primitives. Currently, the only interrupt allocations of memory are those coming from network devices (like Ethernet interfaces). An optional request signalled by the flag (M_ZERO_IT) fills the requested memory with zero contents, readying it for later use.

4.4.3.2 Improvements to the Current Implementation of malloc()

Suppose a new facility in the kernel which requests memory allocation suddenly goes into a perpetual block, and a check of the status (using **vmstat -m**) shows a very large amount of a particular type of memory being allocated and a number of blocks being accumulated against that type. In this case, one might assume that memory wasn't being freed as it should, and a review of the code is in order.

However, this may be a simplistic assumption. Overallocation and memory leaks are only one class of problems. A far more insidious problem occurs when the memory has been freed but is still in use, since it will corrupt another allocator of the block later on. In this case, it may be hard to tell which user of the allocator is corrupting the arena. This is one key fragility of dynamically allocated systems which a systems designer should be aware of at all times.

One possible future improvement to **malloc()** is that of an optional flag to garbage collect the arena when memory is freed. A "mark and sweep" algorithm is used so that additional references to freed memory could be detected, resulting in a system panic, allowing a programmer to catch the kernel bug before it was masked.[42] This

---

[42] By destroying a data structure for another portion of the kernel.

enhancement could not be done for earlier BSD systems (or 386BSD Release 0.1 either) because these dynamically allocated pointers could and usually did exist in areas of memory that were physically inaccessible to the **malloc()** function.[43]

In 386BSD Release 1.0, all kernel stacks are always visible in unique portions of the kernel address space. This was a major design improvement to the system, since on creation they had to be dynamically relocated upon **fork()**. Now that this is implemented, it is possible to examine all kernel stacks in addition to all kernel memory to discover if the pointers are present in any of the data structures, so the developer can implement a "mark and sweep" algorithm.

4.4.4 What is free()

free() returns a portion of memory allocated by **malloc()** back to the arena. **free()**, like **malloc()**, can be called from anywhere in the kernel. **free()** first checks the address to make sure it belongs to the arena and then replaces that portion of memory back into the arena, accounting for its type usage appropriately. **free()** also attempts to recombine any excessive amounts of memory back into pages and passes them back to the virtual memory allocator where they can be used by all other portions of the system.

... [File: /usr/src/kernel/kern/malloc.c, line: 165]

```
void
free(void *addr, int type)
 ...
```

free() has two arguments: a pointer to the portion of memory being returned; and the type it was allocated as. It returns nothing. The side-effect of **free()** is to return the storage associated with the address back to the free pool of memory, which may either reside in the **malloc()** arena or in the free page queue of the virtual memory system's page allocator. If statistics are defined, another side-effect of **free()** is to update the statistics to reflect the fact that memory has been deallocated that was in use.

4.4.4.1 How is free() Implemented?

... [File: /usr/src/kernel/kern/malloc.c, line: 177]

```
        if (addr < (void *)&end ||
             (vm_offset_t)addr < vm_map_min(kmem_map) ||
             (vm_offset_t)addr > vm_map_max(kmem_map)) {
                  panic("free: outside arena");
        }
 ...
```

free() first checks to see if the address being returned is a valid kernel address corresponding to some part of the memory arena. If it is not, **free()** drops the memory

---

[43] E.g. in a kernel stack that was unmapped.

(which was probably part of the static kernel data section) after issuing a diagnostic message. If the debugger is set, it drops into the debugger so that the problem can be further isolated.

... [File: /usr/src/kernel/kern/malloc.c, line: 183]

```
        kup = btokup(addr);
        size = 1 << kup->ku_indx;
...
```

The usage pointer associated with the address passed back is located and from that the size of the block is determined.

... [File: /usr/src/kernel/kern/malloc.c, line: 193]

```
        kbp = &bucket[kup->ku_indx];
        s = splimp();
        if (size >= MAXALLOCSAVE) {
                kmem_free(kmem_map, (vm_offset_t)addr, ctob(kup->ku_pagecnt));
#ifdef KMEMSTATS
                size = kup->ku_pagecnt << PGSHIFT;
                ksp->ks_memuse -= size;
                kup->ku_indx = 0;
                kup->ku_pagecnt = 0;
                if (ksp->ks_memuse + size >= ksp->ks_limit &&
                    ksp->ks_memuse < ksp->ks_limit)
                        wakeup((caddr_t)ksp);
                ksp->ks_inuse--;
                kbp->kb_total -= 1;
#endif /* KMEMSTATS */
                splx(s);
                return;
        }
...
```

From the recorded bucket index, the bucket list associated with this size of memory allocation is located. If the memory allocation is of large page granularity sized objects,[44] we simply pass its deallocation back to the virtual memory system's memory allocation free routine **kmem_free()**, obtaining the size in units of pages from the usage pointer (*ku_pagecnt*).

If statistics are implemented here, the amount of memory represented by this segment is removed from usage and the number of outstanding in-use requests are reduced, as well as the number of total entries allocated for use with this bucket. If the amount of memory allocated to this type of dynamic memory allocation falls under the limits for this type (and it was over the limit before), any processes waiting for memory allocation of this type are unblocked. Note again that this resource block is on a per-type basis, and that the types are not checked against the allocation type—thus, the

---

[44] Which are not managed by **malloc()** but instead by the virtual memory system.

type might differ during the free. In this case, the statistics would end up being wrong, and any resources blocked for this type would not be unblocked.[45]

During the time that the contents of the bucket are altered, interrupts are blocked that may allocate or free additional memory, so no contention or race conditions are possible in modifying the bucket list. In the case of page granularity units of memory, everything else has been done by the virtual memory system in accepting this back into the free pool of memory—in this case, the process is completed.

... [File: /usr/src/kernel/kern/malloc.c, line: 211]

```
#ifdef KMEMSTATS
        kbp->kb_totalfree++;
        kup->ku_freecnt++;
        if (kup->ku_freecnt >= kbp->kb_elmpercl)
                if (kup->ku_freecnt > kbp->kb_elmpercl)
                        panic("free: multiple frees");
                else if (kbp->kb_totalfree > kbp->kb_highwat)
                     && type != M_MBUF) {
                        caddr_t freepage = kuptob(kup);
                        register caddr_t *cpp, *nxt;
                        int freesize = kup->ku_freecnt * size;

                        ksp->ks_memuse -= size;
                        kup->ku_indx = 0;
                        if (ksp->ks_memuse + size >= ksp->ks_limit &&
                                ksp->ks_memuse < ksp->ks_limit)
                                wakeup((caddr_t)ksp);

    ...
```

If this is a subpage granularity allocation, the total of free buffers, as well as the number of them associated with this particular page and the usage element (since it has now been passed back as free) are all incremented. If the number of usage elements are greater than or equal to the number of elements which would fit in a page, then we might be able to pass back memory to the virtual memory system rather than let it persist in **malloc()**'s buckets.

If there are more elements free than could be present in this page, a panic occurs indicating we have probably freed this page more times than is possible. This panic usually implies a programming error in either **malloc()** or **free()**, or a corrupt arena. On the other hand, if we have the same number of free elements in the page as we have elements in the page, we now have an entirely free page that can be returned. The total amount of free elements allowed to persist in the buckets is checked to see if it is larger than the maximum amount that should persist on the buckets (*kb_highwat*— the high water mark for free elements). The fragments are then reconsolidated and a free page is passed back to the virtual memory system where it can be reallocated.

---

[45] It may not be a good idea to have **free()** pass back the type, but instead record the type as part of the usage element associated with this entry.

... [File: /usr/src/kernel/kern/malloc.c, line: 227]

```
        ksp->ks_inuse--;
        kbp->kb_total -= kbp->kb_elmpercl;
        kbp->kb_totalfree -= kbp->kb_elmpercl;
...
```

The statistics and the contents of the bucket are reconciled by reducing the amount of memory in use and number of elements in use. At the same time, the total amount of free and allocated bucket elements are also reduced by the same amount removed from use. Thus, fewer elements will persist in the **malloc()** hash buckets than were present before. Ironically, we are reducing a total that we just incremented prior to determining we had enough to do the **free()** in the first place.

... [File: /usr/src/kernel/kern/malloc.c, line: 231]

```
        if (−kup->ku_freecnt != 0) {

        /* walk bucket list deleting entries in page freed */
        for (cpp = &kbp->kb_next; *cpp != NULL ; ) {
                nxt = *(caddr_t **)cpp;
                if ((caddr_t)nxt >= freepage
                    && (caddr_t)nxt < freepage + freesize) {
                        while (*nxt >= freepage
                            && *nxt < freepage + freesize) {
                                nxt = *(caddr_t **)nxt;
                                kup->ku_freecnt−;
                        }
                        *cpp = *(caddr_t *) nxt;
                        kup->ku_freecnt−;
                } else if (nxt == NULL)
                        break;
                else
                        cpp = nxt;
        }
...
```

If the memory element we are deallocating is a page size exactly and MAXALLOCSAVE is defined to be greater than a page, we don't need to find all of the elements associated with this entry because there is only one and it has not been reinserted on the free list.

This code in this section becomes very sensitive and difficult to get right if this region of memory is not comprised of a single element. If this region of memory is not comprised of a single element, we must walk the bucket list and only deallocate the entries associated with the page we want to free. Since the bucket list has absolutely no order, it can have entries that are arbitrarily allocated in various orders corresponding to numerous successive frees and allocates—thus, the page we are now freeing might have elements used many times over which just happen to be free at the moment. The list must be searched to find and eliminate them while successively reducing the free count associated with this page incrementally to zero.

Each entry is examined to see if it falls within the bounds of the page we are freeing (*freepage*)—the common case where a chunk of successive entries is adjacent is optimized for here. As each of these entries is found, it is overwritten with the contents of the next successive entry, regardless of whether it belongs to the free block or not. This part of **free()** effectively condenses the bucket list so that the page can be removed from the **malloc()** arena.

... [File: /usr/src/kernel/kern/malloc.c, line: 249]

```
            if (kup->ku_freecnt != 0)
                    panic("free: missing a bucket");
            }
    ...
```

If the number of elements in use of this page is not zero, (i.e., there are no more references to it in the bucket list), a programming error has occurred, resulting in a panic. In this case, somehow during the condensation procedure either the bucket or the arena usage pointers were corrupted.[46]

... [File: /usr/src/kernel/kern/malloc.c, line: 253]

```
            kmem_free(kmem_map, (vm_offset_t)freepage, freesize);
            splx(s);
            return;
    ...
```

Now that there are no more users of this page of memory, it is returned to the virtual memory system for reuse and the function is terminated. This completes the case where a fractional page memory is returned to the virtual memory system.

... [File: /usr/src/kernel/kern/malloc.c, line: 257]

```
        ksp->ks_memuse -= size;
        if (ksp->ks_memuse + size >= ksp->ks_limit &&
            ksp->ks_memuse < ksp->ks_limit)
                wakeup((caddr_t)ksp);
        ksp->ks_inuse--;
#endif /* KMEMSTATS */
        *(caddr_t *)addr = kbp->kb_next;
        kbp->kb_next = addr;
        splx(s);
}
    ...
```

If memory cannot be returned to the virtual memory system, the fragment will be added back onto the bucket list and the statistics of memory usage will be appropriately adjusted (as in the other cases above). The memory list hanging off of the bucket is maintained as a list with the most recently freed entry held in the bucket header entry and all successive entries chained on as elements (using the first word of the address of the region of memory that they describe). Note that the list is thus

---

[46] This is a consistency check.

unterminated and that the bucket count is the only determiner of the size of the bucket list (*kb_totalfree*).

Memory freed will have the first element overwritten—if it is still in use, it will have its first field overwritten with an address on the free list. Otherwise, it will remain unaltered, since in many of the kernel's data structures allocated by **malloc()** and freed by **free()** the first field is usually a pointer to another related element of the kind (like struct proc).

One of the whimsical side effects of this arrangement is that if an additional reference is present after the structure is freed, the arena will occasionally be turned into a sequence of data structures elsewhere in the kernel. As such, a programming error of this kind will result in impossible arrangements of related data structures and is the first tipoff to this kind of dynamic memory allocation bug.

While there exist many clever methods for debugging these dynamic memory allocation bugs, they all present differing benefits and costs. For example, putting in additional debugging facilities at this level is considered a highly subjective area outside of the scope of this project. For 386BSD development, we have chosen to add in debugging facilities as we need them and remove them again when we are done. This allows us to always keep the kernel facilities clean and clear.

4.4.4.2 386BSD free() Design Choices and Trade-Offs

In both Net/2 and 386BSD Release 0.1, **free()** did not return space for fractional page allocation back to the virtual memory system. The lack of this mechanism caused the kernel to essentially overallocate memory for peak-use cases and never pass it back to the kernel. As a result, systems with small amounts of main memory would run much slower because too much memory was fragmented and never returned for reuse to the system. The kernel memory allocator became too expensive to use for certain cases!

Rather than provide a second memory allocator, the **free()** routine was extended to consolidate entries and pass memory back to the virtual memory system, thus eliminating the fragmentation problem. It also had the side-effect of speeding up certain memory allocations because more memory was available to be allocated from the virtual memory system, rather than requiring the pageout daemon to come into play. Once this mechanism was implemented, it also was found that the number of operations necessary to condense the bucket list (the expensive part) was smaller than previously thought if the optimization of looking for successive entries was incorporated.

4.4.4.3 Improvements to the Current Implementation of free()

The semantics of both **malloc()** and **free()** are such that the return of the free segment does not require knowledge of the size of the block being passed back—just the pointer to the region of memory. The size of the allocated portion of memory (which is always known to be larger than or equal to the requested size) is always internally recorded. This means it is impossible to return only a portion of that which was allocated.

Currently, there is no **realloc()** function in the kernel to alter the size of the **malloc()** region, so they are fixed allocated until deallocated. It is debatable if it is desirable to implement **realloc()**, since the few places where it might operate already simply obtain another block of a larger size, allocate it, and free the smaller one. [47]

4.4.5 What is kmeminit()?

kmeminit() is an initialization routine for the memory arena used by **malloc()** and **free()**. It is called from the kernel's **main()** function which initializes the entire kernel and starts system operation.

... [File: /usr/src/kernel/kern/malloc.c, line: 271]

```
void
kmeminit(void)
    ...
```

kmeminit() takes no arguments and returns no value. It has the side-effect of obtaining a private portion of virtual address space for use with the arena, as well as obtaining an array of usage entries per page of virtual address space. Thus, to initialize the arena, only the memory for the usage recording needs to be allocated at this point in time (4 bytes per page). In the case of the default kernel memory of 4 MBytes in virtual arena size, 4 KBytes of memory are allocated to the usage array to record the usage of any pages within the window of virtual address space used by the kernel.

The usage recording is first cleared and the statistics associated with the entries are initialized to reflect the maximum sizes of allocations of each of the hash buckets, both in terms of the high water mark of the amount of space to persist in the buckets[48] and a maximum upper limit before blocking.[49] These numbers are arbitrarily chosen upper bounds, which are in actuality much higher than normally encountered in operation.

Increasing the high water mark will just consume more memory in the hash bucket chains and reduce the number of times the virtual memory system's allocator will be called into play, while increasing the size of the limit placed on all the entries will reduce any blocks on the memory allocation made by overallocation. As such, it is not recommended that these limits be raised, since they are set so large to begin with. Any "improvement" that requires the raising of this limit should be carefully examined for programming errors.

---

[47] See **allocbuf()** in **fs/bio.c** on the **386BSD Reference CD-ROM** for more information.
[48] Five times the number of elements per page allocation.
[49] 60% of the maximum size of the kernel memory arena.

4.4.5.1 How is kmeminit() Implemented?

... [File: /usr/src/kernel/kern/malloc.c, line: 286]

```
        npg = VM_KMEM_SIZE / NBPG;
        kmemusage = (struct kmemusage *) kmem_alloc(kernel_map,
                (vm_size_t)(npg * sizeof(struct kmemusage)), 0);
        memset((caddr_t)kmemusage, 0, npg * sizeof(struct kmemusage));
...
```

The virtual memory system's allocator is first used to allocate an array of usage elements, each corresponding to a page of virtual address space in the arena. This array is initialized to zero, as no pages are in use to begin with.

... [File: /usr/src/kernel/kern/malloc.c, line: 290]

```
        kmem_map = kmem_suballoc((vm_size_t)(npg * NBPG), FALSE);
        kmembase = (caddr_t) vm_map_min(kmem_map);
        kmemlimit = (caddr_t) vm_map_max(kmem_map);
...
```

A region of the kernel's virtual address space is set aside for use as the arena of the **malloc()** memory allocator. This is accomplished by allocating a submap[50] of the main kernel map of the appropriate size. The region of virtual memory is bounded by two kernel variables (*kmembase, kmemlimit*) that describe the starting and ending addresses in the global kernel address space.

... [File: /usr/src/kernel/kern/malloc.c, line: 294]

```
#ifdef KMEMSTATS
        for (indx = 0; indx < MINBUCKET + 16; indx++) {
                if (1 << indx >= CLBYTES)
                        bucket[indx].kb_elmpercl = 1;
                else
                        bucket[indx].kb_elmpercl = CLBYTES / (1 << indx);
                bucket[indx].kb_highwat = 5 * bucket[indx].kb_elmpercl;
        }
        for (indx = 0; indx < M_LAST; indx++)
                kmemstats[indx].ks_limit = npg * NBPG * 6 / 10;
#endif
...
```

The statistics are initialized by iterating through the statically allocated bucket header array. The number of elements per page allocation and the high water mark for the maximum number of persistent allocations are then set. Note that for buckets exceeding the size of MAXALLOCSAVE, the high water mark is meaningless, since memory is always returned to the virtual memory system's allocator. For buckets less than this, however, the high water mark indicates how many elements may persist

---

[50] A submap is a very limited indirect map that segments a portion of virtual address space in the kernel. It sets this address space aside for private use. See *Kinds of Maps* in the **vm/map.c** discussion in **Volume II** of this series for more information.

before any more are passed back as whole pages to the virtual memory system's allocator.

After initializing the bucket, the statistics static array is initialized to record the maximum limit of memory that can be allocated to each type. Since both the bucket and memory statistics arrays are statically allocated in the kernel, the remaining fields are already initialized to zero as a result of the bootstrap, which loaded the kernel which initialized its program's bss segment to zero.

4.5 Why Use Kernel Dynamically Allocated Memory?

The real, original UNIX did not use a dedicated kernel memory allocator, per se. Instead it used buffers, with everything arranged in compile-time arrays of tables. To change the number of processes on the system, for example, one had to recompile the entire system after changing the parameter in the table. One of the earliest changes to 4BSD was to parameterize the size of the arrays so that one could reconfigure the kernel on bootup—there was still a fixed size array, but the size was fixed at boot time, not compilation time.

One of the banes of these early UNIX systems was that everything was dependent on conditional compilation. 2.8BSD was the height of conditional compilation, having more than 44 different separate conditional compilation variables, many of which were interdependent, so it was easy to create an impossible configuration which could not work—thus increasing the support load. The justification for all this conditional compilation was that, if done correctly (a significant caveat), it allowed one to choose precisely the amount of resource dedicated to a particular function. For example, if your system configuration had 10 terminals, with 10 processes per terminal typically opening 20 files per process, it could be tailored to fit. However, if the usage changed, one had to modify the program to change the limits.[51]

While conditional compilation and conditional sizing of parameters are still part of other BSD systems,[52] the same problems of scalability and manageability are issues. For example, to use a SCSI driver properly one might have to define enough of a resource so all of the devices can share it; otherwise, configuration problems might arise which exhaust the ability of the user to diagnose them.

---

[51] The problems with 2.8BSD conditional compilation were anticipated and hotly debated by the author, but it was promoted for, believe it or not, "marketing" reasons. If you think it was hard to use, imagine how miserable it was to implement knowing full well the downsides. For those who like to think that only commercial companies place nontechnical, even self-defeating, marketing demands on operating systems, we've always found this little parable quite instructive. Even research systems are buffeted by "trendy" poorly justified ideas.

[52] Primarily for speed considerations—this is why quite a few drivers still have fixed size tables in them.

SOURCE CODE SECRETS: THE BASIC KERNEL

It is not enough to allow the limits to be easily changed by the end user. For example, systems like Solaris, which allow the user to adjust the limits with configuration files, spawn a second problem—now that the controls are placed where the user can get to them, how do you educate the user on how best to use them? In addition, the burden of system administration and management for the user has been increased—not decreased. As such, it seems that as fast as configuration files are going in, they are also now being taken out and replaced with dynamic algorithms which determine the tradeoff of resource size and utilization via heuristics.

Even the "simple" DOS CONFIG.SYS files contain many parameters which must be carefully set. For example, if there is plenty of RAM in the system but this file is set incorrectly, it may demand more RAM in one of three or four different places before everything works—in the meantime, one still has to manipulate the system so that the rest of it still functions while one is attempting to make a particular item work. The key irritation in all this is that the system itself knows what the problem is, but won't handle it because it doesn't have the control mechanisms built into DOS or Windows to achieve the result, nor does the vendor want to put in such a mechanism because that would place on the operating system the responsibility of asserting that the change in configuration works for all the software used by the operating system. In essence, it would become responsible for all the dependencies of even weird DOS real-mode drivers—something that is impossible given the system design itself.[53]

In modern times, compiling or changing a program on demand has become extremely expensive, since one needs knowledgeable personnel around to set the parameters correctly (if you can really anticipate them)—and even so, there are times when you must go beyond the bounds, so to speak. Unfortunately, in this age of personal systems such as PCs and workstations used by one or a handful of people, the centralized systems administration expertise assumed in all UNIX systems designs is no longer available to most people.

The value of a dynamically allocated system now becomes quite clear, since the cost savings of efficiently using the memory by statically determined amounts is trivial in comparison to the time lost by the computer system when it is unable to respond because the resources it has in abundance cannot be used if they weren't reserved ahead of time.[54] Hence, heuristics determination by the system itself is the wave of the future in operating systems design. If one still must have a bunch of control knobs for the operator, it must be kept to a very limited number to be useful.

---

[53] The reason for the introduction of virtual device driver interfaces, like those used in Chicago, is to get control of the situation again, by reducing configuration dependencies and making it more an interface specification—no analog of this problem exists on the UNIX side right now.
[54] In fact, this dynamic problem rears its head throughout every aspect of a UNIX system's design and is the Achilles' heel in an otherwise aesthetically pleasing system.

Exercises

4.1 Why is the topic of hardware configuration a subset of software configuration?

4.2 **a)** How do 386BSD **.config** configuration files achieve order-independence?
b) Why is this important?

4.3 What are the trade-offs in adding another memory allocator to the kernel?

4.4 **malloc()** reduces fragmentation lost on sub-page sized allocations.
a) Assuming all sub-page sized allocations have occurred just once each, how much fragmentation loss (in bytes) would occur?
b) What advantages and disadvantages would a Knuth buddy allocator have over this one?

4.5 If fewer memory allocators are usually better, why not use just one?

4.6 **a)** What are the costly operations (instructions) of **malloc()** and **free()**?
b) How can the impact of these operations be minimized?
c) Would this always be desirable?

5 THE LIFE CYCLE OF A PROCESS (kern/fork.c, kern/exit.c)

The most basic concurrent object visible to the user in 386BSD is the *process*. This chapter discusses the two most significant events in the life cycle of a process: *creation* and *destruction*.

Processes are implied throughout 386BSD, in books, hypertext, and source code. However, with the significant exceptions of machine-dependent creation/destruction (see **Chapter 3**), and multiprogramming (see **Chapter 8**), the presumption is that of a relative context in which we are running.

Creation and destruction of a process are unique in that we can't describe them in quite the same way; while they appear complementary, they are actually asymmetric operations. To create a process, a new object must carefully be constructed from the information of the old alongside it, while with destruction, the terminating process gracefully relinquishes its resources until it withers away to a mere wisp, and then is gone. Not to get melodramatic, but it does closely parallel birth and death so much that "life cycle" is an appropriate term.[1]

These operations are implemented in the two files **kern/fork.c** and **kern/exit.c**. Currently, process creation only occurs explicitly with the POSIX **fork()** primitive, implemented in 386BSD as a system call. Process destruction can either occur explicitly via a POSIX **exit()** primitive (implemented again as a system call), or implicitly as a terminal exception (see **Chapter 6**) either originating from the processor (for example, an invalid memory fault) or from another process.

5.1 The Structure of Process Creation: kern/fork.c

Process creation is handled on three levels of abstraction:

1. the program interface,

2. the kernel process state replication and kernel subsystems instances copy,

3. and the kernel thread generation and machine-dependent thread generation.

---

[1] This is beginning to sound like a Disney movie...

The topmost layer is made up of system calls that provide a POSIX program interface to copy explicitly the current process and return the process ID of the new child, with the child process receiving a "0" to differentiate it from the parent.[2] Below this layer lies the kernel's mechanism to replicate process state as needed to generate a new copy, by replicating any subsidiary portions of the process as needed (including the user program address space), generating a new kernel thread to allow the process to run along with the machine-dependent generation of the kernel thread itself. At the bottom level, a *naked* kernel-resident control thread allows multiprogramming. This is generated through a combination of machine-independent and machine-dependent code.

When the process eventually terminates, this thread must be disassembled, so the process termination mechanism **exit()** (see **kern/exit.c**) is quite intimate with this process creation mechanism. In turn, both of these are intimate with the context switch mechanism—the primitive upon which *multiprogramming* relies.

5.1.1 The Strategy Behind Thread/Process State Structure

One design goal in 386BSD is to possess a single multithreaded kernel, with the ability to create both independent kernel threads for use in managing kernel subsystems, and process-dependent user threads for application use. However, accomplishing this goal relies heavily upon a careful strategic understanding of the structure of thread and process state. In 386BSD, threads have thread state (proc and kernel stack) at a unique virtual address space in the kernel program.[3] Entirely independent of the kernel threads themselves are the additional characteristics of the user program, POSIX program interface state, and other characteristics of the process. The virtual memory system, in contrast, functions in terms of address spaces, where the entire kernel is one address space and user programs are in other address spaces. Thus, multiprogramming is entirely independent of the virtual memory system.

This approach differs markedly from earlier BSD implementations that context-switched the per-process information located at a fixed kernel virtual (or user virtual) address space and intertwined the two to reduce kernel address space demands. This design change was made because, since all modern processors now have large kernel virtual address spaces, the need to minimize them is now moot.[4] In sum, creating a new kernel thread no longer requires interaction with the virtual memory system other than for storage allocation.

---

[2] Since it's otherwise an exact copy.
[3] This is shared in a shared memory multiprocessor, with the unique virtual address used as a part of the synchronization and exclusive access mechanism.
[4] And can be dealt with in other ways, such as via recursive page maps.

5.1.2 The POSIX Process ID, Group ID, and Session

Processes are identified (or named) by a *process ID*. A process ID is a unique positive integer in the range of [1..PID_MAX] with an internal discrete NO_PID value used to identify a non-named process. Since many applications programs use a process ID as a unique key and assume a successive ordering, the process creation and destruction mechanism ensures this uniqueness at all times. If a process does not have an ID, it cannot be referenced and thus does not exist. Therefore, a process begins to exist when it gains an ID and is considered not to exist when it no longer has an ID.

Processes belong to groups so that a collection of processes can be controlled as if they were a single process.[5] This *process group ID* is named with the process ID of the first (and thus youngest) process in the process group referred to as the *process group leader*.

Each controlling console is assigned a *process session* that contains one or more process groups. Processes need not be connected to terminals—in this case, they are not assigned a process session. Sessions contain one (or more) process groups. Sessions were added because older versions of BSD had overloaded the semantics of process groups with job control semantics, creating an obscure security hole.[6] This hole was closed in POSIX by adding this new layer of grouping.

5.1.3 The POSIX Definition of Process Hierarchy

Processes create new processes by means of a copy operation, with the original termed the *parent* and the nascent process the *child*. A parent can have many children, with the siblings ordered by time of creation (youngest to oldest). Each of these children can in turn spawn more children, thus creating a *hierarchy* of processes. When a child process terminates, it reports its termination status and statistics to the process that created it. If a process in the middle of this hierarchy is terminated, its children will become orphaned.[7] These processes are inherited by the first process *(init)* so as to not clog the system with endless process corpses waiting to return process status to non-existant parents.

5.1.4 Functions Contained in the File kern/fork.c

The file **kern/fork.c** contains machine-independent code to implement the mechanism for *replicating* a process or thread, the basic concurrent objects in a POSIX-based system created explicitly by other user processes. The kernel creates the very first user

---

[5] E.g., a pipeline "**grep foo /bar | wc | more**".

[6] Sessions were not in the original UNIX system; the function they performed was entirely subsumed into process groups. The security hole was that process groups were globally named, and could be interfered with by assigning processes to other process's process groups. By providing another layer to surround process groups, job control could be isolated from this unintended "covert channel."

[7] In general, it is an unusual condition when child processes have no parent to report to.

process by simulating a static **fork()**, and uses **fork()** internally to generate system processes for dedicated functions (scheduling and virtual memory page reclamation). Processes either terminate themselves explicitly via the **rexit()** system call handler, or implicitly terminate themselves on receipt of a terminating signal (see **sigexit()** in the **kern/sig.c** discussion).

This file relies on the primary functions:

fork()

vfork()

fork1()

fork() and **vfork()** are applications program interfaces to the POSIX function and BSD interfaces, respectively, to the system call handlers which they implement, while **fork1()** is the *common* code used to create a process relied upon by both. Earlier UNIX systems used a simplified version of this same mechanism. The current POSIX **fork()** is just an elaboration based on additional characteristics of both BSD and System V UNIX.

5.1.5 What is fork()?

fork() is a system call handler that implements the functionality of a POSIX **fork()** function entirely. It is the way a process explicitly copies itself. There is no implicit process creation nor "virgin birth" process spawn operation in POSIX.

... [File: /usr/src/kernel/kern/fork.c, line: 49]

```
fork(p, uap, retval)
        struct proc *p;
        void *uap;
        int retval[];
    ...
```

fork() conforms to the calling conventions of a system call handler. The system call implemented has no arguments and returns the value of the created process ID to its caller. Since by semantic definition it creates an exact copy of itself, it returns twice— once in the parent (or original process) and once in the child (the fresh copy). To indicate the difference between these otherwise identically-appearing copies, the return value is set to zero (which is an invalid process ID) in the child process.

5.1.5.1 How is fork() Implemented?

fork() relies entirely on the common code kernel function **fork1()** to create the new process.

... [File: /usr/src/kernel/kern/fork.c, line: 55]

```
        return (fork1(p, 0, retval));
    ...
```

In addition to passing the current process and return value arguments, **fork1()** accepts a type of process to create argument, which in this case requests a POSIX *heavy-weight* process copy.

5.1.6 What is vfork()?

vfork() is a system call handler that implements the functionality of a BSD **vfork()** function entirely. It is actually a shorthand version of **fork()**, handling process creation by borrowing the resources and address space of the parent (including the parent's stack!) and using them until either a new process image is loaded or the child process exits, whereupon the parent is returned its resources.

Successful use of **vfork()** by an application program relies on considerable care taken by the programmer to restore any alterations made on the state of the process before an **execve()** or **exit()** system call occurs—otherwise the parent will be damaged (since actually it is the parent running under the assumed name of the child). **vfork()** is potentially a low-cost mechanism because it attempts to avoid copying or bookkeeping overhead by simply not doing it. As such, it typically is used to implement embedded process spawn mechanisms in library functions.[8]

... [File: /usr/src/kernel/kern/fork.c, line: 58]

```
vfork(p, uap, retval)
      struct proc *p;
      void *uap;
      int retval[];
...
```

vfork() conforms to the calling conventions of a system call handler. The system call implemented has no arguments and returns the value of the created process ID to its caller. Since by semantic definition it creates an exact copy of itself, it returns twice— once in the parent (or original process) and once in the child (the fresh copy). To indicate the difference between otherwise identically appearing copies, the return value is set to zero (which is an invalid process ID) in the child process.

5.1.6.1 How is vfork() Implemented?

vfork() relies entirely on the common code kernel function **fork1()** to create the new process.

... [File: /usr/src/kernel/kern/fork.c, line: 64]

```
      return (fork1(p, 1, retval));
...
```

---

[8] Such as in the user program C library **system()** function.

In addition to passing the current process and return value arguments, **fork1()** accepts a type of process to create argument. In this case, it requests a BSD **vfork** process copy simulation.

5.1.7 What is fork1()?

fork1() is the common kernel interface to create a process. It is called by program interfaces to perform explicit creation of different types of processes (see **fork()** and **vfork()**). **fork1()** is a function that returns twice—once in the user process that called it and another time in the child process it creates as a side-effect.

... [File: /usr/src/kernel/kern/fork.c, line: 67]

```
int
fork1(struct proc *p1, int isvfork, int *retval)
...
```

The function is called with a pointer to the process to be copied (*p1*). Integer values describe what kind of process copy to perform (*isvfork*), as well as the parameters to be returned to both child and parent (*retval*). The function will either return a termination status to the parent process, or success to both child and parent process.

5.1.7.1 How is fork1() Implemented?

fork1() generates new processes by replicating the state of the current process (*p1*) and initializing resources unique to the new process. The new process has a unique process ID, proc entry, kernel stack, and various auxiliary structures (like *p_stat*, the process statistics; *p_vmspace*, the user program address space; *p_fd*, the file descriptors allowing access to files, and so forth).

Processes are created in a highly regulated way, since almost any user-level activity is allowed to create them at length. Since they can be rapidly recycled, care must be taken to avoid resource constipation during process creation and contention for shared resources.

... [File: /usr/src/kernel/kern/fork.c, line: 80]

```
redo:
        if (nprocs >= maxproc ||
            (haspriv = use_priv(p1->p_ucred, PRV_NO_UPROCLIMIT, p1)) &&
            nprocs >= maxproc + 1) {
                tablefull("proc");
                return (EAGAIN);
        }
    ...
```

Pragmatic limits are placed on the entire system for all processes, to forestall the case of *runaway* process creation. The last process is preserved for use by processes that hold the "ignore per-user process limit" privilege. This *last* process can sometimes be

---

used to rectify a process overflow situation.[9] Since this global limit takes priority over the per-process limit, it occurs first.

... [File: /usr/src/kernel/kern/fork.c, line: 90]

```
        if (haspriv == 0) {
                uid_t uid = p1->p_ucred->cr_uid;
                int count = 0;

                for (p2 = allproc; p2; p2 = p2->p_nxt)
                        if (p2->p_ucred->cr_uid == uid)
                                count++;
                for (p2 = zombproc; p2; p2 = p2->p_nxt)
                        if (p2->p_ucred->cr_uid == uid)
                                count++;

                /* if too many processes for process limit, return error */
                if (count > p1->p_rlimit[RLIMIT_NPROC].rlim_cur)
                        return (EAGAIN);
        }
...
```

Along with global process limits, limits on the number of processes per user are imposed on processes without the limit privilege. These are implemented by walking the process lists of active and dead processes (the only ones with valid process IDs) and tallying the number of processes with the same user ID credential. If the process's process limit is exceeded, the process creation attempt is terminated.

In either case of process limits, an EAGAIN error is returned to the caller to indicate that no process is created and that the request can be retried with possible success. Since triggering a process limit is currently the only reason a process cannot be created, the only way a retry will be successful is if one of the user's processes is terminated (and **wait()**ed for—zombies still count) in the case of the per-user limit, or if any other process on the system terminates in the case of the global limit. Thus, the *softness* of this error depends on factors external to the kernel and the creating process. At this point, there is no kernel interface to determine the event of "having a process come available."

... [File: /usr/src/kernel/kern/fork.c, line: 110]

```
        nextpid++;
retry:
        /* process id wrapped around */
        if (nextpid >= PID_MAX) {
                /* restart assuming low numbered pids are immortal */
                nextpid = 100;
                pidchecked = 0;
        }
```

---

[9] Usually by killing off the aberrant process-creating process.

```
        /* no more unused pids, scan active & zombie queues for another run */
        if (nextpid >= pidchecked) {
...
```

Processes are uniquely identified by a positive integer ID number in the range of [1..PID_MAX).[10] A range of known unused process IDs (from *nextpid*+1 through *pidchecked*-1) is ready for immediate allocation. In most cases, the process ID is just the value of *nextpid*++. If the process ID overflows the valid range, or the "run" of process IDs is exhausted, a new run must be found. This heuristic takes advantage of the knowledge that processes are usually generated in successive groups (e.g., pipelines of commands) that are short-lived. Exceptions to this rule are the *eternal* server processes that are started up at boot time, and hence have low numbers. These process IDs are skipped over by a fixed-guess number (100) to avoid needless work. One consequence of this is that some process IDs are never available again to user processes, so a program that constantly forks (and exits) itself to probe for the existence of other processes will find more processes active than there actually are.

... [File: /usr/src/kernel/kern/fork.c, line: 121]

```
              int doingzomb = 0;

              /* scan active process queue to find if pid is used. */
              pidchecked = PID_MAX;
              p2 = allproc;
again:
              for (; p2 != NULL; p2 = p2->p_nxt) {
                     pid_t pid = p2->p_pid, pgid = p2->p_pgrp->pg_id;

                     if (pid == nextpid || pgid == nextpid) {
                            nextpid++;
                            if (nextpid >= pidchecked)
                                   goto retry;
                     }
...
```

A linear scan of the active (*allproc*) and dead (*zombproc*) process queues is conducted to find another non-zero length "run" of process IDs. During this scan, the bottom value (*nextpid*) of the prospective run sequence is successively raised, while the top value (*pidchecked*) past the end of the sequence is lowered. The top value corresponds to the lowest valid process ID above the prospective unallocated base process ID. The search looks for the first successive unallocated process ID, skipping over allocated ones (at the bottom) while simultaneously looking for the lowest allocated process above the bottom (at the top).

[10] Actually, process ID 0 is used by the system for the pageout system process, which inherits the statically created bootstrap process context created by the kernel's **main()** program. Note that it is impossible to affect it (e.g., kill) because the process ID of 0 has special meaning; thus, it cannot be used in the conventional sense.

In searching for unallocated process IDs, both process ID and group ID are checked since the process ID is used for both process ID and process group ID.[11] If during the scan the prototype base of the new run is found, successive ones are also examined until the end of the sequence is encountered. If this end-of-sequence wraps over the end of the range, the search will be restarted by the overflow case mentioned above. However, if the end of sequence is non-wrapping, an out-of-order process ID has been detected and the scan will be restarted on the next successive ID.

... [File: /usr/src/kernel/kern/fork.c, line: 136]

```
            if (pid > nextpid && pidchecked > pid)
                    pidchecked = pid;
            if (pgid > nextpid &&  pidchecked > pgid)
                    pidchecked = pgid;
    }
...
```

The end of the run of unallocated process IDs (*pidchecked*) is found by looking for successively smaller process IDs still larger than the current unallocated process ID (*nextpid*).

... [File: /usr/src/kernel/kern/fork.c, line: 142]

```
    if (!doingzomb) {
            /* scan zombie process queue to find if pid is used. */
            doingzomb = 1;
            p2 = zombproc;
            goto again;
    }
...
```

Having checked the active process list, the zombie list is also scanned. A pass through both lists without either wrapping the process ID number or having an order conflict will need to occur to acquire the next run of unallocated process IDs. This loop will terminate with the range [*nextpid..pidchecked*] of intact unused IDs, containing at least one usable process ID that will be used.[12]

... [File: /usr/src/kernel/kern/fork.c, line: 155]

```
    mypid = nextpid;
    MALLOC(p2, struct proc *, sizeof(struct proc), M_PROC, M_WAITOK);
    if (mypid != nextpid) {
            FREE(p2, M_PROC);
            goto redo;
    }
...
```

[11] The first process in a process group has its process group ID set to its process ID.
[12] This algorithm relies on the sparse allocation of process IDs (30,000) to the number of valid processes (in the hundreds), and the (usually) successive ordering of process IDs in the process queues.

Next, a new process proc entry is obtained to hold the core kernel state of the new process. Since this may block, the process ID is checked to ensure that another process has not reallocated the process ID. While this occurrence is almost impossible, if it does happen the **fork1()** operation is started from scratch again, as the conditions may have changed (e.g., more processes to count or someone else has "my" process ID).

... [File: /usr/src/kernel/kern/fork.c, line: 163]

```
        p2->p_stat = SIDL;
        p2->p_flag = SSYS;
        p2->p_pid = mypid;

        /* assemble minimal process state, from parent or from 0 */
        p1->p_cred->p_refcnt++;
        (void) memset(&p2->p_startzero, 0,
            (unsigned) ((caddr_t)&p2->p_endzero - (caddr_t)&p2->p_startzero));
        (void) memcpy(&p2->p_startcopy, &p1->p_startcopy,
            (unsigned) ((caddr_t)&p2->p_endcopy - (caddr_t)&p2->p_startcopy));

        /* process exists, make it visable to kernel to reserve PID */
        p2->p_nxt = allproc;
        p2->p_nxt->p_prev = &p2->p_nxt;        /* allproc is never NULL */
        p2->p_prev = &allproc;
        allproc = p2;
        nprocs++;
...
```

The process entry is minimally initialized with its identification (*p_pid*), ownership credentials,[13] and non-runable state (SIDL), and is placed on the active queue where it can be found.[14] Since the process is now visible to other portions of the kernel, its state must be set not to interact with the rest of the system (SSYS). The process is not yet assembled, so we mark it as "idle" as we fill it out to prevent it from being made runable by the scheduler.

The process ID inherits and shares its credentials from its parent, until any of the processes alter its credentials, at which point a private copy is generated. A reference count is kept to account for the degree of sharing of the process credentials, which, in turn, contain user credentials which are shared with other kernel subsystems (filesystems). Thus, there is a two-level hierarchy between process credentials that are sharable among processes of like capability (in, for example, a login session) and the user credentials that are sharable among low-level kernel objects (like disk buffers, pages, or packets) that may be holding data associated with a pending I/O transaction since a change in the generating process's capabilities.

Many of the fields in the process entry are initialized to zero, and these are grouped into a region so that they can be initialized with a single block clear instruction.

---

[13] **p_cred** containing the user ID. See **kern/cred.c** in **Chapter 7**.
[14] The process ID is allocated and reserved for use, since other concurrent fork operations can discover its presence.

Likewise, many of the other fields in the process entry are inherited from the parent process directly without alteration, and these are grouped into a region so that they can be copied with a single block move instruction.

... [File: /usr/src/kernel/kern/fork.c, line: 182]

```
        retval[0] = p1->p_pid;
        retval[1] = 1;
        if (cpu_tfork(p1, p2)) {
                /* record start time and begin child process context */
                p2->p_stats->p_start = time;
                return (0);
        }
...
```

Associated with every process is a single kernel thread of execution, which consists of a kernel stack and place to store kernel register state (*u_pcb*). In this implementation, for our convenience, it is stored at the bottom of the kernel stack. In this way both can be deactivated and unmapped or swapped to recover physical memory in one action. In addition, both a variable-sized portion of thread state (the kernel stack) and a fixed-size object (context switch state) can be co-located with a single pointer.

Kernel thread state is mandated to be at a unique kernel virtual address per thread, and is visible to all processors in a shared-memory multiprocessor. Thread scheduling relies on the fact that only one processor in a multiprocessor has access to a thread. Since during the generation of a new thread the old kernel stack is copied to a new kernel virtual address, any pointers to stack frame-resident objects will be stale in the new copy of the stack (they will point to within the "old" stack). The return value (*retval*) is kept in such a buffer. Instead of relocating the pointer manually, the return value is set in the parent process prior to child kernel stack generation.

... [File: /usr/src/kernel/kern/fork.c, line: 191]

```
        p1->p_pgrpnxt = p2;
        p2->p_pptr = p1;
        p2->p_osptr = p1->p_cptr;
        if (p1->p_cptr)
                p1->p_cptr->p_ysptr = p2;
        p1->p_cptr = p2;
...
```

With the process entry and kernel stack in place, the process is attached into the hierarchy of processes of which it is a part. It is joined to its parent and to the process group of its parent as well as to the list of siblings that its parent may already possess.

By this point the process is complete from the basic kernel perspective, since it has a name, can be context switched, has an owner, is linked into the process hierarchy, and can be terminated. But processes need to hold other state information implied by the POSIX semantics implemented in the higher layers of level of abstraction in the system. So, the next phase of process creation is to reconcile the additional state information needed by our POSIX-flavored processes, by adding the state semantics of file descriptors, address space, resource limits, statistics, exception handling, and system call tracing. While other system applications program interfaces will have these items as well, the exact semantics vary in detail.[15] Thus, this area must be revised to export non-POSIX characteristics with multiple operating system personality support.

... [File: /usr/src/kernel/kern/fork.c, line: 204]

```
        p2->p_fd = fdcopy(p1);
    ...
```

File descriptors need to be propagated to the new process. In this implementation, they are unconditionally copied instead of used as a shared object. The file descriptor mechanism is passed this responsibility.

... [File: /usr/src/kernel/kern/fork.c, line: 207]

```
        /* if (p1->p_limit->p_lflags & PL_SHAREMOD)
                p2->p_limit = limcopy(p1->p_limit);
        else { */
                /* otherwise, share same limits */
                p2->p_limit = p1->p_limit;
                p2->p_limit->p_refcnt++;

                /* if creating a shared thread, mark shared modification */
                /* if (uthread)
                        p2->p_limit->p_lflags |= PL_SHAREMOD;
        } */
    ...
```

Process resource limits are next copied by reference, as they will be shared in the common case until modified by the process. If user threads are implemented and a thread has requested a complete process fork, a unique copy is forced. This is done because threads share a common set of limits, even for modification, and a unique copy is necessary to detect further sharing by reference modification attempts.

.. [File: /usr/src/kernel/kern/fork.c, line: 220]

```
        MALLOC(ps, struct pstats *, sizeof(struct pstats), M_ZOMBIE, M_WAITOK);
        memset(&ps->pstat_startzero, 0, (unsigned)
                ((caddr_t) &ps->pstat_endzero - (caddr_t)&ps->pstat_startzero));
    ...
```

Process statistics are next replicated. Some of these fields are copied from the parent process, since they describe the current parameters of the replicated program that the child inherits, while others are zeroed (like running time) because the child has yet to consume the resource. The statistics buffer is a unique part of the process, as it will

---

[15] Process hierarchy and naming/ownership also fall into this category; however, this is more of a "gray zone" between underlying implementation and top level representation that can be dealt with in other ways, like object embedding.

preserve the run-time characteristics past the active life of the process. It and the process entry, process ID, and credentials will form the process corpse that will remain long after the process exits, persisting until a parent process reclaims the statistics with a **wait4()** system call.

... [File: /usr/src/kernel/kern/fork.c, line: 228]

```
    p2->p_vmspace = vmspace_fork(p1->p_vmspace, p2);
...
```

The user program virtual address space is next copied by reference by the virtual memory system. This is the sole mandatory interaction with the virtual memory system, since the allocation of space for the kernel thread could be done statically by the kernel. This clear separation between the virtual memory subsystem and the basic kernel is well-defined; the virtual memory system remains a kernel subsystem. However, how the address spaces are implemented is left to the virtual memory system, not the basic kernel.[16]

... [File: /usr/src/kernel/kern/fork.c, line: 232]

```
    if (p1->p_traceflag)
            ktrace_fork(p1, p2);
...
```

If kernel operation tracing is present for the parent process, it is determined here if the child should inherit it as well.

... [File: /usr/src/kernel/kern/fork.c, line: 237]

```
    p2->p_sigacts = &p2->p_addr->u_sigacts;
    *p2->p_sigacts = *p1->p_sigacts;
...
```

Process exception handling state is replicated from the parent. It is currently stored in the kernel stack, since in this implementation of 386BSD it is only referred to in the context of the process. As such, it can be deallocated when the process is no longer active.[17]

... [File: /usr/src/kernel/kern/fork.c, line: 241]

```
    p2->p_flag = SLOAD;
    if (p1->p_session->s_ttyvp != NULL && p1->p_flag & SCTTY)
            p2->p_flag |= SCTTY;
    if (isvfork)
            p2->p_flag |= SPPWAIT;
...
```

---

[16] Earlier versions of BSD were less portable because process creation and virtual address space construction were interwoven, forcing the machine-dependent parts of both to interact.

[17] This will not be the case when full POSIX signal processing is implemented, since that will require a variable-sized signal buffer that must be allocated at all times when a signal may occur.

Process flags are set to reflect the characteristics of the newly assembled process. Its process state is in core, ready for a context switch (SLOAD) if it is connected to a controlling terminal (as opposed to being run by or as a daemon, SCTTY). **vfork()**ed processes are marked to have the parent wait for the child before running (SPPWAIT).

... [File: /usr/src/kernel/kern/fork.c, line: 253]

```
        enterpidhash(p2);
    ...
```

The child process can be found by searching the active queue, or by its attachment to a parent or group. To make it findable by name, it is entered in the hash queue used by **pfind()**. This is held off until the process is about to run, making it impossible to send a signal or other name-related action at a sensitive time during construction.

... [File: /usr/src/kernel/kern/fork.c, line: 256]

```
        (void) splclock();
        p2->p_stat = SRUN;
        p2->p_rlink = 0;
        setrq(p2);
        (void) spl0();
    ...
```

The child process, now fully constructed and visible by all kernel subsystems, can leave the constructing state (SIDL) and run (SRUN) once it is added to the process run queue. Since the run queue is manipulated by clock interrupts to reprioritize, it is made exclusive by means of an interrupt mask. The child process will run as soon as the next block by this process, or by a reschedule trap instigated by a clock interrupt, causing a reschedule. Generally, the parent returns before the child runs. When the child begins to run, it will appear as if the **cpu_tfork()** function returned a true value (see the above).

... [File: /usr/src/kernel/kern/fork.c, line: 263]

```
        if (isvfork) {
                while (p2->p_flag & SPPWAIT)
                        (void) tsleep((caddr_t)p1, PWAIT, "ppwait", 0);
                /* put address space recovery from child here */
        }
    ...
```

If the child process was created with a **vfork()**, the parent will wait for the child process to exit before returning. This is currently done to simulate the semantics of **vfork()**, but if the operation was to implement the semantics fully, the parent process would reacquire its address space from the child at this point, since that is the original reason why it needed to wait.[18]

---

[18] E.g., it "loaned" its address space to the child to avoid copying the address space.

```
        retval[0] = p2->p_pid;
        retval[1] = 0;
        return (0);
    ...
```

At this point, the fork operation has succeeded and is complete, and the process ID of the child is returned to the parent, along with an additional return value to indicate that this is the parent process. The system call stub routine in the user program will notice the second return value to ensure that the first is passed back as the function's return value.

5.1.8 Improvements to the Process Creation Mechanism

Many enhancements to process creation are possible. The most obvious one is to implement **vfork()** address space passing to the child, as was done in "older" versions of the BSD virtual memory system to compensate for the fact that it did not have a way to implement copy-on-writes (as it lacked the data structures to implement the bookkeeping required).[19] By passing the address space to the child, the child could avoid the copy of a large address space and instead create a new one for the new process and pass back the old one to the parent.

With the later substitution of the old BSD virtual memory system with a virtual memory system which implemented the bookkeeping for copy-on-write, ordinary **fork()** operations were sped up dramatically. However, this change also increased the bookkeeping for address spaces in **vfork()**. While a **vfork()** mechanism is still cheaper than a copy-on-write **fork()**, the effect is much less dramatic, while the complexity of implementation has risen. It is now questionable whether this feature is worth the added cost in complexity. In fact, the benefits might be so small as not to be interesting on a minimalist system (as 386BSD represents).

A more mundane observation about this current implementation is that it does not handle the case of resource overload particularly well. The only return present is in a process limits case; if memory and/or processor time is overloaded, the parent process will discover this only by being uninterruptably blocked waiting for memory. Since the current use of this system does not make intensive demands on the number of processes, and since memory is not at a premium, this is not a priority problem. If it were, however, the function would have to be reimplemented to allow for failure to create a process due to not obtaining requisite state. This "improvement" would make the function a great deal more complicated, since it would have to "back out" of

---

[19] Another factor was that some of the most popular machines to run it on, like the VAX 750, had microcode bugs that prevented reliable restarting of certain faults. Ironically, the Intel 80286's fancy segmentation unit also had a similar botch for not-present segments, and this was later to doom it for use with certain operating systems like OS/2 V1.0.

partial process creation. The two main reasons that this has not been attempted yet is the lack of a generalized interruptable memory allocation scheme in the kernel (this is under development) and a method to distinguish temporary memory shortfall transients from indefinite resource blocks (a more subtle and far-reaching problem given I/O buffering demands). If these cases are not dealt with fully, the creation might not be aborted or might be spuriously aborted due to a memory shortfall lasting a fraction of a second.[20]

It is also possible to avoid the linear searches of the process lists by maintaining more information about associations of processes. For example, user credentials might have a reference count that directly corresponds to the number of processes on the system. This would require a much more complicated bookkeeping arrangement for credentials, since one would have to join and separate process sessions. User credentials would also have to be split between user and group fields to account for **setgid**[21] programs. It is unclear if this would provide much of a benefit, or just move the problem to a different part of the system.

Finally, another area for possible improvement is to finish the remaining modifications for support of shared substructures necessary for shared user threads. Shared access to file descriptors and statistics must be added as well.[22] Process limits and credentials should be used to see how this is currently done. It may be wise to centralize control of such sharing into a process entry field like *p_shareflags*, with a bit per structure denoting which element is shared for modification. Again, this may sound a lot like support for variable weight processes which don't appear to be desired at the moment.

5.2 Future Issues in Process Creation

One area to be considered here is the degree to which reference counts to a process are necessary. Currently, no reference count to the process entry itself is present, yet the entry is referenced in many ways, with **fork1()** and **exit()** left the responsibility for creating and deleting all of these references. One problem found with 386BSD Release 0.1 was that **select()** calls on other process objects (for example, network pseudo ttys) could hold references to processes that no longer existed.[23] This problem was a holdover from earlier BSD systems that implemented proc entries in an array. In the

---

[20] This might not be a catastrophic problem if a user program is written in a well-behaved way and retries the **fork()**—unfortunately, not all of them do so.

[21] See **Chaper 7** on **kern/cred.c** and **Chapter 9** on **kern/execve.c**.

[22] Statistics are debatable, as they are more a question of interpretation for user threads.

[23] I.e., a network login session shell would terminate before its server, **rlogind**, would terminate, leaving it **select()**ing on a nonexistent process.

current version of 386BSD, deallocated proc entries go back to the memory allocator and are reused for things other than process entries.[24]

The question, however, remains whether it is more costly in use to industriously reference count process entries, or to force external references through a lookup step (e.g. **pfind()**). This question has architecture-dependent ramifications, because a reference count dropping to zero implies the freeing of the process entry. This is a delicate operation which must be performed in context, and not necessarily where the reference count has dropped to zero logically. A middle case of letting stylized process references and an interlocking termination convention be present may be possible, allowing zombie persistence to terminate things like dead selects. However, performance measurement needs to be done to determine its value, as this "optimization" may actually make the kernel both larger and slower.

The kernel thread fork case is very interesting. This change would result in different return conventions—no system call return pointer (*retval*), but instead only a returning child/parent indication (or EAGAIN error). Nor would it copy any user state (vmspace, fd, stats), since it would just be another kernel thread.[25] The user thread fork case is also interesting in that user threads share everything, but are marked for unsharing when any thread does a POSIX **fork()**.[26] This change would also require modifications to **exit()**, as well as a user stub to allocate a separate stack to which to switch.[27] Finally, the statistics sharing/nonsharing problem will need to be resolved[28] along with debugging issues.

Other larger issues which are under consideration for future 386BSD releases include:

1. The concept of a remote process object and its replication is necessary for network cluster process formation. The remainder of the system has been structured for considering the process as an abstraction where operations may be performed either locally or remotely on it.

2. Shared memory multiprocessing also requires the introduction of mutual exclusion locks to surround the shared state during process creation and scheduling here. This is not yet a part of the main release.

3. Multiple operating systems personalities need to fit into the process creation scheme. The problem is just where do we draw the line—how much of the semantics should be embedded in the personality implementation (e.g. the way in which the

---

[24] By having **select()** use **pfind()** to determine if the process was still allocated, with selectors holding process IDs instead of process pointers.

[25] Either allocated by a related user process or by the kernel process, process 0.

[26] With threads, there are different semantics for subsequent fork operations—do you copy them all, or one to the new instance?

[27] Since thread packages all handle this differently.

[28] This has not yet been resolved in commercial thread implementations, so don't worry.

underlying implementation works, like inside a file descriptor), and how much should be present outside in the core kernel subsystem? This is a difficult but exciting architectural dilemma to explore.

4. Finally, what is the best overall architecture to achieve these conflicting needs? Should it be done by parallel low-level systems, one per need, or by a single one that has an attached set of object calls (like vnode operations and process operations) that implement these functions. If so, how do we negotiate operation between programs of different personalities working with a shared resource (file, memory, socket, stream)?

Many of these issues are quite deep and far reaching. They represent the groundwork of the next generation of systems. We hope to explore some of the more provocative ones in our future releases.

5.3 The Structure of Process Termination: kern/exit.c

Process termination is handled on three levels of abstraction:

1. the program interface,

2. the process state teardown, and

3. the machine-dependent thread termination.

The topmost layer is made up of system calls that provide a POSIX program interface to explicitly terminate the current process returning status, and receive the status of any terminating child processes in the parent. Below this layer lies the kernel's functional interface to the termination of a process, used by the kernel for both explicit and implicit process termination. This machine-independent code examines the process to see if any subsidiary structures are present[29] and whittles the process down to a *naked* kernel thread (kernel stack and register state). Not all processes have all of the fields implemented in a process.

If the process has statistics, it will leave a zombie process entry lying in the process structure, with minimal information allocated so that the status can be returned to another process after this one is terminated. To recover these statistics, a POSIX **wait4()** function is implemented as a system call handler, allowing a parent process to poll for the existence of a terminated child process.

The bottom-most layer of process termination is thread termination. Each process has minimally a single kernel thread as the basic concurrent object upon which all else is based. This thread of execution in the kernel is both created and destroyed in a machine-dependent manner[30] that can widely differ between machines.[31] This layer

---

[29] And reclaims them if they are present.
[30] See cpu_tfork() and cpu_texit(), respectively, in **Chapter 3** of i386/cpu.c.
[31] See **i386/cpu.c**.

SOURCE CODE SECRETS: THE BASIC KERNEL

only deals with the kernel program address space and the particular processor on which it is to execute. Since it must reschedule the processor, **cpu_exit()** is closely integrated with the context switch mechanism **swtch()**.

5.3.1 Antecedents to the POSIX exit() Interface

Earlier UNIX systems used a simplified version of this mechanism. Not present in these earlier versions were the elaborate options for **wait4()** actions (flags), and the ability to return process statistics. These appeared when job control was added to BSD.[32]

One considerable difference between UNIX and BSD systems in this area was that zombie processes[33] were actually allowed to run in original UNIX systems. The **wait()**ing parent would see the zombie child process, return status and mark its entry (in a linear array), and then continue the parent. At some time in the future, the zombie child would run, notice that the entry was now changed, and then exit allowing the process table *slot* to be reused. Thus, an indeterminate time would pass before the zombie was reclaimed. Particularly active systems or those with parents that did not wait for child processes would get clogged with a process table full of zombie processes and freeze. Finally, the extended wait (called **wait3()**) could not return usage state of stopped processes, because the child process's process statistics could not be referenced.[34] As a result, programs like the command shells could not obtain the statistics of running processes by stopping them.

In older versions of this code, a buffer was temporarily allocated to hold process usage statistics in the process corpse **wait()**ed for by the parent. In the last few versions of BSD, this "deathwatch" was held in all sorts of buffers (mbufs, proc table entry, ...), because the information held in the per-process or kernel stack was deallocated with process exit, so it no longer existed when **wait()** was called. In the current version of 386BSD, statistics are allocated off the kernel heap as a substructure. This is done as part of a transitional scheme to a more modern thread state arrangement, so that kernel memory demands will be decoupled from concurrent objects and the virtual memory system.

5.3.2 Functions Contained in the File kern/exit.c

The file **kern/exit.c** contains machine-independent code to implement the mechanism for terminating a process or thread. POSIX processes may be terminated explictly by a function call from the process being terminated itself, or implicitly, either as a result of a processor exception or of a signal sent by another process.

---

[32] See **kern/sig.c** in **Chapter 6**.
[33] Used only to pass a status word back.
[34] They were not in the kernel address space, and in some cases not in RAM memory.

Within this file are contained the following functions:

rexit()

exit()

wait4()

reclaimproc()

rexit() and **wait4()** correspond to the POSIX function interfaces that the system call handlers implement, while **exit()** is the internal kernel interface to the termination of a process. Finally, **reclaimproc()** is a local function to this module which does the final reclaimation of a process entry.

5.3.3 What is rexit()?

rexit() is a system call handler that implements the entire functionality of a POSIX **exit()** function. It is the way a process explicitly terminates itself.

... [File: /usr/src/kernel/kern/exit.c, line: 53]

```
int
rexit(p, uap, retval)
        struct proc *p;
                struct args {
                int      rval;
        } *uap;
        int *retval;
    ...
```

rexit() conforms to the calling conventions of a system call handler. The system call implemented has one argument that will be passed to the parent process upon termination, and it never returns.

5.3.3.1 How is rexit() Implemented?

rexit() relies entirely on the internal kernel interface **exit()** to terminate the process.

... [File: /usr/src/kernel/kern/exit.c, line: 59]

```
        exit(p, W_EXITCODE(uap->rval, 0));
    ...
```

W_EXITCODE() builds an exit status that has no terminal signal to distinguish it from implicit terminations. This is passed to **exit()** for it to incorporate in the soon-to-be terminated process corpse.

5.3.4 What is exit()?

exit() is the internal kernel interface to terminate a process. It is called by progam interfaces to perform explicit termination of a process (see **rexit()**) and via exception mechanisms in the kernel to perform implicit termination (see **Chapter 6**, **sigterm()** in **kern/sig.c**). **exit()** is a volatile function that never returns. It relieves the process of any resources it may have acquired, passes it the remaining kernel thread and continues on to the machine-dependent layer for final reclaimation.

... [File: /usr/src/kernel/kern/exit.c, line: 74]

```
void volatile
exit(struct proc *p, int rv)
    ...
```

The function is first called with a pointer to the process to be terminated and an integer return value to be returned as termination status to the process's parent.

5.3.4.1 How is exit() Implemented?

Exiting a process relies on a four-step procedure: isolation, stripping application interface state and kernel multiprogramming state, determination of process final resting state, and termination of the underlying kernel thread.

Somewhat like the death of HAL in "2001, A Space Odyssey", a process loses its capabilities incrementally until it ceases to exist. The "higher" level of abstraction functions are first lost, since the process may need to block during this procedure.[35] This, of course, makes perfect sense if one thinks about it, since the higher-level of abstraction services are built out of lower-level of abstraction services, so one would expect them to dissassemble in the reverse order as the dependencies are undone.

The lowest level function is the concurrent kernel thread on which this code is actively running, providing the multiprogramming capability inherent to the basic kernel. In dissassembling the running kernel thread, this multiprogramming capability is lost by the terminating process. Thus, it can no longer block as the kernel state that would need to be referenced to restart it no longer exists. In the final step it reaps its own running thread, completing its dissolution.

... [File: /usr/src/kernel/kern/exit.c, line: 90]

```
        p->p_flag &= ~STRC;
        p->p_flag |= SWEXIT | SSYS;

        /* cancel any pending signals, ignore all of them */
        p->p_sigignore = ~0;
        p->p_sig = 0;

        /* clear interval timer (if present) */
        untimeout(realitexpire, (caddr_t)p);
    ...
```

During this procedure, the process must be isolated from outside interference. Since the process may block during exit and control revert to other processes, the process is protected from external blocks or alterations. Debugging (STRC) is also disabled so that the exiting process cannot be stopped by a parent. Other kernel subsystems are

---

[35] N.B. They had better not block indefinitely.

conditioned by the SWEXIT flag to understand that the process is preparing to exit.[36] In addition, since the system is now in control of this process, no statistics gathering is allowed on the process (SSYS). All signals are blocked to prevent delivery of asynchronous events to the exiting process.[37] If an interval timer is present that might signal during **exit()** (or worse, after), it is cancelled.

... [File: /usr/src/kernel/kern/exit.c, line: 107]

```
    if (p->p_fd)
            fdfree(p);
...
```

With the process now isolated, we proceed to free and reclaim process state. Various fields are allocated off the process structure for use with the POSIX interface layer.[38] Any open files of the process will have caused a file descriptor structure to be allocated (p_fd). If present, they are freed by the file subsystem, which closes off the associated files and underlying vnodes. In some cases (such as devices), it may take an indefinite period of time to close a file, and a number of resource requests and releases may occur during the processing of this request.

... [File: /usr/src/kernel/kern/exit.c, line: 111]

```
    if (p->p_pgrp) {
            /* if a POSIX session leader process, abandon session. */
            if (p->p_session && SESS_LEADER(p))
                    exitsessleader(p);
            fixjobc(p, p->p_pgrp, 0);
    }
...
```

If it resides in a process group, we must check if there is a POSIX session associated with this process (p_session), and if we are the session leader, process the case of the session leader ending.[39] Next, the process group membership "reference count" is reduced in preparation for this process leaving the group (which it can only do when the process ID is released). This responsibility is spread across **exit()** and **wait4()**; otherwise the process group membership may fall to zero before the process corpse itself has been delivered to its **wait()**ing parent process.

... [File: /usr/src/kernel/kern/exit.c, line: 120]

```
    if (p->p_tracep)
            ktrace_exit(p);
...
```

---

[36] Key among these, swap scheduling and process priority shifting are suspended since the process resources will shortly be freed.

[37] For example, in the case of the 386, the SIGFPE signal from the NPX. (numeric processor extension, or floating point unit)

[38] And potentially other operating system interfaces.

[39] By informing other members and revoking the console access for all session members.

If the process has its kernel actions traced, we must terminate kernel tracing on this process. This may cause a kernel trace file to have its contents written and closed.

... [File: /usr/src/kernel/kern/exit.c, line: 129]

```
    if (p->p_vmspace)
            vmspace_free(p->p_vmspace);
...
```

If any user address space is associated with this process, the address space is released. Since portions of the address space are shared with other processes and the kernel, some of the virtual memory system's data structures[40] may block on gaining exclusive access or on waiting for I/O operations to complete on mapped pages. In any case, even though the only action is to free the address space, the operation may block.

Having performed all blockable operations in disassembling the process, we next move on to removing the parts of the process used to work multiprogramming in the kernel. From this point on, if the process blocks it can never be rescheduled to finish its termination, and it will just hang.

... [File: /usr/src/kernel/kern/exit.c, line: 143]

```
    curproc = NULL;
    leavepidhash(p);
    if (*p->p_prev = p->p_nxt)
            p->p_nxt->p_prev = p->p_prev;
...
```

The first operation here is to make the process invisible and unschedulable. By zeroing *curproc*, the process rescheduling mechanism is defeated.[41] *curproc* is used to identify the running process to trap and interrupt functions.[42] Next, the process is removed from the hash queue used to find it by *name*[43] and is removed from the main process queue into which it is linked.[44] At this point, the process can only be found by its siblings and parent, as no global mechanisms can reference it in the kernel.

... [File: /usr/src/kernel/kern/exit.c, line: 149]

```
    if (p->p_limit && —p->p_limit->p_refcnt == 0)
            FREE(p->p_limit, M_SUBPROC);
...
```

---

[40] For example, vm_objects. See **Chapter 5** in **386BSD From the Inside-Out**.
[41] See **hardclock()** in **kern/clock.c**.
[42] One key item to note here—the combination of *curproc* set to zero and SWEXIT as a flag is required, otherwise the scheduling mechanism cannot tell the difference between an idle process waiting for a current process that is on a run queue and an exiting process not on a queue.
[43] E.g., the process ID using **pfind()**.
[44] Via *allproc*, used by the kernel to walk the list of active processes.

With the process deactivated, the process resource limits substructure is examined for deallocation, since the limit structure is shared[45] among processes.[46]

... [File: /usr/src/kernel/kern/exit.c, line: 153]

```
        if (p->p_stat) {
                /* record exit status in zombie process */
                p->p_stats->p_status = rv;

                /* make process a zombie */
                if (p->p_nxt = zombproc)
                        p->p_nxt->p_prev = &p->p_nxt;
                p->p_prev = &zombproc;
                zombproc = p;
                p->p_stat = SZOMB;
                p->p_pptr->p_flag |= SZCHILD;
        }
    ...
```

If the process has a statistics buffer, it must be made a zombie process to hold the status until the parent notices. We save the status return value of the process termination, composed of either an abnormal termination code (implicit exit) or an application-supplied code (explicit exit). The child's usage statistics are passed to the parent, by linking it on the "zombproc" so that it will be visible as a process corpse (thus preventing reallocation of its process ID). The parent process is then marked as having at least one zombie child.

... [File: /usr/src/kernel/kern/exit.c, line: 167]

```
        if ((p->p_flag & SZCHILD) != 0 && p->p_cptr) {
                wakeup((caddr_t) initproc);
                p->p_flag &= ~SZCHILD;
        }
    ...
```

If this process itself has a zombie child, we must inform the *init* process that there are more unreclaimed zombie processes that it must reclaim.[47]

... [File: /usr/src/kernel/kern/exit.c, line: 173]

```
        for (q = p->p_cptr; q != NULL; q = nq) {
                nq = q->p_osptr;
                if (nq != NULL)
                        nq->p_ysptr = NULL;

                /* init inherits them as additional children */
                if (initproc->p_cptr)
                        initproc->p_cptr->p_ysptr = q;
                q->p_osptr = initproc->p_cptr;
                q->p_ysptr = NULL;
```

[45] With a manual "copy-on-write" mechanism.
[46] Frequently there is one limit structure allocated for a user's processes in a single login session.
[47] They were hiding behind the exiting process but not waited for by the exiting process.

```
                initproc->p_cptr = q;
                q->p_pptr = initproc;

                /* kill off any traced processes unconditionally */
                if (q->p_flag&STRC) {
                        q->p_flag &= ~STRC;
                        psignal(q, SIGKILL);
                }
        }
        p->p_cptr = NULL;
...
```

The list of all child processes is now walked through to locate ones about to be orphaned to pass them off to the *init* process for reclamation. The child process list is walked from youngest to oldest child processes on the sideways link between sibling processes. Any child processes will be successively "adopted" by the *init* process as new youngest child processes, with each child process now receiving *init* as its parent. If any of these child processes were in a debugged state, they are killed outright to avoid a stopped (possibly perpetual) condition.[48] In practice, this occurs only if a terminal's process group has been shot out from under a debugger running a process.

The final step is to fix up the details of the process's destiny. Either the process will be a POSIX process returning usage statistics to a parent in a zombie process corpse, or it is not a POSIX process that will be immediately reclaimed.

... [File: /usr/src/kernel/kern/exit.c, line: 201]

```
        if (p->p_stats) {
                p->p_flag &= ~SPPWAIT;
                psignal(p->p_pptr, SIGCHLD);
                wakeup((caddr_t)p->p_pptr);
        } else
                reclaimproc(p);
...
```

If statistics are present, the parent process is then signalled that the child process is terminated and is awakened if it is awaiting termination in **wait4()**.[49] Once the parent process is restarted, the parent process block is removed (SPPWAIT). This flag is used to implement a hidden implied **wait()** inside of **vfork()** to simulate the sequential order of its semantics. **vfork()** (see **kern/fork.c**) itself is not implemented, but since many programs expect it to be present it is simulated using **fork()** with an implicit block. This block is interposed because **vfork()** steals the address space of the parent for use in the child, then puts it back in the parent when the child finishes with it.[50]

---

[48] As an alternative, *init* could be taught to clean them up specially, but this provides no great advantage.

[49] N.B. Some processes only "reap" child processes with a **wait()** after receiving a signal (SIGCHLD), while others ignore the signal and always **wait()** immediately after child process creation.

[50] With either **exit()** or **execve()**.

During the time that the parent does not have an address space, it is blocked.[51] **vfork()** as implemented does not pass the address space around because the cost of the bookkeeping exceeds the benefits (see **kern/fork.c**). However, the semantics are preserved in user program to allow the interface to remain present for possible reintroduction.[52] For convenience, **vfork()** waits on the parent process address, like **wait()** does awaiting child termination.

If statistics are not required, the process is immediately reclaimed for use by **reclaimproc()**. This is the case with kernel-only threads and with other operating system interface concurrent objects.

... [File: /usr/src/kernel/kern/exit.c, line: 200]

```
        cpu_texit(p);
    ...
```

With nothing now left but the "naked" kernel thread, we end the **exit()** function by passing control to **cpu_texit()** to handle the machine-dependent thread termination, which will then pass control back to the process scheduler after delicately freeing the last remaining state.

5.3.4.2 Improvements to the Current Implementation of exit()

exit() is written independent of the need to run in the context of the process it is terminating.[53] The remainder of the kernel has yet to exploit this capability, however. One use of this generic capability of all system calls[54] is to be able to treat processes as objects that may be local (on this processor) or distant (on a different processor). To this end, system calls could be embedded in messages that are sent to the processor where the process is located. This concept of a *network process* can be used as the basis of loosely coupled multiprocessing, called *processor clustering*.

One should also note that with a uniform implementation of this capability, context switches themselves could be minimized, so that process debugging and signalling, among other functions, could be performed in the context of the sender/parent instead of requiring a mandatory context switch. It is debatable if this is cheaper than a context switch with local processes on the current hardware—however this may not always be the case, and this alternative should be kept in mind.

---

[51] Unlike **fork()**, where both are concurrent.
[52] N.B. In the first two versions of 386BSD, **vfork()** was fully implemented in an "older" virtual memory system.
[53] As is also the case with **cpu_texit()**.
[54] Process creation and termination are the essential ones for this to function.

Another improvement to this design would be to add back in support for **vfork()**. For example, in the case of **exit()**[55] the address space (p_vmspace) must be passed back to the parent:

```
if (p->p_vmspace) {
        if ((p->p_flag & SPPWAIT) != 0)
                vmspace_pass(p, p->p_pptr);
        else
                vmspace_free(p->p_vmspace);
}
```

5.3.5 What is wait4()?

wait4()is a system call handler that implements a superset of POSIX and BSD **waitXXX()** functions. The system's object library has various versions of **wait()** which can request a portion of the arguments present in the **wait4()** system call, to perform a specific function. **wait4()** will scan for stopped or terminated processes on which to return information, or possibly wait for termination of a child process. Among the information that can be returned is the process ID, status, and resource usage statistics.

... [File: /usr/src/kernel/kern/exit.c, line: 218]

```
int
wait4(q, uap, retval)
        struct proc *q;
        struct args {
                int     pid;
                int     *status;
                int     options;
                struct  rusage *rusage;
        } *uap;
        int retval[];
...
```

wait4(), as its name implies, uses four arguments for the system call it handles. It returns the process ID as a return value, and optionally two other records of information pointed at by the arguments.

5.3.5.1 How is wait4() Implemented?

wait4() is very intimate with the way **exit()** builds a zombie process for **wait4()** to find, and the way that the signal facility and **ptrace()** create stopped processes.

... [File: /usr/src/kernel/kern/exit.c, line: 234]

```
        if (pid == 0)
                pid = -q->p_pgid;
...
```

If a zero process is requested, this is interpreted as a match of any process in the current process's process group. Since process IDs are small, positive IDs and negative IDs can be used to signify process group IDs.

---

[55] During parent process block.

... [File: /usr/src/kernel/kern/exit.c, line: 234]

```
if (uap->options &~ (WUNTRACED|WNOHANG))
        return (EINVAL);
...
```

We must then check the options flag to see if any option is implemented (otherwise it returns an EINVAL error). In this implementation, only two options are present: WUNTRACED (see any "non-traced" processes as well as traced ones), and WNOHANG (don't wait for a child process to terminate or stop).

... [File: /usr/src/kernel/kern/exit.c, line: 242]

```
loop:
        nfound = 0;
        for (p = q->p_cptr; p; p = p->p_osptr) {
...
```

The child process list for this process is walked, youngest to oldest, to find a process that matches the sought-for pattern. If child processes are present but not stopped or terminated, and options are allowed, **wait4()**will sleep, waiting for a process to terminate so that it may loop and recheck the process list.

... [File: /usr/src/kernel/kern/exit.c, line: 247]

```
if (pid != WAIT_ANY && p->p_pid != pid && p->p_pgid != -pid)
        continue;
...
```

Child processes are matched against three patterns: any child process, a specific child process ID, or any child process in the process group that the current process resides within.

... [File: /usr/src/kernel/kern/exit.c, line: 251]

```
if (p->p_stat == SZOMB) {
        retval[0] = p->p_pid;
...
```

If the matching child process is a zombie, its process ID is returned.

... [File: /usr/src/kernel/kern/exit.c, line: 255]

```
ru = p->p_stats->p_ru;
ru.ru_stime = p->p_stime;
ru.ru_utime = p->p_utime;
ruadd(&ru, &p->p_stats->p_cru);
...
```

The child's usage statistics are then copied to a temporary buffer, and user/system times[56] are updated. These statistics are summed with the accumulated statistics of all

---

[56] For the child process stopped when *curproc* was cleared in **exit()**.

prior descendant processes run (p_cru) to obtain a single total to return (calculating the cost in resources of this process).

... [File: /usr/src/kernel/kern/exit.c, line: 261]

```
            if (uap->status && (error = copyout(q,
                (caddr_t)&p->p_stats->p_status,
                (caddr_t) uap->status, sizeof(status)))))
                    return (error);

            /* if resource usage vector, return it */
            if (uap->rusage && (error = copyout(q, (caddr_t)&ru,
                (caddr_t)uap->rusage, sizeof (struct rusage)))))
                    return (error);
    ...
```

If status or process usage statistics are requested, they are recovered from the process corpse and returned. Note that if an error occurs on returning either of these, the zombie remains unchanged on the list of child processes.

... [File: /usr/src/kernel/kern/exit.c, line: 272]

```
            ruadd(&q->p_stats->p_cru, &ru);
            FREE(p->p_stats, M_ZOMBIE);
    ...
```

Having succeeded in returning usage information (if requested), the total process usage statistics are incorporated in the parent process's accumulated child process field (p_cru).

... [File: /usr/src/kernel/kern/exit.c, line: 276]

```
            if (*p->p_prev = p->p_nxt)
                    p->p_nxt->p_prev = p->p_prev;
            reclaimproc(p);
            return (0);
    ...
```

With the statistics and status extracted, the process can now be removed from the zombie queue (zombproc) and reclaimed, returning to the user program.

... [File: /usr/src/kernel/kern/exit.c, line: 283]

```
            if (p->p_stat == SSTOP && (p->p_flag & SWTED) == 0 &&
                (p->p_flag & STRC || uap->options & WUNTRACED)) {
    ...
```

However, if the child process has been stopped and not yet seen by wait, it can be sampled by **wait4()** if the process is **ptrace()**ed (STRC) or if the WUNTRACED flag is set to see all stopped processes. This second case allows job control to learn of newly stopped process.[57]

---

[57] The command shell *csh* uses this to notify the user of a stopped process.

... [File: /usr/src/kernel/kern/exit.c, line: 287]

```
                p->p_stats-p_status =
                        W_STOPCODE(p->p_sigacts->ps_stopsig);
    ...
```

For the status, a special stop code containing a pending signal to the stopped process is returned from the signal structure.[58]

... [File: /usr/src/kernel/kern/exit.c, line: 291]

```
            if (uap->status && (error = copyout(q,
                (caddr_t)&p->p_stats->p_status,
                (caddr_t)uap->status, sizeof(status))))
                    return (error);
    ...
```

As in the terminated process case discussed above, if the status and/or the process usage is requested, they will be extracted from the process and returned to the user if the address is valid in the user process. In this case, however, the process is not a dead body holding status, but a live process temporarily stopped.

... [File: /usr/src/kernel/kern/exit.c, line: 297]

```
            if (uap->rusage) {
                    ru = p->p_stats->p_ru;
                    ru.ru_stime = p->p_stime;
                    ru.ru_utime = p->p_utime;
                    ruadd(&ru, &p->p_stats->p_cru);
                    if (error = copyout(q, (caddr_t)&ru,
                        (caddr_t)uap->rusage,
                        sizeof (struct rusage)))
                            return (error);

            }
    ...
```

For process usage statistics, the accumulated children statistics of the child are summed against the current statistics and returned. As the process successively executes and stops, the statistics will grow.

... [File: /usr/src/kernel/kern/exit.c, line: 310]

```
            p->p_flag |= SWTED;
            retval[0] = p->p_pid;
            return (0);
        }
    ...
```

The process ID of the stopped child will then be returned and marked with a waited for flag so that it will not be redundantly found. If the same process is restarted and stopped again, this flag will be cleared and the process polled by **wait()** yet again. The system call can then return successfully with its catch.

---

[58] See **stop()** in **kern/sig.c, Chapter 6**.

... [File: /usr/src/kernel/kern/exit.c, line: 314]

```
                nfound++;
        }

        /* wait with no children to wait for */
        if (nfound == 0)
                return (ECHILD);
...
```

If the child process is neither stopped or terminated, it must be counted. These processes are in a running or soon to be running state that may terminate or stop. If none of them exist, an error (ECHILD) is returned because there are no child processes to be **wait()**ed for.

... [File: /usr/src/kernel/kern/exit.c, line: 322]

```
        if (uap->options & WNOHANG) {
                retval[0] = 0;
                return (0);
        }

        /* wait for a child process to exit, signal or wakeup this parent */
        if (error = tsleep((caddr_t)q, PWAIT | PCATCH, "wait", 0))
                return (error);
        goto loop;
...
```

Otherwise, if there are child processes that may eventually terminate or stop, the current process will sleep waiting for the child. Before sleeping, the WNOHANG option is checked to avoid blocking by returning no process ID (0). If the sleep occurs, it is interruptable so that the current process can see the delivered signal as it returns from the **wait4()** system call handler. Note that the signal may be conditioned with a signal action option to not interrupt the system call. In that case it will actually restart the scan of child processes and is indistinguishable from the process being awakened on a child terminating or stopping.

5.3.6 What is reclaimproc()?

reclaimproc() is a function private to this module that reaps a process and allows the process ID to be recycled.

... [File: /usr/src/kernel/kern/exit.c, line: 334]

```
static void
reclaimproc(struct proc *p)
...
```

reclaimproc() is called with one argument of the process to be deallocated. It returns nothing.

5.3.6.1 How is reclaimproc() Implemented?

The last remaining references to the proc entry are removed and the entry is freed.

... [File: /usr/src/kernel/kern/exit.c, line: 340]

```
    if (-p->p_cred->p_refcnt == 0) {
            crfree(p->p_cred->pc_ucred);
            FREE(p->p_cred, M_SUBPROC);
    }
...
```

First, the process credentials see cred.c, **Chapter 7** (a shared, manually "copy-on-write" structure) are dereferenced and possibly deallocated. They are left on the process until the last minute to control access to other kernel systems and this process. In addition, the process must be identified by its owner up to the end for utilities like **ps** to work.

... [File: /usr/src/kernel/kern/exit.c, line: 346]

```
    leavepgrp(p);

    /* unlink process from its related queues */
    if (q = p->p_ysptr)
            q->p_osptr = p->p_osptr;
    if (q = p->p_osptr)
            q->p_ysptr = p->p_ysptr;
    if ((q = p->p_pptr)->p_cptr == p)
            q->p_cptr = p->p_osptr;
...
```

The process is then detached from the process group and its related sibling processes. The sibling list is a doubly-linked list that must be maintained by editing out the entry being reclaimed. If there is a younger process, any older siblings are also linked as the younger process's new older siblings. Likewise, any older siblings receive the younger process as their new younger sibling. The p_cptr points to the youngest sibling process in the list; if this is the process being deleted, then the next oldest sibling is selected as the youngest sibling.

... [File: /usr/src/kernel/kern/exit.c, line: 357]

```
    FREE(p, M_PROC);
    nprocs-;
...
```

Finally, the process instance is freed, and the number of active processes reduced.

Exercises

5.1 **a)** Why is the virtual memory system separate from the basic kernel?
b) How does this separation of function impact process creation and destruction?

5.2 Why don't we put "multiprogramming" in a separate module external to the kernel as well?

5.3 What element of a process persist longest prior to the entire process being reclaimed, and why does it persist so long?

5.4 What is the first element of a new process that is created and why?

5.5 Why are kernel threads "self-reclaiming"?

6 PROCESS EXCEPTIONS VIA SIGNALS (kern/sig.c)

The file **kern/sig.c** contains the machine-independent code to implement the POSIX signal mechanism for passing software interrupts to processes. The signal events can be generated by either processor exceptions, kernel subsystems, or other processes. The signal mechanism accepts events from any level of abstraction in the kernel and passes them to their associated process or thread. These events can be either synchronous or asynchronous to the process.

The receiving process accepts the signal in the form of a software interrupt. The POSIX signal mechanism is in effect a simulation of the hardware interrupt, complete down to its ability to postpone an event until past a critical section of code which could be compromised by a untimely event arriving. Thus, this machine-independent event notification mechanism allows for elaborate control of events in a open industry standard way.[1]

An effect on the receiving process of this software interrupt is called an *action*. An action can have many different effects, ranging from causing a user signal handler function to execute, to being blocked and left pending while another signal is in process, ignored entirely, or forcing the abnormal termination of the process.

6.1 POSIX Definition of Signals

Modern UNIX systems all implement the POSIX specification of this standard event interface. The original UNIX system used a much simplified version of this interface primarily for exception handling (via the **signal()** function interface). Both 2BSD and 4BSD systems added a more elaborate and robust version of this (via the **sigvec()** interface). In the POSIX standard, the semantics of this interface are defined to include all of the capabilities of BSD and AT&T signals mechanism for a generalized number of signals in yet another version (via the **sigaction()** interface). The 386BSD kernel contains an implementation for a significant portion of this mechanism, with the remainder of the implementation present in the system's user program libraries.

---

[1] See **i386/locore.s** in **Chapter 2** for a complete discussion of the machine-dependent hardware interrupt mechanism.

All of this mechanism could have been implemented in the kernel. However, the design choice of splitting it between user and kernel is justified by convenience, backward compatibility with older Berkeley systems, and performance.

6.1.1 Signal Structure Layers of Abstraction

Signals are implemented in three layers of abstraction:

1. the program interface,

2. the event generation mechanism, and

3. the signal mechanism.

The topmost layer is made up of system calls that provide a program interface to manipulate a process's signal semantics and gain guarded access to signal event generation. Below this layer lies the kernel signal generation mechanism. This can be used by any portion of the kernel to generate a signal event to a process or processes. At the bottom layer is the signal mechanism itself, where signals are discovered for a process and their actions effected on a process.

6.1.2 Signal Number

The POSIX specification allows for more than the 32 signals present in most UNIX implementations; yet, as with most implementations, this version only implements the 32 signals mentioned. The standard is a little vague in places beyond this basic group, so it should be taken with a grain of salt stretching it beyond the 32 contained in *sigset_t*. Signals are denoted as integer indexes starting from one.[2] In this implementation, 31 of the 32 possible signal numbers are implemented.

6.1.3 Signal Actions

The signal interface associates an *action* with each signal. If a signal is sent to the process, the action will occur in the process. An action can occur inside a process address space if unmasked[3] or it can affect the process externally.[4] It can also do absolutely nothing (the signal is ignored). Certain signals have specific default actions present in program entry or by selection.

---

[2] Older UNIX implementations had the amusing characteristic that signal zero would reschedule a process at improved priority, so that it was possible to signal a process to provide preferential service.

[3] E.g., a signal will be caught by a user program signal handler.

[4] E.g., terminate or suspend a process, or mark it for later delivery to the process when it becomes unblocked.

6.1.4 Maskable Signals

Signals may be masked to postpone their effect until they are unmasked. Like hardware interrupts, a POSIX implementation may not wish to receive signals during a critical section of code. For example, a command shell may wish to block signals when spawning a new command, postponing signal delivery until after a new process has been launched.

Masking a signal does not alter its delivery semantics; it just postpones them. Earlier signal interface mechanisms achieve the same effect by altering the state of the signal handler (by reloading the action on interrupt). Unfortunately this meant that a set of signals could not atomically be blocked in a single system call. This made the interface fragile and expensive to use for anything other than as an exception handling mechanism.

6.1.5 Unmaskable and Uncatchable Signals

Some signals are not maskable or catchable. They exist as signals to allow control of the process itself—so it would defeat the effect if they were maskable or catchable. Among them, SIGKILL unconditionally terminates a process, SIGSTOP unconditionally stops a process (preventing it from becoming runable), and SIGCONT unconditionally restarts a stopped process.

6.1.6 Pending Signals

A signal that has been sent but masked is recorded as *pending*. Pending signals await delivery by the process unmasking the signal. Processes can explicitly discover them by use of the *sigpending* request, or implicitly discover them by signal action effect (e.g., the user program handler entry or user process termination).

6.1.7 Stopped/Traced Processes

Processes are independent entities that can be debugged by transparently suspending the process in a STOP state and compelling it to accept as a slave commands from a master process holding a debugger. The **ptrace()** process tracing facility (see **kern/ptrace.c**) allows a debugger to control a child process in this manner, so that the debugger can alter the characteristics of the process (start, stop, modify, set breakpoints, ...) without the direct involvement of the child process.[5]

Stopped processes in the original UNIX system had the sole purpose of supporting debugging; in BSD versions this was extended to allow multiplexing of many processes from a command processor by "job control", which could suspend or restart

---

[5] E.g., it does not need to be compiled with the debugger itself embedded within, as systems prior to UNIX sometimes required.

processes running from the command processor. Both job control and **ptrace()** interact heavily with signals, which mediate control among related processes in a process group.

6.1.8 Process Pausing Awaiting a Signal

A process can suspend itself waiting for a signal to occur, relinquishing the processor explicitly and allowing only a specific set signal to signal it. When the signal occurs, the process is reactivated and its previous set signal allowed to signal the process. By atomically controlling the mask set during this interaction, potential signal delivery race conditions can be eliminated in the signal interface.

6.1.9 Signals and vfork()ed Processes

This portion of code treats processes created by **vfork()** differently in many respects as a consequence of implementation.[6] Since a **vfork()**ed process passes its context to the child process for the extent of its execution, care must be taken to prevent either deadlock or corruption of the shared context.

6.2 Antecedents to the POSIX Signal Interface

Early UNIX systems used a simplified version of this same mechanism. Not present were the elaborate options for signal actions (flags), signal masks, suspendable processes and the like. Signals were used principally as exception handlers in user program. However, due to the lack of a general purpose mechanism to allow asynchronous I/O between processes, signals began to be used as a "dataless" message between processes, usually to indicate that data was now available at a known place.

Since this mechanism only had a single program interface either to set or return the value of a signal action, it was not reliable in all cases—the signal event might be missed if the receiving process was either already receiving a different signal event, or if the event came as the receiving process was altering its signal action.

Early BSD systems implemented a more elaborate signal mechanism that made up for many of these shortcomings. This mechanism was in essence "imported" from Jim Kulp's *job control* terminal process multiplexing feature implemented at IIASA in Vienna, Austria. Limited terminal asynchronous I/O capabilities were also added at that time, creating a terminal interface not unlike the older Tenex/TOPS-20 systems.

This mechanism was later extended and refined for network sockets, making a reliable signal interface for use with a general purpose interprocess communications facility in 4.2BSD. 4.3BSD addressed reverse compatibility with the previous unreliable interface

---

[6] N.B. 386BSD does not yet implement **vfork()**, so this is inconsequential as of yet.

that had been mandated as an de facto industry standard of the time, while NET/2 brought about the culmination of this signal implementation by adopting the POSIX definition for the interface.

One can think of the PL/1 "on condition" mechanism as the predecessor to the UNIX signal mechanism, although almost all minicomputer operating systems had exception (usually arthemetic) call-back functions as well.

6.3 kern/sig.c Functions and File Organization

Within the file **kern/sig.c** are contained the following functions:

cansignal()

sigaction()

sigprocmask()

sigpending()

sigsuspend()

sigstack()

kill()

killpg()

sigreturn()

nosys()

psignal()

issig()

psig()

coredump()

trapsignal()

siginit()

execsigs()

pgsignal()

sigexit()

stop()

Some of these names correspond to the POSIX function interfaces of which the system calls in part or fully implement. Others are well-known inside the kernel for implementing the signal mechanism or accepting and/or controlling events.

These functions are organized into five functional sections: internal inlines, system call handlers, kernel POSIX signal mechanism, internal kernel interfaces to the signal mechanism, and private functions used in this signal implementation. The first function, **cansignal()**, is an internal inline function used to evaluate the permission of one process to send a signal to another process. It is the only internal inline used in this file.

There are eight system call handlers used in this file. **sigaction()** implements the system call handler used to program the POSIX signals action of the calling process and install a signal action into a process. **sigprocmask()** implements the system call handler that allows access to the process's signal mask. **sigsuspend()** implements the system call handler that suspends a process until a signal occurs. **sigstack()** implements the system call handler which provides an interface to a BSD extended signal feature of taking signals on a separate stack. **kill()** is a system call handler used to allow programs to generate signals to other processes, while **killpg()** is an internal function used by **kill()** that implements a broadcast to groups of processes, or potentially to all processes. **sigreturn()** is a hidden system call interface to a machine-dependent function to recover the signal handler from the end of a user program. Finally, **nosys()** is a dummy system call used as a placeholder for unimplemented system calls that force an error if called.

psignal() is the principle kernel interface to generate a signal event to a process. It implements the external aspects of the signal to a process. **issig()** and **psig()** implement the internal aspects of the signal to a process. **coredump()** is a kernel interface function that saves an abnormal terminating process's image into a file. **trapsignal()** is a kernel interface function that handles process exception traps that must be directly dispatched to the program without delay. **siginit()** initializes the very first process with an appropriate signal state for all others to inherit. **execsigs()** adjusts signal state to be appropriate at the start of a new program execution within a process. **pgsignal()** provides a shorthand way of signalling process groups.

And finally, there are two private functions used in this signal implementation. **sigexit()** forces a process to terminate as a result of a signal action, while **stop()** forces a process into a stopped state to freeze it out when suspended by job control.

6.3.1 What is cansignal()?

cansignal() is a private inline function used only by the POSIX signal mechanism implemented in this file. Its purpose is to determine if a process has the permission to send a specific signal to another process. **cansignal()** must evaluate a process's credentials to determine if the signal can be sent. The comparison is almost symmetrical, and involves the process credentials of both processes.[7]

... [File: /usr/src/kernel/kern/sig.c, line: 68]

```
extern inline
int cansignal(struct proc *p, struct proc *q, int signo)
...
```

---

[7] See **kern/cred.c** in **Chapter 7** for more detailed information.

---

cansignal() has three arguments: the pointer of the process sending the signal (*p*); the pointer of the process receiving the signal (*q*); and the signal being sent. It returns true if the signal is permitted to be sent, and false otherwise.

6.3.1.1 How is cansignal() Implemented?

... [File: /usr/src/kernel/kern/sig.c, line: 73]

```
        if (pc->pc_ucred->cr_uid == 0 ||
            pc->p_ruid == qc->p_ruid ||
            pc->pc_ucred->cr_uid == qc->p_ruid ||
            pc->p_ruid == q->p_ucred->cr_uid ||
            pc->pc_ucred->cr_uid == q->p_ucred->cr_uid ||
            (signo == SIGCONT && q->p_session == p->p_session))
                return 1;
        else
                return 0;
    ...
```

A signal can always be sent by a user with the proper privilege (normally the root user ID: uid == 0) or if the processes have the same real user ID. Otherwise, if the effective user ID of the processes agree or intersect with the real user ID, then the signal is allowed. If none of these are successful, the signal is disallowed.

If the signal is a process continuation and it is being sent within the same session,[8] it is allowed to go through since we always allow a stopped process to be restarted within a session regardless of credentials. If this were not the case, someone within a root user ID shell, for example, could end up suspending the shell and never be able to restart it (a common occurrence).

6.3.1.2 Improvements to the Current Implementation of cansignal()

cansignal() does not really belong to this routine, since it is in effect a check of process credentials and privilege (an embedded **use_priv()**) that belongs to the POSIX process protection mechanism.[9] Since the scope of use of this function is currently limited to this module, its inline implementation is most convenient for minimizing signal overhead.

As an improvement, it might be preferable to reimplement this as two separate inlines in the process or process credentials header file that compare ownership of processes and check for the privilege of signalling another process regardless of ownership, with the signal comparison occurring only in the inline, thus:

```
extern inline int
cansignal(struct proc *p1, struct proc *p2) {

        if (usepriv(p1->p_ucred, PRIV_SIGNAL, p1) || compare_cred(p1, p2) ||
            (signo == SIGCONT && q->p_session == p->p_session))
                return (1);
```

---

[8] A session is a group of processes corresponding effectively to a user's login—see *The POSIX Process ID, Group ID, and Session* in **Chapter 5** and **kern/proc.c** for more information.
[9] See **kern/priv.c** in **Chapter 7** for more information.

```
        else
                return (0);
}
```

6.3.2 What is sigaction()?

sigaction() is a system call interface that implements the POSIX specification for signal handling. It allows the user program to retrieve the signal action state held by the kernel about the desired signal and/or stores new signal action state about the same signal. **sigaction()** has the regular requirements of a POSIX system call in terms of calling arguments and return values. The arguments include a reference to a POSIX set of arguments that a POSIX **sigaction()** function receives.

... [File: /usr/src/kernel/kern/sig.c, line: 89]

```
int
sigaction(p, uap, retval)
        struct proc *p;
        struct args {
                int signo;
                struct sigaction *nsa;
                struct sigaction *osa;
        } *uap;
        int *retval;
    ...
```

The function is called with the POSIX system call internal handler convention of pointer to the process/thread generating the call, a pointer to the encapsulated arguments of the POSIX function implemented, and a pointer to the POSIX function's return value. Any error in the handler's processing of the system call will be passed back as the return value of this function.

The POSIX **sigaction()** call passes three arguments: signal number or index; the pointer to receive the old state of the signal; and the pointer to supply the new signal state to the system. Either signal state pointer is optional, as a null valued pointer will be disregarded without error. Errors in processing the system call can occur if the information supplied is inconsistent or out of bounds.

6.3.2.1 How is sigaction() Implemented?

This implementation uses a fixed number of signals, currently limited by the number of bits in an integer (32), although the POSIX functional description allows for a potentially arbitrary number.

... [File: /usr/src/kernel/kern/sig.c, line: 105]

```
        if (sig <= 0 || sig >= NSIG)
                return (EINVAL);
        bit = sigmask(sig);
    ...
```

First, the signal number index (sig) is checked to see if it references a valid signal. The index must be in the bounds of the implemented signal set (1 through 31), otherwise an EINVAL error is returned immediately.

... [File: /usr/src/kernel/kern/sig.c, line: 110]

```
if (uap->osa) {
        sa->sa_handler = ps->ps_sigact[sig];
        sa->sa_mask = ps->ps_catchmask[sig];

        /* assemble flags */
        sa->sa_flags = 0;
        if ((ps->ps_sigonstack & bit) != 0)
                sa->sa_flags |= SA_ONSTACK;
        if ((ps->ps_sigintr & bit) == 0)
                sa->sa_flags |= SA_RESTART;
        if (p->p_flag & SNOCLDSTOP)
                sa->sa_flags |= SA_NOCLDSTOP;

        if (copyout(p, (caddr_t)sa, (caddr_t)uap->osa, sizeof (vec)))
                return (EFAULT);
}
...
```

Next, the "old" signal action pointer (osa) is checked to see if it is not null, and thus able to receive the old signal information before it may be reloaded from the "new" signal action pointer (if present). The signal action state visible to the user program is assembled into a temporary POSIX signal action structure buffer (*vec*, referenced by *sa*) from the portions spread over the process's structure, which is arranged differently to speed signal implementation.[10] The temporary buffer is then passed back to the requesting process via **copyout**[11] which may not be successful and thus force the system call to terminate prematurely with an EFAULT error.

... [File: /usr/src/kernel/kern/sig.c, line: 128]

```
if (uap->nsa) {
        sig_t act;

        /* valid signal number? */
        if (bit & sigcantmask)
                return (EINVAL);

        /* can we obtain the action from the process? */
        if (copyin(p, (caddr_t)uap->nsa, (caddr_t)sa, sizeof (vec)))
                return (EFAULT);
...
```

After potentially saving the "old" signal action, the "new" signal action pointer (*nsa*) is checked to see if it is not null, and thus can provide a new signal action state. The

---

[10] Signal action option flags are implemented as word bit vectors in the process.
[11] In the case of the 386, **copyout** is performed in **i386/locore.s**.

---

signal index is checked to find if it is allowed to have an action set by a user process; otherwise, the system call is prematurely terminated with an EINVAL error.

The signal action state is imported from the user process by means of **copyin()** to supply to a temporary POSIX signal action structure buffer (again *vec*, referenced by *sa*).

... [File: /usr/src/kernel/kern/sig.c, line: 140]

```
                    act = sa->sa_handler;
                    if (act != SIG_DFL && act != SIG_IGN && act != BADSIG
                        && vmspace_access(p->p_vmspace, (caddr_t)act, sizeof(int),
PROT_READ) == 0)
                            return (EFAULT);
    ...
```

This portion of code is the converse of the previous section, as it will disassemble the POSIX state into the internal signal implementation arrangement. Before attempting this, the temporary buffer is examined for validity before being accepted by the kernel as a valid signal action. Actions without POSIX semantics (e.g., not valid user process addresses or "special" meaning) cause premature termination of the system call with an error (EFAULT).

... [File: /usr/src/kernel/kern/sig.c, line: 146]

```
                    (void) splhigh();
                    ps->ps_sigact[sig] = act;
                    ps->ps_catchmask[sig] = sa->sa_mask &~ sigcantmask;

                    /* decode signal action flag into processes signal state */
                    if ((sa->sa_flags & SA_RESTART) == 0)
                            ps->ps_sigintr |= bit;
                    else
                            ps->ps_sigintr &= ~bit;
                    if (sa->sa_flags & SA_ONSTACK)
                            ps->ps_sigonstack |= bit;
                    else
                            ps->ps_sigonstack &= ~bit;
    ...
```

Having ensured that the signal can be accepted into the kernel signal implementation, the temporary buffer is disassembled into the process signal implementation data structures. This is done in such a way to avoid race conditions with interrupt-driven functions that may wish to send a signal at the exact moment we alter the status of the signal, by holding off all interrupts.

... [File: /usr/src/kernel/kern/sig.c, line: 161]

```
                    if (sig == SIGCHLD) {
                            if (sa->sa_flags & SA_NOCLDSTOP)
                                    p->p_flag |= SNOCLDSTOP;
                            else
```

```
                                  p->p_flag &= ~SNOCLDSTOP;
              }
   ...
```

The SIGCHLD signal has its own private option flag (SA_NOCLDSTOP), which
selectively allows BSD verses System V semantics on handling the action of this signal.
With BSD semantics, the parent process receives a SIGCHLD when the child process is
stopped for any reason (see **stop()**, pg. 319), while with System V semantics, the parent
will be signaled if stopped due to the child being traced. (see **issig()**, pg. 302

... [File: /usr/src/kernel/kern/sig.c, line: 169]

```
            if (act == SIG_IGN ||
                (sigprop[sig] & SA_IGNORE && act == SIG_DFL)) {
                    p->p_sig &= ~bit;

                    /* don't ignore SIGCONT, allow psignal to un-stop it */
                    if (sig != SIGCONT)
                            p->p_sigignore |= bit;
                    p->p_sigcatch &= ~bit;
            } else {
                    p->p_sigignore &= ~bit;
                    if (act == SIG_DFL)
                            p->p_sigcatch &= ~bit;
                    else
                            p->p_sigcatch |= bit;
            }
            (void) splnone();
      }

      return (0);
   ...
```

Another optimization of signal handling is achieved by the encoding of ignored and
non-default signals as word bit vectors (*p_sigignore* and *p_sigcatch*). If the signal is to be
ignored, either explicitly by action or implicitly by default, a bit is set in *p_sigignore* to
bypass evaluation of the signal action if the signal is sent. Any outstanding signal is
cleared, as it will never be seen.

An exception is made in the case of SIGCONT.[12] While its semantics to the process are
ignored, it still must ensure that the process left the suspended state to have its net
result occur. While this could be done by a separate mechanism, the current
implementation subsumes this as part of the special intertwined semantics of stopped
and sleeping processes. Thus SIGCONT is a signal that is never delivered, but just
forces a process out of the STOP state.[13]

p_sigcatch records if the process requires delivery of the signal to a user process
handler. If the action is default, its effect will be limited to the kernel's processing of

---

[12] A "job control" signal used to restart a stopped process.
[13] That was entered by another signal, like SIGTSTP.

---

the signal.[14] Thus, the high-speed path of passing the signal to the process directly can be chosen by the signal implementation directly.[15] After the state changes caused by this new signal state addition have occurred, the lockout of asynchronous interrupts is removed, new signal state addition concludes, and the system call finishes successfully.

Improvements to the Current Implementation of sigaction()

The current signal implementation is highly optimized to the current 32-signal implementation. However, the POSIX standard actually allows for an arbitrary number of signals. Should in the future it become desirable to support either more signals than would fit in a word or an indefinite variable number of signals, the optimizations that rely on fixed bit vectors need to be rethought. It may be the case that simply using the POSIX **sigaction()** representation directly in such cases may be possible. Alternatively, one could implement the first 32 signals by the current mechanism, and remaining ones by extracting bits out of the action structures on demand.

Another problem with the current implementation is that it makes no allowance for non-POSIX system coexistence, since the system only currently implements POSIX semantics. If foreign system semantics were to be needed, the signal implementation would need to be stratified into kernel mechanism and POSIX interface more effectively.[16]

6.3.3 What is sigprocmask()?

sigprocmask() is a system call interface that implements the POSIX specification for masking signals. It allows the user program to retrieve and alter the signal mask of the process. **sigprocmask()** has the regular requirements of a POSIX system call in terms of calling arguments and return values. The arguments include a reference to a POSIX set of arguments that are used to implement a POSIX **sigprocmask** function in a user program.

... [File: /usr/src/kernel/kern/sig.c, line: 197]

```
int
sigprocmask(p, uap, retval)
        struct proc *p;
        struct args {
```

---

[14] Usually abnormal termination and recording the contents of a process in a "core" file for examination by a debugger.

[15] This is desirable when the signal is effectively a time-sensitive message telling the program that an external event (like data becoming available to be read on a socket or device) has occurred.

[16] Earlier implementations of this function supported two interfaces for different UNIX-like systems—unfortunately still relying on UNIX-like low-level semantics.

```
            int how;
            sigset_t mask;
    } *uap;
    int *retval;
...
```

The function is called with the system call internal handler convention of pointer to the process/thread generating the call, a pointer to the encapsulated arguments of the POSIX function implemented, and a pointer to the POSIX function's return value. Any error in the handler's processing of the system call will be passed back as the return value of this function.

The **sigprocmask** system call handler[17] passes two arguments: operation request; and a signal mask. This system call handler will operate on the process signal mask as requested using the arguments, and return the previous mask value. If the operation request is unknown, an EINVAL error will be returned.

This handler does not have the semantics of the POSIX function, which passes the user program masks by reference instead of value. Since this is a frequent[18] system call, the cost of indirectly referencing the words in the user program using **copyin_** and **copyout_** (see **Chapter 2** on **i386/locore.s**) would be more costly than the rest of the resulting system call. Thus, the optimization here is to perform the indirection in the system call stub routine instead, where it corresponds to a single instruction rather than a function call.

6.3.3.1 How is sigprocmask() Implemented?

This handler only needs to return the value of the mask, operate on the current mask as desired and return.

... [File: /usr/src/kernel/kern/sig.c, line: 207]

```
    *retval = p->p_sigmask;
...
```

The mask value is unconditionally returned as the sole return value.

... [File: /usr/src/kernel/kern/sig.c, line: 210]

```
    switch (uap->how) {
    case SIG_BLOCK:
            p->p_sigmask |= uap->mask &~ sigcantmask;
            break;

    case SIG_UNBLOCK:
            p->p_sigmask &= ~uap->mask;
            break;

    case SIG_SETMASK:
            p->p_sigmask = uap->mask &~ sigcantmask;
```

---

[17] Which has different arguments and semantics than the POSIX **sigprocmask()** function.
[18] It is used in the main loop of a command shell.

```
                break;

        default:
                return(EINVAL);
                break;
        }
        return (0);
...
```

One of three operations is performed on the process signal mask; otherwise, an EINVAL error is returned. All of the operations involve applying the second argument mask to the process mask. Signals to be blocked can be added to the mask with the SIG_BLOCK request, or signals to be unblocked can be removed from the mask with SIG_UNBLOCK. The signal mask can be forced to a value with SIG_SETMASK.

To effectively return the value of the mask without modification, the handler can be directed to use SIG_BLOCK with a mask argument of 0. Note that in any event, certain signals can't ever be allowed to become masked—these exceptions are silently ignored.

6.3.3.2 386BSD sigprocmask()
Design Choices and Trade-Offs

One design consideration with **sigprocmask()** is how to avoid interaction with interrupt-level code that may also wish to alter the mask on delivery of the signal. Since **sigprocmask()** is heavily used by command shells, masking interrupts to ensure that no modification occurs between the time the signal mask is sampled and the time the signal mask is altered impacts overhead. Since most signals are processed on the return to user mode of the process, there is no need to protect the signal mask in this manner for the majority of hardware-induced signals.

The only exception to this is the occurrence of exceptions that must always be delivered—in the case of the 386, a coprocessor exception falls into this category. Since the floating point coprocessor runs asynchronous to the main processor when delivering what would otherwise be a synchronous exception, conceivably it may need to be masked to avoid upsetting the mask. But this problem actually is far deeper, since not only could the exception come at any time during the processing of the process, but it could also arrive in the context of another process altogether. To make matters worse, on the 486 and Pentium systems this asynchronous event may come in the form of a processor exception which cannot be masked at all as an ordinary hardware interrupt. Thus, special code is used to deal with this architecture-specific case in the trap handling code.[19]

---

[19] See **i386/trap.c** in **Chapter 3** and **npx/npx.c** for further information.

6.3.4 What is sigpending()?

sigpending() is a system call interface that implements the POSIX specification for returning to the user program the status of any pending signals for it. **sigpending()** has the regular requirements of a POSIX system call handler in terms of calling arguments (there are none) and return values (the pending set of signals). A POSIX set of arguments are used to implement a POSIX **sigpending()** function.

... [File: /usr/src/kernel/kern/sig.c, line: 237]

```
int
sigpending(p, uap, retval)
        struct proc *p;
        void *uap;
        int *retval;
...
```

The function is called with the system call internal handler convention of pointer to the process/thread generating the call, a pointer to the encapsulated arguments of the POSIX function implemented (one, the signal mask), and a pointer to the POSIX function's return value.

This handler does not have the semantics of the POSIX function, which passes the user program pending set by reference instead of value. For consistency with the other ones using masks (which are frequent system calls), the mask is passed by value, with the indirection in the system call stub routine instead.

6.3.4.1 How is sigpending() Implemented?

... [File: /usr/src/kernel/kern/sig.c, line: 244]

```
        *retval = p->p_sig;
        return (0);
...
```

Analogous to **sigprocmask()**, **sigpending()** returns the value of a set of pending signals for the process (p_sig). It then returns successfully.

6.3.5 What is sigsuspend()?

sigsuspend() is a system call handler that implements a part of the POSIX specification for pausing the process awaiting a signal. **sigsuspend()** has the regular requirements of a system call handler in terms of calling arguments and return values. A POSIX set of arguments are used to implement a POSIX **sigpending()** function. This system call is unusual in that it always returns an error (EINTR), since that is the only way it can return from an interrupt (otherwise, it would stay suspended).

... [File: /usr/src/kernel/kern/sig.c, line: 254]

```
int
sigsuspend(p, uap, retval)
        struct proc *p;
```

```
        struct args {
                sigset_t mask;
        } *uap;
        int *retval;
...
```

The function is called with the system call internal handler convention of pointer to the process/thread generating the call, a pointer to the encapsulated arguments of the POSIX function implemented (one, the signal mask), and a pointer to the POSIX function's return value.

This handler does not have the semantics of the POSIX function, which passes the user program masks by reference instead of value. Since this is a frequent[20] system call, the cost of indirectly referencing the words in the user program using **copyin_** would be more costly than the rest of the resulting system call. Thus, the optimization here is to perform the indirection in the system call stub routine instead, where it corresponds to a single instruction rather than a function call.

6.3.5.1 How is sigsuspend() Implemented?

This handler needs to mask interrupts, sleep until interrupted by a signal, and arrange for the signal mask to be restored.

... [File: /usr/src/kernel/kern/sig.c, line: 265]

```
        ps->ps_oldmask = p->p_sigmask;
        ps->ps_flags |= SA_OLDMASK;
...
```

The first order of business is to arrange to have the current mask restored on conclusion of this system call. This needs to be done before the current mask is altered. The problem that arises here is determining where to store the mask and how to have it restored, since by the way system calls are implemented signals will be processed on the way out after the system call returns. This means that, for example, saving the mask in the frame of this handler would cause the wrong effect, since the signal would be masked before it was discovered. On the other end, a stack frame could be inserted in the user process to intercept the return to user code to cause another system call to reset the mask, but this would leave a window of time during which the mask would be inconsistent. Thus, the only way to deal with this is to embed a feature inside the signal implementation to deal with this problem. In this case, an alternate signal mask is returned on completion of this system call.

... [File: /usr/src/kernel/kern/sig.c, line: 269]

```
        p->p_sigmask = uap->mask &~ sigcantmask;

        /* pause. if woken for any reason other than a signal, pause again. */
        while (tsleep((caddr_t) ps, PPAUSE|PCATCH, "pause", 0) == 0)
                ;
```

[20] It is used in the main loop of a command shell.

```
        return (EINTR);
  ...
```

The signal mask supplied in the argument is made the current mask, taking care not to allow any unmaskable signals to be masked. Then the process sleeps forever at a low priority, waiting for a signal to be caught.

When the signal is caught (PCATCH), **tsleep()** (see **Chapter 8** on **kern/synch.c**) is called so that the sleep will be interruptible by a signal. When the function returns, its return value is checked to see if the return was due to the process being awakened for some other reason or if a signal had occurred. If a signal had occurred, **tsleep()** returns with an error value. If the process is awakened for any other reason, it will immediately return to its slumbers. This is done to maintain the POSIX semantics of the suspend function—otherwise, a **sigsuspend()** could return prematurely.

The **sigsuspend()** handler always returns an error (EINTR) value, since the only way it will terminate is when it is interrupted by a signal. Note that if the signal is terminal (e.g., SIGKILL), the process will be terminated; thus, the the signal returning from the system call may never make it back. If the signal does not terminate the process, however, in processing the signal action the *oldmask* feature will reload the previous signal mask back into the process on conclusion of the **sigsuspend()** call. Note that while the process mask will be immediately restored[21], the caller of the **sigsuspend()** function will not necessarily immediately be run on return from this system call— instead, the signal handlers associated with the signals will be run first.

6.3.6 What is sigstack()?

sigstack() is the system call handler function that implements the BSD option to do signal handling on a separate signal stack to process signals instead of on the user program's active stack. This is a non-standard extension to the POSIX signal mechanism useful in certain special case applications programs.[22] **sigstack()** has the regular requirements of a system call handler in terms of calling arguments and return values. The BSD **sigstack()** interface functionally resembles the **sigaction()** arrangement by having separate in/out system call arguments for the signal stack state.

... [File: /usr/src/kernel/kern/sig.c, line: 283]

```
int
sigstack(p, uap, retval)
        struct proc *p;
```

---

[21] And therefore available to any nested signal handlers that may be instantiated on the user process as a result of the process being signalled.
[22] It is not generally useful to implement spaghetti stacks; however, it can come in handy, for example, in threaded-code interpreter/compilers.

```
struct args {
        struct sigstack *nss;
        struct sigstack *oss;
} *uap;
int *retval;
```
...

The function is called with the system call internal handler convention of pointer to the process/thread generating the call, a pointer to the encapsulated arguments of the BSD function implemented (two—one to the new signal state and one to the old signal state), and a pointer to the BSD function's return value. Any error in the handler's processing of the system call will be passed back as the return value of this function. The BSD **sigstack()** call passes two arguments: the pointer to receive the old state of the signal, and the pointer to supply the new signal state to the system. Either signal state pointer is optional, as a null valued pointer will be disregarded without error.

Errors in processing the system call can occur if the information supplied is out of bounds. Note that the contents of the signal stack are not checked at this point— instead, an illegal signal stack is specified. This will be discovered when a signal is delivered to the process; in this case, since the process cannot deliver the signal, it will kill the process outright.

6.3.6.1 How is sigstack() Implemented?

... [File: /usr/src/kernel/kern/sig.c, line: 296]

```
if (uap->oss && (error = copyout(p, (caddr_t)&p->p_sigacts->ps_sigstack,
    (caddr_t)uap->oss, sizeof (struct sigstack))))
        return (error);
```
...

If there is an old signal state pointer in the arguments, the current **sigstack()** state will be returned to the caller by means of the inline function **copyout()**, and the old state will be (optionally) returned prior to loading in a new state. If an error occurs in returning the old state, the error is immediately returned and the new state is not loaded.

... [File: /usr/src/kernel/kern/sig.c, line: 301]

```
if (uap->nss && (error = copyin(p, (caddr_t)uap->oss, (caddr_t)&ss,
    sizeof (struct sigstack))))
        p->p_sigacts->ps_sigstack = ss;

return (error);
```
...

If a new signal state pointer is present in the arguments, the new signal state is copied into a temporary buffer on the stack via the inline function **copyin()**. If an error is encountered, the stack buffer is not copied into place, and an error code is returned. Otherwise, the new signal state becomes the current process's signal stack state.

SOURCE CODE SECRETS: THE BASIC KERNEL

6.3.7 What is kill()?

kill() is the system call handler that implements the POSIX kill() function to deliver signals generated by a process to another process. It is the only way that a process can explicitly force another process to receive a signal. kill() has the regular requirements of a POSIX system call in terms of calling arguments and return values. The arguments include a reference to a POSIX set of arguments that a POSIX kill() function receives.

... [File: /usr/src/kernel/kern/sig.c, line: 312]

```
int
kill(cp, uap, retval)
        struct proc *cp;
        struct args {
                int pid;
                int signo;
        } *uap;
        void *retval;
...
```

The function is called with the POSIX system call internal handler convention of pointer to the process/thread generating the call, a pointer to the encapsulated arguments of the POSIX function implemented (two), and a pointer to the POSIX function's return value. Any error in the handler's processing of the system call will be passed back as the return value of this function. The POSIX kill() call passes two arguments: the process ID to be signalled, and the signal to pass to that process ID. Errors in processing the system call can occur if the information supplied is inconsistent or out of bounds.

6.3.7.1 How is kill() Implemented?

... [File: /usr/src/kernel/kern/sig.c, line: 324]

```
        if ((unsigned) uap->signo >= NSIG)
                return (EINVAL);
...
```

The supplied signal number (signo) is checked to determine if it lies within the prescribed bounds of acceptable signals implemented in this system. Note that the nonexistent signal number of zero is passed through as a valid value, but will have no effect; thus, this "null" signal will be silently passed through the function with no action performed.

... [File: /usr/src/kernel/kern/sig.c, line: 328]

```
        if (uap->pid > 0) {

                /* locate the process */
                p = pfind(uap->pid);
                if (p == 0)
                        return (ESRCH);

                /* do we have permission to send the signal? */
                if (!cansignal(cp, p, uap->signo))
```

```
                return (EPERM);

        /* do we have a signal to send? */
        if (uap->signo)
                psignal(p, uap->signo);

        return (0);
   }
...
```

In the case of a single process signalled (where the process ID is a positive number), the process is located by use of the **pfind()** inline function (see **proc.h**) which returns the process pointer to a process with the desired ID. If no process is present with that ID, the handler terminates immediately, returning an error (ESRCH) indicating that a search for the process failed. If the process is found, however, the inline function **cansignal()** is called to see if the current process calling the handler can send the process located the signal (already bounds checked). If it cannot send the signal, the handler returns an error (EPERM) indicating that it does not have permission to send the signal. If it can send the signal, however, and that signal is not the null signal, the **psignal()** function is called to pass the process the signal. The system call handler then returns successfully.

... [File: /usr/src/kernel/kern/sig.c, line: 347]

```
        switch (uap->pid) {
        case -1:  /* broadcast signal */
                return (killpg(cp, uap->signo, 0, 1));
        case 0:   /* signal own process group */
                return (killpg(cp, uap->signo, 0, 0));
        default:  /* negative explicit process group */
                return (killpg(cp, uap->signo, -uap->pid, 0));
        }
...
```

If the process ID is not a positive number, the semantics of the POSIX **kill()** function dictate that we are sending a special signal to a group of processes. In this case, for convenience, the remainder of this system call is implemented in the helper function **killpg()** to issue a broadcast signal to the appropriate process group. A value of "-1" for the process ID argument indicates that a signal should be sent to all processes in all groups, while a process ID of zero indicates that the signal should be sent to all processes in the current process's process group. Any other negative value indicates that a signal should be sent to all processes within the absolute value of the argument (e.g. a "-2" means to send a signal to all processes in process group "2").

6.3.8 What is killpg()?

killpg() is a shorthand function to simplify the implementation of the **kill()** system call handler. It is the common code used to implement the portions of the **kill()** system call handler that scans all processes for delivery of broadcast and process group signals.

This function locates all processes that should receive the signal and summarily passes the signal to each of them.

... [File: /usr/src/kernel/kern/sig.c, line: 361]

```
static int
killpg(struct proc *cp, int signo, int pgid, int all)
...
```

killpg() has four arguments: a pointer to the current process issuing the signal; the signal number sent; a process group ID the signal is sent to (optional); and a flag indicating if the signal should be sent to all processes (optional). The function returns either an error value or zero if successful.

6.3.8.1 How is killpg() Implemented?

... [File: /usr/src/kernel/kern/sig.c, line: 369]

```
        if (all)
                /*
                 * broadcast - walk the list of all processes,
                 * selecting candidates not system processes, init, or
                 * self.
                 */
                for (p = allproc; p != NULL; p = p->p nxt) {
                        if (p->p_pid == 1 || p->p_flag & SSYS ||
                            p == cp || !cansignal(cp, p, signo))
                                continue;
                        nfound++;
                        if (signo)
                                psignal(p, signo);
                }
...
```

If the "all" argument option is indicated, **killpg()** scans the list of all processes and evaluates each of them to determine if it should receive the signal.[23] If the process being evaluated is a system process (SSYS) or the initialization or page daemon process (processes zero and one, respectively), these processes are explicitly ignored. If the process scanned is the current process or if it does not have permission to signal the process evaluated, it is also ignored. The inline function **cansignal()** is used to determine if the signal can be passed from the current process to the scanned process.

If the signal can be sent to a process, the count of processes successfully signalled is tallied. **psignal()** is then called to send the signal (excluding the null signal) to the processes on the list we are evaluating.

... [File: /usr/src/kernel/kern/sig.c, line: 383]

```
        else {
                /* zero pgid means send to my process group. */
                if (pgid == 0)
```

---

[23] N.B. No zombies are present on the "allproc" process list.

```
                    pgrp = cp->p_pgrp;
        else {
                    pgrp = pgfind(pgid);
                    if (pgrp == NULL)
                            return (ESRCH);
        }
...
```

If the "all" option was not enabled, then a process group is selected to send the signal. If the process group ID option is set to zero, then the current process group of the current process (cp -> p_pgrp) is sent the signal. Otherwise, the process group is located using the **pgfind()** function (in **kern/pgrp.c**). If no process group exists for that process group ID, an error (ESRCH) is immediately returned, avoiding the **kill()** function.

... [File: /usr/src/kernel/kern/sig.c, line: 395]

```
        for (p = pgrp->pg_mem; p != NULL; p = p->p_pgrpnxt) {
                if (p->p_pid == 1 || p->p_flag & SSYS ||
                    p->p_stat == SZOMB || !cansignal(cp, p, signo))
                        continue;
                nfound++;
                if (signo)
                        psignal(p, signo);
        }
    }

    return (nfound ? 0 : ESRCH);
...
```

The process group member list is successively walked, with each process evaluated for possibly sending it the signal. As in the broadcast case, if the process being evaluated is a system process (SSYS) or the initialization or page daemon process (processes zero and one, respectively), these processes are explicitly ignored. If the process scanned is a zombie process or if it does not have permission to signal the process evaluated, it is also ignored. The inline function **cansignal()** is then used to determine if the signal can be passed from the current process to the scanned process. If the signal can be sent to a process, the count of processes successfully signalled is tallied. **psignal()** is then called to send the signal (excluding the null signal) to the processes on the list we are evaluating.

Upon completion of either a process group list walk or the "all" process list walk, an error or success value is returned (depending on whether any processes were found and signalled). If no processes were found or signalled, an error (ESRCH) is returned indicating that the **killpg()** request was unable to find any processes to signal within the defined parameters.

6.3.8.2 386BSD killpg() Design Choices and Trade-Offs

The current arrangement of system processes used with the kernel results in the redundant examination of the single signal process *process zero* during both the checking process of the process ID and in the existence of the system flag. This redundancy introduces flexibility in dealing with arbitrary numbers of system processes (not yet implemented at this time).

One should always keep in mind a few caveats. First, system processes are processes that only have a kernel context and have no user program or user address space. Secondly, as far POSIX is concerned, the process ID of zero does not really exist, since process IDs can only be positive integers (1,..,*maxpid*). Thirdly, unlike a broadcast signal sent to all processes which specifically avoids the sending process, process groups at this time may have the current process signalled if it falls within the process group. And finally, the process group list broadcast is not sent to zombie processes, since they can't receive a signal anyways.

6.3.9 What is sigreturn()?

sigreturn() is a system call handler to a hidden system call embedded in the signal implementation. The signal implementation arranges to have this system call entered after the signal has concluded so that the signal's stack frame may be removed. This allows the signal state to be synchronized between the kernel and the user program.

sigreturn() provides a machine-independent interface to a machine-dependent mechanism to allow the return from a signal. The sole point of this function is to embed in the standard system call handler mechanism a call which tunnels through to the machine-dependent layer. Thus, **sigreturn()** is a system call handler function that encapsulates a machine-dependent return from the signal function—the exact semantics of which depends highly on the particular architecture on which it is run. Alternatively, an entirely machine-dependent mechanism could have been implemented outside of the machine-independent portion of the kernel. However, since all separate machine implementations would then require such a feature, it is more sensible to standardize the interface across all implementations of the kernel on all architectures.

... [File: /usr/src/kernel/kern/sig.c, line: 415]

```
int
sigreturn(p, uap, retval)
        struct proc *p;
        void *uap;
        int *retval;
    ...
```

sigreturn() is called with the POSIX system call internal handler convention of pointer to the process/thread generating the call, a pointer to the encapsulated arguments of the POSIX function implemented, and a pointer to the POSIX function's return value. The function passes no arguments. Any error in the handler's processing of the system call will be passed back as the return value of this function.

---

sigreturn() is an artifact of the BSD signal implementation. IBCS2, in contrast, does not use such a mechanism; instead, by convention, any calls to alter the signal handlers pass a pointer to a portion of code in a process to implement the delivery of a signal. By doing this, it avoids the need to devise a way of returning from the signal, because it is picked up by the kernel when the signal handler is engaged. In addition, a separate call gate is assigned to the body of code used to return from the signal. Thus, a private independent system call facility is used in place of BSD's **sigreturn()**.

6.3.9.1 How is sigreturn() Implemented?

... [File: /usr/src/kernel/kern/sig.c, line: 421]

```
        return (cpu_signalreturn(p));
    ...
```

The machine-dependent function **cpu_signalreturn()** (see **Chapter 3** on **i386/cpu.c**) is called with the current process as its argument. This function serves to recover from the process's stack the previous signal context, remove it, and restore the state prior to the presence of the signal. It then returns, passing any error return value back to the system call handler itself. This function implicitly takes as an argument the current stack frame of the user process.

6.3.10 What is nosys()?

nosys() is a placeholder function for unimplemented system calls. It returns an error (ENOSYS) if any of these unimplemented system calls are invoked and also sends a signal (SIGSYS) to the process to make it aware it has issued an invalid system call.

nosys() sends a signal as well as returns an error because many system calls never check the error value in the first place, while an uncaught SIGSYS signal will cause the program to terminate. Even if the signal is blocked (usually when all signals are set to the ignore state), the ENOSYS error still has a chance to be seen. The function has the regular requirements of a POSIX system call in terms of calling arguments and return values. There are no arguments.

... [File: /usr/src/kernel/kern/sig.c, line: 431]

```
int
nosys(p, args, retval)
        struct proc *p;
        void *args;
        int *retval;
    ...
```

nosys() is called with the system call internal handler convention of pointer to the process/thread generating the call, a pointer to the encapsulated arguments of the POSIX function implemented (none, since it is not implementing a system call), and a pointer to the system call's return value (again, none). An ENOSYS error will be passed back as the return error of this function.

Note that any attempt to invoke an invalid system call should actually be audited as a potential violation of security (as a program which searches a system for holes will inevitably execute nonexistent system calls).

6.3.10.1 How is nosys() Implemented?

... [File: /usr/src/kernel/kern/sig.c, line: 438]

```
      psignal(p, SIGSYS);
      return (ENOSYS);
   ...
```

The current process is signalled with the SIGSYS signal, and the system call handler returns with the ENOSYS error. The signal action will take place on return from the system call to the user process program.

6.3.11 What is psignal()?

psignal() sends a process a signal. It is the principal mechanism of the signal implementation, and is responsible for the external (e.g., outside of the signalled process context) semantics of a signal, including changing the state of the process, entering a signal into the process's pending signal set, and arranging for the process to discover the signal in its context.

psignal() can be called by any part of the kernel to instigate a signal on a process. The process is described by a pointer to a process structure that is usually located by using the **pfind()** function (see **kern/proc.h**). **psignal()** is the root mechanism for sending signals—all other signal generating functions eventually make use of this function.

... [File: /usr/src/kernel/kern/sig.c, line: 456]

```
void
psignal(struct proc *p, int sig)
   ...
```

psignal() has two arguments: the process pointer of the process to be signalled, and the signal number or index of the signal being sent to the process. No return value is provided, and there is no way of determining if the signal actually was sent or when it will have its desired effect. Thus, there is no feedback to the generator of the signal stating if anything happened at all. **psignal()** does not check for permission to send a signal. That is the responsibility of the caller.

psignal() alters the external (e.g., outside of the signalled process) state of a process to suit the semantics of the signal. Among other things, it must arrange for the process to discover the signal and act upon it in its context. The signalled process may be in a variety of different states that **psignal()** will need to negotiate through in order to have the desired action occur; thus it must be intimate with the details of the rest of the kernel's implementation of event handling, process blocks, exception handling, and kernel-user process communication.

6.3.11.1 How is psignal() Implemented?

psignal() gets its marching orders for signal semantics by indexing the *sigprop* table of signal properties (see **include/signalvar.h**). The property for the signal (*prop*) and the bit associated with this signal in all of the signal bit masks (*bit*) will be referenced throughout **psignal()**.

... [File: /usr/src/kernel/kern/sig.c, line: 473]

```
        if (p->p_flag & STRC)
                action = SIG_DFL;
        else {
                /* abandon ignored signals, except for SIGCONT case */
                if (p->p_sigignore & bit)
                        return;

                /* hold blocked signals, catch ones with handlers */
                if (p->p_sigmask & bit)
                        action = SIG_HOLD;
                else if (p->p_sigcatch & bit)
                        action = SIG_CATCH;
                else
                        action = SIG_DFL; /* SIGCONT only */
        }
    ...
```

First, the class of action of this system call must be determined. Traced processes that make use of the **ptrace()** mechanism are treated as if the action is the default one, as this is the path through the code that deals with traced processes. This path allows the parent process to learn about the signal by stopping the child process and returning control to the parent before the signal is honored in the child process. This also allows the debugger grace time before the process abruptly terminates or alters the state of the process, as well as allowing the debugger to catch induced exception traps like breakpoints where they can be removed and the signal eliminated from view by the child process.

Non-**ptrace()**ed signals are classified by the *p_sigignore, p_sigcatch*, and *p_sigmask* bit masks of the process. These bit masks encode the treatment of the signal by the underlying action and handler. Ignored signals are detected by checking *p_sigignore* and immediately dropped. Blocked signals are detected in *p_sigmask*, and queued for later delivery (SIG_HOLD) when they become unblocked. Caught signals are known to have a handler in the process that needs to be activated. The signalled process thus must become active to discover them and have the handler inside the process run.

SIGCONT, a special case, is one of the controlling signals that causes a stopped process to unconditionally start running again. It is implemented along the default processing path regardless of its action. To simplify implementation, it is not allowed to be ignored by the **sigaction()** system call handler that allows a program to alter signal operation.

... [File: /usr/src/kernel/kern/sig.c, line: 490]

```
if (p->p_nice > NZERO && (sig == SIGKILL ||
    sig == SIGTERM && !(p->p_flag&STRC || action != SIG_DFL)))
        p->p_nice = NZERO;
```
...

Signals known to terminate the process are promoted in priority (if they are running at a degraded priority) to the topmost priority of normal user processes (NZERO) so as to have the resources of the process reclaimed quickly. These processes generally have been degraded in priority because they have made excessive use of processor resources already and are thus promoted so as to have them leave more quickly.

... [File: /usr/src/kernel/kern/sig.c, line: 495]

```
if (prop & SA_CONT)
        p->p_sig &= ~stopsigmask;
```
...

Signals that will continue a process remove any pending stop signals, so that a continue effect will be felt regardless of any other stop signals that may be present at the time the continue occurs. Thus any continue will take priority over outstanding stop signals.

... [File: /usr/src/kernel/kern/sig.c, line: 499]

```
if (prop & SA_STOP) {
        /* terminal stops don't affect orphaned process groups */
        if (prop & SA_TTYSTOP && p->p_pgrp->pg_jobc == 0 &&
            action == SIG_DFL)
                return;
        p->p_sig &= ~contsigmask;
}
```
...

Similarly, if a stop signal occurs, it clears all pending continue signals. Thus any stop will take priority over outstanding continue signals. With both of these, the process is either going to be stopped or continued consistently. There is never an intermix of both sets of signals. A special case of stop signals initiated by the tty driver (SA_TTYSTOP) directed to an orphan process group with default action is disallowed, so that those processes cannot be accidentally stopped before they can be reaped elsewhere in the system. (see **exit()** in **Chapter 5**)

... [File: /usr/src/kernel/kern/sig.c, line: 508]

```
p->p_sig |= bit;
```
...

The signal is marked in the process's signal pending mask. It now exists for processing by the remaining parts of the signal implementation.

... [File: /usr/src/kernel/kern/sig.c, line: 514]

```
        if (action == SIG_HOLD && ((prop & SA_CONT) == 0 || p->p_stat != SSTOP))
                return;
    ...
```

If the signal is blocked (and not a continue of a stopped process), signal processing is finished and the signal will dwell on the process waiting for the mask to be removed for this signal (discovered in **syscall()** following cal to unmask, processes by **issig()/psig**), **Chapter 3**.

... [File: /usr/src/kernel/kern/sig.c, line: 518]

```
        s = splhigh();
        switch (p->p_stat) {

        case SSLEEP:
                /* process not interruptable, wait till return to user */
                if ((p->p_flag & SSINTR) == 0)
                        goto out;

                /* process is traced, run it so it can notice signal */
                if (p->p_flag&STRC)
                        goto run;
    ...
```

Process state is next altered as a result of the signal. To ensure no race conditions exist, exclusive access to the process *proc* entry is asserted. If the process is sleeping uninterruptibly, processing is completed and the signal will only be discovered after the sleep is over and the process returned to user mode. This might occur only after a prolonged (possibly infinite) time if either condition is not met (as, for example, might result in the case that a block device like a floppy was opened and the media was not ready). However, if the sleep is interruptable, traced processes are just allowed to run so that they can discover the signal.

... [File: /usr/src/kernel/kern/sig.c, line: 531]

```
        if ((prop & SA_CONT) && action == SIG_DFL) {
                p->p_sig &= ~bit;
                goto out;
        }
    ...
```

If the property of this signal is simply to do a continuation as the default action, the pending signal bit is cleared and the process is left waiting to be awakend. Continuing a sleeping process does not wake it.

... [File: /usr/src/kernel/kern/sig.c, line: 537]

```
        if ((prop & SA_STOP) != 0 && action == SIG_DFL) {
                p->p_sig &= ~bit;
                stop(p, 0, sig);
                goto out;
```

```
        } else
                goto runfast;
...
```

Next we have the case of converting a sleeping process to a stopped state. If the property of this signal is to stop in the default case, the pending bit is removed and the process is forced into the stopped state and presented the signal before continuation by means of the worker function **stop()**. Note that a sleeping process is converted into a stopped state without altering the characteristics of the sleeping state, so that it may be restored to the sleeping state again when it is continued with a SIGCONT signal. Note also that since **psignal()** can be called either when not in the context of a process or when not safe to switch contexts, the process is not rescheduled (an option to the **stop()** function).

Otherwise, if the signal is going to be delivered into the context of the process to be handled by a nondefault action (e.g., if it is caught or will terminate the process), the process will be promoted (if it has been degraded in priority) so that the signal may be delivered as expeditiously as possible (e.g., since in either of these two cases the process may be terminated, either explicitly or implicitly and the resources returned to the system).

... [File: /usr/src/kernel/kern/sig.c, line: 544]

```
    case SSTOP:
            /* kill signal always sets processes running */
            if (sig == SIGKILL)
                    goto runfast;

            /* signal a traced process: no action needed */
            if (p->p_flag&STRC)
                    goto out;
...
```

In the case of a stopped process receiving the signal, the uncatchable signal SIGKILL is checked for. If it is found, we immediately schedule the process to be run so that it may be terminated.[24] If the stopped process is traced, no additional work is required as the process is merely being awakened out of its stopped state so that it may discover an action pending. The remainder of the implementation will take place between **issig()** and **psig()** in the process itself.

... [File: /usr/src/kernel/kern/sig.c, line: 554]

```
    if (prop & SA_CONT) {
            /* if default or ignored, cancel pending */
            if (action == SIG_DFL)
                    p->p_sig &= ~bit;
            /* otherwise, handle it in the context of the process */
            if (action == SIG_CATCH)
```

---

[24] UNIX processes terminate by suicide—they must be in the context of the process in order to notice they are terminated.

```
                    goto runfast;
        /* if it was running before, runt it again */
        if (p->p_wchan == 0)
                    goto run;
        /* otherwise, return it to sleeping state */
        p->p_stat = SSLEEP;
        goto out;
}
```
...

If the property of the signal is to continue the stopped process, the action of the stopped function is reversed. Since processes may be stopped while they are sleeping or running, both cases must be dealt with and the process placed back into the same state it was in before it was stopped.

If the signal to be continued has a default action, the pending signal is removed and the process set to its previous state, since delivery in the context is not required. Otherwise, if the signal is caught, it must be run at a potentially boosted priority (as occurred in the previous case) so that the signal can be discovered and dispatched to the appropriate signal handler in the context of the process.

If the process was running prior to it being stopped, there will be no event that it is waiting for, since by convention the field of the process that identifies the event (*p_wchan*) is left unchanged when a process is stopped. Thus, with no waiting event, the process is restarted as a running process without altering its priority. Note that the effect of not having the process go into the intermediate sleep state while stopped has ramifications for scheduling—the priority of a stopped process will not improve in rank (unlike a sleeping process) since it may have been alternating between stopped and run state.[25] Thus, the stopped state is merely a special case of the run state.

If the process has a event for which it is waiting, it is placed back into the sleeping state and the function is exited without waking up the process. Thus, a process can go from sleeping to stopped to sleeping again without ever being scheduled or having its context referenced in any way. For example, if a program running in the shell is waiting for terminal output that is stopped with the terminal suspension character (usually cntl-Z) and restarted again by the shell,[26] the process itself will be restored from stopped state to sleeping.

... [File: /usr/src/kernel/kern/sig.c, line: 570]

```
        if (prop & SA_STOP) {
                p->p_sig &= ~bit;
                goto out;
        }
```
...

---

[25] See *Process Priority* in **Chapter 8** for a discussion of process ranking and priority.
[26] As in **csh** and **fg**.

If the property of a signal is to stop an already stopped process, the pending signal we just put on prior to the switch statement is cancelled and we exit without doing any additional work, in effect cancelling the signal.

... [File: /usr/src/kernel/kern/sig.c, line: 576]

```
        if (p->p_wchan && p->p_flag & SSINTR)
                unsleep(p);
        goto out;
...
```

If there is a signal to be delivered on the process, the process is examined to see if it is waiting for an event and if the wait is interruptible. If so, we reverse the effect of the process going into the sleeping state to allow it to run and discover the signal. Note that we cannot reverse the effect of a sleep if the sleep is not interruptible, since the whole point of delivering a signal is to interrupt a process. Thus, if a signal is sent to a stopped process, the signal will only be noticed when the process is continued again or if it is returned to an interruptible sleep and reversed back into a running process so that the signal will be discovered.

... [File: /usr/src/kernel/kern/sig.c, line: 580]

```
    default:
            /* force signal evaluation */
            cpu_signotify(p);
            goto out;
    }
...
```

In all other process states (e.g., running or getting ready to run), the process must be notified of the existence of the signal. This is done via the machine-dependent function **cpu_signotify()** (see **i386/cpu.h**). On the 386, the process is marked to simulate an asynchronous system trap (AST)—a form of software interrupt which requires the signal to be honored the next time the process attempts to return to user mode from the kernel. This is the earliest point at which the signal can be noticed by the process. Its effect is to force the process to evaluate the signal implementation in the trap and system call handlers when it is safe to access the process in its context. This case ends the discussions on altering the process state for each kind of process state.

... [File: /usr/src/kernel/kern/sig.c, line: 586]

```
runfast:
        /* give priority to deliver a signal inside a process */
        if (p->p_pri > PUSER)
                p->p_pri = PUSER;
run:
        setrun(p);
out:
        splx(s);
...
```

---

psignal() terminates in one of three ways. Firstly, if it is known that a signal will be delivered or will terminate the process, the function ensures that the process will be raised to the highest process user priority so that delivery may occur and not be postponed by whatever low priority the process may have eroded to (runfast).

The second way to leave **psignal()** is to set the process running at the priority it was set to before being signalled (run). This is done to stopped processes that were previously running so that they do not gain an advantage merely by using the tracing or stopped state, but instead remain at a constant priority since in these cases the process may not be terminating quickly but may instead be hanging on, alternating between states for some time. If this were not done, a timesharing system with lots of users might find that running the debugger on processes would make them run ahead of others, breaking the fairness doctrine.[27]

The last way to leave **psignal()** is to lose the exclusive hold on the processor obtained at the beginning of the switch statement so as to gain exclusive access to the *proc* entry that we have been altering (out). In this case, the process has not been forced into the run state, but is just left in the state as provided for by the signal property examined above.

6.3.12 What is issig()?

issig() ("is a signal present") is an internal kernel function used on (re)entry to a process's context to examine the pending signals of a process. **issig()** examines any pending unmasked signals. Ignored and stopped signals will have their effect implemented and removed from the mask. Caught or default termination signals will be returned to the associated function **psig()** for processing.

issig() is typically used to locate signals for **psig()** to take action on one-by-one. Both **issig()** and **psig()** are only used at the end of trap and system call processing when the process is returning to user mode to implement the semantics of the signal action. **issig()** deals with transparent signals like stops and ignores and tracing, leaving termination or caught signals to **psig()**.[28]

issig() is not used directly but is instead used as part of the macro **CURSIG** (see **include/signalvar.h**) which checks the ignore and held mask against the pending signals, thus avoiding an unnecessary evaluation of the signals by **issig()** for signals which don't require immediate action. Since this is the common null case, the buffering of calls to **issig()** by **CURSIG** reduces the number of unnecessary system

---

[27] This is less critical on a single-user system, however.

[28] N.B. In System V, stop signals are actually implemented in the **psig()** function and not considered to be transparent. In the original UNIX system, **issig()** was actually a trivial function used only to locate a signal for **psig()** to process; thus, the name "psig" stands for "process a signal in its process context" and "issig" stands for "is a signal present."

calls which would otherwise increase the overhead of trap, signal, and system call handling mechanisms. While this was not germane to the PDP-11, this was especially important on the VAX with its horribly slow function call instruction ("calls"), but on the 386 this is not such a big deal. On the Pentium, however, while branch flow is optimized, the effect is to avoid the need for two branches and a cache line reload, so this mechanism still has a value but for an entirely different reason. With even more elaborate processors, this mechanism is probably still valid.

As such, the function is used only in the context of the signalled process. If the signal requires a special kernel action (like tracing, stopping or continuing a process), it implements the action entirely and removes the pending bit. If the signal requires a user program action or termination, it returns a signal index to be passed to the **psig()** function to process the signal.

... [File: /usr/src/kernel/kern/sig.c, line: 612]

```
int
issig(struct proc *p)
...
```

issig() has one argument: the pointer to the process. It returns the value of an outstanding signal to be processed. If there is no signal to be processed, the function returns zero. Note that it is mandatory that if the function returns a signal to be processed, the signal must be processed since it has changed the state of the process in certain ways in anticipation of processing the signal. **psignal()**, **issig()**, and **psig()** are each written with intimate knowledge of the others' actions.

6.3.12.1 How is issig() Implemented?

... [File: /usr/src/kernel/kern/sig.c, line: 617]

```
        for (;;) {
                mask = p->p_sig &~ p->p_sigmask;
                if (p->p_flag & SPPWAIT)
                        mask &= ~stopsigmask;
                if (mask == 0)    /* no signal to send */
                        return (0);
                sig = ffs((long)mask);
                bit = sigmask(sig);
                prop = sigprop[sig];
...
```

The process is first examined for signals.[29] If the process being signalled is doing a **vfork()** operation (see **kern/fork.c**) where it is running off of the parent's context, stop signals are disallowed regardless of the contents of the process's signal mask since such processes are not allowed to stop.

---

[29] Pending signals are checked against the current mask of held signals.

If the resulting set of masked signals do not contain a signal to be evaluated, the function immediately returns zero.[30] If there is a signal in the mask to be examined, the most significant signal in the set, along with its associated bit and properties, are located for use in evaluating the signal.

... [File: /usr/src/kernel/kern/sig.c, line: 631]

```
if (bit & p->p_sigignore && (p->p_flag & STRC) == 0) {
        p->p_sig &= ~bit;
        continue;
}
```
...

If the signal is present in the ignored signal mask and the process is not being traced, then the signal is removed from the signal mask, and the signal mask is reexamined for any other pertinent pending signals.[31]

... [File: /usr/src/kernel/kern/sig.c, line: 636]

```
if ((p->p_flag & (STRC|SPPWAIT)) == STRC) {
        /*
         * If traced, always stop, and stay
         * stopped until released by the parent.
         */
        psignal(p->p_pptr, SIGCHLD);
        do
                stop(p, 1, sig);
        while (!procxmt(p)
            && (p->p_flag & (STRC|SPPWAIT)) == STRC);
```
...

If the process is being traced and is not a **vfork()**ed child, we implement transparently the effect of the signal allowing the parent to gain control of the process. The parent process is informed of the change in status of the child by sending it a signal (SIGCHLD) and the process is stopped with the **stop()** helper function.

When the child is awakened, it will execute the **procxmt()** function (see **kern/ptrace.c**) which receives actions sent by the parent to perform in the context of the child.[32] Effectively, the stopped and traced process is turned into a kind of slave which accepts control requests from the parent process and implements them one per context switch. This continues until the command to the child is sent to either allow the process to continue or allow the process to leave the traced state (usually by terminating).

---

[30] Since this case is checked for in the **CURSIG** macro before **issig()** is called, this happens when the signals in the mask have been eliminated by **issig()** (or **psignal()**).

[31] This generally should not happen, since the **CURSIG** macro checks the ignore mask. However, the condition of entering the trace state may have resulted in this oddity, so we remove it as ignored signals should not be evaluated by **issig()**.

[32] This is how the **ptrace** mechanism gains control of a process.

... [File: /usr/src/kernel/kern/sig.c, line: 653]

```
if ((p->p_flag & (STRC|SPPWAIT)) != STRC)
        continue;
```
...

If the process has either lost the trace state or is attempting to implement a **vfork()** operation (which is how we left the previous loop), we restart the evaluation of signals at the beginning of this function, since there may be more signals with different signal actions now present and our information and local variables may now be stale.

... [File: /usr/src/kernel/kern/sig.c, line: 661]

```
p->p_sig &= ~bit; /* clear the old signal */
sig = p->p_sigacts->ps_stopsig;
if (sig == 0)
        continue;
```
...

The signal that caused us to enter **issig()** is now removed from the pending mask and the value associated with this previously stopped signal is checked to see if it is no longer present in this process. If so, we have no signal to deliver in the context of this process and we restart our scan of signals at the beginning of this function. This is the part of the signal implementation that is incestuously tied with the **ptrace** mechanism which allows the parent process (in this case a debugger) to decide whether or not the signal may be seen by the child process to be signalled. Since breakpoints are noticed by signals, this is usually a case which is rendered transparent to the traced process by means of the debugger removing the breakpoint and the signal when it allows the process to be continued (which would be the case here). Another case which may arise occurs when the interrupt signal is sent to the traced process or a floating point exception (SIGFPE); in this case, the debugger will notice this event of the process being debugged, sample the state of the process, and allow the signal to be delivered to the child process. The effect of the interrupt or floating point exception will be noticed in the child process as well.

... [File: /usr/src/kernel/kern/sig.c, line: 671]

```
bit = sigmask(sig);
p->p_sig |= bit;
if (p->p_sigmask & bit)
        continue;
```
...

In the case cited above of allowing the child process to see the signal, the signal is placed back into the set of pending signals. If the signal is masked, the start of the signal search loop is begun again. Otherwise, we now consider the case of a signal we must process in **issig()**.

... [File: /usr/src/kernel/kern/sig.c, line: 682]

```
switch ((int)p->p_sigacts->ps_sigact[sig]) {

case SIG_DFL:
        /*
         * Don't take default actions on system processes.
         */
        if (p->p_flag & SSYS)
                break;  /* == ignore */
...
```

The action of the signal we are evaluating is checked. Firstly, we ignore any attempts
to perform default actions (this means termination) on any system processes (SSYS).

... [File: /usr/src/kernel/kern/sig.c, line: 698]

```
if (prop & SA_STOP) {
        if (p->p_flag & STRC ||
            (p->p_pgrp->pg_jobc == 0 &&
            prop & SA_TTYSTOP))
                break; /* == ignore */
        stop(p, 1, sig);
        break;
} else if (prop & SA_IGNORE) {
        /*
         * Except for SIGCONT, shouldn't get here.
         * Default action is to ignore; drop it.
         */
        break;  /* == ignore */
} else
        return (sig);
...
```

If the default action is to send a stop signal and the process is being traced, it will be
stopped using the **stop()** helper function and its action will be satisfied by this function
entirely. If the stop action originates from a terminal stop on an unconnected process
left in an orphan process group, the signal is ignored as are any signals left with the
property of ignore. If neither case it true, the signal must be delivered. The value of the
signal number is returned where it is passed summarily to **psig()** for processing. All
default and transparent cases have now been evaluated.

... [File: /usr/src/kernel/kern/sig.c, line: 727]

```
default:
        /* This signal has an action, let
         * psig process it.
         */
        return (sig);
}
p->p_sig &= ~bit;  /* take the signal! */
}
...
```

In the case that a signal is caught in this process, no further evaluation is necessary
and the value is returned for **psig()** to process, since it is known that the process will

---

catch the signal. In the case of transparent signals that have fallen out of the switch statement that we have just evaluated, the signal is removed from the pending mask (as **issig()** has processed it) and we reenter the evaluation for other signals at the top of this loop.

6.3.13 What is psig()?

psig(), "process a signal in its process context," is an internal kernel function used in association with **issig()** to process signal actions that result in either the default termination of a process or signal delivery to a user program's signal handler in a process. **psig()** implements signal catching or termination. If the process is being terminated by the signal, **psig()** will never return. Otherwise, **psig()** will arrange to have the process user context altered so that it will receive the caught signal. The function will also be responsible for masking the signal during the time it will be caught by the signal handler so that the signal will only be delivered once.

psig() performs these actions in the context of a user process, honoring the associated pending signal bit and then removing it. Between **psignal()**, **issig()**, and **psig()**, all of the semantics of the signal mechanism are implemented.

... [File: /usr/src/kernel/kern/sig.c, line: 744]

```
void
psig(int sig)
    ...
```

psig() has one argument: the signal to be delivered. It returns nothing. The side-effect of this function is to either terminate the process or deliver a signal. It is implicit that the signal is being processed in the current running process.

6.3.13.1 How is psig() Implemented?

... [File: /usr/src/kernel/kern/sig.c, line: 757]

```
        p->p_sig &= ~bit;
    ...
```

The pending signal bit is first removed as the signal is being processed.

... [File: /usr/src/kernel/kern/sig.c, line: 766]

```
        if (action == SIG_DFL)
                sigexit(p, sig);

        /* Otherwise the action is to process a caught signal. */
        else {
    ...
```

In the case of a default signal, the process is terminated by the helper function **sigexit()** which will handle all of the necessary details upon termination of the process.

... [File: /usr/src/kernel/kern/sig.c, line: 784]

```
        if (ps->ps_flags & SA_OLDMASK) {
                returnmask = ps->ps_oldmask;
                ps->ps_flags &= ~SA_OLDMASK;
        } else
                returnmask = p->p_sigmask;
        p->p_sigmask |= ps->ps_catchmask[sig] | bit;
        p->p_stats->p_ru.ru_nsignals++;

        /* deliver signal, if any error, terminate process */
        if (cpu_signal(p, sig, returnmask))
                sigexit(p, SIGILL);
        ps->ps_code = 0; /* XXX for core dump/debugger */
    }
...
```

In the case of delivering a signal to the process, the process signal mask must be updated. Normally, the signal mask will be masked during the time the signal handler is run. Upon return from the signal back through the kernel it will be restored to what it was prior to the occurrence of the signal. However, in order to implement the **sigsuspend()** POSIX function, an alternate mask will be returned upon conclusion of the signal. In effect, **sigsuspend()** is just shorthand for implementing a common case of a signal handler entirely within the bounds of the kernel. Typically, the effect of restoring the mask is done in concert with the user mode code.[33] The mask to be reinstated is passed to the signal delivery function so that it may be recorded in the user process and reinstated either by reentry into the kernel (via **sigreturn()**) or by being manually reloaded (see **sigprocmask()**) by the user mode handler doing a nonlocal goto back to top-level code within the user program.

psig() adds any masked signals associated with the action of the signal that will be atomically masked on delivery of this signal. It also accounts for a delivered signal in the statistics of the process (*ru_nsignals*). Finally, a specific code associated with the signal is cleared—this is an artifact of the earlier VAX implementation as an extension of the signal type so that it was possible for a debugger to isolate the exact reason a signal was generated. This mechanism was required due to the class of faults on the VAX which could cause certain signals. It is in actuality an incomplete hack that is nonstandard.[34]

6.3.14 What is coredump()?

coredump() is an internal kernel function which pretty much does what its name implies—it records an abnormally terminating process's image in a file so that it can be examined to find why the process died. It is used by both a terminating signal and

---

[33] Which in this case is bypassed in the kernel with the *oldmask* feature—see **sigpending()**.
[34] What is actually required is a way to identify the machine-dependent properties associated with signals in a machine-independent standard way.

---

by the **ptrace** mechanism to save away the contents of a process's image prior to reclaiming it. A side-effect of this function is to create and open a file to hold the contents of the running image's private data stack and per-process information. The point of **coredump()** is to allow for post-mortem debugging.[35]

... [File: /usr/src/kernel/kern/sig.c, line: 804]

```
int
coredump(struct proc *p)
   ...
```

coredump() has one argument: the process whose image must be dumped. It returns either zero indicating success or an error code if unsuccessful. In keeping with the standard format for UNIX system core files (known widely by public-domain debuggers), the core file is recorded as a specially formatted kernel stack containing the details of the running process, followed by the data and stack segments of the running program.

6.3.14.1 How is coredump() Implemented?

... [File: /usr/src/kernel/kern/sig.c, line: 817]

```
        if (pcred->p_svuid != pcred->p_ruid ||
            pcred->p_svgid != pcred->p_rgid)
                return (EPERM);
    ...
```

First, the process's credentials are checked to see if the program is running under an assumed group or user ID. For security reasons, we disallow core dumps of setuser ID and setgroup ID processes on the off-chance that the information contained within or the action of writing the core file may be used to subvert the system. If either is true, the function fails with an error (EPERM).

... [File: /usr/src/kernel/kern/sig.c, line: 822]

```
        if (ctob(UPAGES + vm->vm_dsize + vm->vm_ssize) >=
            p->p_rlimit[RLIMIT_CORE].rlim_cur)
                return (EFAULT);
    ...
```

Next, a check of the size of the prospective core file is made to see if it falls within the bounds of the resource limit on the size of core files that can be made (see **kern/resource.c**). If it is out of the range of the savecore file bounds, then the attempt to core dump fails with an error (EFAULT).

Note that no check is made for disk storage sufficient to store the file—this should actually be done here as well. Earlier versions of the kernel did not have the ability to

---

[35] Although this function has also been used as a way to simulate a checkpoint and later restart a process.

check for space present, but current and future versions of 386BSD now have this ability. This extension has been left as a simple exercise for the reader.

... [File: /usr/src/kernel/kern/sig.c, line: 827]

```
        sprintf(name, "%s.core", p->p_comm);
        nd.ni_dirp = name;
        nd.ni_segflg = UIO_SYSSPACE;
        if (error = vn_open(&nd, p, O_CREAT|FWRITE, 0644))
                return (error);
    ...
```

We attempt to create the file to hold the image of the process. The name used to hold the core file is created out of the first sixteen characters of the command name with ".core" appended to the end. This file is given permissions appropriate for it to be read and written by the owner and read by all others. If a file of this name cannot be created, then the **coredump()** function terminates immediately with an error from the vnode layer explaining why it could not be created.

... [File: /usr/src/kernel/kern/sig.c, line: 834]

```
        vp = nd.ni_vp;
        if (vp->v_type != VREG || VOP_GETATTR(vp, &vattr, cred, p) ||
            vattr.va_nlink != 1) {
                error = EFAULT;
                goto out;
        }
    ...
```

The now created file is checked to see if it is a regular file that has only one link to it.[36] In order to obtain information on the attributes of the file that would have the link count information, the vnode operation **VOP_GETATTR** is used to obtain the filesystem-independent attributes. Should it be impossible to confirm that a file is of the appropriate type, an error (EFAULT) is returned and the **coredump()** terminated. Since the file has been created and locked, it is incorrect to return immediately, so termination is done by exiting from the bottom of the function where the vnode is released back for reuse.

... [File: /usr/src/kernel/kern/sig.c, line: 842]

```
        VATTR_NULL(&vattr);
        vattr.va_size = 0;
        VOP_SETATTR(vp, &vattr, cred, p);
    ...
```

The attributes of the file are cleared in preparation for the unlinking of the file if we don't succeed in writing the entire contents of the core file.

---

[36] E.g., it is not a directory nor linked to yet another file—this was an old-fashioned method used to get the system to destroy a third party's file.

... [File: /usr/src/kernel/kern/sig.c, line: 849]

```
        memcpy(&p->p_addr->u_kproc.kp_proc, p, sizeof(struct proc));
        fill_eproc(p, &p->p_addr->u_kproc.kp_eproc);
...
```

A snapshot of the process is recorded in the process's kernel stack and the related
fields of the process are loaded into an extended process structure by the function
fill_eproc() (see **kern/kinfo.c**). The extended process structure makes up for the fact
that there is no conventional "u.", which by definition of the core file format is a fixed
record of all of the fields—this is now implemented in an entirely different and novel
manner in modern BSD systems.

... [File: /usr/src/kernel/kern/sig.c, line: 853]

```
        error = vn_rdwr(UIO_WRITE, vp, (caddr_t) p->p_addr, ctob(UPAGES),
            (off_t)0, UIO_SYSSPACE, IO_NODELOCKED|IO_UNIT, cred, (int *) NULL,
p);
        if (error)
                goto out;
...
```

The process's kernel stack containing the per-process information described by the
new extended process structure is written as the first segment of information into the
core file. If there is a problem in writing this segment out to the core file, the function
aborts, releasing the core file's vnode for reuse, and an error is signalled. Note that the
vnode read/write (vn_rdwr) is called with flags denoting that the operation is
occurring from kernel space and is operating on an already locked vnode so it won't
attempt to lock the vnode again, resulting in a deadlock.

The credentials used to write the file are the credentials of the process that is
terminating. Note that the accumulated time taken to write the core file (which may be
considerable) will be accounted to the dying process even though the resources
recorded in the core file's image of the extended process won't show this total, since
the extended process has already been sampled prior to the I/O operation performed.
Thus, the resource usage in the core file will not match the resource usage reported to
the parent process upon termination of the process. A niggling point perhaps, but to
fix this the per-process has to be written last even though it is at the beginning of the
file. This has been left as an interesting and nontrivial exercise for the reader—this is
not as simple as it appears, by the way, as there are some humorous subtleties which
can result if improperly done.

... [File: /usr/src/kernel/kern/sig.c, line: 860]

```
        error = vn_rdwr(UIO_WRITE, vp, vm->vm_daddr,
            (int)ctob(vm->vm_dsize), (off_t)ctob(UPAGES), UIO_USERSPACE,
            IO_NODELOCKED|IO_UNIT, cred, (int *) NULL, p);
        if (error)
                goto out;
...
```

Next, the data segment of the process is written out following the per-process area in the core file. The text segment of a process need not be written, since it can be recovered from the executable file itself unaltered. Like the characteristics of the write done above, the operation is performed in a locked vnode. If an error occurs the vnode must be released before the error is returned. Unlike the previous write, however, the write occurs from the user space of the process—not the kernel space.

... [File: /usr/src/kernel/kern/sig.c, line: 867]

```
    error = vn_rdwr(UIO_WRITE, vp,
        (caddr_t) trunc_page(vm->vm_maxsaddr + MAXSSIZ
            - ctob(vm->vm_ssize)),
        round_page(ctob(vm->vm_ssize)),
        (off_t)ctob(UPAGES) + ctob(vm->vm_dsize), UIO_USERSPACE,
        IO_NODELOCKED|IO_UNIT, cred, (int *) NULL, p);
...
```

Finally, the core file is given the stack segment as the last portion of a core file written. The stack segment is special in that it is a variable sized segment (that may be as large as MAXSSIZ) which generally only has a portion of it allocated (*vm_ssize*) starting at the extreme end of the reserved region of space. Only the allocated portion of the stack is written to the core file. Note that if pages of either the data or the stack are not in core at the time, they will be paged into the user process from swap space in order to write out the core file. Thus, the virtual memory system is very much active at this point in time—a side-effect of having a core dump is that all pages in the stack and data are force-loaded into memory; thus, upon dying, the process frequently grows to its largest size, forcing other processes to be paged out unnecessarily. Another exercise left to the reader is why this is of concern, and ways this side effect can be avoided.

... [File: /usr/src/kernel/kern/sig.c, line: 873]

```
out:
        /* release the file */
        VOP_UNLOCK(vp);
        error1 = vn_close(vp, FWRITE, cred, p);
        if (error == 0)
                error = error1;
        return (error);
...
```

In either the case of success or an error, the vnode is released and the file closed. If any of the vnode operations have returned an error, an error is passed from this function indicating that the **coredump()** was not successful. Note that currently the unsuccessful core dump file is still left allocated in the filesystem, even though it is useless.

6.3.14.2 Improvements to the Current Implementation of coredump()

The **coredump()** function is an anomalous and incomplete portion of the current system. It is primarily concerned with recording the contents of the process into a particular file, both of which are set by specifications that are really external to the kernel and subject to interpretation by different standards in different ways. Like the multitude of executable file formats (see **Chapter 9**) there are many different core dump formats in use in modern systems today. In addition, other problems exist which have not been dealt with. For example, it should be possible to checkpoint a process into an executable file (save all of the state of the file so that it can be reactivated later), but we cannot do this (yet) in this function.

While this function could be expanded by simplistic hacking to glue on yet another bit of functionality (as is done in other versions of **execve()**), **coredump()** would grow excessively. Developing a framework to communicate just how **coredump()** should choose to vary its mode of operation would alone become a considerable undertaking.

Most of the problems encounted in creating a modern **coredump()** function are similar in nature to the problems discussed in doing an extensible and minimalist **execve()**. As such, we suggest that, like **execve()**, this work be done outside of the kernel in the emulator program.[37] Extensions and refinements to the features of **coredump()** (just like the features of **execve()**) could be done and tested entirely independently of the version of the kernel upon which it is running. In addition, as an incentive, many of the security problems outlined above would vanish since now there would be nothing special about writing a core file as differing from writing any other file—they both would fall under the guidelines of the security model of the kernel in a uniform way.

Finally, it should be noted that while an argument might be made that **execve()** is a part of the kernel that should be optimized for speed because of its ability to be used in a large timesharing system very frequently, and thus is relevant to the kernel proper, no such argument exists for **coredump()**. The **coredump()** function is an anomaly of principal use in debugging programs. Thus, there is no excuse whatsoever not to lift it out of the kernel. What is more likely the case is that no one has ever bothered to develop the interfaces to lift it out of the kernel—it's just another unfinished portion of the system.

6.3.15 How Improvements to coredump() Impact Shared Libraries

An imperative towards making the changes discussed here is that there is no support in this kernel for shared libraries or for arbitrary memory mappings of the user process. Note that only one data segment is supported in BSD, while each shared library has its own private data segment. In general, all of the changes to support a new object file format or shared library implementation must have a corresponding entry in the **coredump()** generation—thus, the two are matched hand-in-hand.

While it is possible to finesse this with a data structure in the kernel that tracks the application of regions of virtual memory, this approach also leads to increased

---

[37] See *The 386BSD Executable File Format Emulator* in **Chapter 9**.

complexity in the kernel and its own coherence problems. By passing responsibility for the management of regions of virtual address space entirely to the emulation library which has control of the application interface to the operating system, one can neatly isolate the semantics of the application interface from the core kernel operational functionality. Thus, the operating system standard specifications can be independently applied in separate emulators, as they are intended. Thus, a windows emulator, for example, can be responsible for the semantics of virtual address space usage as necessary to support that operating system while a POSIX emulation library can support its view or version of the address space semantics separately. It is in fact this approach that we are using to allow the system to run with many different application interfaces without increasing the kernel size or complexity.

6.3.16 What is trapsignal()?

trapsignal() is an internal kernel function used as an alternative interface to **issig()** and **psig()**. It is used to process cpu processor exception traps. **trapsignal()** either processes the supplied signal in the context of the process present or arranges it to be processed at an appropriate point in time. The function ensures that the state associated with the signal will be maintained even though the signal may not be immediately acted upon by the user program. In the case where a signal cannot be delivered, the process will be terminated.

... [File: /usr/src/kernel/kern/sig.c, line: 890]

```
void
trapsignal(struct proc *p, int sig, unsigned code)
    ...
```

trapsignal() has three arguments: the pointer to the process receiving the signal; the signal sent; and an optional per-trap code. It returns nothing. The side-effect of this function is that it either handles the signal or makes it pending.

Exception traps differ from software-generated traps in that they can be generated by hard errors that cannot be ignored. Worse, they can occur as a result of handling a signal.[38] Finally, processor exceptions may also have associated additional information about a trap missing from a software-generated signal that frequently must be delivered to the handler before the condition is lost. Another aspect of some processors like the 386 is the asynchronous delivery of signals (as in the case of the floating point coprocessor). However, this is not completely implemented in a machine-independent manner in this edition of the software.

---

[38] For example, the recursive case of an exception in a signal associated with an exception.

6.3.16.1 How is trapsignal() Implemented?

... [File: /usr/src/kernel/kern/sig.c, line: 896]

```
        ps->ps_code = code; /* XXX for core dump/debugger */
    ...
```

A per-trap code supplied is saved in the signal action structure of the process. This is an artifice used to serve in place of a more general source description mechanism for the signal.

... [File: /usr/src/kernel/kern/sig.c, line: 909]

```
        if (p == curproc  && sig == SIGSEGV
            && vmspace_access(p->p_vmspace, (caddr_t)ps->ps_sigact[SIGSEGV],
sizeof(int), PROT_READ)
            == 0)
                sigexit(p, sig);
    ...
```

If the signal sent is in the current process and the signal is due to an invalid address reference (SIGSEGV) and if the signal action will be to attempt to reference an invalid handler address (e.g., we are about to experience a potentially recursive signal), then the process is terminated with **sigexit()**.

... [File: /usr/src/kernel/kern/sig.c, line: 918]

```
        if (p == curproc && (p->p_flag & STRC) == 0 &&
            (p->p_sigcatch & bit) != 0) {

                /* if signal not already blocked, pass to user program ... */
                if ((p->p_sigmask & bit) == 0) {
                        p->p_stats->p_ru.ru_nsignals++;
#ifdef KTRACE
                        if (KTRPOINT(p, KTR_PSIG))
                                ktrpsig(p->p_tracep, sig, ps->ps_sigact[sig],
                                        p->p_sigmask, code);
#endif
                        /* if failed to deliver, force process termination */
                        if (cpu_signal(p, sig, p->p_sigmask))
                                sigexit(p, sig);

                        ps->ps_code = 0; /* XXX for core dump/debugger */
                        p->p_sigmask |= ps->ps_catchmask[sig] | bit;
                }
                /* ... otherwise force process termination. */
                else
                        sigexit(p, sig);
        }
    ...
```

If the process signalled is the untraced current process and it has the ability to be caught, then the signal will be processed by this function. If the signal is not held, then the delivery of the signal to the user program is directly implemented by bypassing **psig()** and directly using the machine-dependent function **cpu_signal()** (see **i386/cpu.c**) to deliver the signal. If **cpu_signal()** cannot deliver the signal because of an illegal memory reference that could cause the function to recurse, the process is halted by calling **sigexit()**. The signal is then accounted for as being processed.

After being engaged, the per-trap code is cleared so as to not confuse it with a successive signal that may occur on the process. The signal mask is then updated to correspond to all of the signals that should be masked atomically on the occurrence of this signal along with the signal that has just been engaged.

If this unmaskable signal has been masked by the process, the process is terminated outright since in effect a default termination is asserted (it is impossible to continue processing of a held terminal signal), as might occur if the process were to set the SIGTRAP signal to be masked and then execute a breakpoint instruction. Without this mechanism, the breakpoint signal would be ignored and instead returned back to the user process, where the breakpoint would be again generated and would loop back again. In 386BSD, such signal loops would result in termination of the process rather than continuing an endlessly looping process.

... [File: /usr/src/kernel/kern/sig.c, line: 941]

```
        else
                psignal(p, sig);
    ...
```

If the signal is sent to a process that is not the current process, **psignal()** is used to add the signal to the process's set of pending signals, potentially causing the process to become the current process and have the signal be delivered or have its default effect occur.

6.3.17 What is siginit()?

siginit() is an internal kernel function which is used to set the first process's signal state to a known state so that it may run successfully. It also causes all ancestor processes to inherit a default state if otherwise uninitialized. **siginit()** consults the properties of all of the signals and sets the signal bitmasks in the process to the appropriate values for default evaluation of signals in a process. It is known that the structure has already been zeroed prior to call.

... [File: /usr/src/kernel/kern/sig.c, line: 951]

```
void
siginit(struct proc *p)
    ...
```

siginit() has one argument: the pointer to the process. It returns nothing.

6.3.17.1 How is siginit() Implemented?

... [File: /usr/src/kernel/kern/sig.c, line: 956]

```
    for (i = 0; i < NSIG; i++)
        if (sigprop[i] & SA_IGNORE && i != SIGCONT)
            p->p_sigignore |= sigmask(i);
...
```

The property array is scanned for all of the signals in the implementation, and the appropriate ignored signals (not including SIGCONT) are added to the *p_sigignore* mask of the process. Note that the continuation signal can never be ignored.

6.3.18 What is execsigs()?

execsigs() is an internal kernel function which is used in the late stages of the **execve()** system call handler to prepare the new process image's signals appropriately. **execsigs()** turns any caught signals in the old process image into the default cases and disables the signal stack.

... [File: /usr/src/kernel/kern/sig.c, line: 964]

```
void
execsigs(struct proc *p)
...
```

execsigs() has one argument: the pointer to the process. It returns nothing. The side-effect of this function is to reset all the signals to the default case. Since it is unlikely that the new process image's signal handlers are at the same location as the old, any caught signals are reset to the default case. Also, the alternate signal stack mechanism is cleared and thus disabled, since its location in the new image also does not make sense.

6.3.18.1 How is execsigs() Implemented?

... [File: /usr/src/kernel/kern/sig.c, line: 975]

```
    while (p->p_sigcatch) {
        signo = ffs((long)p->p_sigcatch);
        bit = sigmask(signo);
        p->p_sigcatch &= ~bit;
        if (sigprop[signo] & SA_IGNORE) {
            if (signo != SIGCONT)
                p->p_sigignore |= bit;
            p->p_sig &= ~bit;
        }
        ps->ps_sigact[signo] = SIG_DFL;
    }
...
```

The process's mask of catchable signals is evaluated and each signal in the mask is summarily eliminated with the corresponding action set to the default state. The properties of each signal are then examined to see if it should be ignored. If it should,

---

the pending signal mask is also adjusted to remove any corresponding signal left pending by the old process.

... [File: /usr/src/kernel/kern/sig.c, line: 990]

```
        ps->ps_onstack = 0;
        ps->ps_sigsp = 0;
        ps->ps_sigonstack = 0;
        ps->ps_stopsig = 0;
    ...
```

The signal stack feature is defeated by selecting that the signals be performed on the normal user process stack. In addition, the values of the old signal stack pointer and state are also cleared so that if the feature is enabled, it will point at an invalid portion of memory.[39] This will catch accidental invocation of the signal stack feature by a contrived signal stack frame. Finally, the value of the stop signal is cleared so that upon the first attempted trace operation any leftover signal from the previous process context won't spuriously be recorded.

6.3.19 What is pgsignal()?

pgsignal() is an internal kernel function which walks the process group list and uses **psignal()** to deliver a signal to each process in the group. An optional argument limits the delivery to processes that have a controlling terminal (or console).

... [File: /usr/src/kernel/kern/sig.c, line: 1001]

```
void
pgsignal(struct pgrp *pgrp, int sig, int checkctty)
    ...
```

pgsignal() has three arguments: the pointer to the process group; the signal to be delivered; and an option requiring that the signal only be delivered to processes that are connected to the controlling terminal (e.g., they are not background daemons that may have been started in the process group). It returns nothing.

6.3.19.1 How is pgsignal() Implemented?

... [File: /usr/src/kernel/kern/sig.c, line: 1006]

```
        if (pgrp)
            for (p = pgrp->pg_mem; p != NULL; p = p->p_pgrpnxt)
        if (checkctty == 0 || p->p_flag & SCTTY)
                psignal(p, sig);
    ...
```

If the process group is present, all processes in the process group are successively examined. If the controlling terminal option is present and the process has a

---

[39] E.g., the instruction space starting out at the bottom of the program address space, thus generating an error.

---

controlling terminal (SCTTY) or if the option is not present, the process is signalled with the **psignal()** function.

6.3.20 What is sigexit()?

sigexit() is a private function used only in this file which forces a process to terminate as a result of a signal. It examines the properties of the signal to determine if a core dump should be generated or if the signal should exit silently and arrange to have the process terminate with the appropriate error code. This function never returns.

The signal causing the termination may require a core dump to be generated prior to termination. The process contents are saved for post-mortem debugging prior to the process being forced to terminate (by calling the **exit()** system call handler—see **Chapter 5** on **kern/exit.c**)).

... [File: /usr/src/kernel/kern/sig.c, line: 1021]

```
static volatile void
sigexit(struct proc *p, int sig)
...
```

sigexit() has two arguments: the pointer to the process, and the signal that is terminating the process. It returns nothing since it never returns.

6.3.20.1 How is sigexit() Implemented?

... [File: /usr/src/kernel/kern/sig.c, line: 1025]

```
        if (sigprop[sig] & SA_CORE) {

                /* If dumping core, save the signal number for the debugger. */
                p->p_sigacts->ps_sig = sig;

                /* if successful, record for exit code that a core was made. */
                if (coredump(p) == 0)
                        sig |= WCOREFLAG;
        }

        /* exit with appropriate status, never to return */
        exit(p, W_EXITCODE(0, sig));
...
```

If the signal requires a core dump to be performed as one of its properties, it records in the process's signal action structure that the terminating signal is the one supplied and requests a core dump by calling the **coredump()** function. If the core dump was successful, this function records this fact in the exit code composed and passed to the **exit()** function that terminates this process. The exit code will ultimately be returned to the parent process via the **wait4()** system call handler (see **kern/exit.c**).

6.3.21 What is stop()?

stop() is a private function used only in this file which puts a process into the stopped state. It is used by both job control and process tracing. If the process can be stopped, **stop()** arranges to place it into the stopped state, optionally informing the parent before forcing it into that state. This function may also optionally force the process to abandon the processor so that the parent can be immediately informed of the change in state of the child process.

... [File: /usr/src/kernel/kern/sig.c, line: 1043]

```
static void
stop(struct proc *p, int swtchit, int sig)
...
```

stop() has three arguments: the pointer to the process being stopped; an option of forcing the process to give up the processor; and the signal associated with the stop request. It returns nothing.

stop() may be called either from the context of the currently running process (in which case it will request to abandon the processor) or from another process (in the case where the process is not the running process and hence will not need to abandon the processor). In the second case, the signal is being processed on the context of the process currently running—not the one getting the signal.

6.3.21.1 How is stop() Implemented?

... [File: /usr/src/kernel/kern/sig.c, line: 1048]

```
        if (p->p_flag&SPPWAIT)
                return;
...
```

If the process has done a **vfork()** operation (see **kern/fork.c**) and has loaned its context to its child, any stopping is disallowed since the process does not have a context on which to honor a stop and would instead result in a deadlock (since we would in effect be stopping the child). **vfork()**ed processes from traced or potentially stopped processes are viewed as if the entire **vfork()** operation of the child running was one big uninterruptible instruction. This artifice allows us to avoid many unpleasant cases associated with the fact that the process entry is not viable until its parts are no longer shared by the child.

... [File: /usr/src/kernel/kern/sig.c, line: 1052]

```
        if ((p->p_flag & STRC) == 0 && (p->p_pptr->p_flag & SNOCLDSTOP) == 0)
                psignal(p->p_pptr, SIGCHLD);
...
```

If the process is not being traced, the parent process is checked to see if it has the no child stop option (SNOCLDSTOP) present. In System V the parent process is not signalled on a stop[40] but signalled only in the case that a trace operation is present. In the BSD variant, the parent is signalled when a process stops.[41] The POSIX definition permits both behaviors by allowing the signal to be optionally sent if an option is selected via the signal's action flags, since many programs rely on this mechanism. A process flag is implemented via the signal action option flag to select this mode of operation (see **sigaction()** for more information). If the parent signal is permitted, it is signalled.

... [File: /usr/src/kernel/kern/sig.c, line: 1056]

```
        p->p_stat = SSTOP;
        wakeup((caddr_t)p->p_pptr);
...
```

The process is placed into the stopped state and the parent process is awakened.

... [File: /usr/src/kernel/kern/sig.c, line: 1060]

```
        p->p_sigacts->ps_stopsig = sig;
        p->p_flag &= ~SWTED;
...
```

The signal associated with the stop request is recorded in the signal action structure for the process and the process flag to indicate that the signal that has been waited for is cleared (SWTED). This flag bit will be set when this stop signal has been evaluated by **issig()**. This is done so that it is possible to identify when successive stop signals may be sent to a process and thus tell when yet another one may be adjacent.

... [File: /usr/src/kernel/kern/sig.c, line: 1064]

```
        if (swtchit) {
                swtch();
                (void) splnone();
        }
...
```

If requested, the processor is abandoned by calling the context switch operation **swtch** (see **i386/locore.s**). When the process is next rescheduled, the interrupt level is reset to the base level so that interrupts may be processed normally without being masked. Since processes may be stopped from interrupt level via **psignal()**, **stop()** both cannot and should not **swtch** away from the current process in stopping a process.

[40] As would be expected when used with **ptrace()**.
[41] As would be expected when a job control signal stops a child of a command shell.

Exercises

6.1 Why might it be desirable for user process signal handlers to make use of a separate stack?

6.2 Why doesn't **psignal()** check for permission to send a signal?

6.3 Why is a process promoted in priority to deliver a default signal?

6.4 **a)** Why do some processes appear to be "unkillable", even by the root superuser?
b) How could this be avoided?

6.5 Core dump files save much of the process state for postmortem debugging. Suppose one wished to restart a process from a **coredump()**. What information in general is not saved?

7 CREDENTIALS AND PRIVILEGES (kern/cred.c, kern/priv.c)

In a multi-user operating system, users are identified by a registered set of characteristics known as *credentials*. Akin to a driver's license or passport, these items are used by the operating system to authenticate access to shared objects. In addition to gating access, some users may be granted extended *privileges* to perform extraordinary operations. Privileges may be either granted for all time or revocable for a given implementation. In the current system, they are not revocable in use.[1]

Note that strictly speaking, a separate discussion of the credentials system calls themselves should appear in the last chapter of this book, since they are extremely specific to a POSIX system. However, since it is essential to the discussion of privilege and credentials in the general case of a low-level of abstraction protection mechanism in the kernel, and since POSIX-styled credentials are so utterly primitive anyway,[2] we examine them in lieu of a more general version of credential semantics.

7.1 Process Protection Mechanism: kern/cred.c

The file **kern/cred.c** contains the machine-independent code responsible for implementing the process protection mechanism, which allows multiple individual users to share access to the system while providing distinct protections via controlled access to system resources. It accomplishes this by implementing a group of credentials and privileges that are mediated by checks and controls throughout the rest of the high level of abstraction kernel. While this file itself operates at the top level of abstraction of the system, it implements a mechanism relied upon by all levels of the system. **kern/cred.c** uses a high-level interface which allows the process's credentials to be read or in some cases modified, as well as low-level primitives accessible by all layers of the system to check if the process credentials allow a privileged operation to occur.

7.1.1 User Credentials

Many of the POSIX program interface operations are conducted relative to a particular user identification, since the UNIX systems it standardizes are multi-user timesharing

---

[1] Although this may change, affecting the way in which credential sharing occurs in the future.

[2] In comparision to the much more elaborate protection models offered by other systems, including MULTICS. Since UNIX is pretty much a modern implementation of CTSS, we're talking basic survival tools for a campus timesharing system.

---

systems requiring protection between individual users. UNIX per-user protection is a simplified version of the earlier grander MULTICS scheme[3] which identified users by an (account, project) two-tuple. In UNIX, this is a user ID and group ID.

7.1.1.1 User ID and Group ID(s) in User Credentials

User credentials are broken up into two dimensions; *user ID* and *group IDs*. A group is akin to a defined administrative unit[4] where a group of users might share files, for example, via separate permissions, similar to the earlier MULTICS "projects." In earlier versions of UNIX, while logged in as a particular user ID, one would change to other permitted groups with the **newgrp** command.

There is only one user ID for each user credential, but there can be more than one group ID for each user credential, set with a manifest constant (NGROUPS), where the very first group member is always present. While the current implementation in 386BSD has a fixed number of groups, this item could easily be modified to allow an arbitrary number of groups (see **crget()** and **crfree()**).

7.1.2 Process Credentials

Process credentials, a superset of user credentials, contain the current user credentials as well as any privileges that may have been acquired or used during execution of a process. As such, process credentials directly relate to the process's capabilities at any given point in time, as does occur, for example, when we are allowed to write a file because our enclosed user credential allows us to do this, or when a privilege is present such as an ability to override file protections. The superuser in UNIX systems is the holder of all privileges.

Process credentials are only effective on process-related operations, such as process creation[5] or during process ID changes (using the **execve()** *setuserid* feature). Process credentials sit at a higher level of abstraction than user credentials. As such, lower level user subsystems (such as filesystems, protocols, drivers, and so forth) focus on user credentials, while in the process layer the kernel focuses primarily on process credentials. In sum, process credentials ask the question "Can this process do this process operation?", while user credentials ask the question "Can this operation be performed with this user credential?" Since user credentials act relative only to the operation being performed, such as doing a write of buffer, it may be that the operation performed no longer has an associated process.

Process credentials act relative to the lifetime of the process itself—in other words, it is valid only while the process exists. Many of the operations performed in checking

---

[3] Actually, it's almost identical to the MULTICS predecessor, CTSS.
[4] Like in a company, which is broken up into units such as engineering, sales, administration, and so forth.
[5] Note there are limits on the number of processes.

credentials often relate to the structural problems of user credentials associated with processes, and resolving issues if the process no longer exists.

7.1.3 Credentials in Older UNIX Implementations

Older UNIX systems using the concept of the group ID and user ID would first check the operation and then, if appropriate, initiate the operation. Since the operation could actually take a considerable period of time, the process itself might have ceased to exist before it finished. As such, credentials did not exist during the time it was processed. There was no concept of a user credential that could live on after the process died—once the operation had been checked, it was performed. This caused difficulty for filesystems like NFS. In order for NFS to perform its operation on another filesystem, it would have to have the credentials to negotiate with the other side, but since the credentials no longer existed, it could not proceed with the negotiation.

7.1.4 Credentials and Reference Counts

To avoid the overuse of memory, a *reference counted object* is shared by the process credentials and all other operations that may reference these particular credential sets. The credentials themselves are all kept in a compact data structure.[6] These objects may have many different references pointed to them at one time. For example, a write in progress to a file must have at least two references present—one reference to the process credential that the user credential is held within and one reference to the particular file or vnode written at that point in time. Since the file write operation may go through many suboperations which may themselves additionally reference credentials, the reference count on credentials may climb as references are made or drop as the operations involved in writing the file complete and the references evaporate.

In all cases related to user credentials the reference count is strictly observed. One cannot create a group or user ID without a reference count, nor destroy either without a zero reference count. The effects of a common user credentials programming mistake is to either leave many copies of credentials allocated but unused (the reference count was larger than actually present), or free the credentials to early, leaving a reference outstanding to a set of credentials passed back to the memory allocator and possibly reused for an entirely different purpose (the reference count was somehow too small). Since this is one of the primary dangers of dynamic memory allocation in the kernel, the number of interfaces which make use of creating and destroying credentials is kept intentionally small to minimize this problem.

---

[6] **struct ucred** for user credentials and **struct pcred** for process credentials.

An analogous macro used with user credentials is **crhold()**, which simply increments the reference count by one in the case where an additional reference is made to the credential. Such code obviously should arrange to (eventually) **crfree()** the selfsame credentials when the reference is relinquished.

7.1.5 Supplementary Groups

The addition of BSD *supplementary groups*[7] in 4 BSD was a small enhancement done to allow more latitude in file access control. In MULTICS, access control lists allowed one to specify exactly what accounts and projects could access a file and the kind of access allowed. This very general and complicated mechanism meant that one could share data or programs with a variety of other users while having greater control over the access to a category.[8] In general, access control lists are usually implemented in secure systems, and POSIX subspecifications address this area. However, interestingly enough, no secure systems implement the POSIX access control lists at this time.

While earlier versions of BSD used only one group ID, requiring the use of the **newgrp** command to switch groups to obtain file access, BSD supplementary groups allowed a program to access files via a number of different groups directly. This mechanism, unlike the MULTICS access control lists, is not a general solution, however, but instead a quick hack. For example, one cannot control access to a file on a per-user basis—just a per-group basis.

File permissions typically fall into three categories: 1) user or owner, 2) group, and 3) other. This primitive mechanism suffices in many cases when one can manage to segregate items into enough individually managed groups. BSD supplementary groups are the set of all possible groups to which a particular process belongs. Supplementary groups are generally set at login time and can be seen with the **groups** command.[9]

7.1.6 Sharing of Credentials

Sharing is an important part of the credentials process, and many of the mechanisms associated with privileges and credentials are concerned with the sharing and unsharing of objects. Sharing is associated only with a reference to a particular credential with a lower level object, so the operations themselves reference the process credentials and not the process itself. Sharing also reduces the cost of operations. Instead of allocating a new set of credentials in terms of memory, this same portion of memory with a reference count is used for possibly dozens of references conducted.

---

[7] Analogous to MULTICS access control lists.

[8] For example, you could allow other people to read your report and selectively enable one person to add to the report but everyone else on that timesharing system could not access the file.

[9] See **setgroups()**, **getgroups()**, and **groupmember()** for further information.

As an alternative, one could avoid sharing by allocating separate portions of memory; however, the resource cost associated with doing these write operations is very costly and hence to be avoided.

7.1.6.1 Sharing of User Credentials

Sharing of user credentials allow us to get around another serious dilemma, to wit, what if an operation is started (such as a write) and the process then changes its identification?[10] If reference checking on credentials was not done, we would have a bad situation arise where the older operation (our write) is done with the older credentials, not the new credentials. With reference checking, as the process credential changes, the process itself disowns its older credential. When the (write) operation completes on the last operation before the change in credential occurs, the old credentials' reference count drops to zero and is reclaimed (freed), while the new credentials inserted in the process are not seen by any of those old operations, because they're looking at the old credentials. This is why user credentials are a shared object.

7.1.6.2 Sharing of Process Credentials

Sharing of process credentials is a new addition to 386BSD as part of the work done to make a more efficient kernel. Process credentials sharing reduces the cost of creating and destroying a process by reducing the number of memory allocations and deallocations required to create a process.

It has been observed that in average use most processes are created in groups (not typically one or two) at a time, such as when a user fires up a **make** or a pipeline[11] command, creating 5-10 processes which cooperate and have exactly the same process and user credentials. Instead of creating a unique set of process credentials, we now use a reference count system to track the number of references to a single set of process credentials held by all of the user's processes. In general, process credentials tend to be one set of credentials for the literally hundreds of processes which a single user may be using. One benefit of this mechanism is that we no longer have to do memory allocations and deallocations for every one of these processes, but instead need only refer to the shared process credentials.[12]

This mechanism does not come for free. In the case where the process credentials are modified[13] we must be able to selectively unshare and create a unique copy of user and process credentials. One of the oddities about this case is that, since process credentials are now shared and contain within them a possibly shared user credential, we now have a *recursively* shared object. This unusual case is dealt with in this implementation.

---

[10] Via changing the user ID or user credentials via the **execve()** *setuserid* feature.
[11] For example "**ls | grep "^foo" | wc**".
[12] See **kern/fork.c** and **kern/exit.c** in **Chapter 5** for more on process creation and destruction.
[13] Such as when **setuserid** programs are run which have different process credentials.

7.1.7 How Credentials Impact Secure Systems

If a secure system requires additional credentials, the situation is greatly complicated. In this case, a secure system must inherently negotiate a more rigorous scheme of credentials which may conflict. For example, in the case of a program allowed to proceed with an operation that is later found illegal, it is difficult to determine if at this point it should be allowed to complete or disallowed for security reasons (breaking the semantics of the procedure). If the item is resource-related (such as disk space allocation), a nasty situation can develop, such as writing a block on a server and not knowing to whom this block is associated.

7.1.8 Scope of Authority in UNIX Systems

Privileges on standard UNIX systems are consolidated into one user ID called the *superuser*. If the system asks for privileged operation, it is done by the superuser and all lumped in one category. This is not desirable for secure systems.

The argument for separation of privileges is a good one, but how this is best handled in a practical way without adding a considerable amount of complex code is a subtle issue. In part, one must divide up secure portions of the system's functionality into zones that do not overlap. This choice of zones is complicated by the fact that one might wish to maintain systems over the network, yet it's via the network system administration interface that most systems are compromised in the first place.

As a first small attempt at accomplishing this, **setuid** programs should be allowed to be executed by incoming network communications, but with all administrative functions stripped out of the superuser function set. In this case, one could only do administration locally,[14] but we would no longer be worried about subversion via the network. Instead, a configuration-dependent file **kern/priv.c** looks for the privilege associated with the process credentials.

7.1.9 Functions Contained in the File kern/cred.c

The functions in the file **kern/cred.c** implement the process and user credential abstraction, which is the means of internally authenticating processes and the users on whose behalf they operate. Actual privileges are implemented in an independent subsystem (see **kern/priv.c** for details). This file contains the following functions:

> **modpcred()**
> **getuid()**
> **geteuid()**
> **getgid()**
> **getegid()**

---

[14] I.e., someone manning the console.

getgroups()

setuid()

seteuid()

setgid()

setegid()

setgroups()

groupmember()

crget()

crfree()

crdup()

getlogin()

setlogin()

Kernel process credential modification is accomplished with **modpcred()**. The **getXX()** and **setXX()** functions are system call handlers used along with the internal kernel function **groupmember()** to access credentials. The **crXX()** functions contain the kernel credential propagation primitives. Finally, the functions **getlogin()** and **setlogin** are BSD system call handlers used to access the login account name.

7.1.10 What is modpcred()?

modpcred(), short for *modified process credentials*, is an internal kernel interface used to detect if the process or user credentials are shared. If the process has shared credentials, **modpcred()** will unshare them and create unique copies. This function is called before the process credentials are modified. If the process credentials are only singularly referenced, however, then the function simply returns. This is the only routine which reconciles the sharing of any credentials.

modpcred() is called by the higher level portions of the kernel and only in the context of a process—usually, but not always, the process it is modifying. Since this function may block allocation of memory, it must not be called from interrupt level. **modpcred()** does not check the veracity of the process. It relies upon the caller to know that the process passed to it has credentials in the first place.

... [File: /usr/src/kernel/kern/cred.c, line: 48]

```
struct pcred *
modpcred(struct proc *p) {
   ...
```

modpcred() accepts a process as its only argument and returns the value of the credentials for this process. Since the credentials may have been modified by this function, any local copies of the credential's pointer for the process called may wish to

---

be updated with the value returned by **modpcred()**. Note that the user credentials are in the process credentials, so any reference to them may also need to be refreshed.

7.1.10.1 How is modpcred() Implemented?

modpcred() is implemented as a staggered set of unsharing calls, depending on the user credential allocation and deallocation functions.

... [File: /usr/src/kernel/kern/cred.c, line: 53]

```
if (pc->p_refcnt != 1) {
        MALLOC(pc, struct pcred *, sizeof(struct pcred),
        M_SUBPROC, M_WAITOK);
        *pc = *p->p_cred;
        pc->p_refcnt = 1;
        p->p_cred->p_refcnt--;
        p->p_cred = pc;

        /* user credentials now referenced by both */
        crhold(p->p_ucred);
}
...
```

modpcred() first checks to see if the process credential reference count is not one—this implies that there is someone else sharing a reference to this set of process credentials. In this case, it allocates a new portion of memory to hold the credential and copies the existing ones into that new region of memory, setting the reference count to one. The reference count of the older credential is reduced by one and the process's process credential pointer is overwritten with the new process credential. In sum, we have exchanged the old shared process credential for a new unshared process credential.

Since both the old process credential and the new process credential share the same user credential, we must now increment the reference count on the user credential of the process. At this point, the top-level process credential that encompasses the user credential is unshared, but this is not yet true for the bottom-level user credential (other than increasing the reference count).

... [File: /usr/src/kernel/kern/cred.c, line: 66]

```
if (pc->pc_ucred->cr_ref != 1) {
        /* duplicate the old one */
        struct ucred *newcr = crdup(pc->pc_ucred);

        /* release the old reference */
        crfree(pc->pc_ucred);
        pc->pc_ucred = newcr;
}

return (pc);
...
```

Next, we check to see if the user credentials are shared as well. If so (the reference count is not equal to one), we must duplicate the credentials into a new set by calling the **crdup()** function. We release the old credentials using **crfree()** (if the reference

---

count drops to zero), which may or may not deallocate the references to the user credential as before, and assign new user credentials to this process.

One should note that replication of process credentials implies replication of user credentials, because at the end of replicating the process credential we incremented the reference count. The new unshared process credentials are returned at the end of this function.

7.1.10.2 386BSD modpcred() Evolutionary History

In prior editions of 386BSD and earlier Berkeley UNIX systems, user credentials were shared but process credentials were uniquely allocated. Process credential sharing is slightly more complicated, because process credentials are the last thing deallocated before the process ceases to exist; to wit, if process credentials are deallocated with the rest of the state of the process during **exit()**, utilities such as **ps(1)** would find random memory for values which may or may not have been correct for the user ID and other credentials in the visible zombie processes.[15]

Process credential sharing also reduced the cost of sharing the process. However, this approach is valid only if we don't tend to change or modify process credentials each time we create new a process, as might occur in the case of a server which accepts requests and then forks processes, changing each user ID each time. In this case, managing to share credentials might not be an advantage, since we're now only postponing the copy on creation. However, this singular example is a very unusual situation, and not common practice for other reasons as well.

7.1.10.3 386BSD modpcred() Design Choices and Trade-Offs

The **modpcred()** function effectively subsumed the **crcopy()** function used in earlier versions of the kernel. **crcopy()** selectively replicated and made unique copies of user credentials only, and in a sense reflected a conscious design choice avoiding process credential sharing. As an alternative to this approach, **modpcred()** could have been written as a nesting **crcopy()** (possibly called **pccopy()**). Unfortunately, in this case, every time a **crcopy()** would be done, we would also have needed to check if the process credential had changed as well, thus adding another interface as well as increasing the hierarchy of the design. As such, we chose to do away completely with **crcopy()**, allowing a more direct approach requiring only one interface.

7.1.11 What are getuid(), geteuid(), getgid() and getegid()?

These POSIX system call handlers implement trivial POSIX functions which gain access to the credentials and return a value. While they needn't be implemented in the kernel, they are placed here for convenience purposes only.

---

[15] Since, in effect, the utility has a "reference" to the credentials even if in the kernel there is no reference to them!

The "get" handlers affect the POSIX process's user and group IDs as implemented inside the credentials. These group and user IDs can be either real or effective. The real user ID contains the ownership of the process and its effective powers at any given point in time (access control)—the base level abilities of the process at the moment. The effective user ID is the effective user credentials at that moment in time—the additional privileges it may possess at the moment beyond the base level abilities.

In an ordinary process, the real and effective IDs are the same. If there is a **setuserid** process running, however, the real user ID will have less privileges than the effective user ID.

The "get" functions basically return the user and group IDs of the current process running as a way for the process to find out who it is being run by and what its effective permissions are. It should be noted that **getegid()** and **getgid()** return the very first group only.

7.1.11.1 Real and Effective Privilege Evolutionary History

Older BSD systems had the ability to swap real and effective privileges. By running a program which could alternate between the two, they didn't have to manually remember what user ID was what at any given point in time, or during times when someone wanted the real user ID to appear as someone else's ID.[16] This ability is not allowed in POSIX, and hence is not part of the current 386BSD implementation.

7.1.11.2 What Does the Kernel Expect of getuid()?

getuid() is a system call handler used to implement a POSIX function. It accepts no arguments and returns as a single value the real user ID obtained from the process credential.

... [File: /usr/src/kernel/kern/cred.c, line: 79]

```
int
getuid(p, uap, retval)
        struct proc *p;
        void *uap;
        int *retval;
    ...
```

Like all system call handlers, **getuid()** has three arguments, the second of which doesn't point to any incoming arguments since there are none for this function. The system call handler itself returns no errors (none are possible).

---

[16] The real user ID was who you were logged in as, while the effective user ID was whose operations you were validated as.

7.1.11.3 How is getuid() Implemented?

... [File: /usr/src/kernel/kern/cred.c, line: 86]

```
        *retval = p->p_cred->p_ruid;
        return(0);
...
```

The real user ID is extracted from the process' credentials and returned as the value of the system call, which always returns sucessfully.

7.1.11.4 What Does the Kernel Expect of geteuid()?

geteuid() is a system call handler used to implement a POSIX function. It accepts no arguments and returns as a single value the effective user ID obtained from the process's current user credential.

... [File: /usr/src/kernel/kern/cred.c, line: 91]

```
int
geteuid(p, uap, retval)
struct proc *p;
void *uap;
int *retval;
...
```

Like all system call handlers, **geteuid()** has three arguments, the second of which doesn't point to any incoming arguments since there are none for this function. The system call handler itself returns no errors (none are possible).

7.1.11.5 How is geteuid() Implemented?

... [File: /usr/src/kernel/kern/cred.c, line: 98]

```
        *retval = p->p_ucred->cr_uid;
        return(0);
...
```

The current effective user ID is extracted from the process's user credential and returned as the value of the system call, which always returns sucessfully. Note that **p_ucred** is actually a macro that hides an additional indirection, since the reference to the user credential is embedded in the process credential.

7.1.11.6 What Does the Kernel Expect of getgid()?

getgid() is a system call handler used to implement a POSIX function. It accepts no arguments and returns as a single value the real group ID obtained from the process credential.

... [File: /usr/src/kernel/kern/cred.c, line: 103]

```
int
getgid(p, uap, retval)
struct proc *p;
void *uap;
int *retval;
...
```

Like all system call handlers, **getgid()** has three arguments, the second of which doesn't point to any incoming arguments since there are none for this function. The system call handler itself returns no errors (none are possible).

7.1.11.7 How is getgid() Implemented?

... [File: /usr/src/kernel/kern/cred.c, line: 110]

```
        *retval = p->p_cred->p_rgid;
        return(0);
...
```

The real group ID is extracted from the process's credentials and returned as the value of the system call, which always returns sucessfully.

7.1.11.8 What Does the Kernel Expect of getegid()?

getegid() is a system call handler used to implement a POSIX function. It accepts no arguments and returns as a single value the effective group ID obtained from the process's user credential. By definition, the very first of the supplementary groups is the POSIX effective group ID.

... [File: /usr/src/kernel/kern/cred.c, line: 115]

```
int
getegid(p, uap, retval)
struct proc *p;
void *uap;
int *retval;
...
```

Like all system call handlers, **getegid()** has three arguments, the second of which doesn't point to any incoming arguments since there are none for this function. The system call handler itself returns no errors (none are possible).

7.1.11.9 How is getegid() Implemented?

... [File: /usr/src/kernel/kern/cred.c, line: 122]

```
        *retval = p->p_ucred->cr_groups[0];
        return(0);
...
```

The current effective group ID is extracted from the process's user credential and returned as the value of the system call, which always returns sucessfully. Note that **p_ucred** is actually a macro that hides an additional indirection, as the reference to the user credential is embedded in the process credential. Also, note that the group ID is the first of the array of supplemental group IDs in the credential.

7.1.12 What is getgroups()?

Another function, **getgroups()**, implements the BSD get supplementary groups system call handler. It returns the complete set of group IDs, where the very first ID in this array of group IDs is the POSIX group ID. **getgroups()** is not a POSIX function itself, but oddly enough the supplementary groups are an optional portion of POSIX 1003.1. POSIX defines the function of supplementary groups as alternative groups that might optionally be implemented. This was done so that BSD multiple groups could be used alongside POSIX without having the POSIX membership agree on how to implement this feature entirely.

The **getgroups()** function implements a system call handler which returns either a value or possibly an error code. There are no side-effects to the function.

... [File: /usr/src/kernel/kern/cred.c, line: 127]

```
int
getgroups(p, uap, retval)
        struct proc *p;
        struct  arg {
                u_int   gidsetsize;
                int     *gidset;                    /* XXX not yet POSIX */
        } *uap;
        int *retval;
    ...
```

This function has the same conventions as a system call handler: two arguments and a return value. It will return an error if trying to return more groups than will fit in the buffer (EINVALID) or if an error is encountered in copying back the groups (e.g., such as if asked to return a value to an unallocated portion of memory (EFAULT)). If a group set of zero is asked to be returned, no groups will be returned. Instead, the return value of the system call will be set to the number of groups that are present with this process. In this way, the number of groups can be determined in preparation for allocating a large enough buffer to return all of the group (avoiding an EINVALID). Note that this system call by definition must return all of the groups or none of the groups—we can't return a portion of the groups.

7.1.12.1 How is getgroups() Implemented?

getgroups() first checks for the presence of an adequate buffer and then translates the stored group IDs in the supplementary set into a form appropriate for the definition of the function which it implements.

... [File: /usr/src/kernel/kern/cred.c, line: 144]

```
        if ((ngrp = uap->gidsetsize) == 0) {
                *retval = pc->pc_ucred->cr_ngroups;
                return (0);
        }
    ...
```

One of the two arguments passed is the size of the user's buffer to receive the supplementary group's array, in units of numbers of group ID (i.e., the size of the largest index of the array). If this number happens to be zero (i.e., no space in the array), then the array pointer to the other argument is ignored entirely and the value of the number of groups in the credential is returned immediately. In this case, we have received none of the supplementary groups as a return value but have instead returned the number present. When we get space in the array, the buffer can be rescaled appropriately for a second pass.

... [File: /usr/src/kernel/kern/cred.c, line: 150]

```
    if (ngrp < pc->pc_ucred->cr_ngroups)
            return (EINVAL);
...
```

If the value of the size of the receiving buffer is smaller than the number of groups present, then an EINVALID error code is returned, since the buffer is not large enough to hold all of the groups at once. Note that if the buffer is larger, it will receive only the number of groups present with no modification of the subsequent portions of the buffer.

... [File: /usr/src/kernel/kern/cred.c, line: 154]

```
    ngrp = pc->pc_ucred->cr_ngroups;
    for (gp = pc->pc_ucred->cr_groups, lp = groups; lp < &groups[ngrp]; )
            *lp++ = *gp++;
...
```

Groups in the user credentials are an array of POSIX group type (gid_t), which may or may not be the same size as the BSD specification calling for integer groups. Therefore, we must copy out the credential into the automatic buffer in this function's frame to convert the credential into a format to be received by the BSD system call. Since this is a fixed length buffer, the size of the maximum number of groups is a compile time limit. If an indefinite limit to the number of supplementary groups is desired, modifications to this implementation would occur here.

... [File: /usr/src/kernel/kern/cred.c, line: 159]

```
    if (error = copyout(p, (caddr_t)groups, (caddr_t)uap->gidset,
        ngrp * sizeof (groups[0])))
            return (error);

    /* return number of groups returned */
    *retval = ngrp;
    return (0);
...
```

The temporary group's buffer is then copied to the user program at the second argument's specified location. If there is an error in passing back the information, an error is returned and a partial number of the elements of the user's buffer will have been modified. If the buffer has been successfully copied back, the number of entries copied back into the group buffer is returned as a return value.

7.1.12.2 getgroups() Design Choices and Trade-offs

getgroups() can be rather silly at times—for example, why insist on returning all of the set at any given point instead of just a partial set? In this case, we wouldn't require geteuid(), reducing complexity. Unfortunately, the way **getgroups()** is defined as a BSD interface does not allow this improvement, so that the number of groups could be atomically set at any given point in time. In this implementation, we follow the specification, but we don't necessarily like it.

7.1.12.3 Improvements to the Current Implementation of getgroups

If an indefinite number of supplementary groups was desired, one might avoid the fixed compile time limit by omitting the temporary buffer or work in a small set of groups successively converting. In this case, one would also have to implement a resource limit[17] (rlimit) for the number of groups in use; otherwise system performance might be degraded.

7.1.13 What is setuid()?

setuid() is a function that sets the real user ID of the process. This is the only function that can set the real and effective user ID portion of the process and user credentials. This function implements a POSIX system call handler which has the side-effect of possibly changing the user ID of the process. If it unable to do so, it returns an error.

```
... [ File: /usr/src/kernel/kern/cred.c, line: 169 ]

int
setuid(p, uap, retval)
        struct proc *p;
        struct args {
                int     uid;
        } *uap;
        int *retval;
 ...
```

setuid() has the arguments appropriate for a system call handler. It accepts as a single argument for the system call the (hopefully) new user ID and then returns nothing. It will return an error (EPERM) if it is not privileged to change the user ID. One additional side effect causes the setting of an accounting flag stating that this process has used the privilege if is permitted to change the user ID. Having a privilege doesn't necessarily mean having to use a privilege, however.

7.1.13.1 How is setuid() Implemented?

setuid() is a very simple function which checks for privileges and, if privileged, modifies the process and user credentials to the new user ID. In advance of modify the credential it ensures a unique set of credentials to modify.

---

[17] See **kern/resources.c** for limits.

... [File: /usr/src/kernel/kern/cred.c, line: 182]

```
        if (uid != pc->p_ruid &&
            (error = use_priv(pc->pc_ucred, PRV_SETUID, p)))
                return (error);
    ...
```

First, the privilege is checked to see if we can even perform this operation. In all cases, we can set our own user ID. If the user ID we wish to set is the real user ID anyway, we will also always accept it. This has the interesting effect of allowing us to erase a saved user ID of the process credential which may be different on the execution of a **setuid** program (see **kern/execve.c** in **Chapter 9**). In this way, we have in part avoided the need for a **setreuid()** BSD system call function, which is no longer implemented and not part of the POSIX standard. If we are a privileged user (or superuser) we can then set the real user ID. If we are not a privileged user, then an EPERM error is returned and the system call handler terminates.

... [File: /usr/src/kernel/kern/cred.c, line: 187]

```
        pc = modpcred(p);
        pc->pc_ucred->cr_uid = uid;
        pc->p_ruid = uid;
        pc->p_svuid = uid;

        return (0);
    ...
```

Now that we have the privileges to modify the process and user credentials, we call the **modpcred()** function to ensure we have a unique copy of the process and user credentials so we can modify them. Note that we don't check to see if the modifications we are about to make have no net effect—thus, one of the side effects of this implementation is that if an **setuid()** is done to the selfsame user ID, the process credential will become unshared regardless, ensuring a unique set. After generating a unique set of credentials which may or may not cause a copy to occur (and thus a potential block from memory), we update the user credential with a new user ID and the process credential with the real and saved user ID, and return successfully back from this system call handler.

7.1.13.2 Improvements to the Current Implementation of setuid()

The major improvement is the inclusion of *list role privileges*. Instead of a singular **suser()** function which examines the process's user credentials to see if it is privileged, we implement privileges as a separately enumerated set of grantable privileges on a per-user basis, grouped into a defined set of roles for ease of implementation (see **kern/priv.c** for more information).

7.1.14 What is seteuid()?

seteuid() sets the effective user ID of the process's user credential. This is the only function that can change the effective user ID portion of the user credential. This function implements a POSIX system call handler which has the side-effect of changing the effective user ID of the user credential or, if it is unable to do so, returns an error.

... [File: /usr/src/kernel/kern/cred.c, line: 196]

```
int
seteuid(p, uap, retval)
        struct proc *p;
        struct args {
                int     euid;
        } *uap;
        int *retval;
...
```

The **seteuid()** function has the arguments appropriate for a system call handler. It will return an error (EPERM) if it does not possess the privileges required to change the effective user ID. A side-effect of this procedure causes an accounting flag to be set stating that this process has used a privilege once it receives permission. As noted before, having a privilege doesn't mean having to use a privilege. **seteuid()** accepts as a single argument the hopefully new user ID and returns nothing.

7.1.14.1 How is seteuid() Implemented?

seteuid() is a very simple function which checks for privileges and, if allowed, modifies the user credential to the new user ID. Prior to modifying the user credential, it ensures that it has a unique set of credentials to modify.

... [File: /usr/src/kernel/kern/cred.c, line: 209]

```
        if (euid != pc->p_ruid && euid != pc->p_svuid &&
           (error = use_priv(pc->pc_ucred, PRV_SETUID, p)))
                return (error);
...
```

First, the privilege is checked to see if we can perform this operation. We can set our own user ID in all cases. If the user ID we wish to set is the real user ID anyway, or the saved user ID, it will always accept that as well.

However, occasionally, the saved user ID is different from the real user ID. For example, in the case of executing a **setuid** program, where the saved user ID is the user ID of the file executed (see **kern/execve.c**), the **setuid** program can alternate between setting the older user credentials (e.g. the real user ID) and the newer user credentials (the saved user ID). One is then able to forego privileges and get them back again in the same program.[18]

During the portion of time that the program did not want to use the privileges of superuser, one merely does a **seteuid()** to the real user ID obtained from **getuid()** and

---

[18] For example, if one does a **setuid()** to root, then the saved user ID is root but the real user ID is the user in which root is operating on its behalf.

then operates with the effective credentials of that user. No superuser priviliges work at this time, but if one wished to regain privileges to perform certain operations, it would then **seteuid()** back to the value of the saved user ID (in this case, root).[19] If one is a privileged user or superuser, we can set the effective user ID. Otherwise an error (EPERM) is returned and the system call handler terminates.

... [File: /usr/src/kernel/kern/cred.c, line: 214]

```
        pc = modpcred(p);
        pc->pc_ucred->cr_uid = euid;

        return (0);
    ...
```

Now that we are privileged, we call the **modpcred()** function to ensure we have a unique copy of the user credentials to modify. Note that we don't check to see if the modifications we are about to make have no net effect—thus, one of the side-effects of this implementation is if one does a **setuid()** to the selfsame user ID, one will unshare the process and user credentials regardless and ensure a unique set. After generating a unique set of credentials, which may or may not cause a copy to occur (and thus a potential block from memory), we update the user credentials with a new user ID (the process credentials themselves do not change) and return successfully back from this system call handler.

7.1.15 What is setgid()?

setgid() is a function which sets the real group IDs of the process. This is the only function that can change the real and effective group IDs portion of the process and user credentials. This function implements a POSIX system call handler which has the side-effect of possibly changing the group ID of the process or, if unable to do so, returns an error.

... [File: /usr/src/kernel/kern/cred.c, line: 221]

```
int
setgid(p, uap, retval)
        struct proc *p;
        struct args {
                int     gid;
        } *uap;
        int *retval;
    ...
```

The **setgid()** function has the arguments appropriate for a system call handler. It will return an error (EPERM) if it is unable to obtain the privileges required to change the group ID. In addition, an accounting flag can be set stating that this process has used a

---

[19] N.B. The saved user ID would have been gotten by doing a **geteuid()** before changing the effective user ID the first time.

privilege. As noted before, having a privilege doesn't mean having to use a privilege. **setgid()** accepts as a single argument the hopefully new group ID and returns nothing.

7.1.15.1 How is setgid() Implemented?

setgid() is a very simple function which checks for privileges and, if privileged, modifies the process and user credentials to the new group ID. Prior to modifying the credentials, it ensures a unique set to modify.

... [File: /usr/src/kernel/kern/cred.c, line: 234]

```
        if (gid != pc->p_rgid &&
            (error = use_priv(pc->pc_ucred, PRV_SETGID, p)))
                return (error);
    ...
```

The privilege is first checked to see if we can perform this operation. We can set our own group ID in all cases. If the group ID we wish to set is the real group ID anyway, we will always accept it. This has the interesting effect of allowing one to erase a saved group ID of the process credential which may differ on the execution of a **setgid** program (see **kern/execve.c** in **Chapter 9**). Thus, we avoid in part the need for a non-POSIX **setregid()** BSD system call function, which is no longer implemented in 386BSD. If we are a privileged user or superuser, we can set the real group ID; otherwise an error (EPERM) will be returned and the system call handler terminated.

... [File: /usr/src/kernel/kern/cred.c, line: 239]

```
        pc = modpcred(p);
        pc->pc_ucred->cr_groups[0] = gid;
        pc->p_rgid = gid;
        pc->p_svgid = gid;

        return (0);
    ...
```

Once we are privileged, the **modpcred()** function is called to ensure we have a unique copy of the process and user credentials to modify. Note that we don't check to see if the modifications we are about to make have no net effect—thus, one of the side-effects of this implementation is that if one does a **setgid()** to the selfsame group ID, one will unshare the process credentials regardless and ensure a unique set. After generating a unique set of credentials, which may or may not cause a copy to occur (and thus a potential block from memory), we update the user credential with a new group ID and the process credential with the real and saved group ID.[20] We then return successfully back from this system call handler.

---

[20] Note that the POSIX group ID is always implemented as the first of the supplementary groups in the user credential.

7.1.16 What is setegid()?

setegid() is a POSIX system call handler that sets the effective group ID of the process and user credentials. This is the only function which changes the effective group IDs portion of the user credentials. setegid() changes the effective group ID of the user credentials or, if unable to do so, returns an error.

... [File: /usr/src/kernel/kern/cred.c, line: 248]

```
int
setegid(p, uap, retval)
        struct proc *p;
        struct args {
                int     egid;
        } *uap;
        int *retval;
...
```

The setegid() function has the arguments appropriate for a system call handler. It will return an error (EPERM) if it does not possess the privileges required to change the effective group ID. An accounting flag can then be set stating that this process has used a privilege. As noted before, having a privilege doesn't mean having to use a privilege. setegid() accepts as a single argument the hopefully new group ID and returns nothing.

7.1.16.1 How is setegid() Implemented?

setegid() is a very simple function which checks for privileges and, if privileged, modifies the user credentials to the new group ID. Prior to modifying the credentials, it ensures a unique set of credentials to modify.

... [File: /usr/src/kernel/kern/cred.c, line: 261]

```
        if (egid != pc->p_rgid && egid != pc->p_svgid &&
            (error = use_priv(pc->pc_ucred, PRV_SETGID, p)))
                return (error);
...
```

The privilege is first checked to see if we can perform this operation. We can set our own group ID in all cases. If the group ID we wish to set is real group ID anyway or the saved group ID, this will be accepted as well. If we are a privileged user or superuser we can set the effective group ID, else an error (EPERM) will be returned and the system call handler will terminate.

... [File: /usr/src/kernel/kern/cred.c, line: 266]

```
        pc = modpcred(p);
        pc->pc_ucred->cr_groups[0] = egid;

        return (0);
...
```

Once we have established our privilege to modify the user credentials, we call the modpcred() function to ensure we have a unique copy of the user credentials to modify. Note we don't check to see if the modifications we are about to make have no net effect—thus, one of the side-effects of this implementation is that if one does a **setgid()** to the selfsame group ID, one will unshare the process and user credentials regardless, ensuring a unique set.

After generating a unique set of credentials, which may or may not cause a copy to occur (and thus a potential block from memory), we update the user credentials with a new group ID[21] (the process credentials do not change), and return successfully back from this system call handler.

7.1.16.2 Improvements to the Current Implementation of setegid()

The saved group ID can differ from the real group ID. For example, in the case of executing a **setgid** program (see **kern/execve.c**), where the saved group ID is the group ID of the file executed, the **setgid** program can alternate between setting the credentials of the older group ID (e.g., the real group ID) and the newer group ID (the saved group ID). Since there are no privileges associated with group IDs at the moment, this is of little effect other than to change the relative file access permissions between the previous group ID and the new group ID. However, if privileges were associated with a certain group ID, one could forego privileges and then get them back again in the same program.[22]

Privileges are coupled only with a special user ID and not with a special group ID. This is primarily historical, as older UNIX systems only had one root or superuser. However, one could have special group IDs known by the kernel as well. In this case, the saved group ID would have the same effect of changing privileges as setting the effective user ID, as root does.

7.1.17 What is setgroups()?

setgroups() is a function which changes the BSD supplementary groups as part of the user credentials. This function implements a BSD set supplementary groups system call handler which has the side-effect of altering the group set of this process. Generally, this is only done upon login of a new user, when its group set is obtained from the system's database of user credentials, and remains unchanged from that point on. However, in the case of programs such as the **su** utility, which allow a subshell to be created as a different user, **setgroups()** is also used to set the group credentials of a different user.

... [File: /usr/src/kernel/kern/cred.c, line: 273]

```
int
setgroups(p, uap, retval)
```

[21] Note that the POSIX group ID is implemented as the first of the supplementary group IDs in the user credentials.
[22] See **seteuid()** for a current example of how this works with user IDs.

```
          struct proc *p;
          struct args {
                  u_int    gidsetsize;
                  int      *gidset;
          } *uap;
          int *retval;
  ...
```

The arguments of this function are those of a system call handler. For this BSD supplementary groups system call, two arguments contain the group set size and the pointer to the buffer containing the new group set. No values are returned and an error is signaled if there is inadaquate permission for this operation, if there are too many groups to fit in the buffer, or if the buffer is not accessible.

7.1.17.1 How is setgroups() Implemented?

setgroups() is a privileged BSD system call that will modify the supplementary groups of this process's user credential. It will check for appropriate privileges, and if privileged, check to see that the group set is small enough to be used and if the new group set can be obtained from the user program. It will then unshare any shared credentials and modify the user credentials so that the new group set is put in place atomically.

... [File: /usr/src/kernel/kern/cred.c, line: 288]

```
      if (error = use_priv(pc->pc_ucred, PRV_SETGID, p))
              return (error);
  ...
```

It first checks for the privilege to set supplementary groups, since this is a privileged operation; otherwise, it returns an error (EPERM) and terminates.

... [File: /usr/src/kernel/kern/cred.c, line: 292]

```
      if ((ngrp = uap->gidsetsize) > NGROUPS_MAX)
              return (EINVAL);
  ...
```

A fixed number of supplementary groups are supported. If the number of supplementary groups in this group set exceeds the fixed number, an error (EINVAL) is returned.

... [File: /usr/src/kernel/kern/cred.c, line: 296]

```
      if (error = copyin(p, (caddr_t)uap->gidset, (caddr_t)groups,
          ngrp * sizeof (groups[0])))
              return (error);
  ...
```

The group set is then obtained from the user program and placed into a temporary buffer in this function's frame. If there is an error in obtaining this (EFAULT), the system call is terminated.

```
        pc = modpcred(p);
        pc->pc_ucred->cr_ngroups = ngrp;

        /* convert from int's to gid_t's */
        for (gp = pc->pc_ucred->cr_groups, lp = groups; ngrp-; )
                *gp++ = *lp++;

        return (0);
    ...
```

With the new group set now present, we unshare the process credentials with the **modpcred()** function, update the user credentials to reflect the new supplementary group set,[23] and then return.

7.1.18 What is groupmember()?

groupmember() is an internal kernel function which determines if a group is a member of a specific user credential. Once **groupmember()** evaluates the user credential for the associated group IDs, it returns either true or false.

... [File: /usr/src/kernel/kern/cred.c, line: 312]

```
int
groupmember(gid_t gid, const struct ucred *cred)
...
```

groupmember() has two arguments: a group ID to be checked and a pointer to the user credential that should be examined to see if it belongs to that credential.

7.1.18.1 How is groupmember() Implemented?

groupmember() is an internal kernel interface that checks to see if this supplied group member matches one of the groups in this particular set of user credentials. It iterates through all of the group set looking for this item.

... [File: /usr/src/kernel/kern/cred.c, line: 318]

```
        for (gp = cred->cr_groups; gp < egp; gp++)
                if (*gp == gid)
                        return (1);

        return (0);
    ...
```

It first iterates through the array of supplementary groups, comparing each of the entries with the supplied group ID it's looking for. If it finds it, it returns true; otherwise, if the loop is terminated, it returns false. Generally, the number of groups is small so a linear search is adaquate—the groups themselves are not sorted in any order. Since each process has at least one group and the very first group is the

---

[23] Converting from the BSD array of integers to the POSIX supplementary group types.

principal POSIX group ID, it is ensured that there will be at least one iteration through this loop.

7.1.19 What are crget(), crfree(), and crdup()?

crget(), **crfree()** and **crdup()** are very simple internal kernel interface functions used by a few other files in the system (typically filesystem-related files) which create a set of credentials and release them (as might occur in the case of replicating a unique set for implmenting low-level subsystems). NFS, for example, mediates access to credentials privately.

7.1.19.1 How is crget() Implemented?

... [File: /usr/src/kernel/kern/cred.c, line: 326]

```
struct ucred *
crget()
 ...
```

crget() allocates a fresh zeroed set of credentials (it has no arguments) and returns a pointer to a fresh credential structure. It has the side-effect of possibly blocking for memory allocations, so it should never be called from interrupt level.

... [File: /usr/src/kernel/kern/cred.c, line: 331]

```
        MALLOC(cr, struct ucred *, sizeof(struct ucred), M_CRED, M_WAITOK);
        (void) memset((caddr_t)cr, 0, sizeof(*cr));
        cr->cr_ref = 1;
        return (cr);
 ...
```

crget() simply allocates from the memory allocator a new user credential entry, zeros it, sets its reference count to one, and returns. The reference count is set to one because by asking for a credential you are asserting at least one reference. Since the credentials are going to be evaluated immediately, they must have some value, so their beginning effective value is set to that of the root user (uid=0), with no group ID set at all.

7.1.19.2 How is crfree() Implemented?

crfree() releases a reference to a user credential set. If there is no reference left, then it will free the credential.

... [File: /usr/src/kernel/kern/cred.c, line: 338]

```
void
crfree(struct ucred *cr)
 ...
```

crfree() reduces the reference, and as a side-effect possibly frees the memory associated with the credential to which it has passed a pointer. It is called with one argument, the credential pointer it is freeing, and has no return value.

... [File: /usr/src/kernel/kern/cred.c, line: 342]

```
        if (--cr->cr_ref != 0)
                return;
        FREE((caddr_t)cr, M_CRED);
...
```

The credential reference count is decremented. If it is zero, the function terminates. If the reference count drops to zero, the memory for the credential is freed and returned back to the memory allocator for reuse. It is assumed at this point that the credential is not referenced elsewhere in the system.

7.1.19.3 How is crdup() Implemented?

crdup() replicates a credential set—in this way, it gains access to a unique singly referenced copy of the credential. The point of **crdup()** is to create a unique copy, and is involved with sharing.

... [File: /usr/src/kernel/kern/cred.c, line: 348]

```
struct ucred *
crdup(const struct ucred *cr)
...
```

crdup() has a pointer to the user credential it is replicating and returns the pointer to a unique user credential referenced singly by its caller. Thus, its side-effect is to allocate a new credential.

... [File: /usr/src/kernel/kern/cred.c, line: 353]

```
        newcr = crget();
        *newcr = *cr;
        newcr->cr_ref = 1;
        return (newcr);
...
```

crdup() obtains a new credential by calling **crget()** and copies the old credential onto the new credential with a structure assignment, setting the reference count of the new credential to one and returning the pointer to this new credential.

7.1.20 What are getlogin() and setlogin()?

getlogin() and **setlogin()** are BSD system call handlers which allow the process to be identified by an ASCII name set of characters. **getlogin()** is used to retrieve the name to find the associated account which allowed the user to get access to the computer, regardless of what user ID the user is running under.[24] **setlogin()** is usually used only by programs such as **login** or any of the network login programs (such as **telnetd** and **rlogind**) to attach the account name to the shell process that it activates. Since **setlogin()** is primarily used by programs that engage new users (either from the

---

[24] Even if the user has changed his user ID (uid), the login string would still be unaffected.

network or the console), it passes in a role as part of the credentials evaluation process (see **kern/priv.c**).

7.1.20.1 How is getlogin() Implemented?

... [File: /usr/src/kernel/kern/cred.c, line: 360]

```
int
getlogin(p, uap, retval)
        struct proc *p;
        struct args {
                char    *namebuf;
                u_int   namelen;
        } *uap;
        const int *retval;
    ...
```

getlogin() has the format of a system call handler. It implements the BSD **getlogin()** name function using two arguments: a pointer to a string buffer in the user's program, and the length of the buffer present. The system call returns no value, but may return an error (EFAULT) if there is trouble in copying to that buffer. The side-effect of this function is to return the contents of the login string associated with the session attached to this process. It may return a null login name if there never was a **setlogin()** done to this session.

... [File: /usr/src/kernel/kern/cred.c, line: 371]

```
        if (uap->namelen > sizeof (p->p_pgrp->pg_session->s_login))
                uap->namelen = sizeof (p->p_pgrp->pg_session->s_login);
    ...
```

setlogin() is implemented as a bounds check and limit of the buffer on the size of the string buffered in the session area. If the buffer is larger than the size of the fixed login string, only the number or characters in the string in the login session will be returned. The string is assumed to be null-terminated. One of the idiosyncracies of the way this is implemented is that if there were a longer string here before, the characters of the older pattern may still be present after the trailing null if the new string is less than the size of the buffer. If **getlogin()** is passed a buffer shorter than the size of a login string, it will only return the partial string, and it may not be null terminated.

... [File: /usr/src/kernel/kern/cred.c, line: 375]

```
        return (copyout(p, (caddr_t) p->p_pgrp->pg_session->s_login,
            (caddr_t) uap->namebuf, uap->namelen));
    ...
```

The string buffer located within the process group's session structure is returned. This may be a fraction up to all of the size of the string, depending on the size of the buffer as expressed by the second argument. It then returns the value of the success or failure of the **copyout** function (located in **locore.s**).

7.1.20.2 386BSD setlogin() Evolutionary History

In earlier versions of 386BSD (and BSD systems in general), **setlogin()** was a BSD system call handler which handled in this file all of the privilege granting mechanism. It had a single argument, which pointed to a null-terminated account name string. That has now been moved (and **suser()** deprecated) to **kern/priv.c** .

7.1.20.3 How is setlogin() Implemented?

setlogin() is used to control the privilege granting mechanism. It is a 386BSD internal kernel interface which allows a privileged process to set the user's account name or login ID to be associated with this process. The side-effect of this function is to set the session name associated with this process. No value is returned, and an error (EINVAL) may be returned in the case that the string passed in is larger than will fit in the session structure, or if the string is not obtainable from the user program.

```
... [ File: /usr/src/kernel/kern/cred.c, line: 380 ]

int
setlogin(p, uap, retval)
        struct proc *p;
        struct args {
                char    *namebuf;
                /* int  role; */
        } *uap;
        int *retval;
    ...
```

The 386BSD **setlogin()** version has two arguments: a pointer to a null-terminated account name string (as in the older BSD versions) and a role privilege of a particular user credential (i.e., privileged, daemon,...). The length of the string to be transferred in is determined by the number of characters up to and including the null-terminating character.

```
... [ File: /usr/src/kernel/kern/cred.c, line: 392 ]

        if (error = use_priv(p->p_ucred, PRV_SETLOGIN, p))
                return (error);
    ...
```

First, a check for the privilege to set the login ID is conducted. This can be done only by the privileged user root, else an error (EPERM) is returned.

```
... [ File: /usr/src/kernel/kern/cred.c, line: 396 ]

        error = copyinstr(p, (caddr_t) uap->namebuf,
            (caddr_t) p->p_pgrp->pg_session->s_login,
            sizeof (p->p_pgrp->pg_session->s_login) - 1, (u_int *)0);
        if (error == ENAMETOOLONG)
                error = EINVAL;
    ...
```

The user's program then has its string read out by the **copyinstr** routine (see **locore.s**) which copies a null-terminated string up to a certain maximum length directly into the buffer. The string is copied directly into the session buffer and the session buffer is bounded in size by the fixed size of the array that implements it (less a character for the null byte). If there is an error in copying the string from the user process,[25] it terminates. Note here that if a memory fault occurs during copying, the session buffer may be partially corrupted since no temporary buffer is used to hold the result copied into the buffer.

... [File: /usr/src/kernel/kern/cred.c, line: 403]

```
        if (error == 0) {
                struct pcred *pc = modpcred(p);

                pc->pc_ucred->cr_role = 0 /*role */;
        }

        return (error);
...
```

If no error is present, just before returning from the system call handler **setlogin()** will modify the credentials to assign a new role to this set of credentials. It does this much like the other modifications to credentials by first checking to unshare the process and user credentials with **modpcred()**. It then calls **kern/priv.c** to assign the new role to the user credential and returns.

7.2 What is Role-Based Security?

Role-based security as we define it here is a mechanism orthogonal to password protection. It is actually a kind of *mandatory access control* policy that attempts to deal with the problems, faced by many UNIX systems, which arise by loading all of the privileges and responsibilities on a single superuser privilege.

Like the janitor at a university, the root account on most UNIX systems has access to the "keys" of all of the offices.[26] While we can go back to the old days of splitting up these responsibilities and privileges among many different user IDs to decentralize them (which can be done in this module if one wanted to), it is unclear that this would buy us much advantage. This ability to segregate privileges into multiple accounts was implemented in older systems (like TOPS/20), but all this did, in practice, was create many janitors with keys instead of just one.

One major difference between administering computers versus cleaning university offices is that in the latter case one requires geographic access to compromise security,

---

[25] It either can't read the memory (EFAULT) or the function exceeds the fixed buffer length in the session structure (ENAMETOOLONG which is translated by the system call handler to EINVAL).
[26] Unfortunately, unlike the janitor, however, we can't "bond" root to ensure responsible behavior.

while on a network one does not. This concept of *geographic access* means that someone has to be in a location to use a key (or in this case, a privilege).

Our use of roles provides a degree of *geographic determination* and limits the scope of access based on that determination. Thus, in order to gain fundamental access to the management functions (which is how most computers are subverted), not only must one know the passwords but one must also be in the appropriate geographic setting. This geographic determination makes it a lot more difficult for an intruder because he now has to subvert all of the mechanisms that determine knowledge of geographic location.

At the moment, our principal consideration is based on very simple geographic determination, to wit, "Did the user arrive on the system from a local terminal or via the net?" This kind of determination can be done entirely in the kernel without regard for external programs that could be subverted. Thus, the scope of subvertable entities has gotten very small.

Since this project has only the most minimal goals of demonstration in mind, this approach is adequate for purposes of example and discussion. However, with careful structure, this concept is extensible in a larger sense, constrained by additional subtleties and responsibilities. See **Appendix B**, *A Blueprint for Role-Based Network-Level Security*, for a rigorous discussion of these constraints.

7.3 Process Privileges: kern/priv.c

The file **kern/priv.c** contains the machine-independent code which provides the fine-grain definition for the use of privileges by other portions of the kernel code. It is in essence the "gateway" through which a privileged operation is permitted to be performed.

All operations lying outside of the class of an ordinary user process operation are termed *privileges*. Each privilege has associated with it a unique code that specifically identifies that privilege used within the kernel—even if a function has many similar uses of that privilege which are distinct only by their position in the function. Privileges are requested against the user credentials associated with the operation.[27] User credentials describe the initiator of the operation in terms of *identification* and *role*—two independent properties.

7.3.1 Identification

An *identification* supplies the information of just who is requesting this action to be performed. This identification has in some way already been *authenticated* (usually by allowing user access via login with a password). In many systems this is an adequate

---

[27] See **kern/cred.c** and the associated discussion in this chapter for details of user credentials.

level of control, but nowadays, with the advent of large computer networks, it is insufficient in and of itself since even the best password algorithms can be broken.

Identification may be broken up into many components; in POSIX we use the user ID, group ID, and supplementary group IDs. However, all these IDs can be treated as much the same singular ID since they are all authenticated via some password control mechanism.

7.3.2 Role and Privileges

Independent of identification is the concept of a *role*. A role is akin to that of an actor, in that an actor can function in many ways depending on what character he is asked to play. Similarly, role is used in this privilege mechanism to discriminate between the types of privileges a user may be permitted to access.

The concept of role is used to allow the treatment of IDs to differ depending upon (in this case) how the user gained access to the system. If it is known, for example, that the user gained access to the system via a physical connection (e.g., logged on via the console), we may be able to allow access to all degree of system management functions.[28] However, if that same user gained access to the system from a remote corner of the network, it might be the case that he may never, no matter what he does or what program is compromised, be able to gain access to any system management functions, merely due to the fact that access is originating over the network instead of via a known, physically connected terminal. There are more gradations[29] to role possible than those discussed here, but these two examples graphically demonstrate the concept behind a role-based model.

Another aspect of a role is that it is a part of the user credential independent of the POSIX program interface specification. User processes themselves are only indirectly aware of them. The system itself has extremely limited ways of altering them—it can only set them once per a hierarchy of processes, and then only under very controlled situations, but it can never discover what they are in any case. These restrictions are intended to both minimize the impact of the privilege mechanism on the majority of software used in the system and also to make it impossible for programs to penetrate and subvert.

While this mechanism is by no means an attempt to simulate the security qualifications of elaborate systems used for secure purposes, role-based security can be an effective pragmatic approach to minimizing intrusion by subversion of the system management functions. It is, in sum, the first step down the road towards intrusion-resistant systems through use of a multilevel approach.

---

[28] If all of the passwords necessary for this to occur are present.
[29] See **Appendix B** for other alternatives.

7.3.3 Privilege on Other UNIX Systems

Prior to this release, 386BSD (like other UNIX systems) used a single subroutine called **suser()** to decide if the user credentials qualified as a superuser or privileged user to determine if a privileged operation could be performed. Unfortunately, during the privilege check itself, many different areas of privilege were collapsed into one single concept, thus causing a loss of information. As such, it was impossible from the superuser's perspective to tell just which privilege was being requested, even though the question asked was "Do I have the privilege?" Since superuser only checked the user ID, and the user ID semantics indicated that root must be the one discriminating privilege, the concept of "root" access was wired into the system—thus making root the prime account to attempt to subvert.

Finally, since this subroutine lacked sufficient information surrounding the context, it was impossible to configure it to do other qualifications. Its simplicity (fine in an isolated environment) was no longer satisfactory in a networked environment, thus dooming this mechanism in our eyes.

7.3.4 Enumerated Types of Role and Privilege

Privilege is an *enumerated type* to which arbitrary numbers of new privileges may be added or deleted at any time. Role is also an enumerated type in that as many roles as needed may be assigned. Role is actually an ordered enumerated type—ordered by level of access, which in our implementation takes a geographic bent. Any of these privileges can, in turn, be checked for different combinations of user ID, group ID, or supplementary group ID (if that were desired). At the moment, only the root user ID[30] is used. Thus, not only do the privileges establish role but they could also individually check user ID, group ID, and supplementary group ID.

... [File: kernel/include/sys/privilege.h, line: 21]

```
enum cr_roles {
        ROLE_ALL, /* all privileges are possible (must be first) */
        ROLE_MGMT, /* privileges for system management */
        ROLE_LOCALUSR, /* privileges for local (non-net) user */
        ROLE_DISTANTUSR, /* privileges for non-local (net) user */
        ROLE_NONE, /* no privileges (must be last) */
};
typedef enum cr_roles cr_role_t;
 ...
```

In this file, we implement five basic types of role categories which relate to privileges (described in the file **sys/privilege.h**) based on geographic determination. To initialize the system and allow basic system function to occur, a top-level role is assigned which assigns all privileges (ALL). A second-tier role is established for direct access system management functions—this privilege requires a direct physical connection in order to

---

[30] For backward compatibility with the previous system only.

---

be allowed (MGMT). The third-tier role is that of local area network privileged users (LOCALUSR) and thus requires access to the locally connected network. The fourth-tier role is for privileged users who are on a distant network (DISTANTUSR).

The last tier of role (NONE) is used in the case where the system has no way of knowing what role to assign, either because the information was lost or because it would be impossible to obtain, yet the process must still be run for semantic reasons. In this last case, the process will only be successful as long as it doesn't require any privileges whatsoever to operate. Since the majority of programs work this way anyways (such as anonymous ftp or kermit or ls), typical system use is not unduly affected. For the root account, however, ROLE_NONE is effectively useless.

7.3.5 What is use_priv()?

This file has only one function: **use_priv()**. **use_priv()** is a kernel interface for requesting privileges. It evaluates a credentials structure for use with a requested privilege. The privilege is then granted or not granted as a result of the return value. Optionally, if a process is present, the attempted use or granting of that privilege will be recorded against that process for accounting purposes. As implemented in the current system, part of the credentials involve a role which determines the scope of allowable privileges that a process may have at any given time.

... [File: /usr/src/kernel/kern/priv.c, line: 62]

```
int
use_priv(const struct ucred *cr, cr_priv_t prv, struct proc *p)
...
```

use_priv() has three arguments: the pointer to the user credentials, the privilege requested, and a process to account for the use of this privilege. The process accounting is an optional argument, since a privilege can be requested without one, as might occur, for example, in the case where a process is terminated when a write operation has yet to complete.

This function returns an integer value indicating success or failure to obtain the privilege. The side-effect of this function is possibly to account for success or failure on the use of this privilege. This function can be called from any part of the kernel, including interrupt level.

7.3.5.1 How is use_priv() Implemented?

The privilege request is evaluated in a switch table where every privilege is enumerated. They are clustered into groups allowable at a particular role and from those groups the minimum role to activate the privilege is assigned.[31]

---

[31] Other mechanisms besides this very simple mechanism discussed here are recommended to buttress security. See **Appendix B** for more information.

... [File: /usr/src/kernel/kern/priv.c, line: 69]

```
switch(prv) {
        /* used by int, login and daemons (rlogind, telnetd, ...) */
case PRV_SETLOGIN:
case PRV_REVOKE:
case PRV_ADJTIME:
case PRV_NFS_GETFH:
case PRV_NFS_SVC:
case PRV_NFS_ASYNC_DAEMON:
case PRV_NFS_SRV_CREATE_SPECIAL:
case PRV_NFS_SRV_REMOVE_DIR:
case PRV_NFS_SRV_LINK_DIR:
        minrole = ROLE_ALL;
        rv = (cr->cr_uid == 0);
        break;
...
```

In the case of privileges necessary to initialize the system and to allow basic system function to occur, a top-level role consisting of all this set of privileges outlined is assigned.

... [File: /usr/src/kernel/kern/priv.c, line: 86]

```
case PRV_SWAPON:
case PRV_MOUNT:
case PRV_UNMOUNT:
case PRV_CHROOT:
case PRV_MKNOD:
case PRV_LINKDIR:
case PRV_UNLINKDIR:
case PRV_TIOCCONS1:
case PRV_TIOCCONS2:
case PRV_SETHOSTID:
case PRV_SETHOSTNAME:
case PRV_REBOOT:
case PRV_SETTIMEOFDAY:
case PRV_NO_UPROCLIMIT:
case PRV_RLIMIT_RSS:
case PRV_RLIMIT_MEMLOCK:
case PRV_UFS_QUOTA_CHANGE:
case PRV_SIOCSDARP:
case PRV_SIOCSIFFLAGS:
case PRV_SIOCSIFMETRIC:
case PRV_SLIP_OPEN:
case PRV_RTIOCTL:
        minrole = ROLE_MGMT;
        rv = (cr->cr_uid == 0);
        break;
...
```

This next set of privileges is used in the management of the system by a user logged into the console (and only that console) of the system. Many of the privileges listed here allow the root account to control network access and management of the system, including certain filesystem operations.

... [File: /usr/src/kernel/kern/priv.c, line: 112]

```
        case PRV_RLIMIT_CPU:
        case PRV_RLIMIT_FSIZE:
        case PRV_RLIMIT_DATA:
        case PRV_RLIMIT_STACK:
        case PRV_RLIMIT_CORE:
        case PRV_RLIMIT_NPROC:
        case PRV_RLIMIT_OFILE:
        case PRV_UFS_SETATTR_TIME:
        case PRV_UFS_SETATTR_UID:
        case PRV_UFS_CHOWN:
        case PRV_UFS_CHMOD:
        case PRV_NICE:
                minrole = ROLE_LOCALUSR;
                rv = (cr->cr_uid == 0);
                break;
...
```

A much smaller set of privileges is present for an ordinary local user that may log in via the immediate local area network. The system discriminates between entry on the directly connected network (e.g., Ethernet) versus access from a distant network (via a router). Note that this level could be compromised by access to another local machine not similarly protected. However, even if it is compromised in this manner, access to more powerful roles are still denied (see **Appendix B**). Thus, even access to the root account by this manner of subversion will only allow the spoofing[32] of user IDs.

... [File: /usr/src/kernel/kern/priv.c, line: 129]

```
case PRV_SETUID:
case PRV_SETEUID:
case PRV_SETGID:
case PRV_SETEGID:
case PRV_SETGROUPS:
case PRV_EXECSETUID:
case PRV_EXECSETGID:
        minrole = ROLE_NONE;
        rv = (cr->cr_uid == 0);
        break;
...
```

Finally, just about any user on the system, even arriving from a distant network, can gain access to some privileges if permitted, including the ability to change one's own apparent user ID and group ID. Note that even if this is done, there is a limit to what is obtained by it—only access to certain files and no ability to overrun resources is possible at this point.

Minimally, **setuserid** programs must be run even by the most unprivileged user anyway, because the system itself is written to use privileged programs to provide services. All the roles have done is to limit the *degree* to which the privileges may be used. It does not remove the need for privileges in the first place.

... [File: /usr/src/kernel/kern/priv.c, line: 147]

```
if ((cr_role_t)cr->cr_role > minrole) {

        /* access to sensitive priviledge, warn system manager */
        if (minrole <= ROLE_MGMT)
                log(LOG_WARNING, "uid %d attempted to use priviledge",
                    cr->cr_uid);

        /* record failure if proc present */
        if (p && p->p_acflag)
                acct_priv(p, ACCT_ROLE_FAIL, cr, prv);

        return (EPERM);
}
...
```

Upon leaving this huge switch statement, a minimum role is assigned to the privilege. This role is compared to the credential's role to see if the privilege will be denied solely on the basis of inadequate role for the privilege. This failure is then recorded.[33] If permission has been denied, an error (EPERM) is returned.

---

[32] Spoofing means to masquerade as someone else.
[33] Currently against the accounting flag of the process, if present. This accounting is done in lieu of a more elaborate accounting system yet to be released.

If an attempt by an unauthorized user has been made to access a sensitive privilege, this attempt is logged via the system's logging facility as a warning to the system administrator that a particular user ID attempted to use a sensitive privilege (one that requires a role of management or better).

... [File: /usr/src/kernel/kern/priv.c, line: 162]

```
if (rv && p && p->p_acflag)
        acct_priv(p, ACCT_PRIV_SUCCESS, cr, prv);
else
        acct_priv(p, ACCT_PRIV_FAIL, cr, prv);

return (rv ? 0 : EPERM);
...
```

After we have checked the role to see if such a permission can be granted, the results of this credential check are now reviewed to see if the process has the correct user ID (or group ID, or supplementary group ID) to gain access to the particular privilege. If all is well, the accounting flag is similarly updated to indicate the use of a privilege (if the process present flag is set). Currently, process accounting does not yet allow for more elaborate tracing of privilege use.

The successful granting of the privilege will result in no error passed back. Otherwise, if the credentials were deemed inadequate, an error (EPERM) is returned.

7.3.5.2 386BSD use_priv() Design Choices and Trade-Offs

The reason we started down this path of role-based security is that we wanted to explore other mechanisms which could increase the security of the system without having to rely on encryption or other cryptographic techniques. Among the reasons to avoid encryption as a basis for all security is that it is a sensitive controlled technology that must fall under government restrictions (especially on crossing national boundaries). For a research system like 386BSD with an international audience, these restrictions were deemed too great of a burden. In addition, many cryptographic techniques are susceptible to certain kinds of attacks based on level of knowledge and resource.

In sum, while this particular rathole has been mined for many years, it still remains to be seen just how useful schemes based on encryption might be to the average user who simply wants his system to not be meddled with on a network, and does most of his work directly on the local PC itself. Thus, we began to explore alternative mechanisms which require little to no management but that do regulate access to the system and its resources for our typical end user.

7.3.5.3 Improvements to the Current Implementation of use_priv()

As we stated earlier, **kern/priv.c** is a minimal example of our version of role-based security. We have tried to allow for great flexibility in exploring future direction with this new approach. One major direction to take this mechanism next is to extend this idea down into the filesystems so as to provide a limited mandatory access control policy that includes the role concept as well. In this way, it would become possible to secure file contents as well as process operations. As such, it would no longer matter whether or not an account was compromised, as the intruder still would not be able to gain access to the file contents.

Another interesting direction is that of implementing a real form of process accounting, as an extention of audit handling of privleges. The process accounting used in Berkeley systems is very rudimentary—it was actually born out of a two-night hack done by Ken Thompson on the Cory Hall 11/70 at Berkeley to record a series of records into an inode regarding process termination on what resources and privileges were activated during the process's lifetime. This older accounting system was only intended as a stop-gap measure so that usage statistics could be used to justify greater use of UNIX by the Computer Science Department as a teaching tool. In fact, the Computer Center later added a few more features and used this same system to bill customers in a recharge system. In sum, it was never intended for anything outside of this scope and is inadequate for our needs, but, like many other things in UNIX systems, it persists to this day.

To implement appropriate process accounting, a structure which combines a logging mechanism (like that used by **syslog** to communicate with the kernel) with an architecture for instantiating records (like that used by the existing **ktrace**) could be developed to create an accounting, or better yet, an auditing facility for the system to record activity systemwide.

One key consideration is whether or not such a facility should be intimate with the existing system call tracing (**ktrace**) facility or not. The purpose of adding in this kind of facility would not be to tally up costs for billing (as it would be in the case of a commercial system), but instead be used as a means to gain access to details of how the system is being used and how resources are being parceled out—to get a crow's eye view, if you will, of system operation. An elaborate display program might then make use of this information to provide this view so that the designers and researchers of the system could determine if the system was making as good a use of resources as thought—with one major aspect of this being an understanding of actual privilege usage. This understanding is important, if only because if an inappropriate use of privileges is made on system resources, it is a loss factor on the system, just as unoptimal use of RAM or disk would be.

Exercises

7.1 a) In the case of the kernel, at what times would a reference to a user credential be necessary?
b) Why are these operations problematic?

7.2 Suppose two different users, one privileged and the other unprivileged, modify (or update) the same low-level object.
a) Which set of credentials is used?
b) Can the unprivileged user "sneak" changes into the object using the privileged user's genuine update? Why or why not?

7.3 After initiating an asynchronous operation, the user changes credentials to alter the process privilege. What credentials will be used to decide if the operation will be allowed?

7.4 a) Where is the actual role get/set mechanism used to institute the role-based security scheme?
b) Why is this done?

7.5 a) Why aren't system calls used to manage roles?
b) If system calls are not used, can a program discover if role-based security is presently enforced on a system?

8 PROCESS MULTIPLEXING (kern/synch.c, kern/lock.c)

The interaction of multiple processes is the core of a modern UNIX system, and the chief manner of their operation is that mechanism that sequences them in careful order. Processor time is parceled out to a queue of processes that alternate between running and being blocked for a variety of different events. Organized methods for exclusively possessing sharable resources is necessary for deterministic operation of this concurrent collection of processes. The files **kern/synch.c** and **kern/lock.c** are used for these purposes. The former provides the primitives of process synchronization, while the latter builds a higher level of abstraction mechanism to ensure exclusive access to a data instance with an embedded lock instance.

8.1 Blocking and Scheduling of Processes: kern/synch.c

The file **kern/synch.c** contains the machine-independent code that implements the blocking, unblocking, and scheduling mechanisms used in a *multiprogramming* system. For multiprogramming operation to occur, the processor is passed around a series of programs. In any UNIX-like system such as 386BSD, this effect is achieved by a kernel mode portion of the process running as a *coroutine* to other processes in the system. These coroutines in essence explicitly relinquish the processor to another process's use whenever they must block to perform a function or when asked to relinquish the processor on their own.

8.1.1 Coroutine Operation

Actual *coroutine* "calls" occur only under controlled circumstances. Since the kernel has very limited support for preemption, care must be taken to avoid arbitrary use of these coroutine calls; otherwise, unforeseen deadlocks can occur. The **swtch** function (see **Chapter 2**) is used to implement these coroutine calls between processes and/or threads. **swtch** exchanges the kernel state of one concurrent entity for another.

A concurrent entity in 386BSD consists of at least a process slot and a kernel stack. A kernel stack is used to hold the immediate process context and the stack frame of the particular threaded execution in the kernel that the process is using at the time **swtch** is called. **swtch** in effect replaces this process with the next runable process of highest priority.

8.1.1.1 Priority Queues

swtch locates the next process by means of a *priority queue*. The priority queue contains an array of 32 ordered queues, each containing none to many processes that are waiting to run at a given priority. As the process priorities are altered, the placement in the queue of a process is changed.[1]

8.1.1.2 Fixed-Point Fractional Values

Rather than support floating point operations in the kernel (and increasing the cost of context switching), fractional values can be employed in the integer-only kernel environment by use of fixed-point arithmetic which reserves a portion of an integer for the fraction.[2] A choice of 11 bits of fraction allows a value (associated with the decay) of 5 percent[3] to be approximated adequately, while the remaining 21 bits of integer allow the multiplication of 10-bit integer values without exceeding the representable range.

8.1.2 Basic Scheduling Algorithm

The kernel uses a *round-robin* algorithm to parcel out the processor to each process in *time slices* (with a maximum duration of 0.1 second). It uses a multilevel queue with a feedback term to provide a *fair access* to the processor for all processes by manipulating process priorities.

Process priorities tend to decay from initial high priorities to lower ones as they consume processor resource, and are restored when less active by a feedback term so that they may consume processor resources yet again. This rate of decay is larger when the system has a larger number of competing processes and is lower when there are few processes in competition for resources. Priorities are updated once a second as a pass through all active processes. Processes that become inactive for long periods of time stand to lose their resources, as the memory they consume is put to no use during that inactive period of time.

8.1.2.1 Smoothed Decay

Rather than allow abrupt changes in priority and processor utilization, the sporadic effects of scheduling are smoothed over a larger time interval by a digital decay function.[4] By use of an exponential constant, the contribution of an increment of execution time (in this case, accumulated clock ticks) at a priority can be accumulated to a decaying total sum, such that the added increment will only contribute a fraction

---

[1] The process is removed from the queue and reinserted at the new priority.

[2] A 32-bit number can be split into 21 bits of integer and 11 bits of fraction representing a number in the range of -1,048,576.999 to 1,048,575.999.

[3] Or $\exp(-1/20)$.

[4] This approach is akin to the reasons why cars have shock absorbers, and why capacitors and inductors are added to electronic circuits.

of the total over a time period. Besides decaying processor utilization, a *smoothed decay* algorithm is used to calculate process CPU usage percentages and load averages.

8.1.3 Memory Reclamation

Independent of process scheduling is *memory reclamation*. Memory reclamation is done solely due to demands for memory use, and no difference is seen by the pageout mechanism between that of a single process demanding huge amounts of memory resource and many processes cumulatively demanding resource. In effect, scheduling of resource in the system boils down to the product of memory allocated to a process and the time allotted to a process—as such, using a large amount of either time or memory have the same cumulative effect.

8.1.4 Scheduling and its Applications

386BSD schedules memory and processor by orthogonally dealing with both. Memory is reused on a global basis and scheduled entirely by a LRU-based activation algorithm (FIFO with reclaim). Independent of this is the allocation of processor time by the system. Should the process require a large amount of memory, it will tend to be blocked waiting to page in that missing memory resource. As a result, it will not be able to use the processor, and the longer the time spent in waiting for that memory to become available, the more likely other of its pages will become candidates for reclamation. In the case of a process competing only for processor time use in the system, its time slice will be the factor limiting its ability to command resource, since it will not be blocked with its pages being reclaimed as frequently as an overabundant user of memory. In this case, the quanta effectively determined by the scheduling within this file is the only aspect of multiprogramming that it will see. These scheduling criteria for memory and processor time are adequate for use in a small multiprogramming environment, as occurs on a PC. However, they are inadequate for use in a large timesharing environment, a real-time environment, or an environment that requires massive I/O and memory allocation.[5]

The scheduling *domains* of each of these different scheduling criteria also differ. In timeshared use, a very fine degree of fairness must be enforced across multiple groups of users. For example, fair use schedulers[6] go to great lengths to ensure even-handed access to resource. Real-time systems, on the other hand, are less worried about even-handed access as they are with the guaranteed time to access a resource. It is necessary with real-time systems to guarantee that a response to a need for a kind of resource

[5] As might be necessary for use with very high speed networks.
[6] I.e., IBM's AIX system.

will be responded to in a deterministic period of time. The current system is not structured for such a need, although it could be adapted fairly readily to that end.[7]

However, both these cases differ (because of the timeliness constraint) to that of the case where a huge amount of memory may need to be created for doing vast amounts of disk I/O.[8] The issue is no longer timeliness but the scheduling of disk bandwidth to memory that buffers the disk.[9] In this case, the scheduling criteria are the arrival times of the requests for transfers, and the ability to assign memory resource and relinquish it rapidly enough to keep up with the scheduled transactions to the secondary storage units. Thus, *queuing theory* is used to precisely schedule memory and time interchangeably as a resource. While 386BSD is not yet able to achieve this scheduling criteria, it could easily be made able to perform in this fashion.

8.1.4.1 Multithreaded Scheduling

While not a multithreaded system (yet), 386BSD could find use in parallel processing systems, either via *shared memory multiprocessing*[10] or via *clusters*.[11] One consideration key to creating a system for parallel processing is the scheduling of activity. Some systems (like Solaris) view fine grain scheduling of threads in a multiprocessor as being essential to obtain a scalable use of a shared memory multiprocessor (e.g., to afford maximal utilization of all processors). In this case, since the rescheduling interval may be extremely short, the cost of recalculating priorities may become a dominant factor in using such as multithreaded system.

This approach, of course, presumes that both a fine-grain degree of preemptibility is possible and desirable. Systems like Solaris invert the usual UNIX arrangement of limited preemption by allowing the system to be highly preemptible. However, the cost for this added advantage is to spread all of the contention sites throughout the system instead of concentrating them within a few files, like the one we are discussing here.[12]

In addition to the increased cost of software management, the overhead of fine-grain rescheduling is incurred during operation in all places where the effect is desired. The

---

[7] A special case of real-time systems is those involved with doing very large amounts of I/O (as in the case of a network) where a guaranteed response time many be necessary to ensure a steady stream of data through a protocol and to a network.

[8] Say, for example, to a RAID cluster implementing a commercial database.

[9] Such applications are in effect big move instructions, since all it's really doing is conveying records of one kind from one place in the mass storage to another place in the mass storage as rapidly as possible—and every microsecond counts, down to the positioning of disk arms and platters to shave latency off the operation. The whole reason for the existence of a mainframe is not the processor itself, but this operation—the actual channels.

[10] E.g., On a Compaq Systempro with multiple processors.

[11] Individual machines linked by a very high speed network interconnect.

[12] Only this file, the machine-independent signals file **kern/sig.c**, and the machine-dependent trap file **i386/trap.c** make use of the **swtch** primitive.

---

ultimate benefit of this is to allow a system to be engineered which always has threads busy on every process at any given point in time, so utilization of the processor is as high as possible. The price paid for this approach is extreme complexity coupled with a fixed overhead above that of a coarse-grained system.

It is not mandatory that one have such a scheduling mechanism on a multithreaded system. It is, in fact, possible to have a course-grained multithreaded system that uses the same mechanism for threads as it does processes. The question in this case becomes, however, whether or not an adequate degree of processor utilization can result from such a coarse-grained system. Since UNIX systems in general are limited by the speed of kernel operations, it would seem that adding threads to the kernel to increase processor utilization would be a wise first step towards improving CPU utilization in a coarse-grained system. Thus, in future 386BSD multithreaded development a higher priority is to allow for an architecture that can make use of threads in the kernel in general than to engineer a fine-grain scheduler.

8.1.4.2 Hierarchical Scheduling

In the original UNIX system running on the PDP-11, virtual memory was not present—instead, the PDP-11 had eight base registers per address space used as if they were a single base register segment machine.[13] Processes were allocated with linear segments of memory. If there was not enough memory, the oldest process would be tossed out to swap space to free up more memory and the process unloaded. To reactivate a process that had been swapped, the special swapper process would be awakened at the appropriate time and allowed to schedule the reloading of the process. Thus, scheduling was a two-tiered arrangement, where processes with memory in core could compete for use of the processor until the point that their time in memory was up. Then they were swapped out and idled until their time at bat came up again and they could be reloaded. With the 3BSD kernel, paging was added to support the VAX virtual memory capability. So, instead of using the older coarse-grained swapping which required deactivation of the entire process (for sometimes considerable periods of time), portions of the process could be activated and deactivated.

Since that time, the speed of processors has gone up by more than two orders of magnitude and program size has increased by more than a magnitude, but I/O speeds of disk drives have barely increased by a magnitude. As such, the cost of deactivating a process entirely for swapping is now very high indeed. In the current version of 386BSD, this hierarchy of swapping versus paging has been obsoleted since it now serves no useful purpose.[14]

---

[13] With the user structure or kernel stack kept in a separate base register.
[14] However, variable page clustering that can dump out more than a page at a time is very desirable and is seen as a enhancement to ordinary paging.

Another form of scheduling hierarchy may be found in systems like Solaris, where threads and processes resemble different hierarchies of scheduling as well. In this case, the queue of processors able to accept new threads is an example of a higher precedence scheduling domain than the page scheduling. In effect, hierarchy is thus not dead—it just may be reapplied as a different idea when appropriate.

8.1.4.3 Cluster Scheduling

An example of applying hierarchy one more time might be in the case of a *cluster scheduling* arrangement. In a cluster, processors communicate via a very high speed interconnector bus that is independent of the main bus. Clusters allow for large-grain parallelism without contention, while the concept of running a process split across many processors affords the inverted domain of a thread scheduler. In this case, we would attempt to schedule machines to an abstract network process where the exact number and time demanded of each may differ based on the operation requested of it (e.g., the network system call).

8.1.5 Synchronization

Synchronization involves allowing concurrent objects to gain access to shared resources or to each other. Besides scheduling, this file implements the basic synchronization mechanisms of **tsleep()** and **wakeup()**.[15] These primitives allow a processor thread to block awaiting an event. When the event occurs, the block is removed and the coroutine eventually runs. This mechanism is the simplest mechanism possible—it does not take into account any protection for activation, nor does it prevent processes that should not block from blocking. As currently arranged, the system does not allow blocking from interrupt-level code because interrupts are arranged to work in any context, including the null context, when they appear.[16]

Other systems like MULTICS had a hierarchy of context-switching primitives and allowed for more elaborate preemption, partially as a result of these mechanisms. Since this involved the possibility of deadlocks, deadlock detection and avoidance was also a critical part of that synchronization mechanism. In the future, the simple mechanism present in 386BSD will have to change to allow for more contention and deadlock. It is unclear, however, at this time the best path in changing beyond this simple mechanism.

---

[15] See *Multiprogramming and Multiprocessing I* (September 1991) and *Multiprogramming and Multiprocessing II* (October 1991), **Dr. Dobbs Journal**, for more information on these two functions.
[16] This is not a mandatory requirement for the system to be designed this way—it is a pragmatic implementation choice that the system was designed to work this way.

SOURCE CODE SECRETS: THE BASIC KERNEL

8.1.6 Process Priority

Processes have a *priority* associated with them to establish the order they are to run. The priority of a process is not fixed, but varies with the need of a process. When the process is in the kernel, it uses fixed priority levels that provide order for processes to be awakened to avoid resource deadlocks caused by dependent resource allocations.[17] Otherwise, the process priority is manipulated to achieve the effect of fair access by allowing each process to consume a portion of the processor's time successively without being locked out, either by another process hogging the processor or by an accumulation of processes having the cumulative effect of indefinitely postponing a process's time slice. These effects occur based on a process's user mode priority (p_usrpri), which is always less than any kernel priority. Kernel priorities, in effect, are "real time."

By UNIX convention, higher priorities correspond to lower values, with zero the highest priority and 127 the lowest. To achieve this effect, the priority is adjusted over different time intervals by various mechanisms in the kernel:

Interval: Less Than or Equal to 0.04 Second

As a process runs, its priority erodes linearly with the amount of the processor it consumes over a short term. Every 4 clock ticks (or 40 ms), its priority value is increased by the process rescheduling clock interrupt, making it less likely to be rescheduled relative to other processes using less of the CPU. Since this component of process priority reflects the use of the processor by a process, it is termed the *processor utilization* (p_cpu).

If the process requires resources from the kernel via a trap or system call, access to the resources will block the process (**tsleep()**), allowing others to run that will accumulate clock ticks instead. Since many blocks may occur to satisfy the request, many reschedulings may occur in the 0.05 to 10 ms time interval. These voluntary context switches allow a short-term sleeping process to release the processor until needed again. If a process's priority has eroded enough to warrant that another become a higher priority, an involuntary context switch (**qswtch**, see **Chapter 2**) is used to exchange the current process with the higher priority process on the run queue.

This multilevel queue provides an ordered set of runable processes for the system to context switch between when a current process blocks (**tsleep()**) or reschedules (**qswtch**). When unblocked (**wakeup()**), the process is inserted back onto the run queue at a position ordered by its priority. The formerly running process will execute when (possibly several successive) context switches consume any higher priority processes ordered ahead of it on the run queue until the process is encountered. There

---

[17] Alternatively, priority inversion deadlocks could be avoided by other means.

is no guarantee as to when this will occur; however, since processes lose priority when run, eventually the run queue is sequenced.

Interval: Every 0.1 Second

The round robin event generator forces an event to preempt the current process. Thus, even if a process does not voluntarily relinquish the processor, nor has had its priority erode far enough for competition with another to prompt an involuntary context switch, it will be forced to relinquish involuntarily the processor every 0.1 second. If no process is ready to run, the current process continues. If a higher priority process is present, the kernel will preempt the current process in favor of the higher priority process. This force distributes the processor around to processes waiting for processor cycles and prevents a process from locking out others. The round robin time interval defines the size of the per-process time slice, which may not be entirely consumed by a process, as it may (in)voluntarily reschedule before consuming the time slice.

Interval: Every 1 Second

The process rescheduling clock arranges to recalculate periodically the priorities of processes and thus reorder the processes on the run queue. While the priority of the running process is altered by the shorter term priority operations mentioned above, none of the other process priorities are altered till this point; thus, the order of outstanding processes to be run is not altered any more frequently. In addition, the contribution of non-runable processes are taken into account by this step, since they consume resources as well.

Interval: Every 5 Seconds

In addition to reordering the processes to be run, the priority recalculation decays the priority value gradually by 90 percent over the period of 5 seconds by a smoothed exponential decay function. This has the effect of raising the eligibility of the process to obtain processor cycles. The feedback term gradually restores what the short-term scheduling effect had removed—the process's ability to obtain a slice of processor time.

The choice of 5 seconds means that the effect of a second's worth of CPU usage will be decayed away in that time interval.[18] On a saturated system, this in effect sets the maximum time before a process is ensured another processor time slice. The feedback term favors interactive processes by putting an upper time bound on how long processor utilization will affect a process's ability to be rescheduled.

---

[18] If it is shorter, briefer interactive periods are favored; if longer, it may delay interactive programs.

8.1.6.1 Weighting

In addition to implementing fairness, priorities can be *weighted* separately to favor or disadvantage a process. A process can adjust its own weighting factor via the **nice()** system call, or can alter others by means of the **setpriority()** system call. Weighting is independent of processor utilization and serves to provide a fixed signed ranking to the total process priority as a whole for administrative purposes.

Weighting is of limited usefulness, since a paradoxical set of other processes could effectively preempt higher-weighted processes because of a short burst of (anomalous) activity. Weighting, thus, is not guaranteed to dominate priority.

8.1.7 Functions Contained in kern/synch.c

The file **kern/synch.c** contains the following functions:

roundrobin()

schedcpu()

updatepri()

tsleep()

endtsleep()

unsleep()

wakeup()

rqinit()

setrun()

setpri()

This file implements the primitives used to schedule time slices of fair size among many competing processes that a process uses in turn to determine when it should relinquish the processor. The blocking and unblocking mechanisms are also present— they interact with the scheduling mechanism so as to always provide a level of fair access to the processor among competing needs. In addition, this file contains a routine which causes events to be generated that allow for turnover of the system on a regular basis, so that the system doesn't become bound to any one process for any reason.

8.1.8 What is roundrobin()?

roundrobin() is an interrupt-level function that trivially forces the current running process to be rescheduled every 100 milliseconds. It is implemented by means of the **timeout()** mechanism in **kern/clock.c** which causes it to be run after a period of time expires. **roundrobin()**reschedules itself after requesting the processor to be rescheduled. Since it runs off the interrupt activity of the process rescheduling clock, it achieves the effect of rescheduling by calling a macro, **need_resched**, to set a flag in the current running process (if any) requesting that the process give up the processor by means of a process rescheduling trap (T_ASTFLT—see **Chapter 3** on **trap.c**).

The **roundrobin()** function is initially scheduled by the **main()** routine on system startup. After that point, it reschedules itself by sticking itself back into the timeout queue.

... [File: /usr/src/kernel/kern/synch.c, line: 54]

```
void
roundrobin(void)
 ...
```

roundrobin()has no arguments and returns no value.

8.1.8.1 How is roundrobin() Implemented?

... [File: /usr/src/kernel/kern/synch.c, line: 57]

```
        need_resched();
        timeout(roundrobin, (caddr_t)0, hz / 10);
 ...
```

First **roundrobin()**calls the CPU-specific macro **need_resched** to request that the current process be rescheduled and then reinserts the function in the timeout queue to be called a tenth of a second later. Since **timeout()** (see **kern/clock.c**) supplies an argument, a dummy argument of zero is passed to **roundrobin()**. The function then waits until the next scheduled interval.

8.1.9 What is schedcpu()?

schedcpu() is the interrupt-level function called via the **timeout()** mechanism implemented by the process rescheduling clock to recalculate the priorities of all running processes once a second. **schedcpu()** walks the list of all processes, increasing the time accumulated by them. It increments the time of execution of the process and the time spent by sleeping processes waiting for active running processes or for those that sleep for less than a second. It recalculates the priority for a process against a digital filter which exponentially decays. The decay period itself depends on the load average of the system—the less loaded the system, the slower the decay—such that 90% of the priority will decay away in five times the load average seconds.[19]

... [File: /usr/src/kernel/kern/synch.c, line: 83]

```
void
schedcpu(void)
 ...
```

[19] Since many simultaneous processes divide up the total CPU utilization, the load average expands the time interval to compensate.

This function takes no arguments and returns no value. It has the side-effect of adjusting the priorities of the processes and waking up any processes sleeping on the magic address *lbolt* (short for "lightning bolt"). It also accounts for virtual memory usage and reschedules itself on another interrupt a second later.

8.1.9.1 How is schedcpu() Implemented?

... [File: /usr/src/kernel/kern/synch.c, line: 91]

```
        wakeup((caddr_t)&lbolt);
    ...
```

schedcpu() first issues a wakeup to all processes waiting for the lightning bolt.

... [File: /usr/src/kernel/kern/synch.c, line: 92]

```
    for (p = allproc; p != NULL; p = p->p_nxt) {
        /* Increment time and sleep time. Overflow is ignored. */
        p->p_time++;
        if (p->p_stat == SSLEEP || p->p_stat == SSTOP)
            p->p_slptime++;
    ...
```

The list of all active processes is successively locked and each process is examined in turn. The time associated with each process is incremented, and any sleeping processes or stopped processes are accounted for with a separate time counter. Stopped processes are a special case of sleeping processes in that they can revert to either a running state or a sleeping state, depending on whether they are continued or signalled.[20]

... [File: /usr/src/kernel/kern/synch.c, line: 110]

```
            p->p_pctcpu = (p->p_pctcpu * ccpu) >> FSHIFT;
            /*
             * If the process has slept the entire second,
             * stop recalculating its priority until it wakes up.
             */
            if (p->p_slptime > 1)
                    continue;
            /*
             * p_pctcpu is only for ps.
             */
#if (FSHIFT >= CCPU_SHIFT)
            p->p_pctcpu += (hz == 100)?
                ((fixpt_t) p->p_cpticks) << (FSHIFT - CCPU_SHIFT):
                100 * (((fixpt_t) p->p_cpticks)
                    << (FSHIFT - CCPU_SHIFT)) / hz;
#else
            p->p_pctcpu += ((FSCALE - ccpu) *
                (p->p_cpticks * FSCALE / hz)) >> FSHIFT;
#endif
    ...
```

---

[20] More information on stopped processes is contained in the discussion for **kern/sig.c** in **Chapter 6**.

Since a majority of processes are usually sleeping and have no run queue order to be changed, scheduling overhead can be reduced. Sleeping processes have their priority calculation postponed until they become runable.

The percent CPU field of the process is a fixed-point fractional number calculated to represent the percentage use of the processor by this process.[21] Normally, this calculation could be more simple if the kernel was allowed to use floating point; however, since the floating point unit is not always present on PCs[22] and since the rather considerable state for the floating point unit would have to be exchanged every time the kernel was called, this field is implemented with integer operations using scaled[23] arithmetic. Two methods are selectable for obtaining the result.

... [File: /usr/src/kernel/kern/synch.c, line: 129]

```
                    p->p_cpticks = 0;
                    newcpu = (u_int) decay_cpu(loadfac, p->p_cpu) + p->p_nice;
                    p->p_cpu = min(newcpu, UCHAR_MAX);
                    setpri(p);
                    s = splhigh(); /* prevent state changes */
                    if (p->p_pri >= PUSER) {
#define PPQ (128 / NQS)   /* priorities per queue */
                            if ((p != curproc) &&
                                p->p_stat == SRUN &&
                                (p->p_flag & (SLOAD|SWEXIT)) == SLOAD &&
                                (p->p_pri / PPQ) != (p->p_usrpri / PPQ)) {
                                    remrq(p);
                                    p->p_pri = p->p_usrpri;
                                    setrq(p);
                            } else
                                    p->p_pri = p->p_usrpri;
                    }
                    splx(s);
    ...
```

The number of rescheduling interrupts that have been received on this process is set to zero so that the percent CPU time can be determined over the next time interval that **schedcpu()** is run. The new CPU priority is then obtained by decaying the older process priority through one stage of decay, using the fixed offset of the UNIX *nice*[24] value. This priority representing the CPU utilization is clamped to a maximum value represented in the data type of 127. It is used by the **setpri()** function as the basis to assign a new user priority.[25] A distinction is made between user mode scheduling and kernel mode scheduling in that any kernel activity is favored over any user activity. Thus, a user priority is always a lower priority than a kernel priority. The effect of the decay is to improve process run queue eligibility.

---

[21] This number is displayed in the output of the **ps -aux** command.
[22] Since many require an additional chip to do floating point.
[23] In place of a floating point modulus.
[24] An arbitrary priority weighting used to give preferential treatment to a process.
[25] The priority used in scheduling a process that is in user mode.

With the new user priority set in the process, the process entry is isolated from changes by disabling interrupts to prevent interference from other parts of the kernel interacting with the run queue. In particular, since the interrupt level code may awaken processes and modify the run queue we are already making use of, we must make it exclusive to ourselves while we are using it.

If the priority of the process is a user level priority (e.g., it is not performing system operation), we allow its priority to be checked for changes. If the process is not the current process (it is a running process that is loaded), and if the change in priority causes its position to change from one run queue to another run queue, the process is removed from its old run queue, its new user priority is assigned as its current priority, and it is placed back on the run queue associated with that current priority. Otherwise, the priority field is just updated.

If the process was sleeping, the priority will only become effective the next time it is rescheduled. If the process was the current process (it is not on a run queue), we cannot remove it from the run queue but only change its current priority. In this case, the next time any effect will occur is when the current process is examined for preemption. Since there are more priorities than there are queues, the priority associated with each queue is the minimum granularity of change since the queue location is effectively the most significant portion of the priority field.

A special mention should be made of the test to see if the process is loaded—if the process is exiting, the current process will no longer point to the process entry since the process is no longer schedulable, yet it is still running as it is dismantled and terminated. Thus, to keep this routine from attempting to remove it from the run queue (where it is already not present),[26] the load comparison includes a test for whether the process is waiting to exit.

... [File: /usr/src/kernel/kern/synch.c, line: 148]

```
vmmeter();
timeout(schedcpu, (caddr_t)0, hz);
    ...
```

After examining all processes in this fashion, **schedcpu()** will call the virtual memory system's accounting function **vmmeter()** (in **vm_meter.c**) to tally the usage of virtual memory (with the utility **vmstat**) and then reschedule itself in a second using the **timeout()** feature. Again note that this function is run at interrupt level and takes care to alter the state of (in this case) process entries, but does not make use of any functions which might block.

---

[26] An attempt to remove a process from a run queue which isn't on the run queue will cause a panic.

8.1.9.2 386BSD schedcpu() Design Choices and Trade-offs

The "lightning bolt," part of the original UNIX system, is a quaint old mechanism used to jab drivers that need to be periodically awakened for some service purpose. Earlier UNIX systems relied on character lists (or clists) blocks which caused the tty driver to block waiting for a *lbolt* to arrive so that it could wake up and check to see if there were more clists available. Instead of clists, 386BSD uses ring buffers which are statically allocated. As such, the use of the lightning bolt is not essential for this system, but remains solely as an artifact for older drivers. It can be removed with little effort.

The decay filter that implements the percentage estimation in **schedcpu()** is built out of an algorithm that is sensitive to bit assignments within a fixed-point fractional number. FSHIFT and CCPUSHIFT allow for a different treatment of the portion of an integer field used as the fraction portion of the number. The base value is obtained every rescheduling and accumulated against a decay count based on one of two algorithms which (depending on your view) is either simpler but less accurate or more accurate but more costly in terms of time.

In the case of processes sleeping for longer than a second, it is actually silly to do the second portion of the calculation, since the priority will not erode any further. That and the rest of this routine which concerns itself with repositioning running processes in the queue is not useful for these long sleeping processes.

8.1.10 What is updatepri()?

updatepri() is used to recalculate the priority of a process after it has been sleeping for a while. It is used when a process is reactivated to calculate a sensible priority for it.[27]

... [File: /usr/src/kernel/kern/synch.c, line: 157]

```
void
updatepri(struct proc *p)
   ...
```

updatepri() accepts a process pointer as an argument and returns nothing. It has the side-effect of changing the CPU utilization priority and user priority of the process it is handed as an argument. A process, in effect, is rewarded for sleeping by being made more eligible to run.

---

[27] Since we don't bother to update priorities for long-term sleepers as an efficiency consideration in **schedpri()**.

SOURCE CODE SECRETS: THE BASIC KERNEL

8.1.10.1 How is updatepri() Implemented?

... [File: /usr/src/kernel/kern/synch.c, line: 161]

```
    fixpt_t loadfac = loadfactor(averunable[0]);

    if (p->p_slptime > 5 * loadfac)
            p->p_cpu = 0;
    else {
            p->p_slptime—; /* the first time was done in schedcpu */
            while (newcpu && —p->p_slptime)
                    newcpu = (int) decay_cpu(loadfac, newcpu);
            p->p_cpu = min(newcpu, UCHAR_MAX);
    }
    setpri(p);
...
```

If the process has been sleeping for longer than five times the number of the load factor (in seconds), we don't bother with consuming the time to decay the CPU value—we just drop it to zero immediately. Otherwise, for every second spent sleeping, the CPU utilization factor is decayed by the portion of the load factor that it would have decayed by if we had calculated it during its period of sleep.

Note that since we are sampling the load factor at the end of sleep and not during, these numbers will not be the same. In particular, if the load factor was larger during the sleep, the priority will not erode as much as if the process had run the whole time. One of the oddities of this mechanism is that processes that sleep for small increments lose less of their priorities than ones which sleep for long periods of time or not at all— this is appropriate behavior for an interactive system.

After calculating the new CPU utilization, the user priority is updated with **setpri()** and we are done.

8.1.10.2 386BSD updatepri() Design Choices and Trade-Offs

In a sense, **updatepri()** tries to "catch up" on the priority recalculations that should have been done in **schedcpu()** but were put off until the process was rescheduled. By postponing this cost, the overhead of rescheduling sleeping[28] processes has been reduced. The whole emphasis in the priority calculation and utilization numbers is to keep the overhead of these calculations low. This is especially true in the case of running a large timesharing system with hundreds of processes, where the cost per each process of priority management to implement the multilevel feedback queue scheduling becomes in and of itself a large consumer of cycles.

In the case of a PC running a mere forty or fifty processes, this cost is down in the noise, so this structure is a bit overblown for normal usage. However, if one starts thinking of threads instead of just processes, one can understand why one might want to keep the cost low once again.

---

[28] Which most processes on the system usually are at any given point in time.

8.1.11 What is tsleep()?

tsleep(), the *timed sleep* function, is the blocking mechanism for the kernel. **tsleep()** will suspend the current process until a **wakeup()** is made of the event on which it is blocked. Optionally, it may catch signals, ignore signals, or elect to time out after a period of time.

... [File: /usr/src/kernel/kern/synch.c, line: 205]

```
int
tsleep(caddr_t chan, int pri, char *wmesg, int timo)
...
```

tsleep() has four arguments: the address of the event that **tsleep()** is waiting to be awakened from, the priority to set the sleeping process, and an optional pointer to a string indicating what the sleep is waiting for. Part of the priority field includes a bit (PCATCH) which may be or'd into the priority to indicate that the caller to **tsleep()** elects to catch signals sent to the process. In this case, it must catch the signal and return all the way out to user mode for the signal to be honored, and not reengage **tsleep()**. The string in the optional pointer will appear in the output of the "ps" utility indicating the intent of the sleep and the amount of time to wait before timing out the wait for the signal (in units of rescheduling clock ticks); if it is set to zero, no timeout will be done.

tsleep() returns zero if awakened in a normal fashion. Otherwise, if a signal is caught by means of calling **tsleep()** with PCATCH on, an EINTR error is returned indicating that the signal has aborted the routine, except in the case that it was called by a system call which allowed the signal to be checked—in this case, a ERESTART error is returned. These two choices are made based on the signal treatment specified (see **kern/sig.c** with regards to the SA_RESTART signal action option). Otherwise, if the timeout expires before a wakeup occurs, an error (EWOULDBLOCK) is returned.

8.1.11.1 How is tsleep() Implemented?

tsleep() is written with a great deal of implicit knowledge of context switching, signalling, and scheduling code.

... [File: /usr/src/kernel/kern/synch.c, line: 215]

```
        s = splhigh();
        if (cold || panicstr) {
                /*
                 * After a panic, or during autoconfiguration,
                 * just give interrupts a chance, then just return;
                 * don't run any other procs or panic below,
                 * in case this is the idle process and already asleep.
                 */
                splx(safepri);
                splx(s);
                return (0);
        }
        ...
```

All interrupts are masked during the sleep operation to allow sleep to manipulate the sleep queue exclusively. If the system is being initialized or has a panic terminal condition, it is not allowed to sleep; instead, the interrupt level priority is dropped to a safe level to allow device interrupts to occur, then placed back to its original level. This assures that the interrupt priority is not locked out perpetually by the device interrupts calling **tsleep()** at **splhigh**. No other processes are allowed to run during this time (e.g., **swtch** is not allowed to be called) so that the system will not experience a cascade of panics.

In the case of system initialization, the ability to context switch between processes actually develops after device drivers are configured, since device drivers use sleep and wakeup anyway. By avoiding context switching, the device drivers can configure themselves without requiring any special initialization code, eliding sleeps and wakeups during configuration. The effect of this is that sleep and wakeup will be ignored, and only the side-effects, not the operations that surround them, will be observed by the driver and the interacting portion of the system.[29]

... [File: /usr/src/kernel/kern/synch.c, line: 231]

```
        p->p_wchan = chan;
        p->p_wmesg = wmesg;
        p->p_slptime = 0;
        p->p_pri = pri & PRIMASK;
        qp = &slpque[HASH(chan)];
        if (qp->sq_head == 0)
                qp->sq_head = p;
        else
                *qp->sq_tailp = p;
        *(qp->sq_tailp = &p->p_link) = 0;
        if (timo)
                timeout(endtsleep, (caddr_t)p, timo);
...
```

The event address is recorded in the process's p_wchan field along with the pointer to the message associated with this event. The sleep time is initialized to zero since the process is going to sleep, and the priority is assigned to the process. The process itself is inserted into the sleep queue which has a hash table as its head of queue. The sleep queue is an array of two process pointers per entry indicating the beginning and ending point of a queue of processes waiting on this hash entry. The hash is computed from the address waited for, and the process is added either to the beginning of the queue (if there is nothing on the queue) or to the last entry of the queue. The trailing process's forward link is zeroed to indicate the trailing end of this list of processes for which to search.

---

[29] For example, in **fs/bio.c**, **biowait()** will call **tsleep()** repeatedly; in this case, nothing actually happens but it does allow monitoring of the state of the done bit, set when the disk driver does a **biodone** and issues an non-operational **wakeup()**.

This pointer is also used in a running process to indicate its placement on a run queue. If a mistake is made and the process was left on the run queue when **tsleep()** was called, a panic would ensue the next time the queue entry was activated. If a timeout was requested, the function **endtsleep()** is requested for a timeout called with this process's pointer after the requested period of time.

... [File: /usr/src/kernel/kern/synch.c, line: 252]

```
if (catch) {
        p->p_flag |= SSINTR;
        if (sig = CURSIG(p)) {
                if (p->p_wchan)
                        unsleep(p);
                p->p_stat = SRUN;
        goto resume;
        }
        if (p->p_wchan == 0) {
                catch = 0;
                goto resume;
        }
}
p->p_stat = SSLEEP;
p->p_stats->p_ru.ru_nvcsw++;
swtch();
...
```

The signals are checked to see if any are already pending at the time we entered the sleep. If there are any signals pending, we reverse the effect of the sleep (making the process runable) and resume operation. We do not attempt to context switch the process because the signal has cancelled our attempt at sleeping. This is done because the signals block each other until they are received. Thus, if this procedure was not followed, the signal might never be seen because it got into a race with a call to **tsleep()**, with the signal arriving ahead of the process going to sleep.

If during the check for any current signals a SIGCONT signal was processed, a sleep may have occurred during the check for signals. If we find that the event field we were waiting for is set to zero during our wakened period, no signal has yet occurred, and we continue onwards. Otherwise, we set the state of this process to sleeping, increment the statistics for an involuntary context switch, and then execute the context switch.

... [File: /usr/src/kernel/kern/synch.c, line: 274]

```
resume:
        curpri = p->p_usrpri;
        splx(s);
        p->p_flag &= ~SSINTR;
        if (p->p_flag & STIMO) {
                p->p_flag &= ~STIMO;
                if (catch == 0 || sig == 0)
                        return (EWOULDBLOCK);
        } else if (timo)
                untimeout(endtsleep, (caddr_t)p);
```

```
if (catch && (sig != 0 || (sig = CURSIG(p)))) {
        if (p->p_sigacts->ps_sigintr & sigmask(sig))
                return (EINTR);
        return (ERESTART);
}
return (0);
    ...
```

When this process is resumed[30] the process interrupt level is restored and the interruptible sleep flag is removed. The process's user priority is set to the global variable *curpri* as a value to check against to determine if a higher priority process is present to be run (see **need_resched()** in **machine/cpu.h**). If the timeout flag is indicated on the process flag, a timeout occurred before the **wakeup()** occurred. In this case, if there is no signal caught, an error is returned (EWOULDBLOCK); otherwise, if a timeout had been scheduled but did not come in, the timeout is cancelled by removing it from the timeout queue with the **untimeout()** function call.

If the call to sleep was set to catch signals and a current signal is present or if a check of the outstanding current signals finds a new one present, then the appropriate error value is returned by consulting the signal action state for this signal; otherwise, zero is returned—this is the common case of being awakened. If signals are elected to be caught, the caller must return back to user level to have them honored and unblocked.

8.1.12 What is endtsleep()?

endtsleep() is an internal interrupt level function called from the **timeout()** mechanism of the process timeslice clock. **endtsleep()** notifies the process passed to it as an argument that the sleep has timed out. This will only be called if the sleep is still outstanding, since when the sleep is finished it will otherwise cancel the timeout event scheduled with **endtsleep()**.

... [File: /usr/src/kernel/kern/synch.c, line: 297]

```
static void
endtsleep(struct proc *p)
    ...
```

endtsleep() has one argument: the pointer to the process which has been awakened and marked as having had a timeout occur on it. It returns no value.

8.1.12.1 How is endtsleep() Implemented?

... [File: /usr/src/kernel/kern/synch.c, line: 300]

```
        int s = splhigh();

        if (p->p_wchan) {
                if (p->p_stat == SSLEEP)
                        setrun(p);
```

---

[30] As a result of being awakened by **wakeup()** and having a priority great enough to run.

```
            else
                    unsleep(p);
            p->p_flag |= STIMO;
        }
        splx(s);
    ...
```

endtsleep() disables interrupts for the extent of its operation. If the process is still waiting (it has an outstanding wait event), then the process is checked to see if it has made it into the state for sleeping or if it is stopped. If it is sleeping, it has been context switched and is on the sleep queue. The process is then set to be runable (via a **setrun()** call); otherwise, it is reversed out of sleeping and stuffed back into a stopped state.

In either case, a timeout indication is appended to the process's flag so that when the process is rerun it can discover that a timeout has occurred. Since a sleeping process can encounter a stop signal, it cannot directly be run until it leaves the stop mode.[31] This is the primary reason for **unsleep()**.

8.1.13 What is unsleep()?

unsleep() reverses the effect of a sleep action by withdrawing a process from the sleep queue. By taking the process out of the sleep queue, thus reversing the action of having it enter a sleep, the process may now enter the stopped or run states.

... [File: /usr/src/kernel/kern/synch.c, line: 315]

```
void
unsleep(struct proc *p)
    ...
```

unsleep() has one argument: a pointer to the process that will be removed from the sleep queue. It returns nothing.

8.1.13.1 How is unsleep() Implemented?

... [File: /usr/src/kernel/kern/synch.c, line: 322]

```
        s = splhigh();
        if (p->p_wchan) {
                hp = &(qp = &slpque[HASH(p->p_wchan)])->sq_head;
                while (*hp != p)
                        hp = &(*hp)->p_link;
                *hp = p->p_link;
                if (qp->sq_tailp == &p->p_link)
                        qp->sq_tailp = hp;
                p->p_wchan = 0;
        }
        splx(s);
    ...
```

Like all operations affecting either sleep or run queues, the interrupts are disabled during this operation. If the process is waiting for an event, this event is used to index

---

[31] Stop state is thus a variation on run state.

---

the hash queue where the particular process is searched for, found, and removed from the linked list of processes. The list is a singly-linked list attached to a doubly-linked queue entry. After removing the entry, it erases the event, unblocks its interrupt, and leaves.

8.1.13.2 386BSD unsleep() Design Choices and Trade-Offs

This function is used by the signal mechanism in concert with the process synchronization mechanism. It deals with the added complexity of having a stopped state which in reality is a special type of run state that forces the process to operate under the control of another.

8.1.14 What is wakeup()?

The corresponding function to **tsleep()**, **wakeup()** removes the block that **tsleep()** institutes and schedules the process for execution. **wakeup()** examines the sleep queue to find any and all processes waiting for the event and makes each of them runable, thus removing them from the queue.

... [File: /usr/src/kernel/kern/synch.c, line: 339]

```
void
wakeup(caddr_t chan)
...
```

wakeup() has one argument: the pointer to the event being awakened. It returns nothing. **wakeup()** does not ensure that the process will ever run—that is left to the scheduling of the system. **wakeup()** can be called from anywhere in the system, while **tsleep()** cannot be called from interrupt level (since there is no context to block).

8.1.14.1 How is wakeup() Implemented?

... [File: /usr/src/kernel/kern/synch.c, line: 346]

```
        s = splhigh();
        qp = &slpque[HASH(chan)];
restart:
        for (q = &qp->sq_head; p = *q; ) {
...
```

Like all functions affecting the status of the sleep queue, **wakeup()** blocks interrupts for the length of time it operates. It begins its search for processes to be awakened at the head entry of the queue associated with the hash table entry (hashed on the value of the wakeup event). From this point it examines any entries on this list—the list may be empty or full with every process in the system. A **wakeup()** can be done to a nonexistent address as well, since the address is used only as a rendezvous point. The list itself is a linear list of processes.

... [File: /usr/src/kernel/kern/synch.c, line: 354]

```
                if (p->p_wchan == chan) {
                        p->p_wchan = 0;
```

```
                          *q = p->p_link;
                          if (qp->sq_tailp == &p->p_link)
                                  qp->sq_tailp = q;
    ...
```

If the process examined in the loop has the event we are searching for, the event is
cleared from the process entry and the process is unlinked from the queue it is on.

... [File: /usr/src/kernel/kern/synch.c, line: 359]

```
            if (p->p_stat == SSLEEP) {
                    /* OPTIMIZED INLINE EXPANSION OF setrun(p) */
                    if (p->p_slptime > 1)
                            updatepri(p);
                    p->p_slptime = 0;
                    p->p_stat = SRUN;
                    if (p->p_flag & SLOAD)
                            setrq(p);
                    /*
                     * Since curpri is a usrpri,
                     * p->p_pri is always better than curpri.
                     */
                    /* if ((p->p_flag&SLOAD) == 0)
                            vmspace_activate(p);
                    else */
                            need_resched();
                    /* END INLINE EXPANSION */
                    goto restart;
            }
    ...
```

If this process was in the sleeping state, it is made runable through a variation on the
setrun() routine. If the process had been sleeping for longer than a second, **updatepri()**
is used to quickly implement all of the outstanding priority adjustments which had
been postponed and clear the sleep time field. The process's state is set to run and, if
the process is loaded, it is engaged on the run queue. After waking up this process, we
restart our scan of this list of processes to discover any new entries that may have
arrived during the time that we were processing these entries.

... [File: /usr/src/kernel/kern/synch.c, line: 378]

```
            } else
                    q = &p->p_link;
        }
    splx(s);
    ...
```

If the process examined does not match the wakeup event address, the forward link of
the process is followed to the next entry in the queue and we negotiate down the list. If
there are no other entries to be scanned in this loop, the function terminates, resetting
the interrupt mask back to its prior setting.

8.1.14.2 386BSD wakeup() Design Choices and Trade-Offs

A side-effect of the priority scheme is that when a process is awakened after sleeping,
it runs immediately at a kernel level of priority (since sleep and wakeup are entirely

---

internal to the kernel). As a result, if the processes that were running were not in the kernel, the process just awakened is the process ready to run.

8.1.14.3 Improvements to the Current Implementation of wakeup()

In the current version of the system, processes are always loaded since they are not swapped. This implies that even if they are maximally paged out, process tables[32] and the kernel's stack are still occupying memory. The **vmspace_activate()** and **vmspace_deactivate()** primitives, an unfinished portion of the system, allocate and deallocate all of these resources when the process has become idle for a period of time. In this case, the process will be made active if it had been collapsed, thus effectively unloaded, and then made runable by being incorporated onto the run queue. At the moment, only a rescheduling request is made to indicate that a higher priority process is ready to run.

In the long run, we would like to be able to allow the system to *scale* to very large numbers of processes and threads. At that point, it becomes completely untenable to have any overhead that would not be reclaimable for a process. However, this is a very long-term and comprehensive design consideration. Currently, on the average we may have 40 to 100 processes in use at any time—thus, the additional 160 to 400 KBytes of memory tied down by this additional mechanism is not yet a compelling enough tradeoff considering the current system usage.

The cost of implementing this mechanism is very high because, while it is easy to grab the page tables, it's much harder to get all the other state related to the process. In addition, the problem with factors of thousands is that one must get this contribution down to a small amount; otherwise, you're overwhelmed by trivia. As such, this mechanism which must reclaim and reactivate must be very pervasive—it's not something that one can just hack into the current system overnight. It must interact with all layers of abstraction of the system and subsystems, and thus requires a *fundamental* design shift.

Another item for consideration is the non-atomic nature of both **tsleep()** and **wakeup()**, which require independent checking of the resource and reblocking. With thread-based systems, the cost of waking a thousand threads to pass just one new resource is too excessive.

In sum, while this is an area of long-term design interest, other areas of work which would have a much more immediate effect on the current system usage of 386BSD, such as increasing the I/O bandwidth and improving the page reclamation mechanism, are more strongly encouraged at this time. These are areas of the system which can actually be worked on by the student or small research groups and where

---

[32] And other address translation overhead.

immediate positive results will be seen (if done correctly). Once we find that running thousands of processes is becoming the norm, this issue will be thrust to the fore.

8.1.15 What is rqinit()?

rqinit() initializes the state of the priority queue header so that we may link processes onto it. It is called from the **main()** initialization routine prior to any process multiprogramming. **rqinit()** initializes the run queue with all of its entries pointing back to themselves. These entries are basically sentinels for doubly-linked lists.

... [File: /usr/src/kernel/kern/synch.c, line: 388]

```
void
rqinit(void)
 ...
```

rqinit() has no arguments and returns nothing. Its only effect is the side-effect of initialization.

8.1.15.1 How is rqinit() Implemented?

... [File: /usr/src/kernel/kern/synch.c, line: 393]

```
        for (i = 0; i < NQS; i++)
                qs[i].ph_link = qs[i].ph_rlink = (struct proc *)&qs[i];
 ...
```

The array of run queue headers that implement the priority queue are successively initialized so that their head and tail pointers for forward and reverse links both point to the starting address of each queue header. This is the empty state for every queue—the queues are always initialized as being empty. Note that the queue status variable *whichqs* is statically initialized to zero to indicate that no queues are full.

8.1.16 What is setrun()?

setrun() forces a stopped or sleeping process to be runable. **setrun()** alters the state of the process to make it runable and places it on a run queue if the process can be run. In addition, it will arrange to reschedule the processor if the new process has a better priority than the current running process.

... [File: /usr/src/kernel/kern/synch.c, line: 402]

```
void
setrun(struct proc *p)
 ...
```

setrun() has one argument: the process pointer to be made runable. It returns nothing.

8.1.16.1 How is setrun() Implemented?

... [File: /usr/src/kernel/kern/synch.c, line: 407]

```
s = splclock();
switch (p->p_stat) {

case 0:
case SWAIT:
case SRUN:
case SZOMB:
default:
        panic("setrun");

case SSTOP:
case SSLEEP:
        unsleep(p);   /* e.g. when sending signals */
        break;

case SIDL:
        break;
}
p->p_stat = SRUN;
if (p->p_flag & SLOAD)
        setrq(p);
splx(s);
```
...

Since the run queues are being modified by the function, the clock interrupt is masked so that **schedcpu()** cannot run and collide with the modification of the run queue by changing the state of the process. A check of the process state is made via a case switch. Processes that are in an undefined state or in the wait state, run state, or zombie state should never be made runable; otherwise, a panic is issued. If the process is either stopped or sleeping, it is removed from the sleep queue by **unsleep()**[33] or, in the case of an idled process, it is made runable. With any of these three cases, the process state is upgraded to run and, if the process is loaded, it is inserted into the run queue and the interrupt block removed from the clock.

... [File: /usr/src/kernel/kern/synch.c, line: 429]

```
        if (p->p_slptime > 1)
                updatepri(p);
        p->p_slptime = 0;
        /* if ((p->p_flag&SLOAD) == 0)
                vmspace_activate(p);
        else  */ if (p->p_pri < curpri)
                need_resched();
    ...
```

If the process has been sleeping a long time, the priority is updated to account for the degradation in priority and the sleep time is cleared (since the sleep has been cancelled). If the new process's priority is better than the current process's priority, a reschedule request is made.

8.1.17 What is setpri()?

setpri() recomputes the user priority of a process and determines whether or not the process has a better priority than the current running process. If it does, it signals a rescheduling. The priority value to the process is updated by **setpri()** and assigned to the process supplied. Any outstanding reschedule requests for a better priority process are then issued.

... [File: /usr/src/kernel/kern/synch.c, line: 443]

```
void
setpri(struct proc *p)
    ...
```

setpri() has one argument: the process pointer. It returns nothing.

8.1.17.1 How is setpri() Implemented?

... [File: /usr/src/kernel/kern/synch.c, line: 448]

```
        newpri = PUSER + p->p_cpu / 4 + 2 * p->p_nice;
        newpri = min(newpri, MAXPRI);
        p->p_usrpri = newpri;
        if (newpri < curpri)
                need_resched();
    ...
```

User priorities that **setpri()** creates are always larger than kernel mode priorities, since they are based on the interruptible level of priority (PUSER) as well as the CPU utilization priority. In addition, the "nice" weighting of priority (which is never

---

[33] This is the case when returning from a signal that has been issued.

decayed) is added in to form a base level priority. This new priority is bounded by the maximum priority implemented and assigned to the process. Should the current process have a worse[34] priority than the new one, then rescheduling is requested. If this **setpri()** call is not occurring during another kernel[35] operation, it will not have the effect of rescheduling immediately. Otherwise, if the priority is set during an already long-running (and hence decayed) process, it will cause an immediate rescheduling when the processor attempts to return to user mode, such as after a clock interrupt.

8.2 Process Exclusion: kern/lock.c

The file **kern/lock.c** contains the machine-independent code which implements exclusion locks. These locks, of type *lock_data_t*, are embedded in data abstractions to control access by multiple competing processes and threads. Locks allow for multiple readers while requiring exclusion for write access. The locking primitives which make use of these locks in this file acquire access to the lock and thus the surrounding data structure, either for exclusive modification or for shared read access. An attempt to acquire an already locked lock will cause the second attempt to block until the lock is freed. Since these primitives imply locking, they are primarily meant to be used in the top level of the system and not from interrupt level.

However, some primitives are present that attempt to acquire the lock and, if the attempt would be unsuccessful, return immediately. It is possible to use this subset of primitives to test for the acquisition of an interrupt level lock. Even if the interrupt level code does preserve state from interrupt to interrupt, the lock must be released before the interrupt completes, because the indeterminacy of interrupts makes it impossible to guarantee that locks won't be frozen.

The principal use of these locks in the system is to control access to the shared map entries used in the virtual memory system so that controlled access can be made to them. The only locks used in 386BSD are currently *stateful locks*—meaning that the blocks remain outstanding until they are cleared. Care must be taken to avoid deadlock conditions.

8.2.1 Write Locks Versus Read Locks

Read locks have a lower precedence than *write locks* and many read locks can be present simultaneously. All a read lock is actually is a reference count of the number of current readers of the object. To ensure exclusion, a write lock must wait until there are no readers, and then acquire the lock atomically while disallowing simultaneous access by another write lock.

---

[34] Priority value is the opposite of its computed value; thus, low valued priorities have higher priority values.
[35] User priorities are less than kernel priorities.

If a reader wishes to upgrade from a read lock to a write lock, it must ensure not only that there are no more readers to the region, but also that there are no attempts already underway to upgrade a lock to write status. Otherwise, if the upgrade is in progress and one step ahead of the other upgrade attempt, yet still unable to gain access to the write lock because it cannot get the final read lock outstanding, a deadlock will occur. However, proceeding in the opposite direction and downgrading from a write lock to a read lock implies no conflict at all![36]

8.2.2 Lock Recursion

Locks allow us to gate exclusive access to a data structure that the lock is embedded within, but this can present problems for code that checks the locks at many different levels of abstraction, as is the case in the Mach virtual memory system. So before we continue we must ask the question "How are the underlying layers to know that an object has been locked by higher level layers?" For example, a humorous situation can occur when a lower level routine blocks because a higher level routine has a particular data structure already locked—this type of deadlock can never right itself normally.

To avoid these types of deadlocks, we could pass along, say, a flag as an argument to every layer of subroutines between the top and bottom layers, stating that a particular lock had been locked (so don't bother trying to acquire it again). However, this would only further complicate an already complicated virtual memory system.

An alternative to this dilemma might be to place a mode on the lock which would allow the lock to become stuck in the open position—thus, subsequent attempts at locking and unlocking would always succeed but do nothing. A mode is used because there are times when one needs to determine and block access to oneself.[37] The problem with this approach is that now the pairings of locks and unlocks may become asymmetric, since the software can ignore the significance of the lock.

Thus, a better arrangement would be to record the number of locks so acquired and decrement them as we unlock—in effect using a recursive reference count. In this way, it can be ensured that parity is conserved. At the point when the special recursive mode is removed, the assertion is that all references for recursive locking are no more. A limitation of the current lock mechanism is that read/write locks don't handle recursion independently, since this would significantly complicate implementation. Thus, areas of the kernel avoid the use of this explicitly.[38]

---

[36] Since you can have multiple read locks as long as there isn't a write lock.

[37] In a rare set of cases, true, but still a possibility.

[38] See **vmspace_notpageable()** in **vm/map.c, Volume II** of this series.

8.2.3 Spin Locks

An alternative kind of locking mechanism is a *spin lock*. Spin locks are used in multiprocessor shared memory systems when exclusive access is needed that does not need to exclude access for longer than the time it takes to access a shared variable. In systems such as Mach or Solaris, such locks are common. In fact, since they are a defacto shared resource, locks generally surround access to stateful locks, since the locks themselves require locking primitives (like spin locks) to control access to them. If this sounds a bit like the limerick that "Big ants have little ants upon them, and little ants have littler ants upon them,..." and so on ad infinitum, you can see the creeping effect which results from exposed locking primitives.

In the case of 386BSD, we have chosen to do without mechanisms such as spin locks. In our in-progress work on multithreaded systems, we have instead chosen to use a different mechanism, as well as a fundamentally different approach to thread exclusion.[39]

8.2.4 The Functions of kern/lock.c

The following functions are contained in the file **kern/lock.c**:

lock_init()

lock_write()

lock_done()

lock_read()

lock_read_to_write()

lock_write_to_read()

lock_try_write()

lock_try_read()

lock_try_read_to_write()

lock_set_recursive()

lock_clear_recursive()

8.2.5 What is lock_init()?

lock_init() initializes a lock to the unlocked state. The lock is either statically allocated or embedded in a data structure in place. The lock passed in as an argument to **lock_init()** will be initialized in place and unlocked for either read or write access with recursive mode disabled.

---

[39] Fine grain locks are to be embedded in access to key global data structures only—they are used to control partitioned access to thred/process context relative data structures. The compliler embeds the actual code of the primative entirely (N.B. such locks are never shared).

... [File: /usr/src/kernel/kern/lock.c, line: 93]

```
void
lock_init(lock_t l)
    ...
```

lock_init() has one argument: the pointer to the lock. It returns nothing.

8.2.5.1 How is lock_init() Implemented?

... [File: /usr/src/kernel/kern/lock.c, line: 96]

```
        l->want_write = FALSE;
        l->want_upgrade = FALSE;
        l->read_count = 0;
        l->thread = &nothread;
        l->recursion_depth = 0;
    ...
```

The fields of the lock are initialized to an unlocked condition. A dummy thread is then placed in the thread entry to signal that no recursion is present, and all three fields associated with the write lock are effectively cleared. Since locks are statically allocated and embedded in the structure to which they control access, no allocation of space needs to be done. This is an important point because locks are used to build the dynamic memory allocator.

8.2.6 What is lock_write()?

lock_write() blocks waiting for the write lock to be acquired. After waiting an indefinite period of time for the lock (if it is allocated to another), **lock_write()** arranges to eventually acquire the lock. A write lock implies that when **lock_write()** returns, exclusive access is guaranteed to the associated structure to which the lock belongs.

... [File: /usr/src/kernel/kern/lock.c, line: 104]

```
void
lock_write(lock_t l)
    ...
```

lock_write() has one argument: the pointer to the lock. It returns nothing.

8.2.6.1 How is lock_write() Implemented?

... [File: /usr/src/kernel/kern/lock.c, line: 110]

```
        if (((struct proc *)l->thread) == curproc) {
                l->recursion_depth++;
                return;
        }

        /* wait for write lock */
        while (l->want_write) {
                l->waiting = TRUE;
                (void) tsleep((caddr_t)l, PVM, "lckwrw", 0);
        }
```

```
l->want_write = TRUE;

/* have write lock, wait for readers and upgrades to release. */
while ((l->read_count != 0) || l->want_upgrade) {
        l->waiting = TRUE;
        (void) tsleep((caddr_t)l, PVM, "lckwru", 0);
}
```
...

The lock's thread field is first checked against the value of the current process to determine if it is a part of the recursive lock. If the lock is already set to recursive mode, the lock depth is increased. Otherwise, if a recursive lock is not set, the *want_write* bit is checked to see if the write lock is in use by another. The lock's mode is then set to waiting and a sleep is issued waiting for the write lock to become available.

After the lock becomes available, the *want_write* bit is set true to indicate we have the write lock. With it in hand, we then wait for any upgrading readers to finish with the lock by again reissuing a sleep. When no readers or upgrades continue to hold the lock, we have exclusive access, and hence return with the write lock and exclusive access intact.

8.2.7 What is lock_done()?

lock_done() releases any acquired lock, and wakes up any threads blocked by the lock having been locked. It determines which lock condition was granted and undoes it, thus freeing the lock for use by another. In addition, if there is a process waiting for the lock to become available, it will wake it up and cause it to become unblocked.

... [File: /usr/src/kernel/kern/lock.c, line: 130]

```
void
lock_done(lock_t l)
```
 ...

lock_done() has one argument: the pointer to the lock. It returns nothing.

8.2.7.1 How is lock_done() Implemented?

... [File: /usr/src/kernel/kern/lock.c, line: 134]

```
if (l->read_count != 0)    /* read lock */
        l->read_count--;
else
if (l->recursion_depth != 0) /* write lock: recursive lock */
        l->recursion_depth--;
else
if (l->want_upgrade) /* write lock: upgrade attempt */
        l->want_upgrade = FALSE;
else    /* write lock: write attempt */
        l->want_write = FALSE;

/* someone waiting for lock? */
if (l->waiting) {
        l->waiting = FALSE;
```

```
                    wakeup((caddr_t) l);
        }
    ...
```

The lock is released by determining which condition is present that is responsible for
the lock in the first place, by precedence. If the read count on the lock is not zero, this
indicates that a read lock is present. In this case, the read count is decremented,
releasing the read lock. If the read count is zero, then the recursion depth is checked.

Recursive locks are assumed to be write locks and, as such, if the recursion depth is
not zero, the recursion depth is decremented, releasing the write lock. If the recursion
depth is zero, the upgrade (to writing) is checked to see if it is set true, indicating that
the last lock was an upgrade—if so, then it is cleared. If it is not set then we know that
it was an original write lock attempt that is cleared. This hierarchy indicates in reverse
order the precedence of how locks are acquired. Note there are really only two locking
conditions present here—it's only the methods as to how they are obtained that results
in the need for the different fields.

After releasing the lock, the *lock_waiting* field is checked to see if there someone
waiting for the lock. In this case, the waiting field is set false and a wakeup is done to
relieve the block on any processes waiting for the lock. Note that while many
processes can wait for a single lock, only the first one will get the lock.

8.2.8 What is lock_read()?

lock_read() blocks waiting for a read lock to be obtained. Since many read locks are
possible, the only purpose of this function is to serialize write lock access. **lock_read()**
ensures that no write locks are present to the lock and increments the reference count
associated with the read lock. If any write locks are outstanding it will wait until they
have completed. This function could also have been called "**lock_don't_write()**."

... [File: /usr/src/kernel/kern/lock.c, line: 153]

```
void
lock_read(lock_t l)
    ...
```

lock_read() has one argument: the pointer to the lock. It returns nothing.

8.2.8.1 How is lock_read() Implemented?

... [File: /usr/src/kernel/kern/lock.c, line: 159]

```
        if (((struct proc *)l->thread) == curproc) {
                l->read_count++;
                return;
        }

        /* any write or upgrades request outstanding? */
        while (l->want_write || l->want_upgrade) {
                l->waiting = TRUE;
                (void) tsleep((caddr_t)l, PVM, "lckwru", 0);
```

```
}
/* grab read lock */
l->read_count++;
...
```

If the lock is set to recursive mode, the read lock count is incremented (as the lock is immediately allocated and returned). If the lock is not recursive, a check is made to see if a write lock or write upgrade is outstanding. In these cases, **lock_read()** waits until the write or upgrade lock is no longer held, then increments the read lock count and returns, adding a reference for reading to the lock.

8.2.9 What is lock_read_to_write()?

lock_read_to_write() attempts to upgrade a read lock to a write lock. If it fails, it returns an indication that it has lost its original read lock in the process. If another lock has the upgrade (and possibly is waiting for it), the read lock is passed back so that a deadlock condition is avoided. However, if the upgrade can be obtained, **lock_read_to_write()** waits to ensure that there are no other readers before obtaining exclusive access.

... [File: /usr/src/kernel/kern/lock.c, line: 179]

```
boolean_t
lock_read_to_write(lock_t l)
 ...
```

lock_read_to_write() has one argument: the pointer to the lock. It returns a boolean value indicating true if the upgrade failed. In this case the read lock will be lost and need to be reacquired. The failed call to **lock_read_to_write()** should force its caller to back out all of its other related operations under the assumption that there is competition for the same object. This avoids a deadlock condition which would otherwise occur if one side held a partial set of resources. The loser in the race, in going back to the beginning of the surrounding operations (of which **lock_read_to_write()** is a part), immediately attempts to reacquire the locks, only this time blocking since its contender for the lock has now had the chance to acquire both read and write locks and thus complete its operation while the other waits. This is how *serialization* occurs in upgraded locks.

8.2.9.1 How is lock_read_to_write() Implemented?

... [File: /usr/src/kernel/kern/lock.c, line: 185]

```
l->read_count--;

/* allow recursive lock? */
if (((struct proc *)l->thread) == curproc) {
        /* write lock is implied */
        l->recursion_depth++;
        return(FALSE);
}
```

```
              /* already an upgrade request? */
          if (l->want_upgrade) {
                  /* if waiting for it, let him have it */
                  if (l->waiting) {
                          l->waiting = FALSE;
                          wakeup((caddr_t) l);
                  }

                  /* we lost our read lock and failed the upgrade */
                  return (TRUE);
          }
    ...
```

The read count is decremented on the lock, as the read lock is immediately lost. If the lock is a recursive lock (where the write lock is implied), the recursion depth is incremented and a false value returned since we acquired the lock. If it was not a recursive lock, however, an upgrade might already be present on this lock. A check is thus made to find out whether there is a process waiting for this lock. If so, the condition is cancelled, a wakeup is done, and the read lock is passed to another in an attempt to avoid a deadlock situation. We then return true indicating that the upgrade has failed.

... [File: /usr/src/kernel/kern/lock.c, line: 207]

```
          l->want_upgrade = TRUE;

          /* if any other reader locks, wait for them. */
          while (l->read_count != 0) {
                  l->waiting = TRUE;
                  (void) tsleep((caddr_t)l, PVM, "lkrdwr", 0);
          }
          return (FALSE);
    ...
```

If the upgrade was not in use, we acquire the upgrade and, now holding the write lock, we check to see if there are any read locks outstanding. If so, we wait for them to complete. We then return false, indicating we have exclusive access and that the upgrade did occur.

8.2.10 What is lock_write_to_read()?

lock_write_to_read() downgrades a write lock to a read lock, by acquiring a read lock and giving up its write lock. It also wakes up anyone waiting for the write lock.

... [File: /usr/src/kernel/kern/lock.c, line: 219]

```
void
lock_write_to_read(lock_t l)
    ...
```

lock_write_to_read() has one argument: the pointer to the lock. It returns nothing.

8.2.10.1 How is lock_write_to_read() Implemented?

... [File: /usr/src/kernel/kern/lock.c, line: 223]

```
        l->read_count++;

        /* release write lock */
        if (l->recursion_depth != 0)
                l->recursion_depth--;
        else
        if (l->want_upgrade)
                l->want_upgrade = FALSE;
        else
                l->want_write = FALSE;

        /* anyone waiting for a lock? */
        if (l->waiting) {
                l->waiting = FALSE;
                wakeup((caddr_t) l);
        }
    ...
```

Since we do not have to wait for contention, the read lock count is immediately incremented and the write lock is released from whichever of the three sources (recursion, upgrade, or original write lock) it came from. Anyone waiting for the lock is then awakened.

8.2.11 What is lock_try_write()?

lock_try_write() attempts to obtain the write lock without blocking. This function can be called from interrupt level to attempt to acquire a write lock.

... [File: /usr/src/kernel/kern/lock.c, line: 242]

```
boolean_t
lock_try_write(lock_t l)
  ...
```

lock_try_write() has one argument: the pointer to the lock. It returns a boolean value indicating whether or not it got the lock.

8.2.11.1 How is lock_try_write() Implemented?

... [File: /usr/src/kernel/kern/lock.c, line: 246]

```
        if (((struct proc *)l->thread) == curproc) {
                l->recursion_depth++;
                return(TRUE);
        }

        /* lock in use? */
        if (l->want_write || l->want_upgrade || l->read_count)
                return(FALSE);

        /* grab write lock */
        l->want_write = TRUE;
        return(TRUE);
    ...
```

If the lock is set in recursive mode, the recursion depth is increased and the function immediately returns. If it is not set in recursive mode, it is checked to see if a write upgrade or a read lock is outstanding on the lock. If an outstanding request is present, thus preventing guaranteed exclusion on the lock without waiting, it returns false. However, if it can guarantee exclusion, it grabs the write lock and returns true.

8.2.12 What is lock_try_read()?

lock_try_read() attempts to obtain the read lock without blocking. It can also be called from interrupt level.

... [File: /usr/src/kernel/kern/lock.c, line: 261]

```
boolean_t
lock_try_read(lock_t l)
 ...
```

lock_try_read() has one argument: the pointer to the lock. It returns a boolean value indicating whether or not it got the read lock.

8.2.12.1 How is lock_try_read() Implemented?

... [File: /usr/src/kernel/kern/lock.c, line: 265]

```
        if (((struct proc *)l->thread) == curproc) {
                l->read_count++;
                return(TRUE);
        }

        /* write lock in use? */
        if (l->want_write || l->want_upgrade)
                return(FALSE);

        /* grab read lock */
        l->read_count++;
        return(TRUE);
 ...
```

If the lock is set in recursive mode, the read count is increased and the function immediately returns. If it is not set in recursive mode it checks to see if either the write lock or upgrade is outstanding on the lock. If so, it returns false because a read cannot be allowed during the exclusive access implied by write access. Note that many readers can be outstanding, so that is not checked. If neither a write or upgrade is present, the read lock is grabbed and it returns true.

8.2.13 What is lock_try_read_to_write()?

lock_try_read_to_write() attempts to upgrade a read lock to a write lock without losing the read lock. This function may block if necessary. If it cannot immediately upgrade the lock, it returns false to indicate that the upgrade is in use.

... [File: /usr/src/kernel/kern/lock.c, line: 280]

```
boolean_t
lock_try_read_to_write(lock_t l)
   ...
```

lock_try_read_to_write() has one argument: pointer to the lock. It returns a boolean value indicating if it gets the upgrade (true) or not (false). This routine may block.

8.2.13.1 How is lock_try_read_to_write() Implemented?

... [File: /usr/src/kernel/kern/lock.c, line: 284]

```
        if (((struct proc *)l->thread) == curproc) {
                l->read_count--;
                l->recursion_depth++;
                return(TRUE);
        }

        /* can't get upgrade ? */
        if (l->want_upgrade)
                return(FALSE);

        /* grab upgrade, lose read lock. */
        l->want_upgrade = TRUE;
        l->read_count--;

        /* if other read locks, wait for upgrade. */
        while (l->read_count != 0) {
                l->waiting = TRUE;
                (void) tsleep((caddr_t)l, PVM, "lkrdwr", 0);
        }

        return(TRUE);
   ...
```

If the lock is set in recursive mode, the read lock is dropped by decrementing the read count and the write lock is acquired by incrementing the recursion depth. In this case, the routine immediately returns true. If the lock is not in recursive mode, the *want_upgrade* field of the lock is checked to see if someone else has it; if so, the routine returns false because it cannot acquire the upgrade before losing the read lock.

The whole point of this routine is to never allow the region to become unlocked without a block interceding. If it can get the upgrade lock, it acquires it and drops the read lock, and then checks to see if there are other read locks pending since it cannot use the write lock obtained until all other readers are unlocked. After all readers have been unlocked, it can assure exclusive access and return true.

8.2.14 What is lock_set_recursive()?

lock_set_recursive() sets the lock into recursive mode, allowing multiple lock attempts to succeed for this thread on an already locked lock, while still blocking all others.

... [File: /usr/src/kernel/kern/lock.c, line: 308]

```
void
lock_set_recursive(lock_t l)
   ...
```

lock_set_recursive() has one argument: the pointer to the lock. It returns nothing.

8.2.14.1 How is lock_set_recursive() Implemented?

... [File: /usr/src/kernel/kern/lock.c, line: 312]

```
     if (!l->want_write)
              panic("lock_set_recursive: don't have write lock");

     /* assign lock to thread */
     if ((struct proc *)l->thread != curproc && l->thread != &nothread)
              panic("lock_set_recursive: already set recursive");
     l->thread = (char *) curproc;
   ...
```

The lock is examined to see if the write lock is already engaged; otherwise, a panic occurs since locks can only be set recursive if they are write-locked already. The lock's thread field is also checked to see if it corresponds to the initialized field for a non-recursive lock; otherwise, a panic occurs since a lock is set recursive that has already been set recursive. If everything is correct, then the current process's pointer is assigned to the thread field as a way of identifying the thread on which to allow recursion.

8.2.15 What is lock_clear_recursive()?

lock_clear_recursive() clears the mode set by **lock_set_recursive()**, requiring a lock to block regardless of which thread attempts to lock an already locked lock. It resets the lock's mode to the original non-recursive mode in the case that the recursion depth has been reached.

... [File: /usr/src/kernel/kern/lock.c, line: 322]

```
void
lock_clear_recursive(lock_t l)
   ...
```

lock_clear_recursive() has one argument: the pointer to the lock. It returns nothing.

8.2.15.1 How is lock_clear_recursive() Implemented?

... [File: /usr/src/kernel/kern/lock.c, line: 325]

```
     if (((struct proc *) l->thread) != curproc)
              panic("lock_clear_recursive: wrong thread");

     if (l->recursion_depth == 0)
              l->thread = &nothread;
   ...
```

The lock's thread field is checked to see if it belongs to the process clearing the recursive condition—if not, then a panic occurs since the lock is being cleared on the wrong thread. Otherwise, the recursion depth is checked to see that the number of locks and unlocks have cancelled out. If so, the thread field is reinitialized to point at the *nothread* variable to indicate that the recursion mode is not present.

Exercises

8.1 **a)** Why is priority weighting currently of limited value?
b) How could this factor be made more effective?

8.2 **a)** Can a **tsleep(...,PCATCH,...)** request be reissued if it returns after having been interrupted by a signal? Why or why not?
b) How does this request differ from a ERESTART or EINTR return?

8.3 **a)** What is the processor scheduling algorithm used in the 386BSD kernel?
b) Draw a diagram of the queuing model.

8.4 Are **lock_read_to_write()** and **lock_write_to_read()** symmetric functions to one another? Why or why not?

9 POSIX OPERATING SYSTEM FUNCTIONALITY (kern/execve.c, kern/descrip.c)

In the previous chapters we have examined areas of the kernel that are relatively independent of a given operating system's program interface. However, we cannot indefinitely avoid the characteristics of the given operating system, since efficient implementation requires some degree of close interaction. Two portions of the kernel highly involved with the POSIX/UNIX semantics are *program execution* and *file descriptor operations*. While all operating systems have these facilities, both obvious and subtle semantics significantly govern the operation of a specific implementation of a kind of operating system. Even within the area of UNIX operating system variants, both of these facilities differ greatly among implementations, and represent in a sense the "top of the top" level of abstraction portions of the kernel, which are heavily influenced by the exact semantics of the given operating system application programming interface.

With program loading, the format of an executable file, the arrangement of the image loaded for execution, transfer of arguments, and the semantics of the initiation of the program are all required for the operation to occur. All of these are elements of the POSIX **execve()** program load function, as qualified by both BSD and iBCS specifications—BSD[1] in the file formats and many fine grain details; iBCS in the X86 architecture[2] details.

File descriptors used by UNIX systems are quite similar to other operating systems which use a "handle" to refer to a particular open instance of a file. However, many characteristics of POSIX standardized file descriptors are embedded in the implementation of the kernel. This is an example of a more subtle cast of interface specificity than the obvious case of program loading. Understanding the semantics of the implementation details leads to the fine-grain characteristics necessary for implementing multiple operating system semantics independent of the kernel in an *emulator* mechanism.

---

[1] BSD-based systems have no architecture-specific details for standardization, being just an ad-hoc standard grown out of Bell Labs 32V UNIX.
[2] iBCS specifications define a X86 USL SVR4 system in detail, intentionally ignoring BSD systems in the pursuit of SVR purity of essence.

9.1 The 386BSD Executable File Format Emulator

The *386BSD executable file format emulator* is a new objective for this system, and draws some of its conceptual design from that of the Mach emulation library. In Mach, user program call the system via an emulation library. This emulation library provides a system *personality* mechanism independent of the kernel itself for calling operating system servers running in separate partitions as Mach tasks.[3] These libraries turn user program requests into Mach remote procedure calls which are relayed by the kernel to the appropriate operating system's task that implements that remote procedure call.

In 386BSD, the file format emulator is a conceptually simplified variation of the Mach emulation library concept. It corresponds to a transparent user mode *alter ego* of the operating system. For system calls that are not implemented in the kernel (or are not entirely implemented in the kernel, for that matter), the system call request is passed to an independent program running in the address space of the user process. The 386BSD emulator contains all personalities for a given architecture that may be implemented. Unlike the Mach concept, however, there is one emulator per system.[4]

Currently, the 386BSD file format emulator is implemented as a program-visible portion of the user's address space. However, this merely an implementation-specific detail, and may in the future be replaced by a dynamically created and destroyed entity located somewhere in the address space not necessarily accessible by the user program.[5]

In contrast with the Mach design and implementation, the 386BSD file format emulator is intended to run as a *trusted* program and hence cannot have its integrity violated by other user program nor by other users. Thus, users cannot develop or select their own emulators at this time. However, it is possible for a privileged user to debug the emulator as an ordinary program, by setting breakpoints and examining the contents.

Since the 386BSD emulator is so new, it is only minimally implemented to allow the extension of file execution capabilities. However, the emulator framework has been sufficiently outlined so that the reader can independently expand the concept of the emulator arbitrarily to accommodate a variety of system call interfaces, exception handling, and other characteristics required by specific operating system interface implementations. Note that this area of work is wide open and hence a rather considerable research project. As such, the 386BSD file format emulator will only be implemented to the degree deemed necessary for successive versions of the system.

---

[3] For example, one could have a MS DOS emulation library, a UNIX emulation library, an OS/2 emulation library, and so forth.
[4] As opposed to one per task or process.

9.1.1 Why Executable File Format Emulation as a Design Choice?

Since it is possible to recognize a file and determine the corresponding operating system with which to run it, **execve()** is a typical site to choose the associated operating environment of the program to be executed. However, the required functionality has intentionally not been implemented in this file, since we could end up embellishing it to hold the literally hundreds of different file formats that exist—not only in UNIX-like systems but also MS DOS and other operating systems as well.

We have instead chosen to move these many different file formats outside of the kernel. By working at a higher level of abstraction, we can keep our kernel small rather than compel huge amounts of code to run in its highly constrained environment. As a result of this design choice, the size of this file[6] makes this implementation of **execve()** the smallest in any modern UNIX-like system. At the same time, embellishments in user mode code can be implemented and improved arbitrarily and not impact the kernel proper. Thus, the 386BSD kernel remains the minimalist system desired in the spirit of the original Bell Labs UNIX kernel.

9.1.2 Which Executable File Format(s)?

Another design question which needed to be resolved was whether to implement architecture-independent executable file formats as the base single executable format (each written in machine-dependent code), or to implement a single architecturally "neutral" format written in kernel machine-independent code. The ramifications of this design choice required an examination of its historical roots.

Originally, there was one UNIX executable file format (a.out) that in general was selectively reinterpreted when ported to new platforms. During the 70's and 80's, architectures using UNIX were very diverse, ranging from 8-bit (the original IBM PC) to 64-bit (Cray), supporting various kinds of memory management,[7] shared libraries,[8] debugger symbol formats, and flat or segmented programming environments (286 protected mode). During this time, many attempts were made to support this diversity with a common format that would work for all with varying degrees of success.

This uncontrolled and frequently unecessary diversity was more of a curse than a blessing, since a programmer might have to support split sets of tools and applications just to deal with a handful of different formats on a single platform (sometimes, even within the exact same operating system as well). It boiled down to the fact that

---

[5] The challenging part of implementing this actually lies in the program utilities used to generate such a program and the machine-independent method by which the emulation library is hidden from access by the user program.

[6] Currently 458 lines.

[7] Segmentation, paging, both, and none.

[8] OSF, Sun, numerous variants.

industry people could not agree on a single, spanning file format[9] and so spent more time elaborating formats that they could control and could have a vested interest in maintaining (sometimes even licensing them). This is one of the unnecessary "snake pits" of the UNIX industry, and one example why the UNIX industry lacks cohesion, no matter how COSY it tries to get with itself.

These common file formats, unfortunately, each suffered flaws, from non-uniform implementation[10] to competing allegiances.[11] The net effect, however, is a legacy of a multitude of formats, all different.[12] Recently, however, computer architecture has been moving in the direction of increased similarity. Almost all workstations and PCs tend toward flat 32-bit[13] program virtual address spaces just like the original PDP-11 used with the original UNIX system. The need for architecturally neutral formats is in decline, because architectures are no longer tending to be as different.[14]

Rather than complicate the kernel, we questioned what precluded use of the original a.out format on any modern platform for 386BSD and could not justify an architectural difference. One could, however, justify this on compatibility grounds—however, this is exactly what a executable file emulator is intended for. Thus, we chose to use the a.out format as architecturally independent enough to allow the system basically to function while reserving compatibility extensions for outside of the kernel. This fits with our orginal mandate[15] to not meddle with existing standards, yet avoids the pitfalls encountered by commercial systems that must live in the quagmire of thousands of details inherent in the grand market.

9.1.3 Why do execve() in the Kernel at All?

Another reasonable question might be, why not make the emulator inherit all executable file formats, and move **execve()** to be entirely external to the kernel?[16] This is quite possible, as demonstrated by MACH-US, which runs the system interfaces entirely apart from the kernel itself. However, this topic is still not fully explored by modern systems, and it is hard to ensure that both exactly compatible semantics

---

[9] This argument continues to the present.
[10] Some had different shared library extensions, others none.
[11] OSF vs. UI, now a thing of the past we earnestly hope.
[12] Like the game Zork, "twisty little passages, all alike."
[13] And a few 64-bit.
[14] Perhaps this means that the executable file format champions will have to go back to selling used cars for a living, as they did before, or even maybe soap?
[15] See the original 386BSD software specification *386BSD: A Modest Proposal* (August 1990), **386BSD Reference CD-ROM**, for more information on goals and objectives.
[16] During the early 4BSD working group meetings in what was to become the Computer Systems Research Group, one of the principal architects proposed abandoning **execve()** entirely and have its function subsumed into segment creation primitives that would work via a special object library.

necessary for emulation and appropriate performance can be maintained after this level of abstraction shift occurs. Obviously, this is a topic for further study.

9.2 Binary File Execution: kern/execve.c

The file **kern/execve.c** contains machine-independent code to implement the execution of program machine instruction binary files. It corresponds to the top layer of abstraction of a POSIX 1003.1-based.system by implementing the entire **execve()** functionality of that standard as a single system call.[17] As a consequence, it is the *most* complex of any of the UNIX/POSIX system calls.

Other variations on program file execution are also present in the standard, including **execvp()** and **execl()**. These routines are implemented in the object library as interface routines which call **execve()** as the final step. They are placed outside of the kernel to ease implementation by working at a higher level of abstraction. In addition, by placing these other file execution routines in the object library, the kernel program is kept small by avoiding redundancy.

9.2.1 The Berkeley a.out File Format

The Berkeley 413 a.out file format is a demand load version of the original Bell Laboratories type 410 a.out[18] file format. The only difference between these two file formats is that the header is aligned on the boundaries of a page, so that consecutive pages of text and data start on an even page boundary. This makes the pages of the file correspond one-to-one with pages in memory without overlap.[19]

This executable file format is the only file format processing mechanism contained in this file since at least one is necessary for operation. Other file formats are added only as part of the file format emulator.

9.2.2 The execve() System Call Mechanism in Detail

A user program can either read or map the contents of a file into memory and transfer to execute the code contained within. Thus, the kernel implicitly allows user programs the ability to execute programs. However, the **execve()** system call mechanism is the *only* way that a binary program can be loaded by the kernel explicitly. It is also the only mechanism where the actual format of an application file is known by the kernel.

The first argument in **execve()** is the file pathname of the file to be executed. The **execve()** system call uses the kernel's VFS subsystem and the associated underlying

---

[17] See *Leveraging the POSIX Definition* in **Missing Pieces II** (June 1992), **Dr. Dobbs Journal** for more information.
[18] So named for assembler output.
[19] See *Executable File Format* in **Missing Pieces I** (May 1992), **Dr. Dobbs Journal**, for a complete discussion of the type 413 a.out file format and its historical derivation.

filesystem to gain access to the file contents to allow its execution. Since the file may not exist or may not be appropriate for reference (e.g., an inadmissible file execute permission or file ownership), the attributes of a file must be consulted (using the VFS) for **execve()** to allow execution.

Part of the file contents (usually located at the start of the file) called the *exec header* record describes the format and sizes of portions of the file. **execve()** uses this information to decide if resources are available and then allows the file to be loaded. This same information is also used to configure the process user virtual address space into which the program is loaded.

execve() does more than just execute a file. It builds a fresh execution environment for the new program image, replacing it with the one that issued this system call. Like other programming environments, **execve()** "chains" or overlays functions, so that when it is successful the "old" program is entirely gone. This new environment includes a function stack complete with a list of strings as incoming arguments to the program which are passed by value to the new program.

Also passed by value onto the new program stack are the POSIX environment strings.[20] These strings constitute a configuration database that may be used by applications programs or by parts of the POSIX implementation to adjust its operation accordingly. For example, the PATH environment string[21] is used by the POSIX **execvp()** and **execlp()** functions to specify a search path to locate executable programs described by incomplete path names

A successful **execve()** of a file results in a new program running. It appears as a function call of the file's **main()** function with two vectors (argument and environment) and a count of the number of arguments. To the application program it would appear as:

```
int main(int argc, char *argv[], char *env[])
```

Since some of these characteristics are dependent on the implementation of the program's run-time environment, an interface function in the runtime start off library[22] makes the final adjustment of binary to compiler implementation details, achieving the desired result.

Besides the portions of the program environment directly visible to the user program in its address space, open file descriptors, process authority credentials, and other kernel-resident portions of the process state are adjusted to suit the new program. File descriptors may be set to be closed before the new program runs (CLOSEONEXEC) or

---

[20] Which are inherited from ancestor processes.

[21] E.g. "PATH=:/bin/:usr/bin:".

[22] In the case of C, the object file /usr/lib/crt0.o.

may pass unhindered to the new program.[23] The UNIX **setuserid** and **setgroupid** features may change the effective user ID (or group ID) of the process to the ID set on the file itself, exchanging the credentials of the process for ones relative to the file itself. In UNIX-like systems, this is how privileges are delegated to non-privileged users.[24] As a system call, **execve()** uses only the **syscall()** interface between it and the user program, with the rest of the kernel subsystems residing below it. It is also intimate with the process object historically; otherwise, it is quite independent of implementation.

9.2.3 Unfinished Business

This facility highlights an unfinished portion of the operating system—that of describing the layout of the user-process virtual address space. The remainder of the kernel[25] carefully avoids restricting the contents of the process. However, to maintain the semantics of the user program environment, assignments of the address space, management of stack and "growable" heap, and resource tracking require some kind of structure to be in place for the system to function. Thus, a minimal description of managed virtual address space is compelled into the system, in the form of code that consults a fixed portion of the address space structure (vmspace). This code is embedded throughout the system, and is intended to be removed in future releases. What should be in place is a more generalized memory management interface (e.g., extended **mmap()**) which allows for assignment, control, extension, and statistics of address space. This is not currently implemented.

9.2.4 kern/execve.c Functions and Terminology

Only one function, **execve()**, exists in this file. It is the system call handler for the POSIX **execve()** system call. It may appear a bit confusing to have a function handler of the same name as the function it implements outside of the kernel. The difference between them is that the system call handler must also implement the characteristics of the system call as a way of communicating the arguments, results, and exceptions of a POSIX **execve()** function.

execve() is interesting in that it brings together in one file almost all of the other key portions of the kernel—the virtual memory system, the machine-dependent kernel (i.e., **locore.s**), many functions of the basic machine-independent kernel (e.g., **fork.c**, **exit.c**, **cred.c**, **cpu.c**, and so forth), and the filesystem. In sum, it calls upon so many other key files in the kernel that it is often difficult to obtain a comprehensive

---

[23] For the UNIX IPC to work, both **fork()** (see **Chapter 5**) and **execve()** must preserve file descriptors across operations.
[24] See *User ID and Group ID(s) in User Credentials* in **kern/cred.c** (**Chapter 7**) for more information.
[25] Apart from the virtual memory facility.

understanding of this function. As such, it is an excellent example mechanism to study while referring to the other chapters in this book.

9.2.5 What is execve()?

execve() allows the execution of a file as a program in a user process. **execve()** implements the semantics of a POSIX **execve()** function. As with all 386BSD system calls, it is called with the calling conventions implemented in the **syscall()** function in **i386/trap.c** (see **Chapter 3**).

... [File: /usr/src/kernel/kern/execve.c, line: 92]

```
int
execve(p, uap, retval)
        struct proc *p;
        struct args {
                char *fname;
                char **argp;
                char **envp;
        } *uap;
        void *retval;
    ...
```

execve() has three arguments: the pointer to the process associated with this system call; a pointer to the arguments of the POSIX **execve()** function; and a pointer to the return values (if any) for this system call. It returns only an error value if an error occurs. Otherwise, it has the side-effect of altering the entire address space if it is successful. If it should alter the address space such that it cannot return a value, it will force exit the process by an internal call to the **exit()** system call handler (see **Chapter 5** on **kern/exit.c**).

9.2.5.1 How is execve() Implemented?

... [File: /usr/src/kernel/kern/execve.c, line: 119]

```
        ndp = &nd;
        ndp->ni_nameiop = LOOKUP | LOCKLEAF | FOLLOW | SAVENAME;
        ndp->ni_segflg = UIO_USERSPACE;
        ndp->ni_dirp = uap->fname;
    ...
```

The first step taken is to construct a request to the VFS file path name-to-vnode translation function. Files can only be operated on in the top levels of abstraction in the kernel by means of a special handle known as a *vnode*. The **namei()** file pathname lookup function[26] searches through the directory hierarchy that a file pathname may incorporate, using the *nameidata* structure to decide on how to process the request.

In the case of **execve()**, the operation is a standard request to translate a name into a vnode (LOOKUP). If the file is present, the vnode found at the end of the pathname

---

[26] In **fs/lookup.c**—see the **386BSD Reference CD-ROM** for further information.

will be returned for exclusive access (LOCKLEAF). If any symbolic links are encountered, they will be transparently evaluated (FOLLOW). The name of the file associated with the vnode will be saved (SAVENAME) after the operation if successful.[27] With LOCKLEAF and SAVE, **execve()** takes on the responsibility to manage the *nameidata* structure in place of the **namei()** facility.

The pointer to the directory is then recorded in the *nameidata* structure, along with a flag indicating that the pointer is from the USERSPACE instead of the kernel.

... [File: /usr/src/kernel/kern/execve.c, line: 125]

```
        if (rv = namei(ndp, p))
                return (rv);
...
```

The request is passed to the **namei()** handler. If any error occurs in finding the file, **execve()** terminates and passes back the error.

... [File: /usr/src/kernel/kern/execve.c, line: 129]

```
        rv = EACCES;
        if (ndp->ni_vp->v_type != VREG)
                goto exec_fail;

        /* is the vnode cached already by a previous execve()? */
        pager = (vm_pager_t)ndp->ni_vp->v_vmdata;
        if (pager == NULL)
                vnp = NULL;
        else {
                vnp = (vn_pager_t)pager->pg_data;
                if (vnp->vnp_flags & VNP_EXECVE) {
                        /* avoid redundant I/O by using cached info */
                        hdr = vnp->vnp_hdr;
                        attr = vnp->vnp_attr;
                        goto bypass1;
                }
        }
...
```

The return vnode is checked to see if it is a regular file; if it is not, the file cannot be executed and an error is returned.[28] Before examining the file details, we first check to see if there is an associated pager present for this vnode. If such an associated pager exists, then this program is either being executed by another process or it has already been executed and remains in part of the virtual memory system's cache of executable images. In either case, there is a preloaded executable file header and vnode attributes—we can thus bypass the header and attribute checks entirely.

---

[27] As opposed to freeing the space associated with it after the vnode has been found.
[28] Only regular files can contain executable programs.

This procedure helps avoid redundant[29] operations while not perturbing the cached memory contents of the virtual memory system. The costliest operation (in terms of time) prior actually to mapping the file is the redundant load of the header. However, if the vnode actually changes, this information must be invalidated so that the reload can reestablish the correct values.

... [File: /usr/src/kernel/kern/execve.c, line: 148]

```
        if ((ndp->ni_vp->v_mount->mnt_flag & MNT_NOEXEC) != 0)
                goto exec_fail;
    ...
```

If the vnode is not in the virtual memory's pager cache, we check it to see if it is a reasonable candidate to be executed. First, we see if it belongs to a filesystem where executable files are allowed. The vnode of the found file is returned in the *nameidata* structure (ni_vp), and the filesystem with which it is associated (v_mount) has a set of flags associated with the filesystem when it was mounted.[30] If it is disallowed, an error (EACCES) is returned and the resources of **namei()** returned to the system available pool (exec_fail).

... [File: /usr/src/kernel/kern/execve.c, line: 152]

```
        rv = VOP_GETATTR(ndp->ni_vp, &attr, p->p_ucred, p);
        if (rv)
                goto exec_fail;
    ...
```

The vnode itself contains little state, but is used as the means to access state via the operations on the VFS. **VOP_GETATTR()** obtains the abstract attributes associated with the file, using the context of the process we are working with at the time and the credentials of the process to validate access to the information. If no attributes are available, **execve()** terminates with an error.

... [File: /usr/src/kernel/kern/execve.c, line: 157]

```
        if ((attr.va_mode & VANYEXECMASK) == 0)
                goto exec_fail;
    ...
```

A file must have executable attributes and must be an "ordinary"[31] file to be executable so the file mode of the file must be examined. Normally, this would be accomplished by the use of a VOP_ACCESS. However, the semantics of access in a UNIX system permit the superuser to always obtain access regardless of mode. Thus, to ensure that root can only execute executable files, the mode is checked to see if at

---

[29] Reloading the starting pages of executables that normally are not cached.
[30] Usually, by means of the **mount(8)** command.
[31] E.g., not a "file-like" object such as a directory, socket, device, or named pipe.

least one execute bit is set indicating that this is an executable file; otherwise, an access error (EACCES) is returned and the function terminates.

... [File: /usr/src/kernel/kern/execve.c, line: 166]

```
        rv = vn_rdwr(UIO_READ, ndp->ni_vp, (caddr_t)&hdr, sizeof(hdr),
                0, UIO_SYSSPACE, IO_NODELOCKED, p->p_ucred, &amt, p);

        /* could we obtain a header from the file? */
        if (rv)
                goto exec_fail;
...
```

Another VFS facility, **vn_rdwr()** (see **kern/fs/fs_fops.c**), is then called[32] and the vnode read operations are used to obtain the contents of the header of the executable file. If there is an error in I/O or if the file is too short for a header **execve()** terminates.

... [File: /usr/src/kernel/kern/execve.c, line: 174]

```
        rv = ENOEXEC;
        if (hdr.a_magic != ZMAGIC) {
                /* if already in emulator, fail */
                /* if (p->p_flag & SINEMULATOR) */
                goto exec_fail;
                /* otherwise attempt use of user-mode loader via emulation mech.
*/
                /* em = 1;
                goto bypass2; */
        }
...
```

The header is examined to see if it has the correct magic number as the beginning word of the file.[33] Any other executable file format is passed to an optional user mode program loader via the system call emulation mechanism[34] embedded in this function. A check is first done to see if this system call is already being called from the emulator. If so, then the function fails immediately since the emulator cannot be recursively entered.

Emulation is signalled by setting a variable. Once in emulation mode, the remaining functionality of the **execve()** system call is implemented by a user mode program that is dynamically bounded in the user address space.[35] Since **execve()** also has the function of allowing us to gain access to **setuserid** programs that run with different credentials (see **kern/cred.c**), the emulation program is validated against the new set of

---

[32] Note that this facility is used for convenience, and we could have just called the operations directly.

[33] This implementation of **execve()** system call only implements the operation for one file format—see *The Berkeley a.out File Format* for further information.

[34] See *The 386BSD Executable File Format Emulator* discussed earlier in this chapter.

[35] This is currently accomplished using the static top MByte of user address space because the tools only support statically bound programs—this restriction will be removed once the dynamically bound utilities replace the statically bound ones.

credentials, allowing the change in credentials to take place prior to the completion of the **execve()** function. If the function is traced, the **setuserid** feature is ignored to forestall a system security breach by intercepting the operation of the emulator in user mode.[36]

The remaining portion of **execve()**'s functionality (replacing the current program with a new one and cleaning off the elements of the old context) is left entirely to the user mode handler. Thus, user mode handlers in the emulator are trusted programs that must operate correctly for proper semantics of the **execve()** call to be maintained. Note however that an improperly coded emulator will not lose resources of the system nor interfere with system operation or other processes, as it is still just a user program trusted only to the level that its credentials warrant.

... [File: /usr/src/kernel/kern/execve.c, line: 185]

```
        rv = ENOMEM;
        if (hdr.a_text > MAXTSIZ || hdr.a_text % NBPG
            || hdr.a_text > attr.va_size)
                goto exec_fail;

        if (hdr.a_data == 0 || hdr.a_data > DFLDSIZ
            || hdr.a_data > attr.va_size
            || hdr.a_data + hdr.a_text > attr.va_size)
                goto exec_fail;

        if (hdr.a_bss > MAXDSIZ)
                goto exec_fail;

        if (hdr.a_text + hdr.a_data + hdr.a_bss > MAXTSIZ + MAXDSIZ)
                goto exec_fail;

        if (hdr.a_entry > hdr.a_text + hdr.a_data)
                goto exec_fail;
    ...
```

In the case of a non-emulated (e.g., demand load) a.out format file, the header information is examined. Text, data, and bss segment sizes are checked to see that they fall within sane implementation bounds and that their combined sizes do not overflow the boundaries of the file and the implementation in any combination. In addition, the file is checked to see if it can be mapped correctly, ensuring the protection of the text segment given that the MMU has a page granularity. Finally, the intended entry point into the program must fall within the bounds of the information associated with the program file to be loaded. If any of these conditions are not met, an error (ENOMEM) is returned to indicate that the program cannot be run.

---

[36] However, the breakpoints on the emulator can be set, since it is an ordinary user program anyway.

... [File: /usr/src/kernel/kern/execve.c, line: 204]

```
bypass1:
        rv = ENOMEM;
        if (hdr.a_data + hdr.a_bss > p->p_rlimit[RLIMIT_DATA].rlim_cur)
                goto exec_fail;

        /* don't allow new process contents to exceed memory resources */
        if (chk4space(atop(hdr.a_data + hdr.a_bss + 3*ARG_MAX)) == 0)
                goto exec_fail;
    ...
```

A per-process check for the size of private memory is made to see if it falls within the specified bounds (limit structure) and a global check for availability of swap and/or memory is made to verify that the system will not block attempting to run a program larger than available resources. If either of these cases are true, the **execve()** function aborts with an error (ENOMEM). This is the first function performed for both cached and uncached executables.

... [File: /usr/src/kernel/kern/execve.c, line: 228]

```
        nss = round_page(3*ARG_MAX + NBPG);
        if ((unsigned)vs->vm_maxsaddr + MAXSSIZ + nss < USRSTACK)
                newframe = USRSTACK - nss;
        else
                newframe = ((unsigned)vs->vm_maxsaddr + MAXSSIZ
                    - (vs->vm_ssize*NBPG) - nss);

        /* allocate anonymous memory region for new stack, disable stk limit */
        if (vmspace_allocate(vs, &newframe, nss, FALSE))
                goto exec_fail;
        oss = vs->vm_ssize;
        vs->vm_ssize = 0;
    ...
```

The space necessary to hold the contents of the arguments to be built in the address space of the new program is next calculated. Unlike older BSD systems, the user stack does not remain in the same virtual address space location—instead, a single pass algorithm is used to avoid having to copy all of the strings out of the address space prior to deletion and rebuilding of the entire address space.

Due to the nature of an operation involving replacement of a translated stack in place, the cache contents of an executable program using a large number of arguments would invariably wipe the cache and delay the operation of **execve()**. However, by using a single pass algorithm, a single pass copy results in the smallest impact on the cache since the last series of references to the new stack frame will be the ones that will persist in the successful case of **execve()** completing and the program beginning its execution, while the remaining state in the old stack that will be flushed will never be referenced again and thus will not persist.

The size of the new stack is determined by the maximum number of arguments.[37] The amount of space to map the ARG_MAX bytes of arguments must include the size of the pointer associated with these arguments. The maximum number of arguments that can fit into ARG_MAX bytes is ARG_MAX/2.[38] Since for each two-byte argument we need a four-byte pointer, we require 4*ARG_MAX/2 or 2*ARG_MAX bytes just to hold the space of the pointers. This number of bytes plus the ARG_MAX bytes necessary to record all of the string contents as well as the page of stack contents to hold the initial stack results in the minimal size of the new user program argument stack. Note that this size is only a measure of virtual address space and not actual physical memory.

Minimally, three pages must be allocated for this new program: a page for the actual user program stack (to hold at least its argument count), a page to hold any argument pointers, and a page to hold the argument strings. One side-effect of this arrangement is that these pages are not packed tightly together, but they could have been optionally allocated to fit within one page. However, it was determined that the savings of two pages was not worth the cost in added complexity for this single-pass algorithm.

The existing stack for this process is examined to see if the new stack can be located above or below it. As a direct result of this implementation, there are effectively two stack positions that are present—either at the absolute top of the address space, or immediately beneath that region of address space—and successive **execve()** operations alternate between these two regions. Thus, another cost of this single-pass algorithm is to double the amount of virtual address space consumed by the user program's stack. Again, since there are 4 GBytes of address space to play with, this cost is insignificant.

The current stack's size is held in a local variable and the size associated with this process is cleared. By convention, the stack limit checking mechanism in the trap handler understands this to mean that it should not check for the size violation of a trap exceeding the size of the stack. Since in effect both stacks are valid while we are constructing the new stack frame, we do not do any bounds checking on faults incurred in the regions of the stacks. Finally, the address space for the new stack frame is allocated. Should any address space in this region be allocated for any other purpose, this allocation request will fail and an error will be returned.

... [File: /usr/src/kernel/kern/execve.c, line: 243]

```
argbuf = (char **) (newframe + NBPG);
stringbuf = stringbufp = ((char *)argbuf) + 2*ARG_MAX;
argbufp = argbuf;

/* first, do the args */
```

---

[37] ARG_MAX, a POSIX-defined constant for the number of bytes of arguments.
[38] The minimum length string, one argument, is a single character terminated by a null, hence two characters.

```
        vectp = uap->argp;
        needsenv = 1;
        limitonargs = ARG_MAX;
        cnt = 0;

do_env_as_well:
        if (vectp == 0)
                goto dont_bother;
...
```

The argument and string buffers are initialized as linearly increasing regions of successive virtual address space. The first portion of the address space of the new stack frame is reserved for use in mapping the actual running stack of the program (unused at this point). It is the minimum size of granularity—that of a page. Next comes an array of string pointers corresponding to the "argv" of a user program, followed by space to store the contents of the strings pointed to by the arguments. Each of the regions has a pointer (stringbufp, argbufp) pointing to the consecutively allocated string contents or argument pointer. Since strings can be of varying length, the string pointer will successively increase with respect to the size of the string associated with a particular argument.

This mechanism will be invoked twice: the first time to establish the arguments associated with the **execve()** call and the second time to establish the environment strings (if present) of this same call. Note that this is still a single-pass algorithm, since we will only see the arguments or environment strings once. Note also that an upper bound is placed on the number of arguments by the length of the strings. In this way it can be determined if the **execve()** call is invalid as we build the structure of the new program argument stack in a single pass. If either the arguments or the environment are not present (the supplied pointer is zero), no strings will be added into the the string argument buffers for that region.

... [File: /usr/src/kernel/kern/execve.c, line: 258]

```
        do {
                /* did we outgrow initial argbuf, if so, die */
                if (argbufp == (char **)stringbuf) {
                        rv = E2BIG;
                        goto exec_dealloc;
                }

                /* get an string pointer */
                if (rv = copyin_(p, (void *)vectp++, (void *)&ep, 4))
                        goto exec_dealloc;
...
```

A loop is entered to evaluate the argument strings supplied to the system call, either for the supplied arguments or environment vector. If during this process of constructing the argument frame we run out of argument pointers[39] an error indicating

---

[39] Because the argument buffer now overruns the beginning of the string buffer.

that the argument string is too big is returned and the request terminated. Otherwise, the next string pointer is obtained from the current program in the user process address space. If the string pointer cannot be obtained without an error, the request is terminated with an appropriate error indicating the failure of the attempted fetch of the next argument.

... [File: /usr/src/kernel/kern/execve.c, line: 270]

```
            if (ep) {
                if (rv = copyinoutstr(p, ep, stringbufp,
                    (u_int)limitonargs, (u_int *) &stringlen)) {
                    if (rv == ENAMETOOLONG)
                            rv = E2BIG;
                    goto exec_dealloc;
                }

                (void)copyout_(p, &stringbufp, (void *)argbufp++, 4);
                cnt++;
                stringbufp += stringlen;
                limitonargs -= stringlen;
            } else {
                (void)copyout_(p, &ep, (void *)argbufp++, 4);
                break;
            }
        } while (limitonargs > 0);
    ...
```

If the fetched string argument value is not zero, there is an argument string to process. In this case, the string is copied from its starting location in the current user program to its location in the string buffer for the amount of length that it consumes as a null-terminated string. The **copyinoutstr()** primitive (an inlined function) combines in one both the **copyout()** and **copyin()** primitives. Unlike other previous UNIX implementations, there is no string buffer in kernel address space. Instead, the string is copied into place into the second stack in the user space that will receive the string. Note that the string being copied is of finite length. Should the number of bytes allocated for arguments be consumed, the **copyinoutstr()** function will return an error (E2BIG) and the function will terminate.

It should be noted that modern RISC machines use a single address space to hold both user and kernel address space. As such, for these machines, **copyinoutstr()** is the most efficient way to convey argument state around. In addition, some machines (such as the Intergraph Clipper) which support separate kernel and user address spaces optionally allow the string copy to be performed on a user address space even though the instructions are running in a kernel program. Thus, even though the kernel cannot directly access the user address space, a **copyinoutstr()** function can be written that efficiently performs the argument stack structure.

After moving the contents of the string to the new stack in the user address space, the address of the contents of this new string is used as the address of the next consecutive argument recorded in the argument buffer and copied into place in the user process.

The number of arguments is incremented and the string buffer pointer is updated to point to the next free location in the string buffer space in the argument stack. The remaining number of argument characters is then reduced by the amount consumed by this argument.

If the argument we are processing corresponds to a null string, the null string pointer is copied as the last argument in the list of arguments and the loop terminated. Otherwise, a check is made to see if we still have space left for additional arguments, and if so, additional arguments undergo processing.

... [File: /usr/src/kernel/kern/execve.c, line: 288]

```
dont_bother:
        if (limitonargs <= 0) {
                rv = E2BIG;
                goto exec_dealloc;
        }

        /* have we done the environment yet ? */
        if (needsenv) {
                /* remember the arg count for later */
                argc = cnt;
                vectp = uap->envp;
                needsenv = 0;
                goto do_env_as_well;
        }
    ...
```

If the space reserved for arguments has been exhausted, the **execve()** system call terminates with an error (E2BIG) and falls out of the loop. Otherwise, if the environment set of arguments has not yet been processed (and it is present), the above loop is repeated for those environment vectors. Note that the argument count is saved prior to entering the loop again. There is also no corresponding environment count to be recorded in the argument frame of a POSIX 1003.1 **execve()**.

... [File: /usr/src/kernel/kern/execve.c, line: 319]

```
        vs->vm_ssize =  btoc(nss); /* stack size (pages) XXX */
        vs->vm_maxsaddr = (caddr_t)((unsigned)newframe + nss - MAXSSIZ);
        argbuf-;
        (void)copyout_(p, &argc, (void *)argbuf, 4);
    ...
```

Now that the arguments to the new stack frame are in place, we are committed to loading the new executable image. We update the temporary vmspace description of the stack with the new stack and copy out to the base of the new program frame the number of arguments in the argument frame (e.g., the "argc" of a standard UNIX **main()** program).

... [File: /usr/src/kernel/kern/execve.c, line: 325]

```
        if ((unsigned)newframe + nss < VM_MAX_ADDRESS)
                vmspace_delete(vs, (caddr_t)newframe + nss,
```

```
                VM_MAX_ADDRESS - (unsigned)newframe - nss);

        /* blow away all address space, except the stack */
        vmspace_delete(vs, (caddr_t)VM_MIN_ADDRESS, newframe);
...
```

We next remove the entire address space of the old program and its stack. If the new
stack is not immediately started at the top of address space, everything is removed,
including the old stack lying above the new stack (the old stack was above the new
stack because they alternate). Thus, every other **execve()** does two **vmspace_delete()**[40]
operations to remove the bindings of the old address space, while the other group only
does one (since they alternate).

... [File: /usr/src/kernel/kern/execve.c, line: 333]

```
        addr = 0;

        /* screwball mode — special case of 413 to save space for floppy */
        if (hdr.a_text == 0)
                foff = tsize = 0;
        else {
                tsize = roundup(hdr.a_text, NBPG);
                foff = NBPG;
        }

        /* treat text and data in terms of integral page size */
        dsize = roundup(hdr.a_data, NBPG);
        bsize = roundup(hdr.a_bss + dsize, NBPG);
        bsize -= dsize;

        /* map text & data in file, as being "paged in" on demand */
        rv = vm_mmap(vs, &addr, tsize+dsize, VM_PROT_ALL,
            MAP_FILE|MAP_COPY, (caddr_t)ndp->ni_vp, foff);
        if (rv)
                goto exec_abort;
...
```

With the program space now empty except for the now current argument stack, the
new program contents are mapped into the bottom portion of virtual address space
starting with address zero. Note that the type 413 a.out executable file format is
defined as starting at location zero of the address space. This is somewhat unfortunate
for the 386, since both user and kernel uninitialized pointers reference this point.
However, since this is a part of the definition of the file format, this is a mandatory
requirement.

The size of the text, data, and bss segments are adjusted to reflect their page
granularity (tsize, dsize, bsize). The beginning portion of the file to be mapped (foff) is
determined in two ways: as the page following the header or, in the case of a zero-
length text segment, as the beginning of the file itself.[41] In the first ordinary type 413

---

[40] See **Volume II** on **vm/map.c**.
[41] Since the header is considered to be part of the data region as well.

a.out case, the text segment is rounded up to a page boundary. However, the second case, a variant on type 413 a.out, actually results in a space savings in the text segment that would otherwise be consumed (4 KBytes of header plus possibly 4 KBytes of roundout of the text segment). This second case is somewhat nonstandard but is much more efficient when storing executables on a bootstrap floppy.

The boundary between data and bss segments is not set on a page boundary basis. Thus, since the file is allocated at a lesser granularity than the address space, data size is rounded up to the next boundary prior to it being mapped, and the combination of data and bss (which reflect the total size of the initial program) is lumped together to find the upper bound of anonymous memory which needs to be allocated.

The **vm_mmap()** primitive (see **vm/mmap.c**) is used to map the contents of the file for text and data. At this point, both text and data are accessible for any level of reference, including writes, but in a copy-on-write mode so that any changes will not be made to the master copy.[42] If the file cannot be mapped in this manner, the **execve()** system call handler terminates with an error returned from **vm/mmap.c**. Note that **vm/mmap.c** only builds the bookkeeping information which allows the file to be mapped at this location, but it does not load the contents or even allocate memory in the user program—this will occur later as the memory is referenced for the first time. Thus the execution of all programs is always done via demand load.[43]

... [File: /usr/src/kernel/kern/execve.c, line: 355]

```
        if (tsize) {
                addr = 0;
                rv = vmspace_protect(vs, (caddr_t)addr, tsize, FALSE,
                    VM_PROT_READ|VM_PROT_EXECUTE);
                if (rv)
                        goto exec_abort;
        }
    ...
```

If there are any read-only text pages in this program, the **vmspace_protect()** (see **vm/map.c**) function is called to restrict access to this portion of address space by disallowing writes.

... [File: /usr/src/kernel/kern/execve.c, line: 364]

```
        addr = dsize + tsize;
        if (rv = vmspace_allocate(vs, &addr, bsize, FALSE))
                goto exec_abort;
    ...
```

---

[42] See the discussion *Copy-on-Write* in **vm/map.c**, **Volume II**, for more information.
[43] See *Design Choices and Trade-Offs with the Virtual Memory System* in **vm/object.c**, **Volume II**, for a discussion of the bookkeeping functions of the virtual memory system.

Starting at the end of the data segment, anonymous memory is allocated for bss by use of the **vmspace_allocate()** function (see **vm/map.c**). If there is insufficient memory for this purpose, the function aborts with an out-of-memory error.

... [File: /usr/src/kernel/kern/execve.c, line: 373]

```
        vs->vm_tsize = tsize/NBPG;   /* text size (pages) XXX */
        vs->vm_dsize = (dsize+bsize)/NBPG; /* data size (pages) XXX */
        vs->vm_taddr = 0;   /* user virtual address of text XXX */
        vs->vm_daddr = (caddr_t)tsize; /* user virtual address of data XXX */

        /* close files on exec, fixup signals, name this process */
        fdcloseexec(p);
        execsigs(p);
        nameiexec(ndp, p);
    ...
```

The contents of the user program's address space have now been initialized (well, at least the bookkeeping associated with it has), and all that remains prior to execution are the details. The descriptions of the shape and allocation of the program are recorded in an extension of the vmspace structure. Because the vm_map and vmspace portion of the system is still unfinished, this procedure is only a temporary expedite. An additional set of semantics must be added to map entries to allow for typing of address space corresponding to a specific use (e.g. text, data, bss, and stack).

Any files that have been marked to be closed on execution are requested to be closed by calling the **fdcloseexec()** function (see **kern/descrip.c**). Likewise, signal actions are reverted to default by means of the **execsigs()** function (see **kern/sig.c**). If this were not done, the addresses of the signal handlers outstanding would have no relevance to the new program, and the signal would be passed through a random address in the new program.

Finally, the **nameiexec()** function (see **fs/lookup.c**) is called to label the process with the name of the file that is being executed and free the buffers allocated by **namei()** at the start of this function (SAVENAME). Instead of following this process, many other BSD implementations simply free the structures in **namei()**. This is not advised, however, since there may be other resources associated with **fs/lookup.c** that need to be freed in a coordinated way, as occurs in the case of handling the portal[44] mechanism. It is simply poor design and short-sighted to teach all of the users of the **namei()** facility about all of the details of its internal implementation.

... [File: /usr/src/kernel/kern/execve.c, line: 387]

```
        p->p_flag |= SEXEC;
bypass2:
        if (p->p_pptr && (p->p_flag & SPPWAIT)) {
```

---

[44] See *Improvements to the Current Implementation of namei()* in **fs/lookup.c**, **The 386BSD Reference CD-ROM**, for a discussion of portals.

```
            p->p_flag &= ~SPPWAIT;
            wakeup((caddr_t)p->p_pptr);
    }

    /* implement set userid/groupid */
    if ((attr.va_mode&VSUID) && (p->p_flag & STRC) == 0) {
            p->p_cred = modpcred(p);
            p->p_cred->p_svuid = p->p_ucred->cr_uid = attr.va_uid;
    }
    if ((attr.va_mode&VSGID) && (p->p_flag & STRC) == 0) {
            p->p_cred = modpcred(p);
            p->p_cred->p_svgid = p->p_ucred->cr_groups[0] =
                attr.va_gid;
    }
    /* if (em)
            return(EEMULATE); */
...
```

The process is now marked as having an exec operation performed on it.[45] At this point, the emulated executables are processed as well as the normal unemulated case. For emulated processes, the **setuserid** operation and **vfork()** (see **kern/fork.c**) synchronization are permitted but nothing else, as everything else is done by the emulator. This implies that the emulator must relinquish the setuserid capability if it actually does not succeed in executing the program—this is simply one aspect of its trusted nature.

If there is a parent process and it is waiting for this process, the parent process is awakened and the indication of the wait is cleared. This is used to signal to a **vfork()**ed process that the parent may continue since the child is now underway. **vfork()** infers order of execution, with the child always coming before the parent. This is an artifact of earlier Berkeley systems, where **vfork()** was fully implemented (as an alternative to copy-on-write) to allow a child process to temporarily use the resources of the parent process in lieu of copying them. Since **vfork()** is not used in lieu of copy-on-write in this system (and hence not fully implemented as in earlier BSD systems), this procedure has the effect of merely enforcing the synchronization of the processes but it does not give any resources back since it does not use any of the parents resources.[46]

If either the **setuserid** or **setgroupid** attribute is set on the file being executed, the credentials of the process will be updated to correspond to the user and/or group ID of the file. This is done only in the case that the process is not **ptrace**'d (STRC) to forestall a user from using the debugger to gain inappropriate privileges and thus bypass authentication. If either **setuserid** or **setgroupid** is invoked, the credentials of the process must be modified. In this case, a modification request is sent to the credentials module via the **modpcred()** function in **kern/cred.c** to guarantee a unique

---

[45] This feature is currently unused, but could be used in the future to detect processes that fork but don't do a successive exec.
[46] An additional complication arises in how parent and child resources can be shared in the case that the emulators, if more than one, are symmetric.

set of credentials. Once a unique set of credentials are in hand, the credentials are updated for the current and saved user and group ID. The saved user and group IDs are used to relinquish privileges by the **setuserid** program.

If this user of **execve()** is actually being emulated, the processing in this file has been completed and the system call entry handler is instructed to continue processing in the emulator by means of an internally implemented error (EEMULATE).

... [File: /usr/src/kernel/kern/execve.c, line: 408]

```
        cpu_execsetregs(p, (caddr_t)hdr.a_entry, (caddr_t) (argbuf));

        /*
         * if tracing process, pass control back to debugger so
         * breakpoints can be set before the program "runs"
         */
        if (p->p_flag & STRC)
                psignal(p, SIGTRAP);

        /* cache information in vm system. */
        if (vnp == NULL) {
                pager = (vm_pager_t)ndp->ni_vp->v_vmdata;
                vnp = (vn_pager_t)pager->pg_data;
                vnp->vnp_hdr = hdr;
                vnp->vnp_attr = attr;
                vnp->vnp_flags |= VNP_EXECVE;
        }

        return (0);
...
```

The non-emulated demand load **execve()** continues its initialization by setting the registers (both stack and program counter) with the machine-dependent **cpu_execsetregs()** function in **i386/cpu.c**. This function will set the initial location to execute and the machine-specific characteristics of the stack. The signal trampoline code bounces a POSIX signal into user space. It is loaded at the extreme top of the stack with a block copy operation. This tiny handler is documented in **i386/locore.s**.

If the process is being **ptrace**'d (STRC), a signal is sent to the process indicating that it should enter the traced state before returning. This allows the debugger to run before the program executes so that it is possible to set breakpoints in the early stages of program execution. If there was no cached information present at the beginning of the **execve()** function that we now have, the header and attribute information are assigned into the beginning of the associated vnode's pager so that we may benefit from it the next time this executable is run. We then return successfully having completed this **execve()** operation.

... [File: /usr/src/kernel/kern/execve.c, line: 428]

```
exec_dealloc:
        /* remove interim "new" stack frame we were building */
        vmspace_delete(vs, (caddr_t)newframe, nss);
```

```
                /* reengauge stack limits */
                vs->vm_ssize =  oss;

exec_fail:
                /* release namei request */
                nameiexec(ndp, (struct proc *)0);

                return(rv);
       ...
```

Should a failure have occurred during the later stages of processing the **execve()** operation, the stack frame we were building must be deallocated before we can return to the previous program which attempted the **execve()**. The stack size field is updated, if necessary, to reinstitute stack bounds checking and the outstanding **namei()** resources are freed. Since the operation was not successful, the process should not be relabeled, so a zero process pointer is used to signal this fact. The reason for failure is then returned as the error.

... [File: /usr/src/kernel/kern/execve.c, line: 441]

```
exec_abort:
                /* sorry, no more process anymore. exit gracefully */

                /* release namei request */
                nameiexec(ndp, (struct proc *)0);

                exit(p, W_EXITCODE(0, SIGABRT));

                /* NOTREACHED */
                return(0);
       ...
```

If an error occurred after the contents of the address space was destroyed, there is no viable program to which to return. In this case, the resources for **namei()** are released as in the previous section and a call is made to the **exit()** system call handler (see **kern/exit.c**), to indicate that the current process should be terminated and any resources reclaimed. This will then pass an exit code back to the parent process and never return.

9.2.5.2 386BSD execve() Evolutionary History

To accomplish the execution of a file as a program in a user process, early UNIX systems used overlays, multiple kinds of executables, and/or multiple file formats.[47] For 386BSD Release 0.0, a bare-bones implementation of **execve()** (see **Missing Pieces II**) was written in the space of a week simply to make the system usable for more work and recompilation.[48] The actual code for this function was written in user mode on another UNIX system to simulate its operation. This first version of **execve()** was a simple one, with a fixed buffer that would allow a process to be loaded and run. No

---

[47] See *Choices of Implementation* in the article **Missing Pieces II** (June 1992), **Dr. Dobbs Journal**.
[48] At this point there was no other **execve()** available.

attention was paid to the finer details of POSIX semantics or to implementing an arbitrarily large number of arguments.

In 386BSD Release 0.1 (released three months later), the functionality of **execve()** was expanded and the concept of multiple user stack frames was introduced as an alternative to the older UNIX approach. More POSIX functionality was also added.[49] Executable shell scripts (shell files that start with "#!") were intentionally not implemented in Release 0.1, since we realized this would soon be implemented by users either in the exec functions in the C library or in the loader as suggested.

After the release of 0.1, there was a great demand for expanded support for different file formats. Rather than elaborate **execve()** to implement arbitrary file formats, we began seriously to reconsider the older UNIX approach of stuffing more support in the kernel. Instead, we proposed that the best way to expand the support for file formats might be to use a loader program in user space (but we did not formally indicate how this might be done at that time). In addition, growable stacks and adjacent allocation of successive **execve()** stacks were done to improve the quality of the work, and to avoid unnecessary consumption of address space.

The **execve()** function for Release 0.1 had been designed so that other architectures (such as RISC) could easily benefit.[50] However, while these benefits might appear obvious now, the concept was too novel at the time for the many UNIX users lacking a broad understanding of different processor architectures and porting techniques.

9.2.5.3 386BSD execve() Current Design Choices and Trade-offs

In 386BSD Release 1.0, we attempted to remedy some of the flaws inherent in the older Release 0.1 implementation while still cleaving to our minimalist design goals that have always been the basis of 386BSD.[51] For example, this implementation is quite tractable to multiple architecture implementation. Note however that we are still using the same a.out format implemented on all of these different architectures with all of its restrictions in place and not reinterpreting this for each architecture.[52] This change was intended to be fairly minor since the characteristics of a.out and the class of processors we are using are fairly uniform. Thus, this function should not require much more than ifdefs to run the standard type 413 a.out format on other processors.

The other major change is that of supporting arbitrary file formats. An example of the interface to the emulator has been implemented which allows other file formats to be implemented in a user program. Since we had no time to arbitrarily embellish this

---

[49] Although some of the missing details were still not present, again due to time limitations.
[50] See the discussion on **copyinoutstr()** in *How is execve() Implemented?*.
[51] And the original Bell Laboratories UNIX as well. If you have divined from this discussion that we come from the original minimalist school of thought on UNIX design, you are dead on the money.
[52] Per-architecture file formats should always be implemented in the emulator program and not in the kernel.

example, we have chosen only to implement the aforementioned shell script execution format (see the system source). In this example, the emulator is called by **execve()** to handle a foreign format and the emulator is solely responsible for translating the new format into a series of system calls that it then performs to execute the shell script format. While this example in no way demonstrates every possible use of this facility (such as the creation of new argument stack frames—the understanding of this is left as an exercise to the reader), it minimally demonstrates to the reader where and how to expand functionality

The purpose of implementing a low-level program load facility for simple file formats such as a.out is not as a prelude to a more elaborate kernel **execve()** function but is instead intended as a bootstrap which allows the implementation of a much more elaborate loader facility to handle all of the arbitrary formats that cannot necessarily be dealt with in the kernel alone. The number of little changes required in the kernel per file format alone in order to take all the idiosyncrasies into account grows enormously ludicrous and is not an example of good kernel planning and design.

9.2.5.4 Improvements to the Current Implementation of execve()

The emulation facility is unfinished, and we have left plenty of room for independent work and exploration by the reader. It is our earnest hope that this facility will grow into a general purpose facility for multiple operating system emulation—done, of course, outside of the kernel where the tools for developing such facilities are more convenient and where the internal interfaces of the kernel do not have to be arbitrarily altered.

It is important to realize that improving a file execution procedure doesn't necessarily imply improving the portion which lies within the kernel, since it is naive to assume that if an optimization or elaboration occurs at a low level of abstraction (e.g., the kernel), it will inherently be fast. In fact, it is often the case that the cost of calling the kernel is fairly small compared to total operations overhead. With elaborate program file formats, the greatest cost lies in managing the interpretation of the segments of these formats and attaching them to the facilities to which they correspond. As such, the trade-offs of performing a system call for every few hundred operations versus performing one system call and several hundred operations becomes meaningless.

In addition, since it is possible in user mode to employ more elaborate means of directing the implementation of a particular standard of program execution, it is also possible to more conveniently and thoroughly implement a much broader class of executable objects than could ever be achieved in the kernel—even if the kernel was grown by replicating a user level environment within it (thus magnifying the kernel size grossly while defeating the point of separate user and kernel mode environments).

Apart from this caveat, changes to this module which would qualify as valid improvements include those that would strengthen its ability to externalize the interfaces and make them more efficient for access as the bottom level of abstraction of a program execution facility. In this way, the same functionality of this routine can be made more efficient for said use. Another valuable improvement to this function would be to make more efficient the interface to the loader facility in the emulator, improving the emulator's ability to perform its program execution function. Other than these few structural changes, there are no improvements possible with this design, and it will remain primarily unchanged as a result.[53]

9.2.6 The Overall Design Philosophy Reflected in execve()

One undesirable side-effect of any traditional minimalist UNIX design is that it unintentionally encourages the bad notion that elaboration on a theme is a good idea. The extrapolation that if something is simple and good, then more would be even better should be actively discouraged in certain areas of operating systems design, especially with respect to the kernel itself.

The kernel is the kernel, which by its name alone signifies that it works only as the switchyard to more elaborate user-level facilities lying at a completely different level of abstraction. As such, the moronic hack attack approach of elaborating the simple into the obtuse is often fatal in the long run to any good operating system, whether we consider performance, reliability, and even future expandability. Even though it is often more challenging to implement efficiently desired functionality in the correct manner, we cannot stress enough the importance of discipline in maintaining the aesthetic and ultimately the operational properties of the kernel programming environment.

9.3 The File Descriptor Mechanism: kern/descrip.c

The file **kern/descrip.c** contains the machine-independent code used to implement the file and file descriptor mechanisms. It is through this mechanism that low level file-like objects are attached to the POSIX program interface in the system calls which in turn implement all of the POSIX functions used with files.

9.3.1 Files

Files are *instances* of open operations on file-like objects (vnodes and sockets). They record (among other things) the current position of just where a sequential file is being read from, the particular file flags, and other per-open characteristics of a file reference operation. In the case of the file-like object called a socket, the file maintains a count of

---

[53] N.B. If the a.out format itself is abandoned, the program execution facility may not remain in this file, and the emulator will handle all cases. However, a.out has been around for a long time and runs on all architectures, so don't hold your breath.

the outstanding messages associated with the file descriptor, since a socket in a sense exists only when it is open.[54]

Files are a high-level entity which correspond to file references to functions.[55] They connect this high-level object to the next lower level abstraction (e.g., vnodes and sockets) via a series of file operators used to communicate actions to the lower level layer. Thus, to achieve the actual semantics of an operation like a read or write on an open file, the underlying vnode or socket is passed an operation to be performed via a method (e.g. one of these operators).

The concept of being open is that of a *stateful* operation relevant only to the file layer, since the underlying data abstractions are for the most part stateless. As such, since many different processes could have this same file open in different portions of the file performing different operations on that file, the only point of the file abstraction is to provide a place to retain the information unique to this particular open event on a file.

Indeed, even one process can hold the same underlying object open with different file instances (e.g., the file is distinctly opened more than once). The advantage of doing this is that separate file offset pointers can be maintained so that multiple seek operations on a file can be avoided. For example, in dealing with a password data base or other authentication files where different parts of the authentication information in the file are located successively at different offsets of the same file, instead of having one file open and seeking to change the file offset pointer to go back or forward to a different set of records, a handful of file instances are left pointing at the appropriate offset in the file for the next operation so no seeks need be performed—only the implicit seek of the appropriate read or write operation of the requested different file instance. For authentication, there are some kinds of abstractions through which (in having yet a second system call) the seek could provide a covert channel in determining the characteristics of how the authentication mechanism is located or coded on secondary storage. By avoiding the secondary operation, one can hide the physical information.

While file instances can point to a shared object like a vnode or socket, a UNIX oddity is that multiple processes can point to a single file—in effect sharing a file offset. The reason for this oddity is that the pipe interprocess communication mechanism requires a way of passing file descriptors from a parent to a child process. As a result, it must share them to pass them off. This particular characteristic somewhat aggravates attempts to make UNIX a full message-based operating system as would be desirable in a clustered environment, because in sharing this file abstraction across, say, two machines in a processor cluster, we must devise a way to determine just which

---

[54] It does not persist after it is closed.
[55] E.g., open, close, read, write, ioctl, stat, and so forth, as specified in the POSIX 1003.1 specification.

machine should hold onto the shared file instance (since obviously both have the opportunity to change it). Many attempts at doing UNIX clustering simply avoid this special case completely.[56]

9.3.2 File Descriptors

Files themselves in POSIX are attached to a user process by an integer *index* associated with the actual file at the time it is opened. Thus, instead of passing an address around in a user program (either in the kernel or user address space), an index is used to refer to a particular open file or file descriptor. This index indexes a table of files open at any given point in time, but the actual contents of the descriptor (a file pointer) are hidden (in the kernel) from the view of the user program.

To implement this abstraction, a special data structure in the kernel is used to describe a sparsely allocated table. Rather than implement a huge static array of potential file entries, BSD systems allocate these file pointer arrays as *lists* of extents. In this way, the number of file descriptors can be dynamically grown efficiently in clumps[57] at a time. A list of extents is actually a compromised data structure lying somewhere between a list and a static linear table. Through the use of these lists of extents, we reduce the overhead of entry by relying on the fact that files are allocated themselves in clumps.

A process can have many files open at any time when they are run.[58] In 386BSD, the limit on the number of open files is categorized as a resource that can be set as large as needed (see **kern/resource.c**). To allow for a more flexible use of files, 386BSD uses a variable-sized file descriptor instance that allows for a sparse allocation of a large number of files. File descriptors are implemented as lists of extents of files where each extent can add another group of file references to the process's file descriptor arrays.

Within the POSIX 1003.1 set of function specifications, many operations are described that involve only file descriptors. These operations allow for different organization and control of the file descriptors and the files with which they are associated. Many of the characteristics of file descriptors in the implementation in this file are included solely to allow the use of some of these control requests. Files and file descriptors have semantics that are closely bound to the operating system specification of which they are a part.[59]

---

[56] Note that in most UNIX programs this typically involves only the first three open files; stdin, stdout, and stderr.
[57] Since it has been observed that files in UNIX programs tend to occur in clumps as well.
[58] The original UNIX system, in contrast, generally had an upper limit of 20 open files.
[59] There are even a few operating systems that don't have files or file descriptors, but instead use user libraries to implement these abstractions, because they have only lower level abstractions similar to vnodes and sockets.

9.3.2.1 File Descriptor Bit Sets

One of the evolutionary oddities in BSD based systems has to do with the extension of these systems to support an *arbitrary number* of file descriptors. Early UNIX systems generally supported up to only 20 file descriptors. For various internal reasons, many versions always had a fixed upper bound.[60] This limitation had some interesting ramifications—most significantly, it found its way into the applications program interface of BSD systems that supported the **select()** system call.

select() as originally defined in 4.2BSD returned a word bit mask indicating which file descriptor had an event (for example, ready for another input or output request) associated with it. However, a word length of 32 bits inherently set an upper bound on the number of file descriptors one could use. One of the principal goals in 4.3BSD which anticipated the need to support an arbitrary number of open files was to get around this fixed limitation.[61]

The concept of the multiple word bit vector (fd_set) data type was created to reserve a fixed number of words at compile time as a quick way to avoid this limit while retaining compatibility with 4.2BSD programs (which only knew about a maximum 32 file descriptors). One of the interesting problems with this fix was that since it depended on a compile-time constant, kernels and user programs could disagree as to how they were compiled concerning the number of descriptors and the size of the set. This is truly an unresolvable conflict, because the **select()** system call (which is an integral part of multiplexing applications) relies mostly on a compile-time constant allocation arrangement. Thus, it is impossible to fix this conflict by coming up with a dynamic allocation scheme since it would have to be done in the user program.

Unlike DOS, UNIX systems do not have a default standard memory allocator from the system. As such, most UNIX systems rely on possibly different subroutine library memory allocators that subdivide space allocated by either moving the tail of the data segment out further or by using the **mmap()** (see **kern/mmap.c**) primitive to allocate a new segment in virtual address space. Subtle differences in implementation make this something that a system call-level interface cannot rely upon for use. Thus, dynamic bit sets are just not possible while still calling it a UNIX system.

This limitation in the **select()** system call handler is dealt with in an adequate way in the current release. However, while it underlies the fragility of inherent limits in system interfaces, it also illustrates one of the great strengths of the original basic minimalistic UNIX API, since this is the only place that a change in scaling the API to arbitrary numbers was required in the system that has been found.

---

[60] In 4.2BSD/4.3BSD, this was raised to 32.
[61] The **getdtablesize()** system call was added as well.

9.3.2.2 File Descriptor Data Structures

The file descriptor table of each process is implemented in modern versions of BSD as a dense but dynamically growable array. Actually, it is composed of two arrays: an array of file pointers, and an array of file descriptor flags. Since in general file descriptors are allocated as a contiguous group, allocating them in a list structure is both inefficient and wasteful of space, because the overhead of managing even a singly-linked list is comparable to the size of the file descriptor entry itself.[62]

In the current implementation, a fixed data structure is used to represent the beginning of the region of memory allocated to the file descriptor table. The file pointer array is based at a specific value, which is an offset farther into this region of memory (*fd_ofiles*) as is the array of file descriptor flags (*fd_ofileflags*). To grow the file descriptor table, a new portion of memory is allocated larger than the previous portion and the entries are copied into the new region by copying the formerly adjacent two arrays into their new enlarged segments in the new table along with the header of this record.[63]

By keeping the file pointers and file flags distinct and adjacent, no overhead is lost to padding[64] as would otherwise occur in having a substructure for each entry. To postpone the cost of growing the descriptor table, the descriptor table is only grown in clumps large enough to be of significance to the kernel's memory allocator (*ndextent*, corresponding to almost 256 bytes). Since most UNIX processes never use more than a small number of files, a smaller number is allocated by default on the creation of a process (NDFILE). This is done to economize on space. In addition, to minimize the time spent in allocating or locating a file descriptor, indexes are kept for the last allocated and first free file descriptor so as to minimize the time spent in allocating or deallocating file descriptors. Note that this arrangement is convenient for small allocations of file descriptors in a clump, and is especially inefficient where file descriptors are allocated in clumps greater than or equal to NDEXTENT (because each clump of file descriptors would require an allocation copy and free). This is a reasonable design choice, however, since programs don't usually allocate a large number of file descriptors at a time.

9.3.3 Functions Contained in the File kern/descrip.c

The following functions are contained in the file **kern/descrip.c**

getdtablesize()

dup()

dup2()

---

[62] Currently five bytes.
[63] See **fdalloc()** for further information.
[64] With C, we would lose at least three bytes for every entry due to alignment.

---

fcntl()

close()

fstat()

read()

readv()

write()

writev()

ioctl()

select()

selscan()

seltrue()

selwakeup()

fdalloc()

fdavail()

falloc()

ffree()

fdcopy()

fdfree()

fdcloseexec()

closef()

flock()

fdopen()

dupfdopen()

The first ten functions listed above are file descriptor system call handlers, while the next twelve functions are internal kernel functions. The last two functions, **fdopen()** and **dupfdopen()**, are file descriptor pseudodrivers.

9.3.4 What is getdtablesize()?

getdtablesize() is a BSD system call handler. It implements the BSD **getdtablesize()** function that determines the size of the descriptor table, returning the number of file descriptors usable by the process. It was originally put into 4.3BSD to determine how big the descriptor size was per process. Since open files are now a resource, this is implemented for reverse compatibility only.

... [File: /usr/src/kernel/kern/descrip.c, line: 79]

```
int
getdtablesize(p, uap, retval)
        struct proc *p;
        void *uap;
        int *retval;
...
```

getdtablesize() has three arguments: the pointer to the process; the pointer to the arguments to the system call (in this case, no arguments); and the pointer to the return value. It returns the number of file descriptors that can be used to open files.

9.3.4.1 How is getdtablesize() Implemented?

... [File: /usr/src/kernel/kern/descrip.c, line: 86]

```
        *retval = p->p_rlimit[RLIMIT_OFILE].rlim_cur;
        return (0);
...
```

The current resource limit for open files is returned as the value for the size of the file descriptor table. This function always succeeds so it returns a value of zero indicating success. Note that since file descriptors are described as a resource, there is no point to this function other than for reverse compatibility with older BSD systems.

9.3.5 What is dup()?

dup(), an original UNIX system call handler, duplicates a file descriptor. It fully implements the POSIX 1003.1 function as a system call. It accepts a valid file descriptor and creates a new distinct file descriptor that refers to the exact same file as the file of the file descriptor supplied.

... [File: /usr/src/kernel/kern/descrip.c, line: 93]

```
int
dup(p, uap, retval)
        struct proc *p;
        struct args {
                int     i;
        } *uap;
        int *retval;
...
```

dup() has three arguments: the pointer to the process; the pointer to the arguments to the system call (in this case, one—the file descriptor to be duplicated); and the pointer to the return values. It returns zero if successful and an error code if unsuccessful.

9.3.5.1 How is dup() Implemented?

... [File: /usr/src/kernel/kern/descrip.c, line: 105]

```
        if ((unsigned)uap->i >= fdp->fd_nfiles ||
            (fp = fdp->fd_ofiles[uap->i]) == NULL)
                return (EBADF);
...
```

We first check to see if the file descriptor about to be duplicated falls in the range of the number of files allocatable in the file descriptor structure or if the file descriptor is already allocated. If not, the system call handler is terminated with an error (EBADF).

... [File: /usr/src/kernel/kern/descrip.c, line: 109]

```
        if (error = fdalloc(p, 0, &fd))
                return (error);
...
```

A new file descriptor is allocated to the process. If the new file descriptor cannot be obtained, an error signalled by **fdalloc()** is returned. Otherwise, since we are interested in any file descriptor, we start at the very first file descriptor (zero).

... [File: /usr/src/kernel/kern/descrip.c, line: 112]

```
        fdp->fd_ofiles[fd] = fp;
        fdp->fd_ofileflags[fd] = fdp->fd_ofileflags[uap->i] &~ UF_EXCLOSE;
        fp->f_count++;
        if (fd > fdp->fd_lastfile)
                fdp->fd_lastfile = fd;
        *retval = fd;
        return (0);
...
```

The just-allocated file descriptor is made to refer to the file instance of the file descriptor we are duplicating, along with the open file flags of how it was opened. Per POSIX 1003.1 specifications, we don't copy the exclusive close file flag of the old file descriptor, since it must be set separately via a **fcntl()** system call.

The reference count is increased on the now shared file instance and this information is recorded if this is the largest valued file on the set of open files. Note that the data structure field *fd_lastfile* allows us to terminate our scan of open file descriptors early by knowing the last one allocated in sequence. The file descriptor is then returned to the system call handler, and the function returns zero to indicate success.

9.3.6 What is dup2()?

dup2(), another original UNIX system call handler, duplicates a file descriptor when it is to be assigned for a specific use. It fully implements the POSIX 1003.1 function as a system call. It accepts a valid file descriptor and creates a new distinct file descriptor at the supplied file descriptor index. If it cannot duplicate the file descriptor because that particular file descriptor is in use, it will return an error.

... [File: /usr/src/kernel/kern/descrip.c, line: 125]

```
int
dup2(p, uap, retval)
        struct proc *p;
        struct args {
                u_int   from;
                u_int   to;
```

```
        } *uap;
        int *retval;
...
```

dup2() has three arguments: the pointer to the process; the pointer to the arguments to the system call (in this case, two—the file descriptor to be duplicated and which file descriptor it should return as); and the pointer to the return values. It returns zero if successful and an error code if unsuccessful. **dup2()** is used when a specific file descriptor is to be assigned for a specific use.[65]

9.3.6.1 How is dup2() Implemented?

... [File: /usr/src/kernel/kern/descrip.c, line: 139]

```
        if (old >= fdp->fd_nfiles ||
            (fp = fdp->fd_ofiles[old]) == NULL ||
            new >= p->p_rlimit[RLIMIT_OFILE].rlim_cur)
                return (EBADF);
...
```

We first check to see if the file descriptor we are duplicating lies within the range of a valid file descriptor and whether it contains an open file descriptor. If neither are true, or if the file descriptor we would like to duplicate it to lies outside of our set bounds, an error (EBADF) is returned and the function is terminated.

... [File: /usr/src/kernel/kern/descrip.c, line: 144]

```
        *retval = new;
        if (old == new)
                return (0);
...
```

The value of the new file descriptor is returned as the return value of the system call. If the descriptor is the same as the one we are duplicating, we return successfully (zero) immediately, since the file descriptors are already identical.

... [File: /usr/src/kernel/kern/descrip.c, line: 148]

```
        if (new >= fdp->fd_nfiles) {
                if (error = fdalloc(p, new, &i))
                        return (error);
#ifdef DIAGNOSTIC
                if (new != i)
                        panic(dup2: fdalloc);
#endif
        } else if (fdp->fd_ofiles[new]) {
                if (fdp->fd_ofileflags[new] & UF_MAPPED)
                        (void) munmapfd(p, new);
                /* dup2() must succeed even if the close has an error.*/
```

---

[65] In the POSIX/UNIX arrangement, the first three file descriptors serving the function as stdin, stdout, and stderr reside at the first three file descriptors 0, 1, and 2, respectively. **dup2()** is used to force the use of one of these three file descriptors.

```
                (void) closef(fdp->fd_ofiles[new], p);
        }
...
```

If the new file descriptor that we request to use lies out of bounds of the current file descriptor range allocated, **fdalloc()** is called to expand and allocate a larger pool of file descriptors to hold the file descriptor desired—it returns a file descriptor starting with the desired file descriptor. This function is guaranteed to work if it can expand the table since this file descriptor is known not to have been allocated yet. If **fdalloc()** cannot expand the table, an error is returned, and the function is terminated.

If the requested file descriptor we are copying to lies in the allocated range already, we check to see if it is already associated with a file. If it is, then the file is closed, but the descriptor is left allocated. If the file has been mapped, the file is forced unmapped prior to being closed.

... [File: /usr/src/kernel/kern/descrip.c, line: 162]

```
        fdp->fd_ofiles[new] = fp;
        fdp->fd_ofileflags[new] = fdp->fd_ofileflags[old] &~ UF_EXCLOSE;
        fp->f_count++;
        if (new > fdp->fd_lastfile)
                fdp->fd_lastfile = new;
        return (0);
...
```

The file associated with the file descriptor to be duplicated is now associated with the desired file descriptor, and its flags are copied. The reference count is increased on the now shared file instance, and this information is recorded if this is the largest valued file on the set of open files. Note that the data structure field *fd_lastfile* allows us to terminate our scan of open file descriptors early by knowing the last one allocated in sequence. The file descriptor is then returned to the system call handler and the function returns zero indicating success.

9.3.7 What is fcntl()?

fcntl() is a POSIX system call handler which implements the POSIX 1003.1 function to perform various operations on file descriptors. During the implementation of the **fcntl()** system call handler, the supplied file descriptor has the supplied command and argument applied to it, resulting in either success or an error value returned. The side-effect of this function is that it performs the desired operation on the file descriptor.

... [File: /usr/src/kernel/kern/descrip.c, line: 174]

```
int
fcntl(p, uap, retval)
        struct proc *p;
        struct args {
                int     fd;
                int     cmd;
                int     arg;
```

```
        } *uap;
        int *retval;
...
```

fcntl() has three arguments: the pointer to the process; the pointer to the arguments to the system call (in this case, three—the file descriptor, the command to be performed by **fcntl()**, and the argument to be used with the command); and the pointer to the return values. It returns zero if successful or an error if unsuccessful.

9.3.7.1 How is fcntl() Implemented?

... [File: /usr/src/kernel/kern/descrip.c, line: 191]

```
        if ((unsigned)uap->fd >= fdp->fd_nfiles ||
            (fp = fdp->fd_ofiles[uap->fd]) == NULL)
                return (EBADF);
...
```

The file descriptor to be operated on is checked for veracity by seeing if it lies within the bounds of the open file descriptor table and has a file instance associated with it. If it does not, an error (EBADF) is returned.

... [File: /usr/src/kernel/kern/descrip.c, line: 195]

```
        pop = &fdp->fd_ofileflags[uap->fd];
        switch(uap->cmd) {
        case F_DUPFD:
                if ((unsigned)uap->arg >= p->p_rlimit[RLIMIT_OFILE].rlim_cur)
                        return (EINVAL);
                if (error = fdalloc(p, uap->arg, &i))
                        return (error);
                fdp->fd_ofiles[i] = fp;
                fdp->fd_ofileflags[i] = *pop &~ UF_EXCLOSE;
                fp->f_count++;
                if (i > fdp->fd_lastfile)
                        fdp->fd_lastfile = i;
                *retval = i;
                return (0);
...
```

A pointer to the open file flags associated with the file descriptor is saved for common reference among the numerous commands implemented by **fcntl()**. Each command corresponds to a case in a case switch statement that decodes the command requested (uap->cmd).

The first command implemented here is the duplication (F_DUPFD) request which implements an inline variant of the **dup2()** system call. The argument field of **fcntl()** is used to select the desired file descriptor to receive the copy result. If it lies out of the bounds of an allocatable file descriptor, the system call is terminated with an error (EINVAL).

The file descriptor is then allocated at the desired index or at the index following it. If this attempt is unsuccessful, an error is returned. Otherwise, the file descriptor is associated with the file of the file descriptor to be duplicated, and the file descriptor and its flags (except for the close-on-execute flag) are copied to the new file descriptor. The reference count is then increased on the now shared file instance. As with all allocations for file descriptors, the *lastfile* field is updated if this is the largest valued file index allocated, and the file descriptor is returned as the return value with a zero value indicating success.

Note that the semantics of this duplication inline are almost but not exactly like **dup2()**, but the new file descriptor is not closed if it was open—instead we just find the next larger file descriptor to use.

... [File: /usr/src/kernel/kern/descrip.c, line: 210]

```
        case F_GETFD:
                *retval = *pop & UF_EXCLOSE;
                return (0);
...
```

The contents of the file descriptor's flags (sans close-on-execute) are returned.

... [File: /usr/src/kernel/kern/descrip.c, line: 214]

```
        case F_SETFD:
                *pop = (*pop &~ UF_EXCLOSE) | (uap->arg & 1);
                return (U);
...
```

The file's flags are set, preserving the value of the close-on-execute flag.

... [File: /usr/src/kernel/kern/descrip.c, line: 218]

```
        case F_GETFL:
                *retval = OFLAGS(fp->f_flag);
                return (0);
...
```

The file instance flags of the file descriptors are returned as indicated by the **fcntl()** file descriptor arguments.

... [File: /usr/src/kernel/kern/descrip.c, line: 222]

```
        case F_SETFL:
                fp->f_flag &= ~FCNTLFLAGS;
                fp->f_flag |= FFLAGS(uap->arg) & FCNTLFLAGS;
                tmp = fp->f_flag & FNONBLOCK;
                error = (*fp->f_ops->fo_ioctl)(fp, FIONBIO, (caddr_t)&tmp, p);
                if (error)
                        return (error);
                tmp = fp->f_flag & FASYNC;
                error = (*fp->f_ops->fo_ioctl)(fp, FIOASYNC, (caddr_t)&tmp, p);
                if (!error)
                        return (0);
                fp->f_flag &= ~FNONBLOCK;
                tmp = 0;
                (void) (*fp->f_ops->fo_ioctl)(fp, FIONBIO, (caddr_t)&tmp, p);
                return (error);
...
```

The file flags which can be set are set in the file associated with the requested file descriptor. File flags indicating non-blocking I/O (FNONBLOCK) and asynchronous I/O (FASYNC) are communicated to the underlying file-like object by means of the lower level ioctl (fo_ioctl) method to indicate the change in the status of the file instance and its underlying object. If the lower levels cannot implement either or both I/O, a corresponding error will be returned and the function terminates.

If no error is returned on the status change of the file, the function will return successfully. Otherwise, the non-blocking state will be reversed by a succeeding file ioctl call so that the state of the non-blocking I/O status can be disabled, since the asynchronous operation was not allowed to be applied to the file.

This subfunction of **fcntl()** is used to change the file back and forth from asynchronous to synchronous I/O capabilities. This ensures that file write or read operations will take place immediately and not necessarily overlap with another operation or dwell in the cache.

... [File: /usr/src/kernel/kern/descrip.c, line: 238]

```
case F_GETOWN:
        if (fp->f_type == DTYPE_SOCKET)
                cmd = SIOCGPGRP;
        else
                cmd = TIOCGPGRP;
        error = (*fp->f_ops->fo_ioctl) (fp, cmd, (caddr_t)retval, p);
        if (fp->f_type != DTYPE_SOCKET)
                *retval = -*retval;
        return (error);

...
```

The ownership by process group ID of the underlying file is requested from the underlying object with this case (F_GETOWN). Only tty devices and sockets will return successful process group IDs since only these types can have process group IDs associated with them. For sockets, the process group is obtained by casting the pointer to the file's data region to the type of socket. Thus, the code is written to evaluate inline contents of the field. In the case of a tty device, a terminal ioctl is called on the underlying file and its value returned. Since the process groups held by terminals are always negative values, the return value is altered to return the same positive group ID. If the underlying file was not a tty special device, the ioctl will fail with a known return error which will be relayed back as the error terminating this function.

... [File: /usr/src/kernel/kern/descrip.c, line: 248]

```
case F_SETOWN:
        if (fp->f_type == DTYPE_SOCKET)
                cmd = SIOCSPGRP;
        else {
                cmd = TIOCSPGRP;
                if (uap->arg <= 0) {
                        uap->arg = -uap->arg;
                } else {
```

```
                                struct proc *p1 = pfind(uap->arg);
                                if (p1 == 0)
                                        return (ESRCH);
                                uap->arg = p1->p_pgrp->pg_id;
                }
        }
        return((*fp->f_ops->fo_ioctl)(fp, cmd, (caddr_t)&uap->arg, p));
...
```

The ownership is set with this case (F_SETOWN). In the case of a socket, the contents of the socket structure is found by a cast on the file's data pointer and set to the argument supplied. Otherwise, if the argument is a negative number, it corresponds to a process group and is converted in place to a positive number to be attached to the tty special device.

If the argument is positive, it refers to a process whose process group ID we would like to use instead of the supplied argument. The **pfind()** inline function (see **kern/proc.h**) is called to locate the process. If the process cannot be found, an error (ESRCH) is returned. Otherwise, the argument is changed to refer to the process group ID of the process just located and a file ioctl request is made to set the process group of the terminal device with the supplied argument.

... [File: /usr/src/kernel/kern/descrip.c, line: 264]

```
        case F_SETLKW:
                flg |= F_WAIT;
                /* Fall into F_SETLK */

        case F_SETLK:
                if (fp->f_type != DTYPE_VNODE)
                        return (EBADF);
                vp = (struct vnode *)fp->f_data;
        ...
```

Two cases (F_SETLKW and F_SETLK) are used to set locks, either to be waited for or returned immediately if the lock is not granted, respectively. These two cases implement POSIX 1003.1 mandatory file locking. Currently, file locking is only implemented and only makes sense on vnode file objects (not sockets, obviously).

... [File: /usr/src/kernel/kern/descrip.c, line: 274]

```
                error = copyin(p, (caddr_t)uap->arg, (caddr_t)&fl, sizeof (fl));
                if (error)
                        return (error);

                if (fl.l_whence == SEEK_CUR)
                        fl.l_start += fp->f_offset;
        ...
```

The lock structure to be set is obtained from the user process at the address contained in the argument with **fcntl()**. If there is an error in obtaining a lock structure to be set, the system call handler returns immediately with an error (EFAULT). Otherwise, if the

---

position of the lock is relative to the current lock position, the starting address of the lock is updated relative to the current file offset.

... [File: /usr/src/kernel/kern/descrip.c, line: 281]

```
            switch (fl.l_type) {

            case F_RDLCK:
                    if ((fp->f_flag & FREAD) == 0)
                            return (EBADF);
                    p->p_flag |= SADVLCK;
                    return (VOP_ADVLOCK(vp, (caddr_t)p, F_SETLK, &fl, flg));

            case F_WRLCK:
                    if ((fp->f_flag & FWRITE) == 0)
                            return (EBADF);
                    p->p_flag |= SADVLCK;
                    return (VOP_ADVLOCK(vp, (caddr_t)p, F_SETLK, &fl, flg));

            case F_UNLCK:
                    return (VOP_ADVLOCK(vp, (caddr_t)p, F_UNLCK, &fl,
                            F_POSIX));

            default:
                    return (EINVAL);
            }
    ...
```

The lock type is dispatched in a switch statement to encode the three possible requests to instantiate a read lock (F_RDLCK) or a write lock (F_WRLCK) or to remove a lock (F_UNLCK). Each of these requests are passed to the vnode layer using the vnode operation **VOP_ADVLOCK**. Use of the advisory locks is recorded on the process by the setting of the advisory lock bit on the process flag (SADVLCK). Attempts to either write lock a read-only file or read lock a write-only file are explicitly disallowed. Note that locks instantiated with this mechanism follow POSIX file locking rules which differ from BSD advisory locking rules (see **flock()**). If an unimplemented lock type is requested, an error code (EINVAL) is returned.

... [File: /usr/src/kernel/kern/descrip.c, line: 303]

```
        case F_GETLK:
                if (fp->f_type != DTYPE_VNODE)
                        return (EBADF);
                vp = (struct vnode *)fp->f_data;

                /* fetch the lock structure */
                error = copyin(p, (caddr_t)uap->arg, (caddr_t)&fl, sizeof (fl));
                if (error)
                        return (error);
                if (fl.l_whence == SEEK_CUR)
                        fl.l_start += fp->f_offset;
                if (error = VOP_ADVLOCK(vp, (caddr_t)p, F_GETLK, &fl, F_POSIX))
                        return (error);
                return (copyout(p, (caddr_t)&fl, (caddr_t)uap->arg, sizeof
(fl)));
```

```
default:
        return (EINVAL);
}
/* NOTREACHED */
...
```

The get-a-lock status request (F_GETLCK) is next implemented. It currently works on vnode file-like objects. Akin to set-a-lock, the lock structure is copied in from user space and, if relative to the current file's object, the start of the region is relocated using the file's offset pointer. The underlying vnode is accessed via the **VOP_ADVLOCK** primitive to evaluate the lock structure and to return a (possibly overlapping) lock instance in its place, which would then be copied back in place to the lock structure instance read in from the user process.

If an error occurs either during the **copyin** or **copyout** operations, an error value (EFAULT) is returned. If an error occurs from the lower level object, it will be signalled from that layer. If an unimplemented option was requested as a command to **fcntl()**, an error (EINVAL) will be returned.

9.3.8 What is close()?

close(), a POSIX system call handler which implements the POSIX 1003.1 function, closes an open file and releases all resources used in accessing it.

... [File: /usr/src/kernel/kern/descrip.c, line: 328]

```
int
close(p, uap, retval)
        struct proc *p;
        struct args {
                int     fd;
        } *uap;
        int *retval;
...
```

close() has three arguments: the pointer to the process; the pointer to the arguments to the system call (in this case, one—the file descriptor); and the pointer to the return values. It returns zero if successful or an error if unsuccessful.

9.3.8.1 How is close() Implemented?

... [File: /usr/src/kernel/kern/descrip.c, line: 341]

```
        if ((unsigned)fd >= fdp->fd_nfiles ||
            (fp = fdp->fd_ofiles[fd]) == NULL)
                return (EBADF);
...
```

The file descriptor to be operated on is checked for veracity by seeing if it lies within the bounds of the open file descriptor table and has a file instance associated with it. If it does not, an error (EBADF) is returned.

```
        pf = (u_char *)&fdp->fd_ofileflags[fd];
        if (*pf & UF_MAPPED)
                (void) munmapfd(p, fd);
...
```

A pointer to the open file flag associated with this file descriptor is saved and the flag is checked to see if the file descriptor may be mapped into the address space of the program. If so, the file descriptor is forced unmapped prior to it being closed.

... [File: /usr/src/kernel/kern/descrip.c, line: 349]

```
        fdp->fd_ofiles[fd] = NULL;
        while (fdp->fd_lastfile > 0 && fdp->fd_ofiles[fdp->fd_lastfile] == NULL)
                fdp->fd_lastfile--;
        if (fd < fdp->fd_freefile)
                fdp->fd_freefile = fd;
        *pf = 0;
        return (closef(fp, p));
...
```

The file descriptor is closed by overwriting the file pointer of the file descriptor. The last file allocated field is scanned backwards until it finds the last open file. Likewise, the first free file is maintained by checking to see if the file descriptor being freed is smaller than the one previously remembered. Both the last file allocated and the first free file are used to speed allocation and scanning of the file table by only scanning or allocating in a known subrange of the set of allocated file descriptors.

Finally, the flags field is cleared and the underlying file itself is closed using the **closef()** function. Any error returned from this function is passed through **close()** and the function terminates.

9.3.9 What is fstat()?

fstat(), a POSIX system call handler which implements the POSIX 1003.1 function, returns the POSIX file attributes for the file that are attached to a file descriptor. It consults the appropriate low-level function for the low-level file-like object for return of POSIX-specified attribute statistics (struct stat) and passes them back to the caller.

... [File: /usr/src/kernel/kern/descrip.c, line: 361]

```
int
fstat(p, uap, retval)
        struct proc *p;
        struct args {
                int     fd;
                struct  stat *sb;
        } *uap;
        int *retval;
...
```

fstat() has three arguments: the pointer to the process; the pointer to the arguments to the system call (in this case, two—the file descriptor, and a pointer to a buffer to receive a POSIX file attributes stat instance); and the pointer to the return values. It returns zero if successful or an error code if unsuccessful.

9.3.9.1 How is fstat() Implemented?

... [File: /usr/src/kernel/kern/descrip.c, line: 375]

```
    if ((unsigned)uap->fd >= fdp->fd_nfiles ||
        (fp = fdp->fd_ofiles[uap->fd]) == NULL)
            return (EBADF);
...
```

The file descriptor to be operated on is checked for veracity by seeing if it lies within the bounds of the open file descriptor table and has a file instance associated with it. If it does not, an error (EBADF) is returned.

... [File: /usr/src/kernel/kern/descrip.c, line: 379]

```
    error = (*fp->f_ops->fo_stat)(fp, &ub, p);
...
```

The object underlying the file (either a vnode or socket) is instructed to throw the contents of its POSIX stat structure of attributes into a temporary buffer on the stack.

... [File: /usr/src/kernel/kern/descrip.c, line: 381]

```
    if (error == 0)
            error = copyout(p, (caddr_t)&ub, (caddr_t)uap->sb, sizeof (ub));
    return (error);
...
```

If an error was encountered while obtaining the attributes from the lower level object, the function returns the error code. Otherwise, the attributes are copied back to the user program and the function returns successfully. If an error was encountered from the inline function **copyout**, it is returned and passed back through this function as an error value.

9.3.10 What is read()?

read(), a POSIX system call handler which implements the POSIX 1003.1 function, issues a read request on a file. The file associated with the file descriptor used by **read()** is located and a read operation issued to the underlying object. The results are then passed back to the user program. **read()** is essentially a wrapper function used to issue a request to a lower level file-like object (e.g. a vnode or socket).

... [File: /usr/src/kernel/kern/descrip.c, line: 387]

```
int
read(p, uap, retval)
        struct proc *p;
        register struct args {
```

```
                int     fdes;
                char    *cbuf;
                unsigned count;
        } *uap;
        int *retval;
...
```

read() has three arguments: the pointer to the process; the pointer to the arguments to the system call (in this case, three—the file descriptor, a pointer to the area to receive the contents of the file to be read, and the number of bytes to be read from the file); and the pointer to the return values. It returns zero if successful or an error code if unsuccessful.

9.3.10.1 How is read() Implemented?

... [File: /usr/src/kernel/kern/descrip.c, line: 406]

```
        if (((unsigned)uap->fdes) >= fdp->fd_nfiles ||
            (fp = fdp->fd_ofiles[uap->fdes]) == NULL ||
            (fp->f_flag & FREAD) == 0)
                return (EBADF);
...
```

The file descriptor to be operated on is checked for veracity by seeing if it lies within the bounds of the open file descriptor table and has a file instance associated with it. If it does not, an error (EBADF) is returned.

... [File: /usr/src/kernel/kern/descrip.c, line: 411]

```
        aiov.iov_base = (caddr_t)uap->cbuf;
        aiov.iov_len = uap->count;
        auio.uio_iov = &aiov;
        auio.uio_iovcnt = 1;
        auio.uio_resid = uap->count;
        auio.uio_rw = UIO_READ;
        auio.uio_segflg = UIO_USERSPACE;
        auio.uio_procp = p;
...
```

A description of the I/O operation is recorded in a uio (user I/O) structure instance (auio) allocated on the stack. All I/O inside of the kernel is described generically as a uio (even though the kernel can do this from kernel space as well).

... [File: /usr/src/kernel/kern/descrip.c, line: 428]

```
        cnt = uap->count;
        if (error = (*fp->f_ops->fo_read)(fp, &auio, fp->f_cred))
                if (auio.uio_resid != cnt && (error == ERESTART ||
                    error == EINTR || error == EWOULDBLOCK))
                        error = 0;
        cnt -= auio.uio_resid;
...
```

The I/O descriptor is passed off to the low-level object's read method along with its file pointer and credentials. If an error is found it is returned from the read operation. In the case of an error, if the residual count indicates that a portion of the read

---

operation had succeeded and the error indicates that the operation was interrupted for a reason related to a transient condition (e.g., interrupted/restarted and passed an interrupted sleep), the error is ignored so that the **read()** system call may successfully return its contents or be restarted. The residual count is used to determine the amount actually transferred.

... [File: /usr/src/kernel/kern/descrip.c, line: 440]

```
        *retval = cnt;
        return (error);
...
```

The residual count is returned as a return value for the system call, along with any error or success values, and the function terminates.

9.3.11 What is readv()?

readv(), a BSD system call handler which implements the BSD function, issues a read request on a file. **readv()** differs from **read()** in that in place of the single segment read in a descriptor, a count of descriptor elements is used to allow a multiple segment read to take place. Thus, this single system call can read numerous successive portions of a file into discrete segments of the program.

The file associated with the file descriptor used by **readv()** is located and a read operation issued to the underlying object. The results are passed back to the user program. Note that the low level operations all accept a vector of segments. In the case of **readv()**, a vector is loaded from the user space of the program and checked before being passed down to the lower level request. The point of **readv()** is to reduce the cost of such successive reads so that one system call can do a vector of reads at one time— hence **readv()** implies read vector.

... [File: /usr/src/kernel/kern/descrip.c, line: 447]

```
int
readv(p, uap, retval)
        struct proc *p;
        register struct args {
                int     fdes;
                struct  iovec *iovp;
                unsigned iovcnt;
        } *uap;
        int *retval;
...
```

readv() has three arguments: the pointer to the process; the pointer to the arguments to the system call (in this case, three—the file descriptor, a pointer to the area to receive the contents of the file to be read, and the number of bytes to be read from the file); and the pointer to the return values. It returns zero if successful or an error code if unsuccessful.

---

readv() is essentially a wrapper function used to issue a request to a lower level file-like object (a vnode or socket).

9.3.11.1 How is readv() Implemented?

... [File: /usr/src/kernel/kern/descrip.c, line: 469]

```
    if (((unsigned)uap->fdes) >= fdp->fd_nfiles ||
        (fp = fdp->fd_ofiles[uap->fdes]) == NULL ||
        (fp->f_flag & FREAD) == 0)
            return (EBADF);
    ...
```

The file descriptor to be operated on is checked for veracity by seeing if it lies within the bounds of the open file descriptor table and has a file instance associated with it. If it does not, an error (EBADF) is returned.

... [File: /usr/src/kernel/kern/descrip.c, line: 490]

```
    iovlen = uap->iovcnt * sizeof (struct iovec);

    if (uap->iovcnt > UIO_SMALLIOV) {
            if (uap->iovcnt > UIO_MAXIOV)
                    return (EINVAL);
            MALLOC(iov, struct iovec *, iovlen, M_IOV, M_WAITOK);
            saveiov = iov;
    } else
            iov = aiov;

    auio.uio_iov = iov;
    auio.uio_iovcnt = uap->iovcnt;
    auio.uio_rw = UIO_READ;
    auio.uio_segflg = UIO_USERSPACE;
    auio.uio_procp = p;

    if (error = copyin(p, (caddr_t)uap->iovp, (caddr_t)iov, iovlen))
            goto done;
    ...
```

A description of the I/O operation is recorded in a uio (user I/O) structure instance (auio) which is allocated on the stack. All I/O inside of the kernel is described generically as a uio.[66] In the case of **readv()**, the I/O vector is imported along with the I/O vector length (iovec), which describes a vector of segments that will be read in by the read operation. This is the entire point of this BSD system call. If the I/O vector being read is small enough, a buffer on the stack is used to hold the contents—otherwise, a temporary buffer is allocated to hold the contents while it is referenced by the kernel. Should any error be encountered in reading in the I/O vector, the system call is aborted with an error (EFAULT).

---

[66] Even though the kernel can do it from kernel space as well.

```
        auio.uio_resid = 0;
        for (i = 0; i < uap->iovcnt; i++) {
                if (iov->iov_len < 0) {
                        error = EINVAL;
                        goto done;
                }
                auio.uio_resid += iov->iov_len;
                if (auio.uio_resid < 0) {
                        error = EINVAL;
                        goto done;
                }
                iov++;
        }
...
```

The I/O vector imported from the user program is scanned for veracity and the expected residual amount determined from the sum of all I/O lengths.

... [File: /usr/src/kernel/kern/descrip.c, line: 518]

```
        cnt = auio.uio_resid;
        if (error = (*fp->f_ops->fo_read)(fp, &auio, fp->f_cred))
                if (auio.uio_resid != cnt && (error == ERESTART ||
                    error == EINTR || error == EWOULDBLOCK))
                        error = 0;
        cnt -= auio.uio_resid;
...
```

The I/O descriptor is passed off to the low-level object's read method along with its file pointer and credentials. If an error is encountered it is returned from the read operation. In the case of an error, if the residual count indicates that a portion of the read operation had succeeded and the error indicates that the operation was interrupted for a reason related to a transient condition (interrupted/restarted and passed an interrupted sleep, for example), the error is ignored so that the **readv()** system call may successfully return its contents or be restarted. The residual count is used to determine the amount actually transferred.

... [File: /usr/src/kernel/kern/descrip.c, line: 534]

```
        *retval = cnt;
done:
        if (uap->iovcnt > UIO_SMALLIOV)
                FREE(saveiov, M_IOV);

        return (error);
...
```

The count is returned as a return value for the **readv()** system call, along with any error or success. If a buffer was required to hold the copy of the I/O vector contents, the buffer is freed.

9.3.12 What is write()?

write(), a POSIX system call handler which implements the POSIX 1003.1 function, issues a write request on a file. The file associated with the file descriptor used by **write()** is located and a write operation issued to the underlying object. The results are then passed back to the user program.

... [File: /usr/src/kernel/kern/descrip.c, line: 545]

```
int
write(p, uap, retval)
        struct proc *p;
        struct args {
                int     fdes;
                char    *cbuf;
                unsigned count;
        } *uap;
        int *retval;
    ...
```

write() has three arguments: the pointer to the process; the pointer to the arguments to the system call (in this case, three—the file descriptor, a pointer to the area to receive the contents of the file to be written, and the number of bytes to be written from the file); and the pointer to the return values. It returns zero if successful or an error code if unsuccessful.

write() is essentially a wrapper function used to issue a request to a lower level file-like object (a vnode or socket).

9.3.12.1 How is write() Implemented?

... [File: /usr/src/kernel/kern/descrip.c, line: 564]

```
        if (((unsigned)uap->fdes) >= fdp->fd_nfiles ||
            (fp = fdp->fd_ofiles[uap->fdes]) == NULL ||
            (fp->f_flag & FWRITE) == 0)
                return (EBADF);
    ...
```

The file descriptor to be operated on is checked for veracity by seeing if it lies within the bounds of the open file descriptor table and has a file instance associated with it. If it does not, an error (EBADF) is returned.

... [File: /usr/src/kernel/kern/descrip.c, line: 569]

```
        aiov.iov_base = (caddr_t)uap->cbuf;
        aiov.iov_len = uap->count;
        auio.uio_iov = &aiov;
        auio.uio_iovcnt = 1;
        auio.uio_resid = uap->count;
        auio.uio_rw = UIO_WRITE;
        auio.uio_segflg = UIO_USERSPACE;
        auio.uio_procp = p;
    ...
```

A description of the I/O operation is recorded in a uio (user I/O) structure instance (auio) which is allocated on the stack. All I/O inside of the kernel is described generically as a uio (even though the kernel can do it from kernel space as well).

... [File: /usr/src/kernel/kern/descrip.c, line: 586]

```
        cnt = uap->count;
        if (error = (*fp->f_ops->fo_write)(fp, &auio, fp->f_cred)) {
                if (auio.uio_resid != cnt && (error == ERESTART ||
                    error == EINTR || error == EWOULDBLOCK))
                        error = 0;
                if (error == EPIPE)
                        psignal(p, SIGPIPE);
        }
        cnt -= auio.uio_resid;
    ...
```

The I/O descriptor is passed off to the low-level object's write method along with its file pointer and credentials. If an error is present it is returned from the write operation. In the case of an error, if the residual count indicates that a portion of the write operation had succeeded and the error indicates that the operation was interrupted for a reason related to a transient condition (interrupted/restarted and passed an interrupted sleep, for example), the error is ignored so that the **write()** system call may successfully return its contents or be restarted. The residual count is used to determine the amount actually transferred.

If the error was due to a write on a pipe that no longer exists, the process is signalled with the appropriate signal (SIGPIPE). Instead of using an error code, signals are always used with pipes. This is done because while a write on a pipe that has gone away is considered a terminal condition, there are many UNIX programs that ignore simple error values. Pipes are treated specially to avoid terminal conditions where the program would otherwise wait indefinitely.

... [File: /usr/src/kernel/kern/descrip.c, line: 602]

```
        *retval = cnt;
        return (error);
    ...
```

The residual count is returned as a return value for the system call, and any error or success is returned from the **write()** system call hander.

9.3.13 What is writev()?

writev(), a BSD system call handler which implements the BSD function, issues a write request on a file. **writev()** differs from **write()** in that that in place of the single segment write in a descriptor, a count of descriptor elements is used to allow a multiple segment write to take place. Thus, this single system call can write numerous successive portions of a file into discrete segments of the program.

The file associated with the file descriptor used by **writev()** is found and a write vector operation issued to the underlying object. The results are then passed back to the user program. Note that low-level operations all accept a vector of segments. In the case of **writev()**, a vector is loaded from the user space of the program and checked before being passed down to the lower level request. The point of **writev()** is to reduce the cost of such successive writes so that one system call can do a vector of writes at one time—hence **writev** implies write vector.

... [File: /usr/src/kernel/kern/descrip.c, line: 609]

```
int
writev(p, uap, retval)
        struct proc *p;
        register struct args {
                int     fdes;
                struct  iovec *iovp;
                unsigned iovcnt;
        } *uap;
        int *retval;
    ...
```

writev() has three arguments: the pointer to the process; the pointer to the arguments to the system call (in this case, three—the file descriptor, a pointer to the area to receive the contents of the file to be written, and the number of bytes to be written from the file); and the pointer to the return values. It returns zero if successful or an error code if unsuccessful.

writev() is essentially a wrapper function used to issue a request to a lower level file-like object (a vnode or socket).

9.3.13.1 How is writev() Implemented?

... [File: /usr/src/kernel/kern/descrip.c, line: 631]

```
        if (((unsigned)uap->fdes) >= fdp->fd_nfiles ||
            (fp = fdp->fd_ofiles[uap->fdes]) == NULL ||
            (fp->f_flag & FWRITE) == 0)
                return (EBADF);
    ...
```

The file descriptor to be operated on is checked for veracity by seeing if it lies within the bounds of the open file descriptor table and has a file instance associated with it. If it does not, an error (EBADF) is returned.

... [File: /usr/src/kernel/kern/descrip.c, line: 637]

```
        iovlen = uap->iovcnt * sizeof (struct iovec);
        if (uap->iovcnt > UIO_SMALLIOV) {
                if (uap->iovcnt > UIO_MAXIOV)
                        return (EINVAL);
                MALLOC(iov, struct iovec *, iovlen, M_IOV, M_WAITOK);
                saveiov = iov;
        } else
                iov = aiov;
```

```
auio.uio_iov = iov;
auio.uio_iovcnt = uap->iovcnt;
auio.uio_rw = UIO_WRITE;
auio.uio_segflg = UIO_USERSPACE;
auio.uio_procp = p;

if (error = copyin(p, (caddr_t)uap->iovp, (caddr_t)iov, iovlen))
        goto done;
```
...

A description of the I/O operation is recorded in a uio (user I/O) structure instance (auio) which is allocated on the stack. All I/O inside of the kernel is described generically as a uio (even though the kernel can do it from kernel space as well). In the case of **writev()**, the I/O vector is imported along with the I/O vector length (iovec), which describes a vector of segments that will be written by the write operation. This is the entire point of this BSD system call.

If the I/O vector being written is small enough, a buffer on the stack is used to hold the contents—otherwise, a temporary buffer is allocated to hold the contents while it is referenced by the kernel. Should any error be encountered in writing the I/O vector, the system call is aborted with an error (EFAULT).

... [File: /usr/src/kernel/kern/descrip.c, line: 655]

```
auio.uio_resid = 0;
for (i = 0; i < uap->iovcnt; i++) {
        if (iov->iov_len < 0) {
                error = EINVAL;
                goto done;
        }
        auio.uio_resid += iov->iov_len;
        if (auio.uio_resid < 0) {
                error = EINVAL;
                goto done;
        }
        iov++;
}
```
...

The I/O vector imported from the user program is scanned for veracity and the expected residual amount determined from the sum of all I/O lengths.

... [File: /usr/src/kernel/kern/descrip.c, line: 679]

```
cnt = auio.uio_resid;
if (error = (*fp->f_ops->fo_write)(fp, &auio, fp->f_cred)) {
        if (auio.uio_resid != cnt && (error == ERESTART ||
            error == EINTR || error == EWOULDBLOCK))
                error = 0;
        if (error == EPIPE)
                psignal(p, SIGPIPE);
}
cnt -= auio.uio_resid;
```
...

The I/O descriptor is passed off to the low-level object's write method along with its file pointer and credentials. If an error is present it is returned from the write operation. In the case of an error, if the residual count indicates that a portion of the write operation had succeeded and the error indicates that the operation was interrupted for a reason related to a transient condition (interrupted/restarted and passed an interrupted sleep, for example), the error is ignored so that the **writev()** system call may successfully return its contents or be restarted. The residual count is used to determine the amount actually transferred.

If the error was due to a write on a pipe that no longer exists, the process is signalled with the appropriate signal (SIGPIPE). Instead of relying on error values, signals on pipes are used because while a write on a pipe that has gone away is considered a terminal condition, there are many UNIX programs that ignore error values. Pipes are treated specially to avoid terminal conditions where the program would otherwise wait indefinitely.

... [File: /usr/src/kernel/kern/descrip.c, line: 698]

```
        *retval = cnt;
done:
        if (uap->iovcnt > UIO_SMALLIOV)
                FREE(saveiov, M_IOV);

        return (error);
...
```

The count is returned as a return value for the system call, and any error or success is returned from the **writev()** system call hander. If a buffer was required to hold the copy of the I/O vector contents, the buffer is freed.

9.3.14 What is ioctl()?

ioctl(), a POSIX system call handler which implements the POSIX 1003.1 function, issues a control operation on a file-like object. The file associated with the file descriptor used by **ioctl()** is located and an ioctl operation issued to the underlying object. The results are then passed back to the user program. Operations may pass information down to the underlying object and/or return information from the underlying object.

... [File: /usr/src/kernel/kern/descrip.c, line: 710]

```
int
ioctl(p, uap, retval)
        struct proc *p;
        register struct args {
                int     fdes;
                int     cmd;
                caddr_t cmarg;
        } *uap;
        int *retval;
...
```

---

ioctl() has three arguments: the pointer to the process; the pointer to the arguments to the system call (in this case, three—the file descriptor, the command to be performed on the underlying file, and a pointer to a portion of data to be used with the command in the user program's address space); and the pointer to the return values. It returns zero if successful or an error code if unsuccessful.

ioctl() is essentially a wrapper function to issue a request to a lower level file-like object (a vnode or socket). Note that there are generic file ioctls that are performed in concert with the file and the underlying object (where state of the file flags is involved).

9.3.14.1 How is ioctl() Implemented?

... [File: /usr/src/kernel/kern/descrip.c, line: 730]

```
    if ((unsigned)uap->fdes >= fdp->fd_nfiles ||
        (fp = fdp->fd_ofiles[uap->fdes]) == NULL)
            return (EBADF);
    if ((fp->f_flag & (FREAD|FWRITE)) == 0)
            return (EBADF);
...
```

The file descriptor to be operated on is checked for veracity by seeing if it lies within the bounds of the open file descriptor table and has a file instance associated with it. If it does not, an error (EBADF) is returned. An EBADF error is also returned in the case that the file is not open for reading or writing.

... [File: /usr/src/kernel/kern/descrip.c, line: 736]

```
    com = uap->cmd;
    if (com == FIOCLEX) {
            fdp->fd_ofileflags[uap->fdes] |= UF_EXCLOSE;
            return (0);
    }
    if (com == FIONCLEX) {
            fdp->fd_ofileflags[uap->fdes] &= ~UF_EXCLOSE;
            return (0);
    }
...
```

If the command is either to set (FIOCLEX) or unset (FIONCLEX) the close-on-execute bit of the file descriptor flags, the flags for the file descriptor are changed appropriately. One of the historical oddities of UNIX systems is that since the **fcntl()** (file control) system call came after the **ioctl()** system call, it sets all but the close-on-execute bit of the file descriptor flags. These two specific commands terminate successfully immediately following their interception.

... [File: /usr/src/kernel/kern/descrip.c, line: 751]

```
    size = IOCPARM_LEN(com);
    if (size > IOCPARM_MAX)
            return (ENOTTY);
    if (size > sizeof (stkbuf)) {
            memp = (caddr_t)malloc((u_long)size, M_IOCTLOPS, M_WAITOK);
```

```
                data = memp;
        }
        if (com&IOC_IN) {
                if (size) {
                        error = copyin(p, uap->cmarg, data, (u_int)size);
                        if (error) {
                                if (memp)
                                        free(memp, M_IOCTLOPS);
                                return (error);
                        }
                } else
                        *(caddr_t *)data = uap->cmarg;
        } else if ((com&IOC_OUT) && size)
                /*
                 * Zero the buffer so the user always
                 * gets back something deterministic.
                 */
                (void) memset(data, 0, size);
        else if (com&IOC_VOID)
                *(caddr_t *)data = uap->cmarg;
...
```

The ioctl's parameter, either referring to a field of bytes or an integer value, is imported into kernel space for use. BSD systems do not implement a separate length on the ioctl's parameter fields. Instead, they encode the length of the object pointed to by the optional argument and the direction (read in or written out or both) from a portion of the command field. As such, this portion of code breaks up the high-order portion of the command field into a size length, and either fetches or clears a buffer that may either be read in or read back to the user program. Note that the buffer can be used both ways. Also note that the length of the parameter is thus limited and if the parameter length exceeds a valid size an error (ENOTTY) is returned. This rather lame method of indicating an invalid **ioctl()** is always problematic but is inherent to an arrangement which tries to maintain reverse compatibility across three generations of UNIX systems.

The parameters use a stack temporary buffer (stkbuf) if small enough; otherwise, a temporary buffer is dynamically allocated. It should be noted that along with a parameter being used as a pointer to a field of data, a command can also use the argument as a value (IOC_VOID).

... [File: /usr/src/kernel/kern/descrip.c, line: 777]

```
        switch (com) {

        case FIONBIO:
                if (tmp = *(int *)data)
                        fp->f_flag |= FNONBLOCK;
                else
                        fp->f_flag &= ~FNONBLOCK;
                error = (*fp->f_ops->fo_ioctl)(fp, FIONBIO, (caddr_t)&tmp, p);
                break;
...
```

Various file ioctls are implemented partially in this handler in concert with the lower-level file-like objects. This case switch statement filters these command requests. The first of these commands, FIONBIO, requests that the file be set into non-blocking I/O mode where the filesystem call handlers will return a special error (EWOULDBLOCK) if an operation were to occur that necessitates the process to become blocked for an indefinite time. The state of this property is retained in a file flag bit (FNONBLOCK). The low-level file-like object underneath the file is requested to change the state via its ioctl method (**fo_ioctl()**). Note that the request is blind; if the lower-level object cannot change, the flag bit does not revert. Note also that both **fcntl()** and **ioctl()** use the lower-level ioctl method call (**fo_ioctl()**) and share a single vocabulary of low-level commands.

... [File: /usr/src/kernel/kern/descrip.c, line: 787]

```
case FIOASYNC:
        if (tmp = *(int *)data)
                fp->f_flag |= FASYNC;
        else
                fp->f_flag &= ~FASYNC;
        error = (*fp->f_ops->fo_ioctl)(fp, FIOASYNC, (caddr_t)&tmp, p);
        break;
...
```

The FIOASYNC command requests that the file be set into asynchronous I/O mode, sending a signal (SIGIO) when the operation is satisfied. The state of this property is retained in a file flag bit (FASYNCH). The low-level file-like object underneath the file is requested to change the state via its ioctl method (**fo_ioctl()**). Note that this request is blind; if the lower-level object cannot change, the flag bit does not revert.

... [File: /usr/src/kernel/kern/descrip.c, line: 795]

```
case FIOSETOWN:
        tmp = *(int *)data;
        if (fp->f_type == DTYPE_SOCKET)
                cmd = SIOCSPGRP;
        else {
                cmd = TIOCSPGRP;
                if (tmp <= 0) {
                        tmp = -tmp;
                } else {
                        struct proc *p1 = pfind(tmp);
                        if (p1 == 0) {
                                error = ESRCH;
                                break;
                        }
                        tmp = p1->p_pgrp->pg_id;
                }
        }
        error = (*fp->f_ops->fo_ioctl) (fp, cmd, (caddr_t)&tmp, p);
        break;
...
```

The FIOSETOWN command (identical to the **fcntl()** F_SETOWN command) sets the process group ownership of a tty special file or socket. In the case of a socket, the contents of the socket structure are found by a cast on the file's data pointer and set to the argument supplied. Otherwise, if the argument is a negative number, it corresponds to a process group ID and is converted in place to a positive number to be attached to the tty special device.

If the argument is positive, it refers to a process whose process group ID we would like to use instead of the supplied argument. The **pfind()** inline function (see **kern/proc.h**) is called to locate the process. If the process cannot be found, an error (ESRCH) is returned. Otherwise, the argument is changed to refer to the process group ID of the process just located, and a file ioctl request is made to set the process group of the terminal device with the supplied argument.

... [File: /usr/src/kernel/kern/descrip.c, line: 815]

```
        case FIOGETOWN:
                if (fp->f_type == DTYPE_SOCKET)
                        cmd = SIOCGPGRP;
                else
                        cmd = TIOCGPGRP;
                error = (*fp->f_ops->fo_ioctl)(fp, cmd, data, p);
                if (fp->f_type != DTYPE_SOCKET)
                        *(int *)data = -*(int *)data;
                break;
    ...
```

The FIOGETOWN command (identical to the **fcntl()** F_GETOWN command) requests the ownership by process group ID of the underlying file from the underlying object. Only tty devices and sockets will return successful process group IDs, since only these items can have process group IDs associated with them. For sockets, the process group is obtained by casting the pointer to the file's data region to the type of socket. Thus, the code is written to evaluate inline contents of the field. In the case of a tty device, a terminal ioctl is called on the underlying file and its value returned. Since the process groups held by terminals are always negative values, the return value is altered to return the same positive group ID. If the underlying file was not a tty special device, the ioctl will fail with a known return error which will be relayed back as the error terminating this function.

... [File: /usr/src/kernel/kern/descrip.c, line: 825]

```
        default:
                error = (*fp->f_ops->fo_ioctl)(fp, com, data, p);
                if (error == 0 && (com&IOC_OUT) && size)
                        error = copyout(p, data, uap->cmarg, (u_int)size);
                break;
        }
    ...
```

All other ioctl commands are passed to the lower-level file-like object's ioctl method (fo_ioctl) unchanged. If the command returns any parameters, the buffer is copied back if the request was successful.

... [File: /usr/src/kernel/kern/descrip.c, line: 832]

```
        if (memp)
                free(memp, M_IOCTLOPS);
        return (error);
...
```

If a temporary buffer was dynamically allocated to hold the parameters (because they were larger than would fit on the stack), the buffer is freed prior to the conclusion of this handler. The return or success is then passed back from the function, as no return values will be present.

9.3.15 What is select()?

select(), a BSD system call handler which implements the BSD select function, tests for the presence of an event on the underlying file attached to a file descriptor(s). The file associated with the file descriptor used by **select()** is located and a select operation issued to the underlying object. The results are then passed back to the user program. **select()** is unique in that it accepts vectors of file descriptors to check for events associated with input, output, and exceptions that may occur during a brief space of time. **select()** is an attempt to bridge the gap between the synchronous nature of UNIX file I/O by allowing a process to be able to test for the presence of an I/O-related event to see if a synchronous read or write operation should be performed.

... [File: /usr/src/kernel/kern/descrip.c, line: 842]

```
int
select(p, uap, retval)
        register struct proc *p;
        register struct args {
                int     nd;
                fd_set  *in, *ou, *ex;
                struct  timeval *tv;
        } *uap;
        int *retval;
...
```

select() has three arguments: the pointer to the process; the pointer to the arguments to the system call (in this case, five—the number of descriptors, pointers to the bit vectors of file descriptors for input, output or exception events, and the pointer to the interval of time associated with the attempt to check the status of the file descriptor); and the pointer to the return values. It returns zero if successful or an error code if unsuccessful.

select() is essentially a wrapper function to issue a request to a lower level file-like object (a vnode or socket). Note that **select()** is implemented with its framework at the top level and only a sensing function of the appropriate event at the lower levels. The **select()** system call handler uses the **selscan()** helper function to perform the scan in the lower level objects.

In the case of a multithreaded user program, one would generally not use something like **select()**, but would instead just let the operation stall a particular thread. However, the effect of multithreaded operation can still be simulated in a user application with **select()** by checking which of the possible file descriptors has an appropriate state for another I/O operation—thus selecting the particular thread of operation to be executed at that moment.

9.3.15.1 How is select() Implemented?

... [File: /usr/src/kernel/kern/descrip.c, line: 856]

```
        (void) memset((caddr_t)ibits, 0, sizeof(ibits));
        (void) memset((caddr_t)obits, 0, sizeof(obits));
        if (uap->nd > p->p_fd->fd_nfiles)
                uap->nd = p->p_fd->fd_nfiles;
        ni = howmany(uap->nd, NFDBITS);
    ...
```

The prospective temporary bit vectors used to scan the file descriptors are zeroed prior to use. In addition, the number of descriptors is bounded by the size of the number of allocated descriptors. This partially deals with the consequences resulting from the fact that the bitmap's space reserved in the program calling this system call handler has set its size at compile time, while the system is set to have a variable number of files that may be selected—thus, technically we have an error (EBADF) that should be signalled or a case where truncation could result in an error on **copyout**.[67] This is dealt with pragmatically by quietly bounding the length of the scan.[68] The number of integer mask words to be scanned is then converted into a number of bits to be examined in the bit fields.

... [File: /usr/src/kernel/kern/descrip.c, line: 862]

```
#define getbits(name, x) \
        if (uap->name) { \
                error = copyin(p, (caddr_t)uap->name, (caddr_t)&ibits[x], \
                        (unsigned)(ni * sizeof(fd_mask))); \
        if (error) \
                goto done; \
        }
        getbits(in, 0);
        getbits(ou, 1);
        getbits(ex, 2);
#undef getbits
    ...
```

The file descriptor bit sets are loaded from their pointers in the list of arguments for the **select()** system call with a macro that conveniently checks if the bit field is being used in this invocation. If it is, the bit vector is fetched from the user program using the inline function **copyin** to return the contents into a stack temporary. Stack

---

[67] If too large, causing a possible EFAULT or corruption of adjacent data.
[68] N.B. There are other potential minor problems here—can the reader figure them out?

---

temporaries are only assumed in this function if FDSETSIZE is so large as to consume a large portion of the kernel stack. This code should be rewritten so that (like other system call handlers) a temporary buffer is dynamically allocated and freed to hold the copy in kernel mode. This has been left as an exercise to the reader.

If an error occurs in reading any of the bit vectors, the function returns prematurely with an error (EFAULT). The input, output, and exception bit vectors are possibly used as part of the three-tuple bits (which had previously been zeroed)—the lack of any of these in the argument will result in a null selection. The macro is then defeated to prevent its accidental use further down in the source.

... [File: /usr/src/kernel/kern/descrip.c, line: 874]

```
if (uap->tv) {
        error = copyin(p, (caddr_t)uap->tv, (caddr_t)&atv,
                sizeof (atv));
        if (error)
                goto done;
        if (itimerfix(&atv)) {
                error = EINVAL;
                goto done;
        }
        splclock(); timevaladd(&atv, &time); splnone();
        timo = hzto(&atv);
} else
        timo = 0;
...
```

An optional treatment for **select()** (actually all of this function's arguments are optional) is to select a timeout based on a supplied time value (tv). If it is present, the value is used during an interruptible sleep to keep the file descriptors in a state of readiness. If an event occurs during that time, the sleep will be abandoned, the events discovered and scanned, and the file descriptors returned to the user. Thus, in this case, the bits are effectively scanned twice—once before the sleep and once after the sleep. The first scan catches bits set at the time that the system call was first engaged and the second scan finds any outstanding events which had to be waited for during the sleep. If the events don't happen in the set time interval during which the timeout occurred, the system call returns prematurely.

If no time interval is supplied, the file descriptor event bits will be scanned only once and their results returned. The time value supplied is adjusted with the value of the current time to determine the number of clock ticks required to suspend while waiting for the events to become ready (by using **tsleep()**—see **kern/synch.c** in **Chapter 8**). Note that due to the assumptions of 32-bit arithmetic, the select interval cannot be arbitrarily large. The time value is loaded from the program's address space with the inline function **copyin**, which returns early with an error (EFAULT) if unsuccessful. The supplied time value is normalized to an acceptable level by the function **itimerfix()** (see **kern/time.c**).

If the value is out of range for use as an interval time, an error is returned (EINVAL); otherwise, the relative time is converted into an absolute time by adding the current time to the time interval, then further converted into a number of clock ticks which are recorded in the timeout variable (timeout).

```
... [ File: /usr/src/kernel/kern/descrip.c, line: 888 ]

retry:
        ncoll = nselcoll;
        p->p_flag |= SSEL;
        error = selscan(p, ibits, obits, uap->nd, retval);
        if (error || *retval)
                goto done;

        splhigh();
        /* this should be timercmp(&time, &atv, >=) */
        if (uap->tv && (time.tv_sec > atv.tv_sec ||
            time.tv_sec == atv.tv_sec && time.tv_usec >= atv.tv_usec)) {
                p->p_flag &= ~SSEL;
                /* error = EWOULDBLOCK; */
                splnone();
                goto done;
        }
        if ((p->p_flag & SSEL) == 0 || nselcoll != ncoll) {
                splnone();
                goto retry;
        }
        p->p_flag &= ~SSEL;
        error = tsleep((caddr_t)&selwait, PSOCK | PCATCH, select, timo);
        splnone();

        if (error == 0)
                goto retry;
done:
    ...
```

The main loop for **select()** is this sequence of code which first samples the number of select collisions present in a local variable. Since **select()** can be active while the state of the events that it may need to consult are also active and changing, collisions (better known as races) are possible. To avoid the condition of having a bit come ready just after it is tested, the number of outstanding cases where an event has been waited for and potentially missed is tracked. If during our wait the number has changed (the number is global for all selects across all processes), then we know that there is potentially a lost event which must be rescanned for. We then mark the process as being involved in a select operation (SSEL) and call the helper function **selscan()** to implement the scan of the file descriptor events.

If an error or any events are found after this scan, we branch out of this loop. Otherwise, we check the time to see if we have already during the process of scanning exceeded the time limit of the timeout (if a timeout was present), as well as check to see if any collisions are present or if the process is no longer selecting. If we have exceeded the time limit, we remove the select bit from the process flags and return to interrupt base level and leave the loop.[69]

If any collisions are present or if the select bit is off, we restart the select loop. If the process has lost the select bit, this means that the events waited for have occurred since the time that the **selscan()** function was called (we just missed seeing them). If the number of collisions differs, we potentially have the condition where someone else is looking for the same event in another process, which caused us to miss seeing the event. In both these cases, a retry is necessary.

During the period that these checks are being performed, interrupts are disabled to avoid the race conditions of either the time changing or the select event changing state during the comparisons to determine if a race has occurred. This is an example of a *critical* section of code.

The select bit is removed and the process is allowed to sleep waiting for the event or (optionally) a timeout to occur. **select()** sleeps interruptibly (PCATCH) so that signals may force it awake. Note that the design of interruptible sleeps requires that a caught signal be interpreted and **tsleep()** not immediately be reentered. Thus, the error returned by a PCATCH will force a select to return prematurely so that the caught signal can be implemented and possibly result in terminating or issuing a signal to a user mode process.

The sleep occurs at a fixed priority (PSOCK) for wakeup appropriate for either socket or vnode operations. The priority lies above that of waits, locks, or pauses in the system, since the availability of a resource in effect may also be an event. On return from the sleep, the interrupt level is returned to the base level (no interrupts masked). If there have been no errors returned from sleep (we haven't timed out or been signalled), a rescan is conducted. Otherwise, this core signal loop is completed.

... [File: /usr/src/kernel/kern/descrip.c, line: 917]

```
        if (error == ERESTART)
                error = EINTR;
        if (error == EWOULDBLOCK)
                error = 0;
    ...
```

Since **select()** does not honor restarting after signals are sampled, the ERESTART error is turned into EINTR error to indicate that the system call was interrupted. **select()** must not restart because the signal will need to be honored in the user process before

---

[69] Note that the error is set to zero at this point, which is appropriate since this is a timeout which will be turned into an ignored error—we are effectively doing an EWOULDBLOCK error. The net effect is the same, whether we have the additional instruction or not, so it is left in but commented out.

the scan for signals is reissued. Thus, only in the user program can it be successively reissued. In addition, the timeout case of EWOULDBLOCK is silently ignored.

... [File: /usr/src/kernel/kern/descrip.c, line: 922]

```
#define putbits(name, x) \
        if (uap->name) { \
                int error2 = copyout(p,(caddr_t)&obits[x],(caddr_t)uap->name, \
                        (unsigned)(ni * sizeof(fd_mask))); \
                if (error2) \
                        error = error2; \
        }
        if (error == 0) {
                putbits(in, 0);
                putbits(ou, 1);
                putbits(ex, 2);
        }
#undef putbits

        return (error);
...
```

A macro is used to return the bit vectors corresponding to the scanned file descriptor bit sets for each of the fields implemented on this instantiation of the call. This is only done in the case where no error was encountered. After its use, the macro is undefined to prevent its accidental reuse. The error or success of the system call handler is then returned.

9.3.16 What is selscan()?

selscan() is a private helper function used by select() which scans sets of file descriptors to discover if any events are present. It checks each of the file descriptors encoded into the bit masks to determine if an event is present. If the event is not present, the bit set in the file descriptors will be cleared; otherwise, it will be left set to indicate that the event is present. The number of found events will then be returned from selscan() in a pointer as well as an error value if the attempt to select the file has resulted in an error.

... [File: /usr/src/kernel/kern/descrip.c, line: 939]

```
static int
selscan(struct proc *p, fd_set *ibits, fd_set *obits, int nfd, int *retval)
...
```

selscan() has five arguments: the pointer to the process on which the select is being performed: the pointer to a vector of file descriptor sets to be checked; a pointer to a vector of file descriptor sets to be written back; the accumulated number of file descriptors in the sets to be checked; and a pointer to a value to receive the number of file descriptors that indicate a true select case. It returns a value of zero upon success or an error (EBADF) if the file descriptor does not exist.

9.3.16.1 How is selscan() Implemented?

... [File: /usr/src/kernel/kern/descrip.c, line: 949]

```
for (which = 0; which < 3; which++) {
        switch (which) {

        case 0:
                flag = FREAD; break;

        case 1:
                flag = FWRITE; break;

        case 2:
                flag = 0; break;
        }
...
```

The three cases (input, output, exception) of file descriptor bit vector sets are successively scanned for by the outermost for loop. The associated flag with each of the cases is chosen by the switch statement. Note that the flag for the exception case is zero (or no flag).

... [File: /usr/src/kernel/kern/descrip.c, line: 961]

```
for (i = 0; i < nfd; i += NFDBITS) {
        bits = ibits[which].fds_bits[i/NFDBITS];
        while ((j = ffs(bits)) && i + --j < nfd) {
                bits &= ~(1 << j);
                fp = fdp->fd_ofiles[i + j];
                if (fp == NULL) {
                        error = EBADF;
                        break;
                }
                if ((*fp->f_ops->fo_select)(fp, flag, p)) {
                        FD_SET(i + j, &obits[which]);
                        n++;
                }
        }
    }
}
...
```

From the least significant word to the most significant word, each word of bits in the bit mask is examined to find any bits (least significant to most significant) that are set in the word. The bit offset is converted into a file descriptor index used to locate a file pointer. If the file pointer is null (the file is not open), an error (EBADF) is returned. If it is not null, a file descriptor's select method (fo_select) is used to check to see if the event has occurred on the lower level file-like object. Every low-level object may in turn pass this request down subsequent layers to determine if the exception is present.

The exception is again selected using the value of the flag as set above. If the event has been found, the associated bit in the output bit vector is set to indicate that the event on that file descriptor has been found and a counter of the number of found events is incremented. Note that the bit vectors are scanned entirely regardless of the number of found events. Thus, scanning one thousand file descriptors (even though events on only the first three would occur) result in three thousand and nine unnecessary checks. These three encased loops eventually terminate. Note also that no waiting is allowed on the select path; however, for a large number of file descriptors this can still consume a large amount of time.

... [File: /usr/src/kernel/kern/descrip.c, line: 977]

```
        *retval = n;
        return (error);
    ...
```

Upon completion of the loop, the number of found events is returned as well as any error code or success. The only error code which can be returned occurs in the case of a closed file in the set of file descriptors.

9.3.17 What is seltrue()?

seltrue() is a driver support routine that implements a dummy select operation. It will always return a successful select state. The point of this function is to allow a driver that cannot or did not implement the select feature to work sensibly when someone invokes a select. Since it will always return true (one), the applications program will perform the appropriate I/O or exception operation without delay since it will always be ready.

... [File: /usr/src/kernel/kern/descrip.c, line: 982]

```
int
seltrue(dev_t dev, int which, struct proc *p)
...
```

seltrue() has three arguments: the device number; the select flag type; and the pointer to the process performing the select. It always returns true.

9.3.17.1 How is seltrue() Implemented?

... [File: /usr/src/kernel/kern/descrip.c, line: 986]

```
        return (1);
    ...
```

seltrue() returns the value one indicating readiness for select operations.

9.3.18 What is selwakeup()?

selwakeup(), a kernel internal function, is used to wake up a sleeping select call. It is called from either the top level or interrupt level of the kernel to wake up a sleeping select call so that **selscan()** can be called to observe that an event has occurred. It in effect cuts short the time of a select operation so that the event may be immediately noticed by the associated process.

... [File: /usr/src/kernel/kern/descrip.c, line: 990]

```
void
selwakeup(pid_t pid, int coll)
...
```

selwakeup() has two arguments: the process ID of the process to be awakened; and a flag indicating if a collision has occurred. It returns nothing. The side-effect of this function is that it wakes up the process waiting for the select.

Note that **selwakeup()** can be called asynchronously to the selection of a file descriptor. Note also that since the file descriptor may be shared across two processes, one of the processes may go away during the time that the select operation has started. For example, with telnet or login servers that communicate to the login shell with a pseudo tty device, a situation can occur where the selected process no longer exists. In this case, how can we use a process pointer to a process which no longer exists? One way to handle this is to not use a process pointer, but instead use the user process index and **pfind()** (see **kern/proc.h**) to discover if the process still exists and, if it does, determine what its process pointer is. Thus, we avoid the need to place a reference count on a process. This is a subtlety missing in earlier versions of UNIX and 386BSD.

9.3.18.1 How is selwakeup() Implemented?

... [File: /usr/src/kernel/kern/descrip.c, line: 995]

```
        if (coll) {
                nselcoll++;
                wakeup((caddr_t)&selwait);
        }
    ...
```

If a collision is indicated in the arguments, the global collision counter (*nselcoll*) is incremented and a broadcast wakeup is issued to all processes waiting for selects. This mechanism notifies all processes that are using the **select()** function that a collision has occurred and that they should rescan their file descriptors for events.

... [File: /usr/src/kernel/kern/descrip.c, line: 1000]

```
        if (pid && (p = pfind(pid))) {
                int s = splhigh();

                if (p->p_wchan == (caddr_t)&selwait) {
                        if (p->p_stat == SSLEEP)
                                setrun(p);
                else
                                unsleep(p);
                } else if (p->p_flag & SSEL)
                        p->p_flag &= ~SSEL;
                splx(s);
        }
    ...
```

If there is a process ID associated with this call and the process ID has a process associated with it (found by using **pfind()**, see **kern/proc.h**), the process is checked to see if it is involved in a select operation. While the process is being checked, interrupts are masked so that other interrupts (including the clock interrupt) don't alter the state of the process's status. If the process is waiting for the global selection event (*selwait*), the process is checked to see if it is sleeping or stopped and, if so, is restored to the run state by use of **setrun()** if it is sleeping or **unsleep()** if it is stopped (see **kern/synch.c**).

Otherwise, the process is known already to be in the run state so the selecting bit is checked (ssel). If the ssel bit is removed, this indicates that during the time that select was scanning for events an event came in (so this process may have just missed the event). If not, this function restores the interrupt priority level it was called with and returns.

9.3.19 What is fdalloc()?

fdalloc() is an internal kernel function which allocates a file descriptor for the process. It examines the existing file descriptor associated with the process and allocates a file descriptor at or above the index number requested. If there is no free descriptor that can be allocated in the existing table, the table will be grown if the upper bound has not yet been reached. The upper bound itself is setable as a resource (see **kern/resource.c**).

... [File: /usr/src/kernel/kern/descrip.c, line: 1017]

```
int
fdalloc(struct proc *p, int want, int *result)
    ...
```

fdalloc() has three arguments: the process in which we will be allocating a new file descriptor; the desired file descriptor to be allocated; and the pointer to the location to receive the new file descriptor. It returns a zero if successful or an error code (EMFILE) if unsuccessful in allocating a new file entry.

9.3.19.1 How is fdalloc() Implemented?

... [File: /usr/src/kernel/kern/descrip.c, line: 1031]

```
            lim = p->p_rlimit[RLIMIT_OFILE].rlim_cur;
            for (;;) {
                    last = min(fdp->fd_nfiles, lim);
                    if ((i = want) < fdp->fd_freefile)
                            i = fdp->fd_freefile;
                    for (; i < last; i++) {
                            if (fdp->fd_ofiles[i] == NULL) {
                                    fdp->fd_ofileflags[i] = 0;
                                    if (i > fdp->fd_lastfile)
                                            fdp->fd_lastfile = i;
                                    if (want <= fdp->fd_freefile)
                                            fdp->fd_freefile = i;
                                    *result = i;
                                    return (0);
                            }
                    }
    ...
```

fdalloc() checks for the first free descriptor, starting at the greater of the desired descriptors or at the last descriptor known to be free. It will continue to scan until the end of the amount of file descriptors allocated or until the resource limit of file descriptors has been reached—whichever comes first. A file descriptor is reusable if its file field is null. If such a descriptor is found, the flags are cleared, the last and first file descriptor bounds are updated, and the descriptor is returned via the parameter's pointer with a success indicated by a zero return value.

... [File: /usr/src/kernel/kern/descrip.c, line: 1049]

```
        if (fdp->fd_nfiles >= lim)
                return (EMFILE);
        if (fdp->fd_nfiles < NDEXTENT)
                nfiles = NDEXTENT;
        else
                nfiles = (2 * fdp->fd_nfiles) % lim;
   ...
```

If the file descriptor was not found in the currently allocated array, we check to see if we are already at the limit of allocatable file descriptors for this process. If we are, we return an error (EMFILE) indicating we have no more file descriptors to allocate. Otherwise, we set upon allocating more file descriptors by extending the file descriptor pointer and file arrays adjacently allocated in a single block of memory (see *File Descriptor Data Structures*). If this is our first extension, we extend the number of files up to the first group (ndextent). Otherwise, we estimate the number of files we are going to use.[70]

... [File: /usr/src/kernel/kern/descrip.c, line: 1056]

```
        MALLOC(newofile, struct file **, nfiles * OFILESIZE,
            M_FILEDESC, M_WAITOK);
        newofileflags = (char *) &newofile[nfiles];
   ...
```

A new array buffer is dynamically allocated by the kernel's memory allocator to hold the enlarged arrays, and the new file pointer and file flag arrays are allocated and held in temporary pointers.

... [File: /usr/src/kernel/kern/descrip.c, line: 1064]

```
        (void) memcpy(newofile, fdp->fd_ofiles,
            (i = sizeof(struct file *) * fdp->fd_nfiles));
        (void) memset((char *)newofile + i, 0,
            nfiles * sizeof(struct file *) - i);
        (void) memcpy(newofileflags, fdp->fd_ofileflags,
            (i = sizeof(char) * fdp->fd_nfiles));
        (void) memset(newofileflags + i, 0, nfiles * sizeof(char) - i);
   ...
```

---

[70] Double the number of files we currently have allocated bounded by the number of files possible within the limits.

The old file pointer array is copied at the base of the new file pointer array, and the expanded region following it is zeroed to mark the new descriptors as unallocated. Similarly, the new file flags are also copied from the old file flag's array and the unused ones zeroed.[71]

... [File: /usr/src/kernel/kern/descrip.c, line: 1072]

```
        if (fdp->fd_nfiles > NDFILE)
                FREE(fdp->fd_ofiles, M_FILEDESC);
    ...
```

The first set of allocatable file descriptors (ndfile) are implemented as a portion of the file descriptor structure itself and is never freed or reused. Any expansion above this number indicates that the previous file table was dynamically allocated, so we free the old table and pass it back to the kernel memory allocator for reuse.

... [File: /usr/src/kernel/kern/descrip.c, line: 1075]

```
        fdp->fd_ofiles = newofile;
        fdp->fd_ofileflags = newofileflags;
        fdp->fd_nfiles = nfiles;
    }
    ...
```

The new file pointer array and file descriptor flag array are installed in the file descriptor structure, along with the new size and number of file descriptor entries in the file descriptor size field. The for loop is reentered at the top with the now larger array, and, as its new empty entries will now satisfy the request, it successfully returns from the request for the file descriptor.

9.3.20 What is fdavail()?

fdavail() is an internal kernel function which ensures that enough file descriptors are present that can be allocated with **fdalloc()**. It simply checks to see if the desired number of file descriptors are still available for allocation in the desired process.

... [File: /usr/src/kernel/kern/descrip.c, line: 1085]

```
int
fdavail(struct proc *p, int n)
    ...
```

fdavail() has two arguments: the pointer to the process in which the file descriptors will be allocated; and the number of file descriptors to be checked for availability. It returns the value one (true) if the file descriptors can be allocated and zero (false) if they cannot be allocated.

---

[71] This is redundant since file flags are already cleared before a file is allocated.

fdavail() exists because currently there is no convention for **fdalloc()** to allocate atomically a number of file descriptors. In general, **fdavail()** is used to ensure that there are the requisite number of file descriptors, whereupon **fdalloc()** can be used to allocate them.

9.3.20.1 How is fdavail() Implemented?

... [File: /usr/src/kernel/kern/descrip.c, line: 1092]

```
        if ((i = p->p_rlimit[RLIMIT_OFILE].rlim_cur - fdp->fd_nfiles) > 0 &&
            (n -= i) <= 0)
                return (1);
    ...
```

If there are enough remaining file descriptors that can be allocated given the resource limits versus the number of files already allocated, such that the number of files can be satisfied by expanding the file table alone, the function returns true. This quick check suffices in most cases since the file descriptor table is usually densely allocated.

... [File: /usr/src/kernel/kern/descrip.c, line: 1096]

```
        fpp = &fdp->fd_ofiles[fdp->fd_freefile];
        for (i = fdp->fd_nfiles - fdp->fd_freefile; --i >= 0; fpp++)
                if (*fpp == NULL && --n <= 0)
                        return (1);
        return (0);
    ...
```

If an expansion alone won't guarantee us the desired number of file descriptors,[72] a linear search is made for the number of files starting with the first free file. If the requisite number of file descriptors are found before the linear scan completes, a true value is returned, indicating we can allocate these file descriptors. If the scan completes without the required number of free file descriptors found, a false is returned.

9.3.21 What is falloc()?

falloc() is an internal kernel function that allocates a file instance and attaches it to an allocated file descriptor within a process. It is the first step in completing an **open()** operation on a file-like object (see **fs/fs_sys.c**). It obtains a file descriptor (using **fdalloc()**) and attaches it to a freshly allocated file instance. The file instance has been initialized to retain the information of an empty file, with its offset pointer located at the beginning of the object. In addition, the file will retain a reference count on the credentials of the process so that any file operations will reference these credentials for determining from the user ID the authorization for the appropriate related user of the operations.

---

[72] E.g., the file descriptors are sparsely allocated, having been expanded, opened, and closed possibly a number of times with free entries sprinkled about.

... [File: /usr/src/kernel/kern/descrip.c, line: 1107]

```
int
falloc(struct proc *p, struct file **resultfp, int *resultfd)
    ...
```

fdalloc() has three arguments: the pointer to the process to which the file will be allocated; a pointer to receive the pointer to the file instance that will be returned; and a pointer to the value to receive the file descriptor index. It returns a zero value if successful, an error (EMFILE) if no file descriptors are available for this process, or an error (ENFILE) if there are too many files already allocated.

9.3.21.1 How is falloc() Implemented?

... [File: /usr/src/kernel/kern/descrip.c, line: 1113]

```
    if (error = fdalloc(p, 0, &i))
            return (error);
    if (nfiles >= maxfiles) {
            tablefull("file");
            return (ENFILE);
    }
    ...
```

fdalloc() is called to supply a file descriptor to be used with the file. Since files can only be accessed via file descriptors, even if we have files we cannot use them if we don't have a file descriptor to attach to them. If we have no file descriptor, the function returns with an error (EMFILE).

A check is made to see if the number of file instances already allocated is at or above its maximum. If it is, a file exhaustion message is sent to the system administrator via the kernel's console **printf()** and error logging message **tablefull()**, and an error (ENFILE) is returned. Even though the files are now dynamically allocated on the list, the function used to record their paucity refers back to earlier versions of the system when this table was a statically allocated array.

... [File: /usr/src/kernel/kern/descrip.c, line: 1126]

```
    nfiles++;
    MALLOC(fp, struct file *, sizeof(struct file), M_FILE, M_WAITOK);
    if (fq = p->p_fd->fd_ofiles[0])
            fpp = &fq->f_filef;
    else
            fpp = &filehead;
    p->p_fd->fd_ofiles[i] = fp;
    if (fq = *fpp)
            fq->f_fileb = &fp->f_filef;
    fp->f_filef = fq;
    fp->f_fileb = fpp;
    *fpp = fp;
    ...
```

A new file instance is allocated using the kernel's memory allocator, and the global count of how many files are allocated is increased. The newly allocated file instances are enqueued on a global file list which is grouped with sublists associated with each process which have a sequence of files allocated. In this way, all of the files associated with a process can be found by following the pointer from the first file descriptor on through successive file instances as successive forward pointers. Thus, the file instances are linked in a two-tiered arrangement, with the first file of a process on the global list and every subsequent file instance of that process linked onto that entry alone. This arrangement allows programs such as **fstat** to locate all of the files associated with a process.

The file list is a doubly-linked list with a reverse pointer referring to the prior entry to which the entry was linked. This allows the entries on the list to become unlinked merely by adjusting the pointers of an element within, instead of having to scan the doubly-linked list. The file descriptor allocated earlier is then attached to the file instance by assigning its array value. (Note that it is assumed that the first file descriptor zero is always the first one allocated. If a process starts out with no file descriptors, does a **dup2()** operation, and allocates a non-zero file descriptor first, you will get a different result—what exactly happens is left as an exercise for the reader; however, this is most assuredly a pathological case).

... [File: /usr/src/kernel/kern/descrip.c, line: 1139]

```
        fp->f_count = 1;
        fp->f_msgcount = 0;
        fp->f_offset = 0;
        fp->f_cred = p->p_ucred;
        crhold(fp->f_cred);

        if (resultfp)
                *resultfp = fp;
        if (resultfd)
                *resultfd = i;
        return (0);
...
```

The file instance is initialized with a single reference and no messages attached to it (for sockets). The file offset is initialized to start at zero (for vnodes), and a reference to the user credentials is asserted for the file. (Note that file credentials for reading and writing will derive from the process's user credentials. In a non-UNIX system where the credentials may be different on every file, or in a secure operating system, this credential reference has additional meanings).

If the file descriptor or file pointer has been requested to be returned by the arguments of this function, the values are summarily returned. In some cases, only the file descriptor is interesting to users of this function, since it is implied that a file pointer is already present, while in other cases the reverse is actually true. The function then returns successfully with a value of zero.

9.3.22 What is ffree()?

ffree() is an internal kernel function that frees a file instance for reuse. It unlinks the file instance from the global file list, strips it of its credentials, and returns it to the free pool of memory used by the kernel's memory allocator (see **kern/malloc.c** in **Chapter 3**).

... [File: /usr/src/kernel/kern/descrip.c, line: 1155]

```
void
ffree(struct file *fp)
 ...
```

ffree() has one argument: the pointer to the file instance being freed. It returns nothing.

9.3.22.1 How is ffree() Implemented?

... [File: /usr/src/kernel/kern/descrip.c, line: 1161]

```
        if (fq = fp->f_filef)
                fq->f_fileb = fp->f_fileb;
        *fp->f_fileb = fq;
 ...
```

The file instance is removed from the global file list by adjusting the doubly-linked list's pointers to bypass this entry.

... [File: /usr/src/kernel/kern/descrip.c, line: 1171]

```
        crfree(fp->f_cred);
        nfiles--;
        FREE(fp, M_FILE);
 ...
```

The reference to the credentials associated with the file is then released and the number of files counter is decremented prior to the file instance being returned to the kernel's memory allocator.

9.3.23 What is fdcopy()?

fdcopy() is an internal kernel function used by the **fork1()** operation (see **kern/fork.c**) to replicate a file descriptor in the new process. It allocates a new file descriptor structure for use in another process and initializes it to point at all of the file and vnode references shared with its original copy.

... [File: /usr/src/kernel/kern/descrip.c, line: 1179]

```
struct filedesc *
fdcopy(struct proc *p)
 ...
```

fdcopy() has one argument: the pointer to the process from which it will copy the file descriptor. It returns a pointer to the fresh copy of the file descriptor table. Note that as implemented **fdcopy()** may require two memory allocations. This function could be improved to require a single memory allocation by reorganization and restructuring, increasing the speed of a fork operation.

9.3.23.1 How is fdcopy() Implemented?

... [File: /usr/src/kernel/kern/descrip.c, line: 1186]

```
        MALLOC(newfdp, struct filedesc *, sizeof(struct filedesc0),
            M_FILEDESC, M_WAITOK);
        (void) memcpy(newfdp, fdp, sizeof(struct filedesc));
        newfdp->fd_refcnt = 1;
    ...
```

A new file descriptor data structure is dynamically allocated to hold the contents of the new copy of the file descriptor information to be copied. The contents of the entry are copied from the process supplied, as the argument and the reference count is asserted as one.

... [File: /usr/src/kernel/kern/descrip.c, line: 1191]

```
        VREF(newfdp->fd_cdir);
        if (newfdp->fd_rdir)
                VREF(newfdp->fd_rdir);
    ...
```

A reference is added to the vnode describing the current directory of the old process. This is done to account for the new reference of the copy. If there is a root directory vnode in use as well, the root directory vnode reference is also increased.

... [File: /usr/src/kernel/kern/descrip.c, line: 1201]

```
        if (newfdp->fd_lastfile < NDFILE) {
                newfdp->fd_ofiles = ((struct filedesc0 *) newfdp)->fd_dfiles;
                newfdp->fd_ofileflags =
                    ((struct filedesc0 *) newfdp)->fd_dfileflags;
                i = NDFILE;
        } else {
    ...
```

If the number of files currently open in the old process that we are copying is enough to be satisfied by the arrays already present in the file descriptor structure, the file pointer array and file flag array are adjusted to point at the fields within the newly allocated file descriptor, and the number of file descriptors is set as the default number of the immediately allocated group (ndfile).

... [File: /usr/src/kernel/kern/descrip.c, line: 1212]

```
                i = newfdp->fd_nfiles;
                while (i > 2 * NDEXTENT && i >= newfdp->fd_lastfile * 2)
                    i /= 2;
                MALLOC(newfdp->fd_ofiles, struct file **, i * OFILESIZE,
                    M_FILEDESC, M_WAITOK);
                newfdp->fd_ofileflags = (char *) &newfdp->fd_ofiles[i];
    ...
```

Otherwise, the number of files in use is used to estimate to the nearest NDEXTENT number of files how big the table should be. This allows a process that uses a large number of file descriptors for brief periods of time the opportunity to create child processes that have a smaller number of file descriptor entries.

A memory segment is next allocated to hold the file pointer array and the number of descriptors in the extended form with the file flags array following immediately adjacent to it. This mechanism works well just as long as they are not spread out, since an open file descriptor at the end of a sequence of empty file descriptors cannot be relocated adjacent to the other allocated file descriptors. The child process knows only that the file descriptor is at its fixed location—such are the limitations of assigning absolute indexes as a user interface mechanism. This half-hearted attempt to allow some degree of control for processes with large number of file descriptors in use is not deterministic. We cannot guarantee they are all contiguous and can be saved.

For example, user processes like the shell clear all descriptors other than the ones they use, as in the case of a pipeline of processes forked from a shell forked in turn from a process with a large number of file descriptors (as would be the case in the use of the C-library system function). While the shell would have a large number of files due to the process replication, its children would not because the number of files in active use by the shell would be fewer than the minimum used by the earlier case. Note also that the close-on-execute feature still would not help in resolving this, since the **copyin** allocation of the file descriptors will occur as part of the fork operation and the descriptors will be closed following the allocation. There seems to be no easy way around shrinking the table short of shrinking it upon freeing the file descriptors.

... [File: /usr/src/kernel/kern/descrip.c, line: 1220]

```
newfdp->fd_nfiles = i;
(void) memcpy(newfdp->fd_ofiles, fdp->fd_ofiles,
    i * sizeof(struct file **));
(void) memcpy(newfdp->fd_ofileflags, fdp->fd_ofileflags,
    i * sizeof(char));
fpp = newfdp->fd_ofiles;
for (i = newfdp->fd_lastfile; i-- >= 0; fpp++)
        if (*fpp != NULL)
                (*fpp)->f_count++;

return (newfdp);
```

...

The file descriptor structure is updated to indicate the number of files that can be allocated in the current arrays, and the old file pointer and flag arrays are copied into the new file pointer and flag arrays in the new file descriptor structure. For all allocated files in the new file descriptor structure, each file instance that is open has its reference count increased to account for the file sharing with the new copy, and the new file descriptor structure's address is returned.

9.3.24 What is fdfree()?

fdfree() is an internal kernel function used by **exit()** (see **kern/exit.c**) that frees all file descriptors prior to the termination of a process. It releases the reference to the file descriptors and closes them off successively. It also releases any references to root and current directories before ultimately releasing the file descriptor structure back to free kernel memory.

... [File: /usr/src/kernel/kern/descrip.c, line: 1234]

```
void
fdfree(struct proc *p)
 ...
```

fdfree() has one argument: the pointer to the process whose file descriptors are being freed. It returns nothing. The side-effect of this function is that it reclaims all file descriptors and the files to which they are attached.

9.3.24.1 How is fdfree() Implemented?

... [File: /usr/src/kernel/kern/descrip.c, line: 1242]

```
        if (--fdp->fd_refcnt > 0)
                return;
 ...
```

A reference count is decremented for file descriptors. If the file descriptors are still referenced, the function returns immediately. This is done to allow processes that share address space and file descriptors to terminate without freeing their reference to the file descriptors. Since shared address space processes are not present yet, the feature is not currently used, so fd_refcnt is always one.

... [File: /usr/src/kernel/kern/descrip.c, line: 1245]

```
        fpp = fdp->fd_ofiles;
        fdfp = fdp->fd_ofileflags;
        for (i = 0; i <= fdp->fd_lastfile; i++, fpp++, fdfp++)
                if (*fpp != NULL) {
                        if (*fdfp & UF_MAPPED)
                                (void) munmapfd(p, i);
                        (void) closef(*fpp, p);
                }
 ...
```

A file descriptor array is successively freed. Any open files are closed with a check made to see if the descriptor needs to be unmapped from the address space prior to closing. The file instance is then closed using the **closef()** function.

... [File: /usr/src/kernel/kern/descrip.c, line: 1254]

```
        if (fdp->fd_nfiles > NDFILE)
                FREE(fdp->fd_ofiles, M_FILEDESC);
 ...
```

The extended file descriptor segment is freed in the case that there are more than the number of files that can be implemented in the file descriptor instance. Unlike incremental closes, **fdfree()** frees the space for the file descriptors en mass.

... [File: /usr/src/kernel/kern/descrip.c, line: 1257]

```
        vrele(fdp->fd_cdir);
        if (fdp->fd_rdir)
                vrele(fdp->fd_rdir);
    ...
```

The references on the current directory vnode and possibly the root directory vnode are released. Root directories are optional and are only present in the case that the process is the ancestor of a process that did a **chroot()** system call (see **fs/fs_sys.c**).

... [File: /usr/src/kernel/kern/descrip.c, line: 1261]

```
        FREE(fdp, M_FILEDESC);
    ...
```

The file descriptor structure itself is finally freed as all references and subsidiary structures have been removed.

9.3.25 What is fdcloseexec()?

fdcloseexec() is a kernel internal function defined in the POSIX 1003.1 specification used to see if any files need to be closed while doing an **execve()** system call (see **kern/execve.c**). It inspects the file descriptors for the presence of any files that have been marked with the close-on-execute flag (UF_EXCLOSE). It then forces those files closed before the new program is executed.

... [File: /usr/src/kernel/kern/descrip.c, line: 1265]

```
void
fdcloseexec(struct proc *p)
    ...
```

fdcloseexec() has one argument: the pointer to the process being scanned and having files closed. It returns nothing. The side-effect of this function is that any marked files are closed.

9.3.25.1 How is fdcloseexec() Implemented?

... [File: /usr/src/kernel/kern/descrip.c, line: 1273]

```
        fpp = fdp->fd_ofiles;
        fdfp = fdp->fd_ofileflags;
        for (i = 0; i <= fdp->fd_lastfile; i++, fpp++, fdfp++)
                if (*fpp != NULL && (*fdfp & UF_EXCLOSE)) {
                        if (*fdfp & UF_MAPPED)
                                (void) munmapfd(p, i);
                        (void) closef(*fpp, p);
                        *fpp = NULL;
                        *fdfp = 0;
```

```
              if (i < fdp->fd_freefile)
                      fdp->fd_freefile = i;
      }
  ...
```

The file array of the file descriptor is scanned up to the last allocated file. Allocated files are checked to see if their open file flag has a close-on-execute (UF_EXCLOSE) flag present. If so, a close is done on the file and the file descriptor. As with all close operations, if a file is marked as being mapped, it is unmapped from the address space prior to being closed. Next, the file instance is closed with **closef()** and the descriptor itself is marked for reuse. The first free file is updated if the newly freed file is less than the last free file index.

... [File: /usr/src/kernel/kern/descrip.c, line: 1286]

```
      while (fdp->fd_lastfile > 0 && fdp->fd_ofiles[fdp->fd_lastfile] == NULL)
             fdp->fd_lastfile--;
  ...
```

Finally, the last allocated file field is updated by scanning backward for empty entries in the trailing set of possibly allocated entries.

9.3.26 What is closef()?

closef() is a private function used only in this file to perform the close operation on a file instance. It releases a reference to the file instance as used in the given process. If it is the last file reference, the function will close the file and free the file instance. Since closing a file is distinctly different from just closing a file descriptor, these two functions are implemented differently, since file descriptors are not normally shared but file instances frequently can be shared across processes.

... [File: /usr/src/kernel/kern/descrip.c, line: 1294]

```
int
closef(struct file *fp, struct proc *p)
  ...
```

closef() has two arguments: the pointer to the file instance; and the pointer to the process which has the file open. It returns zero if the file close has been successful and an error if it has been unsuccessful. The side-effect of this function is that the file descriptor may be closed and the underlying file object deactivated and possibly reclaimed.

9.3.26.1 How is closef() Implemented?

... [File: /usr/src/kernel/kern/descrip.c, line: 1301]

```
      if (fp == NULL)
              return (0);
  ...
```

If the file instance is already closed, the function returns successfully.

... [File: /usr/src/kernel/kern/descrip.c, line: 1309]

```
if ((p->p_flag & SADVLCK) && fp->f_type == DTYPE_VNODE) {
        lf.l_whence = SEEK_SET;
        lf.l_start = 0;
        lf.l_len = 0;
        lf.l_type = F_UNLCK;
        vp = (struct vnode *)fp->f_data;
        (void) VOP_ADVLOCK(vp, (caddr_t)p, F_UNLCK, &lf, F_POSIX);
}
if (--fp->f_count > 0)
        return (0);
...
```

Otherwise, if the process is using advisory locks and the low level file-like object underneath is a vnode, an unlock request is passed through to the vnode using the **VOP_ADVLOCK** method to unlock any locks associated with the contents of the file. This will only be honored by POSIX locks (f_POSIX), while BSD file locks will be ignored. The reference count for the file is then reduced. If the file is still referenced by another, the function will return, allowing the remainder of the close to complete when the last reference is removed.

... [File: /usr/src/kernel/kern/descrip.c, line: 1324]

```
if ((fp->f_flag & FHASLOCK) && fp->f_type == DTYPE_VNODE) {
        lf.l_whence = SEEK_SET;
        lf.l_start = 0;
        lf.l_len = 0;
        lf.l_type = F_UNLCK;
        vp = (struct vnode *)fp->f_data;
        (void) VOP_ADVLOCK(vp, (caddr_t)fp, F_UNLCK, &lf, F_FLOCK);
}
...
```

In the case of a BSD file lock (F_FLOCK), a file marked with a BSD file lock in its flag (FHASLOCK) corresponds to a vnode that must have all of its locks released prior to the file structure being freed. This is done with a **VOP_ADVLOCK** method on the vnode. Obviously one of the differences between POSIX and BSD locks is that POSIX locks are relative to every file reference by a process while BSD locks are relative to all file references.

... [File: /usr/src/kernel/kern/descrip.c, line: 1333]

```
error = (*fp->f_ops->fo_close)(fp, p);
ffree(fp);
return (error);
...
```

The underlying low-level file-like object's close method (fo_close) is called to perform the closing action on the now unreferenced object. Any error present is saved for return to the caller. The file instance is freed for reuse with the **ffree()** function, and the error (if any) or success is returned to the caller. Note that the use of an error value on a close is of indeterminate value.

9.3.27 What is flock()?

flock(), a BSD system call handler which implements the BSD function, is a BSD advisory file lock system call that may insert or remove an exclusive or shared lock on a file-like object (currently vnodes only). **flock()** is a historical BSD file locking primitive from earlier BSD versions which has since been supplanted by POSIX record locking primitives (using mandatory locks instead of advisory locks). It is implemented only for reverse compatibility.

... [File: /usr/src/kernel/kern/descrip.c, line: 1346]

```
int
flock(p, uap, retval)
        struct proc *p;
        struct args {
                int     fd;
                int     how;
        } *uap;
        int *retval;
    ...
```

flock() has three arguments: the pointer to the process; the pointer to the arguments to the system call (in this case, two—the file descriptor, and the command indicating just how **flock()** should process the file descriptor); and the pointer to the return values. It returns zero if successful or an error code if unsuccessful.

9.3.27.1 How is flock() Implemented?

... [File: /usr/src/kernel/kern/descrip.c, line: 1361]

```
        if ((unsigned)uap->fd >= fdp->fd_nfiles ||
            (fp = fdp->fd_ofiles[uap->fd]) == NULL)
                return (EBADF);
        if (fp->f_type != DTYPE_VNODE)
                return (EOPNOTSUPP);
    ...
```

The file descriptor to be operated on is checked for veracity by seeing if it lies within the bounds of the open file descriptor table and has a file instance associated with it. If it does not, an error (EBADF) is returned. If the file type does not correspond to a vnode (DTYPE_VNODE), then an error (EOPNOTSUPP) is returned because **flock()** does not work on anything but vnodes.

... [File: /usr/src/kernel/kern/descrip.c, line: 1367]

```
        vp = (struct vnode *)fp->f_data;
        lf.l_whence = SEEK_SET;
        lf.l_start = 0;
        lf.l_len = 0;
    ...
```

The vnode pointer is extracted from the cast of the file instance's data field, and a lock instance covering the size of the file is prepared for use. Note that unlike POSIX file record locks, a BSD **flock()** operation covers the entire file.

... [File: /usr/src/kernel/kern/descrip.c, line: 1372]

```
if (uap->how & LOCK_UN) {
        lf.l_type = F_UNLCK;
        fp->f_flag &= ~FHASLOCK;
        return (VOP_ADVLOCK(vp, (caddr_t)fp, F_UNLCK, &lf, F_FLOCK));
}
...
```

If the request to **flock()** is to unlock the file, the unlock request is set into the lock operation and the flag's lock status bit is removed. The vnode is asked to unlock itself by calling the vnode method **VOP_ADVLOCK**, selecting the BSD lock semantics only (F_FLOCK).

... [File: /usr/src/kernel/kern/descrip.c, line: 1378]

```
if (uap->how & LOCK_EX)
        lf.l_type = F_WRLCK;
else if (uap->how & LOCK_SH)
        lf.l_type = F_RDLCK;
else
        return (EBADF);
...
```

The lock request field is checked to decode which kind of lock request is outstanding. If an exclusive lock is requested, a write lock is acquired. If a shared lock is requested, a read lock is acquired. If neither lock is requested, an unimplemented lock request or no lock request is being indicated—this is an illegal request which is signalled back to the caller with an error (EBADF).[73]

... [File: /usr/src/kernel/kern/descrip.c, line: 1385]

```
fp->f_flag |= FHASLOCK;
if (uap->how & LOCK_NB)
        return (VOP_ADVLOCK(vp, (caddr_t)fp, F_SETLK, &lf, F_FLOCK));
return (VOP_ADVLOCK(vp, (caddr_t)fp, F_SETLK, &lf, F_FLOCK|F_WAIT));
...
```

The file's lock status flag is set (FHASLOCK) and **VOP_ADVLOCK** is called on the vnode to engage the lock (F_SETLK). If the lock request has been requested not to block, the operation will not be allowed to wait for it to complete (F_WAIT); otherwise, it will wait until completion.

9.3.28 What is fdopen()?

fdopen() is a driver open routine that coupled with **dupfdopen()** has the effect of implementing a pseudo-device driver interface to the file descriptors themselves. Thus, the file descriptors of a process can be identified and opened as if they were ordinary files. **fdopen()** arranges (by means of a kludge) to signal that an open request

---

[73] This should probably be an EINVAL error but is left as is for compatibility with past mistakes.

will be satisfied at a higher level of abstraction of the kernel by substituting the reference to the driver special file with a reference to the file descriptor associated with the minor device (associated with this special device). It does this by means of always returning an error while recording separately a nonzero value in a reserved field inside the process's proc structure (p_dupfd).

... [File: /usr/src/kernel/kern/descrip.c, line: 1401]

```
static int
fdopen(dev_t dev, int mode, int type, struct proc *p)
...
```

fdopen() has four arguments: the device number; open mode; open type; and the pointer to the process opening the file. It always returns an error (ENODEV). This special case error is generated to hide a message for the file descriptor layer.

9.3.28.1 How is fdopen() Implemented?

... [File: /usr/src/kernel/kern/descrip.c, line: 1413]

```
        p->p_dupfd = minor(dev);
        return (ENODEV);
...
```

The minor device number is extracted from the device number and recorded in a special field of the proc structure. This field is then used along with the ENODEV error to send a message to the higher level layers of the system that the file descriptor associated with the minor device number's value should be used as the source of the file attached to the open file descriptor attempting to open the file descriptor pseudo-device.

9.3.28.2 386BSD fdopen() Design Choices and Trade-Offs

The reason why this action is done with a kludge is because passing the reference off to another separate file (via a transparent **dup2()**) actually occurs at a much higher level of abstraction than that of devices.[74] In a sense, what we are doing is sending a message up the level of abstraction ladder so that it may be acted upon at that level.

9.3.29 What is dupfdopen()?

dupfdopen() is an internal kernel function used by the file open primitive **open()** (see fs/fs_sys.c) to implement the effect of the message generated by **fdopen()**. It is a special case duplication function that opens the file descriptor referenced by the driver message and transparently allocates and initializes a new file descriptor to point to the desired file, reusing the existing file descriptor that had opened the file descriptor pseudo-device.

---

[74] Devices lie below vnodes, and vnodes lie below files and file descriptors in level of abstraction.

... [File: /usr/src/kernel/kern/descrip.c, line: 1435]

```
int
dupfdopen(struct filedesc *fdp, int indx, int dfd, int mode)
    ...
```

dupfdopen() has four arguments: the pointer to the file descriptor table of the process; the index of the file descriptor to be reused; the index to the file descriptor derived from the driver; and the mode of the open special device used to gain access to the file descriptor. It returns zero if successful, an error code (EBADF) if the file descriptor was not open to begin with or already is the file descriptor used to open the special device, or an error (EACCES) if the underlying file has not already been opened in a compatible way with the open request on the file descriptor.

9.3.29.1 How is dupfdopen() Implemented?

... [File: /usr/src/kernel/kern/descrip.c, line: 1448]

```
    fp = fdp->fd_ofiles[indx];
    if ((u_int)dfd >= fdp->fd_nfiles ||
        (wfp = fdp->fd_ofiles[dfd]) == NULL || fp == wfp)
    ...
```

The descriptor returned from the file descriptor pseudo-device driver **open()** message is checked to see if it falls within the bounds of a valid file descriptor. If it doesn't or if it is not open or does not correspond to the file descriptor already open to the device (a recursive evaluation is in progress), an error (EBADF) is returned and the function terminates.

... [File: /usr/src/kernel/kern/descrip.c, line: 1457]

```
    if (((mode & (FREAD|FWRITE)) | wfp->f_flag) != wfp->f_flag)
            return (EACCES);
    ...
```

The mode of the attempted open is checked against the flags of the file associated with the indirectly referenced file descriptor to ensure that the access modes are compatible or a subset.

... [File: /usr/src/kernel/kern/descrip.c, line: 1459]

```
    fdp->fd_ofiles[indx] = wfp;
    fdp->fd_ofileflags[indx] = fdp->fd_ofileflags[dfd];
    wfp->f_count++;
    if (indx > fdp->fd_lastfile)
            fdp->fd_lastfile = indx;
    return (0);
    ...
```

The file descriptor's file pointer for the formerly open descriptor to the pseudo-device is now overwritten with the file pointer of the file descriptor determined from the minor device number of the file descriptor pseudo-device open, along with the file flags from the same descriptor. The reference count on the now shared file is then increased to account for the new reference. Since a file descriptor has been allocated, a check is made to see if the newly allocated file descriptor is the largest allocated file index. If so, the last file index is updated and the function returns successfully.

Exercises

9.1 Many programs are run repeatedly, so a cache of executable images is kept. What information is cached in the current implementation? What items might also be cached to enhance **execve()**'s efficiency?

9.2 **a)** Does an operating system kernel itself need file descriptors for operation?
b) If management of files and file descriptors were moved to a system call emulator, what problem would surface in maintaining compatibility?

9.3 Assume an application is written two different ways: [A] a single process using select on a set of file descriptors, and [B] multiple threads with one blocked on each file descriptor.
a) Assuming a single processor, if all file descriptors become active at once, compute and compare the minimum overhead possible for system calls and context switches.
b) Same as **a)** but assuming multiple processors (4).

9.4 What is the affect of using the **readv()** and **writev()** system calls to handle requests with a small number of I/O vectors?

9.5 Contrast mandatory file locking versus advisory file locking.

APPENDIX A: THE 386BSD KERNEL PROGRAM SOURCE ORGANIZATION

Starting with Release 1.0, the 386BSD kernel has been radically changed. Utilizing the lessons learned in modular design, the kernel is now composed of independent *modules* that may be included into the kernel program simply by adding a line into a parameterized makefile describing a system (e.g. odysseus.mk).

A kernel is just a collection of modules. Each module (for example, ./**kern**) is entirely contained within a single directory in the master kernel directory, and may be composed of many source files and organized into a hierarchy of directories within it, such as ./**kern/i386**, /**kern/vm**, and so on. The configuration makefiles are located in the ./**config** directory, which also contains common subsystem parameterized makefiles that may be included as shorthand descriptions of commonly chosen sets of modules (e.g., config.inet.mk).

Each module contains code, private common header files, and mechanisms for construction. Optionally, machine-dependent code can be conditionally present (e.g., **inet/in_cksum_i386.c**) to handle internal optimizations for a specific architecture; however, extensive use of this is discouraged as such might more properly belong in the architecture-dependent portion of the kernel as a standard interface for all modules.

The Core Kernel Module

The core kernel ./**kern** is itself a module that is composed of basic operating system mechanisms, subsystems, and interfaces to other modules. While most of the kernel is architecture-independent, all architecture-specific code is located within an architecture directory (ex:./**kern/i386**). The kernel module is unique in exporting interfaces to both other kernel modules and user program, as all other modules have private contents and are only visible to other modules via registration with the kernel module on a particular kernel interface.

Substantial subsystems of the kernel also have separate directories that allow implementation to be divided into multiple source files to facilitate decomposition into smaller component parts (e.g., ./**kern/fs**, ./**kern/vm**). A subroutine directory

---

(**./kern/subr**) contains general purpose functions that may be used by any part of the kernel.

Common Interface and Data Structure Include Files

The kernel interacts with the user program and other kernel modules to achieve its function as a kind of level of abstraction "traffic cop." It shares interfaces and data structures in an organized fashion via the C language **#include** files. To minimize unnecessary interdependence, files are shared only on a *need to know* basis by means of scope. Include files that are *private* to a subsystem are contained within the subsystem's directory of source files, and are not included by any other source files lower or higher in the directory hierarchy. Thus, no directory paths are incorporated into the source files themselves.[1]

The Role of Other Kernel Modules

The kernel module, while independent in interface, is *not* able to function on its own as a standalone program in the computer system. It requires additional modules to adapt its software interfaces for use with the particular collection of hardware on which it is to be run.

A Bird's Eye View of the Entire System

Low-level device driver modules (e.g., **./wd, ./pccons**) perform these functions, along with other higher level drivers (e.g., **./ufs, ./termios**) that further adapt the device-independent interface (**devif_XXX**) layer of functionality into program-manageable abstractions (files, directories, terminal devices). The program-manageable abstractions are themselves made visible to user-mode programs running on top of the kernel (**/bin/sh**) via applications program interfaces. API's, in turn, adapt to a higher level environment for running applications programs for the computer's user.

The composition of all of these different entities, operating on different levels of abstraction, form the operating system proper. An operating system is just a contrivance for running applications programs, supplying a top level of abstraction to an applications environment for the computer's user.

Why a Modular Kernel?

Our perspective is that *hierarchy* and *levels of abstraction* afford a way of compartmentalizing portions of the software architecture, such that the extension of function can be managed efficiently. Fewer interface contradictions arise when the

---

[1] Except for *well-known* names incorporated already into the programming environment by means of a *standard*.

correct layering of abstraction is maintained—thus, modular decomposition can be beneficial for reducing the inherent costs of a software architecture.

Modularity in itself is not universally a positive value. It can be an irrelevant straight-jacket for performance or implementation and can also increase the cost of a software architecture to maintain. The art of choosing an appropriate architecture comes hand-in-hand with the choice of appropriate solutions for the problems presented, while revisiting the overall architecture occasionally to see that it still remains relevant for the use it is applied.

Tailoring the 386BSD Kernel to a Non-standard Configuration

The 386BSD kernel programs configure modules by evaluating simple symbolic scripts embedded in each module.[2] It presumes a standard *safe* configuration for each module. If the required configuration is different, these scripts can be overridden by the contents of the system's configuration file (/.**config**), located in the booted root filesystem. Modules can be defeated or logically reassigned new parameters. The primary function of this file is to compensate for configuration conflicts as a secondary avenue to the embedded configuration of each module.

Since IBM PC peripheral configuration can itself easily allow for cases where automatic configuration can be fooled or, worse yet, potentially jam the system, default automatic configuration is intentionally limited to the *safe* cases described by manufacturers as the standard defaults. In some cases (like Ethernet cards), even these safe cases can contain potentially *unsafe* cases; thus, any of these options are considered an exceptional case that must be handled in the system's configuration file.

The naive user should not toy with this file idly, as little is gained while much can be lost. Nor should the compulsive system programmer view this as a place to put ultimate configuration information—the proper place for such is in user mode configuration and control programs, where enough "elbow room" already exists to work on serious configuration and conflict resolution. The point of this file is to deal with the "Gordian Knot" problems that cannot otherwise be addressed. Specifically, this file is *not* destined to be another CONFIG.SYS file, and thus its syntax, role, and deployment is intentionally kept minimal. It is much more valuable as a *simple feature*.

Building a Kernel Program

In use, this arrangement is much akin to the layout of utilities in the rest of the system. To build a stock kernel out of the stock release, type "**make**" in the kernel directory **/usr/src/kernel**. The stock kernel simply selects the modules necessary to run the system on a ordinary IBM clone PC. This defacto industry standard is a system with a

---

[2] See each module's manual entry for details and "man config" for the overall arrangement and strategy.

video display, IDE drive, floppy, serial and parallel ports. Other "ready-made" configurations are available in the configuration subdirectory, by copying one to the computer's host name file (e.g., host "foo" would use the **config/foo.mk** file). Custom configurations may be made by editing the file with a text editor.

On initial (re)configuration, the configured kernel should have its compilation dependencies set by issuing a "**make depend**." A stale set of object files can be erased by issuing a "**make clean**" prior to recreating a kernel.

Testing a New Kernel Program

A freshly made kernel can be tested by installing it with the "**make install**" command, which places it in the root as the file **/386bsd.alt**. This file can be booted selectively by the system bootstrap (see "**man bootstrap**"). Alternatively, a bootable floppy (see "**man floppy**") can be used to hold the new kernel and its dedicated root filesystem to check out a new kernel in isolation from the main system.

The *-debug* and *-specify* flags can be used with the bootstrap to invoke run time diagnostic facilities to illustrate kernel operation on the console as a means to allow fault isolation.

Installing a New Kernel Program

After arriving at a satisfactory new kernel, it can be exchanged with the existing kernel's file **/386bsd** prior to a reboot to bring the system up with the new kernel as the installed kernel. It may be desirable to save the last installed kernel (e.g., **/386bsd.old**) for an indefinite period of time until the new kernel has proven that it is correctly configured for use as the installed kernel.

Should a newly installed kernel fail to boot the system successfully, proper operation can be restored by booting the last installed kernel manually. Should no usable copy of the kernel be available or the root filesystem be damaged, either a bootable floppy or the distribution master CD-ROM can be booted to repair or reinstall the software.

Debugging a New Kernel Program

In addition to the default diagnostics of the kernel program, the kernel debugger can be incorporated into the kernel program to allow *ordinary* program debugging facilities (breakpoints, single-stepping of code, stack back traces) to be performed on the system (see "**man ddb**"). Also, system panic postmortem memory dumps can be captured (via the **savecore** command executed in **/etc/rc** on system reboot in the directory **/var/crash**) and examined.[3] To look at a running system, "**gdb -k /386bsd**

---

[3] Via the **gdb** debugger by type, such as **gdb -k /var/crash/system**.N **/var/crash/ram**.N, for the Nth dump you wish to examine.

/dev/mem" can be used. In addition, the in-kernel debugger can be entered at any time while the system is operating by typing CTRL, ALT, and ESC keys simultaneously. Finally, **printf()**s can be scattered in the kernel for debugging, just as in ordinary user program.

Debugging the kernel, as with kernel programming in general, is not done lightly. Prior to attempting this, you may wish to familiarize yourself with the other existing **386BSD Reference CD-ROM** source code documentation,[4] articles,[5] and books in this series.

Adding a Module to a Kernel

One can obtain a new kernel module for use with the kernel by receiving a set of files that will be placed in the kernel directory under a uniquely named subdirectory. To incorporate it into a kernel, reconfigure the configuration makefile associated with the system (e.g., **config/myhost.mk**), update dependencies ("**make depend**"), and rebuild. Some options may require the system's configuration file (**/.config** or **CONFIG.BSD**) to be altered to tailor the kernel for configuration conflicts or additional resources.[6]

Creating a New Module for the Kernel

To write a new device driver, examine an existing similar device driver to see how it makes use of the existing interfaces. In addition, **kern/config.c** (see **Chapter 4**) can be examined for hints on configuration details of implementation and other interfaces that may be better employed in the proposed new driver. Finally, the device-independent interface is documented briefly in the manual (see "**man devif**").

You should choose a new directory for the module, as well as a unique set of identifiers (major numbers and character string ID). If you would like to incorporate your driver in the next release of 386BSD, contact the authors so that we can register the names and numbers for unique use with your driver.

---

[4] The **386BSD Reference CD-ROM** (November, 1994), Miller-Freeman Inc., contains a complete bootable system and source code as well as 386BSD on-line manuals and other reference materials.
[5] The **Porting UNIX to the 386** series (January-November 1991, February 1992-July 1992) and follow-on articles on 386BSD appearing in **Dr. Dobbs Journal**. This series is available as part of the **386BSD Reference CD-ROM**.
[6] See *An Example Configuration Script* in **Chapter 4**.

Kernel Source Directory Hierarchy

Here is a brief description of the existing kernel program source tree.

Individual Kernel Build Description (makefiles):

config/	Configuration-dependent files

Kernel Module (kern):

kern/	Core kernel module subsystems & interfaces
kern/fs	Virtual file system interface
kern/i386	i386 machine-dependent kernel
kern/net	Network interface
kern/opt	Optional subsystems of the core kernel module
kern/opt/compat43	Remaining 4.3BSD compatibility
kern/opt/ktrace	Kernel tracing mechanism
kern/opt/shm	System V shared memory
kern/socket	BSD sockets subsystem
kern/subr	Internal subroutine library of the kernel
kern/vm	Virtual memory subsystem

Kernel Module Interface Description (to other modules and user/system programs):

include	Kernel global include files
include/dev	Device driver related include files
include/domain	Communication domain related files include files
include/fs	Filesystem related include files
include/i386	Public 386 machine-dependent include files
include/i386/inline	386 machine-dependent inline functions
include/ic	Integrated circuit defined register include files
include/portable	Public shared machine-dependent include files
include/sys	Public operating system interface include files

Other independent kernel modules:

ddb	DDB kernel debugger module
isa	[E]ISA/VLB/PCI Bus driver
as, aux, com, ed, fd,	Peripheral Device Drivers
is, lpt, mcd, npx, pccons,	Other Drivers
wd, wt, ...	
bpf, devtty, log,	Software Pseudo Drivers
loop, pty, mem	
slip, termios	Line Disciplines
fifo, isofs, mfs,	Filesystems
nfs, ufs, ...	
inet, raw, route,	Communications Domains and Networking
un, ...	

Multiple Simultaneous Kernel Compilation Directories

By default, the stock 386BSD system only has a single kernel compilation directory. This is done for convenience and simplicity, since in most cases, only a single configuration is ever used. In addition, since the kernel is migrating to a run-time configuration arrangement, it is counterproductive to have compile-time and run-time configuration competing for use. However, sometimes it is valuable to have a vector of different kernel configurations, often in private user directories. By setting the system base variable to the path of the desired kernel source tree ($S in a copy of **/usr/src/kernel/Makefile** into the compilation directory), multiple compilation directories can be placed anywhere in the system.

Alternatively, one can use a directory of symbolic links to point to the unmodified module directories in an alternative kernel base directory which has a different module complement. This can be helpful in gradually transitioning from a particular set of modules to a different set of modules incrementally.

Future Work on Modular Configuration

Appropriately for Release 1.0 of 386BSD, the modular kernel configuration done thus far is only the first step in the process of turning 386BSD into a modern modular kernel. Much other work is still in progress (and hence not contained in this release), since the work contained within is still predicated on the existing kernel architecture. Hopefully this other work will become available in later releases:

- Filesystem and communications domain modular interfaces.
- Complete elimination of outmoded, non-modular dependencies.
- Separate compilation, relocation, and dynamic loading/unloading.
- Module interface registration and dynamic scoping.
- New stackable link layer socket interface to packet drivers.
- Dynamically bound system call/exception handlers.

Other longer term design goals affecting 386BSD modular kernel design are under consideration in the indefinite future. Given adequate future resource, the following areas may be explored in further work:

- Emulation libraries for multiple operating system personalities.
- Externalization of kernel executable file formats.
- Replacement of special devices with portals.

As with any complicated and long-term project, these items will appear only if there is continued interest in 386BSD. Up to this point, there has been a gratifying pronouncement of encouragement from the research, educational, and professional communities with respect to exploring novel areas of operating systems design. We hope that this will continue.

With the recent availability of inexpensive or freeware INTERNET UNIX-like systems running TCP/IP on PC's, the number of INTERNET hosts (now standing at 3.8 million) has increased dramatically, with a third quarter 1994 overall growth rate of 21% and a projected *100 million* hosts by 1999[2]! However, connecting to the net brings its own problems, as the now famous Morris worm demonstrated.

While there are many facilities and packages which can mitigate this risk, they are usually comprehensive approaches requiring a great deal of additional overhead to implement and administer. However, since most PC environments are now managed by only one person (typically, the user of the system), this system management overhead cannot easily be spread among many systems and networks. Hence, the user-administrator, who has neither the time nor the expertise to properly implement and maintain these facilities, is left to fend for himself. Since the minimal desire of a typical user-administrator connected to the INTERNET is just that certain files and facilities never be accessible, either from outside of the PC, outside of the group, or outside of the company or institution, a different approach is required—one which introduces network-level security on a intuitive basis, yet is still actually robustly *secure.*

Role-based security is a mechanism orthogonal to authentication, encryption, and threat detection mechanisms. It is a minimal mandatory access control (MAC) policy that restricts access with a low-level of abstraction mechanism that is hard if not impossible to bypass, yet requires little in the way of knowledge or maintenance overhead from the user. Role-based security derives its name from the concept of *roles* used to simplify the description of allowable access characteristics of an host's user. Coupled with the concept of *access path*, roles provide a degree of geographic classification (where the user is located) in order to determine a specific role. As a consequence, roles directly determine the scope of access of a user to files and privileged operations.

[1] This article appeared in a shorter fom as *Role-Based Network Security*, in **Dr. Dobbs Journal** (May 1995).
[2] *INTERNET Domain Survey*, Mark Lottor, **Connexions** (November 1994).

Conventional Approaches to Securing Systems

Balancing the need to provide a secure environment with that of a convenient and accessible one is always difficult. Typically, the routes to access are mediated by locks requiring a combination.[3] Account passwords provided a reasonable degree of security when machines were relatively isolated—however, with network access and some work, an intruder can now attempt to either pick the combination of an account or intercept the use of the password as it transits the network. An intruder can also case large numbers of network host computers looking for vulnerabilities (stale/common passwords, alterable system control files, and so forth) with relative ease. As such, machines can be compromised even though the intruder may have no idea where the machine resides or what it looks like, as he will never gain physical access to it (see **Drive-by Casualties on the Information Highway**).

Many existing facilities and packages have been developed to help the user cope with this increased threat, beginning with the most fundamental (Kerberos, COPS, and so forth). These additions seek to plug the holes through which vermin might enter by beefing up existing authentication mechanisms and attempting to discover vulnerabilities before the bad guy does. Kerberos-extended network utilities (like **rlogin**, **ftp**, and **telnet**) also encrypt communications to avoid passing information in clear text where it might be intercepted.

Drive-by Casualties on the Information Highway

Putting a PC on the INTERNET is akin to having a a highway constructed right behind a formerly quiet rural homestead. Most Windows-based PCs only support on-ramp client programs (like **mail**, **ftp**, **telnet**, **mosaic**, ...) to obtain network service manually. In contrast, more powerful UNIX and UNIX-like systems (such as Solaris, Windows NT, 386BSD, and so on) also provide server programs (i.e., **telnetd**, **ftpd**, **sendmail**). These programs act as off-ramps to the network, allowing wayward travellers and snoops the possibility to look over the fence and into your PC's backyard.

If a PC is used to serve information (even if only to a few friends and yourself when at work), then the security of your electronic doors and windows must be of paramount concern. Just as it is a shock to come home and find it ransacked, it's just as bad to log into the system and find your personal electronic files tampered, destroyed, or posted on the network for all to see. Even if a computer is used only to consume service, security is still a

---

[3] Password authentication and file access mode discretionary access control, also known as DAC.

[4] A bit vector of all the privileges.

[5] 386BSD has more than 50 distinct privileges.

Unfortunately, these solutions require additional administrative overhead by the user, because they are yet another facility which must be maintained. Worse yet, this overhead increases with the sophistication of the security mechanisms and the model of security that it attempts to reach. Failure to attend to the system management details required to keep such systems current may compromise the integrity of the entire system—thus, defeating the purpose of these facilities in the first place.

Network-Level Security Elements

Like network gateway firewalls, role-based security is simple to employ yet hard to bypass. In effect, the firewall is integrated into the operating system so that it surrounds files, sockets and system facilities. Unlike a gateway firewall, it does not require administration and monitoring to review new access requirements and intrusion attempts.

The role-based security model consists of four key elements: *roles and privileges*, *access path*, *transparency*, and *mandatory access control*. Each of these elements is critical to creating a comprehensive yet simple approach to network-level security.

The First Element: Roles and Privileges

In many secure systems, privileges are recorded as bits set in a *list of privileges*.[4] The lion's share of privileges revolve around system management functions, such as manipulating or add new devices, reformatting disks, changing the access or protection or ownership of a file, and so forth. As a system is enhanced more privileges are usually added, so this number of privileges may become large and varying. Indeed, one

concern, since the organization and management of the information exchanged with the network becomes a significant issue. (You wouldn't want to inadvertently incorporate a file containing your credit card numbers into a broadcast electronic letter sent to a news group, would you?)

Unlike a real house, however, the door to our electronic analog can also become a casualty of an expert lockpicking machine (like a supercomputer) despite our best efforts at securing it, or an electronic neighbor might take a snapshot of our combination as we unlock the door. Worse yet, these techniques (along with others even more sinister) can be automated and launched by a bad guy from anywhere in the world. In sum, while your little PC might not have a high profile, no one wants to be a drive-by casualty on the information superhighway.

While your PC (like your house) can be secured with good locks, alarmed, and even may be watched by a security patrol, it may still be compromised if a consistent security management policy has not been put in place to maintain the integrity of the security system itself. Locks and keys must be rotated, alarm systems must be expanded if an addition is added, alarms must be responded to, and security patrols must be reviewed and

might even create privileges merely due to the existence of other privileges as a way of enabling groups of them or offering special treatment. At some point, the management or control of literally hundreds of privileges itself becomes a formidable task.[5]

Rather than affording such a fine-grain and difficult-to-manage concept, the older list of privileges model can be replaced by a *role* model. A role is akin to an actor's assigned character. Unlike traditional UNIX systems (which have one ultimate privilege called the superuser or root account), systems using role-based security identify the use of privileges inside the kernel on a case-by-case basis. The role concept is essential to compressing the complexities of the model of security, much as the description of a character at the beginning of a book provides an intrinsic understanding of that character over the course of the story.

Roles compress the notion of privilege. If new privileges or file access rights are added to the system, they are added only to suit the needs of roles—the roles themselves generally do not change. This means that as our security needs and environment in the operating system become more elaborate, the model still stays simple from the user perspective.

Unlike UNIX set user ID / set group ID features that allow another group or user ID to be used as a proxy, roles are set once by the access path and never allowed to change—they are independent of these user/group ID concepts. These are then used by lower levels of the kernel to bound access.

The Second Element: Access Path

A user makes access to information or services from the computer via an *access path*. This may

overseen. And since computers, unlike houses, can be entered through an amazing number of contrived ways (akin to a thief coming down a chimney, squeezing through the sewer line, or hanging from a tree), providing adequate coverage can itself become a full-time job (which may even require its own oversight in turn). If the computer is left to handle all this, we might work down the costs a bit, but we will still be stuck with managing the process, and if we are not careful the bad guy might still compromise our computer security system (just like bypassing the wires to an alarm system). Short of defending your computer with **Home Alone** bear traps, what is an already overloaded computer user to do? The answer lies in restructuring the problem intrinsically.

Role-based security is like having a house with a door opening onto a public back entrance which intrinsically restricts access, while access via the front door (unreachable from the public side) remains unrestricted. Thus, even if authentication is broached, certain privileges cannot be obtained and certain files are never accessible. Thus, administration can be reduced to the bare minimum—that of labelling restricted files so that the system can know what information cannot leave the premises.

SOURCE CODE SECRETS: THE BASIC KERNEL

be done through physical access to the computer's console or through an attached serial line, or via network communications. Roles are defined by the access path to the computer; thus, the way in which the information is accessible may differdepending where the information may be traveling to. Since the mechanisms that determine path are extremely low-level, the bad guy must find ways to imitate access, either by gaining physical access or by contriving to simulate physical access.

By using a role-based model, the scope of access is limited without increasing system management overhead.[6] For example, to gain fundamental access to management functions (the method by which most computers are subverted), one must know not only the passwords but also the appropriate required setting. This geographic determination makes it far more difficult for an intruder, because he must now attempt to subvert *all* of the mechanisms that determine knowledge of geographic location. Thus, access path qualifies a user to access restricted privileges and files, in the same way that a password is used to authenticate a user.

The Third Element: Transparency

Many attempts at improving the level of security of an operating system pervasively affect both the operating system and the host on which it is installed.[7] As such, it may be almost impossible to remove the security mechanism when needed because it is interwoven into the system, making security mechanisms less desirable to employ.[8] With our role-based model, a high degree of transparency is a paramount requirement, because otherwise it would be too troublesome for a 386BSD user to consider employing it. The demand for transparency affects all areas of the role-based security design, to wit:

1. The role-based security implementation is located in the kernel program entirely (except for a single utility program), requiring no changes in utility or application programs.

2. There are no external interfaces for programmers to subvert or oversee. There are no conflicts with existing industry standards, either defacto or official.

3. It is entirely independent of other security facilities (encryption, authentication, intrusion detection).

4. It requires no change to system operation, network management, or other procedures, and minimal knowledge to manage in use.

---

[6] E.g., no user account profile need be maintained.
[7] If not the entire environment of the network on which it is used as well.
[8] Like adding, removing, or changing a padlock, for example.

The Fourth Element: Mandatory Access Control

Another requirement for a secure system is that it provide a mechanism which can guarantee that certain sensitive files can only be accessed by certain characters playing these roles—even if a more trusted role is tricked by a lesser one.[9] A Mandatory Access Control (MAC) policy is thus used to maintain the integrity of the information by ensuring that any files that may contain *elements* of the information will be kept at the same restricted access as that of the original file. Thus, the system is *mandatory* in that the computer, not the user, maintains the restrictions in all cases so that a user who may not be aware of a program's scope of vulnerability does not inadvertently compromise the information.

With role-based security, files can be marked so that contents cannot be sent outside of a specified geographic zone.[10] Once marked, even if a privileged account is compromised, the information of a file so marked cannot be obtained outside of its restricted zone. Files created by programs using such restricted files are defacto restricted as well, avoiding the accidental release of information outside of the zone. This effect is achieved without alteration of the user program environment or interfering with existing industry standards (like POSIX). Thus, it can be added (or removed) from a system without affecting any existing programs other than the kernel.

Mandatory Access Control is complementary to Discretionary Access Control (DAC), which in a UNIX system corresponds to the permission attributes of read/write/execute access methods across user, user's group, or system-wide access.[11] The great virtue of Mandatory Access Control is the fact that it is automatically managed—the user need not be aware of it. Many UNIX systems, in contrast, are compromised simply because the user does not manually set the access permission bits properly so that other users cannot read or write a file. With MAC, the operating system automatically supplies the restriction.

By reducing management of restricted files to one simple operation that is further managed by the system automatically in a fail-safe way, the user obtains the benefits of a secure environment without having to intimately manage such details. Since the mechanism is implemented at the lowest levels of abstraction in the system, it is difficult if not impossible to subvert directly.

---

[9] E.g., asked to hand over a file or run a program that passes out the information indirectly.

[10] Currently, host, local network, and external network.

[11] N.B. Many UNIX systems extend this concept still further with the MULTICS-like concept of an Access Control List or **acl**, which allows access rights to be specified on a per-user basis—this mechanism also presents advantages and problems of an extreme sort.

An Example of Simple Network-Level Security Using 386BSD

In the 386BSD Release 1.0 implementation of role-based security, there are four roles. The primary[12] role controls the lion's share of administrative privileges. The secondary role has access to most of the privileged files, and also has the ability to mark/unmark files as being privileged. The third role can obtain access and mark as privileged a much lesser grade of files, and also has the ability to go between systems on the immediate local area network to which the computer is attached. The last role is the least trusted. Since the only thing we know for certain is that he has come in from somewhere outside the LAN, we don't trust him with anything privileged. Thus, any attempts to invoke any substantive privilege or access to a privileged file will not be successful. What is common among all of these roles is that the way in which we identify them is done solely by the way in which they gain access to our system, each in varying degrees of trusted path, with the last trusted the least.

With 386BSD role-based security, a user who is assigned either the second or third role can indicate a file is sensitive by setting a mode on a directory in which that files lies. A file so marked cannot be referenced outside of the scope of access allowed to those two roles. Thus, a file may not have its contents sent by any user across the network if it marked in this manner. If the file is copied to another file or incorporated into a portion of another file, the new file by default will likewise be marked at the level of the most sensitive part incorporated into it.

With this implementation of network-level role-based security, files can be restricted to remaining on the host computer (when information should be restricted to a user's own PC) or within the immediate local area network (when the LAN is considered to be adequately secure, yet the information should not be accessible or distributed outside of the LAN organization).

Advantages and Drawbacks to a Simple Role-Based Model

While role-based security can be extended into a more elaborate arrangement, its primary advantage is one of simplicity:

1. It is a model which can be easily fit into any extant modern operating system.

2. It is easy to understand and administrate, yet hard to subvert because it remains so fundamental.

One key problem resulting from creeping featurism in security that this approach avoids is that as the complexity increases, the possibility of holes develop which may

---

[12] Purposely put into the background.

ultimately defeat the entire point. Through simplicity, one avoids those nasty corner cases.

One other advantage of this simple arrangement is that, since one must be physically present to install an operating system (like 386BSD) anyways, it is possible to incorporate security at this point without requiring the user to go through additional administrative hurdles to gain access to the most simple and straightforward of procedures. Easing the decision-making burden for the user during installation in a safe way is critical, since it is at this time that a user will know the least about what items to secure. For example, a naive user wishing to prevent any possible disclosure of personal files whatsoever need only mark the home directory of his account as being not accessible over a wide area network—the computer itself takes care of sensitive system-related files automatically.

The chief drawback of this approach is its own advantage—that of inflexibly binding privilege and access rights with the path of access. This mechanism is so low-level in terms of level of abstraction that it is difficult (if not impossible) to bypass. However, because it is so low-level, it can also get in the way during times that one might really want to read a privileged file via the network. With clarity of definition, flexibility is usually lost.

Likewise, remote system management is also impeded. However, since a user-administrator generally does his own system administration on-site (there really are no good network-based system management tools intended for a single user-administrator yet), this is not considered a problem at this time.

Removing Restrictions on Sensitive Files

There are times when one might like to remove the restrictions on a particular file, and as such a utility is provided to allow restrictions to be removed by a user with the appropriate role. This utility, however, requires authorization directly from the console through what is called a *known secure path*. If the authorization is not supplied, the restriction is not removed. For example, suppose the bad guy had somehow gotten a user running with a privileged role to execute something useful for him—in this case, the console would suddenly spout an unexpected request for authorization. This particularly quaint attempt at subversion could then be tracked down and the bad guy revealed, all without any loss of integrity.[13]

Subverting Role-Based Security

Any security mechanism can be subverted, and exclusive reliance upon any one of these measures should always be taken with a grain of salt. Role-based security, like

---

[13] Note that this is the only violation of our mandatory access control policy possible and it is again tightly controlled—it is a convenience for operation only.

other security mechanisms, is not fool-proof.[14] However, it is possible to characterize all of these ways by how the mechanism works—the roles provide the scope of access to privileges and restricted files, and the roles are governed solely by access path. Clearly. the easiest way to compromise the system is to gain access to a trusted path (e.g., another host directly connected to the same network or physical access to the machine's console). Thus, role-based security is not intended to deal with insider related threats. The implicit assumption in role-based security is that physical access to the machine itself is trusted and access to the immediate LAN is trusted within limits.

Why the Need for Simple Network-Level Security?

For the many people planning to put their PC or workstation on the network, security considerations usually get lost in the difficulty of just installing the software, connecting to the network, and learning the ropes. We ourselves have noted with concern the great increase in hosts on the INTERNET which have not been properly secured, or are running versions of software with known security holes, and we believe it is only a matter of time before another another bad guy tries to one-up the Morris worm.

However, we also understand that it is extremely difficult to maintain, much less create and install, a secure environment. Less than ten years ago, this was not a great problem, since at that time only major sites (with their own full-time administrators) provided network access of any kind. However, with the increase in hosts, there has been no real decrease in administrative overhead.[15] Thus, we have scoped role-based security for their needs.

Role-based security as implemented is not intended as a complete answer for all security needs. For example, a different set of rules employing this mechanism mentioned here might be more appropriate if we wanted to deal with inside or internal threats. This leads to a much thornier problem of who watches the watchers. However, we hope it gives the Morris wanna-be's a harder time and saves users a lot of aggravation. By the way, it wouldn't hurt to get a burglar alarm or a dog for your house—that way, physical access to your PC and your home is protected too.

---

[14] We ourselves have already devised ways to subvert it, as in the example mentioned above.
[15] Especially with UNIX systems, but this can also be said of OS/2 and Windows 95.

APPENDIX C: A DYNAMIC MAKE ENVIRONMENT FOR LARGE SCALE APPLICATIONS DEVELOPMENT

As the complexity of software development environments has increased, the elaborations upon just how to construct a program have grown as well—not only among programs composed of multiple modules but even within modules created either automatically or by another module or tool. For example, a DOS/Windows applications developer may commonly deal with programs involving twenty to as many as five hundred source files, when only five years ago this was not usually the case.

Since the speed of all software development is ultimately linked to the compile/edit/debug route, the faster one can regenerate the program, find the problem in the new version, alter the source, and regenerate it yet again for another test directly determines the quality and timeliness of the product. As such, mechanisms to speed development while easily managing large amounts of code become an economic as well as personal necessity. Reusable common code, usually in the form of libraries, is one way that a developer can mitigate these costs, while honing techniques with existing programming tools is yet another.

A dynamic **make** environment for large scale programming is one extremely important yet often underutilized[1] mechanism which can minimize the time spent in the regeneration of an application under development—hence, reducing the cost. By better applying the latent capabilities of **make** to create programs from shared rules to inherit configuration dependencies from unrelated modules, redundant configuration information is eliminated. The makefile size is reduced as well, since **make** is essentially creating its own program internally. Finally, clever use of these shared rules can allow us to develop extensible make *libraries* where hundreds of programs can invoke this shared information base merely by inclusion.

Earlier Uses of Make

Prior to the development of the original UNIX **make** facility at Bell Laboratories, UNIX shell scripts (like their DOS cousin's batch files) were used to mechanically recreate

---

[1] And frequently underdocumented.

software regardless of whether various parts had changed or not. Using defined rules and a dependency graph, the standard **make** facility allowed software developers to recreate only the portions of software whose source files had changed. This meant that if only one or two modules had changed during a debugging cycle, for example, only those modules would be recompiled and merged into the master program instead of recompiling all modules.

Make was used with statically defined makefiles containing a set of targets and rules used to build and consolidate them. These files were written and altered manually when the configuration changed. On the average, a programming system[2] would only have a dozen or so makefiles total. However, it was the popularity at that time of **yacc** and **lex** which made **make** usage an imperative for program development, since debugging and recompiling these interdependent automatically created modules would otherwise become too great a burden. **Make** shortened this development cycle time considerably.

Since software development on all current programming systems is much more demanding than even five years ago, the standard **make** facility has found its way in one form or another onto a variety of other programming environments. It has even been incorporated into the very structure of large applications themselves. For example, the X Windows System uses its own version of the

The Ultimate Make: A Look at X Windows

One example of a large programming environment that makes great use of makefiles is the X Consortium's X Windows system. More than 180 makefiles are used by the core X11 implementation. Because this system is supported on literally thousands of widely different configurations, it was not possible to use a single set of makefiles that could address all the different characteristics of all the supported architectures along with the different ways they implemented various tools. To resolve this dilemma, the developers chose to use an extended version of make, the **imake** tool, which uses a macro preprocessor to create makefiles and adapt them to a specific configuration described by a given architecture which one wishes to compile X for. When a pass is made over all of the **imake** files (using the **imake** utility), a per-host configuration file is used to write every single makefile prior to their execution.

---

[2] Such as the Version 7 UNIX system.

[3] In fact, on some programming systems the makefiles can grow larger than the code they describe.

[4] N.B. Many existing program development environments for Windows-based applications are inherently not scalable.

make facility (called **imake**) and static makefiles to deal with the complexity inherent in a windowing programming environment (see **The Ultimate Make: A Look at X Windows**).

Limitations in the Use of Make

While the standard **make** facility with static makefiles have caught on so widely as to be almost universal, its use can itself create problems. Firstly, the make facility is actually just a little programming language which must be incorporated into yet another file. Since generally the size of this file increases at a linear or better rate with every module used within it, these makefiles can grow quite large.[3] Secondly, these makefiles contain configuration-dependent information that must be managed along with the configuration information in the program itself. Thus, static makefiles increase the number of files and size of information which must be managed.

Finally, it should be noted that many makefiles in a software distribution contain the same or very similar information. As such, if some element of this information is changed, all of the makefiles with this related information must also be manually changed by an editing program to revise them—thus defeating the whole point of **make** to begin with.

The root problem with **make** is simply that it is typically used only at the lowest level of abstraction. An analysis of large makefiles shows that most of the contents are dedicated to manifests of filenames, dependency graphs (that can be generated by **make** itself), and redundant rules for the generation of similar objects. Usually any differences between makefiles of similar programs are only arbitrary or erroneous. This technique becomes, in sum, unscalable and hence

The Fly in the Ointment

While this approach has been successful in allowing the use of X Windows on a variety of platforms and configurations, it has also introduced additional complications—in particular, we now have yet another database of information to maintain (the static makefiles) while still having the responsibility for making sure that the imake files themselves operate correctly prior to use. Thus, we haven't really reduced our development time cycle costs through the use of make, but have only made the problem a bit more manageable by coming up with an organized updating procedure to separate out configuration dependent characteristics. In addition, this process requires a writable source file tree to hold the macro-expanded makefiles in place (e.g., you can't compile X sources directly off a CDROM), presenting the potential defect of the information becoming out-of-phase (information in the conglomeration of imakefiles vs. information in the makefiles themselves).

Problems Encountered with X Imake on 386BSD

These defects do impact the developer in the real world, as we ourselves found while incorporating X into 386BSD. During this project, most of the battle cen-

unsuitable for large scale programming.

Instead of creating a custom makefile for every case, we would prefer that **make** somehow construct or locate portions as needed, and, when possible, link to a single instance (and not redundantly copy common portions). By breaking up the makefile into separate parts (most of which are shared with other programs), the responsibilities for providing contents would then also be separated. Since the shared portions are built by use of abstract descriptions, which are realized by pattern substitution into **make** targets, the nonshared portions now lie at a higher level of abstraction since they program the shared portions to achieve the net result.

Makefiles and the Scaling Dilemma

In addition to the limitations described above, the larger issues of reducing time and effort creating and maintaining these large programming environments is also a key consideration. One way to achieve this goal is to use *scaling* to reduce the cost of maintaining multiple programs to that of a single program, by using the exact same operation for each of N instances. Like a Xerox machine or an assembly line, anything repeatable in time or space (or, in the case of computers, composition) reduces the cost or complexity of a larger assemblage. While scaling in both hardware and software can be used in many different ways, we are concerned here with scaling program construction management overhead.[4]

tered around deciphering the idiosyncrasies surrounding the master configuration file driving the construction of all makefiles by **imake**. Since a hidden configuration dependency on an option could negatively affect one of the window system's numerous tendrils, fiddling with this file becomes a necessary but extremely expensive operation (... here be dragons ...), as all of the makefiles must be re-expanded each time. Worse yet, if an inconsistent state is introduced (perhaps by an incomplete build, which often occurs during the porting stage), stale information may be used in the creation of the makefiles which in turn can lead to a pathologic condition. Since at this point one cannot consistently diagnose and eliminate bugs, the project can go spinning out of control—the ultimate developer's nightmare.

The net advantage to the developer of this approach is to focus and unify program construction mechanisms so that they may be scaled across many programs. For example, if each program is constructed with different makefiles composed of different procedures, mechanisms, and rules, then each must be managed separately—hence, no scaling is possible. However, if all programs are generated via the same procedures, mechanisms, and so forth, then changes in this shared set result in a global effect on all of the programs impacted. This is an entirely scalable mechanism.

Scaling with Make: Dynamic Makefiles

Dynamic makefiles are makefiles that have been restructured to use a *shared* programming base. Thus, instead of directly invoking rules, dependencies, and other low-level portions of **make**, a single shared makefile contains all of the rules and relationships for an entire programming *system* while the makefiles for every subsystem contain only that part unique to that portion of the programming system.[5] All other information resides in a shared makefile driven off the definitions in the per-program makefiles. Thus, these makefiles rely on the composition of many other makefiles to *dynamically* construct the resulting fully-fleshed out makefile that will effectively be used.

With this approach, instead of using external facilities to implement macro expansion, pattern match, and replication, and a single location for configuration-dependent parameters, internal **make** facilities already present are used to perform all of these operations. These makefiles are composed of other included makefiles, each of which defines only the small portion describing that part or step of the process. As such, we greatly reduce the bulk of all of the makefiles in the programming subsystem, allowing for read-only software distributions.[6] Finally, since the effective makefile is constructed on the fly each time, it always remains current to the state of all subsidiary makefiles, reducing software management costs.

The 386BSD Kernel
Dynamic Makefile Environment: An Example

Prior to Release 1.0, 386BSD used a large C program (**config**) to macro-expand a common makefile (**i386/conf/Makefile.i386**) symbolically from a per-host description file (i.e. **i386/conf/MYHOST**). This would then statically configure a kernel program by creating numerous program files and a large makefile in a per-host directory (i.e. **compile/MYHOST**). **Config**, like **imake**, generated makefiles that would have to be regenerated manually[7] if the configuration description changed. Since Release 1.0 allows the configuration to change dynamically, this arrangement[8] was no longer suitable.

In Release 1.0, the makefile for the kernel program was transformed into its own *configuration file.* A kernel program is described (see **Listing 1**) as a set of manifest

---

[5] In the simplest case, this is a manifest or list of the source modules themselves to be used to create the program.
[6] For example, we can now compile software directly off CDROM-resident source filesystems.
[7] Again with **config**.
[8] Which had been strained for years due to its inherent inflexibility.

global symbol definitions and a set of subsystems which are selected by including the makefile that describes them. For convenience, the configuration directory holds collections of commonly used subsystem components like **config/config.std.mk**—(see **Listing 2**). An example subsystem, in this case the core kernel module kern (located in **kern/Makefile.inc**—see **Listing 3**), describes the files and subsystems of which it is composed and incorporates the rules by which its class of components may be constructed (located in **config/kernel.kern.mk**—see **Listing 4**). After incorporating all component definitions and rules, the master makefile for all 386BSD kernels (located in **config/kernel.mk**—see Listing 5) is invoked to dynamically glue together the file names, dependencies, and rules to the mechanisms used to generate the effective makefile itself to be employed.

The power of this approach can be demonstrated when one wishes to add new facilities, modules, or source files to the kernel program. In this example, only the makefiles referencing the changes need be altered or created. For the most part, these makefiles are little more than program manifests, as the mechanisms for construction are present in the component class and master makefiles.[9] Thus, a new facility can be added and used solely by adding new files, and not by requiring a rewrite of the config program or any of its dependent files. Alternatively, if the kernel program were to be instrumented with a new tool, a single modification to the master makefile would allow the new tool to be usable on all generated kernels without changing the rest of the program environment. Thus, it is now possible to *scale* the program construction environment.[10]

Why Doesn't Everyone Use Dynamic Makefiles?

Since the usefulness and cost-effectiveness of dynamic makefiles is very obvious, and since scalable extensions to the original **make** facility were made in more recent versions, including SVR4 make, GNU make, and Berkeley pmake (used in 386BSD), why isn't everyone using this facility already? Unfortunately, while the potential for scalability using dynamic makefiles already exists, most developers still make use of only the oldest most primitive features of **make** and have not restructured their systems or usage to scale their development more efficiently.

In sum, the use of dynamic makefiles implies shifting our perspective from that of a single, large, unstructured file to a structured library of smaller composed reusable files. This shift in perspective on how to better use an old tool is often times more difficult for a developer than the actual programming work required to implement the changes to use it differently.

---

[9] N.B. the only reason for component class makefiles is to allow special treatment of a class of components, like providing different pre- or post- processing.

[10] See **Appendix A** and the discussion in **Chapter 4** on **kern/config.c** for further information.

The Past and Future of Dynamic Makefiles

Since most BSD utilities require five or fewer line makefiles that indirectly invoke a single included makefile (**bsd.prog.mk**), the new work[11] we did in creating the 386BSD kernel dynamic makefile environment was intended to simplify software management of the entire BSD utility source tree, and has been highly effective. However, other extensions to the **make** environment are also possible, including ones that can adapt various and potentially conflicting programming environments on a case-by-case basis.[12] This concept can even be extended by examining certain common cases and creating default makefiles by inspection of the sources themselves—even allowing for cases where no makefiles need be present at all.

While the default use of **make** (such as **imake**) is still valuable in many instances, the need to scale software development will be the deciding factor that pushes the increased usage of dynamic makefiles and extended **make** facilities. Integrated development environment products will need to exploit dynamic **make** programming to manage the large numbers[13] of programs required. In sum, better use and understanding of tools and techniques such as **make** is not just good business—it's also good sense.

```
#
# 386BSD operating system kernel for network host "odysseus".
#

KERNEL=        386bsd                                  # kernel program name
IDENT= -Di486 -DTCP_COMPAT_42 -DDIAGNOSTIC             # static options
S=/usr/src/kernel                      # location of source tree

# standard kernel with INTERNET protocols
.include "$S/config/config.std.mk"
.include "$S/config/config.inet.mk"

# additional options
.include "$S/ppp/Makefile.inc"                         # point-to-point protocol
.include "$S/bpf/Makefile.inc"                         # packet filter
.include "$S/fpu-emu/Makefile.inc"      # math emulator
.include "$S/mcd/Makefile.inc"                         # mitsumi cdrom
.include "$S/wt/Makefile.inc"                          # wangtec cartridge tape
.include "$S/ed/Makefile.inc"                          # NE2000 ethernet
.include "$S/ddb/Makefile.inc"                         # kernel debugger
.include "$S/kern/opt/ktrace/Makefile.inc"  # BSD ktrace mechanism
.include "$S/isofs/Makefile.inc"            # ISO-9660 CDROM filesystem
.include "$S/dosfs/Makefile.inc"            # DOS FAT filesystem
```

[11] Inspired by some prior work done by Keith Bostic while at UC Berkeley.
[12] Viz., the **NONSTD** feature in 386BSD.
[13] Hundreds to thousands.

```
.include "$S/mfs/Makefile.inc"                    # BSD memory-based filesystem

.include "$S/config/kernel.mk"
```

Listing 1: Sample 386BSD Kernel

```
#
# Standard 386BSD kernel configuration.
#

# kernel
.include "$S/kern/Makefile.inc"

# residual 4.3BSD compatibility
.include "$S/kern/opt/compat43/Makefile.inc"

# standard socket IPC (BSD - UNIX communications domain)
.include "$S/un/Makefile.inc"

# standard pseudo devices
.include "$S/mem/Makefile.inc"
.include "$S/log/Makefile.inc"
.include "$S/termios/Makefile.inc"
.include "$S/devtty/Makefile.inc"

# standard filesystems
.include "$S/ufs/Makefile.inc"

.if ${MACHINE} == i386
#
# Standard PC/AT complement of devices
#

# standard bus
.include "$S/isa/Makefile.inc"

# standard devices
.include "$S/pccons/Makefile.inc"
.include "$S/aux/Makefile.inc"
.include "$S/wd/Makefile.inc"
.include "$S/fd/Makefile.inc"
.include "$S/com/Makefile.inc"
.include "$S/lpt/Makefile.inc"
.include "$S/npx/Makefile.inc"
.endif
```

Listing 2: Sample 386BSD Kernel Configuration

```
#
# Makefile for the kernel of the kernel (kern) module. -wfj
#
# $Id: Makefile.inc,v 1.1 94/10/20 00:02:43 bill Exp $

.PATH:  $S/kern
KERN_SRCS+= \
        clock.c config.c cred.c descrip.c execve.c exit.c fork.c sysent.c \
        host.c kinfo.c lock.c main.c malloc.c physio.c priv.c \
        proc.c prof.c ptrace.c reboot.c resource.c sig.c synch.c time.c \
        ldisc.c

SYMBOLS+= kern.symbols
MAN9+=          malloc.0 # kinfo.0 io.0 priv.0 process.0 config.0 lock.0
#         host.0 time.0 memory.0
MAN5+=          core.0
MAN4+=          fd.0 # ldisc.0 kern.0

.include "$S/kern/fs/Makefile.inc"
.include "$S/kern/$(MACHINE)/Makefile.inc"
.include "$S/kern/net/Makefile.inc"
.include "$S/kern/socket/Makefile.inc"
.include "$S/kern/subr/Makefile.inc"
.include "$S/kern/vm/Makefile.inc"

# .include <bsd.kernel.mk>
```

Listing 3: Sample Kernel Makefile

```
#
# kernel module make rules
#

KMODULE=kern
KERNEL_C?=      ${CC} -c ${CFLAGS} ${PROF} ${DEBUG} ${.IMPSRC} -o
${.TARGET}
KERNEL_C_C?= ${CC} -c ${CFLAGS} ${PROF} ${PARAM} ${DEBUG} ${.IMPSRC} \
                -o ${.TARGET}
MACH_C?=       ${CC} -c -I$S/kern/${MACHINE} ${CFLAGS} ${PROF} ${DEBUG} \
                ${.IMPSRC} -o ${.TARGET}
MACH_AS?=      ${CPP} -I. -I$S/kern/${MACHINE} -DLOCORE ${COPTS} ${.IMPSRC}
| \
                ${AS} ${ASFLAGS} -o ${.TARGET}

.SUFFIXES: .${KMODULE}o .${KMODULE}co .${KMODULE}mo

OBJS+= ${KERN_SRCS:R:S/$/.${KMODULE}o/g}
```

```
OBJS+= ${KERN_SRCS_C:R:S/$/.${KMODULE}co/g}
OBJS+= ${MACH_SRCS:R:S/$/.${KMODULE}mo/g}
OBJS+= ${MACH_SRCS_S:R:S/$/.${KMODULE}mo/g}

.c.${KMODULE}o:
        ${KERNEL_C}

.c.${KMODULE}co:
        ${KERNEL_C_C}

.c.${KMODULE}mo:
        ${MACH_C}

.s.${KMODULE}mo:
        ${MACH_AS}

DEPEND+= depend_kern depend_mach

depend_kern: ${KERN_SRCS}
        mkdep ${COPTS} ${.ALLSRC}
        mv .depend /tmp/dep
        sed -e "s;.o :;.kerno:;" < /tmp/dep >depend_kern
        rm -rf /tmp/dep

depend_mach: ${MACH_SRCS}
        mkdep ${COPTS} ${.ALLSRC}
        mv .depend /tmp/dep
        sed -e "s;.o :;.kerno:;" < /tmp/dep >depend_mach
        rm -rf /tmp/dep
```

Listing 4: Sample Kernel Make Rules

```
#
# This make file incorporates the generic 386BSD kernel program makefile,
# kernel.mk. Copyright (C) 1990-1994 W. Jolitz, All Rights Reserved.
# $Id:$
#

.SUFFIXES: .symbols .9 .8 .7 .6 .5 .4 .3 .2 .1 .0

TOUCH?=         touch -f -c
LD?=    /usr/bin/ld
CC?=    cc
CPP?=   cpp

# XXX overkill, revise include scheme on a per file basis
INCLUDES= -I$S/include

COPTS+=         ${INCLUDES} ${IDENT} -DKERNEL -Di386 -DNPX
```

```
DEPEND= depend_mk

ASFLAGS= ${DEBUG}
CFLAGS=        -O ${COPTS}

# locate the kernel at a different virtual address base?
.if defined(KERNBASE)
CFLAGS+= -DKERNBASE=0x${KERNBASE}
BASE= -DKERNBASE=0x${KERNBASE}
.else
KERNBASE=FE000000
.endif

# setup the compilation directory if parts are missing
.if !exists(machine)
FOO!=ln -s $S/include/$(MACHINE) machine
.endif

# principal targets
.MAIN:  all

ALLMAN=        ${MAN1} ${MAN2} ${MAN3} ${MAN4} ${MAN5} ${MAN6}
${MAN7} ${MAN8} ${MAN9}

KOBJS = ${FIRSTOBJ} ${OBJS}

_KERNS=               ${KERNEL}
.if defined(DDB)
_KERNS+=       ${KERNEL}.ddb
.endif
.if defined(PROFILE)
_KERNS+=       ${KERNEL}.prof
.endif
.if defined(KGDB)
_KERNS+=       ${KERNEL}.kgdb
.endif

all: ${_KERNS}   ${ALLMAN}

assym.s: $S/include/sys/param.h $S/include/buf.h $S/include/vmmeter.h \
        $S/include/proc.h $S/include/msgbuf.h machine/vmparam.h \
        $S/config/genassym.c
        ${CC} ${INCLUDES} -DKERNEL ${IDENT} ${PARAM} ${BASE} \
                $S/config/genassym.c -o genassym
        ./genassym >assym.s

.include "$S/config/kernel.kern.mk"
.include "$S/config/kernel.dev.mk"
.include "$S/config/kernel.fs.mk"
.include "$S/config/kernel.domain.mk"
```

```
SRCS= ${KERN_SRCS} ${MACH_SRCS} ${DEV_SRCS} ${FS_SRCS}
${DOMAIN_SRCS}

${KERNEL}: Makefile symbols.sort ${FIRSTOBJ} ${OBJS}
        @echo loading $@
        @rm -f $@
        @$S/config/newvers.sh
        @${CC} -c ${CFLAGS} ${PROF} ${DEBUG} vers.c
.if defined(DEBUGSYM)
        @${LD} -z -T ${KERNBASE} -o $@ -X ${FIRSTOBJ} ${OBJS} vers.o
.else
        @${LD} -z -T ${KERNBASE} -o $@ -x ${FIRSTOBJ} ${OBJS} vers.o
.endif
        @echo rearranging symbols
        @symorder ${SYMORDER} symbols.sort $@
.if defined(DBSYM)
        @${DBSYM} $@
.endif
        @size $@
        @chmod 755 $@

.9.0 .8.0 .7.0 .6.0 .5.0 .4.0 .3.0 .2.0 .1.0:
        nroff -mandoc ${.IMPSRC} > ${.TARGET}

clean:
        rm -f eddep 386bsd* tags ${OBJS} errs linterrs makelinks

depend: ${DEPEND}
        cat ${DEPEND} >> .depend

depend_mk: assym.s
        mkdep ${COPTS} ${.ALLSRC}
        mkdep -a -p ${INCLUDES} ${IDENT} ${PARAM} $S/config/genassym.c
        mv .depend depend_mk

symbols.sort: ${SYMBOLS}
        grep -hv '^#' ${.ALLSRC} | sed 's/^   //' | sort -u > symbols.sort

.if !target(install)
.if !target(beforeinstall)
beforeinstall:
.endif

realinstall: beforeinstall

install: afterinstall
afterinstall: realinstall maninstall
.endif
```

```
.if !target(tags)
tags: ${SRCS}
        -cd ${.CURDIR}; ctags -f /dev/stdout ${.ALLSRC:M*.c} | \
          sed "s;\${.CURDIR}/;;" > tags
.endif

.include <bsd.man.mk>
```

Listing 5: Sample Kernel Master Makefile

ANSWERS TO EXERCISES

2.1 a) Traps are used to indicate an unusual situation (an exception). Apart from pathologic cases (like a program that generates a page fault or overflow every instruction), traps only occur sporadically during system operation. However, since system calls are used for external communication (I/O) by the program in addition to resource allocation and various control functions, they occur very frequently throughout the system.

b) Interrupts usually indicate the completion of a hardware operation. Since the operating system is used to transform high-level program requests to low-level hardware operations, typically many low-level operations (interrupts) are performed for every high-level operation (e.g. system calls).

2.2 Because they are not maskable since they have no hardware mask to disable them.

2.3 Due to processor implementation. On the X86, a system call is done via a protected procedure call mechanism. Unlike traps and interrupts, procedure calls don't normally save processor status, so one word is missing from its hardware frame. Interrupts differ from traps only in that interrupts retain the former interrupt level information for recovery after processing of the interrupt concludes.

2.4 a) The page directory element corresponding to the "PTmap" refers to itself; thus, the directory elements are interpreted as page table entries, allowing the contents of the page tables to be referenced directly in this region. Since the location of the table entries is found in the same manner as that done by the processor's MMU, the 4 MByte region contains all 1024 4 byte table entries in consecutive order.

b) This is useful because it takes a two-level deep table and represents it as a single-level sparse linear table. Finding the correspondence between address and pte (and the converse) is now fast and simple. This is a common operation used in maintaining an address space (see **pmap.c** in **Volume II** of this series).

2.5 An address fault trap occurs with no initialized trap handling table. On the X86, this causes a processor shutdown (e.g. akin to pressing the "reset" or power switch on the computer).

2.6 In the case where process priority changes considerably, 32 run queues are more efficient than one single run queue. A priority-sorted list is too expensive to implement in the kernel (see **synch.c** in **Chapter 9**). as would also a linear search on process priority in **swtch**. By segregating run queues by priority level, one comparison finds the highest priority process queue. A design compromise has been made here in not having a process queue for each priority level, so only 32 levels are discrete.

3.1 To allow for more "graceful" error recovery handling in the kernel. One way to achieve this is to have the process's *md_onfault* field instantiate a list of error handlers that "catch" an exception as the process's kernel stack is incrementally unwound. (Each element would contain a stack frame and program counter reference locations, as well as a convention to return state of the exception recovery method used). Each handler has the opportunity to alter kernel state before "throwing" control to a higher-level handler. With error handling arranged in this manner, most 386BSD panics would be recoverable.

3.2 The virtual memory system must "filter" the fault first, as it may be rectified (e.g. allocate and/or load/copy a page from disk) transparently prior to consideration as a hard fault.

3.3 We would fail to discover the signal and return it to the user. Also, the user signal code must execute prior to reissuing the system call, and this only occurs when the system call is restarted from the user program itself.

3.4 A unique kernel stack, proc instance, and pcb.

3.5 *exit_tss*. The moment another thread is ready to execute, the "ljmp" to the next process will "free" it for use with another exiting thread, as the processor switches to a new TSS (see **swtch** in **Chapter 2**).

4.1 Hardware devices are accessed through software device drivers. It is through the configuration software that the hardware is successfully configured and used. Since the software driving the hardware is typically much more complex than the hardware itself (containing different features, capabilities, and so forth), configuration in software is the greater challenge.

4.2 a) A module parses the file each time from start to end, gleaning only the parts that match its requirements. This differs from an order-dependent arrangement where the file may be processed once in the order of the file contents (line-by-line) and the information then applied to the modules. Note that the contents of the files are ordered with respect to each module scanning it (thus, symbolic reassignment is order-dependent for a module), but since modules are not initialized in a specific order, this has no effect relative to other modules.

b) Eliminating configuration order dependence results in an unambiguous definition of shared state. Programs that manage such state are simpler to write and maintain (otherwise, such programs grow too quickly in size and complexity). In addition, future systems will expect configuration or reconfiguration will be possible without taking the entire system out-of-service. In this case, we will not be able to ensure that a given configuration order will be maintained.

4.3 Memory allocators should only be added if a novel advantage is gained which was not present in the other kernel memory allocators. This advantage must also be great enough to offset the cost of splitting management of free memory resource. For example, reducing the overhead to allocate and free memory could not only be done by adding another memory allocator but could also be done by modifying **malloc()** and **free()**; thus, it is not unique. **kmem_alloc()** is unique in that it allocates address space and memory from the virtual memory system— which supplies both with page granularity. **MCLGET** allocates packet buffers that are copied by reference; thus, the same physical memory is logically used as if it were multiple instances. Another example of a potential additional memory allocator might be **alloca()** (see the **386BSD User Manual**).

4.4 a) 16, 32, 64, 128, 256, 512, 1024, 2048 buckets have at least one 4 KByte page. Of 32 KBytes total (8 * 4KBytes), 4080 bytes are used (16 + 32 + 64 + 128 + 256 + 512 + 1024 + 2048) with 28688 bytes unused.

b) A buddy allocator would waste less space but consume more processor overhead. If efficient space use of tiny allocations is required, it is a better choice. (For example, a fraction of the space in the above example would be wasted).

4.5 Because then the optimal case for each would not be possible. The smallest "spanning set" of allocators is determined by expressed needs which may conflict with one another. The objective here is to determine what the needs actually are, to serve them to the best combined advantage, and to set rules for addition of allocators (if ever).

4.6 **a)** For **malloc()**, adding new memory to the bucket chain. For **free()**, reclaiming surplus memory and returning it to the virtual memory system.

b) By using a lazy mechanism. **malloc()** can postpone page allocation to the bucket chain by exaggerated over-allocation of memory to the chain. **free()** does not have to return memory to the virtual memory system but instead lets the virtual memory system call a reclaim function to examine the bucket chain and return needed memory when resource exhaustion occurs.

c) No. This approach varies in success depending on the resource utilization of a system. For example, if the system is always "tight" on pages but not limited by existing **malloc()** and **free()** costs, this optimization might thrash between overallocation and reclamation, slowing the system.

5.1 **a)** The kernel program is divided up into subsystems which interact only with each other in predictable ways, thus making it tractable in debugging the overall kernel as it is extended. The virtual memory system (or main store manager) is a central component of the kernel and thus is a key separate facility of the kernel.
b) Process creation/destruction are structured so that memory and address space allocation are disjoint from the multiprogramming primitives and the POSIX semantics of a process. Conceivably, the kernel could operate without a full virtual memory system by simply allocating portions of memory posted into regions of address space. One reason this might be done is to allow the kernel to load the virtual memory system itself from the filesystem as a separate module.

5.2 Multiprogramming is a mechanism which permeates the design of the basic kernel. As such, it cannot be externalized. The presence of processes in the basic kernel allow much of the operating system's functionality to be built out of processes instead of being rooted in the basic kernel.

5.3 The proc instance **struct proc**, which is reclaimed after the parent process's recovery status (see **wait4()**) is signalled following an **exit()** of the child. It persists so long because it must convey termination status and process statistics back to the parent.

5.4 The process's unique process ID. It appears after we are permitted to create a new process. A process ID is required by a proc instance.

5.5 Kernel threads are created by various kernel modules (drivers, filesystems, etc.) in response to requests by user program. Since there is no "parent" to inform or status to return, kernel threads have nothing corresponding to POSIX semantics to maintain. In addition, since many kernel threads only last until the next context switch, self-reclamation is the lowest overhead arrangement possible.

6.1 There are a number of reasons: 1) The "standard" stack may actually be a list of many "shallow" stacks, with a single "deep" signal stack holding state for common error recovery of the multiple user threads; 2) If as a part of error recovery the running stack must be altered or exchanged, the current signal stack itself does not need to be relocated (this would otherwise be a very expensive operation).

6.2 **psignal()** sends a signal only—it relies on callers to determine if the signal should be sent. Since **psignal()** can be called from low-level or interrupt level code or from other processes, it may not be possible for it to otherwise locate the credentials associated with the requestor (e.g., the association may be at a higher-level of abstraction). There are also many "corner-cases" where the rules of permission require special exceptions. These exceptions may not be expressible or efficiently checked in a general-purpose way.

6.3 Default signals result in the normal or abnormal termination of a process, usually within a deterministic time. Since this signal results in the release of resources, it is desirable that this procedure be expedited to obtain the resources.

6.4 **a)** UNIX processes die by arranged suicide. In order for the process to recognize the request to die (e.g., a **kill()** or **psignal()**), it must return from kernel mode to user mode (see **trap()** and **syscall()** in **Chapter 3**). If it cannot return to user mode, the request cannot be seen and hence not honored.
b) If the signal was recognized internally and termination manually forced, some special termination cases could be rectified. However, in the general case, various kernel resources must be relinquished by other parts (layers) of the operating system as well. One way to achieve this is through use of a nested exception handling mechanism.

6.5 The most obvious information still missing is the state of open files (names, seek indexes, other file/driver state), address space additions, and signal state.

7.1 **a)** When an interrupt level (or other low-level) service must validate whether a requestor can perform an operation.
b) In general, such operations have no way to locate the associated process. Worse yet, the operation which is being checked may occur after the process has terminated.

7.2 **a)** The user credentials bound to each object reference or modification request.
b) No. Each request is considered solely on the basis of supplied credentials for the corresponding operation—e.g., there is never a case that an operation has multiple credential sets to be considered. In addition, user credential references are not allowed to persist across operations. Hence, changes cannot bypass credential checks.

7.3 The credentials present when the operation was requested. Note these are not necessarily the same credentials present when the operation is executed.

7.4 **a)** While the role-based security mechanism is itself embedded in the basic kernel, there is no mechanism in the basic kernel which gets/sets roles.
b) The access paths alone govern roles. Access paths are determined solely by modules external to the basic kernel (e.g., device drivers, networking, filesystems). As a process references less-secure paths, its role restricts access accordingly.

7.5 **a)** System calls would require a standard interface to maintain and protect along with the associated management and control surrounding the interface. Hence, no system calls are used.

b) The lack of system calls does not prevent one from determining that role-based security is present. A program can deduce that this mechanism is present if, for example, it has root privilege yet cannot modify files or perform certain activities from less-secure access paths.

8.1 a) Weighting provides a different constant bias to the process's priority in the selection of a run queue. Other factors, such as CPU utilization, can also skew the priority of other processes, so that the effect of weighting may be rendered ineffective. Hence, weighting has more of a stochastic than deterministic effect.

b) One way that this mechanism could be made more effective would be to alter the effect of either the CPU utilization accumulation or the priority decay by basing them on weight—resulting in a cumulative effect on processor resource usage. This would eliminate the stochastic behavior of weighting by ensuring that process will only get scheduled ahead of others based on the effective weighting and not other transitory factors.

8.2 a) No. The signal must be processed by returning the process to user mode so that the signal can be discovered and delivered.

b) In the case of ERESTART, after signal delivery the system call will reoccur, returning control back to where the **tsleep()** request occurred—thus, completing the loop (potentially). In the case of EINTR, the system call returns an interrupted system call error and is now responsible for error recovery. The difference is one of transparent versus mandatory handling of the given system call signal delivery.

8.3 a) Preemptive scheduling with multilevel feedback on a round-robin basis.
b)

Queueing Model (note: three levels of feedback):

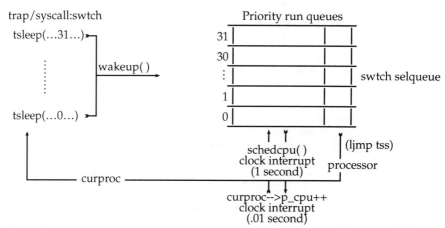

8.4 No. Upgrades and downgrades of locks are not symmetric. A write lock implies no readers (exclusive). One can always downgrade an exclusive write lock to hold a read lock since read locks are not exclusive. The converse is not true, however, since in order for a read lock to upgrade to a write lock it must obtain exclusive access to it and hence it may have to block waiting for exclusive access.

9.1 Currently, the header and file attributes are cached. Since this information is not managed directly by the virtual memory system cache, they compete for a place in the file buffer cache (at present). Since each program will load like the first time, setting up the address space is an identical operation. So caching a dummy address space for each executable and then performing an address space copy to the current address space could eliminate all address space related details (except argument processing).

9.2 **a)** No. The file descriptors can be implemented outside of the kernel, since the kernel never directly uses them.
b) File descriptors are not shared, but files can be shared. To implement **pipe()** semantics, a file is shared across descriptors in both child and parent.

9.3 **a)** [A] 1+NFD system calls, 0 context switches. [B] NFD system calls, NFD context switches.
b) [A] 1+NFD system calls, 0 context switches. [B] NFD system calls, NFD/4 context switches. N.B. The point here is that the benefits of a multithreaded system may not be as pronounced as expected, since we might simply shift the burden to another portion of the system. This very simple example illustrates this point without resorting to the fine-grain analysis that would otherwise be necessary (e.g., factoring in relative overhead and synchronization costs).

9.4 Most of these requests have few segments to scatter/gather data to/from. By avoiding the allocation of a buffer, the overhead is reduced for frequent cases.

9.5 Mandatory locks ensure data integrity by forestalling any out-of-order changes to locked data by other processes. Advisory locks allow an application additional control (i.e. it can override the lock) at the price of not guaranteeing data integrity.

INDEX

malloc(), 33, 144, 218–35, 238, 521–2
Mandatory Access Control, 500
memory allocation, 94, 157, 220, 224–9, 233–4, 254, 327, 329, 348, 365, 475
memory allocator, 7, 24, 33, 91, 157, 218–24, 228, 233–8, 255, 327, 348–9, 392, 431, 469–70, 472, 474, 521
memory allocators, 91, 221
minimalism, 219
modified process credentials, 331
modpcred(), 331–3, 340, 342–4, 347, 352, 423
modscaninit(), 174–5, 186
multiprogramming, 23, 239–40, 259, 261, 271, 363, 365, 386, 522

N

nameidata structure, 410–12
network cluster, 255
Network File System. *See* NFS
NFS, 327, 348
nosys(), 126, 277, 278, 296, 297

O

outer stack frame, 96

P

page granularity, 144, 223–30, 414, 420, 521
panic, 71, 82, 104–8, 111–5, 119, 188–200, 206–8, 224–32, 375, 378–80, 387, 400–1, 436, 490
parent, 130, 140, 144, 240–4, 248–67, 283, 298, 305–7, 313, 321–3, 423, 425, 429, 525
Peripheral Device Interrupts, 35, 77–8
pgsignal(), 277–8, 320
plug and play, 160, 171–2
portal, 170–1, 500
POSIX, 26, 133, 241, 257, 273, 276, 403
primitive, 8, 23, 104, 124, 146, 160–1, 239–40, 325, 328, 366, 418, 421, 431, 443, 481, 483, 510
privileges, 26, 325–6, 328, 330, 334, 339–46, 352–61, 409, 423, 496–501, 503
proc instance. See process slot
Process, 133
    blocking and scheduling, 363
    creation, 239, 253–4
    credentials, 326, 329
    priority, 369
    privileges, 353
    protection, 325
    termination, 256
    threads vs., 133

process protection mechanism, 279, 325
process slot, 363
Process Termination, 256
processor exception, 31, 35, 74, 76, 77, 78, 101, 102, 103, 116, 257, 273, 286, 316
program execution, 23, 278, 403, 424, 427, 428
psig(), 277, 278, 301, 304, 305, 308, 309, 310, 316, 317
psignal(), 277, 278, 292, 293, 297, 298, 301, 304, 305, 306, 309, 318, 320, 321, 323, 324, 522, 523
ptrace, 106, 115, 125, 141, 154, 265, 267, 275, 276, 298, 306, 307, 311, 323, 423, 424, 513

Q

qswtch, 31, 34, 72, 73, 369

R

Read locks, 389, 390, 394, 396, 399, 524
read(), 174, 193–4, 204, 206–7, 391, 394–8, 433, 445–7
readv(), 433, 447–9, 485
reclaimproc(), 258, 264, 269
recursively shared object, 329
reloc, 34–5, 38–9, 41, 43–4, 49, 51–2
rexit(), 242, 258
rfillkpt, 34–5, 44–6, 51–3
Role and Privileges, 354
roundrobin(), 371, 372
rqinit(), 371, 386

S

scalable, 366, 385, 506, 509–10
schedcpu(), 69, 371–7, 387
Secure Systems, 330
security, 127, 150, 241, 297, 311, 315, 330, 352, 354, 356, 360, 362, 414, 495–503, 523–4
select(), 195–6, 204, 254–5, 431, 459–64, 467
selscan(), 459, 462–5
seltrue(), 466
selwakeup(), 466, 467
set processor level, 31, 90
setegid(), 331, 344–5
seteuid(), 331, 340–1, 345
setgid(), 331, 342–5
setgroupid, 25, 409, 423
setgroups(), 328, 331, 345–6
setlogin(), 331, 349–52
setpri(), 371, 374, 377, 388
setrun(, 303, 371, 381–7, 468

Other fine books by Peer-to-Peer Communications

Operating System Source Code Secrets Series
Volume 2: Virtual Memory Source Code Secrets
William F. Jolitz & Lynne Greer Jolitz
Available early 1996, ISBN 1-57398-027-7

One of Berkeley UNIX's lead developers teaches the inner workings of modern, high-performance operating systems (e.g. Windows NT, UNIX, Mach) via complete line-by-line source code annotations. Based on a port of Berkeley UNIX, with advanced non-UNIX features added, profiled in a 17-part *Dr. Dobb's Journal* serialization.

The PCMCIA Software Developer's Handbook
Dana L. Beatty, Steven M. Kipisz and Brian E. Moore
335 pages, $49.95, ISBN 1-57398-010-2

Foreword by the chairman of the PCMCIA technical committee, 1990-1993. A comprehensive treatment of programming and debugging PC Card devices. Covers the new 1995 PC Card Standard. Includes a diskette containing program templates, utilities, and other development aids. The authors are IBM's project lead and staff programmers responsible for PCMCIA implementation for PowerPC.

Ethernet Configuration Guidelines
Charles Spurgeon
156 pages, $19.95, ISBN 1-57398-012-9

Ethernet works with a huge variety of media types; specifications are scattered throughout a mass of IEEE's 802.x standards. These guidelines overcome the complexity and bring all the configuration rules together in a single, convenient reference (includes 100BASE-T "Fast Ethernet"). Anyone who administers, installs, supports, or designs Ethernet LAN's will appreciate this practical, hands-on professional quick reference.

Packet Communication
Bob Metcalfe
224 pages, $39.95, ISBN 1-57398-033-1

A reprint of Bob Metcalfe's 1972 groundbreaking Harvard Ph.D. dissertation that not only led to the development of Ethernet by Metcalfe at Xerox PARC, but also provided much of the conceptual underpinnings for TCP/IP. Foreword by Vint Cerf. Metcalfe is now the publisher of *InfoWorld*.

Special Offer on 386BSD Reference CD-ROM 1.0!

Readers of the Operating System Source Code Secrets™ series may purchase the companion software for only **$74.95—25% off the CD-ROM's list price**. This bootable* CD-ROM (can be sampled without being installed!) gives you 574 Mbytes of source, binaries, and documentation:

* high-performance UNIX-like 386BSD operating system (multi-tasking kernel, role-based security, interprocess communications, advanced virtual memory subsystems, fast file systems, dynamic driver configuration, and much much more)

* online 386BSD manual, also hyper-linked documentation (arranged in Windows help files) explains key kernel code line by line

* C and C++ libraries, X11R5, hundreds of tools and utilities, tens of thousands of source files, a variety of UNIX and Internet applications

* source code of Mosaic, WAIS, and gopher

* mountable as a UNIX filesystem (Rockridge), all code viewable in DOS/Windows (ISO-9660)

* the complete 17-part *Dr. Dobb's* 386BSD article series and excerpts from the not-yet-published **386BSD from the Inside Out**.

The 386BSD CD-ROM gives you an unparalleled environment in which to explore and analyze operating system design and anatomy. You can even recompile the system itself. Do software development on 386BSD... or just hack the kernel!

* on select supported PC configurations

To receive your copy of the 386BSD CD-ROM at the reduced price of $74.95 (checks and money orders in US dollars only), please provide us with shipping instructions & payment information:

Name _____

Address _____
    (please include zip code/postal code, also mailstop/routing info. if necessary)

_____

_____

Credit Card# _____ Expiration _____

Signature _____ Date _____

_____ Please indicate the total number of CD-ROMs ordered

_____ California purchasers, please add appropriate sales tax

_____ Shipping/Handling Charge: $5 US and Canada, $12 elsewhere

Send Orders to:

Peer-to-Peer Communications, Inc.   Fax : (408) 435-0895
PO Box 640218   Phone : (408) 435-2677
San Jose, CA 95164-0218 USA   Email : info@peer-to-peer.com

Thank you for your order!